T0318193

Commitment in Organizations

Accumulated Wisdom
and New Directions

Commitment in Organizations

Accumulated Wisdom and New Directions

Edited by
Howard J. Klein • Thomas E. Becker • John P. Meyer

Routledge
Taylor & Francis Group
New York London

First issued in paperback in 2013
Routledge
Taylor & Francis Group
605 Third Avenue,
New York, NY 10017

Routledge
Taylor & Francis Group
2 Park Square, Milton Park
Abingdon, Oxon OX14 4RN

© 2009 by Taylor & Francis
Routledge is an imprint of Taylor & Francis Group, an Informa business

ISBN 13: 978-0-41584-669-1 (pbk)
ISBN 13: 978-1-84872-830-1 (hbk)

Library of Congress Cataloging-in-Publication Data

Commitment in organizations : accumulated wisdom and new directions / [edited by] Howard J. Klein , Thomas E. Becker, John P. Meyer.
    p. cm.
    ISBN 978-1-84872-830-1 (hbk.)
    1. Organizational commitment. 2. Organizational behavior. 3. Employee loyalty. I. Klein, Howard J., 1935- II. Becker, T. E. (Thomas E.) III. Meyer, John P., 1950-

HD58.7.C6258 2009
302.3'5--dc22   2008035327

The Organizational Frontiers Series

The Organizational Frontiers Series is sponsored by The Society for Industrial and Organizational Psychology (SIOP). Launched in 1983 to make scientific contributions to the field, the series has attempted to publish books on cutting-edge theory, research, and theory-driven practice in Industrial/Organizational psychology and related organizational science disciplines.

Our overall objective is to inform and to stimulate research for SIOP members (students, practitioners, and researchers) and people in related disciplines including the other subdisciplines of psychology, organizational behavior, human resource management, and labor and industrial relations. The volumes in the Organizational Frontiers Series have the following goals:

- Focus on research and theory in organizational science, and the implications for practice
- Inform readers of significant advances in theory and research in psychology and related disciplines that are relevant to our research and practice
- Challenge the research and practice community to develop and adapt new ideas and to conduct research on these developments
- Promote the use of scientific knowledge in the solution of public policy issues and increased organizational effectiveness

The volumes originated in the hope that they would facilitate continuous learning and a continuing research curiosity about organizational phenomena on the part of both scientists and practitioners.

The Organizational Frontiers Series

SIOP Organizational Frontiers Series

Series Editor

Robert D. Pritchard
University of Central Florida

Lord/Klimoski/Kanfer: (2002) Emotions in the Workplace

Drasgow/Schmitt: (2002) Measuring and Analyzing Behavior in Organizations

Feldman: (2002) Work Careers

Zaccaro/Klimoski: (2001) The Nature of Organizational Leadership

Rynes/Gerhart: (2000) Compensation in Organizations

Klein/Kozlowski: (2000) Multilevel Theory, Research and Methods in Organizations

Ilgen/Pulakos: (1999) The Changing Nature of Performance

Earley/Erez: (1997) New Perspectives on International Industrial/Organizational Psychology

Murphy: (1996) Individual Differences and Behavior in Organizations

Guzzo/Salas: (1995) Team Effectiveness and Decision Making

Howard: (1995) The Changing Nature of Work

Schmitt/Borman: (1993) Personnel Selection in Organizations

Zedeck: (1991) Work, Families, and Organizations

Schneider: (1990) Organizational Culture and Climate

Goldstein: (1989) Training and Development in Organizations

Campbell/Campbell: (1988) Productivity in Organizations

Hall: (1987) Career Development in Organizations

For Julius and Charlotte for all of their love and commitment,

and to my favorite and strongest commitment targets—

Sheryl, Josia, and Leland.

H. J. K.

To LuAnn, Jake, and Charlie for teaching me the real meaning of

commitment—and to all the managers who realize

that employee commitment must be earned.

T. E. B.

To Natalie Allen—an inspiration from the beginning—and all my

former and current graduate students whose questions, ideas, and

enthusiasm kept the research alive and made the process enjoyable!

J. P. M.

Contents

Section 4   Methodological Issues and Challenges

Section 5   Integration and Future Directions

Series Foreword

This is the 29th book in the Organizational Frontiers Series of books. The overall purpose of the series volumes is to promote the scientific status of the field. Ray Katzell first edited the Series. He was followed by Irwin Goldstein, Sheldon Zedeck, and Neal Schmitt. The topics of the volumes and the volume editors are chosen by the editorial board, or individuals propose volumes to the editorial board. The series editor and the editorial board then work with the volume editor(s) in planning the volume.

The success of this series is evident in the high number of sales (now over 50,000). Volumes have also received excellent reviews, and individual chapters as well as volumes have been cited frequently.

This volume, edited by Howard Klein, Thomas Becker, and John Meyer, is important because it presents current thinking and research on the topic of organizational commitment. It is a major synthesis of the new research and thinking on commitment and updates us on what is known in this important area. The volume has a number of strengths. The organization of the volume is done with a clear conceptual structure including a theoretical focus on the commitment literature. It offers the reader an up-to-date comprehensive picture of what we know about commitment and what we need to know with future research. Chapter authors were asked to address a series of questions: What do we know now? What are existing theories/models, and how well do they facilitate our understanding of commitment? How useful is what we know? What do we still need to know and do? In answering these questions, authors used an interdisciplinary focus and tried to consider not only the I/O psychology literature but also theory and research in other areas. The volume also offers a multilevel perspective, identifying issues at the individual, team/group, and organizational levels of analysis. Finally, the authors do a very nice job of identifying research needs that should have a significant impact on commitment research for years to come. The editors and authors have indeed provided inspiration for researchers to explore a broader set of issues with a wider range of multidisciplinary approaches.

The editors and chapter authors deserve our gratitude for clearly communicating the nature, application, and implications of the theory and research described in this book. Production of a volume such as this involves the hard work and cooperative effort of many individuals. The editors, chapter authors, and editorial board all played important roles in this endeavor. As all royalties from the series volumes are used to help support SIOP, none of the editors or authors received any remuneration. The editors and authors deserve our appreciation for engaging a difficult task for the sole purpose of furthering our understanding of organizational science. We also want to express our gratitude to Anne Duffy, Senior Editor Psychology Press/Routledge, who has been a great help in the planning and production of the volume.

Robert D. Pritchard
University of Central Florida
Series Editor
September 2, 2008

Preface

This book about workplace commitments originated from a small conference on commitment held at The Ohio State University in October 2005. The impetus for this conference was the realization that commitment was being studied relative to a wide variety of workplace concerns and in different disciplines without much cross-communication or fertilization of ideas. Our objective for writing this book is to provide an up-to-date review and cutting-edge thinking on theory, research, and research methodology as it pertains to all aspects of commitment in organizational contexts. We also wanted this book to address how the realities of the modern workplace are changing the way we need to think about and study commitment in organizations and to provide a future research agenda for advancing our understanding of the development, operation, and consequences of commitment and the resulting implications for organizational policies and practices. To achieve that end, this book brings together the collective wisdom of many of the major theorists and researchers in the field—individuals who have spent many years examining workplace commitments. In the chapters that follow, they summarize, synthesize, and critique existing theory and research, and share their views on the future.

This book meets an important need for the accumulation and integration of a burgeoning literature on workplace commitments. It is primarily aimed at academic faculty and graduate students who study commitment in all of its various contexts and who teach courses that focus on or include commitment. The book can serve as the core reading for a graduate seminar as well as an excellent source of reference. The primary disciplines of interest are industrial and organizational psychology, organizational behavior, and human resources management. Other relevant disciplines include decision making (commitment to decisions), industrial relations (union commitment), organizational design (commitment to change), strategy (commitment to a strategy), marketing (customers' commitment to products), counseling psychology (interpersonal commitment), sports psychology (commitment to exercise and conditioning routines), and political science (commitment to positions, candidates, parties). The primary focus of the book is theory and research rather than practice, but the content of this book should also appeal to practitioners interested in retention, turnover, loyalty, engagement, job performance, organizational citizenship and counterproductive work behaviors, and other important organizational consequences of commitment.

One of the strengths of this book is its diversity, both in terms of issues addressed and perspectives taken. We have tried to balance that diversity with a sense of continuity and integration by asking the contributing authors to consider and address the following five questions as they pertain to their topic in preparing their chapters: (1) What do we know now? (2) How useful is what we know? (3) Are current commitment theories adequate, and if not, what theoretical developments are needed? (4) What can we learn from relevant theory and research outside of commitment within I/O psychology, and from theory and research on commitment outside of I/O psychology? (5) What do we need to know and do?

In answering the "what we know" question, we worked with authors to achieve a balance of breadth and depth of coverage. With respect to "usefulness," we encouraged authors dealing with substantive issues (chapters 4–10) to critique the literature in terms of actionable implications for both worker well-being and organizational effectiveness. For the authors of more conceptual or methodological chapters (chapters 1–3, 11–12), the focus is on usefulness to researchers. To address the "theoretical analysis and development" theme, each author was asked to provide a theoretical critique and to evaluate the applicability of the current theoretical models presented in chapter 1 to the particular domain they cover. With regard to the interdisciplinary theme, authors were asked to consider theory and research in related areas of I/O psychology, in other fields of psychology (e.g., social, developmental, counseling, sports, and evolutionary), and in other disciplines (e.g., sociology, political science, industrial relations, marketing). Authors were given considerable leeway in addressing the final theme, "What do we need to know and do?" but they were asked to consider how commitment is affected by the myriad changes in the workplace (e.g., alternate work forms and relationships, changing demographics), and the implications these have for key theoretical and empirical issues that need to be studied.

To avoid potential confusion, a few key terms are clarified here as to how they are used throughout the book. First, *affective, continuance,* and *normative* commitment are referred to as mindsets (not types or kinds of commitment). In addition, although the term *dimensions* has sometimes been used to refer to such mindsets, it is only used if referring to factor analytic results or when distinguishing between uni- and multi-dimensional models. Second, the different things to which one can be committed (e.g., organizations, goals, supervisors, career) are referred to as either *commitment foci* or *targets*.

This book is organized into five sections: The Meaning and Relevance of Commitment, Multiple Foci of Commitment, Building and Maintaining Commitments, Methodological Issues and Challenges, and Integration and Future Directions. The content covered within each of these sections is briefly summarized below.

The first section contains three chapters. Chapter 1, by Klein, Molloy, and Cooper, provides a brief history of the study of commitment and addresses the different ways commitment has been conceptualized and defined. This chapter presents the conceptual foundation for the book and discusses a set of representative theories that are evaluated by subsequent chapter authors. Chapter 2, by Meyer, explores the relevance of commitment in a turbulent environment where the nature of work and work relationships change frequently. Convincing arguments are presented that commitment continues to be important in the modern workplace, but that the nature, terms, and focus of commitments may differ from that in the past. This section concludes with chapter 3, by Riketta and Van Dick, which discusses commitment's place in the literature by positioning commitment as a unique concept within the broader I/O psychology literature. In doing so, commitment is differentiated from related constructs (e.g., identification) and discussed as both an independent and dependent variable in the study of other I/O psychology topics (e.g., performance, withdrawal).

The second section of the book also contains three chapters, each focusing on the set of commitment targets at a different level. Chapter 4, by Vandenberghe, addresses commitment to organizations and other macro-level entities. These include commitment to one's employing organization, organizational subunits, client organizations, unions, professional associations, and career commitment. Chapter 5, by Becker, addresses interpersonal commitments to both small groups and individuals, including supervisors, subordinates, customers, coworkers, work teams, and top management. The final chapter in this section, chapter 6, by Neubert and Wu, focuses on action commitments. Action commitments include commitments to goals, strategies, decisions, job tasks, ideologies, and change initiatives. Each chapter within this section discusses the similarities and differences among the different commitment targets discussed within the chapter as well as the distinctions between those commitments and those at the other levels discussed in this section.

Section three of this book, Building and Maintaining Commitments, contains four chapters, each focusing on the antecedents of commitment at a different level. Chapter 7, by Bergman, Benzer, and Henning, focuses on individual-level antecedents to commitment, particularly need satisfaction, attachments, and dispositions, and the processes through which individual differences influence commitment. Chapter 8, by Wayne, Coyle-Shapiro, Eisenberger, Liden, Rousseau, and Shore, focuses on social antecedents to commitment and the processes through which group and social influences affect commitment with an emphasis on leader-member exchange, perceived support, and psychological contracts. In chapter 9, by Wright and Kehoe, organizational-level antecedents and correlates of commitment are examined, including organizational culture, strategy and structure, and human resource management practices and the processes through which organizational influences impact commitment.

This section concludes with chapter 10, by Wasti and Önder, which examines the cultural influences on commitment, and critically examines the growing cross-cultural commitment literature and the extent to which the nature of commitment is culturally dependent.

The fourth section of this book contains two chapters addressing methodological issues and challenges. Chapter 11, by Jaros, focuses on the measurement of commitment. This chapter evaluates existing measures of commitment and discusses several measurement issues. The implications of those issues for the interpretation of past research findings and future research needs, including measurement development, are also addressed. The other chapter in this section, chapter 12, by Vandenberg and Stanley, highlights the methodological challenges that need to be addressed in order to significantly advance our understanding of commitments in the workplace. Latent growth modeling (LGM), latent profile analysis (LPA), and latent class growth modeling (LCGM) are given particular attention as tools to help meet these challenges.

The final section, Integration and Future Directions, contains a single chapter by the editors, summarizing the accumulated wisdom on workplace commitments and presenting an agenda for future research. This is accomplished by summarizing and integrating the answers provided within this volume to the five questions we asked each author to address, with emphasis placed on the issue of what we still need to know. It is our conclusion that the topic of employee commitment remains a relevant and vibrant topic of research and a continuing practical concern. We further believe that changes in the nature of organizations and the employment relationship have made commitment more pertinent than ever, though the most relevant target for that commitment may not be the employing organization.

Acknowledgments

We are most grateful to our contributing authors. This book is not a compilation of papers that were already planned or written. Each author was asked to address a specific set of issues and review and comment on a particular aspect of commitment relative to those issues. To do so, authors had to draw upon their expertise and, in some cases, expand their expertise. In all cases, they delivered chapters that are thought provoking, provide comprehensive treatments of the current literature, and offer valuable directions for future research. We have very much enjoyed working with one another and with this talented and insightful group of contributors. We have learned a tremendous amount from them through this process and cannot thank them enough for their effort and willingness to address yet one more set of constructive comments. This Frontier Series volume was made possible by their time, talent, and contributions. We also wish to acknowledge the untimely passing of one of our authors, Michael Ritetta. Michael was a dedicated scholar whose work has influenced our own, and whose contribution will be missed by the I/O community.

The ideas for this book emerged from the 2005 Conference on Commitment that we organized. We recognize and appreciate the contributions of the presenters and attendees at that conference, not all of whom could be included as authors. We would also like to acknowledge the hundreds of researchers in numerous disciplines who have researched and written about commitment in so many different contexts and from such diverse perspectives. The breadth and depth of the literature was somewhat daunting, but mostly inspiring, as it presented a wealth of information for us and the chapter authors to mine and augment. We are also grateful to the Society for Industrial and Organizational Psychology (SIOP) Frontier Series Editorial Board for their guidance and encouragement. Their feedback helped us refine our vision for this volume and strengthened the end result. Finally, we thank Anne Duffy, Senior Editor Psychology Press/ Routledge, for her continuous support, guidance, and expertise and for keeping us on track and (mostly) on schedule.

H. J. K.

T. E. B.

J. P. M.

Contributors

Thomas E. Becker is a professor of management in the Lerner College of Business at the University of Delaware. He received his Ph.D. in I/O psychology from Ohio State University in 1990. His primary research interests are employee commitment, integrity, motivation, job performance, and research methods. He has published in most of the better journals and some of the underappreciated ones, and is currently on the editorial boards of *Human Performance* and *Organizational Behavior and Human Decision Processes*. He has won several research and teaching awards but is most proud of the lofty title he held on his last sabbatical: the Belgian International Francqui Chair in the Human Sciences.

Justin K. Benzer is a post-doctoral fellow at the Center for Organization, Leadership, and Management Research. He received his M.S. (2006) from Texas A&M University and his B.A. (2008) from the University of Massachusetts at Amherst. His current research focuses on multi-level influences on individual and group motivation.

Mindy E. Bergman is an Assistant Professor of Psychology at Texas A&M University. She earned her Ph.D. (2001) and A.M. (1999) in I/O psychology from the University of Illinois at Urbana-Champaign. Her research has appeared in journals such as *Journal of Applied Psychology, Journal of Occupational Health Psychology,* and *Journal of Organizational Behavior.* Her research focuses on commitment, occupational health, sexual and racial harassment and discrimination, organizational climate (with an emphasis on safety climate, in particular), and situational judgment tests.

Joseph T. Cooper is a doctoral candidate in organizational behavior and human resources at the Fisher College of Business at Ohio State University. He earned his B.S. in Civil Engineering in 1997 and his M.B.A. in 2003, both from Case Western Reserve University. His research interests center around organizational roles, commitment, and work motivation.

Jacqueline A-M. Coyle-Shapiro is a professor of organizational behavior in the Department of Management at the London School of Economics and Political Science (LSE), where she received her Ph.D in 1996. Her research interests include employment relationships, psychological contracts, perceived organizational support, organizational justice, organizational citizenship behavior, and communal relationships. She is senior editor at the *Journal of Organizational Behavior* and is on several editorial review boards. Her work has been published in outlets including the *Academy of*

Management Journal, Journal of Applied Psychology, Journal of Organizational Behavior, Journal of Vocational Behavior, and *Journal of Management Studies.*

Robert Eisenberger is a professor of psychology at the University of Delaware. His research on motivation and organizational behavior has appeared in such journals as the *Psychological Review, Psychological Bulletin, American Psychologist, Journal of Applied Psychology,* and *Journal of Personality and Social Psychology.* His work has been the focal topic of symposia at the annual meetings of the Society for Experimental Social Psychology and the Society for Industrial and Organizational Psychology. Dr. Eisenberger received the Psi Chi Distinguished Lectureship and is a fellow of the Association for Psychological Science, Divisions 1, 6, 14, and 25 of the American Psychological Association, and the Society for Industrial and Organizational Psychology. Two special reports focusing on his research were carried nationally on National Public Radio, and reports on his research have appeared in the *American Psychological Association Monitor, Encyclopedia Britannica Science, Future Yearbook, Science News, Report on Educational Research,* and *School Board Notes.*

Jaime B. Henning is an assistant professor of psychology at Eastern Kentucky University. She earned her B.S. and M.S. from Missouri State University, and her Ph.D. in industrial/organizational psychology is from Texas A&M University. Her research interests include employee volunteerism and prosocial behaviors, work-life balance, and organizational commitment.

Stephen Jaros is professor of management in the Department of Management, Marketing, and E-Business at Southern University and A&M College. He received his Ph.D. from the College of Business at the University of South Florida. His scholarly interests include commitment, employee retention, the philosophy of science, and the study of value-added and labor processes in organizations. His research has appeared in such journals as the *Academy of Management Journal, Journal of Vocational Behavior, Organization, International Studies of Management and Organization,* and the *Journal of Workplace Rights.* He is the past chair of the Critical Management Studies interest group in the Academy of Management.

Rebecca R. Kehoe is a Ph.D. student in human resource studies in the School of Industrial and Labor Relations at Cornell University. She holds a B.S. in communication and applied economics and management and an M.S. in industrial and labor relations from Cornell University. Her research interests include strategic human resource management, equifinality in HR systems, business strategy, organizational design, organizational commitment, and diversity management in organizations.

Howard J. Klein is a professor of management and human resources in the Fisher College of Business at Ohio State University. He received his Ph.D. in organizational behavior and human resource management from Michigan State University. His research interests center on improving individual and team performance through the use of selection, socialization, commitment, goal setting, performance management, and training. Professor Klein has authored more than 40 articles and book chapters on these and other topics. Professor Klein has received awards for his research, teaching, and service. He serves on several editorial review boards including the *Human Resources Management Review, Journal of Applied Psychology, Journal of Organizational Behavior,* and *Organizational Behavior and Human Decision Processes.* He is a fellow of Society for Industrial and Organizational Psychology and has held elected positions in the HR division of the Academy of Management and on the SHRM Foundation Board of Directors.

Robert C. Liden (Ph.D., University of Cincinnati) is professor of management at the University of Illinois at Chicago, where he is director of the OB/HR doctoral program. He has served as a visiting professor at the Chinese University of Hong Kong and at the University of Toulouse, France. His research focuses on interpersonal processes as they relate to such topics as leadership, groups, career progression, and employment interviews. He has won awards (all with coauthors) for the best article published in the *Academy of Management Journal* during 2001, the best article published in *Human Resource Management* during 2001, and the best organizational behavior article published in any journal during 2005 by the Organizational Behavior Division of the Academy of Management. He serves on the editorial boards of *Human Relations, Journal of Applied Psychology, Journal of Management,* and *Leadership Quarterly,* and from 1994 to 1999 served on the *Academy of Management Journal* board. He was the 1999 program chair and 2000–01 division chair for the Academy of Management's Organizational Behavior Division.

John P. Meyer is a professor and chair of the graduate program in I/O psychology at the University of Western Ontario. His research interests include employee commitment, work motivation, leadership, and organizational change. He has published in leading journals in the fields of I/O psychology and management, and coauthored two books: *Commitment in the Workplace* and *Best Practices: Employee Retention.* He is a fellow of the Canadian Psychological Association, the American Psychological Association, and the Society for Industrial and Organizational Psychology, and a member of the Academy of Management.

Janice C. Molloy is a doctoral candidate in labor and human resources at Ohio State University's Fisher College of Business. Her M.B.A. is from the University of Rochester, and her research interests are in strategic human resource management.

Mitchell J. Neubert is the Chavanne Chair of Christian Ethics in Business and holds the H. R. Gibson professorship in management development at the Hankamer School of Business at Baylor University. He received his Ph.D. from the University of Iowa. The focus of his teaching and research is to equip principled leaders to effectively lead individuals, teams, and organizational change. Dr. Neubert has published in several academic and practitioner journals including *Leadership Quarterly, Personnel Psychology, Journal of Applied Psychology, Human Relations, Journal of Business and Psychology, Human Performance, Journal of Business Venturing,* and *Journal of Applied Behavioral Science.*

Çetin Önder completed his Ph.D. in management at Sabanci University, Turkey, in 2006. His research interests include organizational ecology of entrepreneurship and political-institutional influences on organizations. Dr. Önder is currently an assistant professor of management at Başkent University in Turkey. He is a member of the European Group for Organizational Studies.

Michael Riketta was a lecturer in work and organizational psychology at Aston Business School, Aston University, Birmingham, United Kingdom up until his untimely death in November 2008. He received his Ph.D. in social psychology from the University of Mannheim, Germany. His research focused on job attitudes, social identity, and self-esteem and appeared in outlets including *Journal of Applied Psychology, Journal of Vocational Behavior, Journal of Organizational Behavior,* and *European Journal of Social Psychology.*

Denise M. Rousseau is the H. J. Heinz II professor of organizational behavior and public policy at Carnegie Mellon University's H. John Heinz II School of Public Policy and Management and the Tepper School of Business. She was the 2004–2005 president of the Academy of Management. Rousseau received her A.B., M.A., and Ph.D. from the University of California at Berkeley with degrees in psychology and anthropology. Her research focuses upon the impact workers have on the employment relationship and the firms that employ them. It informs critical concerns such as worker well-being and career development, organizational effectiveness, the management of change, firm ownership and governance, and industrial relations.

Lynn M. Shore is a professor of management at San Diego State University. She was previously on the faculty at University of California, Irvine, and Georgia State University. Her primary research areas are on the employment relationship and workforce diversity. Her research on the employment relationship focuses on the influence of social and organizational processes on the employee-organization relationship, and effects of this relationship on employee attitudes and behavior. Dr. Shore's work on diversity has examined the impact that composition of the work group and employee/supervisor dyads has on the attitudes and performance of work groups and individual employees. She has published numerous articles in such journals as *Academy of Management Journal, Academy of Management Review, Journal of Applied Psychology, Journal of Organizational Behavior,* and *Personnel Psychology.* Dr. Shore was an associate editor for the *Journal of Applied Psychology* from 2003 to 2008.

Laura J. Stanley is a doctoral candidate in organizational behavior at the Terry College of Business at the University of Georgia. She earned her B.S. in business administration in 1996 and Master of Accounting in 1997, both from the University of North Carolina at Chapel Hill. She earned a Master of Education in human resource and organizational development from the University of Georgia in 2005. Her research interests include organizational commitment, identification, and emotions.

Rolf Van Dick is a professor of social psychology at the Goethe-University Frankfurt (Germany) and currently serves as associate dean of the Institute of Psychology. Prior to his current position he was professor of social psychology and organizational behavior at Aston Business School Birmingham (UK). He received his Ph.D. in social psychology from Philipps-University Marburg (Germany). His research interests center on the application of social identity theory in organizational settings. In particular, he is interested in identity processes in teams and organizations which are highly diverse, he is applying identity research in the area of mergers and acquisitions, and is currently investigating leadership and identity in the field and the laboratory. Rolf served as associate editor of the *European Journal of Work & Organizational Psychology* and is editor-in-chief of the *British Journal of Management.* He has published and edited seven books, more than 20 book chapters, and more than 60 papers in academic journals published in outlets including the *Academy of Management Journal, Journal of Applied Psychology, Journal of Marketing, Journal of Organizational Behavior, Journal of Vocational Behavior,* and *Journal of Personality and Social Psychology.*

Robert J. Vandenberg is a professor of management in the Terry College of Business at the University of Georgia. He teaches in the undergraduate,

M.B.A., and Ph.D. programs, including courses in organizational behavior, leadership, change management, research methods, and structural equation modeling. Articles from his substantive and methodological research streams have appeared in the *Journal of Applied Psychology, Journal of Management, Journal of Organizational Behavior, Human Resource Management, Organization Sciences, Group and Organization Management, Organizational Behavior and Human Decision Processes,* and *Organizational Research Methods.* His article coauthored with Charles Lance on measurement invariance received the 2005 Robert McDonald Award for the best published article to advance research methods given by the Research Methods Division of the Academy of Management. He has served on the editorial boards of the *Journal of Applied Psychology, Journal of Management, Organizational Behavior and Human Decision Processes,* and *Organizational Research Methods.* Bob is currently editor-in-chief of *Organizational Research Methods.* He is past division chair of the Research Methods Division. In addition, he is a fellow of the Society for Industrial and Organizational Psychology, the American Psychological Association, the Southern Management Association, and the Center for the Advancement of Research Methods and Analysis at Virginia Commonwealth University, at which he conducts annual methods workshops. Finally, and vastly more important, he is married to Carole; has three children, Drew, Kaity, and Jackson; and rides his Harley with a passion every day.

Christian Vandenberghe is a professor of organizational behavior at HEC Montreal. He is the holder of a Canada Research Chair in the management of employee commitment and performance. His research interests include multiple commitments in the workplace, perceived support and organizational justice, leadership, and employee motivation and well-being. His work has appeared in such journals as *Journal of Applied Psychology, Journal of Organizational Behavior, Journal of Vocational Behavior,* and *Group and Organization Management.* He is currently division editor of the Organizational Behavior and Human Resource Management Division at the *Canadian Journal of Administrative Sciences.*

S. Arzu Wasti is an associate professor of management and organization studies at the Faculty of Management, Sabanci University, Turkey. She received her Ph.D. in industrial relations and human resource management from University of Illinois at Urbana-Champaign. Her cross-cultural research on organizational commitment, sexual harassment, organizational trust, and organizational culture has appeared in such journals as *Journal of Applied Psychology, Journal of Management, Journal of Personality and Social Psychology, Journal of International Business Studies,* and *Leadership Quarterly.* She is a recipient of several research awards, including the International Academy of Intercultural Relations's *Best Dissertation Award,* the Academy of Management's *Lyman Porter and Carolyn Dexter Best Paper Awards*, and the Turkish Academy of Sciences' *Encouragement Award*.

Sandy J. Wayne is professor of management at the University of Illinois at Chicago and Director of the University of Illinois (Chicago and Urbana-Champaign campuses) Center for Human Resource Management. She received a Ph.D. in management from Texas A&M University. She has received a number of awards for her research, including the S. Rains Wallace Dissertation Award, the Yoder-Heneman Human Resource Management Research Award, and the Ulrich & Lake Award for Excellence in HRM Scholarship. She is a fellow of the Society for Industrial and Organizational Psychology. Her research focuses on relationships in the workplace including employee-supervisor relationships and employee-organization relationships, and the antecedents and consequences of these relationships for organizations and their members. Her articles have appeared in *Academy of Management Journal, Journal of Applied Psychology, Personnel Psychology, Organizational Behavior and Human Decision Processes, Journal of Management, Journal of Organizational Behavior, Leadership Quarterly*, and *Research in Personnel and Human Resources Management*.

Patrick M. Wright is the William J. Conaty GE professor of strategic human resources and director of the Center for Advanced Human Resource Studies in the School of Industrial and Labor Relations, Cornell University. He holds a B.A. in psychology from Wheaton College and an M.B.A. and a Ph.D. in organizational behavior/human resource management from Michigan State University. Professor Wright teaches, conducts research, and consults in the area of strategic human resource management (SHRM), particularly focusing on how firms use people as a source of competitive advantage. Dr. Wright served as the chair of the HR Division of the Academy of Management, and has served on the Board of Directors for SHRM Foundation, World at Work, and Human Resource Planning Society. He was also inducted as a fellow in the National Academy of Human Resources.

Cindy Wu is assistant professor of management at the Hankamer School of Business at Baylor University. She received her Ph.D. from the University of Illinois at Urbana-Champaign. Her current research interests include leadership, employee motivation, cross-cultural studies, and strategic human resource management. Wu has published research papers in a number of prestigious academic journals, including *Journal of International Business Studies, Leadership Quarterly, Journal of Business Venturing, International Journal of Human Resource Management, Journal of Cross-Cultural Psychology*, and *Journal of Applied Behavioral Science*. She also serves on the editorial board of *Organizational Behavior and Human Decision Processes*.

Section 1

The Meaning and Relevance of Commitment

1

Conceptual Foundations: Construct Definitions and Theoretical Representations of Workplace Commitments

Howard J. Klein, Janice C. Molloy, and Joseph T. Cooper
Ohio State University

Commitment is one of the most frequently examined constructs in the study of organizational phenomena. This is likely due to commitment being a relatively convenient outcome to assess as well as the impact workplace commitments have been shown to have on individual-level outcomes important to organizations, such as absenteeism, turnover, motivation, performance, and prosocial behaviors (Cooper-Hakim & Viswesvaran, 2005; Mathieu & Zajac, 1990; Meyer & Allen, 1997; Meyer, Becker, & Vandenberghe, 2004; Mowday, 1998). Commitment is also frequently studied outside of the workplace in numerous other disciplines, suggesting that commitment is a fundamental concept for understanding human behavior.

Most dictionaries provide multiple definitions of commitment. The commitment literature provides even more variation with respect to the nature and meaning of commitment. Some of that variation is due to the changing nature of work and work relationships as discussed by Meyer in chapter 2. Most of the variation, however, is due to differences in perspective, with different authors approaching the study of commitment from different foundational literatures and/or with a focus on different phenomena relating to commitment (e.g., turnover, motivation, decision making, behavioral consistency). Consistent with Weick's (1989) depiction of the evolutionary stages in theory development, such variation is an important initial stage in construct development. However, continued variation and the absence of consensus on the definition of commitment leads to confusion surrounding the terminology, nature, and function of commitment. We feel the commitment literature has matured to a point where such variation creates more problems than benefits and suggest that it is time to move from variation to selection (i.e., consensus).

Chapter Overview

The primary purpose of this chapter is to provide the conceptual basis for this book so that other chapters need not provide extensive discussions of the history, nature, or theories of commitment. Central to that purpose, this chapter summarizes the different ways commitment has been conceptualized and defined in the literature. The focus of this chapter is the study of workplace commitments over the past half-century within the organizational behavior (OB) and industrial/organizational (I/O) psychology literatures. That focus is not limited to organizational commitment, although this is the dominant target covered, given that it has been the most widely researched, has the longest and richest history, and has often been borrowed from by those studying commitment to other targets. In terms of structure, the chapter begins by providing a brief history of the study of commitment. We then discuss the various definitions of commitment found in the literature and provide our assessment of those conceptualizations. A small set of theories representing the various perspectives found in the literature is then presented. As a whole, the chapter provides the necessary background so that other authors can evaluate the commitment literature in light of the available theories and conceptualizations outlined in this chapter.

Historical Perspective

Prior to 1960. It is not our intention to provide an exhaustive history of the study of commitment but rather to present a timeline to recognize the sequencing of oft-cited works and to highlight some of the shifts in focus that have occurred over the past half-century. The explicit study of commitment was largely absent from the workplace literatures prior to the early 1960s. Before then, the study of commitment was found primarily in the fields of psychology and sociology. There were exceptions; for example, Simon, Smithburg, and Thompson (1950) noted that commitment to the organization is distinct from commitment to that organization's specific values, policies, and goals. In the psychology and sociology literatures, even when notions of commitment were central to the research, the term *commitment* was not defined but instead, as H. S. Becker (1960) noted, "treated as a word requiring no such definition" (p. 32).

An example of the early work from this era is Whyte's (1956) classic book, which examined the loyalty of individuals who not only worked for an organization but also obtained a sense of social belongingness from the organization and subordinated their personal goals and desires to conform to the demands of the organization. In general, the interests of psychologists and sociologists at this time centered on how individuals could engage in collective action (e.g., strikes, negotiations) through commitment to social institutions (e.g., employers, unions, workgroups) to cope with power differentials between workers and management, enhance social welfare, and move between social classes (e.g., Commons, 1908; A. W. Gouldner, 1948; Roethlisberger & Dickson, 1939).

1960–early 1970s. From about 1960 forward, the commitment construct began to receive considerably more attention in the workplace literatures. One stream of research has viewed commitment as the propensity to engage in consistent lines of activity and exchanges. For example, H. S. Becker (1960), focusing on "loyalty" to employers, studied the mechanisms through which commitment to a course of action may occur. Specifically, Becker examined how side-bets and prior choices commit the individual to future actions that are consistent with those prior choices. Kiesler (1971; Kiesler & Sakamura, 1966) also studied commitment to future actions but took more of a psychological perspective based on the attitude and attitude change literatures. In this work, Kiesler defined "commitment as a pledging or binding of the individual to behavioral acts" (Kiesler & Sakamura, 1966, p. 349). Other examples from this time period include Grusky (1966), who examined how the rewards received and the difficulty experienced in attaining rewards influenced organizational attachment, and Greenwald (1965), who suggested that individuals who commit in writing to a particular stance are less likely to be persuaded from that stance.

The origins of other views of commitment also developed during this time and can be found in work that identified multiple bases of commitment. For example, H. P. Gouldner (1960) distinguished between cosmopolitan integration and organizational introjection. Etzioni (1961) developed a typology of involvement based upon the types of organizational control and use of power to manage employees (i.e., moral involvement with normative power, calculative involvement with remunerative power, and alienative involvement with coercive power). Kanter (1968) provided a similar typology, although it differed in several respects. First, unlike Etzioni, who viewed his bases of involvement as distinct, Kanter viewed her different bases of commitment as highly interrelated. Second, Kanter's typology was based on her study of social groups such as utopian communities and focused on how the behaviors that groups require of members influenced commitment and the survival of the social group (i.e., norms and control commitment, investments and continuance commitment, and renunciation of relationships with outsiders and cohesive commitment). Taken together, the work from this period provided important insights into the phenomena of commitment and established the foundation for studying both multiple bases of commitment and commitment from different perspectives (e.g., economic, social, behavioral, psychological).

Early 1970s–mid-1980s. Work born out of the behavioral, investment, and exchange views continued through the 1970s and beyond, as evidenced by extensions of H. S. Becker (1960) and Kiesler's (1971) work (e.g., Hrebiniak & Alutto, 1972; Salancik, 1977) and research on the escalation of commitment (e.g., Staw, 1981; Staw & Fox, 1977). More significantly, however, another perspective became prevalent during this period, an attitudinal view of commitment that would inform much of the subsequent research on commitment. The attitudinal perspective focuses on how individuals identify or relate to the commitment target. Examples of work in this area at this time include Porter, Steers, Mowday, and Boulian's (1974) study of commitment and turnover, Buchanan's (1974) suggested components of commitment (identification, involvement, loyalty), and Steers's (1977) test of a model of commitment antecedents and outcomes. It was also during this time frame that the Organizational Commitment Questionnaire (OCQ) was first published (Mowday, Steers, & Porter, 1979) and gained wide acceptance. Mowday, Porter, and Steers's (1982) book summarized the early work on this perspective. This time period essentially marked the emergence and wide acceptance of organizational commitment as an important outcome variable, a construct of importance to employees and organizations that managers could measure and attempt to influence.

Mid-1980s–2000. In the mid-1980s commitment researchers rediscovered and focused greater attention on understanding commitment to multiple targets (not just the employing organization) along with the multiple bases of commitment. For instance, the work of Morrow (1983), Reichers (1985), and T. E. Becker (1992) was foundational in the study of multiple commitment targets. In terms of bases of commitment, O'Reilly and Chatman (1986) offered a taxonomy reminiscent of earlier works by Etzioni (1961) and Kanter (1968). A considerable amount of research followed, examining commitment to targets other than the employing organization (e.g., Blau, 1985; Hollenbeck, Williams, & Klein, 1989), multiple commitment targets (e.g., Fukami & Larson, 1984; Zaccaro & Dobbins, 1989), multiple bases of commitment (e.g., Allen & Meyer, 1990; Dunham, Grube, & Castaneda, 1994), and both multiple commitment targets and bases (e.g., T. E. Becker & Billings, 1993; Clugston, Howell, & Dorfman, 2000). During this time, and consistent with the broader trend in psychology, greater attention was also given to the role of cognition in explaining the formation and influence of commitment (e.g., Hollenbeck & Klein, 1987; Wiener, 1982). Also in this period, Meyer and Allen (1991) introduced their typology of three commitment mindsets (affective, normative, and continuance) resulting from multiple bases of commitment, a typology that has risen to predominance in the study of workplace commitments, along with measures for assessing each mindset (Allen & Meyer, 1990). Consistent with Weick's (1989) model of theoretical evolution, this era was marked by considerable expansion and variation in the breadth of commitment-related concepts with numerous frameworks presented to try and make sense of the dizzying array of workplace commitments being studied.

Recent research. Most recently, research on workplace commitments has focused on construct clarification and integration. Examples of this include the integrative models presented by Meyer and Herscovitch (2001) and Klein, Brinsfield, and Molloy (2006). Efforts have also been directed toward better distinguishing and articulating the linkages between commitment and related constructs such as identification (e.g., Meyer, Becker, & Van Dick, 2006; Riketta, 2005) and motivation (e.g., Meyer et al., 2004). There have also been efforts to quantitatively summarize the growing commitment literature (e.g., Cooper-Hakim & Viswesvaran, 2005; Meyer, Stanley, Herscovitch, & Topolnytsky, 2002). Those studies documented both substantial convergences and important distinctions among the various bases and targets of commitment studied in the workplace literatures. A final trend evident in recent commitment research is the recognition of the multiple commitments present in today's work environment and attempts to understand the most relevant targets of commitment for different types of workers given the changes in the nature of work and work relationships (e.g., Liden, Wayne, Kraimer, & Sparrowe, 2003; McElroy, Morrow, & Laczniak, 2001). The sections that follow provide a more detailed discussion of the many conceptualizations of commitment that have been presented in the literature over the years as well as a summary of the primary theories put forth to explain and examine workplace commitments.

Definitions and Conceptualizations of the Commitment Construct

As noted, many definitions and conceptualizations of commitment have emerged over the past half-century. Based on our review of those conceptualizations, we identified eight distinct conceptualizations of commitment. Related to the issue of construct variation discussed at the beginning of this chapter, we have chosen a scheme for organizing those conceptualizations that reflects our assessment of the commitment construct and its boundaries. That is, rather than taking an inclusive approach (see, for example, Macey and Schneider's (2008) treatment of engagement) and describing commitment in a manner that encompasses all of the different ways people have defined and discussed commitment, we believe that the commitment literature is best served at this stage of its development by taking a construct refinement approach (i.e., moving from variation to selection). In evaluating these eight conceptualizations, we concluded that commitment has, in many cases, been described in a manner that is confounded with the antecedents or consequences of commitment. Therefore, we have organized our description of each of those eight conceptualizations using three categories: conceptualizations of commitment that we believe are not confounded, conceptualizations that we view as confounded by antecedents of commitment, and conceptualizations that we view as confounded by commitment outcomes.

Conceptualizations of Commitment That Are Not Confounded

Commitment as an attitude. Commitment is often referred to as an attitude (e.g., Solinger, Van Olffen, & Roe, 2008) and it is commonly presented as a work attitude in OB and I/O psychology textbooks. It is notable that although Mowday et al. (1982) did use the term *attitudinal commitment* in differentiating the psychological aspects of commitment from the economic (e.g., H. S. Becker, 1960) and behavioral (e.g., Salancik, 1977) views of commitment, they defined commitment as identification and involvement (as discussed below), not as an attitude per se. Examples of definitions of commitment as an attitude include Chusmir's (1982) depiction of job commitment as an "attitude or orientation toward the job" (p. 596), and Blau's (1985) definition of career commitment as "one's attitude toward one's profession or vocation" (p. 278). Depicting commitment in this manner results in an extremely vague conceptualization. Such definitions convey the category in which the construct is thought to belong (i.e., an attitude) but does not specifically describe the construct or sufficiently distinguish commitment from other work-related attitudes (e.g., satisfaction).

Defining commitment as an attitude is also problematic because, as noted by Allen and Meyer (1990) and others, commitment does not fit the current depiction of attitudes in the psychology literature. The tripartite (affect-behavior-cognition) view of attitudes (e.g., Breckler, 1984) has been supplanted in the psychology literature by the view of attitudes as *summary evaluations* (Ajzen & Fishbein, 2000; Eagly & Chaiken, 1998; Petty, Wegener, & Fabrigar, 1997). Specifically, as noted by Ajzen (2001), "There is general agreement that an attitude represents a summary evaluation of the psychological object captured in such attribute dimensions as good-bad, harmful-beneficial, pleasant-unpleasant, and likable-dislikable" (p. 28). As such, the currently used definition of attitudes (i.e., summary evaluations) does not, in our opinion, appropriately describe the construct of commitment. Being committed to a target is distinct from the summary judgment of how favorable (or unfavorable) one views that target. Indeed, one need not have a favorable view of a target to be committed to that target.

Commitment as a force. The literature also contains depictions of commitment as a binding force. These conceptualizations of commitment hold that the antecedents of commitment create pressure, experienced as mindsets, binding the individual to the target (e.g., Meyer & Allen, 1991; Meyer & Herscovitch, 2001). Scholl (1981), for example, in differentiating commitment from motivation, defined commitment as a force that maintains behavioral direction. Brown (1996) defined commitment as an "obliging force," and Meyer and Herscovitch (2001) defined commitment as "a force that binds an individual to a course of action of relevance to one or more targets" (p. 301). In the following chapter, Meyer refines this definition by clarifying that this force is internal, residing within the individual. Our concerns with conceptualizing commitment as a force are discussed later in this section.

Commitment as a bond. In contrast to viewing commitment as a force that creates a bond, depictions of commitment as a bond also permeate the literature. Central to this view is the position that commitment is a psychological state reflecting how strongly one is bound (or psychologically attached) to the commitment target. Buchanan (1974), for example, defined commitment as attachment to the organization for its own sake, above and beyond any instrumental (i.e., economic) value the organization may provide. O'Reilly and Chatman (1986) defined organizational commitment as one's "psychological attachment to an organization—the psychological bond linking the individual and the organization" (p. 492). Other scholars portraying commitment as a bond or attachment include Mathieu and Zajac (1990) and T. E. Becker, Billings, Eveleth, and Gilbert (1996). Commitment to other targets has similarly been defined in terms of a bond or attachment, including career (Darden, Hampton, & Howell, 1989), union (Sjoberg & Sverke, 2001), organizational units (Mueller & Lawler, 1999), job (Rusbult & Farrell, 1983), team (Pearce & Herbik, 2004), goal (Locke, Latham, & Erez, 1988), and change initiatives or specific programs (Neubert & Cady, 2001).

A distinction can be made between conceptualizations of commitment as a *bond in general* and conceptualizations of commitment as a *particular type of bond*. Some authors (e.g., T. E. Becker et al., 1996; Klein et al., 2006) have defined commitment simply as a perceived bond or psychological attachment to the target. When defined in this manner, commitment does

not need to be intentional or even consciously recognized, as perception is often automatic (Bargh & Chartrand, 1999). Also, because broadly
defining commitment as a bond or attachment does not differentiate
commitment in terms of how individuals experience or make sense of
that perceived bond, secondary concepts such as bases (e.g., O'Reilly &
Chatman, 1986), mindsets (e.g., Meyer & Allen, 1991), or rationales (Klein
et al., 2006) are required to account for those differences. In contrast, commitment has also been more narrowly defined as a particular type of
bond. Scholars taking this view (e.g., Brown, 1996; Kiesler & Sakamura,
1966; Lee, Carswell, & Allen, 2000) tend to define commitment as an intentional, conscious choice to accept or take responsibility for one's bond to
the target and to actively dedicate or pledge oneself to that target. From
this perspective, there are different types of perceived bonds, and not all
are commitment. As such, multiple accompanying mindsets or rationales
may not be needed as, depending upon how the bond is defined, not all
attachments would be viewed as commitment. Identification, for example,
is an attachment characterized by the psychological merging of the self
with the target. Similarly, it has been argued that attachments reflecting
compliance or alienative bases or a continuance mindset should be considered distinct from commitment (see chapter 13 for more on this issue).

Force versus bond. Although subtle, there are important differences
between conceptualizing commitment as a force versus as the perceived
bond resulting from that force. Commitment as a force holds that commitment antecedents or bases create an intangible "pressure," experienced
as mindsets, binding the individual to the target (e.g., Meyer & Allen,
1991; Meyer & Herscovitch, 2001). From a psychological perspective, we
believe that perceptions are more discernible than forces or "intangible
pressures" and that defining commitment as a perceived bond better recognizes the role of social cognition and the considerable variance known
to exist in how different people can perceive the "same" situation (e.g.,
Weick, 1995). In addition, although conceptualizing commitment as a
force does not necessarily confound commitment with its antecedents and
consequences, it does, in our opinion, blur the boundaries. For example,
portraying commitment as a force makes it difficult to distinguish the
"commitment force" from other forces operating on one's emotions, cognitions, and behavior such as motivation, which is further discussed below.
Moreover, viewing commitment as a force that creates a bond suggests
that the resulting bond is more proximal to commitment outcomes and a
key mediator, yet theory and research taking this view does not address
what that resulting bond is or its role in the commitment process. It is thus
our conclusion that, of the three conceptualizations of commitment that
we evaluated here as not confounded, commitment is best conceptualized
as a bond.

Conceptualizations of Commitment Confounded by Antecedents

Conceptualizations of commitment that we believe should be viewed as determinants of commitment include commitment as exchanges and/or investments, identification, and goal and/or value congruence. In all three cases, it is our opinion that defining commitment in these terms confounds the commitment construct with factors that lead to commitment.

Commitment as investments/exchange. Workplace commitments have long been conceptualized within the context of either investments (e.g., H. S. Becker, 1960) or exchanges (e.g., Barnard, 1938). The nature of the investment or exchange can be economic, behavioral, social, or a combination thereof. The main difference between investments and exchanges is that in the case of exchange, the individual is expecting or has already received something of value from the commitment target, with commitment resulting from an obligation to reciprocate and/or the desire to retain that thing of value. In the case of investments, there is no obligation to reciprocate but there is the expectation of some future valued outcome that will be lost or diminished if the behavior or relationship is not continued. Although views of commitment as investments or exchanges are common in the literature, such depictions are problematic in that both investments and exchanges are antecedents of commitment. That is, the accrual of investments and exchanges lead to commitment but is not, in our opinion, commitment itself.

Distinctions are sometimes drawn between the behavioral and economic views of commitment, but we view both as forms of investment. Commitment as an investment was first depicted by H. S. Becker (1960), who suggested that "commitments come into being when a person, by making a side-bet, links extraneous interests with a consistent line of activity" (p. 32). Side-bets occur when individuals involved in a specific course of action stake some other valued aspect of their lives upon that course of action continuing, for example, someone purchasing a home close to a new job. If that employment ended, the perceived value of that new home to its owner (i.e., the extraneous interest linked to the course of action) would be lost or reduced. The desire to avoid such potential loss creates what Becker termed "commitment by default" (p. 38). Side-bets represent an accrual process during which previous actions and rewards become intertwined such that the individual loses degrees of freedom in possible future behaviors. Under certain conditions, past actions make it difficult for one to disengage from a line of activity or reverse one's decisions (Kiesler, 1971). According to Salancik (1977), for example, one's commitment is influenced by the extent to which the behavior is perceived to be explicit, revocable, volitional, and visible. Bielby (1992) provides another example of commitment viewed primarily in terms of invested behaviors. Similarly, Hrebiniak and Alutto (1972) viewed commitment as "a structural phenomenon which occurs as a result of individual-organizational transactions and alterations in side-bets or investments over time" (p. 271).

Related to Becker's notion of side-bets is the sunk-costs phenomenon studied in commitment to decisions (e.g., Staw, 1981). Here, decision makers have invested resources toward some desired goal, and despite negative feedback about progress and increasing uncertainty about the likelihood of achieving that goal, they maintain or escalate their commitment (i.e., "invest more") rather than "cut their losses" (e.g., Staw, 1981; Brockner, 1992). In this context, commitment is the "continued investment in a failing course of action or a non-promising exchange" (Staw, 1981, p. 580). One difference worth noting between the conceptualizations of H. S. Becker (1960) and Staw (1981) is that Becker focused on the "awareness" of the costs of discontinuing an action, whereas Staw focused on processes that can occur subconsciously. Other conceptualizations of commitment based at least in part on an individual's interest in protecting investments include Etzioni's (1961) calculative involvement, Kanter's (1968) continuance commitment, O'Reilly and Chatman's (1986) compliance dimension, and Rusbult and Farrell's (1983) investment model.

Exchanges can be viewed as investments with returns that are expected or have already been received. The work of Angle and Perry (1981) is a good example of a study including social as well as economic aspects of exchange. Angle and Perry (1981) define commitment as "one's reciprocation for the organization satisfying important past, present, and future needs, including intangible social needs (e.g., work relationships, pride from membership)" (p. 291). In support of this position, Gaertner and Nollen (1989) found that more favorable perceptions of organizational employment practices were associated with stronger organizational commitment. In essence, research showing positive organizational support as an antecedent of organizational commitment (e.g., Eisenberger, Fasolo, & Davis-LaMastro, 1990; Yoon & Thye, 2002) is consistent with commitment reflecting a social exchange. The mechanisms through which investments/ exchange lead to commitment can thus operate at either the conscious or subconscious level and take several forms including cognitive (e.g., conscious analysis of the costs/benefits of alternatives), social (e.g., wanting to appear consistent, not wanting to admit a mistake, obligation to reciprocate), or psychological (e.g., cognitive dissonance, wanting to be internally consistent) processes; but the commonality is that something of value that has been received, promised, or accrued through one's engagement with a target would be lost or diminished if one withdrew from the target. To reiterate, however, it is our opinion that those received, promised, or accrued benefits (i.e., what has been invested, received, or exchanged) are antecedents to commitment and not commitment itself.

Commitment as identification. Another common conceptualization defines commitment in terms of identification or internalization. This view was popularized by Porter et al. (1974) and Mowday et al. (1982), who in part defined organizational commitment as the strength of an individual's identification with a particular organization. They were not the first to do so, however, as Sheldon (1971), for example, defined commitment as an attitude toward the organization that links or attaches the identity of the person to the organization. Others have since offered variations of this view. Bielby (1992), for example, defined commitment as "an attachment that is initiated and sustained by the extent to which an individual's identification with a role, behavior, value, or institution is considered to be central among alternatives as a source of identity" (p. 284). Mowday et al.'s (1982) definition of commitment as identification has been widely adopted in defining commitment relative to other targets, including professional commitment (e.g., Aranya, Pollock, & Amernic, 1981), career commitment (e.g., Colarelli & Bishop, 1990), workgroup commitment (e.g., Bishop & Scott, 2000), union commitment (e.g., Fukami & Larson, 1984), and external organizational commitment (e.g., McElroy et al., 2001). Similarly, Reichers (1985), in discussing multiple targets, defined commitment as "a process of identification with the goals of an organization's multiple constituencies" (p. 465).

The concern with defining commitment as identification is that identification has come to be viewed as a separate and distinct construct (Van Dick, Becker, & Meyer, 2006). Although commitment and identification are both aspects of attachment (Meyer et al., 2006) and are often highly related (Riketta, 2005), identification is both deficient and contaminated as a construct definition of commitment. That is, there are unique aspects of commitment not captured by identification and characteristics of identification that are not part of commitment. For example, although identification (like commitment) has been defined in various ways, central to identification is the "forming of oneness" with the target, or the notion that the target becomes part of the individual's self-concept or image (Mael & Tetrick, 1992; Riketta, 2005; Van Dick, Wagner, Stellmacher, & Christ, 2004). Others have further detailed the conceptual differences and the need to better differentiate these two constructs (see Mael & Ashforth, 1992; Meyer et al., 2006; Van Dick et al., 2004; Van Knippenberg & Van Schie, 2000). Interested readers are directed to a special 2006 issue of *Journal of Organizational Behavior* devoted entirely to this topic (Van Dick et al., 2006). In sum, there is both conceptual and empirical evidence supporting the distinctiveness of the two constructs (Riketta, 2005) and suggesting that social identities are antecedents to commitment rather than commitment itself (Meyer et al., 2006).

Commitment as congruence. Commitment is also sometimes conceptualized in terms of the congruence between the goals and/or values of the individual and the commitment target. An early example of this view is the moral-involvement dimension from Etzioni's (1961) typology, which was defined in part as the internalization of organizational goals and values. Porter et al. (1974) and Mowday et al. (1982), while defining commitment as identification, stated that organizational commitment is characterized in part by the belief in and acceptance of organizational goals and values. Another example is O'Reilly and Chatman's (1986) internalization dimension of organizational commitment, which "occurs when influence is accepted because the induced attitudes and behaviors are congruent with one's own values; that is, the values of the individual and the group or organization are the same" (p. 493). It is worth noting that in these examples, congruence is a part of what creates and/or characterizes commitment but does not completely define commitment. Like other commitment conceptualizations, congruence conceptualizations are not limited to organizational commitment. Professional commitment, for example, has been equated with the importance an individual places on professional values (Jauch, Glueck, & Osborn, 1978), and union commitment has been viewed as congruence with the goals of organized labor (e.g., Gordon, Philpot, Burt, Thompson, & Spiller, 1980).

As with identification discussed above, we believe that congruence is more appropriately viewed as an antecedent of commitment rather than as commitment itself. This conclusion is based on two arguments. First, congruence implies a fit between the goals, values, or other characteristics of the individual and the characteristics of the commitment target. Thus, congruence is a function of a particular configuration of what are typically considered antecedents of commitment — individual and target characteristics. This merging of antecedents and commitment is evidenced in O'Reilly and Chatman's (1986) depiction of congruence, compliance, and identification as both bases for commitment and as "separate dimensions of commitment" (p. 493). That is, the three dimensions are at once said to be commitment—and also processes for becoming committed. In our opinion, this definitional overlap confounds commitment with its antecedents. In addition, it is possible to be committed to a target without having congruent values or goals. Although congruence can facilitate commitment, it is not a necessary condition for commitment. Therefore, value and/or goal congruence between the individual and the commitment target is best depicted as an antecedent of commitment rather than as commitment itself.

Conceptualizations of Commitment Confounded by Outcomes

Conceptualizations of commitment that in our opinion should be viewed as consequences of commitment include motivation and continuance. In both of these cases, we believe that defining commitment in these terms confounds commitment with outcomes that commitment should predict.

Commitment as motivation. Motivation is typically defined as a set of internal and external forces that initiate behavior and determine its form, direction, intensity, and duration (Pinder, 1998). Because commitment is also sometimes defined as a force (e.g., Meyer & Herscovitch, 2001; Brown, 1996), as noted previously, the demarcation between commitment and motivation is sometimes unclear. One example of a conceptualization of commitment as motivation is the framework provided by Wiener (1982). Wiener portrayed commitment as a motivational phenomenon and used Fishbein's behavioral-intentions model (Fishbein & Ajzen, 1975) to contrast attitudinal commitment (viewed as internalized normative beliefs) with side-bets (viewed as instrumental beliefs). More recently, Meyer et al. (2004) proposed a model that presents motivation and commitment as related yet distinguishable concepts, with commitment being one of several energizing forces that constitute motivation. Indeed, numerous authors have implicitly or explicitly defined commitment in motivational terms. For example, career commitment has been defined as one's motivation to work in a chosen vocation (e.g., Carson & Bedian, 1994; Colarelli & Bishop, 1990) and as "the strength of one's motivation to work in a chosen career role" (Hall, 1971, p. 59). Similarly, team commitment has been defined as one's willingness to exert effort on behalf of the team (Bishop & Scott, 2000); commitment to strategy defined as the "willingness of the person to put forth effort to enact the strategy" (Weissbein, Plamondon, & Ford, 1999, p. 381); and commitment to change effort goals defined as the consistent, persistent pursuit of the change goal, the rejection of courses of action not consistent with that goal, and a willingness to expend resources in pursuit of the goal (Conner & Patterson, 1982).

It is our conclusion that motivation is an outcome of commitment and not commitment itself. A number of definitions of commitment have been offered thus far in this chapter, and few if any are redundant with commonly accepted definitions of motivation such as Pinder's (1998), provided above. If commitment is a part of motivation, not only should conceptual definitions exhibit greater overlap, but the two constructs should also demonstrate a high degree of covariation. There clearly are interrelationships between commitment and motivation, but one can be highly committed and minimally motivated. Stated differently, high commitment often results, but does not necessarily result, in the increased willingness to exert effort in support of the commitment target and persistence in maintaining that effort over time (i.e., motivation). For example, one can be highly committed to writing a book chapter yet not be highly motivated to actually sit down and work on that chapter. Moreover, there are important differences among the primary antecedents and consequences of commitment and motivation, further supporting the distinctiveness of the constructs. In sum, defining commitment as motivation merges commitment with one of its outcomes and confounds attempts to examine the relationships between the two constructs.

Commitment as continuance. Finally, commitment has often been defined in terms of continuance—the desire or intention to continue, or an unwillingness to withdraw from the target. Note that this grouping of conceptualizations is not referring to Allen and Meyer's (1990) continuance mindset.[1] The emphasis on continuance extends back to early efforts to understand the relationship between job attitudes and turnover (e.g., Brayfield & Crockett, 1955; Herzberg, Mausner, & Peterson, 1957; Porter & Steers, 1973). Mowday et al. (1982), for example, characterized commitment as including "a strong desire to maintain membership in the organization" (p. 27). Researchers studying other targets have similarly defined commitment along these lines, including commitment to jobs (Rusbult & Farrell, 1983), commitment to decisions (Staw & Ross, 1978), commitment to goals (Campion & Lord, 1982), and commitment to teams (Bishop & Scott, 2000).

However, like motivation discussed above, commitment and the unwillingness to withdraw from a target are distinct phenomena. Using Meyer and Allen's (1991) typology, different mindsets tend to be differentially related to withdrawal behaviors (turnover, absenteeism, tardiness) (Cooper-Hakim & Viswesvaran, 2005; Mathieu & Zajac, 1990; Meyer et al., 2002). Common patterns of withdrawal would be expected for all commitment mindsets if commitment were not distinct from continuance. It is our conclusion that one's desire to continue with a target is an outcome of commitment and not an element of commitment itself. Indeed, empirical research frequently uses commitment to predict whether or not individuals will continue a course of action. Similarly, a major criticism of the OCQ is that some items assess the desire to stay (e.g., Bozeman & Perrewe, 2001). The inclusion of either the desire or intentions to continue within the commitment construct (or within measures of commitment) confounds commitment with one of its primary outcomes. Desire and intentions are both important for understanding the linkages between commitment and behavior, but they are distinct both from each other (one can desire an outcome and yet have no intention to strive for that outcome) and from commitment. Persistence, loyalty, dedication, and unwillingness to withdraw from or abandon the target are all indicators of commitment, but such indicators are not commitment itself.

Summary

In this section we have summarized eight alternative conceptualizations of commitment found in the literature. We recognize that our categories result in some overlap. For example, there are some overlaps among the conceptualizations of commitment as an attitude, identification, and congruence, as identification and congruence are sometimes viewed as part of the basis for the attitudinal view of commitment. These overlaps can be traced in part to the fact that many early and influential descriptions of commitment defined the construct in multiple ways (e.g., Etzioni, 1961; Kanter, 1968; Mowday et al., 1982; O'Reilly & Chatman, 1986). Although such overlaps among our categories are regrettable, in our opinion there is not a more meaningful classification offering less conceptual overlap. In addition to describing the different ways in which commitment has been defined, we have also distinguished among those depictions that, from our perspective, in light of the accumulated evidence, are best viewed as either antecedents or consequences of commitment and not part of commitment itself. Of the conceptualizations not contaminated by antecedents or consequences, conceptualizing commitment as a bond is most viable in our opinion as it most clearly differentiates commitment from its antecedents, consequences, and related but distinct constructs (Klein et al., 2006).

Theoretical Perspectives

The previous section presented the various ways commitment has been conceptualized within the workplace literatures without detailing specific models or theories of commitment. Space does not permit a comprehensive review of all of the theories and models of commitment presented in the literature, but in this section we present a small set of theories to represent the various perspectives that have been used to understand workplace commitments. Specifically, we provide exemplar models representing the investment/exchange (Staw, 1981), attitudinal (Gordon et al., 1980), and cognitive (Hollenbeck & Klein, 1987) views. The cognitive view, not explicitly addressed previously, focuses on a rational, calculative approach, regardless of conceptualization, though it is most closely associated with conceptualizations of commitment as motivation. In addition, several integrative models (e.g., Klein et al., 2006; Meyer & Herscovitch, 2001; Reichers, 1985) are presented.

Investment/Exchange View

As noted previously, scholars examining commitment as investments or exchanges have focused on economic, behavioral, and social factors. In terms of exchange, many scholars have recognized that employment relationships are fundamentally economic and social exchanges between an employee and employer (e.g., Rousseau, 1997) and that throughout the course of employment individuals make psychological, social, behavioral, and financial investments in workplace targets. Exchange theory is relevant to workplace commitments based on the logic that employees offer commitment in return for the receipt (or anticipated receipt) of rewards from the organization or work context (Oliver, 1990). Investments need not involve any reciprocal benefit but are similar in that something of value would be lost or diminished if the behavior or relationship is not continued. Theories based on behavioral or economic views of investment/ exchange emanate from H. S. Becker's (1960) research on side-bets and subsequent work by Kiesler (1971; Kiesler & Sakamura, 1966). Staw's (1981) model of escalation of commitment is discussed below as an example of the investment/exchange view. Although this model is typically applied to the study of overcommitment to decisions or courses of action, it can be applied to other targets. Other models of investment/exchange include Salancik (1977), Angle and Perry (1981), Brockner and Rubin (1985), and Bielby (1992).

Staw's (1981) model, illustrated in Figure 1.1, views commitment, particularly the escalation of commitment to a course of action, as a complex, multistage process involving both psychological and economic factors. This model embraces the fallibility of decision makers and the complexity of decision making by highlighting three factors that influence commitment: prospective rationality, modeling, and retrospective rationality. In this model, commitment decisions are not isolated choices, but rather decisions influenced by past as well as anticipated future events. Thus, commitment decisions are not based solely on an interest in attaining future outcomes (as economic theory might suggest) but also on justifying past outcomes and decisions. Economic determinants of commitment, namely the probability and value of future outcomes, influence the prospective rationality of decisions to continue investing in a course of action. Staw's primary interest was not, however, the economic justification and net-present value of decisions, but rather the contextual antecedents and noneconomic factors (e.g., ego protection) that influence commitment to a course of action.

As depicted in Figure 1.1, the antecedents of a decision maker's need to justify previous decisions lie in the extent to which there are negative consequences of previous choices—and how responsibility for such consequences is perceived by others. In this model, the combination of consequences of the decision, perceived responsibility for the outcome, and decision maker's psycho-social needs influence one's motivation to justify previous investments in the course of action. Psycho-social needs, specifically, one's need to protect self-esteem and maintain perceptions of one's competence (to oneself and others), result in retrospective rationality—the

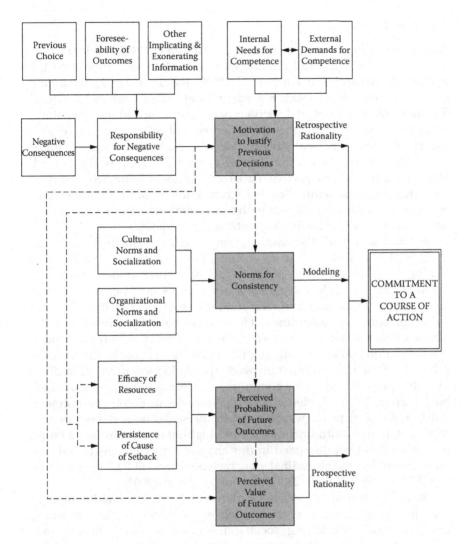

FIGURE 1.1
Staw's (1981) model of escalation of commitment. *Note.* From "The Escalation of Commitment to a Course of Action," by B. M. Staw, 1981, *Academy of Management Review, 6*(4), p. 582. Copyright 1981 by the Copyright Clearance Center. Reprinted with permission.

post hoc rationalizations of previous investments. The final factor Staw (1981) identified as influencing commitment is organizational or societal norms for behavior, as individuals would be influenced by, and likely "model," commonly held expectations of the "right" or best course of action in specific situations.

Attitudinal View

With its roots in the early work of A. W. Gouldner (1957), Etzioni (1961), and Kanter (1968), the attitudinal approach is often associated with the work of Buchanan (1974), Porter et al. (1974), and Steers (1977). For a time there was considerable debate regarding the attitudinal versus behavioral (i.e., investment/exchange) depictions of commitment and the compatibility of these views. Although some differences of opinion remain regarding which is more predominant (e.g., Mowday et al., 1982, versus Salancik, 1977), there is consensus that the two views are reciprocally related. Depending on the perspective, either commitment influences behavior with that behavior reinforcing one's commitment (attitudinal view), or behavior results in commitment with that commitment leading to the continuation of the behavior (investment/exchange view).

As noted above in discussing different conceptualizations, commitment is often referred to as an attitude, yet such definitions are often lacking in specificity, which carries over to attitudinal models of commitment. In these models, categories of antecedents (e.g., personal characteristics, structural characteristics, and experiences) are identified, as are valued outcomes of commitment. However, as noted by Oliver (1990), the nature of commitment as well as "the mechanism by which the 'inputs' affect commitment are usually implicit rather than explicit, although the principle of exchange is often invoked" (p. 20). Indeed, in the attitudinal view, the process underlying commitment is left as somewhat of a "black box" (Oliver, 1990). Gordon et al.'s (1980) model of union commitment, illustrated in Figure 1.2, was selected for presentation here because it is representative of attitudinal models and highlights a commitment target (i.e., unions) not yet discussed in this chapter. Other models of commitment that reflect the attitudinal view include Steers (1977), Mowday et al. (1982), Blau (1985), Cohen (2007), and Solinger et al. (2008).

Like many attitudinal models, Gordon et al. (1980) identified individual (e.g., demographic, work experience), job (e.g., satisfaction, characteristics), and contextual variables (e.g., social influences) thought to influence commitment to a target. In this particular model, the target is the union, and demographic factors include education, age, father's occupation, sex, race, and tenure. Other individual factors include job grade and tenure with the employer. The socialization category recognizes the impact of both early and recent socialization relative to unions and includes socialization relating to unions both inside and outside of work. The final category of antecedents, which reflects experiences, captures both past and present union affiliation and participation. Together, these antecedents predict one's union commitment (attitude toward unionism), and commitment, in turn, predicts behavioral intentions and behaviors. In the case of union commitment, the outcomes specified by Gordon et al. (1980) are indicators

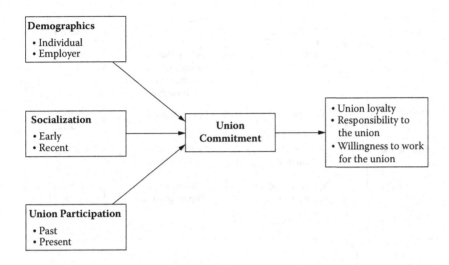

FIGURE 1.2
Gordon, Philpot, Burt, Thompson, and Spiller's (1980) model of union commitment. *Note.*
Figure based on depiction provided in "Commitment to the Union: Development of a
Measure and an Examination of Its Correlates," by M. E. Gordon, J. W. Philpot, R. E. Burt,
C. A. Thompson, and W. E. Spiller, 1980, *Journal of Applied Psychology, 65*(4), pp. 479–499.

of commitment and include one's union loyalty, responsibility to the
union, and willingness to work for the union.

Cognitive View

Cognitive views of commitment are focused on the conscious, rational
determination of commitment to targets through one's perception, intu-
ition, reasoning, and acquisition of information. Such views emphasize
a calculative and nonaffective approach to explaining commitment (e.g.,
Crosby & Taylor, 1983), although the nonaffective descriptor is not entirely
accurate. Hollenbeck and Klein's (1987) model of goal commitment is
discussed below as one example of the cognitive view. Katz (1992) provides another example of a cognitive model. It should be recognized that
there is some overlap in our categorization as some models best viewed
as investment/exchange conceptualizations, and discussed previously in
that category, are highly rational and calculative in nature and thus also
could be argued to fit our description of cognitive views.

The Hollenbeck and Klein (1987) model, presented in Figure 1.3, combined antecedents of commitment identified in the goal-setting literature
with antecedents identified in the organizational commitment literature
and interpreted those antecedents through an expectancy theory (e.g.,
Vroom, 1964) framework. Hollenbeck and Klein further explicated sets of

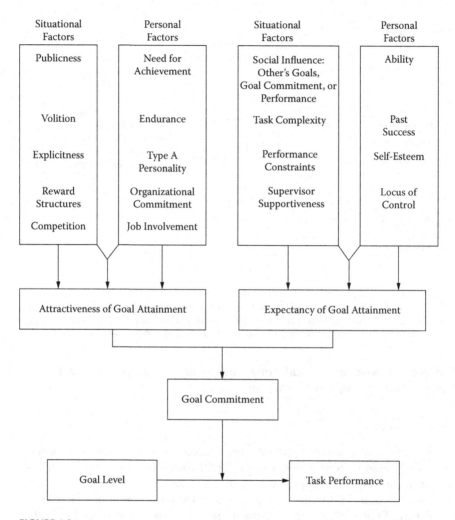

FIGURE 1.3
Hollenbeck and Klein's (1987) model of goal commitment. *Note.* From "Goal Commitment and the Goal-Setting Process: Problems Prospects, and Proposals for Future Research," by J. R. Hollenbeck and H. J. Klein, 1987, *Journal of Applied Psychology, 72*(2), p. 215. Copyright 1987 by the American Psychological Association. Reprinted with permission.

situational and personal factors thought to impact goal commitment and hypothesized not only main effects, but also person-situation interactions. Those personal and situational factors (and their interactions) were viewed as impacting either the attractiveness of goal attainment or the expectancy of goal attainment, and the attractiveness and expectancy of goal attainment constructs, in turn, were proposed to determine goal commitment. In this model, goal commitment is viewed as a motivational construct and defined as such (i.e., in terms of persistence). As noted above, our position is that motivation is more appropriately viewed as an outcome rather than as a component of commitment.

The primary role of goal commitment in the Hollenbeck and Klein model is to moderate the relationship between goal difficulty level and task performance. Klein, Wesson, Hollenbeck, and Alge (1999) subsequently documented the moderating role of goal commitment, demonstrating that goal commitment is necessary for a difficult goal to result in high task performance. That meta-analysis also confirmed that the attractiveness of goal attainment, expectancy of goal attainment, and motivational force (the product of expectancy and attractiveness) were all significantly related to goal commitment, as were several of the more distal individual and situational antecedents suggested by the Hollenbeck and Klein (1987) model. Supporting our arguments that commitment and motivation are distinct constructs, the Klein et al. (1999) meta-analysis reported average sample weighted correlations between commitment and the examined motivational constructs to range from .26 to .32, indicating that although significantly related, goal commitment is not redundant or interchangeable with attractiveness, expectancy, or motivational force. Although this may be surprising given that goal commitment is defined in motivational terms in this model, the self-report measures typically used to assess goal commitment (Klein et al., 2001) are closer to other commitment scales than measures of motivation.

Integrative Views

Multiple targets. It has long been recognized that individuals have multiple commitments to a variety of targets (e.g., policies, goals, individuals, teams, units) within a work organization (e.g., T. E. Becker, 1992; Simon et al., 1950). Further, individuals have commitments to targets (e.g., the family, professional organizations, political parties, and religious organizations) outside of work (Morrow, 1983; Randall, 1988; Reichers, 1985; Zaccaro & Dobbins, 1989). Research suggests that individuals can simultaneously commit to multiple targets and that such commitments need not be in conflict (Randall, 1988). There are limits on an individual's resources (e.g., time, attention), however, suggesting that even though the amount of commitment that an individual can have across targets need not be limited, conflict is likely to result when multiple commitments create incompatible demands (Ilgen & Hollenbeck, 1991). Reichers (1985) built upon and expanded prior work on commitments to multiple targets to develop the model of multiple organizational commitments presented in Figure 1.4. Examples of other multiple target models include Morrow (1983), Randall and Cote (1991), T. E. Becker (1992), Hunt and Morgan (1994), and Cohen

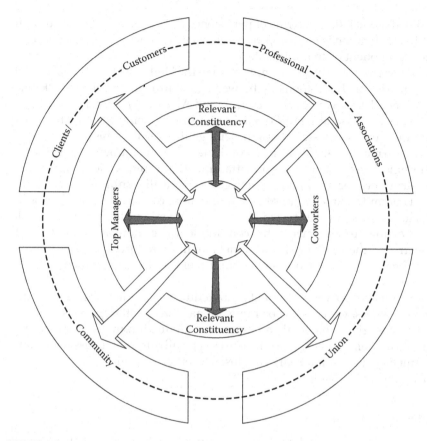

FIGURE 1.4
Reicher's (1985) model of organizational commitments. *Note.* From "A Review and Reconceptualization of Organizational Commitment," by A. E. Reichers, 1985, *Academy of Management Review, 10*(3), p. 472. Copyright 1985 by the Copyright Clearance Center. Reprinted with permission.

(2003). Some of these models, however, mix commitment targets with other constructs that are distinct from commitment (Klein et al., 2006).

Reichers' (1985) model clarified that the "organization" in organizational commitment is not an abstract, monolithic, depersonalized entity, but rather a composite of "coalitions and constituencies, each of which espouses a unique set of goals and values that may be in conflict with the goals and values of other organizational groups" (p. 470). Thus, organizational commitment can be understood as a "collection of multiple commitments to various groups" (p. 469). At the center of this collection (see Figure 1.4) is the individual, as Reichers asserted that commitment must be understood and evaluated from the standpoint of those who are committed. Surrounding the individual are top managers, coworkers, and other "relevant constituencies." These constituencies are connected to the individual with short arrows to reflect that such commitments are psychologically closer than constituents in the outer circle of Figure 1.4. The more distal constituents include professional associations, unions, community, and customers/clients. Encompassing this outer circle is a dotted line that represents the permeable boundary of the organization, as workplace commitments may be to both external and internal constituents.

Multiple bases. Whereas the Reichers (1985) model focused on multiple workplace commitment targets, others have focused on the multiple bases of commitment. Bases of commitment have long been viewed as multidimensional. Early examples include Etzioni's (1961) moral, calculative, and alienative bases of involvement and Kanter's (1968) continuance, cohesion, and control commitments. More recently, O'Reilly and Chatman (1986), drawing from Kelman's (1958) taxonomy of the bases of attitude change, proposed compliance, identification, and internalization bases of commitment. The typology that is currently most widely used is that provided by Meyer and Allen (1991). Empirical tests of such conceptualizations of commitment include Penley and Gould (1988), Bar-Hayim and Berman (1992), Jaros, Jermier, Koehler, and Sincich (1993), Dunham et al. (1994), and Clugston et al. (2000). The Meyer and Allen (1991) model was expanded by Meyer and Herscovitch (2001), whose model is provided in Figure 1.5 and is presented here as an example of a multiple bases model.

In Meyer and Herscovitch's (2001) model, three different bases of commitment are positioned around the perimeter (see Figure 1.5). These bases reflect different processes by which commitment can develop. Each basis is associated with a different mindset, a different way an individual may perceive their singular commitment (defined as a binding force). Specifically, the desire basis is associated with the affective commitment mindset, whereas perceived cost is associated with the continuance mindset, and felt obligation is associated with the normative mindset. The circle on the right side of the model represents the behavioral outcomes of commitment. Whereas Meyer and Allen's (1991) model focused on organizational commitment, the model presented by Meyer and Herscovitch (2001) is described as applicable to all targets. Meyer and Herscovitch (2001) also explicate the different types of behavior that can be expected given the different mindsets characterizing the commitment and given the bases involved in creating those mindsets.

Further integration. Lastly, we present another integrative model developed by Klein et al. (2006). This model was based on a thorough review of commitment targets studied within as well as outside of the workplace. The conclusion was that, regardless of target or context, the general nature and function of commitment is largely the same, with commitment having the same general outcomes and resulting from the same general categories of antecedent variables. The resulting model, presented in Figure 1.6, was

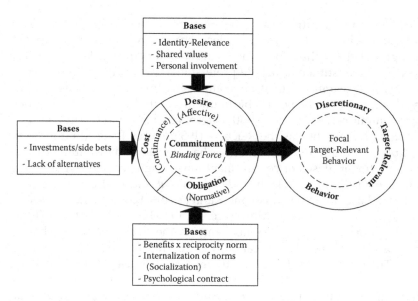

FIGURE 1.5
Meyer and Herscovitch's (2001) general model of workplace commitment. *Note.* From "Commitment in the Workplace Toward a General Model," by J. P. Meyer and L. Herscovitch, 2001, *Human Resource Management Review, 11*(3), p. 317. Copyright 2001 by Elsevier. Reprinted with permission.

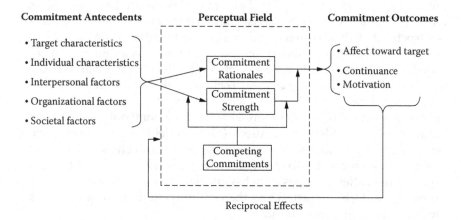

FIGURE 1.6
Klein, Brinsfield, and Molloy's (2006) heuristic model of workplace commitments.

aimed at bringing greater coherence to the study of commitment through construct clarification and a general, heuristic framework applicable to all workplace commitments. Klein et al. (2006) assert that much of the confusion in the literature stems from (a) definitions of commitment that are often confounded with the antecedents and consequences of commitment, as discussed earlier in this chapter, and (b) the failure to adequately distinguish between three distinct elements of commitment: target, strength, and rationales. The boxes in Figure 1.6 labeled commitment strength and commitment rationales (along with the specific target being considered) thus constitute commitment in this model. The target is not shown, as the model depicts one's commitment to a specific target and is applicable to any target. Klein et al. (2006) define commitment as a bond and specifically define commitment strength as the degree to which an individual perceives that they are bound to a specific target. In contrast, commitment rationales are the different possible self-explanations one may have for feeling bound to a given target. These distinctions recognize that how securely someone is attached (commitment strength), that to which someone is attached (the target), and why someone believes they are attached (commitment rationales) are three distinct elements of commitment that need to be defined and examined as such.

As noted above, commitment rationales reflect how an individual makes sense of their perceived bond and, as such, are somewhat analogous to attributions. Just as attributions may not reflect the "actual" causes of performance, commitment rationales may not reflect the actual bases or antecedents of commitment. Yet it is these rationales, not the actual causes of commitment, which determine the individual's reactions and responses. Commitment rationales have parallels to Allen and Meyer's (1990) mindsets in that both are psychological states, individuals can have multiple mindsets or multiple rationales for any given commitment, both can change over time, and both have important implications for commitment consequences (i.e., different rationales will lead to different cognitive, emotional, and motivational reactions). Yet rationales and mindsets differ in several important respects. First, mindsets are more closely and directly linked to the different bases and antecedents of commitment (e.g., Meyer & Herscovitch, 2001), whereas rationales reflect how people make sense of their commitment and may or may not reflect the actual causes of that perceived bond. Second, mindsets confound how individuals view their commitment with how strongly they are committed. Third, rationales more clearly convey that there is a singular commitment that can be viewed in multiple ways, whereas mindsets have been widely misinterpreted in the literature as being different dimensions, types, or forms of commitment. Finally, consistent with arguments made elsewhere in this chapter, rationales more clearly differentiate commitment from both its antecedents and consequences than mindsets (which reflect, in part, both the reasons for and the consequences of being committed). Specifically, mindsets blur those boundaries in terms of the labels used (i.e., affective, continuance), how they are defined (i.e., desire, obligation, or cost), and how they are measured (see chapter 11).

This Klein et al. (2006) model describes the general antecedent categories and outcomes common to all workplace commitments and illustrates the differentiation and relationship between commitment strength and rationales. The model also explicitly recognizes the perceptual nature of commitment and the existence and influence of competing commitments. In this model, commitment strength and rationales are posited as occurring simultaneously and likely influence each other reciprocally, although how one rationalizes being bound to a target is not dependent on how strongly one feels bound to that target or vice versa. Both commitment strength and commitment rationales are depicted as resulting from past and current perceptions of the various antecedent factors. Although they share the same general antecedents, Klein et al. (2006) posit that those antecedents differentially relate to commitment strength and rationales. The model further holds that the relationships between commitment and its outcomes cannot be fully understood without consideration of both commitment strength and commitment rationales, which are proposed to interact in determining commitment outcomes. Finally, a feedback loop is depicted extending from commitment outcomes back to the perceptual field to reflect the fact that commitment is dynamic and evolves over time and to recognize that prior emotions, cognitions, and actions relative to a target and the environment surrounding that target influence how that target and environment are subsequently perceived.

Summary

This chapter provided a brief history of the study of workplace commitments, reviewed the different ways commitment has been conceptualized and defined in the literature, and presented a small set of conceptual models to represent the various perspectives found in the literature. In preparing this chapter, several themes emerged. One observation is that despite the overlap that exists between perspectives and definitions of commitment, there is little consensus on the definition of the construct. There are two factors that have likely contributed to this situation. First, several early writers (e.g., H. S. Becker, 1960; Etzioni, 1961; Kanter, 1968; Porter et al., 1974) defined commitment in multiple ways, as having multiple bases, and/or as being characterized by multiple indicators. Second, subsequent researchers have often only focused on certain aspects of these early writers' definitions or have intertwined elements from various conceptualizations in ways that have obfuscated important distinctions regarding the precise nature of the commitment construct. The result has been considerable conceptual confusion, a problem that has been regularly acknowledged in the commitment literature (e.g., Meyer & Allen, 1991; Mowday et al., 1982; O'Reilly & Chatman, 1986; Reichers, 1985; Stebbins, 1970; Vandenberg, Self, & Seo, 1994) yet, in our opinion, still persists. Although there are exceptions, the lack of attention to construct definition has resulted in a lack of precision, which, as discussed by Jaros in chapter 11, has important implications for the measurement of commitment as well as its relation to other constructs. Addressing these definitional, theoretic, and measurement issues is critical for commitment research to continue to progress.

A second observation is that the conceptualizations and models that have shaped the commitment literature have been developed predominantly in the North American context. Our objective in this chapter was to summarize how commitment has been conceptualized and defined in the literature across time, traditions, targets, and cultures. With respect to culture, we were surprised and disappointed by the limited number of conceptual articles we located that reflected cultures outside of North America. There are exceptions, of course, including the research on lifetime commitment in Japan (Abegglen, 1958; Marsh & Mannari, 1977) and the conceptual work that has come out of the Israeli context (e.g., Cohen, 2003; Wiener, 1982). It should also be recognized that numerous researchers have conducted comparative and single-country studies using and testing the concepts and models reviewed in this chapter. We have included references to such studies when relevant, and momentum appears to be gaining for cross-cultural research on commitment. In chapter 10, Wasti and Önder provide a more thorough review of the cross-cultural commitment literature along with suggestions for how researchers should approach the study of commitment across cultures in the future.

Our final set of observations concerns the impressive range, scope, and volume of the commitment literature. Although volume does not necessarily equate with importance, we feel the breadth, diversity, and longevity of commitment research point to the recognition that commitment has tremendous value as a key theoretical mechanism for influencing critical employee and organizational outcomes. Furthermore, as discussed by Meyer in chapter 2, the importance of commitment transcends changes in the nature of work and work relationships. It is also our sense that over time a greater appreciation has emerged in the literature for the complexity of the phenomenon of workplace commitments.

This chapter has not attempted to resolve all of the conceptual issues relating to workplace commitments, but we have asserted our views on how commitment should be conceptualized. In doing so, we have provided the background necessary for the discussion of these issues throughout the remainder of this volume as the other authors evaluate the commitment literature in light of the theories and definitions highlighted in this chapter. Authors of the chapters in sections 2 and 3 of this volume were asked to consider and critique the theoretical perspectives presented here relative to their respective domains. These theories will be revisited at the end of this volume in chapter 13.

Note

1. In presenting these conceptualizations of commitment, we have not referred specifically to any of Meyer and Allen's (1991) three mindsets because all three are defined as psychological states reflecting different ways commitment (defined as a binding force) can be experienced. In other words, we do not view Meyer and Allen's mindsets as conceptualizations of commitment per se. The various commitment mindsets are thought to result from different bases of commitment and relate differentially to outcomes, including the unwillingness to withdraw, which we refer to here as continuance.

References

Abegglen, J. C. (1958). *The Japanese factory*. New York: Free Press.

Ajzen, I. (2001). Nature and operation of attitudes. In S. Fiske, D. Schacter, & C. Zahn-Waxler (Eds.), *Annual Review of Psychology, 52*, 27–58. Palo Alto, CA: Annual Reviews.

Ajzen, I., & Fishbein, M. (2000). Attitudes and the attitude-behavior relation: Reasoned and automatic processes. In W. Strobe & M. Hewstone (Eds.), *European Review of Social Psychology*. New York: John Wiley & Sons.

Allen, N. J., & Meyer, J. P. (1990). The measurement and antecedents of affective, continuance and normative commitment to the organization. *Journal of Occupational Psychology, 63*(1), 1–18.

Angle, H. L., & Perry, J. L. (1981). An empirical assessment of organizational commitment and organizational effectiveness. *Administrative Science Quarterly, 26*(1), 1–14.

Aranya, N., Pollock, J., & Amernic, J. (1981). An examination of professional commitment in public accounting. *Accounting, Organizations & Society, 6*(4), 271–280.

Bargh, J., & Chartrand, T (1999). The unbearable automaticity of being. *American Psychologist, 54*(7), 462–479.

Bar-Hayim, A., & Berman, G. S. (1992). The dimensions of organizational commitment. *Journal of Organizational Behavior, 13*(4), 379–387.

Barnard, J. (1938). *The functions of the executive*. New York: McGraw Hill.

Becker, H. S. (1960). Notes on the concept of commitment. *American Journal of Sociology, 66*(1), 32–40.

Becker, T. E. (1992). Foci and bases of commitment: Are they distinctions worth making? *Academy of Management Journal, 35*(1), 232–244.

Becker, T. E., & Billings, R. S. (1993). Profiles of commitment: An empirical test. *Journal of Organizational Behavior, 14*(2), 177–190.

Becker, T. E., Billings, R. S., Eveleth, D. M., & Gilbert, N. L. (1996). Foci and bases of employee commitment: Implications for job performance. *Academy of Management Journal, 39,* 464–482.

Bielby, D. D. (1992). Commitment to work and family. *Annual Review of Sociology, 18*(1), 281–302.

Bishop, J. W., & Scott, K. D. (2000). An examination of organizational and team commitment in a self-directed team environment. *Journal of Applied Psychology, 85*(3), 439–450.

Blau, G. J. (1985). The measurement and prediction of career commitment. *Journal of Occupational Psychology, 58*(4), 277–288.

Bozeman, D. B., & Perrewe, P. L. (2001). The effect of item content overlap on Organizational Commitment Questionnaire—turnover cognitions relationships. *Journal of Applied Psychology, 86,* 16–25.

Brayfield, A. H., & Crockett, W. H. (1955). Employee attitudes and employee performance. *Psychological Bulletin, 52,* 396–424.

Breckler, S. J. (1984). Empirical validation of affect, behavior, and cognition as distinct attitude components. *Journal of Personality and Social Psychology, 47,* 1191–1205.

Brockner, J. (1992). The escalation of commitment to a failing course of action: Toward theoretical progress. *Academy of Management Review, 17*(1), 39–61.

Brockner, J., & Rubin, J. (1985). *Entrapment in escalating conflict: A social-psychological analysis.* New York: Springer-Verlag.

Brown, R. B. (1996). Organizational commitment: Clarifying the concept and simplifying the existing construct typology. *Journal of Vocational Behavior, 49,* 230–251.

Buchanan, B. (1974). Building organizational commitment: The socialization of managers in work organizations. *Administrative Science Quarterly, 19*(4), 533–546.

Campion, M. A., & Lord, R. G. (1982). A control systems conceptualization of the goal-setting and changing process. *Organizational Behavior & Human Performance, 30*(2), 265–287.

Carson, K. D., & Bedeian, A. G. (1994). Career commitment: Construction of a measure and examination of its psychometric properties. *Journal of Vocational Behavior, 44*(3), 237–262.

Chusmir, L. H. (1982). Job commitment and the organizational woman. *Academy of Management Review, 7*(4), 595–602.

Clugston, M., Howell, J. P., & Dorfman, P. W. (2000). Does cultural socialization predict multiple bases and foci of commitment? *Journal of Management, 26*(1), 5–30.

Cohen, A. (2003). *Multiple commitments in the workplace: An integrative approach.* Mahwah, NJ: Lawrence Erlbaum.

Cohen, A. (2007). Commitment before and after: An evaluation and reconceptualization of organizational commitment. *Human Resource Management Review, 17,* 336–354.

Colarelli, S. M., & Bishop, R. C. (1990). Career commitment. *Group & Organization Studies, 15*(2), 158–176.

Commons, J. R. (1908). Is class conflict in America growing and is it inevitable? *American Journal of Sociology, 13*, 756–783.

Conner, D. R., & Patterson, R. W. (1982). Building commitment to organizational change. *Training & Development Journal, 36*(4), 18–30.

Cooper-Hakim, A., & Viswesvaran, C. (2005). The construct of work commitment: Testing an integrative framework. *Psychological Bulletin, 131*(2), 241–259.

Crosby, L. A., & Taylor, J. R. (1983). Psychological commitment and its effects on post-decision evaluation and preference stability among voters. *Journal of Consumer Research, 9*(4), 413–431.

Darden, W. R., Hampton, R., & Howell, R. D. (1989). Career versus organizational commitment: Antecedents and consequences of retail salespeople's commitment. *Journal of Retailing, 65*, 80–106.

Dunham, R. B., Grube, J. A., & Castaneda, M. B. (1994). Organizational commitment: The utility of an integrative definition. *Journal of Applied Psychology, 79*(3), 370–380.

Eagly, A. H., & Chaiken, S. (1998). Attitude structure and function. In D. T. Gilbert, & S. T. Fiske (Eds.), *The Handbook of Social Psychology* (Vol. 2, pp. 269–322). Boston: McGraw-Hill.

Eisenberger, R., Fasolo, P., & Davis-LaMastro, V. (1990). Perceived organizational support and employee diligence, commitment, and innovation. *Journal of Applied Psychology, 75*(1), 51–59.

Etzioni, A. (1961). *A comparative analysis of complex organizations.* New York: Free Press.

Fishbein, M., & Ajzen, I. (1975). *Belief, attitude, intention, and behavior: An introduction to theory and research.* Reading, MA: Addison-Wesley.

Fukami, C. V., & Larson, E. W. (1984). Commitment to company and union: Parallel models. *Journal of Applied Psychology, 69*(3), 367–371.

Gaertner, K. N., & Nollen, S. D. (1989). Career experiences, perceptions of employment practices, and psychological commitment to the organization. *Human Relations, 42*(11), 975–991.

Gordon, M. E., Philpot, J. W., Burt, R. E., Thompson, C. A., & Spiller, W. E. (1980). Commitment to the union: Development of a measure and an examination of its correlates. *Journal of Applied Psychology, 65*(4), 479–499.

Gouldner, A. W. (1948). Industrial sociology: Status and prospects. *American Sociological Review, 13*(4), 396–400.

Gouldner, A. W. (1957). Cosmopolitans and locals: Toward an analysis of latent social roles. *Administrative Science Quarterly, 2*, 281–306.

Gouldner, H. P. (1960). Dimensions of organizational commitment. *Administrative Science Quarterly, 4*(4), 468–490.

Greenwald, A. G. (1965). Effects of prior commitment on behavior change after a persuasive communication. *Public Opinion Quarterly, 29*(4), 595–601.

Grusky, O. (1966). Career mobility and organizational commitment. *Administrative Science Quarterly, 10*(4), 488–503.

Hall, D. T. (1971). A theoretical model of career subidentity development in organizational settings. *Organizational Behavior & Human Performance, 6*, 50–76.

Herzberg, F., Mausner, B., & Peterson, R. (1957). *Attitudes: Review of research and options.* Pittsburgh, PA: Psychological Service of Pittsburgh.

Hollenbeck, J. R., & Klein, H. J. (1987). Goal commitment and the goal-setting process: Problems, prospects, and proposals for future research. *Journal of Applied Psychology, 72*(2), 212–220.

Hollenbeck, J. R., Williams, C. R., & Klein, H. J. (1989). An empirical examination of the antecedents of commitment to difficult goals. *Journal of Applied Psychology, 74,* 18–23.

Hrebiniak, L. G., & Alutto, J. A. (1972). Personal and role-related factors in the development of organizational commitment. *Administrative Science Quarterly, 17*(4), 555–572.

Hunt, S. D., & Morgan, R. M. (1994). Organizational commitment: One of many commitments or key mediating construct? *Academy of Management Journal, 37*(6), 1568–1587.

Ilgen, D. R., & Hollenbeck, J. R. (1991). The structure of work: Job design and roles. In M. Dunnette & L. Hough (Eds.), *Handbook of Industrial & Organizational Psychology*: 165–207. Palo Alto, CA: Consulting Psychologists Press.

Jaros, S. J., Jermier, J. M., Koehler, J. W., & Sincich, T. (1993). Effects of continuance, affective, and moral commitment on the withdrawal process: An evaluation of eight structural equation models. *Academy of Management Journal, 36,* 951–994.

Jauch, L. R., Glueck, W. F., & Osborn, R. N. (1978). Organizational loyalty, professional commitment, and academic research productivity. *Academy of Management Journal, 21*(1), 84–92.

Kanter, R. M. (1968). Commitment and social organization: A study of commitment mechanisms in utopian communities. *American Sociological Review, 33*(4), 499–517.

Katz, J. A. (1992). A psychosocial cognitive model of employment status choice. *Entrepreneurship: Theory and Practice, 17,* 29–37.

Kelman, H. C. (1958). Compliance, identification, and internationalization: Three processes of attitude change. *Journal of Conflict Resolution, 2,* 51–60.

Kiesler, C. A. (1971). *The psychology of commitment: Experiments linking behavior to belief.* New York: Academic Press.

Kiesler, C. A., & Sakamura, J. (1966). A test of a model for commitment. *Journal of Personality and Social Psychology, 3,* 349–353.

Klein, H. J., Brinsfield, C. T., & Molloy, J. C. (2006). *Understanding workplace commitments independent of antecedents, foci, rationales, and consequences.* Paper presented at the Academy of Management Annual Meeting, Atlanta, GA.

Klein, H. J., Wesson, M. J., Hollenbeck, J. R., & Alge, B. J. (1999). Goal commitment and the goal-setting process: Conceptual clarification and empirical synthesis. *Journal of Applied Psychology, 84*(6), 885–896.

Klein, H. J., Wesson, M. J., Holenbeck, J. R., Wright, P. M., & DeShon, R. D. (2001). The assessment of goal commitments: A measurement model meta-analysis. *Organizational Behavior and Human Decision Processes, 85,* 32–55.

Lee, K. L., Carswell, J. J., & Allen, N. J. (2000). A meta-analytic review of occupational commitment: Relations with person- and work-related variables. *Journal of Applied Psychology, 85,* 799–811.

Liden, R., Wayne, S., Kraimer, M., & Sparrowe, R. (2003). The dual commitments of contingent workers: An examination of contingents' commitment to the agency and the organization. *Journal of Organizational Behavior, 24*(5), 609–625.

Locke, E. A., Latham, G. P., & Erez, M. (1988). The determinants of goal commitment. *Academy of Management Review, 13*(1), 23–39.

Macey, W. H., & Schneider, B. (2008). The meaning of employee engagement. *Industrial and Organizational Psychology: Perspectives on Science and Practice, 1,* 3–30.

Mael, F. A., & Ashforth, B. E. (1992). Alumni and their alma mater: A partial test of the reformulated model of organizational identification. *Journal of Organizational Behavior, 13,* 103–123.

Mael, F. A., & Tetrick, L. E. (1992). Identifying organizational identification. *Educational & Psychological Measurement, 52*(4), 813–824.

Marsh, R. M. & Mannari, H. (1977). Organizational commitment and turnover: A prediction study. *Administrative Science Quarterly, 22*(1), 57–75.

Mathieu, J. E., & Zajac, D. M. (1990). A review and meta-analysis of the antecedents, correlates, and consequences of organizational commitment. *Psychological Bulletin, 108*(2), 171–194.

McElroy, J. C., Morrow, P. C., & Laczniak, R. N. (2001). External organizational commitment. *Human Resource Management Review, 11*(3), 237–256.

Meyer, J. P., & Allen, N. J. (1991). A three-component conceptualization of organizational commitment. *Human Resource Management Review, 1*(1), 61–89.

Meyer, J. P., & Allen, N. J. (1997). *Commitment in the workplace: Theory, research, and application.* Thousand Oaks, CA: Sage.

Meyer, J. P., Becker, T. E., & Vandenberghe, C. (2004). Employee commitment and motivation: A conceptual analysis and integrative model. *Journal of Applied Psychology, 89*(6), 991–1007.

Meyer, J. P., Becker, T. E., & Van Dick, R. (2006). Social identities and commitments at work: Toward an integrative model. *Journal of Organizational Behavior, 27,* 665–683.

Meyer, J. P., & Herscovitch, L. (2001). Commitment in the workplace: Toward a general model. *Human Resource Management Review, 11*(3), 299–326.

Meyer, J. P., Stanley, D. J., Herscovitch, L., & Topolnytsky, L. (2002). Affective, continuance, and normative commitment to the organization: A meta-analysis of antecedents, correlates, and consequences. *Journal of Vocational Behavior, 61,* 20–52.

Morrow, P. C. (1983). Concept redundancy in organizational research: The case of work commitment. *Academy of Management Review, 8*(3), 486–500.

Mowday, R. T. (1998). Reflections on the study and relevance of organizational commitment. *Human Resource Management Review, 8*(4), 387–401.

Mowday, R. T., Porter, L. W., & Steers, R. M. (1982). *Employee-organization linkages: The psychology of commitment, absenteeism, and turnover.* New York: Academic Press.

Mowday, R. T., Steers, R. M., & Porter, L. W. (1979). The measurement of organizational commitment. *Journal of Vocational Behavior, 14,* 224–247.

Mueller, C. W., & Lawler, E. J. (1999). Commitment to nested organizational units: Some basic principles and preliminary findings. *Social Psychology Quarterly, 62,* 325–346.

Neubert, M. J., & Cady, S. H. (2001). Program commitment: A multi-study longitudinal field investigation of its impact and antecedents. *Personnel Psychology, 54*(2), 421–448.

Oliver, N. (1990). Rewards, investments, alternatives and organizational commit-ment: Empirical evidence and theoretical development. *Journal of Occupational Psychology, 63*(1), 19–31.

O'Reilly, C., & Chatman, J. (1986). Organizational commitment and psychological attachment: The effects of compliance, identification, and internalization on prosocial behavior. *Journal of Applied Psychology, 71*(3), 492–499.

Pearce, C. L., & Herbik, P. A. (2004). Citizenship behavior at the team level of anal-ysis: The effects of team leadership, team commitment, perceived team sup-port, and team size. *Journal of Social Psychology, 144*(3), 293–310.

Penley, L. F., & Gould, S. (1988). Etzioni's model of organizational involvement: A perspective for understanding commitment to organizations. *Journal of Organizational Behavior, 9*(1), 43–59.

Petty, R. E., Wegener, D. T., & Fabrigar, L. R. (1997). Attitudes and attitude change. *Annual Review of Psychology, 48*, 609–647.

Pinder, C. C. (1998). *Motivation in work organizations.* Upper Saddle River, NJ: Pren-tice Hall.

Porter, L. W. & Steers, R. M. (1973). Organizational, work, and personal factors in employee turnover and absenteeism. *Psychological Bulletin, 80*, 151–176.

Porter, L. W., Steers, R. M., Mowday, R. T., & Boulian, P. V. (1974). Organizational commitment, job satisfaction, and turnover among psychiatric technicians. *Journal of Applied Psychology, 59*(5), 603–609.

Randall, D. M. (1988). Multiple roles and organizational commitment. *Journal of Organizational Behavior, 9*, 309–317.

Randall, D. M., & Cote, J. A. (1991). Interrelationships of work commitment con-structs. *Work and Occupations, 18*(2), 194–211.

Reichers, A. E. (1985). A review and reconceptualization of organizational commit-ment. *Academy of Management Review, 10*(3), 465–476.

Riketta, M. (2005). Organizational identification: A meta-analysis. *Journal of Voca-tional Behavior, 66*, 358–384.

Roethlisberger, F. J., & Dickson, W. J. (1939). *Management and the worker.* Cambridge, MA: Harvard University Press.

Rousseau, D. M. (1997). Organizational behavior in the new organizational era. In J. T. Spence, J. M. Darley, & D. J. Foss (Eds.), *Annual review of psychology* (Vol. 48, pp. 515–546). Palo Alto, CA: Annual Reviews.

Rusbult, C. E., & Farrell, D. (1983). A longitudinal test of the investment model: The impact on job satisfaction, job commitment, and investments. *Journal of Applied Psychology, 68*(3), 429–438.

Salancik, G. R. (1977). Commitment and the control of organizational behavior and belief. In B. M. Staw & G. R. Salancik (Eds.), *New directions in organizational behavior.* Chicago: St. Clair Press.

Scholl, R. W. (1981). Differentiating organizational commitment from expectancy as a motivating force. *Academy of Management Review, 6*(4), 589–599.

Sheldon, M. E. (1971). Investments and involvements as mechanisms produc-ing commitment to the organization. *Administrative Science Quarterly, 16*(2), 143–150.

Simon, H. A., Smithburg, D. W., & Thompson, V. A. (1950). *Public administration.* New York: Knopf.

Sjoberg, A., & Sverke, M. (2001). Instrumental and ideological union commitment: Longitudinal assessment of construct validity. *European Journal of Psychological Assessment, 17*, 98–111.

Solinger, O., Van Olffen, W., & Roe, R. A. (2008). Beyond the three-component model of organizational commitment. *Journal of Applied Psychology, 93*, 70–83.

Staw, B. M. (1981). The escalation of commitment to a course of action. *Academy of Management Review, 6*(4), 569–577.

Staw, B. M., & Fox, F. V. (1977). Escalation: The determinants of commitment to a chosen course of action. *Human Relations, 30*(5), 431–450.

Staw, B. M., & Ross, J. (1978). Commitment to a policy decision: A multi-theoretical perspective. *Administrative Science Quarterly, 23*(1), 40–64.

Stebbins, R. A. (1970). On misunderstanding the concept of commitment: A theoretical clarification. *Social Forces, 48*, 526–529.

Steers, R. M. (1977). Antecedents and outcomes of organizational commitment. *Administrative Science Quarterly, 22*(1), 46–56.

Vandenberg, R. J., Self, R. M., & Seo, J. H. (1994). A critical examination of the internalization, identification, and compliance commitment measures. *Journal of Management, 20*(1), 123–140.

Van Dick, R., Becker, T. E., & Meyer, J. P. (2006). Commitment and identification: Forms, foci, and future. *Journal of Organizational Behavior, 27*(5), 545–548.

Van Dick, R., Wagner, U., Stellmacher, J., & Christ, O. (2004). The utility of a broader conceptualization of organizational identification: Which aspects really matter? *Journal of Occupational & Organizational Psychology, 77*(2), 171–191.

Van Knippenberg, D., & Van Schie, E. C. M. (2000). Foci and correlates of organizational identification. *Journal of Occupational & Organizational Psychology, 73*(2), 137–147.

Vroom, V. H. (1964). *Work and motivation.* New York: Wiley.

Weick, K. E. (1989). Theory construction as disciplined imagination. *Academy of Management Review, 14*(4), 797–806.

Weick, K. E. (1995). *Sensemaking in organizations.* In D. Whetten (Series Ed.), *Foundations for organizational science.* Thousand Oaks, CA: Sage.

Weissbein, D., Plamondon, K., & Ford, J. K. (1999). Linking commitment to work behaviors: Commitment to a strategy. *Journal of Community Policing, 1*, 47–64.

Whyte, W. H. (1956). *The organization man.* New York: Doubleday.

Wiener, Y. (1982). Commitment in organizations: A normative view. *Academy of Management Review, 7*, 418–428.

Yoon, J., & Thye, S. R. (2002). A dual-process model of organizational commitment: Job satisfaction and organizational support. *Work & Occupations, 29*(1), 97–124.

Zaccaro, S. J., & Dobbins, G. H. (1989). Contrasting group and organizational commitment: Evidence for differences among multilevel attachments. *Journal of Organizational Behavior, 10*(3), 267–273.

2

Commitment in a Changing World of Work

John P. Meyer
The University of Western Ontario

About a decade ago I coauthored a book on workplace commitment (Meyer & Allen, 1997). When I mentioned this project in conversation with a senior executive, I was somewhat taken aback by his reply: "I guess it will be a short book." It turned out that this was becoming a fairly widespread sentiment that I had perhaps overlooked or denied as a result of my own enthusiasm for the topic. The major threat to commitment was *change*. Among other things, changes in technology, global competition, and consumer demands were placing pressure on organizations for improved efficiency. Organizations responded in a variety of ways, many of which involved the elimination of jobs (e.g., mergers and acquisitions, downsizing, outsourcing, reengineering). In a review of downsizing trends, Emshoff (1994) cited a Conference Board survey in 1992 indicating that 90% of large corporations in the U.S. had downsized in the preceding five years. He further noted that several companies had downsized more than once in a given year. Reichheld (1996) observed that many such downsizings occurred among companies that were profitable at the time. Indeed downsizing had become a corporate strategy that was often rewarded by overnight increases in stock price.

Another increasingly common strategy in the 1990s for achieving flexibility and efficiency was greater reliance on a contingent workforce, even at the professional and senior management ranks (Ettorre, 1994). Perhaps no organization made it clearer to employees that their relationship would be short-term than Apple Computer, who provided all full-time employees with the following written contract:

> Here's the deal Apple will give you: here's what we want from you. We're going to give you a really neat trip while you're here. We're going to teach you stuff you couldn't learn anywhere else. In return ... we expect you to work like hell, buy the vision as long as you're

here... We're not interested in employing you for a lifetime, but that's not the way we are thinking about this. It's a good opportunity for both of us that's probably finite.

Ettorre, 1994, p. 15

Conditions such as this fueled the perception that employers were becoming increasingly unable, or unwilling, to make long-term commitments to their employees (Mowday, 1998). Without such a commitment, it is difficult or impossible for organizations to expect commitment from employees (Baruch, 1998; Cappelli, 1999). Indeed, researchers at the time were demonstrating that commitment is a two-way street and that one of the strongest predictors of employee commitment to the organization was the perception of their employer's commitment to them (e.g., Eisenberger, Huntington, Hutchison, & Sowa, 1986; Eisenberger, Fasolo, & Davis-LaMastro, 1990). Not surprisingly, therefore, numerous books and articles were beginning to appear that urged employees to take control of their own careers and to view their relationships with employers as temporary (e.g., Bridges, 1994). So, by the late 1990s there was an increasingly widespread belief that employee commitment was dead, or at least terminally ill!

My own response to this situation was an increasing interest in organizational change and its impact on employer-employee relations. As I read the academic and practitioner literatures on change, I found a common theme—a theme reflected nicely in the following statements:

If there is one generalization we can make about leadership and change it is this: No change can occur without willing and committed followers.

Bennis, 2000, p. 117

Successful change is rooted in commitment. Unless key participants in a transition are committed to both attaining the goals of the change and paying the price those goals entail, the project will ultimately fail.

Connor, 1993, p. 146

I was struck by the apparent paradox—organizational change has the potential to undermine employee commitment, but commitment is essential for the successful implementation of change. I have spent the last decade exploring this paradox and have come to the conclusion that commitment in the workplace is neither dead nor terminally ill. Indeed, commitment is quite relevant in the changing world of work. However, it can take different forms, and these differences have important implications for theory, research, and management.

To illustrate how I came to this conclusion, I first address two key questions: "What *is* commitment?" and "What makes commitment *relevant?*" I then turn to a discussion of major threats to relevance and potential counterforces to these threats. I conclude with a summary of the challenges associated with managing commitment in an era of change and offer an agenda for future research.

What Is Commitment?

Unfortunately, despite more than 40 years of theory development and research, there is still no easy answer to this question. Klein, Molloy, and Cooper (chapter 1) provide a brief history of the field and identify eight distinct conceptualizations that have guided research. This lack of consensus in conceptualization may be due, in part, to the complexity of the construct itself. It undoubtedly also reflects the fact that theorists and researchers have come at the problem of understanding commitment from a variety of perspectives due to, among other things, differences in training, philosophies of science, and research questions. One of the objectives of this book is to work toward greater consensus, but until that objective is achieved, it is important for authors to be clear about the perspective they are taking for the purpose at hand. Therefore, the following describes my view of commitment and the focus I will take as I discuss its relevance in a changing world of work.

Like Klein et al., I view commitment as residing within the individual. In my own work (see Meyer & Allen, 1997; Meyer & Herscovitch, 2001), I have found it useful to think of commitment as an internal force that binds an individual to a target (social or nonsocial) and/or to a course of action of relevance to that target. Although it can be influenced by factors within (e.g., personality, values) or outside (e.g., norms, work experiences) the person, the force itself is experienced as a conscious "mindset." This mindset can be one of desire (affective commitment), obligation (normative commitment), perceived cost (continuance commitment), or some combination of these (Allen & Meyer, 1990). The nature of the mindset has important implications for the quality of the relationship with a target and/or of the ensuing behavior. For example, the quality of a relationship is arguably stronger when the parties commit to one another out of desire rather than obligation or the fear of what they have to lose. Similarly, individuals should be more willing to go beyond the specific "terms" of a commitment (Brown, 1996) when they freely choose to pursue a course of action than when they feel pressured or trapped.

Although I consider commitment to be characterized by a conscious mindset, I do not rule out the possibility that there may be unconscious influences (Bargh & Chartrand, 1999). In some of the theoretical perspectives reviewed by Klein et al., commitment is presumed to develop in an effort to justify previous decisions (e.g., Staw, 1981) and/or to maintain a stable self-image (Salancik, 1977). These objectives may require that the true reason for the commitment remain unconscious. However, according to Staw and Salancik, the individual develops an attitude that is consistent with the behavior. This attitude can be considered one manifestation of a commitment mindset. These unconscious processes are likely to operate in a changing workplace in the same way they do under more stable conditions. For example, organizational decision makers are just as likely to escalate their commitment to a failing course of action today as they ever were (see Staw, 1997). Therefore, understanding these commitment processes and their implications for behavior continues to be important. However, for present purposes, I focus attention on theory and research involving conscious processes of relevance to the establishment, maintenance, and consequences of commitment to organizations and related foci. Specifically, I define commitment as "an internal force (mindset) that binds an individual to a target (social or nonsocial) and/or to a course of action of relevance to that target." With this definition in mind, we can now turn our attention to the issue of relevance.

What Makes Commitment Relevant?

Early interest in commitment among organizational theorists and researchers was stimulated by its implications for employee retention (see Mowday, Porter, & Steers, 1982). Based on concerns about deteriorating employer-employee relationships and increasing turnover (Whyte, 1956), researchers began to search for solutions. Early efforts to link turnover to job dissatisfaction produced disappointing results and led researchers to focus on commitment to the organization as a contributing factor (e.g., Porter, Crampon, & Smith, 1976; Porter, Steers, Mowday, & Boulian, 1974; Steers, 1977). Retention was not the sole behavioral implication of commitment, however. Mowday et al. (1982) proposed that, in addition to staying, committed employees were also more likely to share the goals and values of the organization and to exert effort on the organization's behalf. Thus, the *relevance* of commitment was that it led to lower levels of turnover and higher levels of effort and performance, all of which were expected to contribute to the overall effectiveness of organizations. Meta-analytic reviews of the early outcome studies revealed that commitment was indeed related to turnover intention and turnover (e.g., Mathieu & Zajac, 1990; Randall, 1990), although not necessarily more strongly than job satisfaction (Tett & Meyer, 1993). Commitment was also found to correlate positively, albeit modestly, with job performance and attendance, and negatively with tardiness (Mathieu & Zajac, 1990; Randall, 1990).

Subsequent research demonstrated that organizational commitment was also linked to outcomes of importance to employees themselves, most notably their own physical and psychological well-being. For example, affective commitment has been found to correlate negatively with psychosomatic symptoms (e.g., Barling & Kelloway, 1996; Richardson, Burke, & Martinussen, 2006), physical health complaints (e.g., Leiter, Clark, & Dunrup, 1994; Wegge, Van Dick, Fisher, West, & Dawson, 2006), mental health complaints, including anxiety and depression (e.g., Wittig-Berman & Lang, 1990; Tucker, Sinclair, & Thomas, 2005), work interference with nonwork (e.g., Cohen & Kirchmeyer, 1995), felt stress and job-related tension (e.g., Irving & Coleman, 2003), and burnout (e.g., Cropanzano, Rupp, & Byrne, 2003; Leiter & Maslach, 1988). There is also some evidence that affective commitment can serve as a buffer against the detrimental effects of stressors on experienced strain (e.g., Begley & Czajka, 1993; Schmidt, 2007), although the findings regarding this buffering effect have been somewhat inconsistent (cf. Irving & Coleman, 2003).

Although the focus here is on organizational commitment, a great deal of attention has been paid recently to employee commitment to other foci including unions (e.g., Fullagar & Barling, 1989; Sverke & Kuruvilla, 1995), careers/occupations (e.g. Blau, 1985; Carson, Carson, & Bedeian, 1995; Meyer, Allen, & Smith, 1993), supervisors and workgroups (e.g., Becker, Billings, Eveleth, & Gilbert, 1996; Vandenberghe, Bentein, & Stinglhamber, 2004), customers and clients (e.g., Redmond & Snape, 2005; Siders, George, & Dharwadkar, 2001), and organizational goals, programs, and change initiatives (e.g., Ford, Weissbein, & Plamondon, 2003; Herscovitch & Meyer, 2002; Klein, Wesson, Hollenbeck, & Alge, 1999; Neubert & Cady, 2001). I discuss these commitments in more detail below, but mention them here to point out that each has been linked to important focus-relevant outcomes (e.g., occupation/union involvement, cooperative behavior, support for organizational goals and policies) that make them relevant to individuals and to the groups and organizations to which they belong.

In sum, if we consider work behavior and employee health and well-being to be important, then the links that have been established with employee commitment clearly attest to its relevance. The question then becomes, is it still possible to build and take advantage of this commitment in an era of change? To answer this question, let us first consider the potential threats to commitment.

Threats to Commitment

As I noted earlier, the most salient threat to organizational commitment is change. But what is it about change that makes it so damaging? Is the damage irreparable? Is the impact really so great that commitment is no longer relevant? To begin to answer these questions, we need to consider how commitment develops. For the purposes of this discussion, I focus primarily on organizational commitment because it has received by far the greatest attention in the academic literature, and because it has been targeted specifically by those who claim that commitment is in decline.

There are many factors involved in the development of commitment, but there are a few that appear to be particularly crucial. That is, they have been shown to have the strongest links to commitment, particularly affective and normative commitment, in recent meta-analyses and/or are theoretically more proximal determinants of commitment. These key factors are perceived organizational support, organizational justice, person-organization fit, and psychological contract fulfillment. Let us consider each in turn, focusing first on the evidence for its role in the development of commitment and then on the potential impact of change on this relationship. We can then consider a few other particularly salient aspects of change that are also likely to affect employee commitment, either directly or through their effects on perceptions of support, justice, fit, or contract fulfillment.

Perceived organizational support (POS). According to organizational support theory (Eisenberger et al., 1986; Rhoades & Eisenberger, 2002), organizations show their support for employees by meeting their socioemotional needs and valuing their contributions. Eisenberger and his colleagues argued that it is through these supportive efforts that organizations demonstrate their commitment to employees. To the extent that employees perceive this support, they are expected to reciprocate with commitment to the organization (see Wayne et al., chapter 8, for more detail).

According to Baruch (1998), one of the major threats to employee commitment is the fact that organizations are less able, or willing, to provide support than was the case in the past. In their efforts to cut costs, increase flexibility, and improve efficiencies, organizations have cut jobs, increased workloads, and made other changes that undermine the trust required to maintain reciprocal commitment from employees. While some organizations have made such changes a part of their corporate strategy—downsizing even when profits are up—others have been forced to make cuts and/or reduce commitments due to uncertainties in their environment (Cappelli, 1999). In either case, such changes threaten to reduce POS and make it difficult for employers to foster, or even expect, affective or normative commitment from their employees.

Organizational justice. Organizational justice comes in many forms, including distributive (i.e., fair distribution of resources), procedural (i.e., fair allocation and decision-making procedures), and interactional (i.e., humane treatment), all of which are expected to influence employee commitment (Colquitt, Conlon, Wesson, Porter, & Ng, 2002). As it does with POS, organizational change has the potential to undermine perceptions of justice. Organizational changes invariably involve shifts in the distribution of valued resources (e.g., jobs, finances, space) that therefore make distributive justice salient. They also sensitize employees to the procedures used in making allocation decisions and to the treatment of those affected by the changes (Gopinath & Becker, 2000; Korsgaard, Sapienza, & Schweiger, 2002). Although the justice literature is replete with suggestions for ways to maintain perceptions of justices in the face of change (see Novelli, Kirkman, & Shapiro, 1995), it is arguably more easily said than done, particularly when organizations face uncertainty and constant pressure for change. Therefore, like lack of POS, perceptions of injustice resulting from change have the potential to undermine employee commitment to organizations.

Person-organization (P-O) fit. According to Schneider's attraction-selection-attrition (ASA) theory (e.g., Schneider, Goldstein, & Smith, 1995), organizations gradually assemble a workforce of like-minded individuals who shape the organization's culture. Employees whose values are compatible with those reflected in the organizational culture will have a better "fit" and should develop a stronger commitment than those whose values conflict (Chatman 1989; Kristof, 1996). It stands to reason, therefore, that any change that threatens an organization's core values has the potential to reduce fit and undermine commitment (Caldwell, Herold, & Fedor, 2004). Some large-scale organizational changes, mergers and acquisitions in particular, almost invariably involve changes in culture. Others, such as changes in strategy (e.g., from a quality focus to a cost focus), can also be interpreted by employees as reflecting a shift in values. Moreover, any change that involves a workforce reduction might be taken as evidence of a decline in the value the organization places on its people. One might argue, therefore, that it is difficult to make any substantial change in an organization without altering culture and potentially threatening P-O fit and employee commitment.

Psychological contract fulfillment. During the recruitment, selection, and socialization processes, new employees develop beliefs about their obligations to the organization and the organization's obligations to them. Rousseau (1995) described this perception of mutual obligations as a "psychological contract." Psychological contracts can take various forms, the most common being transactional contracts and relational contracts. *Transactional contracts* are of relatively limited duration and involve a fairly concrete set of obligations (e.g., employment at a specified rate of pay for effective performance on defined tasks), whereas *relational contracts* are of longer duration with less clearly specified terms that include a promise of mutual caring and support. Because they are longer term and involve a promise of support, relational contracts generally provide a more solid basis for the establishment of a committed relationship (Dabos & Rousseau, 2004). In more stable times, organizations were arguably in a better position to establish such relational contracts with their employees. However, as they encounter pressures for increased flexibility and efficiency, they intentionally or inadvertently violate their contracts in the eyes of employees by eliminating jobs, cutting salaries, increasing workloads, and the like (Rousseau, 1996). Because relational contracts are built on principles of trust and reciprocity, one potential implication of this violation is a reduction in employees' affective and normative commitment to the organization (Meyer, Allen, & Topolnytsky, 1998).

Other salient effects of change. Perhaps one of the most immediate consequences of organizational change, or the threat of change, is uncertainty and insecurity (Cappelli, 1999). Job insecurity resulting from organizational change has been found to contribute to psychological distress and withdrawal (e.g., Dekker & Schaufeli, 1995). Cappelli makes an important distinction between job stability and job security, noting that even employees who retain jobs for a reasonable length of time (i.e., have stable employment) may experience insecurity if the threat of job loss continually hangs over their heads. This suggests that even employees who are currently unaffected by change can experience insecurity due to the ubiquity of change in general. Feelings of uncertainty and insecurity can undermine trust and fuel cynicism about organizations and organizational change initiatives (Reichers, Wanous, & Austin, 1997; Stanley, Meyer, & Topolnytsky, 2005). This, of course, makes it difficult for employees to feel confident in their organization's ability or willingness to sustain a relational contract. The natural consequence might be a reduction in employee commitment to the organization.

Changes that require employees to acquire new knowledge and skills might threaten employees' self-efficacy and perceptions of person-job (i.e., abilities/demand) fit, both of which have been linked to commitment (Meyer, 1997). Changes in the structure of organizations (e.g., flattening the hierarchy) and in staffing policies (e.g., from internal to external recruitment) can reduce development and promotion opportunities for employees and lead them to consider outside opportunities. These and many other changes taking place in modern organizations have the potential to undermine employee commitment to their employers (see Cappelli, 1999, for a more detailed discussion).

Summary. In light of the foregoing discussion, it is easy to see why there is concern about the continued relevance of employee commitment. The seemingly constant demand for change undoubtedly poses a challenge for the development and maintenance of a strong employer-employee relationship. But does this challenge really provide a death blow to commitment? In the following section I argue that it does not, and I provide several explanations to support this view. However, I also acknowledge that the way we think about and study commitment may need revision. In the concluding section, I offer some suggestions for new directions in commitment research.

In Support of the Continuing Relevance of Commitment

There are several reasons why I believe that commitment is still relevant, both as a focus of research and as a management strategy. First, although change *can* lead to reductions in support, justice, P-O fit, and contract fulfillment, it doesn't have to, at least to the point where it completely undermines commitment. Several studies have demonstrated how change can be managed in such a way as to minimize its detrimental effects. Second, although it may make commitment more difficult to achieve, change does not undermine the *potential* benefits of commitment—indeed, the well-established links between commitment and retention, performance, organizational citizenship behavior (OCB), employee well-being, and other important outcomes continue to emerge in ongoing research. Moreover, there are many organizations that are finding ways to maintain highly committed workers despite the turbulent environment, and are reaping the benefits as a result. Third, even if change is making it difficult to build and maintain commitment to *organizations*, it is clear that employees can and do form commitments to many other foci (e.g., occupations, workgroups, customers). These commitments have implications for behavior of relevance to the specific foci as well as to the organization as a whole. Fourth, there is increasing evidence that the success of organizational change initiatives themselves depend on the commitment of those charged with implementing them. Finally, it can be argued that human beings are naturally predisposed to form commitments. Therefore, making commitments more difficult to achieve does not reduce their relevance. To the contrary, it may be more important than ever to understand how the various challenges to commitment will affect employees, employers, and their relationship. Let me elaborate on each of these arguments in turn.

Effective Management of Change

While it may be difficult to maintain perceptions of support, justice, fit, and contract fulfillment under conditions of large-scale organizational change, it is not impossible. Organizations that manage change with due diligence to these important employee concerns may be better able to maintain commitment in spite of the change. To illustrate, here are just a few examples.

Schweiger and DeNisi (1991) conducted a quasi-experimental study to examine the impact of a program of "realistic communications" on employees' reactions (including commitment) subsequent to the announcement of a merger. The investigators found a decline in commitment following the announcement, but also found that commitment tended to stabilize following the introduction of a communication program in the experimental plant. In the control plant, commitment and intention to stay continued to decline over time. A similar pattern of findings was obtained for ratings of uncertainty, stress, and company trustworthiness, suggesting that these may have been mediating mechanisms in the effects of the communication program on commitment.

Korsgaard et al. (2002) investigated the effects of planned change on employees' perception of the psychological contract. They found an overall decline in employees' perception of their obligation to the organization and an increase in intention to leave following the announcement of the plan. However, this effect was mitigated by perceptions of procedural justice. Trust in management was actually found to *increase* following the announcement for those who felt the process was just, leading the authors to suggest that organizational change, if handled properly, could provide an opportunity to build trust among employees.

Fedor, Caldwell, and Herold (2006) investigated how organizational changes in 32 different public and private organizations affected employees' commitment to the organization as well as to the change initiative. Although employees reported a decline in commitment under some conditions, they reported an increase in commitment to the organization when they perceived the change as having benefits for their work unit. The same group of investigators (Caldwell et al., 2004), demonstrated that change *increased* perceptions of P-O fit when it was perceived to benefit the work unit and signal an intention to improve and remain competitive.

Finally, Gopinath and Becker (2000) examined the impact of managerial communication and perceptions of procedural justice for layoffs in the context of divestiture. They found that communication had a positive effect on perceptions of procedural justice pertaining to (a) the decision to divest and (b) the postdivestiture decision to reduce staff. Perceptions of justice, in turn, related positively to employees' commitment to the new organization.

Together, these findings suggest that organizational change, indeed even the announcement of a plan for change, can have a negative impact on employee commitment. However, they also demonstrate that by communicating effectively and taking steps to ensure perceptions of fairness, it is possible to maintain and possibly even build employee commitment to the organization and its new goals and objectives.

Benefits of Organizational Commitment

As I noted earlier, the relevance of commitment can be evaluated in terms of its implications for turnover, job performance, OCB, and employee health and well-being. The results of recent meta-analytic reviews (e.g., Cooper-Hakim & Viswesvaran, 2005; Meyer, Stanley, Herscovitch, & Toplonytsky, 2002; Riketta, 2002; T. A. Wright & Bonett, 2002) suggest that the correlations between organizational commitment and these important outcome variables are as strong, or stronger, than they were in earlier analyses (e.g., Mathieu & Zajac, 1990; Randall, 1990). Moreover, there are new forms of evidence beyond the typical within-time correlation between individual-level measures to demonstrate the benefits of organizational commitment. I focus here on three sources of evidence. The first includes cross-sectional and longitudinal research conducted at higher levels of analysis (e.g., organization, division, work unit). The second involves studies conducted to demonstrate the effects of commitment-oriented human resource management (HRM) systems on organizational effectiveness. Finally, I highlight examples of organizations that have been able to maintain a committed workforce as they adapt to pressures for change. While no single source of evidence is without limitations, together they make a strong case for the continued relevance of organizational commitment.

A few studies have now been conducted to examine the relations between organizational commitment and its hypothesized outcomes at an organization or unit level (e.g., Ostroff, 1992; P. M. Wright, Gardner, Moynihan, & Allen, 2005). Ostroff reported negative correlations between commitment, aggregated to a school level, and high school teacher turnover and student dropout rate. She found positive correlations with administrative performance, student academic achievement, and student satisfaction. Using longitudinal data obtained from 45 business units, Wright et al. found that unit-level affective commitment was positively related to measures of past, concurrent, and future operational performance. Similar patterns of correlations were also obtained in studies (e.g., Koys, 2001; Ryan, Schmit, & Johnson, 1996) using aggregate measures of satisfaction with the organization, a variable likely to be related to affective commitment. A word of caution is in order, however. Wright et al. pointed out that research to date has not yet established a *causal* link between unit-level commitment and performance. It is possible that the correlations observed in both concurrent and longitudinal studies reflect reverse causality (i.e., strong performance leading to enhanced commitment) or are merely spurious (i.e., due to other common causes). This is an important issue that applies as well to individual-level studies and should be addressed in future research.

These organization/unit-level studies are particularly noteworthy for two reasons. First, some investigators (Ostroff, 1992; Ryan et al., 1996) noted that, if anything, the strength of the relations observed between organizational commitment/satisfaction and performance at the organization and unit levels are stronger than those typically reported in individual-level studies. This is due, in part, to increased reliabilities associated with aggregation. However, it may also reflect the fact that commitment can have effects on outcomes (e.g., group synergy and performance) that cannot be detected at an individual level. Second, these studies link organizational commitment to outcomes that are of particular interest to organizational decision makers (e.g., profitability and customer satisfaction). Consequently, they might provide a stronger justification for the investments in the HRM systems needed to foster commitment than will evidence for links between individual-level commitment and behavior, particularly if future research can establish commitment as having causal priority.

A second line of research demonstrating the benefits of commitment is that linking HRM systems to organizational effectiveness (e.g., Arthur, 1994; Huselid, 1995; MacDuffie, 1995). Although these investigators examined direct links between HRM practices and effectiveness, the underlying assumption was that these relationships are mediated by positive employee reactions (e.g., commitment) and behaviors (Ferris et al., 1998; Kopelman, Brief, & Guzzo, 1990). Therefore, I first describe some of the evidence linking HRM systems to organizational effectiveness. I then provide a summary of findings pertaining to the mediating mechanisms presumed to be operating within the "black box" between HRM and organizational outcomes (Bowen & Ostroff, 2004; P. M. Wright & Haggerty, 2005).

In a study conducted with 30 U.S. steel minimills, Arthur (1994) compared the relative effectiveness of two HRM systems: commitment and control. According to Arthur (1994, p. 672):

> The goal of control human resource systems is to reduce direct labor costs, or improve efficiency, by enforcing employee compliance with specific rules and procedures and basing employee rewards on some measurable output criteria (Eisenhardt, 1985; Walton, 1985). In contrast, commitment human resource systems shape desired employee behaviors and attitudes by forging psychological links between organizational and employee goals. In other words, the focus is on developing committed employees who can be trusted to use their discretion to carry out job tasks in ways that are consistent with organizational goals.

Arthur found that mills using commitment strategies had significantly higher performance (i.e., higher labor efficiency and lower scrap rate) and lower turnover compared to those using control strategies.

In a similar study conducted with 62 automotive plants from around the world, MacDuffie (1995) found that the use of high-commitment HRM practices (i.e., focus on openness to learning and interpersonal skills in selection, compensation contingent on plant performance, low status-differential, extensive training) was associated with higher levels of productivity and quality, particularly when appropriately integrated with work systems (e.g., use of work teams, employee involvement in quality control) and production strategies. Finally, Huselid (1995) examined the relations between the use of what he called "high performance work practices" and various indices of corporate performance. These high-performance practices, which corresponded closely to those included in a commitment system as described by Arthur (1994), were found to be associated with lower levels of turnover and higher levels of productivity and corporate financial success.

As noted above, it is commonly assumed that HRM practices contribute to organizational effectiveness at least in part through employee reactions, including commitment (Ferris et al., 1998; Kopelman et al., 1990). Evidence to support this proposition can be pieced together by considering studies that have demonstrated links between HRM practices and perceptions of organizational support, justice, and climate (e.g., Gelade & Ivery, 2003; Meyer & Smith, 2000), between perceptions of organizational justice and support and employee commitment (e.g., Colquitt et al., 2001; Rhoades & Eisenberger, 2002; Tsui, Pearce, Porter, & Tripoli, 1997), between employee commitment and individual-level performance (Meyer et al., 2002; Riketta, 2002), between unit-level commitment and unit-level performance (Ostroff, 1992; P. M. Wright et al., 2005), and between unit-level behavior and unit-level performance (Podsakoff & MacKenzie, 1994). Therefore, although there is no single study that examines all the hypothesized links between HRM practices and organizational effectiveness, the cumulative evidence from studies examining individual links provides considerable support for the key mediating role played by commitment.

As a final piece of evidence for the relevance of organizational commitment, I simply note that there are many very successful organizations, including Cisco Systems, Gillette, Hewlett-Packard, Procter & Gamble, Southwest Airlines, 3M, and Walgreens, to name a few, whose success has been attributed, at least in part, to the efforts they have made to build a strong and committed workforce (see Collins, 2001; Collins & Porras, 1997; O'Reilly & Pfeffer, 2000; and Pfeffer, 1998, for more detailed discussion of these and other successful companies). These companies have encountered the pressures for change discussed earlier, and in some cases, had to respond in ways that had adverse effects for employees. However, in doing so they were able to stick to their core values and maintain a climate of support, justice, and trust. As a complement to these individual success stories, Fulmer, Gerhart, and Scott (2003) compared companies on

Fortune magazine's "100 Best Companies to Work for in America" with a matched group of competitors and found that the best employers were indeed superior in managing human relations and, importantly, that they achieved this superiority without sacrificing effectiveness. In fact, the best companies were found to be as effective as or more effective than their competitors when evaluated in terms of return on assets and market-to-book value.

As an aside, it is interesting to note that there has been a surge of interest recently in "employee engagement" (see Macey & Schneider, 2008, for a review). This interest may have been stimulated, in part, by the publications and success stories described above and/or an increasing awareness of the paradox I described earlier—employers need a committed workforce to implement the changes required to succeed in an increasingly competitive and constantly changing environment. Although commitment and engagement are not the same, they are closely related (Macey & Schneider, in press). Indeed, Macey and Schneider argue that commitment is one facet of the *state of engagement*, which they describe as having "a strong affective tone connoting, at a minimum, high levels of involvement (passion, absorption) in the work and the organization (pride and identity) as well as affective energy (enthusiasm and alertness) and a sense of self presence in work." Thus, the interest in engagement may also signal a renewed awareness of the importance and relevance of commitment. Of course, whether this interest lasts or becomes just another fad will depend on whether it is embraced as part of a long-term business strategy (as in the companies described above) or as a quick fix.

In sum, there is strong evidence from many sources to suggest that employee commitment to organizations is still possible and that organizations can benefit by fostering a strong affective commitment in their workforce. This is not to deny that doing so might be difficult or impossible under some conditions. Even under these conditions, however, a case can be made for the relevance of commitment, albeit commitment to different foci.

Commitments to Other Foci and Their Implications

Organizations are complex entities with multiple nested constituencies (March & Simon, 1958; Reichers, 1985), including divisions, work units, teams, and supervisors. Employees may develop commitments to any or all of these internal constituencies, as well as to various external constituencies such as occupations/professions, unions, customers/clients, or their own personal careers (Becker, 1992; Cohen, 2003; Morrow, 2003). Moreover, they may develop commitments to goals, policies, or projects designed to benefit one or more of these internal or external constituencies. These commitments are discussed in more detail elsewhere in this book (see chapters 4–6), so I provide only a few examples here to illustrate that commitment *is* relevant in a changing world of work, even in the absence of commitment to organizations. Specifically, I focus on commitments to occupations, workgroups and their supervisors, and customers/ clients. I also describe a relatively new but increasingly common situation in which employees are contracted out and therefore have a relationship with both the contracting and client organizations.

As research expanded to include foci other than the organization, one of the first to be considered was career commitment (e.g., Blau, 1985, 1989). Blau and others (e.g., Carson et al., 1995) used the term "career" to refer to an individual's "line of work." More recently, Blau (2003) and others (e.g., Irving, Coleman, & Cooper, 1997; Meyer et al., 1993) have adopted the term "occupational commitment" because it more accurately captures the emphasis on line of work (as opposed to one's career path within or across organizations), and subsumes commitment to a profession (e.g., Wallace, 1995). Therefore, I use the latter term hereafter when referring to research on occupational, career, or professional commitment.

Occupational commitment is of interest in its own right because it has potential benefits for occupational groups/associations and their members. Indeed, research has demonstrated that individuals who are committed to their occupations are less likely to change occupations and more likely to engage in occupation-relevant activities (e.g., reading relevant literature, involvement in associations) than are those who are less committed (Meyer et al., 1993). However, research has also demonstrated links with behaviors benefiting organizations, including retention, job performance, and organizational citizenship behavior (K. Lee, Carswell, & Allen, 2000; Meyer et al., 1993).

McAuley, Zeitz, and Blau (2006) recently conducted a study to determine whether feelings of job insecurity in an organization would contribute to a decline in commitment to the organization and "push" employees toward a stronger commitment to their occupational group. They found that although job insecurity was indeed negatively related to affective and normative commitment to the organization, it did not relate significantly with commitment to the occupation. Rather, they found positive links between "perceived professionalization" of the occupation and affective, normative, and continuance commitment to the occupation. That is, employees who viewed their occupational group as having well-defined standards and requiring specialized knowledge and skills were more likely to be "pulled" toward the occupation as a focus of commitment. Given the evidence for positive relations between occupational commitment and organization-relevant outcomes, McAuley et al. suggested that organizations that are not in a position to foster strong commitment to themselves might nevertheless benefit from efforts to build ties with professionalized occupational groups.

Research on workgroup and supervisor commitment was stimulated in large measure by Reichers' (1985) argument that organizations may be too large and amorphous to be the focus of commitment and that employees might instead focus their commitments on smaller and more proximal entities such as their immediate workgroup or supervisor. Lawler (1992; Mueller & Lawler, 1999) argued that these more proximal entities are also likely to exert a stronger influence on employee attitudes and behavior than more distal foci such as top management or the organization itself. Research has demonstrated that commitments to workgroups and supervisors relate positively to citizenship behaviors of direct benefit to the workgroup (e.g., Becker & Kernan, 2003; Redman & Snape, 2005). However, these commitments were also found to relate positively to outcomes of relevance to the broader organization, including in-role and extra-role performance (Redman & Snape, 2005; Siders et al., 2001) and innovation (Swailes, 2004). Indeed, Becker et al. (1996) and Vandenberghe et al. (2004) found that commitment to the supervisor was actually a better predictor of job performance than was commitment to the organization. This should perhaps not be surprising given Lawler's (1992) argument regarding the influence of proximal foci and the fact that supervisors and workgroups are put in place by organizations to achieve organizational objectives. In any case, it provides further evidence for the relevance of employee commitment.

Recent research on commitment to customers has demonstrated links with outcomes of relevance to customers and, by implication, the organization (e.g., Redman & Snape, 2005; Siders et al., 2001). In two separate studies, one with private sector and one with public sector employees, Redman and Snape found that the commitment of front-line service personnel was positively related to supervisor ratings of customer service behaviors. Similarly, in a study of sales executives from four organizations, Siders et al. found that commitment to the customer was associated with objective measures of market share and product breadth (i.e., number of different product types sold). These findings are particularly noteworthy given recent theory and research linking employee service orientation to customers' loyalty and commitment to products and services (e.g., Allen & Grisaffe, 2001; Bansal, Irving, & Taylor, 2004; Fullerton, 2005). Thus, it is interesting that, in the light of growing concerns about the feasibility of mutual employer-employee commitment in the changing world of work, there appears to be emerging evidence for the importance of mutual commitments between organizations (as reflected in the behavior of front-line employees) and their customers.

Finally, there has been recent growth in "alternative work relationships" (e.g., Coyle-Shapiro & Morrow, 2005; Gallaghar & McLean Parks, 2001) in North America and the United Kingdom. Gallaghar and McLean Parks (2001, p. 185) defined alternative work arrangements as "any job in which the individual does not have an explicit or implicit contract for long-term employment and one in which the minimum hours can vary in a non-systematic manner." One might naturally assume from this definition that such relationships involve a low level of commitment on the part of both employers and employees. However, recent research with employees in one particularly intriguing form of alternate relationship, contracted employment, suggests that this may not be the case (e.g., Connelly, Gallagher, & Gilley, 2007; Coyle-Shapiro & Morrow, 2005; Coyle-Shapiro, Morrow, & Kessler, 2006).

Coyle-Shapiro and her colleagues conducted their research with individuals employed by an agency that contracts their services to a client organization on a relatively long-term basis. This situation has the potential to create a feeling of alienation such that employees have the sense that they do not really belong to either organization. To the contrary, the investigators found that employees can develop a strong affective commitment to both the contractor and client organizations. An important correlate of this commitment was the level of perceived support they received from each. There also appeared to be some spillover in that commitment to the contractor accounted for unique variance in commitment to the client organization. Connelly et al. (2007) obtained similar results with temporary workers rather than long-term contracted employees. Although much more research is need to understand how commitment develops and affects employee behavior in these and other alternative employment relationships, the current findings clearly suggest that commitment continues to be a relevant issue.

In sum, there are numerous targets of commitment in the workplace. These commitments have important implications for the specific target as well as for the broader entities in which they are nested or otherwise connected. I turn now to another focus of commitment that has only recently started to receive research attention and that is at the heart of the paradox I alluded to earlier, namely, commitment to organizational change. Indeed, the very changes that have the potential to undermine commitment to the organization can only succeed if there is commitment by those who initiate, manage, and implement the change (Bennis, 2000; Connor, 1993).

Commitment to Change and Its Implications

Pfeffer (1998) argued that the most important stage in organizational change is implementation—even the most well-developed strategic initiatives will not work if they are not implemented effectively (cf. Klein & Sorra, 1996). Due to the inevitable uncertainties associated with large-scale changes, effective implementation requires a high level of buy-in and support from those who are affected by the change. However, despite the ubiquitous claims by experts concerning the importance of commitment to organizational change, it has only recently become the focus of empirical investigation (e.g., Herscovitch & Meyer, 2002; Neubert & Cady, 2001; Ford et al., 2003). Neubert and Cady demonstrated that affective commitment to a new program initiative was positively related to level of participation in the program and program-relevant performance, both within and across time. They noted that this finding is consistent with, but extends, earlier research demonstrating a strong link between goal commitment and employee effort and performance (e.g., Klein et al., 1999). Similarly, in a study of 11 police departments moving toward a community-policing strategy, Ford et al. found that officers' commitment to the new strategy was positively related to the frequency of their community policing-type behavior.

In a study of commitment to change, Herscovitch and Meyer (2002) adapted Meyer and Allen's (1991) three-component model of commitment and demonstrated that the nature of employees' commitment to a change initiative has important implications for the level of support they are willing to provide. They found that affective, normative, and continuance commitment all related positively to compliance with the requirements for change, but that only affective and normative commitment related positively to willingness to go beyond minimum requirements to make the change work. In a follow-up study, Meyer, Srinivas, Lal, and Topolnytsky (2007) found similar evidence for the benefits of affective and normative commitment. Moreover, by including a measure of "mere compliance," they were able to demonstrate that employees with strong continuance commitment tended to restrict their efforts to those activities required of them by the organization. Finally, Cunningham (2006) found that affective and normative commitment to a change initiative was also negatively related to turnover intentions following the change, whereas continuance commitment was positively related.

In sum, the experiences of change experts and findings from recent empirical investigations attest to the importance of commitment, particularly affective and normative commitment, for the effective implementation of change. Thus, even if commitment to organizations itself is becoming less relevant (despite claims to the contrary above), commitment to the changes organizations are making to remain competitive *is* relevant and requires further investigation.

Commitment as a Basic Human Quality

My final argument in support of the continuing relevance of commitment is based on theory and research drawn from various sources, all of which lead to the conclusion that employees, as human beings, have a natural inclination to make commitments to and expect commitments from others. It follows, therefore, that if commitments between employers and employees are indeed on the decline, then (a) there may be detrimental consequences for both parties, and (b) employees will develop other commitments that are likely to influence their work behavior.

One of the strongest arguments I have encountered in support of the claim that commitment is a natural human tendency was provided in a collection of essays compiled by Nesse (2001a) in *Evolution and the Capacity for Commitment*. In his opening chapter, Nesse (2001b) argues that human beings are motivated by more than "rational" self-interest and that their willingness to make commitments that require personal sacrifice is a function of evolutionary forces. Nesse draws on a diverse body of theory and research from economics, behavior genetics, and evolutionary psychology to demonstrate that the capacity to make commitments had survival value and evolved as a basic human quality. He argues that by making and following through on commitments to act, whether they be threats or promises, individuals are able to influence others to make reciprocal commitments, the benefit of which is increased certainty and predictability. For our ancient ancestors, such behavior had survival value. Today, this inherited capacity for commitment reflects itself in a willingness to behave in ways that benefit others (e.g., caring for a spouse with Alzheimer's, working unpaid overtime), even when it requires sacrificing other things of value (e.g., engaging in more enjoyable or leisurely activities). Of course it can also lead us to make threats (e.g., to quit a job unless things change), even when following through on the threat might have negative consequences for ourselves (e.g., unemployment in a tight economy). Associated with the capacity to make commitments is the capacity to identify and avoid cheaters (i.e., those who take advantage of others for personal gain; see Frank, 2001). Together, these capacities facilitate the development of social structures that serve the collective interests of those who belong to them.

A related set of arguments is provided by Lawrence and Nohria (2000) in *Driven: How Human Nature Shapes Our Choices*. Lawrence and Nohria also draw on an eclectic body of literature to make the case that, through the process of evolution, individuals developed four key drives—to acquire, to bond, to learn, and to defend—which combine to influence our individual behavior and our interactions with others. The authors argue that psychologically healthy individuals are able to achieve balance in the satisfaction of these four drives. Of particular interest for the present discussion is the drive to bond. As noted earlier, forming bonds with social entities is part of the core essence of commitment.

Lawrence and Nohria (2000) are not alone in arguing that humans have a drive (or need) to bond or form relationships with others. Indeed, relationship needs were included in early need theories of motivation (e.g.,

Alderfer, 1972; Maslow, 1943) and continue to be acknowledged in modern theories, most notably Deci and Ryan's (1985; Ryan & Deci, 2000) self-determination theory. Perhaps the strongest body of evidence in support of the argument that human beings have a *need* to form relationships was provided by Baumeister and Leary (1995). They identified a rigorous set of criteria for evaluating the existence of a need (e.g., evidence that people regularly seek to satisfy it, that it is reflected in behavior across cultures, and that there are serious negative psychological consequences of deprivation) and reviewed a broad range of research from different disciplines using a variety of methodologies. Based on this evidence, the authors argued that there is little question that human beings need to form relationships.

There is also a large body of research demonstrating that human beings derive their sense of identity, at least in part, based on their associations with other individuals and groups. According to social identity theory (Tajfel, 1978) and its derivative, organizational identity theory (e.g., Ashforth & Mael, 1989; Pratt, 1998), the tendency to identify with groups and organizations is natural, largely unconscious, and satisfies basic needs for self-esteem and belonging. Although identification and commitment are not synonymous, they are strongly related (Meyer, Becker, & Van Dick, 2006; Riketta &Van Dick, chapter 3). Among other things, individuals who identify with a collective are likely to share (or come to share) the values of that collective and therefore develop a value-based (affective and/or normative) commitment to that group.

There are many other findings that can also be used to support the argument that human beings have a natural inclination to form and benefit from commitments. For example, as mentioned earlier, affective commitment has been found to be positively related to employee health and well-being (e.g., Cropanzano et al., 2003; Wegge et al., 2006), suggesting that it may be associated with the satisfaction of basic human needs. There is also evidence that employees may have a propensity to commit to organizations (T. W. Lee, Ashford, Walsh, & Mowday, 1992) and that they develop strong commitment to organizations well before they have a chance to test the quality of the relationship (e.g., Meyer, Bobocel, & Allen, 1991). Even employees who leave one organization with relatively low commitment report high levels of commitment as they enter new organizations (Kontratuck, Hausdorf, Korabik, & Rosen, 2004). Finally, as noted above, employees develop commitment in nontraditional employment relationships (i.e., contract positions) where it might not be expected (e.g., Connelly et al., 2007; Coyle-Shapiro & Morrow, 2006). Interestingly, a key factor in the development of this commitment is a high level of support from the contracting and client organizations.

Admittedly, the proposition that we have a natural inclination to make commitments is no defense against the argument that the prevalence of change is undermining the ability or desire for employers and employees to enter into a committed relationship. However, it does suggest that the loss of this opportunity could have detrimental effects for both parties and/or that employees will seek substitutes (i.e., shift their commitments to other social foci). In either case, commitments continue to be relevant as a basis for understanding and managing workplace behavior.

The Future of Commitment: A Research Agenda

My objective in this chapter was to provide a case for the relevance of commitment in the changing world of work. Fortunately, there was a large body of theory and research to draw on, and I hope I have convinced the reader that organizations of various forms (business, nonprofit, occupational/ professional associations, unions), their internal and external constituencies, and their employees can all benefit from commitments, particularly those based on mutual trust and support. Nevertheless, traditional employer-employee relationships are being strained, and uncertainty, insecurity, and demands for flexibility and change abound. This provides a challenge not only for those who have to manage these commitments, but also for those who study them. In this closing section I identify what I think are important directions for future research. These are intended to complement the recommendations to be presented throughout this book and focus specifically on addressing the challenges of change.

We know that, where feasible, commitment to organizations is still important. We also know that employees can make commitments to many other constituencies, inside and outside the organization, that have the potential to complement or substitute for organizational commitment. What we don't know enough about is how these commitments relate to one another and interact to influence behavior. There seems to be evidence of a positive manifold (Cooper-Hakim & Viswesvaran, 2005), but the positive correlations among the various commitments vary in strength from weak (e.g., organization and union) to strong (e.g., organization and occupation). It does not appear that any one commitment precludes another or that one is a necessary condition for another. With regard to outcomes, there appears to be some controversy as to whether the effects of more global commitments (e.g., to the organization) mediate the effects of local commitments (e.g., to the supervisor or work team), or vice versa (e.g., Bentein, Stinglhamber, & Vandenberghe, 2002; Hunt & Morgan, 1994; Maertz, Mosley, & Alford, 2002). The existing research provides a good starting point, but we need a much more systematic approach to addressing these important questions. Ideally, this research should include foci that are only beginning to emerge as a result of the changing nature of work, such as contracting and client organizations (Coyle-Shapiro & Morrow, 2006; Gallagher & McLean Parks, 2001); "new organizations" resulting from mergers, acquisitions, or divestitures (Gopinath & Becker, 2000; Schweiger & DiNisi, 1991); and new projects (Neubert & Cady, 2001), strategies (Ford et al., 2006) or other change initiatives (Herscovitch, & Meyer, 2002).

The question raised by McAuley et al. (2006) as to whether uncertainty about one's relationship with the organization necessarily pushes employees to commit to their occupation is also an interesting one. Their findings suggest that, to the contrary, employees are pulled by attractive features of the occupation and will not naturally be inclined to view the occupation as a substitute. However, this is only one study and it needs replication. It would also be interesting to extend the research to other foci such as workgroups, customers, and personal career. It is also important to know how well these alternate commitments serve as substitutes for organizational commitment. For example, recall the contract offered by Apple Computer described earlier. Implicit in this contract was that notion that, despite the temporary nature of the employer-employee relationship, Apple could expect high levels of effort based on employees' commitment to their personal careers (and the benefits of the experience gained at Apple). Do employees who are committed to foci other than the organization perform all organization-relevant tasks as effectively as they would if they had a strong organizational commitment, or are there activities (e.g., organization-relevant OCB) that can only be achieved by establishing a strong link to the organization itself?

Although the vast majority of commitment research has been conducted at an individual level, arguably the most convincing evidence for the relevance of commitment comes from studies demonstrating that unit- or organization-level commitment relates to objective indices of organizational effectiveness. We need more such studies, both on their own and as part of broader research designed to explore the black box between HRM systems and effectiveness. Ideally, we also need cross-level research linking effects at the unit/organization level to those at the individual level and vice versa. Such research would serve to validate the assumption made at the organization level that employee commitment is a key mediator, as well as the assumption made at the individual level that the behavioral consequences of employee commitment ultimately affect the organization's bottom line.

To complement the research on HRM systems and organizational commitment described above, we need research linking organization- or unit-level theory on change management (e.g., Connor, 1993; Klein & Sorra, 1996) with theory linking employee commitment to change (e.g., Herscovitch &

Meyer, 2002; Neubert & Cady, 2001). Again, such research would serve to validate the assumptions made at the organization level that employee commitment is a key mediator in organizational transformation, as well as the assumption made at the individual level that the behavioral consequences of employee commitment is a major determinant of whether or not the change is successful.

Finally, although the majority of research reviewed above focused on the impact of change on affective commitment, it is important to keep in mind that commitment can take other forms (e.g., normative and continuance), each characterized by a different mindset. Indeed, recent research suggests that employee behavior can be better understood by considering how the various mindsets combine within a "commitment profile" (e.g., Gellatly, Meyer, & Luchak, 2006; Herscovitch & Meyer, 2002; Wasti, 2005). Interestingly, these studies provide some evidence that employees demonstrate the highest levels of discretionary effort (e.g., OCB, support for organizational change initiatives) when they have strong affective (desire) *and* normative (obligation) commitment. One possible explanation for this finding is that the combination of desire and obligation creates a *moral imperative* that drives individuals to do whatever it takes to achieve a goal or support the target of their commitment (Meyer, Becker, & Vandenberghe, 2004). While it might seem that this kind of dedication would be particularly difficult to achieve in the face of change, it may be precisely what separates the "great" companies (Collins, 2001) from the rest. Even those organizations that cannot guarantee long-term employment for all might be able to instill a strong commitment to an organizational mission, vision, or ideology that gives work a sense of meaning and purpose (see Thompson & Bunderson, 2003; Collins & Porras, 1997). Therefore, additional directions for future research include examining the impact of change on commitment profiles, and examining the organization's mission/vision as another potential focus of commitment.

Conclusion

Commitment is alive and well and exists in many different forms in the constantly changing world of work. Although change has not undermined the importance of commitment, it has made the management of commitment more complex. This complexity should serve as a challenge to commitment scholars. I have suggested just a few of the important questions that need to be answered. There are undoubtedly many more that will be raised in the following chapters.

References

Alderfer, C. P. (1972). *Existence, relatedness, and growth.* New York: Free Press.

Allen, N. J., & Meyer, J. P. (1990). The measurement and antecedents of affective, continuance, and normative commitment to the organization. *Journal of Occupational Psychology, 63,* 1–18.

Allen, N. J., & Grisaffe, D. B. (2001). Employee commitment to the organization and customer reactions: Mapping the linkages. *Human Resource Management Review, 11,* 209–236.

Arthur, J. B. (1994). Effects of human resource systems on manufacturing performance and turnover. *Academy of Management Journal, 37,* 670–687.

Ashforth, B. E., & Mael, F. (1989). Social identity theory and the organization. *Academy of Management Review, 14,* 20–39.

Bansal, H. S., Irving, P. G., & Taylor, S. F. (2004). A three-component model of customer commitment to service providers. *Journal of the Academy of Marketing, 32,* 234–250.

Bargh, J., & Chartrand, T. (1999). The unbearable automaticity of being. *American Psychologist, 54,* 462–479.

Barling, J., & Kelloway, E. K. (1996). Job insecurity and health: The moderating role of workplace control. *Stress Medicine, 12,* 253–259.

Baruch, Y. (1998). The rise and fall of organizational commitment. *Human Systems Management, 17,* 135–143.

Baumeister, R. F., & Leary, M. R. (1995). The need to belong: Desire for interpersonal attachments as a fundamental human motivation. *Psychological Bulletin, 117,* 497–529.

Becker, T. E. (1992). Foci and bases of commitment: Are they distinctions worth making? *Academy of Management Journal, 35,* 232–244.

Becker, T. E., Billings, R. S., Eveleth, D. M., & Gilbert, N. W. (1996). Foci and bases of commitment: Implications for performance. *Academy of Management Journal, 39,* 464–482.

Becker, T. E., & Kernan, M. (2003). Matching commitment to supervisors and organizations to in-role and extra-role performance. *Human Performance, 16,* 327–348.

Begley, T. M., & Czajka, J. M. (1993). Panel analysis of the moderating effects of commitment on job satisfaction, intent to quit, and health following organizational change. *Journal of Applied Psychology, 78,* 552–556.

Bennis, W. (2000). Leadership of change. In M. Beer & N. Nohria, (Eds.), *Breaking the code of change* (pp. 113–121). Boston: Harvard Business School Press.

Bentein, K., Stinglhamber, F., & Vandenberghe, C. (2002). Organization-, supervisor-, and workgroup-directed commitments and citizenship behaviors: A comparison of models. *European Journal of Work and Organizational Psychology, 11,* 341–362.

Blau, G. (1985).The measurement and prediction of career commitment. *Journal of Occupational Psychology, 58,* 277–288.

Blau, G. (1989). Testing the generalizability of a career commitment measure and its impact on employee turnover. *Journal of Vocational Behavior, 35,* 88–103.

Blau, G. (2003). Testing for a four-dimensional structure of occupational commitment. *Journal of Occupational and Organizational Psychology, 76*, 469–488.

Bowen, D., & Ostroff, C. (2004). Understanding HRM-firm performance linkages: The role of the strength of HRM systems. *Academy of Management Review, 29*, 203–221.

Bridges, W. (1994). *Job shift: How to prosper in a workplace without jobs*. Reading, MA: Addison-Wesley.

Brown, R. B. (1996). Organizational commitment: Clarifying the concept and simplifying the existing construct typology. *Journal of Vocational Behavior, 49*, 230–251.

Caldwell, S. D., Herold, D. M., & Fedor, D. B. (2004). Toward an understanding of the relationships among organizational change, individual differences, and changes in person-environment fit: A cross-level study. *Journal of Applied Psychology, 89*, 868–882.

Cappelli, P. (1999). Career jobs are dead. *California Management Review, 42(1)*, 146–167.

Carson, K. D., Carson, P. P., & Bedeian, A. G. (1995). Development and construct validation of a career entrenchment measure. *Journal of Occupational and Organizational Psychology, 68*, 301–320.

Chatman, J. A. (1989). Improving interactional organizational research: A model of person-organization fit. *Academy of Management Review, 14*, 333–349.

Cohen, A. (1993). Work commitment in relation to withdrawal intentions and union effectiveness. *Journal of Business Research, 26*, 75–90.

Cohen, A. (1999). Relationships among five forms of commitment: An empirical assessment. *Journal of Organizational Behavior, 20*, 285–308.

Cohen, A. (2003). *Multiple commitments at work: An integrative approach*. Hillsdale, NJ: Lawrence Erlbaum.

Cohen, A., & Kirchmeyer, C. (1995). A multidimensional approach to the relation between organizational commitment and nonwork participation. *Journal of Vocational Behavior, 46*, 189–202.

Collins, J. C. (2001). *Good to great: Why some companies make the leap and others don't*. New York: HarperBusiness.

Collins, J. C., & Porras, J. I. (1996). *Built to last: Successful habits of visionary companies*. New York: HarperBusiness.

Colquitt, J. A., Conlon, D. E., Wesson, M. J., Porter, C. O. L. H., & Ng, K. Y. (2001). Justice at the millennium: A meta-analytic review of 25 years of organizational justice research. *Journal of Applied Psychology, 86*, 425–445.

Connelly, C. E., Gallagher, D. G., & Gilley, K. M. (2007). Organizational and client commitment among contracted employees: A replication and extension with temporary workers. *Journal of Vocational Behavior, 70*, 326–335.

Connor, D. R. (1993). *Managing at the speed of change: How resilient managers succeed and prosper where others fail*. New York: Villard Books.

Cooper-Hakim, A., & Viswesvaran, C. (2005). The construct of work commitment: Testing an integrative framework. *Psychological Bulletin, 131*, 241–259.

Coyle-Shapiro, J. A.-M., & Morrow, P. C. (2006). Organizational and client commitment among contracted employees. *Journal of Vocational Behavior, 68*, 416–431.

Coyle-Shapiro, J. A.-M., Morrow, P. C., & Kessler, I. (2006). Serving two organizations: Exploring the employment relationship of contracted employees.
Human Resource Management, 45, 561–583.

Cropanzano, R., Rupp, D. E., & Byrne, Z. S. (2003). The relationship of emotional
exhaustion to work attitudes, job performance, and organizational citizenship behaviours. *Journal of Applied Psychology, 88*, 160–169.

Cunningham, G. B. (2006). The relationships among commitment to change,
coping with change, and turnover intentions. *European Journal of Work and
Organizational Psychology, 15*, 29–45.

Dabos, G. E., & Rousseau, D. M. (2004). Mutuality and reciprocity in psychological contracts of employees and employers. *Journal of Applied Psychology, 89*,
52–72.

Deci, E. L., & Ryan, R. M. (1985). *Intrinsic motivation and self-determination in human
behavior.* New York: Plenum.

Dekker, S. W. A., & Schaufeli, W. B. (1995). The effect of job insecurity on psychological health and withdrawal: A longitudinal study. *Australia Psychologist,
30*, 57–63.

Eisenberger, R., Fasolo, P., & LaMastro, V. (1990). Perceived organizational support and employee diligence, commitment, and innovation. *Journal of Applied
Psychology, 75*, 51–59.

Eisenberger, R., Huntington, R., Hutchison, S., & Sowa, D. (1986). Perceived organizational support. *Journal of Applied Psychology, 71*, 500–507.

Emshoff, J. R. (1994). How to increase employee loyalty while you downsize.
Business Horizons, 37, 49–57.

Fedor, D. B., Caldwell, S., & Herold, D. M. (2006). The effects of organizational
changes on employee commitment: A multilevel investigation. *Personnel
Psychology, 59*, 1–29.

Ferris, G. R., Arthur, M. A., Berkson, H. M., Kaplan, D. M., Harrell-Cook, G., &
Frink, D. D. (1998). Toward a social context theory of the human resource
management–organizational effectiveness relationship. *Human Resource
Management Review, 8*, 235–264.

Ford, J. K., Weissbein, D. A., & Plamondon, K. E. (2003). Distinguishing organizational from strategy commitment: Linking officers' commitment to community policing to job behaviours and satisfaction. *Justice Quarterly, 20*,
159–185.

Frank, R. H. (2001). Cooperation through emotional commitment. In R. M. Nesse
(Ed.), *Evolution and the capacity for commitment* (pp. 57–76). New York: Russell
Sage Foundation.

Fullagar, C., & Barling, J. (1989). A longitudinal test of a model of the antecedents and consequences of union loyalty. *Journal of Applied Psychology, 74*,
213–227.

Fullerton, G. (2005). How commitment both enables and undermines marketing
relationships. *European Journal of Marketing, 39*(11/12), 1372–1388.

Fulmer, I. S., Gerhart, B., & Scott, K. S. (2003). Are the 100 best better? An empirical
investigation of the relationship between being a "great place to work" and
firm performance. *Personnel Psychology, 56*, 965–993.

Gallagher, D. G., & McLean Parks, J. (2001). I pledge my troth ... contingently: Commitment and the contingent work relationship. *Human Resource Management Review, 11,* 181–208.

Gelade G. A., & Ivery, M. (2003). The impact of human resource management and work climate on organizational performance. *Personnel Psychology, 56,* 383–404.

Gellatly, I. R., Meyer, J. P., & Luchak, A. A. (2006). Combined effects of the three commitment components on focal and discretionary behaviors: A test of Meyer and Herscovitch's proposition. *Journal of Vocational Behavior, 69,* 331–345.

Gopinath, C., & Becker, T. E. (2000). Communication, procedural justice, and employee attitudes: Relationships under conditions of divestiture. *Journal of Management, 26,* 63–83.

Herscovitch, L., & Meyer, J. P. (2002). Commitment to organizational change: Extension of a three-component model. *Journal of Applied Psychology, 87,* 474–487.

Hunt, S. D., & Morgan, R. M. (1994). Organizational commitment: One of many commitments or key mediating construct? *Academy of Management Journal, 37,* 1568–1587.

Huselid, M. A. (1995). The impact of human resource management practices on turnover, productivity, and corporate financial performance. *Academy of Management Journal, 38,* 635–672.

Irving, P. G., & Coleman, D. F. (2003). The moderating effect of different forms of commitment on role-ambiguity-job tension relations. *Canadian Journal of Administrative Sciences, 20,* 97–106.

Irving, P. G., Coleman, D. F., & Cooper, C. L. (1997). Further assessment of a three-component model of occupational commitment: Generalizability and differences across occupations. *Journal of Applied Psychology, 82,* 444–452.

Klein, K. J., & Sorra, J. S. (1996). The challenge of innovation implementation. *Academy of Management Review, 21,* 1055–1080.

Klein, H. J., Wesson, M. J., Hollenbeck, J. R., & Alge, B. J. (1999). Goal commitment and the goal-setting process: Conceptual comparison and empirical synthesis. *Journal of Applied Psychology, 84,* 885–896.

Kontratuck, T.B., Hausdorf, P.A, Korabik, K., & Rosen, H.A. (2004). Linking career mobility with corporate loyalty: How does job change relate to organizational commitment? *Journal of Vocational Behavior, 65,* 332–349.

Kopelman, R. E., Brief, A. P., & Guzzo, R. A. (1990). The role of climate and culture in productivity. In B. Schneider (Ed.), *Organizational climate and culture* (pp. 282–318). San Francisco: Jossey-Bass.

Korsgaard, M. A., Sapienza, J. H., & Schweiger, D. M. (2002). Beaten before begun: The role of procedural justice in planning change. *Journal of Management, 28,* 497–516.

Koys, D. J. (2001). The effects of employee satisfaction, organizational citizenship behavior, and turnover on organizational effectiveness: A unit-level, longitudinal study. *Personnel Psychology, 54,* 101–114.

Kristof, A. L. (1996). Person-organization fit: An integrative review of its conceptualizations, measurement, and implications. *Personnel Psychology, 49,* 1–49.

Lawler, E. J. (1992). Affective attachment to nested groups: A choice-process theory. *American Sociological Review, 57,* 327–339.

Lawrence, P. R., & Nohria, N. (2000). *Driven: How human nature shapes our choices.* San Francisco: Jossey-Bass.

Lee, K., Carswell, J. J., & Allen, N. J. (2000). A meta-analytic review of occupational commitment: Relations with person- and work-related variables. *Journal of Applied Psychology, 85,* 799–811.

Lee, T. W., Ashford, S. J., Walsh, J. P., & Mowday, R. T. (1992). Commitment propensity, organizational commitment, and voluntary turnover: A longitudinal study. *Journal of Management, 18,* 15–32.

Leiter, M. P., Clark, D., & Durup, J. (1994). Distinct models of burnout and commitment among men and women in the military. *Journal of Applied Behavioral Science, 30,* 63–82.

Leiter, M. P., & Maslach, C. (1988). The impact of interpersonal environment on burnout and organizational commitment. *Journal of Organizational Behavior, 9,* 297–308.

MacDuffie, J. P. (1994). Human resource bundles and manufacturing performance: Organizational logic and flexible production systems in the world auto industry. *Industrial and Labor Relations Review, 48,* 197–221.

Macey, W. H., & Schneider, B. (2008). The meaning of employee engagement. *Journal of Industrial-Organizational Psychology.*

Maertz, C. P., Mosley, D. C., & Alford, B. L. (2002). Does organizational commitment fully mediate constituent commitment effects? A reassessment and clarification. *Journal of Applied Social Psychology, 32,* 1300–1313.

March, J., & Simon, H. (1958). *Organizations.* New York: Wiley.

Maslow, A. H. (1943). A theory of human motivation. *Psychological Review, 50,* 370–396.

Mathieu, J. E., & Zajac, D. M. (1990). A review and meta-analysis of the antecedents, correlates, and consequences of organizational commitment. *Psychological Bulletin, 108,* 171–194.

McAuley, B. J., Zeitz, G., & Blau, G. (2006). Testing the "push-pull" theory of work commitment among organizational professionals. *The Social Science Journal, 43,* 571–596.

Meyer, J P. (1997). Organizational commitment. In I. T. Robertson and C. L. Cooper (Eds.), *International review of industrial and organizational psychology,* (Vol. 12, pp. 175–228). New York: John Wiley & Sons.

Meyer, J. P., & Allen, N. J. (1991). A three-component conceptualization of organizational commitment. *Human Resource Management Review, 1,* 61–89.

Meyer, J. P., & Allen, N. J. (1997). *Commitment in the workplace: Theory, research, and application.* Newbury Park, CA: Sage.

Meyer, J. P., Allen, N. J., & Smith, C. A. (1993). Commitment to organizations and occupations: Extension and test of a three-component conceptualization. *Journal of Applied Psychology, 78,* 538–551.

Meyer, J. P., Allen, N. J., & Topolnytsky, L. (1998). Commitment in a changing world of work. *Canadian Psychology, 39,* 83–93.

Meyer, J. P., Bobocel, D. R., & Allen, N. J. (1991). Development of organizational commitment during the first year of employment: A longitudinal study of pre- and post-entry influences. *Journal of Management, 17,* 717–731.

Meyer, J. P., Becker, T. E., & Vandenberghe, C. (2004). Employee commitment and motivation: A conceptual analysis and integrative model. *Journal of Applied Psychology, 89*, 991–1007.

Meyer, J. P., Becker, T. E., & Van Dick, R. (2006). Social identities and commitments at work: Toward an integrated model. *Journal of Organizational Behavior, 27*, 665–683.

Meyer, J. P., & Herscovitch, L. (2001). Commitment in the workplace: Toward a general model. *Human Resource Management Review, 11*, 299–326.

Meyer, J. P., & Smith, C. A. (2000). Human resource management practices and organizational commitment: Test of a mediation model. *Canadian Journal of Administrative Sciences, 17*, 319–331.

Meyer, J. P., Srinivas, E. R., Lal, J. B., & Topolnytsky, L. (2007). Employee commitment and support for an organizational change: Test of the three-component model in two cultures. *Journal of Occupational and Organizational Psychology. 80*, 185–211.

Meyer, J. P., Stanley, D. J., Herscovitch, L., & Topolnytsky, L. (2002). Affective, continuance, and normative commitment to the organization: A meta-analysis of antecedents, correlates, and consequences. *Journal of Vocational Behavior, 61*, 20–52.

Morrow, P. C. (1983). Concept redundancy in organizational research: The case of work commitment. *Academy of Management Review, 8*, 486–500.

Mowday, R. T. (1998). Reflections on the study and relevance of organizational commitment. *Human Resource Management Review, 8(4)*, 387–401.

Mowday, R. T., Porter, L. W., & Steers, R. M. (1982). *Employee-organization linkages: The psychology of commitment, absenteeism, and turnover.* New York: Academic Press.

Mowday, R. T., Steers, R. M., & Porter, L. W. (1979). The measurement of organizational commitment. *Journal of Vocational Behavior, 14*, 224–247.

Mueller, C. W., & Lawler, E. J. (1999). Commitment to nested organizational units: Some basic principles and preliminary findings. *Social Psychology Quarterly, 62*, 325–346.

Nesse, R. N. (Ed.) (2001a). *Evolution and the capacity for commitment.* New York: Russell Sage Foundation.

Nesse, R. N. (2001b). Natural selection and the capacity for subjective commitment. In R. M. Nesse (Ed.), *Evolution and the capacity for commitment* (pp. 1–44). New York: Russell Sage Foundation.

Neubert, M. J., & Cady, S. H. (2001). Program commitment: A multi-study longitudinal field investigation of its impact and antecedents. *Personnel Psychology, 54*, 421–448.

Novelli, L., Jr., Kirkman, B. L., & Shapiro, D. L. (1995). Effective implementation of organizational change: An organizational justice perspective. In C. L. Cooper and D. M. Rousseau (Eds.), *Trends in Organizational Behavior* (Vol. 2, pp. 15–36).

O'Reilly, C. A, & Pfeffer, J. (2000). *Hidden value: How great companies achieve extraordinary results with ordinary people.* Boston: Harvard Business School Press.

Ostroff, C. (1992). The relationship between satisfaction, attitudes, and performance: An organizational level analysis. *Journal of Applied Psychology, 77*, 963–974.

Pfeffer, J. (1998). *The human equation: Building profits by putting people first*. Boston: Harvard Business School Press.

Podsakoff, P. M., & MacKenzie, S. B. (1994). Organizational citizenship behaviour and sales-unit effectiveness. *Journal of Marketing Research, 31*, 351–363.

Porter, L. W., Crampon, W. J., & Smith, F. (1976). Organizational commitment and managerial turnover: A longitudinal study. *Organizational Behavior and Human Performance, 15*, 87–89.

Porter, L. W., Steers, R. M., Mowday, R. T., & Boulian, P. V. (1974). Organizational commitment, job satisfaction, and turnover among psychiatric technicians. *Journal of Applied Psychology, 59*, 603–609.

Pratt, M. G. (1998). To be or not to be? Central questions in organizational identification. In D. A. Wheton & P. C. Godfrey (Eds.), *Identity in organizations: Building theory through conversations* (pp. 171–207). Thousand Oaks, CA: Sage.

Randall, D. M. (1990). The consequences of organizational commitment: Methodological investigation. *Journal of Organizational Behavior, 11*, 361–378.

Redman, T., & Snape, E. (2005). Unpacking commitment: Multiple loyalties and employee behavior. *Journal of Management Studies, 42*, 301–328.

Reichheld, F. F. (1996). *The loyalty effect*. Boston: Harvard Business School Press.

Reichers, A. E. (1985). A review and reconceptualization of organizational commitment. *Academy of Management Review, 10*, 465–476.

Reichers, A. E., Wanous, J. P., & Austin, J. T. (1997). Understanding and managing cynicism about organizational change. *Academy of Management Executive, 11(1)*, 48–59.

Rhoades, L., & Eisenberger, R. (2002). Perceived organizational support: A review of the literature. *Journal of Applied Psychology, 87*, 698–714

Richardson, A. S., Burke, R. J., & Martinussen, M. (2006). Work and health outcomes among police officers: The mediating role of police cynicism and engagement. *International Journal of Stress Management, 13*, 555–574.

Riketta, M. (2002). Attitudinal organizational commitment and job performance: A meta-analysis. *Journal of Organizational Behavior, 23*, 257–266.

Rousseau, D. M. (1995). *Promises in action: Psychological contracts in organizations*. Newbury Park, CA : Sage.

Rousseau, D. M. (1996). Changing the deal while keeping the people. *Academy of Management Executive, 10(1)*, 50–61.

Ryan, R. M., & Deci, E. L. (2000). Self-determination theory and the facilitation of intrinsic motivation, social development, and well-being. *American Psychologist, 55*, 68–78.

Ryan, A. M., Schmit, M. J., & Johnson, R. (1996). Attitudes and effectiveness: Examining relations at an organizational level. *Personnel Psychology, 49*, 853–882.

Salancik, G. R. (1977). Commitment and the control of organizational behavior. In B.M. Staw & G.R. Salancik (Eds.), *New Directions in Organizational Behavior* (pp. 1–54). Chicago: St. Clair Press.

Schmidt, K.-H. (2007). Organizational commitment: A further moderator in the relationship between work stress and strain? *International Journal of Stress Management, 14*, 26–40.

Schneider, B., Goldstein, H. W., & Smith, D. B. (1995). The ASA framework: An update. *Personnel Psychology, 48*, 747–773.

Schweiger, D. M., & DeNisi, A. S. (1991). Communication with employees following a merger: A longitudinal field experiment. *Academy of Management Journal, 34,* 110–135.

Siders, M. A., George, G., & Dharwadkar, R. (2001). The relationship of internal and external commitment foci to objective job performance measures. *Academy of Management Journal, 44,* 580–590.

Stanley, P. J., Meyer, J. P., & Topolnytsky, L. (2005). Employee cynicism and organizational change. *Journal of Business and Psychology. 19,* 429–459.

Staw, B. M. (1981). The escalation of commitment to a course of action. *Academy of Management Review, 6,* 569–577.

Staw, B. M. (1997). The escalation of commitment: an update and appraisal. In Z. Shapiro (Ed.), *Organizational decision making* (pp. 191–215). Cambridge: Cambridge University Press.

Steers, R. M. (1977). Antecedents and outcomes of organizational commitment. *Administrative Science Quarterly, 22,* 46–56.

Sverke, M., & Kuruvilla, S. (1995). A new conceptualization of union commitment: Development and test of an integrated theory. *Journal of Organizational Behavior, 16,* 505–532.

Swailes, S. (2004). Commitment to change: Profiles of commitment and in-role performance. *Personnel Review, 33,* 187–204.

Tajfel, H. (1978). Social categorization, social identity, and social comparison. In H. Tajfel (Ed.), *Differentiation between social groups: Studies in the social psychology of intergroup relations* (pp. 61–76). London: Academic Press.

Tett, R. P., & Meyer, J. P. (1993). Job satisfaction, organizational commitment, turnover intention and turnover: Path analyses based on meta-analytic findings. *Personnel Psychology, 46,* 259–293.

Thompson, J. A., & Bunderson, J. S. (2003). Violations of principle: Ideological currency in the psychological contract. *Academy of Management Review, 28,* 571–588.

Tsui, A. S., Pearce, J. L., Porter, L. W., & Tripoli, A. M., (1997). Alternative approaches to the employee-organization relationship: Does investment in employees pay off? *Academy of Management Journal, 40,* 1089–1121.

Tucker, J. S., Sinclair, R. R., & Thomas, J. L. (2005). The multilevel effects of occupational stressors on soldiers' well-being, organizational attachment, and readiness. *Journal of Occupational Health Psychology, 10,* 276–299.

Vandenberghe, C., Bentein, K., & Stinglhamber, F. (2004). Affective commitment to the organization, supervisor, and work group: Antecedents and outcomes. *Journal of Vocational Behavior, 64,* 47–71.

Wallace, J. E. (1995). Organizational and professional commitment in professional and non-professional organizations. *Administrative Science Quarterly, 40,* 228–255.

Wasti, S. A. (2005). Commitment profiles: Combinations of organizational commitment forms and job outcomes. *Journal of Vocational Behavior, 67,* 290–308.

Wegge, J., Van Dick, R., Fisher, G. K., West, M. A., & Dawson, J. F. (2006). A test of basic assumptions of Affective Events Theory (AET) in call centre work. *British Journal of Management, 17,* 237–254.

Whyte, W. H. (1956). *The organization man.* New York: Simon & Schuster.

Wittig-Berman, U., & Lang, D. (1990). Organizational commitment and its out-
    comes: Differing effects of value commitment and continuance commitment
    on stress reactions, alienation and organization-serving behaviors. *Work and
    Stress, 4,* 167–177.
Wright, P. M., Gardner, T., Moynihan, L., & Allen, M. (2005). The HR–performance
    relationship: Examining causal directions. *Personnel Psychology, 58,* 409–446.
Wright, P. M., & Haggerty, J. J. (2005). Missing variables in theories of strategic
    human resource management: Time, cause, and individuals. *Management
    Revue, 16,* 164–173.
Wright, T. A., & Bonett, D. G. (2002). The moderating effects of employee tenure
    on the relation between organizational commitment and job performance: A
    meta-analysis. *Journal of Applied Psychology, 87,* 1183–1190.

3

Commitment's Place in the Literature

Michael Riketta
Aston University, Birmingham, United Kingdom

Rolf Van Dick*
Goethe-University, Frankfurt, Germany

Commitment plays an important role in predicting behavior at the workplace. As many reviews of the literature have shown, commitment correlates with work outcomes such as performance, organizational citizenship behavior, turnover, and withdrawal cognition and thus appears crucial for understanding and enhancing work effectiveness (e.g., Cooper-Hakim & Viswesvaran, 2005; Mathieu & Zajac, 1990; Meyer, Stanley, Herscovitch, & Topolnytsky, 2002; Meyer & Allen, 1997; Mowday, Porter, & Steers, 1982; see also chapters 1 and 2). However, the same can be said of several other psychological constructs, most of which are strongly correlated with commitment, such as satisfaction or identification (e.g., see Cooper-Hakim & Viswesvaran, 2005; Morrow, 1983; Riketta, 2005; Harrison, Newman, & Roth, 2006). Thus, one may wonder what is so special about commitment and would justify studying it as a construct in its own right.

The present chapter tries to answer this question, referring to theoretical, empirical, and practical considerations. The next section compares commitment with related psychological constructs and highlights the unique features of commitment. In particular, we will (a) compare the definitions and measures of commitment and each related construct, (b) briefly review theoretical models specifying causal relations between the constructs, and (c) review empirical research comparing these constructs. Specifically, as to the latter point, we will use findings from previous meta-analyses and selected single studies to (a) provide an estimate of the correlation between commitment and each related construct and (b) compare the profiles of

---

* Michael Riketta was a friendly and helpful colleague I could always rely on. The collaboration on this chapter was the last in a series of joint undertakings. Michael was a determined scholar, committed to a deeper understanding of the phenomena we were both researching. He lost a long battle against cancer and died shortly after correcting the proofs of this chapter. I will miss him and his untimely death is a loss to all who got to know him as a nice human being.

correlations of commitment with the correlation profiles of each other construct. Research lacunae will be pointed out.

Complementing these analyses that point to the distinctness of organizational commitment, in a final section we will present metatheoretical and practical arguments for studying commitment as a construct in its own right. Specifically, we will sketch the importance of commitment for theorizing in industrial/organizational psychology and for management practice.

As detailed in chapter 1, commitment has been defined in many different ways and examined with regard to a variety of targets or foci (e.g., organization, workgroup, career). Because this chapter puts emphasis on reviews of the empirical literature, we adopt conceptualizations of commitment that underlie the measures in most of the research reviewed. By far the most influential conceptualizations of commitment are those by Porter and colleagues (who defined commitment as an inner bond, or attachment, to the target, and coined the term *attitudinal commitment* for this construct; e.g., Mowday et al., 1982; Mowday, Steers, & Porter, 1979) and by Allen and Meyer (e.g., 1990), who distinguish between three commitment mindsets: affective (which largely overlaps with attitudinal commitment as defined by Porter and colleagues), continuance, and normative (see chapter 1 for a detailed discussion and alternative conceptualizations). The large impact of these conceptualizations is evident, for example, from the fact that the huge majority of commitment studies since the 1980s used measures that are based on these definitions (above all, the measures developed by Mowday et al., 1979, 1982; Allen & Meyer, 1990). Further, we agree with Klein and colleagues (chapter 1) that these conceptualizations, compared with most alternatives suggested in the literature, show less overlap with possible antecedents, consequences, and job attitudes (in a narrow sense, i.e., excluding commitment) and thus are preferable from a theoretical perspective. That is, they assign to commitment a relatively clearly specified and unique place in the literature. This renders them useful for the present discussion. Of course, the distinctness of commitment from the constructs discussed below depends on the definitions used.

Reflecting the current emphasis in research, we will pay more attention to the organization than to other targets of commitment. Thus, we will look mainly at affective organizational commitment (AOC), continuance organizational commitment (COC), and normative organizational commitment (NOC).

Commitment in Comparison to Conceptually Related Constructs

This section starts with detailed analyses of three constructs that show substantial conceptual overlap with commitment (especially with AOC) and have been studied frequently enough to enable firm conclusions about their empirical relation to commitment. These constructs are identification, involvement, and satisfaction. As far as possible, we build on meta-analytic evidence to flesh out the empirical differences between commitment and each construct. Finally, we briefly discuss two constructs that are also conceptually related to commitment (work engagement and job embeddedness) but for which only tentative conclusions are possible.

Our discussion draws heavily on meta-analytic results. Table 3.1 gives an overview of the findings we will use in this discussion. To ensure comparable results, we considered only meta-analyses that corrected for sampling error and unreliability. In instances where multiple values on the same relation from different meta-analysis were available, only the values based on the largest number of samples were included in the table.

The data in the table refer to constructs that are frequently included in the nomological net around commitment. We divide these constructs into three categories: job attitudes, work context, and work behavior. In general, researchers tend to view the work context as antecedent to commitment, and work behavior as consequence of commitment (e.g., Mathieu & Zajac, 1990; Meyer et al., 2002). However, evidence on the causal relations between these constructs is scarce, and alternative causal models are plausible (e.g., see Judge, Thoresen, Bono, & Patton, 2001; Riketta, 2008). Thus, we will be cautious with causal interpretations of the reviewed correlations. Where we offer such interpretations, they should be considered preliminary.

In the studies included in the reviewed meta-analyses, as well as in the single studies reviewed below, AOC has almost exclusively been measured with the Affective Commitment Scale (ACS; Allen & Meyer, 1990) or the Organizational Commitment Questionnaire (OCQ; Mowday et al., 1979). Both measures conceptualize commitment as an inner bond or attachment to the organization. Further, all studies on NOC and COC cited in the following used Allen and Meyer's (1990) Normative Commitment Scale and Continuance Commitment Scale, respectively. Thus, the empirical findings discussed in the following refer to the particular conceptualizations of commitment that underlie these scales.

Identification

Identification is the closest conceptual neighbor of commitment, especially of affective commitment. Because identification has almost exclusively been studied with the organization as focus, we concentrate on organizational identification (OI) in the following discussion.

Reflecting the heterogeneous theoretical traditions within this area, many definitions of OI are available (see Edwards, 2005; Riketta, 2005; Van Dick, 2001, 2004). For example, OI has been alternatively defined as the congruence of individual and organizational values (Hall, Schneider,

TABLE 3.1

Meta-Analytic Comparison of the Correlates of Organizational Commitment and Three Other Job Attitudes

Correlates	AOC	NOC	COC	OI	JI	JS
NOC	.64(59)[a] [.61;.67]					
COC	.13(163)[a] [.10;.16]	.19(56)[a] [.16;.22]				
Job Attitudes						
OI	.78(16)[b] [.54;1.00]	n.a.	n.a.			
JI	.50(22)[a] [.38;.62]	.52(5)[a] [.49;.55]	.15(10)[a] [.06;.24]	.61(12)[b] [.55;.67]		
JS	.60(140)[a] [.58;.62]	.36(45)[a] [.33;.39]	.12(79)[a] [.08;.16]	.54(38)[b] [.48;.60]	.35(462)[a] [.33;.37]	
Work Context						
Role conflict	−.30(9)[c] [−.36;−.24]	−.24(5)[c] [−.32;−.16]	.13(8)[c] [.3;.23]	n.a.	−.17(27)[d] [−.22;−.12]	−.35(13)[e] [n.a.]
Role ambiguity	−.39(12)[c] [−.49;−.29]	−.21(7)[c] [−.31;−.11]	.10(11)[c] [.05;.15]	n.a.	−.16(32)[d] [−.23;−.09]	−.25(16)[e] [n.a.]
Transformational leadership	.46(4)[c] [.41;.51]	.27(3)[c] [.17;.37]	−.14(4)[c] [−.23;−.05]	n.a.	.20(5) [.09;.31], .56(9) [.48;.64], .27(9) [.21;.33][d,g]	.18(58)[h] [n.a.]
Autonomy	.32(6)[i] [n.a.]	n.a.	n.a.	n.a.	.23(18)[d] [.15;.31]	.48(20)[j] [n.a]
Skill variety	.18(5)[i] [n.a.]	n.a.	n.a.	n.a.	.37(15)[d] [.27;.47]	.45(22)[j] [n.a.]
Feedback	.41(4)[i] [n.a.]	n.a.	n.a.	n.a.	.28(13)[d] [.21;.35]	.43(20)[j] [n.a.]

Work Behavior

In-role behavior	.18(87)[k] [.15;.21]	.08(17)[a] [.05;.11]	-.12(33)[a] [-.18;-.06]	.17(16)[b] [.10;.24]	.18(85)[a] [.15;.21]	.30(312)[n] [.27;.33]
Extra-role behavior	.25(42)[k] [.21;.29]	.07(6)[c] [.00;.14]	-.05(6)[c] [-.11;.01]	.35(25)[b] [.28;.42]	n.a.	.21 to.28 (5 to 28)[m] [.16;.32]
Absenteeism	-.23(6) [n.a.], -.12(11)[f] [n.a.]	.05(4)[c] [.03;.07]	.06(7)[c] [.06;.06]	-.01(6)[b] [-.06;.03]	-.14(17)[d] [-.20;-.08]	-.10(20) [n.a.], -.24(12) [n.a.][f]
Turnover intention	-.58(97)[a] [-.56;-.60]	-.37(34)[a] [-.35;-.39]	-.19(48)[a] [-.15;-.23]	-.48(34)[b] [-.41;-.55]	-.30(103)[a] [-.28;-.32]	-.58(88)[o] [-.54;-.62]
Turnover	-.33(25)[p] [-.38;-.28]	-.16(6)[a] [-.22;-.10]	-.25(15)[a] [-.33;-.17]	n.a.	-.16(26)[a] [-.15;-.22]	-.25(49)[o] [-.29;-.21]

Note: Sample size weighted and disattenuated mean correlations (number of analyzed samples in parentheses, 95% confidence intervals in brackets). AOC, NOC, and COC: affective or attitudinal, normative, and continuance organizational commitment, respectively. OI: organizational identification. JI: job involvement. JS: job satisfaction. n.a.: not available.

[a] Cooper-Hakim & Visweswaran (2004). [b]Riketta (2005). [c]Meyer et al. (2002). [d]Brown (1996). [e]Fisher & Gitelson (1983). [f]Farrell & Stamm (1988), referring to absence frequency and total time lost, respectively. [g]Correlations for communication, participation, consideration, respectively. [h]Judge & Piccolo (2004). [i]Eby et al (1999). [j]Fried and Ferris (1987). [k]Riketta (2002), confidence intervals calculated from the raw data (unpublished). [m]Organ & Ryan (1995), separately for five facets of extra-role performance; the confidence interval denotes the lowest lower and highest upper bound across all five facets. [n]Judge et al. (2001). [o]Tett and Meyer (1993).

& Nygren, 1970; Pratt, 1998), the "perception of oneness with or belonging-ness to an organization" (Mael & Ashforth, 1992, p. 104), the inclusion of one's organization membership into one's general self-definition (Dutton, Dukerich, & Harquail, 1994; Elsbach, 1999; Rousseau, 1998), the desire to maintain an emotionally satisfying self-defining relationship with the organization (O'Reilly & Chatman, 1986), or a combination of one's aware-ness, evaluation, and emotional significance of one's own organizational membership (e.g., Abrams, Ando, & Hinkle, 1998; Ouwerkerk, Ellemers, & de Gilder, 1999; Tajfel, 1978). The common thread of these definitions is that "the organizational member has linked his or her organizational membership to his or her self-concept, either cognitively (e.g., feeling a part of the organization; internalizing organizational values), emotionally (pride in membership), or both" (Riketta, 2005, p. 361). This definition is used as a working definition of OI throughout this chapter.

What are the conceptual differences of this construct from commit-ment? For one, OI clearly overlaps with AOC, which is commonly defined as "employees' emotional attachment to, identification with, and involve-ment in, the organization" (Allen & Meyer, 1990, p. 1; for a similar defi-nition, see Mowday et al., 1979). According to this definition, OI is one component of AOC. In fact, there is consensus in the literature that OI is a construct related to but narrower than AOC (e.g., Ashforth & Mael, 1989; Mael & Tetrick, 1992; Pratt, 1998).

Further, OI is clearly distinct from continuance organizational commit-ment (COC), which refers to the belief that one has to stay with the organi-zation because of the costs associated with leaving (Allen & Meyer, 1990). Obviously, COC implies neither relevance of organizational membership to self-definition nor emotional bonds to the organization.

Finally, OI appears distinct from NOC, defined as the perceived obliga-tion to remain with the organization (Allen & Meyer, 1990). The feeling of an obligation toward the organization may be a consequence of OI, espe-cially if OI implies the internalization of organizational reciprocity norms. However, NOC may also occur in the absence of OI, for example, as a result of a specific work ethic (see Cooper-Hakim & Visweswaran, 2005).

Based on the above definitions, one would expect that OI (a) correlates strongly with AOC, less strongly with NOC, and not at all with COC and (b) is more similar to AOC than NOC and COC regarding its correlations with overlapping constructs as well as with postulated antecedents and consequences. We now review evidence relevant to these propositions.

Correlations between OI and AOC are typically high. Riketta (2005) reported an average correlation between OI as assessed with a variety of measures and AOC of .78. As evident from Table 3.1, the 95 percent confidence interval of this correlation even includes 1.0 (which is not the case for all other meta-analytic correlations discussed hereafter). That is, the possibility that OI and AOC measures refer to same construct(s) cannot be rejected at conventional levels of significance. When one limits this analysis to studies using the most common OI measure, the Mael scale (Mael & Ashforth, 1992; Mael & Tetrick, 1992), the correlation with AOC is almost the same, $r = .79$, $k = 3$, but the 95% confidence interval excludes 1.0, ranging from .69 to .89 (Riketta, 2005). Thus, at least in its most common operationalization, OI seems highly related to but distinct from AOC. Further, studies using confirmatory factor analysis have also shown the distinctness of AOC and OI as measured with either the Mael scale (Mael & Tetrick, 1992; Van Knippenberg & Sleebos, 2006) or other scales (e.g., Gautam, Van Dick, & Wagner, 2004).

To illustrate the reasons for the strong but not perfect empirical overlap between OI and AOC, let us take a closer look at their measures. The Mael scale consists of items such as "When I talk about this organization, I usually say *we* rather than *they*"; "When someone praises this organization, it feels like a personal compliment"; and "This organization's successes are my successes." Thus, this measure focuses quite narrowly on the link between organizational membership and self-concept—that is, on the essential characteristic of OI. The two most common measures of AOC also include items that refer to OI defined this way, such as "I really feel as if this organization's problems are my own" or "This organization has a great deal of personal meaning for me" from the ACS, or "I really care about the fate of this organization" or "I find that my values and the organization's values are very similar" from the OCQ. These items may contribute to a high correlation between OI and AOC. However, ACS and OCQ contain additional items that refer to constructs such as a positive evaluation of the organization (e.g., "For me this is the best of all possible organizations to work for" from the OCQ; "I enjoy discussing my organization with people outside it" from the ACS), willingness to stay with the organization (e.g., ACS: "I would be very happy to spend the rest of my career with this organization"; OCQ: "There is not too much to be gained by sticking with this organization indefinitely"), or work motivation (OCQ: "I am willing to put in a great deal of effort beyond that normally expected in order to help this organization be successful"; no such items are included in the ACS). These constructs are not definitional components of OI. Thus, such items are absent from the Mael scale and several other OI scales. This may be the reason why, on the average, OI scales correlate far less than perfectly with the ACS and OCQ.

Only a few studies reported correlations of NOC or COC with OI. The available correlations are lower than those for AOC. In particular, Saks and Ashforth (1997) found correlations between OI and NOC of .49 and .52 (at two points in time) in a sample of 216 U.S. graduates. Gautam et al. (2004), in a cross-sectional survey among 450 employees from different organizations in Nepal, found correlations of a revised eight-item version of the Organizational Identification Questionnaire (Cheney, 1983) with COC of $r = .29$ and with NOC of $r = .67$. Thus, as expected on the basis of the definitions of these constructs, NOC and especially COC, relative to AOC, appear more distinct from OI.

Again, the distinctness between these constructs is also apparent from the content of the two common measures of these commitment mindsets. The items of the Normative Commitment Scale refer to the obligation to remain with one's organization (e.g., "I think that people these days move from company to company too often"; "If I got another offer for a better job elsewhere, I would not feel it was right to leave my organization"), while the items of the Continuance Commitment Scale refer to possibilities and consequences of leaving the organization (e.g., "Too much in my life would be disrupted if I decided I wanted to leave my organization now"; "I feel that I have too few options to consider leaving this organization"). These concepts are obviously independent of identification. The reason why the Normative Commitment Scale nonetheless correlates quite strongly with OI may be that OI fosters internalization of organizational reciprocity norms, which in turn may instigate a feeling of obligation toward the organization. It should be noted that the Normative Commitment Scale correlates similarly high with measures of affective commitment as it does with OI measures ($r = .64$, Table 3.1; see also Meyer et al., 2002).

As for the causal relation between identification and commitment, several authors assume that OI is an antecedent of commitment (e.g., Bergami & Bagozzi, 2000, referring to AOC; Meyer, Becker, & Van Dick, 2006, referring to affective, continuance, and normative commitment). However, this still needs to be tested in a conclusive manner, for example, by means of longitudinal designs. At present, no conclusions about the causal ordering of OI and AOC are possible.

To what extent do identification and commitment differ in their relation to other variables? If one looks at theoretical discussions of antecedents and consequences for AOC (Mathieu & Zajac, 1990; Meyer & Allen, 1997; Mowday et al., 1982) and OI (Mael & Ashforth, 1992; Van Dick, 2001), there is remarkable overlap. Still, it is possible that the empirical strengths of the postulated relations differ. One way to answer this question is to compare meta-analytic correlates of OI and AOC (see also Riketta, 2005). Table 3.1 allows such a comparison for two job attitudes (job involvement and job satisfaction) and four work outcomes (in-role and extra-role behavior, turnover intention, and absenteeism).

As can be expected considering the strong conceptual and empirical overlap between AOC and OI, the correlation patterns for these two constructs are very similar, with a few noteworthy differences. For one, OI and AOC differ in their correlations with the job attitudes. Specifically,

AOC overlaps slightly more strongly with job satisfaction (JS) (rs = .60 vs. .54) and less strongly with job involvement (JI) (rs = .50 vs. .61). Although these differences may appear small, Riketta (2005) observed differences of similar magnitude in a slightly smaller dataset and found them to be statistically significant.

What, then, are the reasons for this difference? The higher correlation of OI (relative to AOC) with JI is not surprising given that JI is essentially defined as identification with the job (see next section for details). The difference regarding JS is less obvious considering the definitions of these constructs. The difference can be explained, however, if one looks at the respective measures. Some items of the OCQ and the ACS refer to a positive evaluation of the organization (see the sample items cited above). Such a positive evaluation is likely to indicate or contribute to JS but is not a necessary component of OI. Indeed, comparable items are not included in the common Mael scale and several other OI scales. This may explain why, on the average, AOC correlates more strongly with JS than does OI.

Differences are also evident regarding the correlations with work behavior. AOC, compared with OI, relates more strongly to absenteeism (rs = −.23 vs. −.01) and turnover intention (rs = −.58 vs. −.48) but less strongly to extra-role performance (rs = .25 vs. .35). The correlations with the fourth form of work behavior considered, in-role performance, do not differ remarkably (rs = .18 vs. .17). Again, the differences can be partially explained looking at the measures of OI and AOC. As already mentioned, some items of the OCQ and the ACS refer to willingness to stay with the organization, whereas such items are missing from the Mael scale and several other OI scales. This may explain the higher average correlation of AOC (than OI) with intent to leave. The reason for the differences regarding extra-role behavior and absenteeism are less obvious considering the definitions and the items of the common measures of OI and AOC. Thus, at present, their reasons are unknown.

As already mentioned, most researchers consider work behaviors consequences of AOC and OI. A common argument is that AOC and OI imply an internalization of organizational norms and hence motivate employees to act in line with these norms. Because high performance, attendance at work, and loyalty are among the norms of most organizations, AOC and OI should strengthen these behaviors (for this reasoning, e.g., see Meyer, Becker, & Vandenberghe, 2004; Van Knippenberg, 2000). However, from other theoretical perspectives, the reverse effect is also possible. In particular, employees who behave in accordance with organizational norms for some reason may subsequently develop job attitudes (such as AOC and OI) that are consistent with that behavior. This may be a consequence of dissonance reduction (cf. Festinger, 1957) or self-perception processes (cf. Bem, 1972). Thus, effects between AOC and OI can go both ways.

Only very few studies provided the data necessary to test for the causal direction of these effects (i.e., used a longitudinal design with repeated measurement; cf. Williams & Podsakoff, 1989). A recent meta-analysis of this research (Riketta, 2008) revealed that AOC had a small positive effect on subsequent (in-role and extra-role) performance when initial performance was controlled ($\beta = .08$, $p < .001$, $k = 5$), whereas performance did not affect subsequent AOC when initial AOC was controlled ($\beta = .02$, *ns*, $k = 5$). No comparable data were available for OI. These findings do suggest that AOC is more likely to be a consequence rather than an antecedent of performance. Note that the small number of relevant studies renders this conclusion preliminary and that the meta-analysis did not consider work behaviors other than performance.

In general, unless more research is available that enables such causal analyses, researchers should be very cautious with causal interpretations of correlations of AOC or OI with work behavior. The same caveat applies to all correlations with work behavior as discussed below, although we will not reiterate this point.

Regarding their correlates, COC and NOC differ more strongly from OI than does AOC. Generally, the differences in correlations of OI with NOC or COC resemble the differences of AOC from NOC or COC. Specifically, COC correlates more weakly ($rs < .16$) than both OI and AOC with the two job attitudes considered (satisfaction and involvement) and three of the four work behaviors considered (in-role and extra-role behavior and turnover intention). The only exception is that COC relates more strongly to absenteeism than does OI, and even in the opposite direction ($r = .06$). Yet, the correlation is weaker than the one for AOC.

The correlations for NOC are also weaker than most correlations for both OI and AOC. This is true for the correlations with one of the two job attitudes considered (JS; $r = .36$) and all work behaviors considered (in-role behavior, $r = .08$; extra-role behavior, $r = .07$; absenteeism, $r = .05$; and turnover intention, $r = -.37$). Most correlations were stronger than those for COC. A puzzling exception is that NOC correlates with job involvement even slightly more strongly ($r = .52$) than does AOC, albeit less strongly than OI does.

To conclude, the meta-analytic findings summarized in Table 3.1 suggest that OI is clearly distinct from COC in terms of both intercorrelations and correlations with other variables. The same can be said of OI in comparison with NOC, although differences are less pronounced. There is however strong overlap between OI and AOC. Indeed, the correlation between these two constructs is very high, and the correlations with third variables are rather similar.

In light of these findings, some researchers may call for measures that produce clearer differences between AOC and OI. For example, Meyer et al. (2004) and Meyer et al. (2006) have argued that OI is an antecedent of commitment and not part of it. Testing this assumption requires that identification items be removed from commitment measures. This would not only increase discriminant validity but would also likely alter the correlation profiles of commitment and identification measures. As long as researchers continue to use the most common measures of AOC (the ACS and the OCQ), empirical differences between the two constructs may often turn out to be small and even negligible for many practical and research purposes.

Involvement

Involvement has almost exclusively been studied with the job as target (and more seldom with work in general as target). Thus, in the following discussion, we focus only on job involvement (JI), defined as "psychological identification with one's work" and "the degree to which the job situation is central to the person and his identity" (Lawler & Hall, 1970, pp. 310–311; see also Brown, 1996; Kanungo, 1982; Lodahl & Kejner, 1965).

These quotes suggest that JI overlaps strongly with identification. At the measurement level, however, the common measures of JI refer not only to identification but also to the importance of and preoccupation with the job. (See the following sample items from the 10-item Kanungo, 1982, scale: "To me, my job is only a small part of who I am" [reversed]. "The most important things that happen to me involve my present job." "I live, eat and breathe my job." "Most of my interests are centered around my job." "I like to be absorbed in my job most of the time.") Thus, in its operational form, JI is not wholly redundant with identification but has a slightly broader meaning, partly referring to constructs (importance of the job, effort and time spent on the job) that can be independent from identification. For this reason, and because research on identification and involvement has evolved largely independently, we discuss these two constructs in separate sections.

Similar to OI, the concept of JI is related to, but more specific than, affective commitment. It seems less related to normative and continuance commitment. However, the most comprehensive meta-analysis on the correlations between these variables (Cooper-Hakim & Viswesvaran, 2005; see Table 3.1) revealed similar correlations of JI with AOC (.50) and NOC (.52). The correlation with COC was much weaker (.15).

As to the issue of causality, some authors (e.g., Brown, 1996; Hackett, Lapierre, & Hausdorf, 2001) postulated that JI causes AOC, but this hypothesis still needs conclusive testing. We are not aware of longitudinal studies testing for the causal relationship between JI and commitment. Thus, their causal ordering is still unclear.

Theoretical discussions of AOC and JI show remarkable similarity in the postulated antecedents, correlates, and consequences between these constructs (cf. Brown, 1996; Meyer et al., 2002). Consistent with this, the observed correlations of AOC and JI with other variables are similar in direction (Table 3.1). This tendency is evident across the job attitudes (OI and JS), six work-context characteristics (transformational leadership, role conflict, role ambiguity, autonomy, skill variety, and feedback on the job), and four work behaviors (in-role behavior, absenteeism, turnover intention, and turnover). Despite this similarity in correlation patterns, a few noteworthy differences are evident.

One difference is that AOC, relative to JI, correlates more strongly with OI (rs = .78 vs. .61). This may be surprising considering that involvement is usually defined and measured with reference to identification. One explanation is that this similarity is overruled by overlap in targets. Both AOC and OI refer to the same target (the organization), whereas JI refers to a different target (the job, for which the organization may be the context). Because people may develop different job attitudes toward different targets (Becker, 1992; Cohen, 2003; Riketta & Nienaber, 2007; Riketta & Van Dick, 2005), this may explain why JI is more discrepant from AOC and OI than the latter two are from each other. Another reason may be that JI scales do not focus exclusively on identification but include items referring to distinct constructs, such as effort and time spent on the job (see sample items cited above). This may reduce the correlation with more focused identification scales, such as the Mael scale.

Another difference is that AOC, relative to JI, correlates more strongly with JS (rs = .60 vs. .35). One possible reason is that, as already explained, the common AOC measures may tap a broader range of causes or indicators of satisfaction than do JI measures, which focus less on the evaluation of the job. Another possible reason is that, in the case of JS, the target may be interpreted quite broadly. That is, when people talk about satisfaction with their jobs, they may be referring to the place they work at as well as to the tasks they perform. This is especially likely when JS is measured with global items (referring to the unspecified "job" as a whole, e.g., "How do you feel about your job?"; e.g., Kunin, 1955) rather than with domain-specific items, which refer to satisfaction with single facets of one's job (pay, supervisor, promotion opportunities, etc.; e.g., Smith, Kendall, & Hulin, 1969; Weiss, Dawis, England, & Lofquist, 1967). By contrast, measures of JI refer more clearly to the tasks than to the workplace. Therefore, "job" might more likely be interpreted as overlapping with "organization" in measures of JS (especially in general measures) than in measures of JI. This would create stronger overlap in targets between AOC and JS than between JI and JS.

AOC, relative to JI, also relates more strongly to two negative aspects of the work context, role conflict (rs = −.30 vs. −.17) and role ambiguity

($rs = -.39$ vs. $-.16$). Again, this may be due to the fact that AOC measures seem to refer more strongly to a positive evaluation of the workplace than do JI measures. Thus, for example, negative experiences at the workplace, such as those caused by role conflict and ambiguity, may reduce scores on AOC measures more strongly than scores on JI measures.

Another, more positive, contextual characteristic is transformational leadership (referring to the employees' immediate superior). Note that the available meta-analytic findings are not entirely comparable between AOC and JI because of differences in measurement. Specifically, the analyzed studies on JI measured selected components of transformational leadership separately (communication, participation, and consideration), whereas the analyzed studies on AOC used a conjoint measure of transformational leadership without differentiating between components. Despite these differences in measurement, the findings do suggest substantial positive relationships of both AOC and JI with transformational leadership ($r = .46$ vs. rs between .20 and .56). These correlations are not surprising because transformational leadership aims at increasing workers' passion, identification, and engagement at work (Bass, 1985), which in turn is likely to result in higher AOC and JI.

Moreover, AOC correlates more strongly than JI with two other positive context characteristics, autonomy ($rs = .32$ vs. .23) and feedback ($rs = .41$ vs. .28), and more weakly with a third one, skill variety ($rs = .18$ vs. .37). Whereas this precise pattern is difficult to explain, the positive correlations are in line with the proposition of the Job Characteristics Model (Hackman & Oldham, 1976) that the presence of the mentioned context characteristics leads to more positive job attitudes and higher motivation. This in turn may be reflected in higher AOC and JI.

As to work behaviors, AOC generally correlates more strongly with turnover intention and turnover than does JI ($rs = -.58$ vs. $-.48$, and $-.33$ vs. $-.16$, respectively). Again, this may be due to the fact that some of the items used in the two most common measures of AOC (ACS and OCQ) closely resemble items that could also be used to assess turnover intention (see section on OI), whereas the common JI measures do not include such items (see Brown, 1996; Kanungo, 1982; Lodahl & Kejner, 1965). AOC also correlates more strongly with absenteeism ($rs = -.23$ vs. $-.14$). The correlation for the remaining type of work behavior considered, in-role behavior, is the same for AOC and JI ($r = .18$ each). On the whole, the correlation patterns for AOC and JI are rather similar, although there are some substantial differences (especially regarding the correlation with JS).

COC is clearly distinct from JI regarding its correlations. Most correlations for COC, though weak, are even reversed in their direction compared with the correlations for JI (role conflict, $r = .13$; role ambiguity, $r = .10$; transformational leadership, $r = -.14$; in-role behavior, $r = -.12$; and absenteeism, $r = .06$). From the remaining three correlations, two are weaker than the respective correlations for JI (JS, $r = .12$ vs. .35; and turnover intention, $r = -.19$ vs. $-.30$) and one is stronger (turnover, $r = -.25$ vs. $-.16$). On the whole, the correlation patterns for COC and JI are clearly different. This is not surprising considering both the clearly different definitions of and the low correlation between COC and JI.

By contrast, the correlations for NOC are remarkably similar in magnitude to the correlations for JI. This is true for almost all variables considered; namely, one job attitude (JS, $r = .36$; no data are available for OI), three context characteristics (role conflict, $r = -.24$; role ambiguity, $r = -.21$; transformational leadership, $r = .27$; no data on the other context characteristics are available) and three work behaviors (in-role behavior, $r = .08$; turnover intention, $r = -.37$; and turnover, $r = -.16$). The most remarkable difference is that JI relates negatively to absenteeism ($r = -.14$), whereas NOC, strangely, relates positively, and statistically significantly, to this variable ($r = .05$). Apart from this, the correlation patterns for NOC and JI are hardly distinguishable. This, together with the fact that NOC correlates with JI even more strongly than do the other two commitment mindsets, suggests that of the three commitment mindsets, NOC is most similar to JI regarding its nomological net. This is surprising because the definitional characteristic of NOC (a felt obligation toward the organization) is absent from the definition and common measures of JI. Clearly, this empirical similarity between the two constructs deserves further research attention.

In conclusion, JI appears more distinct from AOC and especially COC than from NOC. In any event, the differences between JI and all three commitment mindsets taken together are more pronounced than in the OI-commitment comparison. One reason may be the differences in targets (organization for OI and commitment vs. job for JI).

Satisfaction

The most often studied work-related target of satisfaction is the job. Thus, this section focuses on this form of satisfaction. According to its most general definition, job satisfaction (JS) is an evaluation of the job as more or less positive or negative (Brief & Weiss, 2002). Other definitions are clearer about the nature of this evaluation, viewing JS as a cognitive appraisal (e.g., satisfaction as the result of perceived discrepancies between actual and desired features of the job; Lawler & Porter, 1967) or, alternatively, as an affective state (cf. the classic definition of JS as "a pleasurable or positive emotional state resulting from the appraisal of one's job or job experiences," Locke, 1976, p. 1300).

A positive evaluation of the target of commitment is more strongly implied in the definitions of affective commitment (e.g., the component "emotional attachment"; Allen & Meyer, 1990) than continuance or normative commitment. Further, as shown above, some items of the common AOC measures do refer to a positive evaluation of the workplace. Thus, similarly to identification and involvement, one would expect a stronger correlation of satisfaction with affective than continuance or normative commitment, especially if they have the same target.

Usually, however, the targets differ, with the organization being the target of commitment and the job being the target of satisfaction. Complicating matters, JS measures differ in their conceptualization of "job." Some measures explicitly refer to the job as a whole (e.g., the Job in General scale of the Job Descriptive Index; Smith, 1985; or the Faces Scale of Job Satisfaction; Kunin, 1955), whereas others refer to satisfaction with specific facets of one's job (such as the supervisor, pay, promotion opportunities, or one's tasks). The latter is true of two of the most often used JS measures, the Job Descriptive Index (Smith et al., 1969) and the Minnesota Satisfaction Questionnaire (Weiss et al., 1967). The selection of job facets differs between the latter two measures. Thus, in its operational form, JS does not refer to an unambiguous and clearly defined target in the way commitment measures do.

Nonetheless, Table 3.1 shows that JS correlates with AOC at $r = .60$, with NOC at $r = .36$, and with COC at $r = .12$. Thus, as expected, AOC is strongly associated with JS, whereas COC is rather independent of it, with NOC showing moderate overlap with JS.

The causal relation between AOC and JS received ample research attention. Several meta-analyses and longitudinal studies addressed this issue, but with inconsistent findings. For example, Brown and Peterson (1993) estimated reciprocal effects with meta-analytic structural equation modeling, based on 59 (mostly cross-sectional) studies using samples of salespeople. The estimated satisfaction →AOC path was much stronger (standardized coefficient = .59) than the reverse path (–.17). In contrast, Bateman and Strasser (1984) in a two-wave longitudinal study among U.S. nurses, as well as Wong, Hui, and Law (1995) in a three-wave panel study among Hong Kong graduates, found that AOC predicted JS but not vice versa. An attempted replication of the Bateman and Strasser study, using another sample of U.S. nurses, did not find evidence for either causal path (Curry, Wakefield, Price, & Mueller, 1986). Similarly, yet another meta-analysis using structural equation modeling suggested no causal relationship between these two variables. In particular, this meta-analysis found that a model in which AOC and JS were independent predictors of turnover generally fitted the data better than models in which AOC and JS were in a causal sequence (Tett & Meyer, 1993). Finally, a three-wave panel study among U.S. Navy recruits (Farkas & Tetrick, 1989) found that the direction of causality changed over time, with JS affecting AOC at Time 1 and Time 3 (2 and 20–21 months after enlistment, respectively) and AOC affecting JS at Time 2 (8–10 months after enlistment). Thus, the available evidence does not suggest a consistent causal relation between satisfaction and commitment. This calls for further research on the moderators of the direction of causality in this relation.

How do JS and commitment differ regarding their correlations with other variables? Relative to AOC, JS overlaps less strongly with OI ($rs =$ .78 vs. .60) and JI ($rs = .50$ vs. .35). This makes sense, considering that in contrast to the other constructs, JS does not include identification as a definitional component. As already mentioned, identification and satisfaction can occur independently of each other.

As to characteristics of the work context, AOC and JS show quite similar correlations with role conflict ($rs = -.30$ vs. −.35) and feedback ($rs = .41$ vs. .43) but differ markedly in their correlations with role ambiguity ($rs = -.39$ vs. −.25), transformational leadership ($rs = .46$ vs. .18), autonomy ($rs = .32$ vs. .48), and skill variety ($rs = .18$ vs. .45). Thus, assuming a causal role of the work context, AOC seems to depend more strongly than JS on certain social factors (especially behaviors of the superior and the clarity of one's roles in the organization) whereas JS, relative to AOC, tends to depend more strongly on characteristics of the work task (especially autonomy and variety). The reasons for these differential correlations of AOC and JS are unknown. Note that they cannot be explained by measurement characteristics alone, because satisfaction with the mentioned task characteristics and the relationship with the supervisor receive roughly equal weight in the most common facet measures of JS (i.e., the Job Descriptive Index and the Minnesota Satisfaction Questionnaire).

As to work behaviors, one remarkable difference is that AOC relates less strongly to in-role behavior than JS ($rs = .18$ vs. .30). One reason might be that in-role behavior can have a variety of targets apart from the organization (e.g., employees may work hard to meet expectations not only of their organization but also of their superior or their colleagues). As explained above, JS measures also refer to a variety of targets, whereas commitment measures have a specific target (such as the organization in the present analysis). Thus, greater overlap in targets may explain the stronger correlation of JS, relative to AOC, with in-role behavior.

Another interesting pattern emerges for absenteeism. The relevant meta-analysis (Farrell & Stamm, 1988) reported separate results for two indicators of absenteeism. It found that AOC, relative to JS, is a better predictor of absence frequency ($rs = -.23$ vs. −.10), whereas the reverse is true for total time absent ($rs = -.12$ vs. −.24). Assuming that absence frequency is more indicative of voluntary absence (skipping work) and that total time absent is more indicative of involuntary absence (e.g., due to longer periods of illness), a tentative interpretation is that AOC is more closely associated with the motivation to attend work, whereas JS is more closely associated with the ability to attend work. Because the results are based on few studies (between 6 and 20) and the direction of causality is unclear, this pattern should not be overinterpreted. Replications within studies and investigations into the underlying processes are necessary to explore the robustness and meaning of this pattern.

Finally, the correlations with the other work behaviors considered are quite similar between AOC and JS (extra-role behavior, turnover intention, turnover; see Table 3.1). In this context, a study is worth mentioning that not only compared AOC and JS regarding their zero-order relations with work behavior but also estimated their unique predictive power (Eby, Freeman, Rush, & Lance, 1999). Using meta-analytic structural equation modeling, this study found that AOC but not JS predicted absenteeism when entered as simultaneous predictors and that AOC and JS simultaneously predicted turnover. This study suggests that AOC predicts work outcomes independently of JS, despite their similarly strong zero-order correlations with work outcomes.

NOC differs more strongly from JS than does AOC regarding its correlates. In particular, NOC correlates more weakly than JS with all five work behaviors considered, as well as with two context characteristics (role conflict and ambiguity). The only exception is that NOC, like AOC, relates more strongly to transformational leadership ($r = .27$) than does JS.

The differences between COC and JS are even more pronounced. COC consistently correlates less strongly than JS with one job attitude (OI), three context characteristics (role conflict, role ambiguity, and transformational leadership) and all work behaviors in Table 3.1 except turnover (as to the latter, $r = -.25$ each; see Table 3.1 for the other correlations). As already mentioned, some of the correlations even differ in their sign between COC and JS.

To conclude, then, the variables included in Table 3.1 seem to play a minor role in the nomological nets of NOC and COC than JS. From these two commitment mindsets, COC is more clearly distinct from JS. The similarity between AOC and JS is greater, but these two constructs still differ in a pronounced and interpretable manner.

Other Constructs Overlapping With Commitment

In this section, we briefly address two other constructs that are conceptually similar to commitment but received less research attention than the three job attitudes discussed so far. In particular, no meta-analyses on these constructs are available. Thus, the following conclusions will be more tentative than most of the above conclusions.

Work Engagement

Work engagement is a relatively recent concept that has been developed in line with the growing interest in positive psychology. It is the conceptual opposite of job burnout (see Schaufeli, Bakker, & Salanova, 2006) and defined as "being charged with energy and fully dedicated to one's work" (Hallberg & Schaufeli, 2006, p. 119) or a "positive-affective-motivational state of fulfillment" (Maslach, Schaufeli, & Leiter, 2001, p. 417). These definitions appear distinct from the definitions of affective, continuance, and normative commitment, although it is plausible to assume that the states defining work engagement are associated with affective commitment. Further, Schaufeli and colleagues distinguish between three dimensions of work engagement, namely, vigor, dedication, and absorption. Overlap between work engagement and commitment seems most likely in the component of dedication than in the other two components.

Hallberg and Schaufeli (2006) investigated whether engagement could be empirically separated from organizational commitment. In a sample of 186 Swedish IT consultants, they found a correlation of .46 between engagement and AOC. Unfortunately, they did not explore the relations with the three dimensions of engagement. In any event, the empirical overlap between work engagement and AOC seems moderate, as could be expected on the basis of their definitions.

In a comprehensive discussion of employee engagement, Macey and Schneider (in press) proposed an alternative conceptualization of this construct, which differentiates between three core elements: (1) engagement as a psychological state, (2) behavioral engagement, and (3) engagement as a trait. Particularly relevant to the present chapter is their conceptualization of state engagement, which they view as a global construct comprising AOC, JS, JI, empowerment, and positive affect. Thus, according to this definition, AOC is one component of work engagement.

To conclude, work engagement seems a broader, and less precisely defined, construct than AOC. According to the sparse evidence available, their empirical overlap is moderate. As we will argue below (see Unique Contribution of Commitment), it depends on one's research aims whether such broad composite constructs are useful or whether it is better to keep related but distinct constructs separate.

Job Embeddedness

The construct of job embeddedness also has a short history (Lee, Mitchell, Sablynski, Burton, & Holtom, 2004; Mitchell, Holtom, Lee, Sablynski, & Erez, 2001; Mitchell & Lee, 2001). This construct "represents a broad constellation of influences on employee retention" (Mitchell et al., 2001, p. 1104). Thus, it denotes the overall extent to which an employee is attached or connected to his or her workplace. Job embeddedness has three components: "individuals' (1) links to other people, teams, and groups, (2) perceptions of their fit with job, organization, and community, and (3) what they say they would have to sacrifice if they left their jobs" (Mitchell et al., 2001, p. 1102). These components can refer to the job itself (on-the-job embeddedness) or the community in which one lives (off-the-job embeddedness). Lee, Mitchell, and colleagues believe that both on-the-job and off-the-job embeddedness are important for explaining work behavior (e.g., Lee et al., 2004).

Research found high correlations between on-the-job embeddedness and AOC (e.g., $r = .71$, Lee et al., 2004; $r = .57$, Crossley, Bennett, Jex, & Burnfield, 2007). This is somewhat surprising considering that most components of the on-the-job embeddedness construct are clearly distinct from AOC, as illustrated by the following sample items from a measure of on-the-job embeddedness: "How long have you worked for this organization?" "How many coworkers do you interact with regularly?" "I would sacrifice a lot if I left this job," "I like my work schedule," "I am well compensated for my level of performance" (Lee et al., 2004; see also the conceptual differentiation between job embeddedness and AOC in Mitchell et al., 2001, p. 1106; and Crossley et al., 2007; Table 3.1). Thus, for unknown reasons, AOC and on-the-job embeddedness are more closely related empirically than their respective conceptualizations may suggest.

By contrast, off-the-job embeddedness shows less empirical overlap with AOC. This can be expected on the grounds of the definitions of these constructs (e.g., $r = .22$, Lee et al., 2004; $r = .21$, Crossley et al., 2007).

Studies using commitment and embeddedness as simultaneous predictors have consistently found that the latter predicts work behavior better than, and over and above, commitment (Lee et al., 2004; Mitchell et al., 2001). For example, Lee et al. (2004) found off-the-job embeddedness to predict turnover and absenteeism and on-the job embeddedness to predict in-role and extra-role performance independently of AOC (measured with six items from the OCQ). AOC did not predict most of these outcomes independently of embeddedness. Thus, job embeddedness seems to be superior to commitment in terms of predictive power.

As in the case of work engagement, we believe that a broad construct such as job embeddedness may indeed be more useful than commitment for certain purposes (e.g., when the goal is merely to predict work behavior). Yet, many research questions require more fine-grained distinctions between concepts. In these cases, we suggest that the construct of commitment be preferred. We elaborate on this point below.

The Relevance of Commitment to Industrial/Organizational Psychology and Management Practice

Unique Contribution of Commitment

The meta-analytical evidence described in this chapter shows that for some of the concepts (e.g., AOC and OI) there is substantial overlap. So, why should we continue using commitment as a separate concept in industrial/ organizational psychology research? Some authors have indeed claimed that the overlap is so substantial that we better give up the construct of commitment and combine it with, for instance, JS as part of a more global construct (e.g., Cooper-Hakim & Visweswaran, 2005; Harrison et al., 2006; Morrow, 1983).

We disagree and think that commitment deserves a place in the literature and continued research in its own right. The first argument we put forward is purely empirical: Even the relation of ADC to its closest conceptual neighbor, OI, is $r = .78$ on average (Riketta, 2005). Although this confirms the strong conceptual similarity between the concepts, it still leaves room for distinctness, because the shared variation is just about two thirds. Moreover, studies have shown that commitment predicts work outcomes over and above its conceptual neighbors (e.g., OI regarding turnover intention as outcome, Cole & Bruch, 2006; Van Knippenberg & Sleebos, 2006; JS regarding absenteeism and turnover as outcomes, Eby et al., 1999; Tett & Meyer, 1993). Thus, commitment did prove to be empirically distinct from conceptually similar constructs.

Secondly, we believe that it depends on the research question whether commitment should be studied separately from related constructs or subsumed under a more global construct. If the goal is, for example, to compare psychological with context-related or demographic predictors of work behavior, a broader construct such as job attitudes, which encompasses commitment and JS (Harrison et al., 2006), may be preferable over a fine-grained distinction for the sake of parsimony and presentational clarity. However, if the goal is an in-depth analysis of the psychological processes underlying work behavior, a more detailed distinction between psychological variables, and hence between commitment, satisfaction, and other related constructs, seems appropriate. In fact, some authors developed models integrating the different constructs with clear hypotheses about their causal ordering and/or interactive effects. For example, Meyer et al. (2006) have attempted to combine identity-related concepts and different mindsets of organizational commitment into an integrated framework. Their model assumes that two forms of identity (surface level or "situated" vs. deep structure identity; see Riketta, Van Dick, & Rousseau, 2006; Rousseau, 1998) precede two broad forms of commitment—exchange-based versus value-based commitment, respectively—which in turn predict work behaviors. Furthermore, attempts have been made to integrate commitment with other concepts, such as satisfaction, via a range of mediating and moderating process variables (e.g., self-regulation, goal setting; Meyer et al., 2004). A test of such hypotheses requires that these constructs are measured separately.

A final reason why we believe that commitment should be maintained as a unique concept is a practical one. Research suggests that increasing commitment is beneficial to in-role and extra-role behaviors (Riketta, 2008). Thus, we believe that practitioners who want to increase the performance of their staff are well advised to pay close attention to commitment. One may argue that this is not a unique feature of commitment because the same effect has been postulated for other job attitudes, such OI (e.g., Van Dick, 2001), JI (e.g., Brown, 1996), and JS (e.g., Judge et al., 2001). Yet, the means to improve commitment may differ from the actions practitioners would take if they want to increase other aspects of employee morale. For example, if one dares a causal interpretation of the correlations referring to the work context in Table 3.1, it seems that transformational leadership is more promising a means for increasing ADC than for increasing JS, whereas increasing autonomy and variety at work is more promising as a means for increasing JS than ADC.

Directions for Future Research

In this chapter we have highlighted some common features of and differences between commitment and related concepts, particularly OI, JI, and JS. We have also mentioned some gaps in the existing literature that prevent us from drawing clearer conclusions as to some of the questions raised. We would like to conclude the chapter with directions for future empirical research and conceptual work.

First, and as pointed out in several places in this chapter, there is a striking dearth of longitudinal studies that would allow cross-lagged analyses to answer questions of causality. It might well be that—if one accepts our above conclusion that commitment is conceptually different from the job attitudes discussed here—commitment is influenced by OI, JI, and JS, as Meyer et al. (2004) suggest for the OI-commitment relation. It might also be the other way round, however, as has been argued for the commitment relation (e.g., Brown & Peterson, 1993). And, of course, it might also be that the variables mutually influence each other over time or that they are influenced by some third variables such as performance, common method bias, and so forth. Only empirical data can help clarify these issues. Thus, we would like to encourage researchers to undertake the often painstaking task of longitudinal data collection.

Second, we have highlighted some overlap in definitions, which is also reflected in overlapping operationalizations. This is probably most apparent for the concepts of OI and commitment. Definitions of commitment sometimes explicitly include identification as a component. Likewise, commitment and OI measures include items that seem to refer to very similar concepts. For the reasons outlined above, we would like to see more clear and "pure" theoretical conceptualizations, followed by measures that assess the defined constructs but nothing else.

Third, we have pointed out difficulties in comparing research findings regarding certain constructs as they address different foci. It might be worthwhile undertaking research trying to examine different concepts but with reference to the same focus. Combined with clearer definitions and operationalizations (see above), this might lead to better answers to the unique aspects (and therefore also unique impact) of each construct.

Finally, interactive effects of different concepts have received much less attention than deserved. We would like to briefly point out the work by Sagie (1998) on interactive effects of OC and JS and by Blau and Boal (1987; see Blau, 1986) on interactive effects of OC and JI. These studies have spawned surprisingly little follow-up research. We believe it would be theoretically interesting and useful for practitioners alike to undertake more systematic efforts in this direction.

Conclusion

We hope that the analyses presented in this chapter have helped to clarify the place of commitment in the nomological net of work-related attitudes. Our analyses have left some questions unanswered and have even raised new questions. Further, it is clear that we must address serious issues in conceptualization and measurement before the field can progress much further. Nevertheless, perhaps our central conclusion is that, despite limitations in theory and past research and acknowledging less than perfect construct validity, the concept of employee commitment still deserves our attention as scholars and practitioners.

Acknowledgments

We are grateful to Johannes Ullrich and Tina Wu for their careful editing and to Tom Becker and John Meyer for their many useful comments on earlier drafts of this chapter.

References

Abrams, D., Ando, K., & Hinkle, S. (1998). Psychological attachment to the group: Cross-cultural differences in organizational identification and subjective norms as predictors of workers' turnover intentions. *Personality and Social Psychology Bulletin, 24*, 1027–1039.

Allen, N. J., & Meyer, J. P. (1990). The measurement and antecedents of affective, continuance and normative commitment to the organization. *Journal of Occupational Psychology, 63*, 1–18.

Ashforth, B. E., & Mael, F. (1989). Social identity theory and the organization. *Academy of Management Review, 14*, 20–39.

Bass, B. M. (1985). *Leadership and performance beyond expectation.* New York: Free Press.

Bateman, T. S., & Strasser, S. (1984). A longitudinal analysis of the antecedents of organizational commitment. *Academy of Management Journal, 27*, 95–112.

Becker, T. E. (1992). Foci and bases of commitment: Are they distinctions worth making? *Academy of Management Journal, 35*, 232–244.

Bem, D. (1972). Self-perception theory. *Advances in Experimental Social Psychology, 6*, 1–62.

Bergami, M., & Bagozzi, R. P. (2000). Self-categorization, affective commitment and group self-esteem as distinct predictors of social identity in the organization. *British Journal of Social Psychology, 39*, 555–577.

Blau, G. J. (1986). Job involvement and organizational commitment as interactive predictors of tardiness and absenteeism. *Journal of Management, 12*, 577–584.

Blau, G. J., & Boal, K. B. (1987). Conceptualizing how job involvement and organizational commitment affect turnover and absenteeism. *Academy of Management Review, 12*, 288–300.

Brief, A. P., & Weiss, H. M. (2002). Affect in the workplace. *Annual Review of Psychology, 53*, 279–307.

Brown, S. P. (1996). A meta-analysis and review of organizational research on job involvement. *Psychological Bulletin, 120*, 235–255.

Brown, S. P., & Peterson, R. A. (1993). Antecedents and consequences of salesperson job-satisfaction: Meta-analysis and assessment of causal effects. *Journal of Marketing Research, 30*, 63–77.

Cheney, G. (1983). On the various and changing meanings of organizational membership: A field study of organizational identification. *Communication Monographs, 50*, 343–362.

Cohen, A. (2003). *Multiple commitments in the workplace: An integrative approach.* Mawah, NJ: Erlbaum.

Cole, M. S., & Bruch, H. (2006). Organizational identity strength, identification, and commitment and their relationships to turnover intention: Does organizational hierarchy matter? *Journal of Organizational Behavior, 27*, 585–605.

Cooper-Hakim, A., & Viswesvaran, C. (2005). The construct of work commitment: Testing an integrative framework. *Psychological Bulletin, 131*, 241–259.

Crossley, C. D., Bennett, R. J., Jex, S. M., & Burnfield, J. L. (2007). Development of a global measure of job embeddedness and integration into a traditional model of voluntary turnover. *Journal of Applied Psychology, 92*, 1031–1042.

Curry, J. P., Wakefield, D. S., Price, J. L., & Mueller, C. W. (1986). On the causal ordering of job satisfaction and organizational commitment. *Academy of Management Journal, 29,* 847–858.

Dutton, J. E., Dukerich, J. M., & Harquail, C. V. (1994). Organizational images and member identification. *Administrative Science Quarterly, 39,* 239–263.

Eby, L. T., Freeman, D. M., Rush, M. C., & Lance, C. E. (1999). Motivational bases of affective organizational commitment: A partial test of an integrative theoretical model. *Journal of Occupational and Organizational Psychology, 72,* 463–483.

Edwards, M. R. (2005). Organizational identification: A conceptual and operational review. *International Journal of Management Reviews, 7,* 207–230.

Elsbach, K. D. (1999). An expanded model of organizational identification. *Research in Organizational Behavior, 21,* 163–200.

Farkas, A. J., & Tetrick, L. E. (1989). A three-wave longitudinal analysis of the causal ordering of satisfaction and commitment on turnover decision. *Journal of Applied Psychology, 74,* 855–868.

Farrell, D., & Stamm, C. L. (1988). Meta-analysis of the correlates of employee absence. *Human Relations, 41,* 211–227.

Festinger, L. (1957). *A theory of cognitive dissonance.* Stanford, CA: Stanford University Press.

Fisher, C. D., & Gitelson, R. (1983). A meta-analysis of the correlates of role conflict and ambiguity. *Journal of Applied Psychology, 68,* 320–333.

Fried, Y., & Ferris, G. R. (1987). The validity of the job characteristics model: A review and meta-analysis. *Personnel Psychology, 40,* 287–322.

Gautam, T., Van Dick, R., & Wagner, U. (2004). Organizational identification and organizational commitment: Distinct aspects of two related concepts. *Asian Journal of Social Psychology, 7,* 301–315.

Hackett, R. D., Lapierre, L. M., & Hausdorf, P. A. (2001). Understanding the links between work commitment constructs. *Journal of Vocational Behavior, 58,* 392–413.

Hackman, J. R., & Oldham, G. R. (1976). Motivation through the design of work: Test of a theory. *Organizational Behavior and Human Performance, 16,* 250–279.

Hall, D. T., Schneider, B., & Nygren, H. T. (1970). Personal factors in organizational identification. *Administrative Science Quarterly, 15,* 176–190.

Hallberg, U., & Schaufeli, W. B. (2006). "Same same" but different? Can work engagement be discriminated from job involvement and organizational commitment? *European Psychologist, 11,* 119–127.

Harrison, D. A., Newman, D. A., & Roth, P. L. (2006). How important are job attitudes? Meta-analytic comparisons of integrative behavioral outcomes and time sequences. *Academy of Management Journal, 49,* 305–325.

Judge, T. A., & Piccolo, R. F. (2004). Transformational and transactional leadership: A meta-analytic test of their relative validity. *Journal of Applied Psychology, 89,* 755–768.

Judge, T. A., Thoresen, C. J., Bono, J. E., & Patton, G. K. (2001). The job satisfaction-job performance relationship: A qualitative and quantitative review. *Psychological Bulletin, 127,* 376–407.

Kanungo, R. N. (1982). Measurement of job and work involvement. *Journal of Applied Psychology, 67,* 341–349.

Kunin, T. (1955). The construction of a new type of attitude measure. *Personnel Psychology, 9,* 65–78.

Lawler, E. E. I., & Hall, D. T. (1970). Relationship of job characteristics to job involvement, satisfaction, and intrinsic motivation. *Journal of Applied Psychology,* 305–312.

Lawler, E. E. I., & Porter, L. W. (1967). The effect of performance on job satisfaction. *Industrial Relations, 7,* 20–28.

Lee, T. W., Mitchell, T. R., Sablynski, C. J., Burton, J. P., & Holtom, B. C. (2004). The effects of job embeddedness on organizational citizenship, job performance, volitional absences, and voluntary turnover. *Academy of Management Journal, 47,* 711–722.

Locke, E. A. (1976). The nature and causes of job satisfaction. In M. D. Dunnette (Ed.), *Handbook of I/O-psychology* (pp. 1297–1349). Chicago: Rand-McNally.

Lodahl, T. M., & Kejner, M. (1965). The definition and measurement of job involvement. *Journal of Applied Psychology, 49,* 24–33.

Macey, W. H., & Schneider, B. (in press). The meaning of employee engagement. *Industrial and Organizational Psychology: Perspectives on Research and Practice.*

Mael, F., & Ashforth, B. E. (1992). Alumni and their alma mater: A partial test of the reformulated model of organizational identification. *Journal of Organizational Behavior, 13,* 103–123.

Mael, F. A., & Tetrick, L. E. (1992). Identifying organizational identification. *Educational and Psychological Measurement, 52,* 813–824.

Maslach, C., Schaufeli,W. B., & Leiter, M. P. (2001). Job burnout. *Annual Review of Psychology, 52,* 397–422.

Mathieu, J. E., & Zajac, D. M. (1990). A review and meta-analysis of the antecedents, correlates, and consequences of organizational commitment. *Psychological Bulletin, 108,* 171–194.

Meyer, J. P., & Allen, N. J. (1997). *Commitment in the workplace.* Thousand Oaks, CA: Sage.

Meyer, J. P., Becker, T. E., & Vandenberghe, C. (2004). Employee commitment and motivation: A conceptual analysis and integrative model. *Journal of Applied Psychology, 89,* 991–1007.

Meyer, J. P., Becker, T. E., & Van Dick, R. (2006). Social identities and commitments at work: Toward an integrative model. *Journal of Organizational Behavior, 27,* 665–683.

Meyer, J. P., Stanley, D. J., Herscovitch, L., & Topolnytsky, L. (2002). Affective, continuance, and normative commitment to the organization: A meta-analysis of antecedents, correlates, and consequences. *Journal of Vocational Behavior, 61,* 20–52.

Mitchell, T. R., Holtom, B. C., Lee, T. W., Sablynski, C. J., & Erez, M. (2001). Why people stay: Using job embeddedness to predict voluntary turnover. *Academy of Management Journal, 44,* 1102–1121.

Mitchell, T. R., & Lee, T. W. (2001). The unfolding model of voluntary turnover and job embeddedness: Foundations for a comprehensive theory of attachment. *Research in Organizational Behavior, 23,* 189–246.

Morrow, P. C. (1983). Concept redundancy in organizational research: The case of work commitment. *Academy of Management Review, 8,* 486–500.

Mowday, R. T., Porter, L. W., & Steers, R. M. (1982). *Employee-organization linkages.* New York: Academic Press.

Mowday, R. T., Steers, R. M., & Porter, L. W. (1979). The measurement of organizational commitment. *Journal of Vocational Behavior, 14,* 224–247.

O'Reilly, C., & Chatman, J. (1986). Organizational commitment and psychological attachment: The effects of compliance, identification, and internalization on prosocial behavior. *Journal of Applied Psychology, 71,* 492–499.

Organ, D. W., & Ryan, K. (1995). A meta-analytic review of attitudinal and dispositional predictors of organizational citizenship behavior. *Personnel Psychology, 48,* 775–802.

Ouwerkerk, J. W., Ellemers, N., & de Gilder, D. (1999). Group commitment and individual effort in experimental and organizational contexts. In N. Ellemers, R. Spears, & B. Doosje (Eds.), *Social identity: Context, commitment, content* (pp. 185–204). Malden, MA: Blackwell Publishing.

Pratt, M. G. (1998). To be or not to be: Central questions in organizational identification. In D. A. Whetten & P. C. Godfrey (Eds.), *Identity in organizations* (pp. 171–207). Thousand Oaks, CA: Sage.

Riketta, M. (2002). Attitudinal organizational commitment and job performance: A meta-analysis. *Journal of Organizational Behavior, 23,* 257–266.

Riketta, M. (2005). Organizational identification: A meta-analysis. *Journal of Vocational Behavior, 66,* 358–384.

Riketta, M. (2008). The causal relation between job attitudes and performance: A meta-analysis of panel studies. *Journal of Applied Psychology, 93,* 472–481.

Riketta, M., & Nienaber, S. (2007). Multiple identities and work motivation: The role of perceived compatibility between nested organizational units. *British Journal of Management, 18,* S61–S77.

Riketta, M., & Van Dick, R. (2005). Foci of attachment in organizations: A meta-analytic comparison of the strength and correlates of workgroup versus organizational identification and commitment. *Journal of Vocational Behavior, 67,* 490–510.

Riketta, M., Van Dick, R., & Rousseau, D. M. (2006). Employee attachment in the short and long run: Antecedents and consequences of situated and deep-structure identification. *Zeitschrift für Personalpsychologie, 5,* 85–93.

Rousseau, D. M. (1998). Why workers still identify with organizations. *Journal of Organizational Behavior, 19,* 217–233.

Sagie, A. (1998). Employee absenteeism, organizational commitment, and job satisfaction: Another look. *Journal of Vocational Behavior, 52,* 156–171.

Saks, A. M., & Ashforth, B. E. (1997). A longitudinal investigation of the relationships between job information sources, applicant perceptions of fit, and work outcomes. *Personnel Psychology, 50,* 395–426.

Schaufeli, W. B., Bakker, A. B., & Salanova, M. (2006). The measurement of work engagement with a short questionnaire: A cross-national study. *Educational and Psychological Measurement, 66,* 701–716.

Smith, P. C. (1985). *Summary report on the Job-in-General scale of the JDI.* Bowling Green, OH: Bowling Green University, Department of Psychology.

Smith, P. C., Kendall, L. M., & Hulin, C. L. (1969). *The measurement of satisfaction in work and retirement.* Chicago: Rand McNally.

Tajfel, H. (Ed.). (1978). *Differentiation between social groups. Studies in the social psychology of intergroup relations.* London: Academic Press.

Tett, R. P., & Meyer, J. P. (1993). Job-satisfaction, organizational commitment, turnover intention, and turnover:Path analyses based on meta-analytic findings. *Personnel Psychology, 46,* 259–293.

Van Dick, R. (2001). Identification in organizational contexts: Linking theory and research from social and organizational psychology. *International Journal of Management Reviews, 3,* 265–283.

Van Dick, R. (2004). My job is my castle: Identification in organizational contexts. In C. L. Cooper & I. T. Robertson (Eds.), *International review of industrial and organizational psychology* (Vol. 19). Chichester, UK: Wiley.

Van Knippenberg, D. (2000). Work motivation and performance: A social identity perspective. *Applied Psychology: An International Review, 49,* 357–371.

Van Knippenberg, D., & Sleebos, E. (2006). Organizational identification versus organizational commitment: Self-definition, social exchange, and job attitudes. *Journal of Organizational Behavior, 27,* 571–584.

Weiss, D. J., Dawis, R. V., England, G. W., & Lofquist, C. H. (1967). *Manual for the Minnesota Satisfaction Questionnaire.* Minneapolis: University of Minnesota, Industrial Relations Center.

Williams, L. J., & Podsakoff, P. M. (1989). Longitudinal field methods for studying reciprocal relationships in organizational behavior research: Toward improved causal analysis. *Research in Organizational Behavior, 11,* 247–292.

Wong, C.-S., Hui, C., & Law, K. S. (1995). Causal relationship between attitudinal antecedents to turnover. *Academy of Management Journal,* 342–346.

Section 2

Multiple Foci
of Commitment

4

Organizational Commitments

Christian Vandenberghe

HEC Montreal

This chapter deals with employees' commitments to macro-level foci, that is, organizational commitments. I will first review commitment to the major macro-level foci that researchers have investigated over the years. These include commitments to the employing organization, to the profession/occupation and career, and to the union. Second, I will briefly review commitments to lesser studied macro-level foci, such as client organizations and organizational subentities. While reviewing the relevant literature, particular attention will be given to the effects of these commitments on work outcomes. Next, I examine the similarities and differences across organizational commitments. In the section that follows, I propose and discuss a model of the mediating processes linking commitment to work behavior. Finally, avenues for future research on organizational commitments are proposed in the last section of the chapter.

Commitment to Macro-Level Foci

Commitment to the Employing Organization

Definition

Although a variety of definitions of the commitment construct have been proposed in the literature, we will adopt Klein and colleagues' view of commitment as a perceived bond between the individual and a given target of interest (Klein, Brinsfield, & Molloy, 2006; Klein, Molloy, & Cooper, chapter 1 of this book). Klein and colleagues were very meticulous in distinguishing the content of the commitment construct from its presumed antecedents and outcomes. Specifically, they asserted that commitment viewed as a bond is distinct from a force, investments, identification, or congruence, which are best viewed as potential antecedents of commitment, and is also distinct from such outcomes as motivation, continuance, and affect toward the target. Klein and colleagues also suggested that commitment can be accompanied by different rationales or "self-explanations" that individuals use for making sense of their commitment.

Consistent with Klein et al. (chapter 1), we define commitment to the employing organization as a perceived *bond* between the individual and the organization. As Klein et al. suggest, that definition is not new, as some past researchers have conceptualized organizational commitment as one's psychological attachment to an organization (e.g., Buchanan, 1974; O'Reilly & Chatman, 1986). However, the view of commitment as a bond differs from Meyer and Herscovitch's (2001) approach to commitment, conceived as a "force that binds an individual to a course of action of relevance to one or more targets" (p. 299), perceiving a bond between oneself and the organization does not incorporate the force(s) that create(s) the bond.

Brief Overview of Multidimensional Commitment Models

Various multidimensional models of commitment have been developed over the years. These models provide depictions of potential rationales or "self-explanations" that can be used by individuals for making sense of their commitment. Such models include O'Reilly and Chatman's (1986) trilogy of *compliance, identification,* and *internalization* as bases for commitment, Mayer and Schoorman's (1992, 1998) dichotomy between *commitment to stay* and *willingness to participate,* and Meyer and Allen's three-component model (Allen & Meyer, 1990; Meyer & Allen, 1991, 1997). According to Meyer and Allen, organizational commitment is composed of three mindsets: *affective commitment* (AC), which represents an emotional attachment to, involvement in, and identification with the organization (e.g., Buchanan, 1974; Kanter, 1968; Mowday, Porter, & Steers, 1982; Porter, Steers, Mowday, & Boulian, 1974); *normative commitment* (NC), which refers to a sense of loyalty driven by a feeling of obligation toward the organization (cf. Wiener, 1982); and *continuance commitment* (CC), which is an attachment derived from the recognition of the costs associated with leaving and/or perceived lack of employment alternatives (Allen & Meyer, 1996; Meyer & Allen, 1991). The three-component model—including "mindsets" rather than "rationales"—will be more closely examined in this chapter given the significant empirical attention this model has received. However, it should be noted that rationales or self-explanations for the commitment are cognitive evaluations of one's commitment, while the three-component model's mindsets potentially reflect both cognitive and affective elements. Thus, rationales or self-explanations should not be confounded with commitment mindsets.

Relationships Between Commitment to the Employing Organization and Work Outcomes

Over a dozen meta-analyses have examined the nomological net of organizational commitment. These reviews provide an interesting insight into the nature and strength of the relationships between organizational commitment and work outcomes.

Turnover and absenteeism. Among the various forms of commitment, AC has been consistently found to be the best predictor of turnover, as meta-analytic reviews have reported (rho = −.20 in Cooper-Hakim & Viswesvaran, 2005; rho = −.23 in Griffeth, Hom, & Gaertner, 2000; rho = −.29 in Mathieu & Zajac, 1990; rho = −.17 in Meyer, Stanley, Herscovitch, & Topolnytsky, 2002). Note, however, that Tett and Meyer (1993) found that the relationship between AC and turnover was nearly totally mediated by withdrawal cognitions. Research has also identified a number of moderators of the AC-turnover relationship, such as time interval between measurement of commitment and turnover (Cohen, 1993; Griffeth et al., 2000), occupational group (Cohen & Hudecek, 1993), or career stage (Cohen, 1991). Compared to AC, NC and CC have been found to be less strongly associated with turnover (rho = −.16 and −.25, respectively, in Cooper-Hakim & Viswesvaran, 2005; rho = −.16 and −.10, respectively, in Meyer et al., 2002).

Researchers have also recently considered the possibility that AC, NC, and CC may interact in predicting intended or actual turnover. For example, Somers (1995) found that AC was more strongly associated with intention to stay when CC was low. In one out of two samples, Jaros (1997) found that the highest levels of turnover intentions were displayed by individuals with low CC and low NC. Finally, Cheng and Stockdale (2003) found that at low levels of NC, CC was more strongly (negatively) associated with turnover intentions, which they interpreted as evidence for the primacy of NC in the Chinese culture (i.e., the influence of the other components emerges when NC is low).

Absenteeism is another withdrawal behavior that has been studied in connection with commitment. Attendance has been found to be positively correlated, albeit weakly, with AC (rho = .12 in Mathieu & Zajac, 1990) while correlations between NC or CC and absenteeism have been found to be close to zero (rho = .06 and .05, respectively, in Meyer et al., 2002). Voluntary absence has also been found to be more strongly (and negatively) associated with AC than involuntary absence (rho = −.22 vs. −.09 in Meyer et al., 2002). The relationship between organizational commitment and absenteeism has also been reported to vary across career stages (Cohen, 1991). Cohen actually found that the relationship between AC and absenteeism was stronger in the late career stage (rho = −.27 among employees tenured 9-plus years vs. −.07 among employees tenured 3–9 years), plausibly reflecting the constraining effect of CC with increased tenure in the organization.

Performance. Meta-analytic reviews have consistently reported modest positive correlations between AC and job performance, be it measured through supervisor ratings (e.g., rho = .13 in Cohen, 1991; rho = .14 in Mathieu & Zajac, 1990; rho = .16 in Meyer et al., 2002; Randall, 1990; rho = .19 in Riketta, 2002) or objective indicators (e.g., rho = .05 in Mathieu & Zajac, 1990; rho = .13 in Riketta, 2002). The correlation has generally been found to be stronger with extra-role performance or organizational citizenship behavior (rho = .23 with altruism and .30 with generalized compliance in Organ & Ryan, 1995; rho = .25 in Riketta, 2002) than with in-role performance (rho = .18 in Riketta, 2002). Relatedly, Jaramillo, Mulki, and Marshall (2005) found the correlation between AC and in-role performance to be stronger for salespeople (rho = .25) than for nonsales employees (rho = .18), which they suggest is due to salespeople having more control over their work outcomes than nonsales employees. Finally, Wright and Bonett (2002) found that the correlation between AC and performance tended to decrease exponentially with increasing tenure, which they interpreted as evidence supporting the notion of a honeymoon effect. As to NC and CC, in Meyer et al.'s (2002) review, NC correlated weakly but positively with job performance (rho = .06), while CC correlated negatively with it (rho = −.07).

Besides results from meta-analytic reviews, a number of authors have enriched the study of the commitment-performance relationship by examining the interplay among commitment mindsets (Chen & Francesco, 2003; Gellatly, Meyer, & Luchak, 2006; Meyer, Paunonen, Gellatly, Goffin, & Jackson, 1989; Randall, Fedor, & Longenecker, 1990). Illustrative of that research is the work by Sinclair, Tucker, Cullen, and Wright (2005), who found that a profile characterized by moderate CC and low AC was associated with the poorest supervisor ratings of performance and organizational citizenship behavior, as well as the highest levels of antisocial behavior. Presumably, individuals included in that commitment profile feel weak emotional attachment to the organization but have accumulated side bets. They would be inclined to leave but know it would be difficult to find a more desirable job and are thus resentful about that. This psychological state is akin to what Becker (2005) calls "alienation."

Stress and health. Stress and health-related variables have been less examined in connection with organizational commitment. Research has reported AC to be negatively and CC positively associated with perceived stress (rho = −.33 for AC in Mathieu & Zajac, 1990; rho = −.21 for AC and .14 for CC in Meyer et al., 2002). However, researchers have not clearly identified the mechanisms through which, and the reasons that organizational commitment and health-related variables could be connected. Different mechanisms may be involved. First, commitment dimensions may exert direct effects on health-related variables. For example, as employees with high levels of AC tend to view organizational values as more compatible with their own, they may be less exposed to conflicts concerning the direction of their behavior at work. This may result in lower stress. In contrast, as noted by Mathieu and Zajac (1990), employees with higher levels of calculative commitment (or CC) may experience more strain because their membership is heavily dependent on side bets. Another potential mechanism is that organizational commitment may play the role of a buffer between stress conditions and outcomes. This is the approach taken by Begley and Czajka (1993), who found that AC reduced the effect of strain on job displeasure in the context of an organizational restructuring. Finally, there might be another way for organizational commitment to affect health or well-being, that is, through interactions between commitment mindsets. Although the following reasoning is exploratory at this point, we suspect that a combination of high NC and high CC may result in individuals perceiving much *external* pressure to behave in accordance with the terms specified in their commitment (e.g., staying). This may lead to increased levels of discomfort, and hence, result in more perceived stress.

We now turn to commitment to other important macro-level entities: first, professions/occupations and careers, and second, unions.

Professional/Occupational and Career Commitment

Definition

Although they can be distinguished, the notions of *profession, occupation,* and *career* appear to share important commonalities, namely, the fact that they all refer to a *particular line of work* (Meyer, Allen, & Smith, 1993). As Morrow (1983, p. 490) noted, professional, occupational, or career commitment "is one of the few commitment concepts that attempts to capture the notion of devotion to a craft, occupation, or profession apart from any specific work environment, over an extended period of time." Professional/ occupational or career commitment is important for two reasons. First, as educational levels increase in many societies and as work becomes more complex and specialized, employees are naturally prone to strengthen their commitment and attachment to a line of work (Lee, Carswell, & Allen, 2000). Second, commitment to an occupational field or to one's career has been a response adopted by employees who wish to maintain employability in the midst of organizational changes (Carson & Bedeian, 1994; Meyer, Allen, & Topolnytsky, 1998).

Dominant Models of Professional/Occupational and Career Commitment

A variety of models of professional/occupational and career commitment have been proposed over the years. Fifty years ago, Gouldner (1957, 1958) distinguished among locals (primarily loyal to the employing organization) and cosmopolitans (primarily committed to their profession), who represented conflicting commitment types. Later, researchers theorized that aside from commitment to the employing organization, employees could develop a commitment to a career, defined as one's motivation to work in a given career (Hall, 1971), the degree of centrality of the career for one's self-identity (Carson & Bedeian, 1994; Gould, 1979), the salience of career values in one's total life (Greenhaus, 1971, 1973), or one's attitude regarding one's profession or vocation (Blau, 1985, 1988; Blau, Paul, & St-John, 1993). More recently, research has also demonstrated the applicability of the three-component model of organizational commitment (Meyer & Allen, 1991) to the occupational domain (Irving, Coleman, & Cooper, 1997; Meyer et al., 1993; Snape & Redman; 2003).

Conceptualizing Professional/Occupational/Career Commitment: Issues and Clarifications

A number of issues arise from the literature reviewed above. First, researchers have often questioned whether professional/occupational or career commitment is actually compatible with commitment to the employing organization. In a meta-analysis of the literature on professional and organizational commitment, Wallace (1993) reported a correlation of .45 between the two measures across 25 samples. A number of moderators were identified, including degree of professionalism, position occupied (managers vs. nonsupervisory employees), and type of measure. In another meta-analytic review, based on 49 samples, Lee et al. (2000) also reported a .45 correlation between AC to the organization and occupational commitment. However, they found the correlation to be stronger for professionals working in professional organizations (rho = .48) than for professionals working in nonprofessional organizations (rho = .23). Overall, these findings suggest there is a positive association between commitment to employing organization and occupational commitment. Lee et al. further demonstrated the compatibility of the two constructs by showing that (a) there is a negative relation between occupational commitment and organizational turnover intention, which is fully mediated by occupational turnover intention, and (b) occupational turnover intention also contributed to organizational turnover intention when the effects of job satisfaction and commitment to employing organization were controlled for. However, I suggest that a more complete picture of the degree of compatibility of the constructs would be gained if one looked at their likely antecedents. For example, it would be worth investigating whether organization-occupation value fit would be related to the strength of the association of the two constructs. Also, is fit more important on some values than others? Such questions remain to be addressed by researchers.

Second, according to the definition of commitment as a perceived bond between the individual and a given target (cf. Klein et al.; chapter 1), it appears that past conceptualizations of occupational or career commitment have often included elements that are rather antecedents or outcomes of the construct. For example, concepts such as "the degree of centrality of the career for one's self-identity" (Gould, 1979) and Greenhaus's (1971, 1973) "career salience" should be viewed as antecedents of career commitment, because these variables represent "forces that bind" individuals to the career. Similarly, the notions of "career planning" and "career resilience," proposed by Carson and Bedeian (1994) as facets of career commitment, or that of "vocational planning activities and thinking" (Hall, 1971) actually represent outcomes of career commitment.

Union Commitment

Definition

The conceptualization of union commitment that still prevails today was first proposed by Gordon, Philpot, Burt, Thompson, and Spiller (1980). Paralleling Porter and colleagues' (Porter et al., 1974; Porter, Crampon, & Smith, 1976) definition of organizational commitment, they defined commitment to the union as "the extent to which a person (a) has a strong desire to remain a member of the union, (b) is willing to exert a high degree of effort for the union, and (c) believes in the objectives of organized labor" (Klandermans, 1989, p. 869). Gordon et al. identified four dimensions of union commitment: *union loyalty*, which reflects a sense of pride in being a member of the union and an awareness of the benefits associated with union membership; *responsibility to the union*, which relates to members' willingness to fulfill day-to-day obligations to the union; *willingness to work for the union*, which refers to the willingness to participate in union activities beyond expectations; and *belief in unionism*, which is a general belief in the value of unionism.

Commitment to Union and Employing Organization: Evidence for a Dual Commitment?

Researchers have long considered commitment to the union to be incompatible with commitment to the employer (e.g., Barkin, 1950; England, 1960; Stagner, 1956; Stagner & Rosen, 1965). Subsequent research has shown this was not the case (e.g., Angle & Perry, 1986; Fukami & Larson,

1984). Magenau, Martin, and Peterson (1988) summarized three conceptual frameworks that have been used to support the notion of a dual commitment to union and organization. First, using cognitive consistency theory, Angle and Perry (1986) asserted that dual commitment will only be possible when a collaborative work climate exists between employers and unions. Several studies reported evidence supporting this contention (Angle & Perry, 1986; Deery & Iverson, 2005; Kim & Rowley, 2006; Reed, Young, & McHugh, 1994; Snape, Redman, & Chan, 2000). A second approach has been proposed by Stagner (1956), who argued that individuals perceive their workplace as a whole, suggesting that commitment to the company and union are two facets of the same phenomenon. However, as noted by Snape et al. (2000), studies have generally found measures of commitment to the organization and the union to be empirically distinguishable. Third, the exchange approach is predicated on the idea that commitment to either company or union develops as a result of independent exchanges between individuals and these two entities. The fact that the average correlation between organizational and union commitment has been reported to be positive yet moderate in meta-analyses (e.g., .41 in Reed et al., 1994) lends support to this conceptualization. The compatibility of union and organizational commitment thus appears to be supported in regard to past research.

The "Over and Above" Effects of Union Commitment and Other Conceptual Issues

Union commitment has been found to be an important predictor of the willingness to participate in union activities (meta-analytically derived $\beta = .53$ in Bamberger, Kluger, & Suchard, 1999). This finding has also been replicated in the context of a 10-year longitudinal study of union commitment and self-reports of participation in union activities (Fullagar, Gallagher, Clark, & Carroll, 2004). Moreover, evidence suggests that participation in union activities is uniquely explained by union commitment, even when the effect of organizational commitment is controlled for (Bamberger et al., 1999; Cohen, 2005; Redman & Snape, 2005). In a related vein, Bemmels (1995) found that union commitment interacted with organizational commitment such that dual commitment was significantly related to shop steward grievance processing behaviors and grievance procedure outcomes, over and above union and organizational commitment. Finally, in a study of an Australian-based multinational banking organization, Deery and Iverson (2005) found that organizational commitment was significantly related to branch productivity and customer service, while union loyalty was negatively related to absenteeism. These findings suggest that union commitment might play an important role in the prediction of organizational outcomes. However, a number of situational characteristics may moderate these effects, including the type of work environment, the union structure, or the industrial relations context (Snape et al., 2000).

Gordon et al.'s (1980) conceptualization of union commitment is questionable in regard to the definition of commitment as a perceived bond with a given target (Klein et al., chapter 1). Conceptually, union loyalty may represent commitment based on an affective self-justification or rationale, while responsibility to the union and willingness to work for the union are better viewed as consequences of the commitment (Kelloway & Barling, 1993). On the other hand, belief in unionism reflects a general belief in the value of unionism and therefore should be treated as an antecedent of loyalty to the union (cf. Bamberger et al., 1999; Snape et al., 2000). Note that union instrumentality, that is, "members' cognitive assessments of the costs and benefits associated with union representation" (Tetrick, Shore, McClurg, & Vandenberg, 2007, p. 820), may represent a calculative variable that is another potential antecedent of union commitment. Overall, much work remains to be done to identify the array of rationales that could be associated with union commitment. For example, individuals could make sense of their commitment to unions out of perceived obligation toward the union or the perceived cost associated with disrupting the affiliation with the union.

We now turn to examining commitment to lesser studied macro-foci: client organizations and organizational subunits.

Commitment to Other, Lesser Studied Macro-Foci

Client Organizations

One of the major changes in the employee-employment relationships is the use of third parties who place employees in client organizations to complete tasks during some period of time and who are the legal employers of such employees (Coyle-Shapiro & Morrow, 2006). These third parties are generally temporary staff organizations (Connelly & Gallagher, 2004) or contracting organizations (Coyle-Shapiro & Morrow, 2006; Olsen, 2007). Although these new forms of employment have generated cost savings and increased the flexibility of organizations (Matusik & Hill, 1998), they also have encouraged research on the consequences of such arrangements on employees' commitment to their employer and client organization. However, it should be noted that while research has largely focused on the "commitment dilemma" of contingent workers (Olsen, 2007), commitment to client organizations is relevant to noncontingent employees as well, particularly for employees who work in boundary-spanning positions. The literature on commitment to client organizations thus has implications for both contingent and noncontingent employees.

Recent research appears to support the distinctiveness of AC to the employer and to the client organization among contingent and contract workers (Benson, 1998; Coyle-Shapiro & Morrow, 2006; Coyle-Shapiro, Morrow, & Kessler, 2006; Feldman, Doerpinghaus, & Turnley, 1995; Liden, Wayne, Kraimer, & Sparrowe, 2003; McClurg, 1999). A few studies reported that contingent workers' commitment to the employer was significantly lower than the commitment of their permanent counterparts (e.g., Van Dyne & Ang, 1998), while other researchers found the opposite (e.g., McDonald & Makin, 2000). As noted by Connelly and Gallagher (2004), one should be cautious in interpreting these findings because the samples of contingent workers examined in these studies have often been heterogeneous. Moreover, contingent workers' commitment to the employing organization may be affected by whether or not the contingent work status has been freely chosen by the individual (Ellingson, Gruys, & Sackett, 1998).

Research has provided some insight as to the extent to which commitment to client organizations is compatible with commitment to the employing organization. For example, in a study of temporary employees, agency commitment was found to spill over to influence managers' perceptions of contingent workers' commitment to the client organization. However, the effect was negative in the view of the client organization's managers, suggesting a potential incompatibility between the two (Liden et al., 2003). In contrast, Coyle-Shapiro and Morrow (2006) found that AC to the contracting organization was positively related to AC to the client organization, even when the effects of the client-based antecedents were controlled for. Finally, based on self-categorization theory (Turner, 1987), George and Chattopadhyay (2005) examined the antecedent variables that should be specifically associated with identification with either contracting or client organizations. An interesting finding was that identification with the employer was found to correlate more strongly with identification with the client organization when the two entities were perceived to be similar on key attributes. A central issue in studying the compatibility between commitments to employing and client organizations may thus be the perceived value congruence between the two organizations, particularly if AC is being studied. Indirect evidence of this is Lievens and De Corte's (2008) study that examined the predictors of HR managers' commitment to an HR outsourcing company. Interestingly, they found that HR managers were more inclined to report AC to the service provider organization if they perceived the values of that organization to fit those of their employing organization. Likewise, investments made in the relationship (Lievens & De Corte, 2008) and perceived obligations resulting from a long-term relationship with a client organization may play an important role in the development of CC and NC to client organizations.

Commitment to Organizational Subentities

Organizational subentities cover a wide range of commitment foci, including local subsidiaries of multinational corporations, divisions, work units, and departments of large organizations, but excluding work teams— which are dealt with in chapter 5, by T.E. Becker, as part of interpersonal commitments. Joint ventures also represent special cases of organizational subentities as they emerge from distinct parent organizations. While interpersonal commitments can be either concrete or abstract, organizational commitments—including commitment to organizational subentities—are almost universally abstract. The properties of commitment are isomorphic in the context of interpersonal commitments, while they are not in the context of organizational commitments. That is, the mindsets associated with commitment apply to both sides of the relationship in the former case—for example, a supervisor may experience AC, CC, or NC toward his or her subordinates and vice versa—suggesting the possibility of *mutual commitments*. In contrast, organizational commitments can only be symmetrical via a process of personification (Levinson, 1965), with the individual ascribing humanlike motives of commitment to the target. In the strict sense of the word, mutual commitments are not possible in the context of organizational commitments.

Different mechanisms are likely involved in the development of commitment to local entities versus the larger organization. For example, Lewin's (1943) field theory posits that elements of the environment that are proximal to individuals are the most influential on their reactions. Along that line, Mathieu and Hamel (1989) argued that variables such as job characteristics should influence employees' reactions more directly than characteristics of the larger organization, which are more distal. Field theory also suggests that elements from the proximal environment will mediate the effect of distal variables on commitment (Mathieu & Hamel, 1989; Mathieu, 1991). If one considers that commitment can be directed toward a variety of foci in the organization (Becker, 1992; Becker, Billings, Eveleth, & Gilbert, 1996) and that it results from social exchanges with the target entities (Meyer & Herscovitch, 2001), it is likely that proximal variables (e.g., task characteristics, leadership in the unit) will primarily affect commitment to the local unit, while more distal variables such as characteristics of the global organization (e.g., supportive human resource management practices, organizational values) will primarily act upon commitment to the global organization. However, because field theory (Lewin, 1943) asserts that distal variables act upon individuals' reactions at least partly through proximal variables, the two commitments should correlate positively, that is, be compatible.

Another mechanism potentially involved in dual commitment to the local entity versus the larger collective has been proposed by Lawler (1992), who posits that individuals tend to develop stronger attachments to local entities or groups than to larger collectives because the local groups tend to strengthen their generalized sense of control. Lawler's (1992) choice-process theory states that (a) greater self-determination or choice results in more positive emotions about the job, (b) these emotions increase the attachment or commitment to groups credited for the sense of control and the positive emotions, (c) attachment to the local group is increased more than attachment to the distant whole because individuals generally give more credit to local entities for their choice or sense of control, and (d) individuals act in the interests of the local group more than in those of the larger collective (Mueller & Lawler, 1999). In other words, the local group has an "interaction advantage" (Mueller & Lawler, 1999) that results in stronger ties with the individual (cf. also Yoon, Baker, & Ko, 1994). In support of this view, employees have been found to identify more strongly with their local subsidiary than with the global organization (Reade, 2001).

A final approach of interest is self-identity theory (Tajfel & Turner, 1986) and self-categorization (Turner, 1987) as applied to organizational identification (e.g., Ashforth & Mael, 1989; Bergami & Bagozzi, 2000; Mael & Ashforth, 1992; Van Dick, Wagner, Stellmacher, Christ, & Tissington, 2005). These theories suggest identification with organizations can fulfill a variety of employee needs, such as self-esteem, uncertainty reduction, or affiliation. Through the process of self-categorization, individuals come to incorporate attributes of a group into their self-identity in a manner that serves their needs (Turner, 1987). The bases of identification can be the degree of prestige of the organization or organizational subentity, its distinctiveness and values, as well as the trustworthiness of relations with management and the degree of attractiveness to colleagues in the organization (George & Chattopadhyay, 2005). It is likely that if these properties are stronger at the organizational than at the local level, then identification with—or commitment to—the global organization will be strengthened; while if these attributes are more emphasized in the local entity, then identification with, or commitment to, the local work unit will dominate.

These theories are not mutually exclusive. For example, employees may develop stronger relationships with their local work unit, and these relationships may lead to stronger identification with the local work unit because they provide employees with greater sense of control over their work environment. Yet, the more distant organizational values may indirectly act upon employees' identification to the local entity and ultimately identification with or commitment to the global organization. This view is consistent with the finding that local commitments contribute to increasing commitment to the global organization (Hunt & Morgan, 1994).

Similarities and Differences Among Organizational Commitments

Table 4.1 provides a list of variables that have generally been considered as antecedents or consequences in the commitment literature and reports their degree of relevance to the different organizational commitments. Note that antecedents and outcomes are conceptually driven by Klein et al.'s (2006) definition of commitment as a "perceived bond" for any target of interest. Commitment rationales and strength, the other elements of Klein et al.'s proposed definition of commitment, are not included in Table 4.1, because the identification of these elements remains an important task for future research on organizational commitments (see next section). However, it is likely that the relevance of antecedents and/or consequences for commitments across targets will be influenced by these elements.

Among antecedents, value congruence appears to be relevant to the development of all macro-foci commitments. Indeed, researchers have theorized and/or demonstrated its relevance to the organization (e.g., Cable & Judge, 1996; O'Reilly, Chatman, & Caldwell, 1991; Ostroff, Shin, & Kinicki, 2005; Verquer, Beehr, & Wagner, 2003), occupation (Aranya, Pollock, & Amernic, 1981), union (Gordon et al., 1980), and organizational subentities (e.g., Werbel & Johnson, 2001). Theoretically, it also makes sense that one's value congruence with a client organization would contribute to increasing commitment to the client (Lievens & De Corte, 2008), but to the best of my knowledge, this hasn't been tested yet. Support from target, as indicative of a social exchange relationship, is also conceptually relevant to commitment across most targets (e.g., Coyle-Shapiro & Morrow, 2006; Kraimer & Wayne, 2004; Rhoades, Eisenberger, & Armeli, 2001; Snape & Redman, 2007). An exception may be occupational commitment because (a) it is unclear whether occupations can be easily personified as the other entities can be, and (b) the borders of occupations are often fuzzy, which can further impede the personification process through which perceptions of support are formed (Eisenberger, Huntington, Hutchison, & Sowa, 1986).

Job characteristics have generally been shown to be associated with commitment across most targets (e.g., Felfe, Schmook, Six, & Wieland, 2005; Mueller & Lawler, 1999; Lee et al., 2000; Mathieu & Zajac, 1990; Meyer et al., 2002). Note that job characteristics may also influence union

TABLE 4.1

Relevance of Commitment Antecedents and Consequences Across Organizational Targets

Variable	Degree of Relevance to Target				
	Commitment to Employing Organization	Occupational Commitment	Union Commitment	Commitment to Client Organizations	Commitment to Subentities
Antecedents					
Value congruence	High	High	High	High	High
Support	High	Low	High	High	High
Job characteristics	High	High	High	High	High
Leadership	High	Low	High	High	High
Investments	High	High	High	High	High
Alternatives	High	High	Low	Low	Low
Instrumentality	Low	Low	High	Low	Low
Individual differences	High	High	High	Low	Low
Consequences					
Organizational turnover	High	High	Low	Low	Low
Absenteeism	High	High	Low	High	High
Job performance	High	High	High	High	High
Service performance	Low/High	High	Low	High	High
Workplace deviance	High	High	High	High	High
Well-being	High	High	High	High	High

commitment, as unions are thought to influence the treatment of job conditions by organizations (Gordon, Barling, & Tetrick, 1995). Leadership is another antecedent variable that may potentially affect commitment across targets (e.g., Felfe et al., 2005; Meyer et al., 2002). However, leadership does not seem to be relevant to occupational commitment, because occupations usually do not possess enough legitimacy and power to influence work conditions and decisions in workplaces. Investments are also relevant to commitments across targets. However, despite the fact that the construct appears to apply to other targets, research on investments has been largely limited to commitment to employing organizations. I would argue that it is in the context of occupations that investments may have their strongest influence, creating "career embeddedness" (Feldman & Ng, 2007). Alternatives are also conceptually relevant to most commitments (e.g., Farrell & Rusbult, 1981; Scholl, 1981), with the exception of union commitment. Indeed, in the case of unions, the evaluation of alternatives implies that other similar organizations would be available for playing the same role in the employment relationship, which is not the case in many countries. Moreover, in many industries, individuals do not even have the choice to unionize or not. In contrast, the notion of union instrumentality has been studied as an important antecedent of union commitment (Bamberger et al., 1999; Tetrick et al., 2007). Perceived union instrumentality refers to "members' cognitive assessments of the costs and benefits associated with union representation" (Tetrick et al., 2007, p. 820). There is something specific to this view of instrumentality that makes it unique to union commitment: the costs and benefits are evaluated in connection with the employment relationship, thereby involving another target than the union itself.

Finally, individual differences may affect commitment as well. For example, the dimensions of the Big Five personality model have been recently examined in relation with commitment to the employing organization (Erdheim, Wang, & Zickar, 2006). Similarly, work ethic is an important predictor of occupational commitment (Lee et al., 2000). Also, union commitment may be rooted in early socialization influences that predispose individuals to positive attitudes regarding unions. On the contrary, individual differences may be less important for commitment to client organizations and organizational subentities because these entities are closer to individuals, hence making the impact of job conditions on commitment more salient and critical, as suggested by Lawler's (1992) choice-process theory.

In the array of commitment's consequences, organizational turnover—which is a primary outcome of commitment to the employing organization (Meyer et al., 2002)—can also be influenced by occupational commitment. Along that line, Lee et al. (2002) reported occupational commitment to be indirectly related to organizational turnover intention and actual turnover via occupational turnover intention. However, there is no evidence to date that commitment to unions, client organizations, or organizational subentities relates to organizational turnover. In all cases, commitment should be negatively related to withdrawal *from the target* but will not necessarily spill over to withdrawal from the employing organization. One can, however, speculate that because subentities are nested within the larger organization, commitment to subentities will particularly relate to organizational turnover when commitment to employing organization is weak. Absenteeism is potentially related to all organizational commitments except union commitment. It is also likely that commitment to more proximal targets (client organizations and subentities) will be particularly important for predicting absenteeism because (a) proximal foci tend to play a major role in the organization of employees' work, and (b) absenteeism is viewed as a reaction to, or coping mechanism that helps dealing with the demands from, the immediate work environment (Bakker, Demerouti, de Boer, & Schaufeli, 2003; Hackett & Bycio, 1996).

Job performance is thought to be potentially influenced by all organizational commitments. The importance of commitments' influence on performance will depend on whether the performance has relevance to the target and on the nature and strength of rationales that sustain the commitment. For example, a nurse who has strong occupational commitment out of desire may want to learn skills that are needed to foster nursing care quality (i.e., an outcome that is emphasized in nursing). Similarly, a unionized worker who has been raised in a family that valued unionization may feel obligated to his or her union and therefore take part in pro-union activities (i.e., performance in union-related activities). Service performance, which is a more specific aspect of in-role and/or extra-role performance, may be of particular relevance to occupational commitment, commitment to client organizations, and commitment to subentities. Its relevance to occupations stems from the fact that sense of service is often part of occupational socialization (Kerr, von Glinow, & Schriesheim, 1977), while its relevance to client organizations derives from service quality being a well-known predictor of customer loyalty in business relationships (e.g., Rauyruen & Miller, 2007). Likewise, service performance can be relevant to organizational subentities, as local work units that are in contact with customers often develop a climate for service that encourages service quality and performance (e.g., Johnson, 1996; Schneider & Bowen, 1985; Schneider, White, & Paul, 1998). Finally, service performance may be related to commitment to employing organizations only if organizational and clients' goals are compatible with one another (Allen & Grisaffe, 2001; Vandenberghe et al., 2007).

Finally, both workplace deviance and employee well-being can be affected by organizational commitments. As workplace deviance can be directed toward different targets (Mitchell & Ambrose, 2007), it is likely that the quality of the relationship with the target, as expressed by the strength of and rationales associated with commitment to that target, will be a critical factor for predicting target-related deviance. Those rationales that result in negative emotions, such as rationales of cost and entrapment in the relationship with the target, should ultimately lead to an increase of target-related deviance because such deviance helps individuals reduce negative emotions (Fox, Spector, & Miles, 2001). Note that from a multiple-commitments perspective, the relationship between commitment and workplace deviance may partly depend on the compatibility among the norms and values regarding acceptable behavior that are endorsed across targets. For example, AC to a local entity will be positively related to deviance if this entity is characterized by values and norms that go against the organization's interests (Becker & Bennett, in press). Finally, commitment rationales that lead to positive emotions should foster individuals' well-being, as it is well established that positive emotions strongly contribute to psychological well-being (Diener, Suh, Lucas, & Smith, 1999).

Overall, Table 4.1 shows important similarities among antecedents and outcomes across organizational commitments. However, as discussed above, there are also some noticeable differences in the degree of relevance of antecedents and outcomes to these macro-foci commitments. On a related matter, the antecedents and outcomes associated with organizational commitments may be relevant to some extent to interpersonal commitments (Becker, chapter 5). According to Becker, interpersonal commitment refers to a bond between an individual and another person or a group of individuals. For my purposes, I will take the example of commitment to the supervisor or the workgroup. The degree of relevance of antecedents and outcomes listed in Table 4.1 can be determined within a *target similarity* framework recently proposed by Lavelle, Rupp, and Brockner (2007) to understand how multifoci social exchange variables are connected with one another. A major assumption of the target similarity model is that individuals try to identify the source of actions directed toward them (e.g., organization, supervisor, coworkers) and primarily react by targeting their behavior toward that source. Applying this framework, such antecedents as value congruence, support, leadership, investments, or alternatives (cf. Table 4.1) will have stronger impact on commitment to a supervisor (or workgroup) if these antecedents are related to the supervisor (or workgroup). Similarly, commitment to a supervisor (or workgroup) should be more strongly related to the outcomes listed in Table 4.1 when the outcomes are directed at the same party or beneficiary. This is what Lavelle et al. (2007) call the *target similarity effect*. Note that *spill-*

over effects across foci are also likely but should be weaker (Lavelle et al., 2007).

Finally, the antecedents and outcomes listed in Table 4.1 have indirect relevance for action commitments (cf. Neubert & Wu, chapter 6). Conceived as "commitment to act toward a particular end," action commitment appears more focused and specific than organizational commitments and does not involve a particular target of commitment. However, it is likely that the broader exchange relationship between an individual and a given macro-target (e.g., the organization) will determine the context within which more specific action commitments take place. For example, strong value congruence between the individual and the organization may lead to stronger affective organizational commitment, which in turn may contribute to stronger commitment to a change project (Herscovitch & Meyer, 2002). Similarly, commitment to a change project may spill over on organization-directed citizenship behavior, which in and of itself would be better explained by commitment to employing organization (cf. target similarity effects model).

A Model of the Mediating Processes Linking Commitment to Work Behavior

Overall, the research findings reviewed in the previous sections suggest work outcomes are not very well explained by organizational commitments. With the accumulation of meta-analytic reviews, some moderators of the commitment-outcomes relationships have been identified, and maybe others will be identified in the future. However, it is unlikely that such work will add much over what we already know. What is needed is further conceptualizing the processes through which commitment influences work behavior. It is indeed striking to note how little we know about these processes. Figure 4.1 proposes a model linking commitment to work behavior through two basic mechanisms: approach/avoidance motivation and state goal orientation. The proposed model is thought to be applicable to any macro-level commitment reviewed in this chapter. The model's mediating processes relate commitment to (a) withdrawal behavior, workplace deviance, and well-being, and (b) performance (in-role, extra-role, creative), respectively. In line with Klein et al. (2006), the model also acknowledges that commitment is characterized by two fundamental aspects: strength and rationales. According to Klein et al., commitment strength refers to the degree to which the individual perceives to be bound to a target, while commitment rationales refer to the self-explanations for why one perceives to be bound to a target.

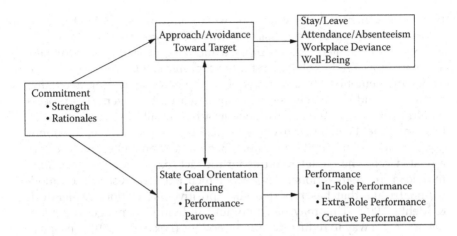

FIGURE 4.1

A general model of the processes linking commitment strength and rationales to work outcomes.

Several observations should be drawn regarding the proposed model. First, there are two distinct mechanisms underlying the links between commitment and behavior. One of those mechanisms reflects the way individuals regulate affect toward the target (Klein et al., 2006). Neuroscientists and personality psychologists (e.g., Carver & White, 1994; Sutton & Davidson, 1997) have demonstrated the existence of two distinct, functionally independent behavioral systems that express individual reactivity to signals of nonpunishment or reward (behavioral activation system, BAS) and nonreward or punishment (behavioral inhibition system, BIS). Activation of the BAS results in individuals experiencing positive emotions and engaging in approach behaviors, while activation of the BIS is associated with negative emotions and emergence of avoidance behaviors (Diefendorff & Mehta, 2007; Gable, Reis, & Elliot, 2000; Gray, 1990). Gable et al. (2000) showed that sensitivities of the two motivational systems are partly shaped by everyday affective experience. That is, positive events tend to activate the BAS, while negative events tend to activate the BIS. Extending these arguments, I argue that commitment strength and rationales provide an important basis as to the extent to which an approach versus avoidance motivation toward the target will be activated (cf. Herrbach, 2006). For example, a combination of rationales of strong affect toward the organization and low cost of membership would provide positive signals about the bond with the organization, leading to the activation of an approach motivation toward the target, which ultimately will reduce turnover and absenteeism.

Another observation is that the model does not presume that commitment is biased toward favorable outcomes exclusively. The existence of two distinct intermediate systems between commitment and withdrawal behavior leaves open the possibility that either approach or avoidance behavior is generated. For example, a rationale of lack of employment alternatives as a self-explanation for the commitment (i.e., bond) may lead to negative emotions (i.e., feelings of entrapment), activating avoidance motivation and ultimately resulting in increased turnover. This process would explain why the subcomponent of lack of alternatives within CC has sometimes been found to correlate positively with turnover intentions (e.g., $r = .10$, $p < .05$, in Stinglhamber, Bentein, & Vandenberghe, 2002). In a related vein, the model accounts for the fact that avoidance motivation may lead to organizational deviance, which parallels research on motivational traits that has reported such positive association (Diefendorff & Mehta, 2007). This may be so because individuals engage in deviant behavior as a way to reduce negative emotions (Fox et al., 2001). On a positive note, approach motivation that likely results from positive rationales associated with commitment should enhance well-being, as positive emotions have generally been found to do so (Diener et al., 1999).

Figure 4.1 also portrays the relationship between commitment and performance as being mediated by state goal orientations. Research in educational settings by Dweck (1986), Dweck and Leggett (1988), and Elliot (1997) has suggested that individuals differ in terms of goal preferences in achievement situations. Individuals with a *learning* goal orientation believe that ability is malleable and can be improved by developing competencies and skills, as well as mastering new situations. Individuals with a *performance-prove* goal orientation are essentially concerned with demonstrating their abilities and getting favorable judgments from their environment. Finally, those who hold a *performance-avoid* goal orientation tend to flee situations where their abilities would be questioned and to avoid negative evaluations from others. Research has also suggested that individuals also hold *state* goal orientations that are shaped by organizational factors (Dragoni, 2005) and more closely associated with performance than *trait* goal orientations (Payne, Youngcourt, & Beaubien, 2007).

Building on this, I suggest that commitment strength and rationales will act upon the state goal orientations of learning and performance-prove, which in turn will influence performance (in-role, extra-role, or creative). Note that I have excluded the performance-avoid component due to its proximity with negative emotions (Payne et al., 2007) and avoidance motivation. For example, as a rationale of affect toward the organization presumably derives from a sense of identification with the organization and is thought to positively relate to effort towards achieving its goals (Meyer, Becker, & Vandenberghe, 2004), it should induce a learning goal orientation, which has typically been reported to relate to the desire to work hard and exert effort (VandeWalle, Brown, Cron, & Slocum, 1999), which in turn should relate to performance. This relationship should be stronger for creative performance, because such performance requires more effort and adaptive responses (VandeWalle et al., 1999). On the other hand, performance-prove orientation is likely to be an important determinant of performance in contexts where creativity and learning are not emphasized or where there is a social pressure toward performance (Rawsthorne & Elliot, 1999).

The model calls for a few more comments. First, it is important to notice that the mechanisms that mediate the relations between commitment strength and rationales and performance are of a different nature than those involved in the emergence of withdrawal behaviors, workplace deviance, and well-being. The regulation of emotions has been found to be central in the use of avoidance-withdrawal strategies (Endler & Parker, 1990; O'Brian & Delongis, 1996; Wong, Yik, & Kwong, 2006), workplace deviance (e.g., Diefendorff & Mehta, 2007), and psychological well-being (Diener et al., 1999). In contrast, goal orientations represent cognitive forms of regulation of "valued propensities" that have high relevance in achievement situations (Wang & Takeuchi, 2007), hence, primarily act on performance. Although the two processes differ, interactions between them may occur, as is illustrated by a two-way arrow connecting them in Figure 4.1. That is, negative emotional states may be related to performance (Wright, Cropanzano, & Bonett, 2007), but their influence should be indirect. For example, it is because negative emotions impede an efficient regulation of cognitive resources (i.e., goal orientations) that performance can deteriorate. Similarly, a performance-prove goal orientation may render individuals liable to experience frustration and anxiety in the face of failure, which can engender negative emotions (Cron, Slocum, VandeWalle, & Fu, 2005) and indirectly elicit withdrawal tendencies.

Second, it is important to note that the model portrayed in Figure 4.1 differs from Meyer et al.'s (2004) integrative model of commitment and motivation in that the latter proposes a unitary process tying commitment to behavior, in which the notion of *goal regulation* (from intrinsic to extrinsic) is central, and thus provides no clear distinction between the regulation of emotions and of cognitive resources. I believe there is value in distinguishing the two mechanisms as they provide different views on how and why people behave the way they do as a result of the self-explanations for and strength of their commitment to macro-foci. Third, as will be discussed below, the processes described in Figure 4.1 are applicable to the other macro-level commitments reviewed in this chapter. For example, they can be applied to interpersonal commitments (cf. Becker, chapter 5). However, I do not see the model being applicable to all commitments. For example, macro-level commitments differ from action commitments (cf. Neubert & Wu, chapter 6) in that action commitment is defined as "commitment to act toward a particular end" (e.g., to act toward the achievement of a goal or project), while macro-level commitments refer to a perceived bond with a target. Our model makes a distinction between the bond itself and the processes and actions that follow. Such a distinction may be difficult to make for action commitments, which assume that commitment and act are inextricably tied to one another. Moreover, macro-level commitments may lead to a variety of actions, which may not be the case for action commitments.

Applicability to Various Macro-Foci Commitments

The processes depicted in Figure 4.1 generalize to all macro-foci commitments reviewed in this chapter. For example, it can be used to model the relationships between occupational or career commitment and withdrawal behaviors and job performance. I will take the case of hospital nurses as an example. It is known that nurses tend to give up their career quite early, presumably due to chronic exposure to stressful work conditions that ultimately reduce their willingness to pursue their career in nursing (Andrews, 2003; Krausz, Koslowsky, Shalom, & Elyakim, 1995; Nogueras, 2006). Using the model in Figure 4.1, it is likely that nurses make sense of their career commitment through feelings of entrapment because of prior investments in their career and strong "career embeddedness" (Feldman & Ng, 2007) that reduces mobility outside the nursing profession. The entrapment rationale then leads to the activation of avoidance motivation directed toward the career, and ultimately results in increased likelihood of withdrawing from the nursing profession. In a similar way, early career commitment through self-justifications as a desire to develop one's abilities and sense of growth may result in stronger learning goal orientation, exemplified by activities that develop one's occupational competencies, and lead to enhanced nursing care performance. Thus, the processes depicted in Figure 4.1 can be applied to describing the paths through which occupational or career commitment influences occupation- or career-related work behavior.

Similarly, several of the mechanisms presented in Figure 4.1 may be involved in how union commitment affects work behavior. For example, a rationale of perceived obligation that accompanies union commitment—plausibly resulting from a history of affiliation to unions in one's family—may result in individuals engaging in a performance-prove orientation toward the completion of union activities. More precisely, a rationale of perceived obligation may reflect some kind of sensitivity to social pressures that easily translates into a performance-prove orientation (i.e., demonstrating one's skills to others), which in turn can influence the performance of union activities. Alternatively, an individual who perceives to be bound to the union out of a rationale of affective attachment may engage in learning goal orientation and end up finding ways to creatively promote the ideas of the union to new affiliates or the company. On a negative note, an individual may feel bound to a union just because he or she fears losing his or her job, thereby experiencing negative emotions and avoidance motivation, which can result in withdrawing from the union once another job is found outside the organization. In sum, the paths described in Figure 4.1 provide different ways through which union commitment can affect work behavior.

The model in Figure 4.1 can also be used to understand how commitment paths may apply in the context of commitment to client organizations. For example, it is likely that a perceived bond with a client organization out of a rationale of affective attachment will encourage the development of a learning goal orientation (i.e., developing skills that are relevant to working with the client organization) that ultimately will lead to client-directed organizational citizenship behavior. As an illustration, an IT professional who works in close relationship with, and experiences an affective attachment to, a client organization may want to learn skills that are relevant to solving IT problems that the client is facing, and thereby go beyond the call of duty to assist the client until the problems are solved. Similarly, commitment associated with a rationale of affective attachment may activate an approach motivation toward the client organization that results in the relationship being pursued on a long-term basis. That is, the IT professional may want to attend to the client organization's needs even after his or her mission is completed. In contrast, if he or she feels trapped in the relationship with the client, he or she may engage in avoidance motivation and ultimately in deviant behavior, such as voluntarily neglecting important aspects of his or her mission, particularly if this cannot be easily detected by the client.

Finally, the principles described in Figure 4.1 also apply to commitment to organizational subentities. However, a major difference here is that organizational subentities are nested within organizations, suggesting that the prediction of behaviors may partly depend on the level of commitment to the employing organization. For example, a low approach toward the local work unit resulting from low affective attachment to the unit may result in (a) one's changing work units *within the same organization* if such possibility exists or (b) leaving the organization if it does not or if affective attachment to the organization is concurrently low. That is, the relationship between approach/avoidance motivation toward the local unit and withdrawal from the organization may be moderated by commitment to the employing organization. On a related matter, commitment to local units out of affective attachment may engender a learning goal orientation—the desire to develop skills and competencies that are related to achieving the goals of the unit—and lead to extra-role behavior directed at helping the unit reach its objectives. Similarly, one may speculate that commitment to the employing organization will moderate the relationship between goal orientations directed at the work unit and organization-directed performance.

٭

Additional Avenues for Future Research

A first avenue concerns the identification of commitment rationales across organizational commitments. Indeed, research has examined multiple mindsets associated with commitment to employing organizations (Meyer & Allen, 1991; Meyer et al., 2002) and occupational commitment (Irving et al., 1997; Meyer et al., 1993; Snape & Redman, 2003) but has not considered the possibility that multiple mindsets—and in Klein et al.'s (2006) terminology, "rationales"—may exist among the other commitments reviewed here. This investigation would be particularly interesting in the area of nested targets because in such instances the prediction of work behavior should be affected by interactions among commitment rationales across targets. For example, an employee who feels committed to a client organization out of perceived obligation and at the same time makes sense of his or her organizational commitment through affective attachment may feel a *moral imperative* (Gellatly et al., 2006) to deliver quality service to the client organization. Another example would be a unionized worker who reasons his or her commitment to the organization as being based on the cost associated with leaving and concurrently experiences an emotional bond to the union. This worker may want to reduce his or her overtime on the job and engage more so in prounion activities.

Second, more research is needed on the potential compatibility of organizational commitments. Particular attention should be given to examining when compatibility can be achieved and when it cannot be. An interesting vehicle for studying compatibility between commitments is value congruence. Although value congruence has been conceptualized and operationalized in a variety of ways (Kristof, 1996; Ostroff et al., 2005), an important aspect is whether its effect on commitment compatibility varies as a function of *value content*. For example, Martin (1992) reasoned that three types of subcultures can be found in organizations: enhancing subcultures, orthogonal subcultures, and countercultures. Enhancing subcultures are characterized by values that are consistent with and reinforce the organization's culture; orthogonal subcultures are defined by values that are not endorsed by but do not conflict with the organization's value system; countercultures are characterized by values that are in conflict with the organization's culture. One may speculate that commitment to subentities defined as countercultures will be the least compatible with commitment to the global organization. Similarly, occupational commitment will be more compatible with commitment to employing organization if there is occupation-organization value congruence on *pivotal* values rather than on *peripheral* values (Schein, 1968). For example, nurses' occupational commitment will be particularly compatible with commitment to a hospital that endorses above all things the value of achieving high care-quality for patients. This is because care quality is critical in nurses' occupational value system.

Third, commitment research has been largely conducted at the individual level, while macro-level commitments may exist at multiple levels of analysis. Moreover, cross-level effects and interactions may occur. For example, it is plausible that business units develop climates for commitment to client organizations that would be characterized by a strong dedication to clients' needs and willingness to serve clients in an efficient manner. Such a climate may help service providers to perceive compatibility between commitment to the organization and the expectations of client organizations. In other words, the individual-level relationship between commitment to the employing organization and service performance may be moderated by a unit-level climate for commitment to client organizations, though the latter may also have a cross-level effect on service performance (cf. Liao & Chuang, 2007). Similarly, occupational commitment may aggregate in some workplaces and create constraints on relationships between other individual-level, organizational commitments and work outcomes. For example, some health care organizations seek to promote professional development of their nursing staff via continuing education, while others do not pursue that objective. This may result in significant variance on occupational commitment across organizations, which in turn may affect patient care quality.

On a related matter, it would be interesting to examine which commitment rationales tend to aggregate at higher-order levels and which do not. For example, commitment based on a rationale of cost may be more easily shared among individuals among the same organizations because the costs associated with organizational membership are assumed to be at least partly influenced by organizational-level human resource management policies (e.g., training, salaries, bonuses). Wright and Kehoe (chapter 9) provide a whole discussion of conceptual issues surrounding the study of commitment at multiple levels of analysis, calling for more efforts at multi-level theorizing that would specify the paths through which commitment impacts broader organizational outcomes and is influenced by organizational variables.

Fourth, commitment research would benefit from building on what we know from social networks in organizations. Social capital theory asserts that the behaviors and attitudes of individuals are influenced by the social networks in which they are embedded (Brass, 2001). A social network refers to the informal relationships between a set of individuals (Koehly & Shivy, 1998). An important characteristic of social networks is the notion of *centrality*, which refers to "the extent to which a given individual is connected to others in a network" (Sparrowe, Liden, Wayne, & Kraimer, 2001, p. 316). Past research has linked the individual's network centrality in the organization to career advancement (e.g., Podolny & Baron, 1997; Seibert, Kraimer, & Liden, 2001), power and influence in decision making (Brass, 1984; Friedkin, 1993), socialization outcomes (Morrison, 2002), and job performance (Sparrowe et al., 2001). Supervisors' network centrality should be particularly important for the development of employees' commitment to the employing organization and to the occupation, because supervisors can use these networks to help their subordinates access resources and information (Seibert et al., 2001) that are important for advancing their career in and out the organization. More generally, relationships that develop between supervisors and organizations may also influence the strength of relationships of social exchange variables (e.g., perceived organizational support and leader-member exchange) with employee commitments (see Wayne et al., chapter 8).

Finally, the advancement of knowledge in commitment research faces other types of challenges. For example, Luchak and Gellatly (2007) demonstrated that the relationships between CC and such outcomes as turnover cognitions, absenteeism, and job performance were better explained by a nonlinear model than by the traditional linear model. Such line of inquiry should be pursued because it is plausible that not all commitment mindsets impact work behavior in a linear fashion. The nonlinearity of effects may be an issue for testing interactions among macro commitments. For example, AC or NC may influence behavior only if CC is maintained at low levels, while at extreme levels of CC, the effects of AC or NC may change direction. Another issue that needs attention is the examination of change processes in commitment across time. We already know that declines in AC and NC are associated with corresponding increases in turnover intentions, which in turn affect turnover (Bentein, Vandenberg, Vandenberghe, & Stinglhamber, 2005). However, we also need to investigate whether such effects occur with other outcomes of importance to organizations (performance, absenteeism, etc.). The study of change in commitment is a contemporaneous issue, given the changing nature of organizations. It would also be interesting to know whether commitments change at a similar pace across targets and mindsets. In a related vein, we need to know whether management practices can influence change in commitment over time, and to identify which practices are most effective in doing so. We also need to know whether declines in commitment may be more likely to occur than increases in commitment, as Bentein et al. suggested, and which management practices are most effective for struggling with declines and/or fostering increases in commitment. Note that change processes involved in relationships between commitment and its antecedents or outcomes may also be nonlinear, which past research has often neglected. (For a review of methodological approaches to the study of change in commitment—linear and nonlinear—see Vandenberg & Stanley, chapter 12). Obviously, although we have learned a lot during the past decades, much remains to be done to improve our knowledge of commitment in the workplace.

References

Allen, N. J., & Grisaffe, D. B. (2001). Employee commitment to the organization and customer reactions: Mapping the linkages. *Human Resource Management Review, 11,* 209–236.

Allen, N. J., & Meyer, J. P. (1990). The measurement and antecedents of affective, continuance and normative commitment to the organization. *Journal of Occupational Psychology, 63,* 1–18.

Allen, N. J., & Meyer, J. P. (1996). Affective, continuance, and normative commitment to the organization: An examination of the construct validity. *Journal of Vocational Behavior, 49,* 252–276.

Andrews, G. J. (2003). Nurses who left the British NHS for private complementary medical practice: Why did they leave? Would they return? *Journal of Advanced Nursing, 41,* 403–415.

Angle, H. L., & Perry, J.L. (1986). Dual commitment and labor-management relationship climates. *Academy of Management Journal, 29,* 31–50.

Aranya, N., Pollock, J., & Amernic, J. (1981). An examination of professional commitment in public accounting. *Accounting, Organizations and Society, 6,* 271–280.

Ashforth, B. E., & Mael, F. (1989). Social identity theory and the organization. *Academy of Management Review, 14,* 20–39.

Bamberger, P. A., Kluger, A. N., & Suchard, R. (1999). The antecedents and consequences of union commitment: A meta-analysis. *Academy of Management Journal, 42,* 304–318.

Bakker, A. B., Demerouti, E., de Boer, E., & Schaufeli, W. B. (2003). Job demands and job resources as predictors of absence duration and frequency. *Journal of Vocational Behavior, 62,* 341–356.

Barkin, S. (1950). A trade unionist appraises management personnel philosophy. *Harvard Business Review, 28,* 59–64.

Becker, T. E. (1992). Foci and bases of commitment: Are they distinctions worth making? *Academy of Management Journal, 35,* 232–244.

Becker, T. E. (2005, October). *Problems of commitment: Three dilemmas regarding the nature of employee attachment.* Presentation at the 2005 Conference on Commitment: Accumulated Wisdom and New Directions. Ohio State University, Columbus, OH.

Becker, T. E., & Bennett, R. J. (in press). Employee attachment and deviance in organizations. In J. Langan-Fox, C. Cooper, and R. Klimoski (Eds.), *Research companion to the dysfunctional workplace: Management challenges and symptoms* (pp. 136–151). Northampton, MA: Elgar.

Becker, T. E., Billings, R. S., Eveleth, D. M., & Gilbert, N. L. (1996). Foci and bases of employee commitment: Implications for job performance. *Academy of Management Journal, 39,* 464–482.

Begley, T. M., & Czajka, J. M. (1993). Panel analysis of the moderating effects of commitment on job satisfaction, intent to quit, and health following organizational change. *Journal of Applied Psychology, 78,* 552–556.

Bemmels, B. (1995). Dual commitment: Unique construct or epiphenomenon? *Journal of Business Research, 16,* 401–422.

Benson, J. (1998). Dual commitment: Contract workers in Australian manufacturing enterprises. *Journal of Management Studies, 35,* 355–375.

Bentein, K., Vandenberg, R. J., Vandenberghe, C., & Stinglhamber, F. (2005). The role of change in the relationship between commitment and turnover: A latent growth modeling approach. *Journal of Applied Psychology, 90,* 468–482.

Bergami, M., & Bagozzi, R. P. (2000). Self-categorization, affective commitment and group self-esteem as distinct aspects of social identity in the organization. *British Journal of Social Psychology, 39,* 555–577.

Blau, G. J. (1985). The measurement and prediction of career commitment. *Journal of Occupational Psychology, 58,* 277–288.

Blau, G. J. (1988). Further exploring the meaning and measurement of career commitment. *Journal of Vocational Behavior, 32,* 284–297.

Blau, G. J., Paul, A., & St.-John, N. (1993). On developing a general index of work commitment. *Journal of Vocational Behavior, 42,* 298–314.

Brass, D. J. (1984). Being in the right place: A structural analysis of individual influence in an organization. *Administrative Science Quarterly, 29,* 518–539.

Brass, D. J. (2001). Social capital and organizational leadership. In S. J. Zaccaro & R. J. Klimoski (Eds.), *The nature of organizational leadership: Understanding the performance imperatives confronting today's leaders* (pp. 132–152). San Francisco: Jossey-Bass.

Buchanan, B. (1974). Building organizational commitment: The socialization of managers in work organizations. *Administrative Science Quarterly, 19,* 533–546.

Cable, D. M., & Judge, T. A. (1996). Person-organization fit, job choice decisions, and organizational entry. *Organizational Behavior and Human Decision Processes, 67,* 294–311.

Carson, K. D., & Bedeian, A. G. (1994). Career commitment: Construction of a measure and examination of its psychometric properties. *Journal of Vocational Behavior, 44,* 237–262.

Carver, C. S., & White, T. L. (1994). Behavioral inhibition, behavioral activation, and affective responses to impending reward and punishment: The BIS/BAS scales. *Journal of Personality and Social Psychology, 67,* 319–333.

Chen, Z. X., & Francesco, A. M. (2003). The relationship between the three components of commitment and employee performance in China. *Journal of Vocational Behavior, 62,* 490–510.

Cheng, Y., & Stockdale, M. S. (2003). The validity of the three-component model of organizational commitment in a Chinese context. *Journal of Vocational Behavior, 62,* 465–489.

Cohen, A. (1991). Career stage as a moderator of the relationships between organizational commitment and its outcomes: A meta-analysis. *Journal of Occupational Psychology, 64,* 253–268.

Cohen, A. (1993). Organizational commitment and turnover: A meta-analysis. *Academy of Management Journal, 36,* 1140–1157.

Cohen, A. (2005). Dual commitment to the organization and the union: A multi-dimensional approach. *Relations Industrielles/Industrial Relations, 60,* 432–454.

Cohen, A., & Hudecek, N. (1993). Organizational commitment-turnover relationship across occupational groups: A meta-analysis. *Group and Organization Management, 18,* 188–213.

Connelly, C. E., & Gallagher, D. G. (2004). Emerging trends in contingent work research. *Journal of Management, 30,* 959–983.

Cooper-Hakim, A., & Viswesvaran, C. (2005). The construct of work commitment: Testing an integrative framework. *Psychological Bulletin, 131,* 241–259.

Coyle-Shapiro, J. A., & Morrow, P. C. (2006). Organizational and client commitment among contracted employees. *Journal of Vocational Behavior, 68,* 416–431.

Coyle-Shapiro, J. A., Morrow, P. C., & Kessler, I. (2006). Serving two organizations: Exploring the employment relationship of contracted employees. *Human Resource Management, 45,* 561–583.

Cron, W., Slocum, J., VandeWalle, D., & Fu, Q. (2005). The role of goal on negative emotions and goal setting when initial performance falls short of one's performance goal. *Human Performance, 18,* 55–80.

Deery, S. J., & Iverson, R. D. (2005). Labor-management cooperation: Antecedents and impact on organizational performance. *Industrial and Labor Relations Review, 58,* 588–609.

Diefendorff, J. M., & Mehta, K. (2007). The relations of motivational traits with workplace deviance. *Journal of Applied Psychology, 92,* 967–977.

Diener, E., Suh, E. M., Lucas, R. E., & Smith, H. L. (1999). Subjective well-being: Three decades of progress. *Psychological Bulletin, 125,* 276–302.

Dragoni, L. (2005). Understanding the emergence of state goal orientation in organizational work groups: The role of leadership and multilevel climate perceptions. *Journal of Applied Psychology, 90,* 1084–1095.

Dweck, C. S. (1986). Motivational processes affecting learning. *American Psychologist, 41,* 1040–1048.

Dweck, C. S., & Leggett, E. L. (1988). A social-cognitive approach to motivation and personality. *Psychological Review, 95,* 256–273.

Eisenberger, R., Huntington, R., Hutchison, S., & Sowa D. (1986). Perceived organizational support. *Journal of Applied Psychology, 71,* 500–507.

Ellingson, J. E., Gruys, M. L., & Sackett, P. R. (1998). Factors related to the satisfaction and performance of temporary employees. *Journal of Applied Psychology, 83,* 913–921.

Elliot, A. J. (1997). Integrating the "classic" and "contemporary" approaches to achievement motivation: A hierarchical model of approach and avoidance achievement motivation. *Advances in Motivation and Achievement, 10,* 143–179.

128   *Commitment in Organizations*

Endler, N. S., & Parker, J. D. (1990). Multidimensional assessment of coping: A critical evaluation. *Journal of Personality and Social Psychology, 58,* 844–854.

England, G. W. (1960). Dual allegiance to company and union. *Personnel Administration, 23,* 20–25.

Erdheim, J., Wang, M., & Zickar, M. J. (2006). Linking the Big Five personality constructs to organizational commitment. *Personality and Individual Differences, 41,* 959–970.

Farrell, D., & Rusbult, C. E. (1981). Exchange variables as predictors of job satisfaction, job commitment, and turnover: The impact of rewards, costs, alternatives, and investments. *Organizational Behavior and Human Performance, 27,* 78–95.

Feldman, D. C., Doerpinghaus, H. I., & Turnley, W. H. (1995). Employee reactions to temporary jobs. *Journal of Managerial Issues, 7,* 127–141.

Feldman, D. C., & Ng, T. W. H. (2007). Careers: Mobility, embeddedness, and success. *Journal of Management, 33,* 350–377.

Felfe, J., Schmook, R., Six, B., & Wieland, R. (2005). Contingent employees' commitment to agency and client organization: Antecedents and consequences. *Zeitschrift Personalpsychologie, 4,* 101–115.

Fox, S., Spector, P. E., & Miles, D. (2001). Counterproductive work behavior (CWB) in response to job stressors and organizational justice: Some mediator and moderator tests for autonomy and emotions. *Journal of Vocational Behavior, 59,* 291–309.

Friedkin, N. E. (1993). Structural bases of interpersonal influence in groups: A longitudinal case study. *American Sociological Review, 58,* 861–872.

Fukami, C. V. & Larson, E. W. (1984). Commitment to company and union: Parallel models. *Journal of Applied Psychology, 69,* 367–371.

Fullagar, C. J., Gallagher, D. G., Clark, P. F., & Carroll, A. E. (2004). Union commitment and participation: A 10-year longitudinal study. *Journal of Applied Psychology, 89,* 730–737.

Gable, S. L., Reis, H. T., & Elliot, A. J. (2000). Behavioral activation and inhibition in everyday life. *Journal of Personality and Social Psychology, 78,* 1135–1149.

Gellatly, I. R., Meyer, J. P., & Luchak, A. A. (2006). Combined effects of the three commitment components on focal and discretionary behaviors: A test of Meyer and Herscovitch's propositions. *Journal of Vocational Behavior, 69,* 331–345.

George, E., & Chattopadhyay, P. (2005). One foot in each camp: The dual identification of contract workers. *Administrative Science Quarterly, 50,* 68–99.

Gordon, M. E., Barling, J., & Tetrick, L. E. (1995). Some remaining challenges. In L. E. Tetrick & J. Barling (Eds.), *Changing employment relations: Behavioral and social perspectives* (pp. 349–366). Washington, DC: American Psychological Association.

Gordon, M. E., Philpot, W. J., Burt, E. R., Thompson, C. A., & Spiller, E. W. (1980). Commitment to the union: Development of a measure and an examination of its correlates. *Journal of Applied Psychology, 65,* 479–499.

Gould, S. (1979). Characteristics of planners in upwardly mobile occupations. *Academy of Management Journal, 22,* 539–550.

Gouldner, A. W. (1957). Cosmopolitans and locals: Toward an analysis of latent social roles. *Administrative Science Quarterly, 2,* 281–306.

Gouldner, A. W. (1958). Cosmopolitans and locals: Toward an analysis of latent social roles. *Administrative Science Quarterly, 3,* 444–480.

Gray, J. A. (1990). Brain systems that mediate both emotion and cognition. *Cognition and Emotion, 4,* 269–288.

Greenhaus, J. H. (1971). An investigation of the role of career salience in vocational behavior. *Journal of Vocational Behavior, 1,* 209–216.

Greenhaus, J. H. (1973). A factorial investigation of career salience. *Journal of Vocational Behavior, 3,* 95–98.

Griffeth, R. W., Hom, P. W., & Gaertner, S. (2000). A meta-analysis of antecedents and correlates of employee turnover: Update, moderator tests, and research implications for the next millennium. *Journal of Management, 26,* 463–488.

Hackett, R. D., & Bycio, P. (1996). An evaluation of employee absenteeism as a coping mechanism among hospital nurses. *Journal of Occupational and Organizational Psychology, 69,* 327–338.

Hall, D. T. (1971). A theoretical model of career sub-identity development in organizational settings. *Organizational Behavior and Human Performance, 6,* 50–76.

Herrbach, O. (2006). A matter of feeling? The affective tone of organizational commitment and identification. *Journal of Organizational Behavior, 27,* 629–643.

Herscovitch, L., & Meyer, J. P. (2002). Commitment to organizational change: Extension of a three-component model. *Journal of Applied Psychology, 87,* 474–487.

Hunt, S. D., & Morgan, R. M. (1994). Organizational commitment: One of many commitments or key mediating construct? *Academy of Management Journal, 37,* 1568–1587.

Irving, P. G., Coleman, D. F., & Cooper, C. L. (1997). Further assessment of a three-component model of occupational commitment: Generalizability and differences across occupations. *Journal of Applied Psychology, 82,* 444–452.

Jaramillo, F., Mulki, J. P., & Marshall, G. W. (2005). A meta-analysis of the relationship between organizational commitment and salesperson job performance: 25 years of research. *Journal of Business Research, 58,* 705–714.

Jaros, S. J. (1997). An assessment of Meyer and Allen's (1991) three-component model of organizational commitment and turnover intentions. *Journal of Vocational Behavior, 51,* 319–337.

Johnson, J. W. (1996). Linking employee perceptions of service climate to customer satisfaction. *Personnel Psychology, 49,* 831–851.

Kanter, R. M. (1968). Commitment and social organization: A study of commitment mechanisms in utopian communities. *American Sociological Review, 33,* 499–517.

Kelloway, E. K., & Barling, J. (1993). Members' participation in local union activities: Measurement, prediction, and replication. *Journal of Applied Psychology, 78,* 262–279.

Kerr, S., Von Glinow, M. A., & Schriesheim, J. (1977). Issues in the study of "professionals" in organizations: The case of scientists and engineers. *Organizational Behavior and Human Performance, 18,* 329–345.

Kim, J. W., & Rowley, C. (2006). Commitment to company and labour union: Empirical evidence from South Korea. *International Journal of Human Resource Management, 17,* 673–692.

Klandermans, B. (1989). Union commitment: Replications and tests in the Dutch context. *Journal of Applied Psychology, 74*, 869–875.

Klein, H. J., Brinsfield, C. T., & Molloy, J. C. (2006). *Understanding workplace commitments independent of antecedents, foci, rationales, and consequences.* Paper presented at the Academy of Management Annual Meeting, Atlanta, GA.

Koehly, L. M., & Shivy, V. A. (1998). Social network analysis: A new methodology for counseling research. *Journal of Counseling Psychology, 45*, 3–17.

Kraimer, M. L., & Wayne, S. J. (2004). An examination of perceived organizational support as a multidimensional construct in the context of an expatriate assignment. *Journal of Management, 30*, 209–237.

Krausz, M., Koslowsky, M., Shalom, N., & Elyakim, N. (1995). Predictors of intentions to leave the ward, the hospital, and the nursing profession: A longitudinal study. *Journal of Organizational Behavior, 16*, 277–288.

Kristof, A. L. (1996). Person-organization fit: An integrative review of its conceptualizations, measurement, and implications. *Personnel Psychology, 49*, 1–49.

Lavelle, J. J., Rupp, D. E., & Brockner, J. (2007). Taking a multifoci approach to the study of justice, social exchange, and citizenship behavior: The target similarity model. *Journal of Management, 33*, 841–866.

Lawler, E. J. (1992). Affective attachments to nested groups: A choice-process theory. *American Sociological Review, 57*, 327–339.

Lee, K. L., Carswell, J. J., & Allen, N. J. (2000). A meta-analytic review of occupational commitment: Relations with person- and work-related variables. *Journal of Applied Psychology, 85*, 799–811.

Levinson, H. (1965). Reciprocation: The relationship between man and organization. *Administrative Science Quarterly, 9*, 370–390.

Lewin, K. (1943). Defining the 'field at a given time'. *Psychological Review, 50*, 292–310.

Liao, H., & Chuang, A. (2007). Transforming service employees and climate: A multilevel, multisource examination of transformational leadership in building long-term service relationships. *Journal of Applied Psychology, 92*, 1006–1019.

Liden, R. C., Wayne, S. J., Kraimer, M. L., & Sparrowe, R. T. (2003). The dual commitments of contingent workers: An examination of contingents' commitment to the agency and the organization. *Journal of Organizational Behavior, 24*, 609–625.

Lievens, F., & De Corte, W. (2008). Development and test of a model of external organizational commitment in human resources outsourcing. *Human Resource Management, 47*, 559–579.

Luchak, A. A., & Gellatly, I. R. (2007). A comparison of linear and nonlinear relations between organizational commitment and work outcomes. *Journal of Applied Psychology, 92*, 786–793.

Mael, F., & Ashforth, B. E. (1992). Alumni and their alma mater: A partial test of the reformulated model of organizational identification. *Journal of Organizational Behavior, 13*, 103–123.

Magenau, J. M., Martin, J. E., & Peterson, M. M. (1988). Dual and unilateral commitment among stewards and rank-and-file union members. *Academy of Management Journal, 31*, 359–376.

Martin, J. (1992). *Cultures in organizations: Three perspectives.* New York: Oxford University Press.

Mathieu, J. E. (1991). A cross-level nonrecursive model of the antecedents of organizational commitment and satisfaction. *Journal of Applied Psychology, 76,* 607–618.

Mathieu, J. E., & Hamel, K. (1989). A causal model of the antecedents of organizational commitment among professionals and nonprofessionals. *Journal of Vocational Behavior, 34,* 299–317.

Mathieu, J. E., & Zajac, D. M. (1990). A review and meta-analysis of the antecedents, correlates, and consequences of organizational commitment. *Psychological Bulletin, 108,* 171–194.

Matusik, S. F., & Hill, C. W. (1998). The utilization of contingent work, knowledge creation, and competitive advantage. *Academy of Management Review, 23,* 680–697.

Mayer, R. C., & Schoorman, F. D. (1992). Predicting participation and production outcomes through a two-dimensional model of organizational commitment. *Academy of Management Journal, 35,* 671–684.

Mayer, R. C., & Schoorman, F. D. (1998). Differentiating antecedents of organizational commitment: A test of March and Simon's model. *Journal of Organizational Behavior, 19,* 15–28.

McClurg, L. (1999). Organizational commitment in the temporary-help service industry. *Journal of Applied Management Studies, 8,* 5–26.

McDonald, D. J., & Makin, P. J. (2000). The psychological contract, organisational commitment and job satisfaction of temporary staff. *Leadership and Organization Development Journal, 21,* 84–91.

Meyer, J. P., & Allen, N. J. (1991). A three-component conceptualization of organizational commitment. *Human Resource Management Review, 1,* 61–89.

Meyer, J. P., & Allen, N. J. (1997). *Commitment in the workplace: Theory, research, and application.* Newbury Park, CA: Sage.

Meyer, J. P., Allen, N. J., & Smith, C. A. (1993). Commitment to organizations and occupations: Extension and test of a three-component conceptualization. *Journal of Applied Psychology, 78,* 538–551.

Meyer, J. P., Allen, N. J., & Topolnytsky, L. (1998). Commitment in a changing world of work. *Canadian Psychology, 39,* 83–93.

Meyer, J. P., Becker, T. E., & Vandenberghe, C. (2004). Employee commitment and motivation: A conceptual analysis and integrative model. *Journal of Applied Psychology, 89,* 991–1007.

Meyer, J. P., & Herscovitch, L. (2001). Commitment in the workplace: Toward a general model. *Human Resource Management Review, 11,* 299–326.

Meyer, J. P., Paunonen, S. V., Gellatly, I. R., Goffin, R. D., & Jackson, D. N. (1989). Organizational commitment and job performance: It's the nature of the commitment that counts. *Journal of Applied Psychology, 74,* 152–156.

Meyer, J. P., Stanley, D. J., Herscovitch, L., & Topolnytsky, L. (2002). Affective, continuance and normative commitment to the organization: A meta-analysis of antecedents, correlates, and consequences. *Journal of Vocational Behavior, 61,* 20–52.

Mitchell, M. S., & Ambrose, M. L. (2007). Abusive supervision and workplace deviance and the moderating effects of negative reciprocity beliefs. *Journal of Applied Psychology, 92,* 1159–1168.

Morrison, E. W. (2002). Newcomers' relationships: The role of social network ties during socialization. *Academy of Management Journal, 45,* 1149–1160.

Morrow, P. C. (1983). Concept redundancy in organizational research: The case of work commitment. *Academy of Management Review, 8,* 486–500.

Mowday, R. T., Porter, L. W., & Steers, R. M. (1982). *Employee-organization linkages: The psychology of commitment, absenteeism, and turnover.* New York: Academic Press.

Mueller, C. W., & Lawler, E. J. (1999). Commitment to nested organizational units: Some basic principles and preliminary findings. *Social Psychology Quarterly, 62,* 325–346.

Nogueras, D. J. (2006). Occupational commitment, education, and experience as a predictor of intent to leave the nursing profession. *Nursing Economics, 24,* 86–93.

O'Brien, T. B., & Delongis, A. (1996). The interactional context of problem-, emotion-, and relationship-focused coping: The role of the Big Five personality factors. *Journal of Personality, 64,* 775–813.

Olsen, K. M. (2007). The role of nonstandard workers in client-organizations. *Relations Industrially/Industrial Relations, 61,* 93–117.

O'Reilly, C. A., & Chatman, J. (1986). Organizational commitment and psychological attachment: The effects of compliance, identification, and internalization on prosocial behavior. *Journal of Applied Psychology, 71,* 492–499.

O'Reilly, C. A., Chatman, J. A., & Caldwell, D. F. (1991). People and organizational culture: A profile comparison approach to assessing person-organization fit. *Academy of Management Journal, 34,* 487–516.

Organ, D. W., & Ryan, K. (1995). A meta-analytic review of attitudinal and dispositional predictors of organizational citizenship behavior. *Personnel Psychology, 48,* 775–802.

Ostroff, C., Shin, Y. Y., & Kinicki, A. J. (2005). Multiple perspectives of congruence: Relationships between value congruence and employee attitudes. *Journal of Organizational Behavior, 26,* 591–623.

Payne, S. C., Youngcourt, S. S., & Beaubien, J. M. (2007). A meta-analytic examination of the goal orientation nomological net. *Journal of Applied Psychology, 92,* 128–150.

Podolny, J. M., & Baron, J. N. (1997). Relationships and resources: Social networks and mobility in the workplace. *American Sociological Review, 62,* 673–693.

Porter, L. W., Crampon, W. J., & Smith, F. J. (1976). Organizational commitment and managerial turnover. *Organizational Behavior and Human Performance, 15,* 87–98.

Porter, L. W., Steers, R. M., Mowday, R. T., & Boulian, P. V. (1974). Organizational commitment, job satisfaction, and turnover among psychiatric technicians. *Journal of Applied Psychology, 59,* 603–609.

Randall, D. M. (1990). The consequences of organizational commitment: Methodological investigation. *Journal of Organizational Behavior, 11,* 361–378.

Randall, D. M., Fedor, D. B., & Longenecker, C. O. (1990). The behavioral expression of organizational commitment. *Journal of Vocational Behavior, 36,* 210-224.

Rauyruen, P., & Miller, K. E. (2007). Relationship quality as a predictor of business-to-business customer loyalty. *Journal of Business Research, 60*, 21–31.

Rawsthorne, L. J., & Elliot, A. J. (1999). Achievement goals and intrinsic motivation: A meta-analytic review. *Personality and Social Psychology Review, 3*, 326–344.

Reade, C. (2001). Dual identification in multinational corporations: Local managers and their psychological attachment to the subsidiary versus the global organization. *International Journal of Human Resource Management, 12*, 405–424.

Redman, T., & Snape, E. (2005). Unpacking commitment: Multiple loyalties and employee behavior. *Journal of Management Studies, 42*, 301–328.

Reed, C. S., Young, W. R., & McHugh, P. P. (1994). A comparative look at dual commitment: An international study. *Human Relations, 47*, 1269–1293.

Rhoades, L., Eisenberger, R., & Armeli, S. (2001). Affective commitment to the organization: The contribution of perceived organizational support. *Journal of Applied Psychology, 86*, 825–836.

Riketta, M. (2002). Attitudinal organizational commitment and job performance: A meta-analysis. *Journal of Organizational Behavior, 23*, 257–266.

Schein, E. H. (1968). Organizational socialization and the profession of management. *Industrial Management Review, 9*, 1–16.

Schneider, B., & Bowen, D. E. (1985). Employee and customer perceptions of service in banks: Replication and extension. *Journal of Applied Psychology, 70*, 423–433.

Schneider, B., White, S. S., & Paul, M. C. (1998). Linking service climate and customer perceptions of service quality: Test of a causal model. *Journal of Applied Psychology, 83*, 150–163.

Scholl, R. W. (1981). Differentiating commitment from expectancy as a motivating force. *Academy of Management Review, 6*, 589–599.

Seibert, S. E., Kraimer, M. L., & Liden, R. C. (2001). A social capital theory of career success. *Academy of Management Journal, 44*, 219–237.

Sinclair, R. R., Tucker, J. S., Cullen, J. C., & Wright, C. (2005). Performance differences among four organizational commitment profiles. *Journal of Applied Psychology, 90*, 1280–1287.

Snape, E., & Redman, T. (2003). An evaluation of a three-component model of occupational commitment: Dimensionality and consequences among United Kingdom human resource management specialists. *Journal of Applied Psychology, 88*, 152–159.

Snape, E., & Redman, T. (2007). The nature and consequences of organization-employee and union-member exchange: An empirical analysis. *Journal of Labor Research, 28*, 359–374.

Snape, E., Redman, T., & Chan, A. W. (2000). Commitment to the union: A survey of research and the implications for industrial relations and trade unions. *International Journal of Management Reviews, 2*, 205–230.

Somers, M. J. (1995). Organizational commitment, turnover, and absenteeism: An examination of direct and interaction effects. *Journal of Organizational Behavior, 16*, 49–58.

Sparrowe, R. T., Liden, R. C., Wayne, S. J., & Kraimer, M. L. (2001). Social networks and the performance of individuals and groups. *Academy of Management Journal, 44*, 316–325.

Stagner, R. (1956). *Psychology of industrial conflict*. New York: Wiley.

Stagner, R., & Rosen, H. (1965). *Psychology of union-management relations*. Belmont, CA: Brooks-Cole.

Stinglhamber, F., Bentein, K., & Vandenberghe, C. (2002). Extension of the three-component model of commitment to five foci: Development of measures and substantive test. *European Journal of Psychological Assessment, 18*, 123–138.

Sutton, S. K., & Davidson, R. J. (1997). Prefrontal brain asymmetry: A biological substrate of the behavioral approach and inhibition systems. *Psychological Science, 8*, 204–210.

Tajfel, H., & Turner, J. C. (1986). The social identity theory of intergroup behavior. In S. Worchel & W. G. Austin (Eds.), *Psychology of intergroup relations* (2nd ed., pp. 7–24). Chicago: Nelson-Hall.

Tetrick, L. E., Shore, L. M., McClurg, L. N., & Vandenberg, R. J. (2007). Model of union participation: The impact of perceived union support, union instrumentality, and union loyalty. *Journal of Applied Psychology, 92*, 820–828.

Tett, R. P., & Meyer, J. P. (1993). Job satisfaction, organizational commitment, turnover intention, and turnover: Path analyses based on meta-analytic findings. *Personnel Psychology, 46*, 253–293.

Turner, J. C. (1987). *Rediscovering the social group: A self-categorization theory*. Oxford, UK: Blackwell.

Vandenberghe, C., Bentein, K., Michon, R., Chebat, J.-C., Tremblay, M., & Fils, J.-F. (2007). An examination of the role of perceived support and employee commitment in employee-customer encounters. *Journal of Applied Psychology, 92*, 1177–1187.

VandeWalle, D., Brown, S. P., Cron, W. L., & Slocum, J. W. (1999). The influence of goal orientation and self-regulation tactics on sales performance: A longitudinal field test. *Journal of Applied Psychology, 84*, 249–259.

Van Dick, R., Wagner, U., Stellmacher, J., Christ, O., & Tissington, P. A. (2005). To be(long) or not to be(long): Social identification in organizational contexts. *Genetic Social and General Psychology Monographs, 131*, 189–218.

Van Dyne, L., & Ang, S. (1998). Organizational citizenship behavior of contingent workers in Singapore. *Academy of Management Journal, 41*, 692–703.

Verquer, M. L., Beehr, T. A., & Wagner, S. H. (2003). A meta-analysis of relations between person-organization fit and work attitudes. *Journal of Vocational Behavior, 63*, 473–489.

Wallace, J. E. (1993). Professional and organizational commitment: Compatible or incompatible? *Journal of Vocational Behavior, 42*, 333–349.

Wang, M., & Takeuchi, R. (2006). The role of goal orientation during expatriation: A cross-sectional and longitudinal investigation. *Journal of Applied Psychology, 92*, 1437–1445.

Werbel, J. D., & Johnson, D. J. (2001). The use of person-group fit for employment selection: A missing link in person-environment fit. *Human Resource Management, 40*, 227–240.

Wiener, Y. (1982). Commitment in organizations: A normative view. *Academy of Management Review, 7*, 418–428.

Wong, K. F. E., Yik, M., & Kwong, J. Y. Y. (2006). Understanding the emotional aspects of escalation of commitment: The role of negative affect. *Journal of Applied Psychology, 91*, 282–297.

Wright, T. A., & Bonett, D. G. (2002). The moderating effects of employee tenure on the relation between organizational commitment and job performance: A meta-analysis. *Journal of Applied Psychology, 87,* 1183–1190.

Wright, T. A., Cropanzano, R., & Bonett, D. G. (2007). The moderating role of employee positive well being on the relation between job satisfaction and job performance. *Journal of Occupational Health Psychology, 12,* 93–104.

Yoon, J., Baker, M. R., & Ko, J. W. (1994). Interpersonal attachment and organizational commitment: Subgroup hypothesis revisited. *Human Relations, 47,* 329–351.

5

Interpersonal Commitments

Thomas E. Becker
University of Delaware

As Klein, Molloy, and Cooper concluded in chapter 1, commitment is a psychological bond. Interpersonal commitment is a bond between an individual and other persons or small groups. Although much attention has been directed toward more macro attachments, such as to organizations and occupations (Lee, Carswell, & Allen, 2000; Meyer, Stanley, Herscovitch, & Topolnytsky, 2002), and more micro ones, such as to goals (Klein, Wesson, Hollenbeck, & Alge, 1999), much less theory and research has addressed interpersonal commitments. Due to the nature of the literature, in this chapter I will focus on supervisors, peers, work teams, top management, and customers as interpersonal foci of commitment. Further, there is evidence that commitments to these targets are empirically distinguishable and that they explain unique variance in workplace outcomes beyond commitment to traditional targets such as organizations (e.g., T. E. Becker, Billings, Eveleth, & Gilbert, 1996; Bishop & Scott, 2000; Stinglhamber, Bentein, & Vandenberghe, 2002; Vandenberghe, Bentein, & Stinglhamber, 2004).

My objectives here are to review the relatively small literature on interpersonal commitments and to suggest several ways that this work can be interpreted and extended. I will concentrate on affective commitment because it has shown to have the strongest, most consistent ties to other variables of interest (Meyer et al., 2002). I'll address the similarities and differences in antecedents, outcomes, and correlates among commitment foci, identify the strengths and weaknesses of the theories discussed in chapter 1, and examine several bodies of work outside I/O psychology. In attempting to further our understanding of interpersonal commitments, I will propose that attitudinal and behavioral effects of commitment to social foci depend on the compatibility between the target of commitment and behavior, and on the level of abstraction and psychological distance of the foci. Directions for future research will be suggested.

Literature Search and Classification of Variables

To find relevant articles I searched the ABI/Inform, Expanded Academic ASAP Plus, and PsychINFO databases for the period from 1985 to 2007, and contacted commitment researchers with whom I am familiar. I chose 1985 as a starting point because this was the year that Arnon Reichers published her influential theory on the importance of multiple commitments. I located 52 scholarly articles, the characteristics of which are summarized in Table 5.1. For the bulk of my review, I focused on 44 of these articles that provided individual-level data across multiple foci.

In identifying the most commonly studied foci, my decision rule was to pay special attention to those for which there were three or more articles. Commitments to five foci met this criterion: commitments to customers (4 articles), peers (5 articles), supervisors (25 articles), teams (36 articles), and top management (6 articles). These don't sum to 44 because some articles examined commitment to multiple foci. Peers differ from teams in that articles including peers as a target did not state or imply that employees had to coordinate their activities to achieve a common goal (e.g., T. E. Becker & Billings, 1997; Redman & Snape, 2005). For the remainder of this chapter, I focus on these five foci. As a point of reference, and due to the historical significance of the topic, I also include commitment to organizations.

To categorize variables into antecedents, consequences, mediators, and moderators, I considered Mathieu and Zajac's (1990) classification scheme. Although these categories were developed based on studies of commitment to organizations, most appear relevant to commitment to other foci as well. For example, age, tenure, and job characteristics seem plausible as antecedents to interpersonal commitments; and job performance, intent to leave, and tardiness seem plausible consequences. (Indeed, the findings support this assumption.) In addition, I considered the treatment of variables by authors.

Consistent with this approach, I will at times use causal language in discussing the results. Note, though, that much of the research in this area is correlational and that caution is called for in making causal inferences. Due to the small number of studies and number of data points per variable, I did not perform a formal meta-analysis. Instead, where multiple correlations existed, I simply calculated median correlations (M_r) to describe the relationships. Where only one study underlies a correlation, I simply report the observed correlation (r). To aid interpretation, I used a slightly modified version of J. Cohen and P. Cohen's (1983) standards to characterize relationships between variables: correlations of 0–.05 in magnitude are negligible, .06–.20 are small, .21–.40 are moderate, and .41 or higher are large.

TABLE 5.1

Summary of Study Characteristics

Study	Customers	Peers	Top Mgt.	Supervisors	Teams	Level of Analysis	Type of Study	Sample
Arnold, 2001					x	team	CS	177 exec MBAs, 42 class teams
Becker, 1992[a]			x	x	x	ind	L1	440 civil service employees
Becker, 1993[a]			x	x	x	ind	CS	same data as '92
Becker, 1995[a,b]		x				ind	CS	112 restaurant workers
Becker, 1996[a]				x		ind	L1	469 university alumni
Becker, 1997-S2[a]		x	x	x		ind	L1	345 university alumni
Becker, 2003[a]				x		ind	L1	188 employed undergrads, MBAs
Bentein, 2002[a]				x		ind	L1	212 French iron and steel workers
Bishop, 2000a[a]					x	ind	CS	463 members of sewing teams
Bishop, 2000b[a]					x	ind	CS	373 employees in 65 teams from an automotive plant
Bishop, 2005[a]					x	ind	CS	902 employees in 4 companies
Boyle, 1997	x	x		x		ind	CS	109 sales reps in US and Sweden
Chan, 2006[a,i]		x		x		ind	CS	145 UK and 283 Chinese unionized manufacturing employees
Chen, 2001[a]				x		ind	CS	333 employees from 36 companies in China
Chen, 2002[a]				x		ind	CS	hundreds of Chinese in multiple companies and 2 studies
Cheng, 2003[a]				x		ind	CS	538 supervisor-subordinate dyads in 59 Taiwanese companies
Clugston, 2000[a]				x	x	ind	CS	156 state employees

(continued on next page)

TABLE 5.1 (continued)

Summary of Study Characteristics

Study	Customers	Peers	Top Mgt.	Supervisors	Teams	Level of Analysis	Type of Study	Sample
Cohen, 2000[a,c,d]					x		L1	283 Israeli nurses from 3 hospitals
Cohen, 2005[a,c,f]					x	ind	CS	564 Arab and Jewish teachers
De Gilder, 2003[a]					x	ind	CS	64 service employees at 2 hotels
Den Hartog, 2007[a,d]				x	x	ind	CS	390 Dutch health care workers and 80 employee-mgr dyads, 2 studies
Ellemers, 1998[a,d]					x	ind	L1	hundreds of Dutch and Belgian employees, 2 studies
Heffner, 2001[a,e]					x	ind	CS	154 MBA students and employees
Howes, 2000[a]					x	ind	CS	136 public employees in 25 teams
Huang, 2002					x	ind	E	240 undergrads in 5-person teams
Hunt, 1994[a]			x	x	x	ind	L1	Becker, 1992 data
Jehn, 1999					x	ind	CS	518 moving company employees in 79 teams
Kirkman, 1999[a]					x	team	CS	111 work teams in 4 companies
Landry, in press				x		ind	CS	162 employed Canadian business students
Law, 2004				x		ind	CS	hundreds of Asian students and employees in 2 studies
Lee, 2002[a,f]				x	x	ind	CS	156 firefighters
Liao, 2005[a]				x		ind, team	CS	231 employees in 44 teams in multiple organizations
Lucas, 1999					x	ind	E	60 undergrads, 2 studies
Park, 2005					x	ind	CS	159 primary school teachers

Study				ind/team	Type	Sample
Pearce, 2003			×	team	CS	197 employees in 71 teams
Pearce, 2004			×	team	CS	same as Pearce, 2003
Porter, 2005			×	team	Lab	80 teams of undergrads
Redman, 2005		×		ind	CS	476 British employees, 3 studies
Siders, 2001[a]	×		×	ind	L1	328 sales executives
Snape, 2006[a]		×	×	ind	CS	223 Chinese manufacturing employees
Stinglhamber, 2002[a,c]	×		×	ind	L1	470 alumni and 186 nurses
Stinglhamber, 2003[a]			×	ind	L2	238 Belgian alumni
Swailes, 2004[a]		×	×	ind	CS	304 public and private accountants
Van der Vegt, 2000			×	ind	CS	114 technological consultants
Van der Vegt, 2003			×	ind	CS	129 telecom employees, 20 teams
Van der Vegt, 2005			×	team	CS	62 teams in the Dutch oil industry
Vandenberghe, 2001[a,c,g]			×	ind	CS	580 European employees
Vandenberghe, 2004[a]			×	ind	L2	709 Belgian employees, 3 studies
Vandenberghe, 2007[a]	×			ind	CS	133 Belgian fast food employees
West, 1991			×	ind	CS	43 health care employees, 14 teams
Workman, 2003[h]			×	ind	CS	261 teleworkers, 21 virtual teams
Zaccaro, 1989[a]			×	ind	CS	203 members of Cadet Corps

Note: For type of study, CS = cross-sectional, L1 = predictors measured at time 1 and outcomes at time 2, L2 = data collected at more than two time periods, E = experimental, Lab = nonexperimental laboratory study.

[a] Also measured commitment to the organization(s)
[b] Also measured commitment to "local management"
[c] Also measured commitment to occupations
[d] Also measured commitment to careers
[e] Also measured commitment to departments
[f] Also measured commitment to job
[g] Also measured commitment to Europe
[h] Also measured commitment to telework
[i] Also measured commitment to union

With respect to relations among commitments to different foci, there is still debate on issues of directionality. Therefore, where relationships among commitments have been found, I have merely listed them as correlates. I further discuss this issue in a later section. In addition, in examining the results of studies, I focused primarily on correlation matrices: if a correlation between commitment and another variable was provided, I included that variable in my list of relationships. An exception was when compelling logic and evidence were provided for a variable either moderating or mediating the effects of commitment. I discuss these kinds of cases in the text.

Antecedents, Consequences, and Correlates of Interpersonal Commitments

Antecedents

Table 5.2 contains a list of antecedents of commitments to the five foci. Very little is known about antecedents of commitment to customers, peers, and top management. It appears older people tend to be slightly more committed to peers ($M_r = .11$) and moderately more committed to top management ($r = .23$) than do younger people, and women seem to develop slightly less commitment to customers than do men ($M_r = -.13$). Students are moderately more committed to customers than are nonstudents ($r = .20$), temporary workers are less committed than full-timers ($r = -.19$), and as employees' perceived organizational support increases, so does their commitment to customers ($r = .32$).

Many more antecedents to commitments to supervisors, teams, and organizations have been identified. There are few discernible differences among demographics and commitment to these foci, and some other variables have similar magnitudes across foci. For example, positive affectivity is moderately and positively correlated with commitment to both supervisors and organizations ($r = .32$ and $.36$, respectively), while commitments to supervisors and teams are negatively and relatively strongly related to interpersonal conflict (correlations of $-.53$ and $-.47$, respectively).

A number of variables have been studied across foci and seem to be more strongly related to one than to others. For example, perceived justice by the supervisor seems to have a stronger tie to commitment to the supervisor ($M_r = .68$) than to commitment to the organization ($M_r = .32$), team cohesiveness appears to have a stronger tie to commitment to teams ($M_r = .61$) than to organizations ($M_r = .23$), and positive exchanges

TABLE 5.2

Antecedents of Interpersonal Commitments

Antecedents	Customers	Peers	Top Management	Supervisors	Teams	Organizations
Demographics						
Age *		.11(2)	.23(1)	.07(11)	.08(5)	.11(9)
Education				−.01(9)	.00(6)	−.02(7)
Gender *	.13(2)	.04(2)		−.01(15)	.04(6)	.01(14)
Married				−.06(1)	−.08(1)	.06(1)
Race	.03(1)			.02(1)	.08(1)	−.03(2)
Tenure, organization	−.01(2)	.08(2)	.09(1)	.02(16)	.02(6)	.05(12)
Tenure, job					.02(2)	.09(2)
Type of contract						
student *	.20(1)					.02(1)
temporary *	−.19(1)		.11(2)	.11(2)	.03(3)	
Psychological Characteristics						
Expectations, met					.43(1)	.57(1)
Justice orientation				.08(1)		.01(1)
Perceived justice, organization focused						
Distributive					−.10(1)	−.16(1)
Informational*				.22(1)		.46(1)
Interpersonal*				.33(1)		.56(1)
Procedural*				.22(1)	.00(1)	.28(2)
Perceived justice, supervisor focused[a] *				.68(3)		.32(3)
Perceived support						
Organization*	.32(1)			.30(2)	.25(8)	.63(9)
Supervisor*					.62(1)	.34(1)
Team*					.59(7)	.30(6)
Of team by organization					.41(1)	.52(1)
Personality						
Affectivity, negative*				−.20(3)	−.11(3)	−.14(3)
Affectivity, positive				.32(3)	.36(3)	.36(3)

(continued on next page)

TABLE 5.2 (continued)

Antecedents of Interpersonal Commitments

Antecedents	Customers	Peers	Top Management	Supervisors	Teams	Organizations
Job Characteristics						
Hierarchical position *				.10(6)	.25(1)	.14(3)
Job conditions						
Extrinsically satisfying*				.00(1)	.17(1)	
Intrinsically satisfying*				.29(1)	.49(1)	
Effective process*				.59(1)	.26(1)	
Interdependence, task					.13(4)	.13(1)
Role States						
Ambiguity *					−.14(2)	−.55(1)
Conflict *					−.39(1)	−.53(1)
Group/Leader Relations						
Cohesiveness, team *				.27(1)	.61(3)	.23(2)
Conflict:						
Interpersonal[b]*				−.53(1)	−.47(3)	−.15(1)
Resource-related*					−.03(1)	−.26(1)
Interaction, social						
Group*					.66(1)	.24(1)
Department					.31(1)	.41(1)
Organization *					.15(1)	.58(1)
Leader-Member Exchange						
Affect/respect*				.66(2)	.12(2)	.32(2)
Contribution				.17(1)	.12(1)	.19(1)
Loyalty *				.12(1)	.46(1)	.36(1)
Leadership behavior[c]*					.46(4)	.20(2)
Organizational Characteristics						
Culture						
Collectivism*				.22(1)	.27(2)	.14 (2)
Power distance				.03(1)	−.05(2)	−.03(2)
Uncertain avoidance*				.01(1)	.04(2)	.26(2)
masculinity*				−.05(1)	.08(2)	−.15(2)

TABLE 5.2 (continued)

Antecedents of Interpersonal Commitments

Antecedents	Customers	Peers	Top Management	Supervisors	Teams	Organizations
Size, organizational	.01(1)			.02(1)		−.05(2)

Note: The numerals in parentheses are the numbers of correlations upon which the estimates are based. Gender was scored so that 0 = woman, 1 = man; race was scored so that white = 1, other = 2; ethnicity was scored so that Jews = 0 and Arabs = 1. An asterisk next to a variable indicates that observed correlations vary across foci, based upon this classification of magnitude: 0–.05 = negligible, .06–.20 = small, .21–.40 = moderate, and > .41 = large. This classification is purely descriptive and not based on significance tests.
[a] Includes informational, interpersonal, and procedural justice. [b] Includes intersender, intrateam, and relationship conflict. [c] Includes consideration, emphasizing teamwork, delegation, initiating structure, supervising, and transformational behaviors.

with supervisors are more strongly related to employees' commitment to supervisors (M_r = .66) than to commitment to their teams (M_r = .12).

Consequences

Consequences of commitment to the five foci are contained in Table 5.3. Compared to the antecedents, multiple variables have been studied for each target and two (citizenship behavior directed toward individuals and intent to quit) have been investigated across all the foci. In addition, a fair proportion of consequences appears to have varying correlations among the foci. For example, organizational citizenship behavior (OCB) directed toward the supervisor seems to have a stronger association with commitment to supervisors (M_r = .28) than to commitment to teams (r = .07), while the reverse is true of OCB directed toward teams (M_r = .40 for commitment to teams, and r = .20 for commitment to supervisors). An employee's "market share" of revenues is predicted by commitment to customers to a greater extent (r = .43) than it is predicted by commitment to supervisors (r = −.01), while commitment to supervisors predicts the number of new accounts (r = .45) better than does commitment to customers (r = .03). Intent to quit the organization is more a function of commitment to organizations (M_r = −.47) than of commitment to teams (M_r = −.25), while intent to leave teams is more a function of commitment to teams (r = −.29) than of commitment to organizations (r = −.05).

Correlates

Table 5.4 reports the relationships between commitments and correlates. The correlations among the five interpersonal foci range from .15

TABLE 5.3

Consequences of Interpersonal Commitments

Outcomes	Customers	Peers	Top Management	Supervisors	Teams	Organizations
Organizational Citizenship						
Intentions, OCB[a]*		.28(2)				.41(2)
OCBI[b]*	.12(3)	.29(10)	.16(2)	.19(24)	.20(17)	.15(22)
OCBO[c]*			.20(3)	.15(16)	.32(13)	.25(13)
OCB toward:						
Supervisor*				.28(2)	.07(1)	.09(2)
Team*			.20(1)	.40(4)	.10(1)	
Local*			.07(1)	.16(2)	.19(2)	.09(2)
Task Performance						
In-role*	.11(3)	.04(2)		.15(13)	.09(5)	.12(12)
Goal achievement			.38(1)	.29(1)	.32(1)	.24(1)
Innovation*			.22(1)	.18(1)	.13(2)	.13(1)
Objective measures						
Customer service*	.16(4)	.11(2)		.23(2)		−.10(2)
Sales growth rate*	.02(1)			.32(1)		.08(1)
Market share*	.43(1)			−.01(1)		−.06(1)
New accounts*	.03(1)			.45(1)		.09(1)
Product breadth*	.21(1)			.03(1)		−.07(1)
Sales volume*	.00(1)			.22(1)		.55(1)
Performance, Team					.30(4)	.07(1)
Union Relations						
Union involvement						
Activism*	.18(1)	.00(1)		.05(1)		
Help, general*	.25(1)	.19(3)		.24(3)		.28(2)
Help, members*	.33(1)	.27(3)		.13(3)		.22(2)
Withdrawal*	−.17(1)	−.14(3)		−.23(2)	.07(1)	−.20(2)

TABLE 5.3 (continued)

Consequences of Interpersonal Commitments

Outcomes	Customers	Peers	Top Management	Supervisors	Teams	Organizations
Withdrawal Intentions and Behavior						
Intent to quit						
Organization*	−.17(5)	−.20(6)	−.31(2)	−.34(18)	−.25(11)	−.47(17)
Team*					−.29(1)	−.05(1)
Job applications					−.18(3)	−.12(3)
Job change					.05(1)	.03(1)
Job search*					−.04(2)	−.14(2)
Overtime work*					.22(1)	.10(1)
Withdrawal behaviors						
Absenteeism					−.06(3)	−.07(3)
Hours worked*					.01(1)	.10(1)
Tardiness*		.29(1)				.09(1)
Turnover*	.02(1)		−.15(3)	−.13(3)	−.16(4)	

Note: The numerals in parentheses are the numbers of correlations upon which the estimates are based. An asterisk next to a variable indicates that observed correlations vary across foci, based upon this classification of magnitude: 0–.05 = negligible, .06–.20 = small, .21–.40 = moderate, and > .41 = large. This classification is purely descriptive and not based on significance tests.

[a] Includes altruism and punctuality. [b] Organizational citizenship behavior directed toward individuals, including altruism, compliance, conscientiousness, consideration, courtesy, and interpersonal helping. [c] Organizational citizenship behavior directed toward organizations, including civic virtue, loyal boosterism, nonidleness, loyalty to the organization, sportsmanship, participating in training, and utilizing "voice" on behalf of the organization.

(commitments to teams and customers) to .47 (commitments to supervisors and top management), with a moderately sized median correlation of .30. Thus, in general, 9% of the variance in commitment is shared among these foci. Correlations between commitments to the five foci and organizational commitment range from .21 (commitment to customers) to .58 (commitment to top management), with a fairly strong mean correlation of .46. Hence, in general, organizational commitment shares about 21 percent of the variance in common with the five interpersonal foci.

Some of the correlates are held in common across the foci and have similar magnitudes. For example, commitment to one's profession is moderately correlated with commitment to customers, supervisors, and teams ($r = .29$ in each case), and employees' attitudes regarding altruism is about equally associated with commitment to peers ($r = .22$) as commitment to organizations ($r = .24$). As with the antecedents and consequences, some

TABLE 5.4

Correlates of Interpersonal Commitments

Correlates	Customers	Peers	Top Management	Supervisors	Teams	Organizations
Correlations Among Foci						
Peers	.20(3)					
Supervisors*	.18(6)	.38(5)	.47(3)			
Teams*	.14(2)		.30(4)	.38(16)		
Organizations*	.21(5)	.55(3)	.58(4)	.46(31)	.37(32)	
Org and mgt*	.34(2)	.19(3)		.56(2)		
Career				.28(2)	.29(5)	.37(5)
Department					.55(1)	.64(1)
Europe*					.27(2)	.54(2)
Job (involvement)*					.34(3)	.49(2)
Occupation*	.25(2)			.18(2)	.37(5)	.53(5)
Profession	.29(1)	.24(1)		.29(1)	.29(1)	.35(1)
Store management*		.35(1)				.57(1)
Union*	.17(2)	.26(5)		.37(4)		.36(2)
Other Commitment Concepts						
Compliance*		.13(1)	.01(2)	−.01(3)	.07(3)	.06(4)
Continuance commitment						
Organizations			−.10(1)	.03(4)	.03(4)	.10(4)
Customers*	.43(1)					.35(1)
Department					.12(1)	.10(1)
Supervisors				.10(1)	.02(3)	.03(3)
Teams*				−.07(1)	.19(2)	.05(2)
Work involvement*					.18(1)	.42(1)
Satisfaction						
Satisfaction, job*	.22(1)	.46(1)	.33(4)	.43(11)	.45(2)	.56(7)
Satisfaction, type						
Extrinsic*			.38(1)	.51(1)	.28(1)	.53(1)
Intrinsic*			.29(1)	.32(1)	.25(1)	.45(1)
Satisfaction with social foci						
Local foci*			.28(1)	.59(2)	.29(2)	.23(2)
Peers*					.63(2)	.22(2)
Supervisors*				.52(2)	.20(1)	.29(3)
Teams*					.68(3)	.13(1)
Satisfaction with nonsocial foci						
Organizations*					.38(2)	.68(2)

TABLE 5.4 (continued)

Correlates of Interpersonal Commitments

Correlates	Customers	Peers	Top Management	Supervisors	Teams	Organizations
Progress*					.39(1)	.56(1)
Promotion*					.35(1)	.53(1)
Work					.55(3)	.56(3)
Other Correlates						
Attitudes re:						
Altruism	.22(1)					.24(1)
Punctuality	.17(1)					.12(1)
Impression management				.11(1)		.07(1)
Subjective norms re:						
Altruism	.15(1)					.17(1)
Punctuality	.22(1)					.23(1)
Trust*					.53(2)	.33(1)

Note: The numerals in parentheses are the numbers of correlations upon which the estimates are based. An asterisk next to a variable indicates that observed correlations vary across foci, based upon this classification of magnitude: 0–.05 = negligible, .06–.20 = small, .21–.40 = moderate, and > .41 = large. This classification is purely descriptive and not based on significance tests.

variables apparently have stronger relations with certain foci. For instance, satisfaction with teams appears to be more strongly correlated with commitment with teams ($M_r = .68$) than commitment to organizations ($r = .13$), while the reverse is true vis-à-vis satisfaction with organizations ($M_r = .68$ for commitment to organizations, and $M_r = .38$ for commitment to teams).

In sum, there are many variables—antecedents, consequences, and correlates—that appear to have differential correlations with commitment foci. These variables are indicated with asterisks in Tables 5.2–5.4. Further, some variables seem to have a unique, stronger relationship with one target than with others. Using the data in Tables 5.2 through 5.4, I have listed these variables in Table 5.5. To be included in the table, at least two summary correlations of a given variable with at least two foci of commitment had to fall into different J. Cohen and P. Cohen (1983) categories of magnitude. It is important to note that this is a descriptive analysis used for purposes of review and theory building, not an inferential analysis used for hypothesis testing.

TABLE 5.5

Variables Appearing Most Strongly Related to One Target

Commitment Foci	Antecedents	Consequences	Correlates
Customers	Gender Type of contract	Market share Product breadth Union activism	Continuance commitment to customers
Peers		Tardiness	
Top management	Age	Innovation	
Supervisors	Justice, supervisor Justice orientation LMX—affect/respect Leader behavior Perceived support—supervisor	Customer service Sales growth rate New accounts OCB toward supervisor	Commitment to • management • organization Continuance commitment to supervisors Satisfaction with • local foci • supervisor
Teams	Cohesiveness, team Hierarchical position Job conditions, process Perceived support—team Social interaction—group	Intent to leave team OCB toward team Overtime work Team performance	Continuance commitment to teams Satisfaction with • peers • teams Trust
Organizations	Conflict, resource-related Culture: uncertainty avoidance Job conditions, satisfying Justice, organizational POS Role ambiguity and conflict Social interaction— organization	Hours worked Intent to quit the organization Job search OCB intentions (general) Sales volume	Commitment to • country (Europe) • job • occupation • store mgt Satisfaction, intrinsic Satisfaction with • the organization • career progress • promotion Work involvement

Moderators and Mediators of Interpersonal Commitments

Moderators

I discovered studies addressing three moderators of commitment-outcome relationships: expertise diversity, supervisor-based self-esteem, and ethnic culture. Van Der Vegt and Bunderson (2005) found that commitment to teams (measured at the team level) interacted with expertise diversity (differences in specialized knowledge and skills within a group) in determining team learning and performance. Specifically, the relations between team commitment and the outcome variables were a function of a non-linear effect of heterogeneity in expertise. Landry and Vandenberghe (in press) defined supervisor-based self-esteem as the self-evaluation of one's worthiness resulting from the relationship with one's supervisor. They found that this variable moderated the relationship between employees' commitment to their supervisors and the level and type of conflict employees had with their bosses. When supervisor-based self-esteem was low, commitment to supervisors was more strongly and negatively related to conflict than when this form of self-esteem was high—apparently because low self-esteem employees are more sensitive to supervisory cues regarding their working relationship, and when commitment is low, they experience more conflicts than do high self-esteem employees.

Finally, there is mixed evidence regarding societal culture as a moderator. Cohen (2005) reported that in-role performance and OCB was a function of 16 complex interactions between commitment foci (including group commitment) and (a) cultural groups (Arabs and Jews in Israel), and (b) Hofstede's (1980) cultural dimensions. For instance, commitment related more favorably to OCB for Arabs than for Jews, but within the two groups the pattern depended on the particular cultural dimension in question. On the other hand, Chan, Tong-quing, Redman, and Snape (2006), in a study including commitments to supervisors, peers, organizations, and unions, found no evidence that differences in culture in the UK and China affected commitment-OCB relationships. A similar finding was reported by Snape, Chan, and Redman (2006), leading them to conclude that there was little support for their "cultural hypothesis." (See chapter 10 for additional discussion of cultural issues.)

Mediators

Research on mediators has been meager. The only reasonably definitive findings are that at the team level of analysis, team learning mediates the effect of team commitment on team performance (Van Der Vegt & Bunderson, 2005), and intent to quit mediates the effects of commitments to supervisors and teams on turnover (A. Cohen, 2000; Stinglhamber et al., 2002; Vandenberghe et al., 2004).

A more debatable hypothesis is that macro commitments, especially commitment to organizations, mediate interpersonal commitments. T. E. Becker (1992) found that commitments to interpersonal foci (supervisors, teams, top management) explained variance in job satisfaction, intent to quit, and prosocial organizational behaviors over and above variance explained by commitment to organizations. In reanalyzing these data, Hunt and Morgan (1994) argued that effects of commitment to interpersonal foci are entirely mediated by commitment to the organization, and others have also adopted this notion (A. Cohen, 2000; Heffner & Rentsch,

2001; Redman & Snape, 2005). However, in another reanalysis of the same data, Maertz, Mosley, and Alford (2002) conducted a more extensive structural equation examination of relations among the commitments in question. These authors found that a partially mediated model fit significantly better than a fully mediated one and had more favorable fit indices. They concluded that their results reconfirmed the original findings that interpersonal commitments can have incremental effects (beyond commitment to organizations) on work-related outcomes. Additional support for this conclusion is provided by T. E. Becker and Kernan (2003), Chen, Tsui, and Farh (2002), Ellemers, de Gilder, and van den Heuvel (1998), Siders, George, and Dharwadkar (2001), and Vandenberghe et al. (2004).

In short, research on moderators has been sparse and, in the case of culture, inconclusive. In addition, hardly any solid empirical work has been done on the processes through which commitment affects employee attitudes and behaviors. To address these concerns and to further analyze potential antecedents and consequences of interpersonal commitments, I now turn to an examination of the broader literature on psychological attachment.

Existing Theory and Interpersonal Commitments

In this section I'll briefly assess the six theories reviewed by Klein et al. (chapter 1). I'll then consider several relevant streams of work outside the field of I/O psychology.

Assessment of the Six Theories

Staw's (1981) model of escalation of commitment. Although Staw's focus was on commitment to a course of action, the three processes he discussed are plausible antecedents to interpersonal commitments as well. Retrospective rationality could exist when employees irrationally decide to maintain commitment to, say, a supervisor. Such a case would exist, for example, if an employee attempted to justify lying to customers by stressing his or her commitment to help a supervisor attain a quarterly financial goal. Modeling could play an important role in the development of commitments as a normal part of socialization, as when a new hire's peers demonstrate a sincere commitment to customers. Finally, prospective rationality may explain certain commitments through a valence-expectancy mechanism. For example, one may become committed to top management when it is clear that this target is likely to steer employees toward valued outcomes (e.g., higher salaries, greater job security). A limitation to this theory is that it doesn't by itself explain the consequences of interpersonal commitment.

Further, as discussed below, there are processes other than those identified by Staw that may drive commitment-related outcomes.

Gordon, Philpot, Burt, Thompson, and Spiller's (1980) model of union commitment. This model also identifies potentially important antecedents. As shown in Table 5.2, demographic variables (e.g., gender, race) have received some attention, though their relations with interpersonal commitments are modest and, without a clear rationale for the effects, psychologically sterile. Socialization (also included in the Staw model) is a potentially interesting driver and is probably underresearched. Limitations of this model for the study of interpersonal commitment are its focus on the union (not in itself an interpersonal foci) and lack of connection to specific behaviors relevant to interpersonal commitment.

Hollenbeck and Klein's (1987) model of goal commitment and Reichers's (1985) model. A key contribution of Hollenbeck and Klein's model is the link from organizational commitment to task performance. Commitment is held to affect the attractiveness of goal attainment, which interacts with expectancy to determine goal commitment. Goal commitment and level interact to drive performance. Considering Reichers's (1985) emphasis on organizational constituencies, and her suggestion that interpersonal foci are psychologically proximal to the individual, a simple extension can be made by including interpersonal commitments in Hollenbeck and Klein's theory. Like commitment to organizations, commitments to particular individuals and groups may affect the attractiveness of goal attainment. Further, commitments to interpersonal foci may also affect expectancy of attainment. For instance, supervisor supportiveness may increase commitment to the supervisor, which, through leader-member exchange, leads the supervisor to be more benevolent. If so, this trade of commitment for resources should increase the expectancy of goal attainment.

A limitation of the Hollenbeck and Klein model is that it does not include a number of relevant commitment concepts (e.g., foci, bases, forms) and goal concepts (e.g., goal regulation, goal mechanisms such as direction and efforts, and moderators such as feedback and ability). A more thorough treatment is provided by Meyer, Becker, and Vandenberge (2004).

Meyer and Herscovitch's (2001) general model. This model significantly advances prior theory by identifying psychological states underlying commitment (desire, cost, obligation), linking them to important antecedents (bases), and specifying discretionary target-relevant behavior as a central outcome. It is a general model and can be directly applied to interpersonal commitments. For example, I might identify with a team of researchers and share their value for organizational science. As a result, I might desire to continue working with them. The authors' view is that this creates a "binding force" that may then lead me to direct discretionary behaviors toward the team.

One limitation to this model is that it does not specify where the actual bond with the target occurs or what role it plays in the process. Including a force that binds but not the bond itself seems odd. Another possible limitation from the perspective of interpersonal commitments is the inclusion of cost as a form of commitment ("continuance commitment"). Space does not permit a full discussion of this issue, but as I've discussed elsewhere (T. E. Becker, 2005), actions based on coercion or necessity don't necessarily constitute a psychological bond with people. Rather, the attachment may be to a goal, behavior, or outcome. This would be so if a professor stayed at a university only because there was too much to lose (e.g., tenure, money) or there weren't jobs elsewhere. We might call this calculative involvement (H. S. Becker, 1960), compliance (O'Reilly & Chatman, 1986), or behavioral commitment (Mowday, Porter, & Steers, 1982), but it does not necessarily require any form of psychological attachment to individuals or groups.

Klein, Brinsfield, and Molloy's (2006) model. One strength of this model is its identification of commitment antecedents. The target characteristics and interpersonal and organizational factors go beyond the "person and situation" set represented in other theories. Other strengths are the recognition of the perceptual field discussed earlier by Lewin (1943) and others (e.g., T. E. Becker et al., 1996), highlighting of the phenomenon of competing commitments suggested by Reichers (1985, 1986), and the notion of reciprocal effects between commitment and other motivational variables (see also Meyer et al., 2004; Meyer, Becker, & Van Dick, 2006). This is a general model of workplace commitments, and these points apply equally to interpersonal foci as to other more micro and macro ones.

Perhaps the most important contribution of the theory is the distinction between commitment strength and commitment rationales. Whether these two variables interact in the way suggested by the authors is an open question. It seems equally plausible to me that they may simply have main effects or that commitment strength is embedded within the rationales. At any rate, this is a potentially critical distinction that deserves careful attention. Limitations of the model are that it doesn't provide a means of easily classifying workplace commitments, and it doesn't specify which foci are likely to be most important under particular circumstances. These limitations are nearly universal, however, and I'll return to them in the section on theory development.

Relevant Theory Outside the Literature on Employee Commitments

There are many places outside of the literature on employee commitments that one might turn to further theorize about interpersonal commitments. To advance thinking in the area, a theorist might focus on individual characteristics, dyadic or group variables, or aspects of the broader context. I will illustrate these paths by discussing attachment theory (with origins in developmental psychology and relevant to individual characteristics affecting interpersonal commitments); work on interpersonal attraction (from social psychology and having implications for group and, especially, dyadic commitments); and the field of evolutionary psychology (with roots in biology and pertinent to the genetic and historical contexts of commitments to individuals and small groups). There are certainly other literatures that may be relevant, such as that pertaining to social exchange. I discuss the exchange perspective at several other places in the chapter, and the interested reader may refer to relevant readings; see, for example, Lawler, Thye, and Yoon (2000, 2006), Rusbult (1983), and chapter 8 of this book. For the current discussion I've chosen the three topics just mentioned based on my personal interest and perceptions of relevance.

Attachment theory. Chapter 7 addresses attachment theory in some depth. Here I will selectively summarize the literature, identifying implications for interpersonal commitments at work. Research on child development has defined *attachment* as "the affectional bond or tie that an infant forms between himself and his mother figure" (Ainsworth, Blehar, Waters, & Wall, 1978, p. 302). Through interactions with caregivers the child develops internal "working models," which include expectations about the caring and responsiveness of the caregiver and beliefs regarding whether the self is worthy of care and attention.

Attachment theory holds that the attachment styles developed in childhood continue to affect the nature of adult bonds (Ainsworth, 1989). Bartholomew (1990) presented a model that described forms of adult attachment along two dimensions: abstract perception of self (self as worthy of love and support or not), and image of others (others as trustworthy and available versus unreliable and rejecting). By crossing these two dimensions, Bartholomew and Horowitz (1991) identified four attachment styles presumed to be relatively stable throughout adulthood. Adults with a *secure attachment style* have positive perceptions of themselves and others. Because they have a sense of worthiness and an expectation that other people are typically accepting and responsive, these adults are comfortable with both relationships and autonomy. Individuals with a *preoccupied attachment style* have positive perceptions of others but view themselves negatively. This combination leads these people to strive for self-acceptance by gaining the acceptance of others.

Adults with a *fearful style* view themselves and others negatively. These people are afraid of relationships because they expect to be rejected by others. By being socially avoidant, they hope to protect themselves against such rejection. Finally, people having a *dismissing style* have a positive self-image but view others negatively. These individuals attempt to protect themselves from disappointment by avoiding relationships and maintaining an image of independence and invulnerability. Adults with this style of attachment are detached from others and see mutual dependence as a personal weakness. (See T. E. Becker, Billings, Eveleth, and Gilbert, 1997, for a discussion of related measurement issues).

Adult attachment theory has been extended to several topics of interest to the fields of management and I/O psychology, including conflict resolution (Simpson, Rholes, & Phillips, 1996), trust (Mikulincer, 1998), and leadership (Bresnahan & Mitroff, 2007). It also seems to have clear implications for interpersonal commitments in the workplace. For example, it is likely that employees with secure or preoccupied attachment styles will more often attempt to develop committed relationships at work than will those with fearful or dismissing styles. It may also be that those with secure styles are more successful than those with preoccupied styles in developing meaningful commitments because the sometimes desperate needs of those with preoccupied styles may scare people away. Unlike pure demographic variables such as age or gender, attachment styles offer a psychologically meaningful way of explaining differences in interpersonal commitments. Also, unlike traits such as the Big Five, attachment styles appear to have a direct and transparent tie to workplace commitment—which, after all, is all about psychological attachment.

Interpersonal attraction. In order for employees to become committed to other individuals or groups, it seems necessary that they must first become attracted to them. In retrospect, it's therefore surprising that, with the exception of several studies involving interdependence, little work on interpersonal commitments has drawn on the literature on interpersonal attraction. Classic research on the topic has identified reliable predictors of attraction, including voluntariness, familiarity, similarity, physical attractiveness, and self-disclosure (Berscheid & Reis, 1998). Further, the nature and reasons for the effects appear to be reasonably understood. This is reflected in the field's well-developed theories, such as the social relations model (e.g., Kenny & La Voie, 1984; Gundlach, Zivnuska, & Stoner, 2006), interpersonal attribution theory (e.g., Fletcher & Fincham, 1991; Forgas & Locke, 2005), and interdependence theory (e.g., Rusbult, 1983; Holmes, 2004).

Recent work continues to expand the knowledge of interpersonal attraction. For example, archival and experimental data now support the notion that individuals gravitate toward those who resemble them because similar others activate individuals' positive, automatic associations about themselves (Jones, Pelham, Carvallo, & Mirenberg, 2004). This is true even when similarities are arbitrary, as with names or numbers. Other examples are a recent twist on the physical attractiveness and familiarity literatures, demonstrating that more familiar faces come to be seen as more attractive (Peskin & Newell, 2004), and that the perceived attractiveness of one's eyes affects the estimation by others of his or her personality (Mescheryakov & Yuschenkova, 2006). Finally, early work on self-disclosure demonstrated that more disclosure typically leads to greater attraction (see Collins & Miller's 1994 meta-analysis), and it now appears that disclosure plays an important role in overcoming negative out-group attitudes (Turner, Hewstone, & Voci, 2007). However, there is also evidence that self-disclosure effects may be more potent when the parties are socially equal (Wanberg, Welsh, & Kammeyer-Mueller, 2007).

In sum, the literature on interpersonal attraction offers us new, psychologically interesting antecedents to interpersonal commitments. If attraction precedes and affects commitments, as seems plausible, then we might hypothesize that employees become strongly committed to another person when their relationship with that person is voluntary and when the other person is a familiar, similar, physically attractive person who self-discloses. This implies that interpersonal commitments may be enhanced by grouping similar people together and encouraging appropriate levels and forms of self-disclosure. In addition, the more current work suggests that grouping by similarity can be done on innocuous grounds (such as names or birth dates), thus avoiding homogeneity of demographics such as gender, age, and race.

Also, the recent work suggests that a top manager might become more attractive to employees by becoming more familiar to them, for example, by doing more walking around or conducting more frequent teleconferences. If the logic holds, greater attractiveness should increase commitment to the manager, both directly and by way of enhanced positive perceptions of his or her personality. Finally, while self-disclosure may not work well from the top down, the recent work also suggests that by increasing trust, self-disclosure may be effective for reducing negative out-group attitudes occurring within work teams. This, in turn, may promote greater commitment to the team by both in-group and out-group members.

The above ideas are largely speculative, and I've offered them primarily to underscore the value to commitment researchers of studying the literature on interpersonal attraction. This work focuses on dyadic relationships and so seems most pertinent to commitments such as employees' relationships with their bosses and individual customers or peers.

Evolutionary psychology. A central premise in evolutionary psychology is that the environmental history of our species has produced a set of genes that interacts with the environment to produce everyday social action (Buss, 1999). Numerous aspects of human behavior—mating, parenting, kinship, and group dynamics—are thus seen as evolved, adaptive responses (Buss, 2005). For example, the development of emotional bonds is explained by reference to mate retention (Campbell & Ellis, 2005), and neurocognitive adaptations are studied as an underlying mechanism of social exchange in groups (Tooby & Cosmides, 1992; Cosmides & Tooby, 2005), the evolution of morality (Krebs, Denton, Vermeulen, Carpendale, & Bush, 1991; Krebs, 2005), the bases for in-group and out-group relationships

(Kurzban & Leary, 2001), and the effects of genetics on dominance, status, and social hierarchies (Cummins, 2005).

Evolutionary psychology has apparent implications for understanding interpersonal commitments. Theory on emotional bonds in mate retention might be extended to emotional bonds at work; research on the adaptive advantage of social exchanges seems relevant to behavioral commitment; literature on the evolution of morality could further elucidate certain bases of commitment, particularly normative commitment; and the research on in-groups, out-groups, dominance, status, and social hierarchies has promise for expanding our understanding of commitment to managers and teams.

Linking interpersonal commitments to evolutionary psychology would allow commitment theorists and researchers to tap a far broader knowledge base. To the extent this base has merit, the explanation of interpersonal commitments would be enriched. For instance, while much of the current literature focuses rather narrowly on interpersonal commitments in a given organization or tries to explain variance in interpersonal commitments within or across organizations, the approach of evolutionary psychology would lead us to investigate broader commonalities. Why do employees need to develop emotional bonds in the workplace? Why are many employees so ready to offer commitment to supervisors? Why do people in work teams attempt to control each other in particular ways? Looking to evolutionary explanations to address such questions may help us better grasp and appreciate the role of work and commitment to the survival of our species.

In conclusion, the above theories have some promise for helping us further understand the development of interpersonal commitments, the corresponding consequences, and the underlying processes. However, they don't seem to offer much in terms of explaining variation in commitment-outcome relations across foci or the nature of connections among commitment foci. In the next section I offer several propositions on these topics.

Compatibility, Level of Abstraction, and Psychological Distance: Review and Propositions

I previously discussed similarities and differences of relationships between commitment and other variables across foci. Some antecedents and consequences appeared unique, or at least more strongly related, to a given commitment focus. Further, evidence suggested that a given target of commitment may sometimes mediate the effects of other commitments and sometimes may not. At this point there is little theory to explain these patterns or to guide future investigations. Therefore, in the following sections I present several ideas that will hopefully advance theory and research in the area of interpersonal commitments.

Compatibility

Fishbein and Ajzen's principle of compatibility holds that a given attitude should be related to behavior only to the extent that the foci of the attitude and behavior are similar (Ajzen, 1989; Fishbein & Ajzen, 1975). In applying a similar rationale to employee commitment, T. E. Becker and Billings (1993) pointed out that commitments to specific foci often have positive implications for those foci but not necessarily for others. Thus, a compatible outcome is one that is believed to benefit the foci to whom one is committed. For example, employees committed to their peers might help the peers when they need it, but cannot necessarily be expected to be helpful to customers unless the employees have a similar commitment to them. These authors' findings that commitments to local, but not global, foci predict local outcomes support the commitment compatibility hypothesis, as do similar results in the area of social exchange.

Brandes, Dharwadkar, and Wheatley (2004) found that compared to global exchanges (with top management and the organization), employees' local exchanges (with supervisors and peers) had a greater effect on performance, certain extra-role behaviors, and employee involvement. Other results supporting the compatibility hypothesis are that commitment to supervisors predicts in-role performance and local citizenship behaviors such as courtesy (outcomes which arguably benefit supervisors in that they are compatible with their goals) (T. E. Becker & Kernan, 2003); commitment to organizations, on the other hand, predicts more organizationally relevant citizenship (such as loyal boosterism), overall job satisfaction, and turnover intentions (Cheng, Jiang, & Riley, 2003); commitment to customers but not commitments to supervisors, peers, or the organization uniquely predicts customer service (Redman & Snape, 2005) and aspects of job performance, such as product breadth, that are relevant to and rewarded by customers (Siders et al., 2001); commitment to peers predicts helping directed toward peers, while commitments to other foci do not (Redman & Snape, 2005).

Compatibility applies to antecedents of commitment as well. For example, group-related variables such as cohesiveness are associated with commitment to teams but not commitment to organizations (Zaccaro & Dobbins, 1989). Further, while perceived support from organizations uniquely predicts commitment to organizations (and job satisfaction and intent to leave the organization), perceived support from one's team uniquely predicts commitment to teams (and team satisfaction, cohesiveness, and intent to leave the team) (Howes, Cropanzano, Grandey, & Mohler, 2000). Also, perceived support of supervisors is a direct antecedent of commitment to supervisors, while perceived support of organizations is not (Stinglhamber & Vandenberghe, 2003). In addition, justice on the part of organizations is more strongly related to commitment to organizations than to commitment to supervisors, while the reverse is true of justice on the part of supervisors (Liao & Rupp, 2005).

The notion of compatibility may apply to levels of analysis issues, too. For instance, because teamwork requires coordination among multiple people, team commitment (that is, overall commitment across team members) may be a better predictor of team performance than is commitment to teams measured at the individual level. However, this is speculative and there is very little research involving data at the team level or higher (for exceptions, see Arnold, Barling, & Kelloway, 2001; Kirkman & Rosen, 1999; Pearce & Herbik, 2004). Therefore, I will restrict my discussion to commitments at the individual level of analysis.

In sum, the above research supports the following proposition regarding compatibility and commitment:

Proposition 1: As compatibility between an antecedent or consequence of interpersonal commitment and the target of commitment increases, so does the strength of the relationship between them.

A related issue of compatibility involves the evidence that certain variables sometimes do and sometimes do not mediate the effects of commitment to a given target on work behavior. For example, as suggested earlier, there is conflicting evidence as to whether commitment to organizations mediates commitments to interpersonal foci and, if it does, under what circumstances. In addition, it appears that, at times, mediational effects may even be reversed. For instance, Bentein, Stinglhamber, and Vandenberghe (2002) reported evidence that commitments to supervisors and workgroups mediated the effect of organizational commitment on organizational citizenship. Vandenberghe et al. (2004) found that commitment to organizations mediated the effect of commitment to supervisors on intent to quit the organization, while commitment to the supervisor mediated the effect of commitment to the organization on job performance.

These kinds of effects are not yet understood. Although in the Vandenberge et al. compatibility study may explain the differential relations of commitments to supervisors and organizations with outcome variables, it doesn't explain why the effects are mediated rather than direct. The relations among commitments are likely to be complex and influenced by multiple variables. For example, a new hire may become committed to her supervisor due to certain traits of the supervisor (e.g., trustworthiness), attributes of the new hire (e.g., agreeableness), and characteristics of the situation (e.g., group norms). If the supervisor is highly committed to the organization, the new hire may develop a similar bond to the company. This could be due to modeling or the effective use of power by the supervisor. It could also be due to what has recently been called *supervisor-organization embodiment*: the extent to which the supervisor and organization are perceived as having a closely overlapping identity (Stinglhamber et al., 2008). When supervisor-organization embodiment is high, employees are believed to experience treatment received from the supervisor as treatment from the organization. Further, the actions of the supervisor are perceived as synonymous with the will of the organization. Therefore, commitment to the supervisor rubs off on the organization. One probable effect of this is that behaviors compatible with commitment to the organization (e.g., loyal boosterism and other organizationally relevant extra-role behaviors) become more likely, as compared to when employees are committed to the supervisor but not the organization.

Different conditions may explain situations where interpersonal commitments mediate the effects of commitment to the organization. For instance, a long-time employee with a history of commitment to the organization might become committed to a new supervisor. This could be due to social exchange between the employee and the organization whereby the employee decides, "The company has been good to me so I'm willing to be loyal to the boss because this will help the company." If the norms in the organization include loyalty to management, commitment to the organization might also rub off on the supervisor via internalization of the norms. Finally, supervisor-organization embodiment may work in both directions: commitment to the supervisor and organization are seen as one and the same, so behaviors compatible with commitment to the supervisor become more likely, as compared to when employees are committed to the organization but not the supervisor.

The above examples are merely illustrative, and it is beyond the scope of this chapter to develop propositions regarding when commitment to various foci can be expected to mediate the effects of other foci. Rather, the point is that mediating effects have been demonstrated by several authors, and it is possible to develop plausible predictions and explanations regarding such effects. In light of this, and consistent with the principle of compatibility, I offer the following two propositions as correlates of Proposition 1. First, where effects of commitment to a target are partially mediated by another variable, such as commitment to another target:

Proposition 2: As compatibility between the target of interpersonal commitment and target of behavior increases, so does the magnitude of direct (unmediated) effects.

Conversely, where commitment to the target mediates the effects of other variables, such as commitments to other foci:

Proposition 3: As compatibility between the target of interpersonal commitment and target of behavior increases, so does the strength of mediation by commitment to the target.

Although compatibility is an essential concept to understanding relationships between commitments and other variables, there may be two other variables central to this topic. I turn to these next.

Level of Abstraction and Psychological Distance

To clarify the nature of workplace foci and to further explain variability in commitment-outcome relationships, I offer the typology shown in Figure 5.1. This scheme classifies interpersonal foci into four categories according to two dimensions. The first is level of abstraction, varying from concrete (specific and tangible) to abstract (general and less tangible). For example, lower-level manufacturing employees directly observe and experience their supervisors and, thus, typically would perceive the supervisor as a concrete target of commitment. On the other hand, these employees likely see the board of directors as abstract because they probably don't have tangible experiences with the board or know particular board members. Although individuals such as supervisors may often be more concrete than groups such as the board, this is not always the case. For example, the manufacturing employees are apt to see the workgroup

| | LEVEL OF ABSTRACTION | |
	Concrete	Abstract
Proximal	MY WORK TEAM	"THE CUSTOMER"
Distal	THE CEO	TOP MANAGEMENT

PSYCHOLOGICAL DISTANCE

FIGURE 5.1
Examples of psychological distance and level of abstraction.

as more concrete than the notion of "the customer" (an individualized abstraction).

The second dimension for describing interpersonal foci is psychological distance, the perceived location, from proximal to distal, within what Lewin (1943) called the psychological field. One could further conceptualize and measure this variable as a function of physical or temporal proximity (e.g., a CEO is usually more distant than one's supervisor and usually spends less time with lower-level employees). In the context of a specific research project this approach may be entirely reasonable. However, one can sometimes feel close to someone physically far away (as with a workplace friend at another location) and distant from someone physically close (as with an abusive manager). Further, spending time with someone is no assurance that psychologically meaningful events occur, and a transformational leader may create such events in a relatively short period of time. Therefore, I'll use perceived frequency of meaningful interaction as a key conceptual indicator of psychological distance. My assumption is that employees who perceive a larger number of meaningful interactions with a target usually see the target as more proximally located in their field than do employees with a smaller number of such interactions.

The foci shown within the cells of Figure 5.1 are illustrative only. Whether a given target (CEO, top management, etc.) is viewed as abstract or concrete, close or distant, likely depends on the characteristics of the employee (e.g., past work experiences), their position (e.g., line worker or top manager), nature of the organization (e.g., flat or multilayered structure), and attributes of the target (e.g., a CEO who is aloof vs. one who reaches out to employees). To illustrate the meaning and possible implications of level of abstraction and psychological distance, in the discussion below I have chosen to classify targets from the perspective of a hypothetical lower-level production worker.

Although both level of abstraction and psychological distance are probably continuous in nature, treating them categorically is useful for organizing and developing the current discussion. The four types of foci are as follows:

1. *Proximal-concrete:* specific, tangible foci, such as an employee's immediate work team, with whom the employee perceives regular interaction.

2. *Proximal-abstract:* general, intangible foci, such as "the customer" (as in "the customer is always right") with whom an employee perceives regular interaction.

3. *Distal-concrete:* specific, tangible foci, such as the CEO, with whom an employee perceives little direct interaction.

4. *Distal-abstract:* general, intangible foci, such as top management, with whom an employee perceives little direct interaction.

Consideration of these dimensions leads to three potential insights. First, compared to commitments to distal foci, commitments to proximal foci often have greater power to influence employees. For example, prima facie, great customer service and the generation of new customer accounts presumably benefit an organization at least as much as they do a given supervisor. However, in Table 5.3, commitment to supervisors is more highly correlated with customer service and new accounts ($M_r = .23$ and .45, respectively) than is commitment to organizations ($M_r = -.10$ and .09, respectively). One potential reason for the greater influence of proximal interpersonal foci is that the level of commitment to these foci may often be greater than that of commitment to distal foci such as top management (T. E. Becker, 1992). As Lawler (1992) argued, proximal foci are more salient and thus have an "interaction advantage" over more distant foci. This gives proximal foci a greater opportunity to affect the working conditions of employees. If these effects are positive, employees feel positive emotions that they attribute to proximal foci, and hence, the proximal foci become objects of affective attachment (Mueller & Lawler, 1999).

However valid this argument may be, two additional points must be acknowledged. One is that levels of commitment to distal foci are not always lower than those to proximal foci. For instance, commitment to organizations, although not an interpersonal commitment, is presumably more distal than to a proximal target like a supervisor. However, commitment to the organization can be as high as or higher than commitment to supervisors (T. E. Becker et al., 1996; T. E. Becker & Kernan, 2003). More important, correlations depend on variability rather than level, so higher levels of commitment to proximal foci cannot account for the differences in observed relationships reported in Table 5.3.

An explanation for the potency of proximal foci is that in most organizations these foci have the primary responsibility for establishing norms regarding behavior and can be more effective than distal foci at monitoring, rewarding, and shaping behavior (T. E. Becker et al., 1996; Bishop & Scott, 2000; Lewin, 1943). This may make a drop of commitment to such foci more powerful than an identical drop of commitment to distal foci. If so, compared to distal foci, commitment to proximal foci could produce stronger effects on behavior even when commitment is somewhat lower. If the hypothesis of varying potency is correct, then the meaning of responses to scale anchors is likely to vary across foci (a lack of metric invariance), as is the pattern of factor loadings (a lack of configural invariance). See Vandenberg & Nelson (1999) and chapter 12 for further discussions of these and related topics.

A second insight that can be gleaned from the typology is that, compared to commitment to abstract foci (e.g., the department), commitments to foci that are more concrete (e.g., team members) may have a greater impact on employees due to greater salience and vividness associated with specific, tangible interaction. For instance, although this would depend to some degree on the particular behavior in question, one would generally expect that interpersonal helping behaviors are at least as beneficial to (compatible with) commitment to customers as commitment to other proximal foci. Table 5.3, though, suggests that interpersonal helping (OCBI in the table) is more strongly related to commitments to peers, teams, and supervisors (M_r = .29, .20, and .19, respectively) than to commitment to customers (M_r = .12). One plausible reason is that the concept of "customers" is often more abstract than are clearly concrete foci such as peers, teams, and bosses.

Finally, for outcomes that are compatible with multiple foci of commitment, psychological distance and level of abstraction may interact. The most likely form of the interaction is that differences in the effects of proximal and distal commitments are lessened, or even reversed, when the foci are concrete rather than abstract. This is because concrete foci, even when they are distal, are likely to be more salient than abstract foci. Further, because concrete foci are specific, tangible entities, they are capable of personal interactions with employees. For instance, although the effect of commitment on an employee's immediate supervisor (a proximal-concrete focus) is likely to be greater than the effect of commitment on top management (a distal-abstract focus), effects of commitment on a specific CEO or founder (a distal-concrete focus) may equal or exceed those of commitment to the supervisor. Examples are the many cases of entrepreneurs and CEOs such as Phil Knight (Nike), Berry Gordy (Motown Records), and Oprah Winfrey (Harpo Productions), all of whom, by force of character and leadership, had a profound influence on the hearts and minds of their employees (Brands, 1999; Locke, 2000). In sum:

Proposition 4: Foci of interpersonal commitment can be empirically distinguished according to level of abstraction and psychological distance.

Proposition 5: Outcomes that are compatible with multiple interpersonal foci are generally more affected by commitments to foci that are proximal, concrete, or both than by commitments to foci that are distal, abstract, or both.

Proposition 6: The magnitude of compatible commitment-outcome relationships is a function of an interaction between level of abstraction and psychological distance. Specifically, the difference in magnitude between the effects of interpersonal commitments to proximal and distal foci decreases, and may reverse, as the level of abstraction becomes more concrete.

Analysis of Progress to Date and Directions for Future Research

Prior research has helped us learn a good deal about interpersonal commitments, including that commitments to a number of different individuals and small groups are empirically discriminable. Further, as evinced in Tables 5.2–5.4, there is reasonably good information regarding some of the likely antecedents, consequences, and correlates of interpersonal commitments, especially commitments to supervisors and teams. We are also beginning to understand which variables tend to vary in their relationships to different foci (see the asterisks in the tables) and which may have relatively unique relations with commitment to a single target (Table 5.5).

That said, there is a good deal left to learn before we will be able to fully grasp the nature of interpersonal commitments and meaningfully predict and influence these commitments and their outcomes. For instance, a number of the findings discussed in this chapter involve correlations based on a single study or a small number of studies. Caution is called for in interpreting these findings, and more research is needed to justify confidence in their generalizability. The following is a list of what I believe to be some of the other most pressing issues for future research in the area.

Antecedents of Commitment to Other Interpersonal Foci

As shown in Table 5.2, we know very little about the variables influencing commitment to customers, peers, and top management. Given that commitments to these foci may be particularly relevant to several significant outcomes (e.g., market share for commitment to customers, innovation for commitment to top management), understanding the corresponding causes is potentially important to theories of commitment and the practice of management.

In discussing the theories from chapter 1, I identified antecedents that could promote the understanding of how interpersonal commitments are formed or maintained. These included modeling and prospective and retrospective rationality from Staw (1981); socialization from Gordon et al., (1980); the psychological bases of desire, cost, and obligation from Meyer and Herscovitch (2001); and individual and target characteristics, and interpersonal, organizational, and societal factors from Klein et al. (2006). These variables are worth studying, but rather than researching a laundry list of antecedents, I urge researchers in the area to tie their work to a strong process theory of interpersonal commitments (e.g., T. E. Becker & Bennett, 2007; Meyer et al., 2004, 2006). This will serve the joint scientific aims of prediction and explanation rather than pursuing prediction alone.

Along the same lines, the literatures on attachment theory, interpersonal attraction, and evolutionary psychology are promising because they each have a rich theoretical and empirical base. At this point, theory on interpersonal commitments is wider than it is deep, and anchoring our conceptualizations to these and other mature fields will be to our advantage.

Due to the paucity of theory and research in the area, it is premature to propose a full-blown model of the formation of interpersonal commitments. I offer the following picture as a possible means of stimulating thought in the area.

New hires bring with them an evolutionary heritage that predisposes them to develop emotional bonds with other individuals and groups. Among other things, they are hardwired to seek social exchanges, form in-groups and out-groups, and organize into social hierarchies characterized by concerns for dominance, status, and a moral order. New hires also bring with them a particular attachment style, formed in their early lives, which will significantly influence the level and nature of their commitments and, thus, their workplace behavior. While they're undergoing socialization, a host of evolved interpersonal factors, including familiarity, similarity, modeling, and physical attractiveness, will influence to whom and to what extent they become committed. Communication practices such as emphasizing similarities and engaging in self-disclosure will also come into play, as will fundamental cognitive processes such as the desire to become committed to various foci, the corresponding assessment of costs, and perceived obligation. In the end, due to their fearful or dismissing attachment styles, some employees won't be able to become committed to anyone. The rest will tend to become committed to foci who offer advantageous social exchanges, status, a sense of dominance, and a moral order; who are perceived to be physically attractive, familiar, and similar and engage in self-disclosure; and who share their values, inspire identification, and foster a sense of obligation.

Moderators and Mediators of Interpersonal Commitments

The effects of interpersonal commitments must depend on a number of factors. For example, an abundance of noncustomer maintenance tasks could increase the relation between commitment to customers and quality of service because only the most committed make time for excellent service. On the other hand, human resources policies that offer generous financial rewards for great customer service could lessen the relevance of commitment to customers because even those low in commitment provide good service in order to obtain the rewards.* Nevertheless, beyond what

---

* Thanks to John Meyer for this example.

I discussed earlier, little is known about how commitment interacts with other variables. Clearly, moderators of relations between interpersonal commitments and their outcomes deserve much more attention.

One place to begin the search for moderators is with compatibility, psychological distance, and level of abstraction. Proposition 1 argues that the relationship between commitment to a target and another variable (antecedent or consequence) depends on the degree of compatibility between the two. Although I discussed some evidence supporting this proposition, formally testing for commitment-by-compatibility interactions across a variety of antecedents and consequences would more rigorously establish whether compatibility is a moderator. Proposition 6 holds that for outcomes compatible with multiple foci, the relation between commitment and outcomes is moderated by level of abstraction and psychological distance. This three-way interaction (commitment level–level of abstraction–psychological distance) is testable by examining commitment-outcome relations across a range of foci varying along the dimensions illustrated in Figure 5.1.

Another promising moderator is level of analysis. It might be predicted that commitment to an interpersonal target is most strongly related to an outcome when the outcome is perceived to benefit the target (the sense of compatibility discussed earlier) and when commitment and outcome are analyzed at the same level (a second sense of compatibility). This would exist, for example, if commitment to a department supervisor is most strongly associated with outcomes that benefit the supervisor (e.g., departmental performance, OCB directed toward the supervisor), especially when the commitment is aggregated to the same level (the department).

Regarding mediators, given the complexity of employee cognitions, emotions, and behavior, commitment effects cannot often be expected to be direct. Thus, commitment theorists have recently recognized target-specific attitudes, subjective norms, perceived behavioral control, goal regulation, goal choice, and goal mechanisms as potential intervening variables (T. E. Becker & Bennett, 2007; Meyer et al., 2004, 2006). Serious investigation of such variables is necessary to understand commitment-outcome processes.

Differential Relationships and Unique Variance Across Foci

Although the factor analytic evidence that commitments to different interpersonal foci comprise separate factors is promising, we must still beware the unnecessary proliferation of foci. It's possible that many commitment foci exist but pay few dividends in terms of variance explained. As discussed earlier, there is evidence that commitment to some foci are differentially related to certain variables, and that commitment to these foci explain variance in outcomes above and beyond commitments to other interpersonal and macro commitments. However, as reflected in the many empty cells in Tables 5.2–5.4, much more needs to be known before we can draw confident conclusions about patterns of relationships across foci. At this time there is currently little reason to believe that commitment to top management by itself accounts for unique variance in commitment outcomes. This may be because for many employees top management is a distal-abstract target and hence has little power to exert influence on day-to-day employee attitudes and behaviors. At any rate, caution is called for as we study this and other foci. We don't want to allow an unreasoned burgeoning of concepts to hinder theory and research in the area.

That being understood, it is possible that some important foci have yet to be sufficiently studied. One use of the typology represented by Figure 5.1 is as an aid in a targeted search for other meaningful foci. Much of the work to date has focused on proximal-concrete foci, including supervisors, peers, team members, and customers. This is fine because this is a condition in which stronger commitment-outcome relations can be expected. While other useful proximal-concrete foci may exist (e.g., workplace friends, romantic partners), the investigation of this cell is well under way. This is less true of the other cells.

Heffner and Rentsch (2001) studied commitment to the department and found that it, along with social interaction among employees at different levels, served as a key link between employee bonds to teams and organizations. This is a rare investigation of a proximal-abstract target. Although I wouldn't expect research on such foci to be extraordinarily fruitful, it is certainly plausible that commitments to departments, strategic business units, and so on could sometimes have important implications. For example, if employees are not structured into teams, a department might be a natural unit around which workers form an in-group. With regard to the distal-concrete cell, I have found no scholarly work on commitments to founders, CEOs, or other distal-concrete foci. Studying commitment to this type of foci could be promising because, as discussed previously, distal-concrete targets may have profound effects.

The remaining cell, representing distal-abstract foci, has not been widely studied and, for the reasons discussed earlier, may not warrant as much attention as the others. There may be exceptions, as in smaller companies where top management has more of a psychological presence. However, in small companies top management may be perceived as more proximal (e.g., because they work in the same physical space as other employees), more concrete (e.g., because the members of top management are known and visible), or both. Therefore, in this case, top management wouldn't belong in the distal-abstract cell. Commitment to distal-abstract foci may be more influential at the organizational or supra-organizational levels. Clearly, people do become committed to foci such as organizations, occupations, professions, and countries, all of which are distal-abstract (see chapters 1, 3, and 4 for further discussion of these foci).

Finally, as I discussed earlier, perceptions of level of abstraction and psychological difference are likely influenced by a variety of individual and situational factors. Thus, as we study different foci, we should probably examine how perceptions of abstraction and distance, within and across targets, affect commitment and its outcomes.

In sum, the search for additional relevant foci should proceed cautiously, driven by grounded theory. Further, this line of inquiry should be accompanied by investigation of underlying perceptual influences that may help explain observed differences in commitment to work-related foci. In this way we can maximize our chances of finding and focusing on relevant foci without needlessly complicating theory.

Testing Propositions

I've offered six propositions about commitment compatibility effects, how these effects may influence the degree of mediation involved in commitment-outcome relationships, and the roles psychological distance and level of abstraction may play in the process. To thoroughly study the propositions, researchers will first need to select representative foci of each of the types shown in Figure 5.1. This could be theory driven, along the lines I've discussed; for example, for most employees, top management is distal-abstract, supervisors are proximal-concrete, and so on. Or foci could be categorized more empirically by having employees rate potential targets on the basis of their psychological distance and level of abstraction. Compatible and noncompatible outcomes would need to be identified, and data on commitment and the outcomes gathered and analyzed. Finally, conventional techniques could be used to determine whether commitment-outcome relations vary in the manner proposed. Researchers taking this course of action will need to be wary of the kinds of methodological concerns discussed by Vandenberg and Stanley in chapter 12.

The Need for Experiments

Most of the work on interpersonal commitments has been correlational. Thus, while logical reasons exist for believing the variables in Tables 5.2 and 5.3 are antecedents and consequences, there is room for doubt. It is very difficult to study commitment to organizations in the lab, because creating a meaningful work organization is usually not feasible. This is not as large a problem with respect to commitments to individuals and small groups. A few intrepid researchers have conducted such studies: Huang, Wei, Watson, and Tan (2002) used a two-by-two factorial design to demonstrate that a group support system with an embedded goal-setting program led to higher commitment to virtual teams; and Lucas (1999) conducted two experiments showing that giving team members a high-status title ("leader") resulted in higher commitment to the team—even when the tasks performed by high-status and lower status members were objectively the same.

We could earn more confidence in our inferences by carrying out more of these kinds of studies, demonstrating experimentally that variables from Table 5.2 do, in fact, increase commitments to certain foci and this, in turn, leads to the expected outcomes. This is basic but essential work and needs to be done so that science in this area can progress—and so field researchers can sleep well at night!

Conclusion

In interpreting research on interpersonal commitments and suggesting a few steps forward, I've described the roles that compatibility, psychological distance, and level of abstraction may play. Much of my analysis has been based on a fairly small body of literature, and the wise reader will treat my explanations and arguments with some skepticism. If such justified doubt serves to provoke further theory development and empirical study, I will be delighted.

References

Ainsworth, M. D. S. (1989). Attachments beyond infancy. *American Psychologist,* *44,* 709–716.

Ainsworth, M. D. S., Blehar, M. C., Waters, E., & Wall, S. (1978). *Patterns of attachment.* Hillsdale, NJ: Erlbaum.

Ajzen, I. (1989). Attitude structure and behavior. In A. Pratkanis, S. Breckler, & A. Greenwald (Eds.), *Attitude structure and function* (pp. 241–274). Hillsdale, NJ: Erlbaum.

Arnold, K. A., Barling, J., & Kelloway, E. K. (2001). Transformational leadership or the iron cage: Which predicts trust, commitment and team efficacy? *Leadership & Organization Development Journal, 22(7),* 315–320.

Bartholomew, K. (1990). Avoidance of intimacy: An attachment perspective. *Journal of Social and Personal Relationships, 7,* 147–178.

Bartholomew, K., & Horowitz, L. M. (1991). Attachment styles among young adults: A test of a four-category model. *Journal of Personality and Social Psychology, 61,* 226–244.

Becker, H. S. (1960). Notes of the concept of commitment. *American Journal of Sociology, 66,* 32–42.

Becker, T. E. (1992). Foci and bases of commitment: Are they distinctions worth making? *Academy of Management Journal, 35(1),* 232–244.

Becker, T. E. (2005). *Problems of commitment: Three dilemmas regarding the nature of employee attachment.* Presented at the first Conference on Commitment, Ohio State University, Columbus, OH.

Becker, T. E., & Bennett, R. J. (2007). Employee attachment and deviance in organizations. In J. Langan-Fox, C. Cooper, & R. Klimoski (Eds.), *Research companion to the dysfunctional workplace: Management challenges and symptoms* (pp. 136–151). New Horizons Management Series (Cary L. Cooper, Ed.). Northampton, MA: Edward Elgar.

Becker, T. E., & Billings, R. S. (1993). Profiles of commitment: An empirical test. *Journal of Organizational Behavior, 14,* 177–190.

Becker, T. E., & Billings, R. S. (1997, May). The development of patterns of commitment: Implications for performance. *United States Army Research Institute Note 97-13.* Alexandria, VA: Army Research Institute.

Becker, T. E., Billings, R. S., Eveleth, D. M., & Gilbert, N. L. (1996). Foci and bases of employee commitment: Implications for job performance. *Academy of Management Journal, 39(2),* 464–482.

Becker, T. E., Billings, R. S., Eveleth, D. M., & Gilbert, N. L. (1997). Validity of scores on three attachment style scales: Exploratory and confirmatory evidence. *Educational and Psychological Measurement, 57,* 477–493.

Becker, T. E., & Kernan, M. C. (2003). Matching commitment to supervisors and organizations to in-role and extra-role performance. *Human Performance, 16(4),* 327–348.

Becker, T. E., Randall, D. M., & Riegel, C. D. (1995). The multidimensional view of commitment and the theory of reasoned action: A comparative evaluation. *Journal of Management, 21(4),* 617–638.

Bentein, K., Stinglhamber, F., & Vandenberghe, C. (2002). Organization-, supervisor-, and workgroup-directed commitments and citizenship behaviors: A comparison of models. *European Journal of Work and Organizational Psychology, 11(3),* 341–362.

Berscheid, E., & Reis, H. T. (1998). Attraction and close relationships. In D. T. Gilbert, S. T. Fiske, & G. Lindzey (Eds.), *The handbook of social psychology: Vol. 2* (pp. 193–281). Boston: McGraw-Hill.

Bishop, J. W., & Scott, K. D. (2000). An examination of organizational and team commitment in a self-directed team environment. *Journal of Applied Psychology, 85(3),* 439–450.

Bishop, J. W., Scott, K. D., & Burroughs, S. M. (2000). Support, commitment, and employee outcomes in a team environment. *Journal of Management, 26(6),* 1113–1132.

Bishop, J. W., Scott, K. D., Goldsby, M. G., & Cropanzano, R. (2005). A construct validity study of commitment and perceived support variables. *Group & Organization Management, 30(2),* 153–180.

Boyle, B. A. (1997). A multi-dimensional perspective on salesperson commitment. *Journal of Business & Industrial Marketing, 12(6),* 354–367.

Brandes, P., Dharwadkar, R., & Wheatley, K. (2004). Social exchanges within organizations and work outcomes. *Group and Organization Management, 29,* 276–301.

Brands, H. W. (1999). *Masters of enterprise.* New York: The Free Press.

Bresnahan, C. G., & Mitroff, I. I. (2007). Leadership and attachment theory. *American Psychologist, 62,* 607–608.

Buss, D. M. (1999). *Evolutionary psychology: The new science of the mind.* Boston: Allyn & Bacon.

Buss, D. M. (2005). *The handbook of evolutionary psychology.* Hoboken, NJ: Wiley.

Campbell, L., & Ellis, B. J. (2005). Commitment, love, and mate retention. In D. M. Buss (Ed.), *The handbook of evolutionary psychology* (pp. 419–446). Hoboken, NJ: Wiley.

Chan, A. W., Tong-quing, F., Redman, T., & Snape, E. (2006). Evaluating the multidimensional view of employee commitment: A comparative UK-Chinese study. *International Journal of Human Resource Management, 17,* 1873–1887.

Chen, Z. (2001). Further investigation of the outcomes of loyalty to supervisor: Job satisfaction and intention to stay. *Journal of Managerial Psychology, 16(8),* 650–660.

Chen, Z. X., Tsui, A. S., & Farh, J. (2002). Loyalty to supervisor vs. organizational commitment: Relationships to employee performance in China. *Journal of Occupational and Organizational Psychology, 75,* 339–356.

Cheng, B., Jiang, D., & Riley, J. H. (2003). Organizational commitment, supervisory commitment, and employee outcomes in the Chinese context: Proximal hypothesis or global hypothesis? *Journal of Organizational Behavior, 24,* 313–334.

Clugston, M., Howell, J. P., & Dorfman, P. W. (2000). Does cultural socialization predict multiple bases and foci of commitment? *Journal of Management, 26(1),* 5–30.

Cohen, A. (2000). The relationship between commitment forms and work outcomes: A comparison of three models. *Human Relations, 53(3),* 387–417.

Cohen, A. (2005). The relationship between multiple commitments and organizational citizenship behavior in Arab and Jewish culture. *Journal of Vocational Behavior, 69,* 105–118.

Cohen, J., & Cohen, P. (1983). *Applied multiple regression/correlation analysis for the behavioral sciences* (2nd ed.). Hillsdale, NJ: Erlbaum.

Collins, N. L., & Miller, L. C. (1994). Self-disclosure and liking: A meta-analytic review. *Psychological Bulletin, 116,* 457–475.

Cosmides, L., & Tooby, J. (2005). Neurocognitive adaptations designed for social exchange. In D. M. Buss (Ed.), *Handbook of evolutionary psychology* (pp. 584–627). Hoboken, NJ: Wiley.

Cummins, D. (2005). Dominance, status, and social hierarchies. In D. M. Buss (Ed.), *Handbook of evolutionary psychology* (pp. 676–697). Hoboken, NJ: Wiley.

de Gilder, D. (2003). Commitment, trust and work behavior: The case of contingent workers. *Personnel Review, 32(5),* 588–604.

Den Hartog, D. N., & Belschak, F. D. (2007). Personal initiative, commitment, and affect at work. *Journal of Occupational and Organizational Psychology, 80,* 601–622.

Ellemers, N., de Gilder, D., & van den Heuvel, H. (1998). Career-oriented versus team-oriented commitment and behavior at work. *Journal of Applied Psychology, 83(5),* 717–730.

Ellemers, N., Spears, R., & Doosje, B. (1997). Sticking together or falling apart: In-group identification as a psychological determinant of group commitment versus individual mobility. *Journal of Personality and Social Psychology, 72(3),* 617–626.

Fishbein, M., & Ajzen, I. (1975). *Belief, attitude, intention and behavior: An introduction to theory and research.* Reading, MA: Addison-Wesley.

Fletcher, G. J. O., & Fincham, F. D. (1991). Attribution processes in close relationships. In G. J. O. Fletcher & F. D. Fincham (Eds.), *Cognition and close relationships* (pp. 7–35). Hillsdale, NJ: Erlbaum.

Forgas, J. P., & Locke, J. (2005). Affective influences on causal inferences: The effects of mood on attributions for positive and negative interpersonal episodes. *Cognition & Emotion, 19,* 1071–1081.

Gordon, M. E., Philpot, J. W., Burt, R. E., Thompson, C. A., & Spiller, W. E. (1980). Commitment to the union: Development of a measure and an examination of its correlates. *Journal of Applied Psychology, 65,* 479–499.

Gundlach, M., Zivnuska, S., & Stoner, J. (2006). Understanding the relationship between individualism-collectivism and team performance through an integration of social identity theory and the social relations model. *Human Relations, 59,* 1603–1632.

Heffner, T. S., & Rentsch, J. R. (2001). Organizational commitment and social interaction: A multiple constituencies approach. *Journal of Vocational Behavior, 59,* 471–490.

Hofstede, G. (1980). *Culture's consequences: International difference in work related values.* Beverly Hills, CA: Sage.

Hollenbeck, J. R., & Klein, J. J. (1987). Goal commitment and the goal-setting process: Problems, prospects, and proposals for future research. *Journal of Applied Psychology, 72,* 212–220.

Holmes, J. G. (2004). The benefits of abstract functional analysis in theory construction: The case of interdependence theory. *Personality and Social Psychology Review, 8,* 146–155.

Howes, J. C., Cropanzano, R., Grandey, A. A., & Mohler, C. J. (2000). Who is supporting whom? Quality team effectiveness and perceived organizational support. *Journal of Quality Management, 5,* 207–223.

Huang, W. W., Wei, K., Watson, R. T., & Tan, B. C. Y. (2002). Supporting virtual team-building with a GSS: An empirical investigation. *Decision Support Systems, 34,* 359–367.

Hunt, S. D., & Morgan, R. M. (1994). Organizational commitment: One of many commitments or key mediating construct? *Academy of Management Journal, 37(6),* 1568–1587.

Jehn, K. A., Northcraft, G. B., & Neale, M. A. (1999). Why differences make a difference: A field study of diversity, conflict, and performance in workgroups. *Administrative Science Quarterly, 44,* 741–763.

Jones, J. T., Pelham, B. W., Carvallo, M., & Mirenberg, M. C. (2004). How do I love thee? Let me count the Js: Implicit egotism and interpersonal attraction. *Journal of Personality and Social Psychology, 87,* 665–683.

Kenny, D. A., & La Voie, L. (1984). The social relations model. *Advances in Experimental Social Psychology, 18,* 142–182.

Kirkman, B. L., & Rosen, B. (1999). Beyond self-management: Antecedents and consequences of team empowerment. *Academy of Management Journal, 42,* 58–74.

Klein, H. J., Brinsfield, C. T., & Molloy, J. C. (2006). *Understanding workplace commitments independent of antecedents, foci, rationales, and consequences.* Paper presented at the Academy of Management Annual Meeting, Atlanta, GA.

Klein, H. J., Wesson, M. J., Hollenbeck, J. R., & Alge, B. J. (1999). Goal commitment and the goal-setting process: Conceptual clarification and empirical synthesis. *Journal of Applied Psychology, 84,* 885–896.

Krebs, D. L. (2005). The evolution of morality. In D. M. Buss (Ed.), *The handbook of evolutionary psychology* (pp. 747–771). Hoboken, NJ: Wiley.

Krebs, D. L., Denton, K., Vermeulen, S. C., Carpendale, J. I., & Bush, A. (1991). The structural flexibility of moral judgment. *Journal of Personality and Social Psychology, 61,* 1012–1023.

Kurzban, R., & Leary, M. R. (2001). Evolutionary origins of stigmatization: The functions of social exclusion. *Psychological Bulletin, 127,* 187–208.

Landry, G., & Vandenberghe, C. (in press). The role of commitment to the supervisor, leader-member exchange and supervisor-based self-esteem in employee-supervisor conflicts. *Journal of Social Psychology.*

Law, K. S., Wong, C., & Song, L. J. (2004). The construct and criterion validity of emotional intelligence and its potential utility for management studies. *Journal of Applied Psychology, 89(3),* 483–496.

Lawler, E. J. (1992). Affective attachments to nested groups: A choice-process theory. *American Sociological Review, 57,* 327–339.

Lawler, E. J., Thye, S. R., & Yoon, J. (2000). Emotion and group cohesion in productive exchange. *The American Journal of Sociology, 106(3),* 616–657.

Lawler, E. J., Thye, S. R., & Yoon, J. (2006). Commitment in structurally enabled and induced exchange relations. *Social Psychology Quarterly, 69(2),* 183–200.

Lee, K., Carswell, J. J., & Allen, N. J. (2000). A meta-analytic review of occupational commitment: Relations with person- and work-related variables. *Journal of Applied Psychology, 85,* 799–811.

Lee, S., & Olshfski, D. (2002). Employee commitment and firefighters: It's my job. *Public Administration Review, 62,* 108–114.

Lewin, K. (1943). Defining the "field at a given time." *Psychological Review, 50,* 292–310.

Liao, H., & Rupp, D. E. (2005). The impact of justice climate and justice orientation on work outcomes: A cross-level multifoci framework. *Journal of Applied Psychology, 90(2),* 242–256.

Locke, E. A. (2000). *The prime movers.* New York: AMACOM.

Lucas, J. W. (1999). Behavioral and emotional outcomes of leadership in task groups. *Social Forces, 78(2),* 747–776.

Maertz, C. P., Mosley, D. C., & Alford, B. L. (2002). Does organizational commitment fully mediate constituent commitment effects? A reassessment and clarification. *Journal of Applied Social Psychology, 33,* 1300–1313.

Mathieu, J. E., & Zajac, D. M. (1990). A review and meta-analysis of the antecedents, correlates, and consequences of organizational commitment. *Psychological Bulletin, 108(2),* 171–194.

Mescheryakov, B. G., & Yuschenkova, D. V. (2006). Eyes as predictors of perceptible physical attractiveness of women's faces. *Cultural-Historical Psychology*, 1, 48–56.

Meyer, J. P., Becker, T. E., & Van Dick, R. (2006). Social identities and commitments at work: Toward an integrative model. *Journal of Organizational Behavior*, 27(5), 665–683.

Meyer, J. P., Becker, T. E., & Vandenberghe, C. (2004). Employee commitment and motivation: A conceptual analysis and integrative model. *Journal of Applied Psychology*, 89(6), 991–1007.

Meyer, J. P., & Herscovitch, L. (2001). Commitment in the workplace: Toward a general model. *Human Resource Management Review*, 11, 299–326.

Meyer, J. P., Stanley, D. J., Herscovitch, L., & Topolnytsky, L. (2002). Affective, continuance, and normative commitment to the organization: A meta-analysis of antecedents, correlates, and consequences. *Journal of Vocational Behavior*, 61, 20–52.

Mikulincer, M. (1998). Attachment working models and the sense of trust: An exploration of interaction goals and affect regulation. *Journal of Personality and Social Psychology*, 74, 1209–1224.

Mowday, R. T., Porter, L. W., & Steers, R. (1982). *Organizational linkages: The psychology of commitment, absenteeism, and turnover*. San Diego, CA: Academic Press.

Mueller, C. W., & Lawler, E. J. (1999). Commitment to nested organizational units: Some basic principles and preliminary findings. *Social Psychology Quarterly*, 62, 325–346.

O'Reilly, C., & Chatman, J. (1986). Organizational commitment and psychological attachment: The effects of compliance, identification, and internalization on prosocial behavior. *Journal of Applied Psychology*, 71, 492–499.

Park, S., & Henkin, A. B. (2005). Teacher team commitment, teamwork, and trust: Exploring associations. *Journal of Educational Administration*, 43(5), 462–479.

Pearce, C. L., & Giacalone, R. A. (2003). Teams behaving badly: Factors associated with anti-citizenship behavior in teams. *Journal of Applied Social Psychology*, 33(1), 58–75.

Pearce, C. L., & Herbik, P. A. (2004). Citizenship behavior at the team level of analysis: The effects of team leadership, team commitment, perceived team support, and team size. *The Journal of Social Psychology*, 144(3), 293–310.

Peskin, M., & Newell, F. N. (2004). Familiarity breeds attraction: Effects of exposure on the attractiveness of typical and distinctive faces. *Perception*, 33, 147–157.

Porter, C. O. L. H. (2005). Goal orientation: Effects on backing up behavior, performance, efficacy, and commitment in teams. *Journal of Applied Psychology*, 90(4), 811–818.

Redman, T., & Snape, E. (2005). Unpacking commitment: Multiple loyalties and employee behavior. *Journal of Management Studies*, 42(2), 301–328.

Reichers, A. E. (1985). A review and reconceptualization of organizational commitment. *Academy of Management Review*, 10(3), 465–476.

Reichers, A. E. (1986). Conflict and organizational commitments. *Journal of Applied Psychology*, 71, 508–514.

Rusbult, C. E. (1983). A longitudinal test of the investment model: The development (and deterioration) of satisfaction and commitment in heterosexual involvements. *Journal of Personality and Social Psychology*, 45, 101–117.

Siders, M. A., George, G., & Dharwadkar, R. (2001). The relationship of internal and external commitment foci to objective job performance measures. *Academy of Management Journal, 44(3),* 570–579.

Simpson, J. A., Rholes, W. S., & Phillips, D. (1996). Conflict in close relationships: An attachment perspective. *Journal of Personality and Social Psychology, 71,* 899–914.

Snape, E., Chan, A. W., & Redman, T. (2006). Multiple commitments in the Chinese context: Testing compatibility, cultural, and moderating hypotheses. *Journal of Vocational Behavior, 69,* 302–314.

Staw, B. M. (1981). The escalation of commitment to a course of action. *Academy of Management Review, 6,* 569–577.

Stinglhamber, F., Bentein, K., & Vandenberghe, C. (2002). Extension of the three-component model of commitment to five foci. *European Journal of Psychological Assessment, 18(2),* 123–138.

Stinglhamber, S., Eisenberger, R., Aselage, J., Sucharski, I.L., Becker, T., & Eder, P. (2008). *Supervisor's organizational embodiment.* Unpublished manuscript, University of Delaware.

Stinglhamber, F., & Vandenberghe, C. (2003). Organizations and supervisors as sources of support and targets of commitment: A longitudinal study. *Journal of Organizational Behavior, 24,* 251–270.

Swailes, S. (2004). Commitment to change: Profiles of commitment and in-role performance. *Personnel Review, 33(2),* 187–204.

Tooby, J., & Cosmides, L. (1992). The psychological foundations of culture. In J. Barkow, L. Cosmides, & J. Tooby (Eds.), *The adapted mind* (pp. 19–136). New York: Oxford University Press.

Turner, R. N., Hewstone, M., & Voci, A. (2007). Reducing explicit and implicit outgroup prejudice via direct and extended contact: The mediating role of self-disclosure and intergroup anxiety. *Journal of Personality and Social Psychology, 93,* 369–388.

Van Der Vegt, G. S., & Bunderson, J. S. (2005). Learning and performance in multidisciplinary teams: The importance of collective team identification. *Academy of Management Journal, 48(3),* 532–547.

Van Der Vegt, G., Emans, B., & Van De Vliert, E. (2000). Team members' affective responses to patterns of intragroup interdependence and job complexity. *Journal of Management, 26(4),* 633–655.

Van Der Vegt, G. S., Van De Vliert, E., & Oosterhof, A. (2003). Informational dissimilarity and organizational citizenship behavior: The role of intrateam interdependence and team identification. *Academy of Management Journal, 46(6),* 715–727.

Vandenberg, R. J., & Nelson, J. B. (1999). Disaggregating the motives underlying turnover intentions: When do intentions predict turnover behavior? *Human Relations, 52(10),* 1313–1336.

Vandenberghe, C., Bentein, K., Michon, R., Chebat, J. C., Tremblay, M., & Fils, J. F. (2007). An examination of the role of perceived support and employee commitment in employee-customer encounters. *Journal of Applied Psychology, 92(4),* 177–187.

Vandenberghe, C., Bentein, K., & Stinglhamber, F. (2004). Affective commitment to the organization, supervisor, and work group: Antecedents and outcomes. *Journal of Vocational Behavior, 64,* 47–71.

Vandenberghe, C., Stinglhamber, F., Bentein, K., & Delhaise, T. (2001). An examination of the cross-cultural validity of a multidimensional model of commitment in Europe. *Journal of Cross-Cultural Psychology, 32(3),* 322–347.

Wanberg, C., Welsh, E. T., & Kammeyer-Mueller, J. (2007). Protégé and mentor self-disclosure: Levels and outcomes within formal mentoring dyads in a corporate context. *Journal of Vocational Behavior, 70,* 398–412.

West, M. A., & Wallace, M. (1991). Innovation in health care teams. *European Journal of Social Psychology, 21,* 303–315.

Workman, M., Kahnweiler, W., & Bommer, W. (2003). The effects of cognitive style and media richness on commitment to telework and virtual teams. *Journal of Vocational Behavior, 63,* 199–219.

Zaccaro, S. J., & Dobbins, G. H. (1989). Contrasting group and organizational commitment: Evidence for differences among multilevel attachments. *Journal of Organizational Behavior, 10,* 267–273.

6

Action Commitments

Mitchell J. Neubert and Cindy Wu

Baylor University

What Are Action Commitments?

Definitions

This book examines and explores commitment to a variety of foci. When discussing commitment that contributes to achievement or organizational excellence, however, the implied focus is commitment to action by which such achievement is attained. For example, a committed workforce plays a critical role in developing and maintaining competitive advantage (Lado & Wilson, 1994; O'Reilly & Pfeffer, 2000). Competitive advantage is realized through commitment to actions such as providing excellent customer service and developing innovative products. Action commitment, as conceptualized in this chapter, is an attachment or bond to an action. This bond to action can be to a particular and identifiable action or to the actions necessary to achieve a particular target. In other words, action commitments can focus on action that is a means to an end as well as the end itself. Action commitments can differ in target level from individual goals to group norms and in the tangibility of the target from intangible individual values to tangible goals for organizational change. In addition, the targets of action commitments can range from broad strategic goals or the organization's culture, to narrow emotional display rules or one's implicit goal orientation. Later in this chapter we discuss four categories of action commitments that differ in the level and tangibility of the target.

Consistent with the arguments presented in chapter 1 by Klein, Molloy, and Cooper, the bond to act, common to all action commitments, parallels the bond of a person to a behavior (Kiesler & Sakamura, 1966; Salancik, 1977), and the attachment to a specified target implying action (Neubert, 1996). The bond to action differs from and occurs subsequent to the "force" Meyer and Herscovitch (2001 p. 301) describe as binding "an individual to a course of action that is of relevance to a particular target." Further, the bond to action is different from, and an antecedent to, the determination (Hollenbeck, Klein, O'Leary, & Wright, 1989) or intention to act (Ajzen, 1991).

Moving beyond definitions, action commitments can be distinguished from commitments to other foci. Action commitments differ from organizational commitments; the latter focus on an organization, not a specific act or target that implies action. Similarly, action commitments differ from interpersonal commitments; the latter is a commitment to a person or persons rather than to action toward an end or a means to an end. Nonetheless, there may be, though not need be, spillover effects where commitment to one or more foci influence commitment to other foci. Organizational and interpersonal commitments can influence action commitments, and the experiences and outcomes of action commitments can affect commitments to the organization and organizational members. For example, the level of commitment to a supervisor may influence commitment to goals he or she assigns. Or, if the goals set by the supervisor represent the best interests of the designated employee(s), goal commitment may influence commitment to the supervisor.

Spillover effects may be most apparent when commitment to the broad organization affects other commitments within the organization (Cohen, 2003; Locke & Latham, 1990). Because commitment to the organization is associated with motivation to contribute positively to the organization (Meyer & Allen, 1997), commitment to the organization likely engenders commitment to goals, changes, and norms when these targets benefit the organization. For example, organizational commitment has been demonstrated to influence goal commitment (Hollenbeck & Klein, 1987) and change commitments (Ford, Weissbein, & Plamondon, 2003; Neubert & Cady, 2001).

On the other hand, the association between commitments is likely to be weaker and may even be negative when a goal, program, or change somehow harms an organization or person, or it alters a preferred status quo. For example, strong commitments to a supervisor or coworkers, or a strong commitment to the organization in its current form, likely result in weak commitment to a change that threatens the jobs of a boss or coworkers. Likewise, change that alters the organization's culture or values, such as may occur when an organization is acquired by or merges with another organization, engenders weaker commitment. In these situations, organizational and interpersonal commitments may be unrelated, or even negatively related, to action commitments that threaten to change or negatively impact the entity or person to which one is committed. In such situations, action commitments are not evaluated exclusively on their own merit, but instead on their impact on other foci of commitment.

Even when commitments align in support of one another, notable differences exist between action commitments and commitments to the organization or interpersonal relationships. For action commitments, a specified end (i.e., a goal or vision) clearly implies action to achieve the end, and a specific means (i.e., a policy or rule) implies action to abide by the means. In contrast, no such clarity is readily apparent when the focus of commitment is an organization, an occupation, a team, or a supervisor. Action commitment necessitates clear and immediate behavioral expectations, whereas other commitments do not immediately imply action.

Conceptualization of Action Commitment

Conceptual understanding of action commitments also requires discussing the dimensionality of the focal constructs. The dimensionality of action commitments has varied from multidimensional conceptualizations of mindsets originating in organizational commitment research (Herscovitch & Meyer, 2002; Meyer & Allen, 1991) to unidimensional conceptualizations originating in goal-setting research (e.g., Hollenbeck et al., 1989; Neubert, 1996). Whereas a unidimensional conceptualization of goal commitment developed to capture a singular motivational attitude toward a goal and the maintenance of that determination (Hollenbeck et al., 1989; Wright, O'Leary-Kelly, Cortina, Klein, & Hollenbeck, 1994), organizational commitment measures have tended to be multidimensional conceptualizations of attitudes or mindsets.

In a comprehensive review of the commitment literature, Cohen (2003) argued for a unidimensional approach to measuring commitment where commitments to a variety of foci are adapted and developed from Meyer and Allen's (1991) affective commitment measure. The basis for his argument is both conceptual and empirical, with the preponderance of evidence indicating the superiority of affective commitment in reviews of construct, content, face, discriminant, and predictive validity (Cohen, 2003). Although Cohen does not review the goal commitment literature, Klein, Wesson, Hollenbeck, Wright, and DeShon (2001) reach a similar conclusion in their meta-analytic review of goal commitment, settling on a unidimensional goal commitment measure. More recently, Klein, Brinsfield, and Molloy (2006) argued for a unidimensional view of commitment but describe commitment as more than summary evaluations of favorability that characterized earlier conceptualizations of commitment.

Following a unidimensional perspective on commitment, action commitments may still have different bases that explain commitment. In this sense, Meyer and Allen's popular three-dimensional conceptualization of commitment mindsets assesses proximal antecedents or bases of commitment such as desires, felt obligations, or perceived costs. According to Klein et al. (2006) and as described in chapter 1 of this book, rationales for commitment exist that differ from mindsets. Rationales are perceived self-explanations that may or may not be fully explained by the mindsets. Further, whereas mindsets take into account objective causes of commitment as well as consequences of commitment, rationales focus primarily on perceived reasons. Even so, as conceptualized, rationales are still predominantly conscious self-explanations or attributions of affective attachments or bonds. The conceptualization of action commitments presented in this chapter is consistent with Klein et al. (2006) in considering mindsets to be antecedents to commitment, but it also enhances their conceptualization of commitment by making the unconscious nature of commitment more salient.

The conceptual assertions that commitment operates both unconsciously and consciously, date back to early research on commitment (e.g., Becker, 1960; Kiesler, 1971). Recently, research has shown that goals can be unconsciously activated and regulate behavior (Bargh, Gollwitzer, Lee-Chai, Barndollar, & Trötschel, 2001; Stajkovic, Locke, & Blair, 2006). Unconscious associations can develop through exposure to a singular intense experience or, over time, in response to recurring stimuli. Similarly, commitment associated with specific goals may be unconscious and evoked when an individual experiences stimuli that were previously associated with past goal pursuits. Although this area is still in its infancy of development, initial empirical evidence suggests that unconscious priming interacts with conscious goal-setting to enhance performance (Stajkovic et al., 2006). In fact, Locke and Latham (2004) suggested that one of the future directions researchers should take to advance the field of work motivation is subconscious motivation. Together, this research points to the existence of unconscious factors underlying psychological phenomena that influence action. As such, we propose that an action commitment is both a conscious and unconscious bond to action. Furthermore, commitment as a bond to action is closely associated with and influences intentions to act, but it is distinct from intentions.

Intentions "capture the factors that influence behavior; they are indications of how hard people are willing to try, of how much effort they are planning on exerting, in order to perform the behavior" (Ajzen, 1991, p. 181). Similarly, in goal-setting theory, Locke, Bryan, and Kendall (1968) argued that the intentions associated with goals are the most immediate determinants of action. Behavioral intention to act has been proposed as the same as commitment, particularly as it relates to change. Fedor, Caldwell, and Herold (2006, p.12), for example, stated that "although recent research has examined other underlying psychological dimensions of change commitment (e.g., Herscovitch & Meyer, 2002), we selected intentions as a representation of commitment due to their established association with actual behavior." In contrast, we make a distinction between commitment and intentions.

In a review of research testing the theory of reasoned action (Ajzen & Fishbein, 1980), the theory of planned behavior (Ajzen, 1991), theories of interpersonal behavior (Triandis, 1977), and subjective probabilities judgments (Jaccard & King, 1977), Davis and Warshaw (1992) asserted that behavioral intentions are "the degree to which a person has formulated conscious plans to perform or not perform a behavior" (p. 392). Moreover, in practice, many intention measures assess conscious desire and self-predictions (e.g., T. E. Becker, Randall, & Reigel, 1995; Davis & Warshaw, 1992; Fishbein & Stasson, 1990). Commitment, on the other hand, has been shown to predict behavior more reliably than intention measures, perhaps due to the more inclusive nature of commitment in capturing both unconscious and conscious processes. Altogether, the conceptual nature and measurement of intention focuses primarily on conscious processes related to formulating plans to act and intentions to persist. In contrast, we propose that action commitment includes both unconscious and conscious processes involving one's psychological bond to the actions necessary to achieve a target.

Overall, action commitment represents a bond to action that is both conscious and unconscious, and it results from bases, mindsets, rationales, emotions, and unconscious influences. Furthermore, action commitment is a proximal antecedent of intentions and subsequent actions.

General Model of Action Commitment

In developing a general model of the antecedents and outcomes of action commitment, we propose that action commitments are informed by both conscious and unconscious factors. In turn, action commitments lead to intentions to act that are proximal to nondiscretionary behavioral outcomes such as explicit target-oriented performance, persistence, and effort, as well as discretionary behavior such as collaboration that is implicitly linked to the target. Figure 6.1 depicts the proposed general model of action commitment.

Antecedents

In this section, we present a framework for the antecedents of action commitment based largely on the theory of planned behavior (Ajzen's, 1991). The framework integrates two antecedents—attractiveness and

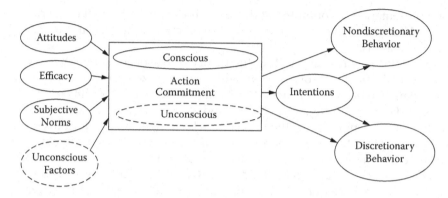

FIGURE 6.1
General model of action commitment antecedents and outcomes.

expectancy—from goal commitment research (Hollenbeck & Klein, 1987; Klein, Wesson, Hollenbeck, & Alge, 1999) with the antecedents of the theory of planned behavior and extends to include unconscious anteced- ents found in other psychological theories of behavior (e.g., Bargh et al., 2001; Winkielman & Berridge, 2004). Although we attempted to include most of the research supporting specific antecedents to action commit- ment, chapters 7 through 9 in this book describe additional research related to individual, social, and organizational influences on commit- ment that also may apply to action commitments.

In the theory of planned behavior (Ajzen, 1991), the antecedents of atti- tudes, perceived behavioral control, and subjective norms mediate the influences of all other variables on intentions. In our general model of action commitments, attitudes toward an action can be influenced by per- sonal and situational factors that affect the attractiveness of achieving the specified end. In our framework, an attitude is a summary evaluation that includes the attractiveness concept from expectancy theory. Personal fac- tors that may influence attitudes include personality, value congruence, emotions, and the spillover of other attitudes toward the organization or one's job. Examples of situational factors that may influence attitudes include competition, participation, visibility, rewards, recognition, and the explicitness of the target (Hollenbeck & Klein, 1987; Salancik, 1977).

The second antecedent, efficacy, subsumes the conceptually similar constructs of expectancy and perceived behavioral control (Ajzen, 2002). Tolman (1932) initiated the concept of expectancy as the probability esti- mate that a behavior or set of behaviors will lead to certain consequences. Vroom (1964) built upon Tolman's work to develop his own expectancy theory. A decade after Vroom, Fishbein, and Ajzen (1975) introduced the concept of perceived behavioral control. Shortly thereafter, Bandura (1977) presented the social learning construct of self-efficacy as an individual's perception of his or her capability to perform a given task, or to perform a task at a specific difficulty level. The constructs of expectancy, perceived behavioral control, and efficacy are related to a large degree and also impact behavior in a similar manner, though each has at times shown marginal unique predictive validity (Ajzen, 2002; Cady, Grey-Boyd, & Neubert, 2001). Efficacy is used here as a broad judgment of one's total capability to perform (Gist, 1989). As a whole, research supports the idea that efficacy constructs are antecedents of action commitments (Klein, 1991; Neubert & Cady, 2001).

Factors influencing efficacy are both personal and situational. For example, personality (i.e., locus of control), personal history, ability, and self-evaluation impact a person's efficacy beliefs (Ajzen, 2002; Klein et al., 1999). Situational factors that influence efficacy include supervisory support, constraints, resources, and the actions' degrees of difficulty or complexity (Gist & Mitchell, 1992; Hollenbeck & Klein, 1987).

A third antecedent from the theory of planned behavior is subjective norms, which are beliefs about the expectations that others have about action (Ajzen, 1991). Although the term subjective norms is rarely used in studies of action commitment, the broader commitment literature supports similar constructs as antecedents of commitment. Scholl (1981) asserted that organizational commitment is influenced by identification with others in the social environment. More specifically, Reichers (1985) noted that organizational commitment relates to identification with the goals of other constituents. In other words, subjective norms capture the influence of the identification one has with others, particularly leaders and peers, and their goals. Furthermore, subjective norms also include organizational sources of expectations such as policies or reward or punishments systems that are codified expectations of leaders. Although a person may not identify with explicit organizational expectations, the perceived consequences associated with these expectations are likely to influence commitment.

A fourth antecedent, which is one not specified in the theory of planned behavior, is the set of unconscious factors that influence commitment. For example, unconscious or implicit emotion can affect cognitions and actions, unbeknownst to the actor (Lazarus, 1991; Winkielman & Berridge, 2004). Unconscious emotional priming, experienced as spontaneous and internally generated reactions to current stimuli, can influence judgments (Clore, Gasper, & Garvin, 2001). Furthermore, when an experience is atypical, complex, or novel, the associated emotions, whether conscious or unconscious, are more likely to be infused in one's judgment and decision making because of this more rigorous information-seeking strategy in information processing (Forgas, 2001). Although research suggests that unconscious emotion influences cognitive processing and motivation, research also is emerging that points to cognitive factors that result in unconscious goal activation (Bargh et al., 2001; Stajkovic et al., 2006). Together, this suggests that unconscious emotions and cognitive factors can influence behavior by means of inducing action commitment.

Outcomes

In this section, we present a framework for the outcomes of action commitment that is rooted in goal commitment research and integrates theory and research from other foci of commitment. Note that, unlike other commitment foci that may show causal relationships with attitudinal or affective variables (e.g., job satisfaction and emotions, respectively), action commitment relates more to actual behavior since an action or series of actions represents the foci of such commitment. Although through the spillover effects action commitment may correlate with certain attitudinal variables (such as change commitment spills over to organizational commitment, which in turn, influences job satisfaction), we do not see theoretical rationale for such direct causal relationships. Furthermore, as specified in Figure 6.1, we expect action commitment to impact behavioral intentions to act and persist, but we view these as proximal to actions that are the foci of commitment. Thus, we do not include other attitudinal and affective outcomes but only discuss two types of behaviors, nondiscretionary and discretionary behaviors, as the focal outcomes of action commitments.

Goal-setting theory has proved to be among the most robust and useful theories in explaining nondiscretionary performance outcomes (Meyer, Becker, & Vandenberghe, 2004). The existence of goal commitment is the essential assumption underlying the effect of goals on performance (Locke & Latham, 1990). Goal commitment moderates the goal difficulty and performance relationship (Klein et al., 1999; Locke & Latham, 1990, 2002) and the feedback-performance relationship (Renn, 2003). Goal commitment also has partially mediated that relationship of conscientiousness to the sales volume and performance ratings of sales people (Barrick, Mount, & Strauss, 1993), and it completely mediated the influence of conscientiousness on learning as measured by test performance (Klein & Lee, 2006). In addition, studies show goal commitment to have a statistically significant main effect on performance after controlling for goal level (Hollenbeck, Williams, & Klein, 1989; Riedel, Nebeker, & Cooper, 1988; Wofford, Goodwin, & Premack, 1992). Commitment to an organization-level goal has a similar effect: individual goal commitment determines one's effort and persistence in implementing organizational goals (Dooley & Fryxell, 1999; Neubert & Cady, 2001; Woodridge & Floyd, 1990).

Goal commitment also has been linked to learning, although the results are equivocal. Klein and Lee (2006) found that in a classroom setting the commitment to a grade goal was related to learning as measured on an exam. In contrast, research indicates that commitment to specific and difficult goals can lead to tunnel vision that detracts from the experimentation and learning that is essential for novel or complex tasks (Seijts & Latham, 2001). In such situations, a learning goal directed toward acquiring specific knowledge or skills is more effective (Locke & Latham, 2006). Even so, commitment to learning goals is, in most cases, a commitment to intermediate or proximal goals that are related to distal performance goals.

Limited evidence exists linking action commitments to discretionary behavior. For example, in a diverse sample of working professionals, commitment to work goals related to task performance but not to organizational citizenship behavior (OCB) (Piccolo & Colquitt, 2006). OCBs are typically discretionary behaviors not explicitly required for task completion or to fulfill an organizational role (Williams & Anderson, 1991). As such, OCB generally would not be expected from action commitments that are directed toward other behaviors. On the other hand, goals for OCBs could be set, making their performance nondiscretionary. Or, as Podsakoff, MacKenzie, Paine, and Bachrach (2000) reasoned, employees may have a broader conception of performance that includes OCB and therefore believe that their leader administers rewards contingent upon both task performance and OCB. However, when the focus of commitment is not an action, such as when it is commitment to the organization, it seems to be more common that affective forms of commitment predict discretionary behavior (Allen & Meyer, 1996; T. E. Becker et al., 1995; Mayer & Schoorman, 1992).

Meyer et al. (2004) argue that self-regulation predicts whether commitment will influence discretionary behavior. Regulatory Focus Theory (RFT) posits that people may self-regulate behavior with a promotion focus or a prevention focus (Higgins, 1997, 1998). Both promotion- and prevention-focus mindsets are goal directed, but they have disparate causes and result in different behaviors (Brockner & Higgins, 2001). Promotion focus is associated with antecedents emphasizing growth and development needs, the achievement of gains, or the attainment of ideals (wishes and aspirations), and therefore, a promotion focus manifests in discretionary behavior such as a taking risks and creativity (Kark & Van Dijk, 2007). In contrast, a prevention focus is associated with antecedents emphasizing security, avoiding losses, or fulfilling obligations, and therefore, a prevention focus manifests in nondiscretionary behavior such as compliance and performing to expectations (Kark & Van Dijk, 2007). To date, most research on action commitments has focused on nondiscretionary behaviors that directly relate to goal accomplishment. Yet, the influence of promotion-oriented antecedents may be an explanation for how discretionary behavior could result from an action commitment.

Categories of Action Commitments

Early in the chapter, an action commitment was described as a bond to a particular and identifiable action or to the actions necessary to achieve a particular target. In other words, action commitments are teleological and can operate at multiple levels. For example, the action could be individually specific, such as reducing errors on a report, or it could be reducing errors on all reports in a department. Antecedents and outcomes may operate at the same levels, such as when individual incentives increase individual goal commitment or group incentives impact group goal commitment (Guthrie & Hollensbe, 2004).

Although some similarities may exist across targets of different levels, the level of the target may influence the array and complexity of the factors that influence action commitments. Perhaps the most notable differences will relate to situational influences on efficacy and subjective norms. For example, team and organizational goal achievement are subject to the competence and commitment of other organizational members. If others with the same goal are perceived to be incompetent or uncommitted, then an individuals' efficacy in achieving the goal is likely to decrease in acknowledgment of the others' control over goal achievement. Furthermore, if an individual perceives others with the same goal to have negative attitudes toward the goal, his or her positive attitudes toward the goal are likely to decrease to avoid dissonance with the group. Therefore, the first distinction we make is one of target level, which may be individual level or group/organization level.

Another distinction that can be made regarding action commitment targets is the extent to which the targets are tangible. That is, targets can be differentiated as being either tangible or intangible. For example, an individual goal can be tangible in being explicitly written into one's performance plans, or intangible in being less concrete and not written down or publicly known. Further, an organization has written, formal goals for action as well as unwritten expectations for action such as informal norms or culture. Differences in tangibility are likely to be a factor in understanding and explaining the relative influence of various antecedents of action commitments as well as the associated outcomes of action commitments. For example, one's commitment to a group norm of continuous improvement (i.e., more intangible) may be influenced more by the level of cohesion of the group. When continuous improvement is institutionalized as a formal program for all the workgroups in the organization (i.e., more tangible), however, one's efficacy or the reward received for continuous improvement may play a more important role in determining the commitment level. For the sake of parsimony, we describe an action commitment as either tangible or intangible.

FIGURE 6.2
Exemplars of four categories of action commitments.

By integrating the two distinctions of target-level focus (individual vs. group/organization) and target tangibility (tangible vs. intangible), we present four categories of action commitments: commitment to tangible individual targets, commitment to tangible group/organizational targets, commitment to intangible individual targets, and commitment to intangible group/organizational targets. Although action commitments may not all fit cleanly or exclusively into one of the four categories, the distinctions are provided to illustrate the similarities and differences of various action commitments. Furthermore, an action commitment described as fitting in one category may over time change to fit in another category, such as when an intangible group or organizational norm becomes formally institutionalized as a tangible organizational goal.

The four categories of action commitments are illustrated in Figure 6.2. In discussing each of the categories, we focus on one exemplar before moving on to discuss other action commitment targets that have received less research attention.

Commitment to Tangible Individual Targets

Goals are common, tangible, individual-level targets for commitment, but this category also includes behavioral targets such as ethics policies and emotional-display rules. Given the considerable research attention directed toward goals (Locke & Latham, 2002), we focus on the antecedents and outcomes of goal commitment as an exemplar of this category before moving on to the discussion of other targets.

Exemplar

Empirical support for a variety of antecedents to goal commitment was assessed in Klein et al.'s meta-analysis (1999). Personal factors contributing to attractiveness (attitudes) that were significantly associated with goal commitment were endurance, organizational commitment, Type A personality, and the need for achievement. Situational factors contributing to attractiveness (attitudes) that were significantly associated with goal commitment were publicness, volition, incentives, explicitness (specificity of goal), and goal stability. Personal factors contributing to efficacy that were significantly associated with goal commitment were ability/past performance, task information/experience, affect, and locus of control. Situational factors contributing to efficacy that were significantly associated with goal commitment were goal level, provision and type of feedback, task complexity, task strategy development, performance constraints, leadership, and supervisor supportiveness (Klein et al., 1999). Leadership and supervisory support also may influence goal commitment through subjective norms in a similar manner as the social influence antecedents that were significantly related to goal commitment in the Klein et al. meta-analysis.

Subsequent research has added to the list of antecedents and explored additional mediating and moderating mechanisms by which antecedent variables influence commitment to goals, although the relationships to the three specified proximal antecedents are unclear. For example, transformational leadership was found to impact goal commitment through core job characteristics (Piccolo & Colquitt, 2006); the relationship of goal assignment (volition) to goal commitment was found to be moderated by the cultural variable of power distance (Sue-Chan & Ong, 2004); and interactional justice was found to mediate the goal rationale-goal commitment relationship (Li & Butler, 2004).

The impact of goal commitment, including its moderating role in the goal-performance relationship and its behavioral outcomes, were discussed in the previous section in the general model of action commitment. In sum, goal commitment is linked primarily to nondiscretionary goal-related behavior, such as performance, persistence, and effort toward goal achievement, as well as learning that either is specified as a goal or is instrumental to goal achievement.

Other Targets

Although individual performance outcomes has been the dominant target of this category of action commitments, other outcomes may relate to individual behavioral targets such as ethics policies or emotional display rules. For example, an organization's written ethics codes fit in this category. Recent ethical scandals in organizations have spurred increasing interest in establishing and enforcing ethical codes and in standardizing procedures for discouraging or dealing with ethical problems (Weaver, Treviño, & Cochran, 1999). Tenbrunsel, Smith-Crowe, and Umphress (2003) propose a framework of ethical practices that includes formal systems of codes, communication, surveillance, and sanctions. Formal systems are defined as practices "that are documented and can be verified by an independent observer" (p. 288). These tangible and explicit practices are devised to influence ethical behavior. However, the empirical evidence supporting the utility of these ethical practices is limited and equivocal (Treviño, Weaver, & Reynolds, 2006). Nonetheless, we propose that commitment to ethical policies may help explain current and future findings related to the utility of various formal interventions in improving ethical behavior. In other words, similar to how goal commitment moderates the effect of goals (Klein et al., 2001), we propose that employee commitment to ethical policies or targets should be considered as a moderator of the relationship of ethical policies to behavior.

In addition to ethics policies, organizations sometimes stipulate emotional display rules for individuals that specify appropriate emotions in various circumstances and in response to different people (Diefendorff & Gosserand, 2003). For example, salespeople are directed to smile, offer warm greetings, and express thanks because behaviors that engender positive affect influence customers' evaluation of the service satisfaction and increase the likelihood of customers returning to the store and recommending it to others (Tsai, 2001; Tsai & Huang, 2002). Gosserand and Diefendorff (2005) found that commitment to emotional display rules, defined as "a person's intention to persist in displaying these emotions over time, and not abandon the display rules under difficult conditions" (p. 1257), strengthens the relationship between emotional display rules and effective emotional display in organizations.

Future research, based on our general model of action commitment, could explore to how employee attitudes toward ethical policies or emotional display rules, efficacy in following such policies or rules, and subjective norms related to complying with the policies or rules, influence the formation of action commitments to these targets.

Commitment to Tangible Group/Organization Targets

Similar to individual targets, action commitments to group- or organization-level targets, such as group goals, organizational strategies, and group or organizational quality or safety standards, have been linked to behavior and performance outcomes. For example, greater safety commitment resulted in fewer accidents in a manufacturing facility (Hofmann &

Morgeson, 1999). Due to the prevalence of change in organizations noted in chapter 2, we focus on change commitment as an exemplar of action commitments to tangible group-/organization-level targets.

Exemplar

The initial change commitment research built upon the theory and research findings for goal commitment (Neubert, 1996; Neubert & Cady, 2001; Neubert, Wong, Hartley, & Hofmann, 2002; Neubert & Wu, 2005), whereas some subsequent research built upon theory related to organizational commitment (Cunningham, 2006; Herscovitch & Meyer, 2002). Studies have investigated action commitments to a continuous improvement program (Neubert, 1996; Neubert & Cady, 2001), new technologies (Neubert et al., 2002), community policing initiatives (Ford et al., 2003), strategic culture change (Jansen, 2004), human resource practices (Neubert & Wu, 2005), structural realignment (Cunningham, 2006), and a variety of other group- or organization-level changes (Fedor et al., 2006; Herscovitch & Meyer, 2002).

Attitudes toward change that might impact change commitment can be influenced by a variety of factors including an individual's organizational commitment, perceived usefulness, and individual differences. In most cases, commitment to the organization positively influences change commitment (Herscovitch & Meyer, 2002; Neubert & Cady, 2001). In the context of new technologies, perceived usefulness of the technology influences acceptance of technology (Davis, 1989; Davis, Bagozzi, & Warshaw, 1989; Morris & Venkatesh, 2000; Venkatesh & Davis, 1996, 2000). Two specific perceptions of the usefulness of an e-procurement initiative—impact on strategic nature of the job and supplier relationships—were significantly related to change commitment (Neubert et al., 2002). Similarly, in another study when changes were perceived to be favorable for the work unit and adaptation at the job level was minimal, change commitment was high (Fedor et al., 2006). In a longitudinal investigation of the antecedents of change commitment to a continuous improvement program, an individual difference variable (teamwork orientation) influenced change commitment (Neubert & Cady, 2001).

Judge, Thoreson, Pucik, and Welbourne's (1999) coping-with-change measure captures another set of more general attitudes toward change that was associated with change commitment in the introduction of novel staffing and performance management practices in China (Neubert & Wu, 2005). Cunningham (2006) also found a relationship between change commitment and coping with change. The interpretation of the findings was that coping with change mediates the relationship of change commitment and turnover intentions, but an alternative interpretation, in which change commitment mediates coping with change attitudes, also fits the data.

The influence of efficacy on change commitment is supported in studies of implementing new technology (Davis et al., 1989; Neubert et al., 2002) as well as novel human resources practices (Neubert & Wu, 2005). Moreover, change efficacy affects change commitment across the duration of a change (Neubert & Cady, 2001). Change efficacy is the confidence an individual has in being able to successfully perform his/her job when it is changed (Neubert, 1996). In a change context, efficacy is related to experience with the implementation and support of the change. Ford et al. (2003) demonstrated that past experience in community policing efforts predicted change commitment. When participants have had a positive experience with the change and the leaders of the change, they are likely to accept and commit to the change (Kavanagh & Ashkanasy, 2006; Reichers, Wanous, & Austin, 1997).

Subjective norms are related to the perceptions a person has regarding what the important people in the work environment, particularly leaders, think about whether the behavior or change is worth doing or supporting (Ajzen, 1991; Fishbein & Ajzen, 1975). The power of subjective norms to influence intentions is moderated by whether social influences have authority to reward or punish behavior, and whether the focal people are instrumental in implementing an initiative (Venkastesh & Davis, 2000). Initial research with subjective norms variables related to the attitudes and behaviors of an individual's immediate leader and coworkers had little or no effect on change commitment (Neubert & Cady, 2001). Alternatively, Reichers, Wanous, and Austin's (1997) measure of cynicism about organizational change (CAOC) has been demonstrated to influence change commitment in the implementation of new technologies (Neubert et al., 2002) and novel human resources management practices (Neubert & Wu, 2005). CAOC assesses employees' perceptions of those responsible for leading a current change and the extent to which the leaders have the ability or motivation to ensure that the change succeeds. As such, CAOC may influence change commitment through individuals' perceptions of their leaders' expectations (subjective norms) as well as competency (efficacy).

The outcomes associated with change commitment have been primarily nondiscretionary performance behaviors. In two field studies involving nurses, affective and normative measures of change commitment were demonstrated to relate to ratings of behavioral support for change (Herscovitch & Meyer, 2002). Similar findings of change commitment influencing specific program-related behavior were found in Ford et al.'s (2003) study of a community policing initiative. Moreover, in a context of a culture change, Jansen (2004) demonstrated in a longitudinal study of a U.S. military academy that change commitment influenced an organizational measure of change momentum. Neubert and Cady (2001) also demonstrated that program commitment was related to participation and performance in a campaign to expand membership in a co-op.

Other Targets

Research on commitment to other group-/organization-level tangible targets has included group goals (e.g., Aube & Rousseau, 2005; Hyatt & Ruddy, 1997; Mulvey & Klein, 1998) and safety standards (Hofmann & Morgeson, 1999; Hofmann & Stetzer, 1996). Initial research in student teams indicates that collective efficacy is related to group goal commitment (Mulvey & Klein, 1998). Although more research is needed on potential antecedents, the subjective norms embedded in safety climate perceptions have been shown to influence the intentions and actual behavior of team members (Hofmann & Stetzer, 1996), and leaders have been shown to influence safety commitment through their safety communication (Hofmann & Morgeson, 1999). As with other targets in this category, safety standards can be set and measured at the group, plant, or organizational level (Nielsen, Carstensen, & Rasmussen, 2006) but also may be individual-level targets. This would make them part of a different category of action commitments.

In addition to commitment to operational targets such as group performance goals and safety standards, another set of strategic targets is an organization's vision or strategic intent. Thoms & Greenberger (1995, p. 212) define vision as "a cognitive image of the future which is positive enough to members so as to be motivating and elaborate enough to provide direction for future planning and goal setting." Hamel and Prahalad (1989, p. 63) say that strategic intent envisions "a desired leadership position and establishes the criteria the organization will use to chart its progress." Both vision and strategic intent can be the targets of action commitments that energize constituents to contribute toward stretching and achieving challenges beyond an organization's existing realities. Commitment to an organizational vision or strategic intent determines one's effort and persistence in implementing organizational goals and is influenced by concerns about implementation as well as individual expectations (Dooley & Fryxell, 1999; Wooldridge & Floyd, 1990). Future research could investigate how collective or group attitudes, collective or group efficacy, and subjective norms relate to action commitments to visions, strategic intentions, and a range of group- or organizational-level targets.

Commitment to Intangible Individual Targets

Commitment to intangible individual goals encompasses action commitments in which the goal is intangible, implicit, and not shared with other members in a social group. Individuals' commitments to values falls into this category and is discussed as an exemplar.

Exemplar

A value is defined as "a person's stable, internalized belief about a desired state, goal, or behavior of how he or she should act, perceive, or judge environmental stimuli" (Hyde & Weathington, 2006, p.153). Studies investigating moral or ethical values argue that when a moral value is central to individuals' self-identity, individuals tend to have ownership over this value; therefore, a sense of commitment and obligation to utilize it in their action is developed, and it holds them accountable for their actions (Hardy & Carlo, 2005; Weaver & Agle, 2002). Although there is not a generally accepted inclusive list of values, some targets of commitment may include achievement, aesthetic, affiliation, benevolence, conformity, economic, hedonistic, power, security, self-direction, status, stimulation, theoretical, and traditional values (Giberson, Resick, & Dickson, 2005; Olver & Mooradian, 2003).

In his classical research on human values, Rokeach (1973) argued that social norms are a primary influence on individual values. The culture in which one is raised, lives, and works impacts value commitments (Schwartz, 1992), but more important, parents, friends, and salient role models such as teachers and organizational leaders shape subjective norms that are likely to influence action commitments to values. Despite the large volume of research on values, there appear to be few studies examining antecedents other than those related to subjective norms. One exception is recent research arguing that personality influences personal values (e.g., Olver & Mooradian, 2003). Our general model of action commitment would suggest that one's attitude toward a specific value, efficacy in being able to demonstrate behaviors congruent with a value, and the strength of the subjective norms may all influence one's commitment to a value.

Rokeach (1973) contended that individuals have the need to align their actions with values. In particular, values determine whether certain decisions or actions are desirable, and consequently, values are of essential importance in determining what actions to take among many possible options. When the level of commitment to a value is high, such a value tends to be a central and integrated part of one's identity, making the value a more salient and accessible criterion for decisions (Hardy & Carlo, 2005). In other words, the higher the commitment to a particular value, the more likely the value-congruent behavior will be shown. For example, one study demonstrated that higher commitment to the value of conventionality is negatively related to the use of illegal drugs, because such behavior is incongruent with conventional values (Liu & Kaplan, 2001).

Other Targets

The goal-orientation hierarchy proposed by DeShon and Gillespie (2005) includes a variety of intangible individual orientations: self-goals (such as esteem and affiliation goals), principle goals (such as growth, social values, and fairness goals), achievement goals (such as performance-approach and mastery-approach goals), achievement goals (such as performance-approach and mastery-approach goals), and action plan goals (such as impression management and feedback-seeking goals). Although these goals can be tangible if one chooses to make these goals concrete by codifying them into written objectives, procedures, or actions to take, they also can be intangible if one simply holds these as unarticulated beliefs that guide and drive behavior. DeShon and Gillespie's model helps identify potential research areas for action commitments to a variety of intangible individual targets.

One intangible target that has received research attention is learning or mastery goal-orientation (E. S. Elliot & Dweck, 1988). In achievement contexts, individuals can have an orientation toward learning and mastering or toward performing and demonstrating competence (Dweck & Leggett, 1988; VandeWalle, 1997). Different targets in goal orientation result in differences in learning (Cannon-Bowers, Rhodenizer, Salas, & Bowers, 1998), feedback-seeking behavior (VandeWalle & Cummings, 1997), and individual performance (VandeWalle, Brown, Cron, & Slocum, 1999). Related research also has established team goal-orientation as a team characteristic that has influence on team performance (DeShon, Kozlowski, Schmidt, Milner, & Wiechmann, 2004). Generally, the relatively intangible orientation toward mastery or learning relates to greater learning, more requests for feedback, and better performance, due largely to more effective self-regulatory processes such as exerting more effort and setting higher goals (VandeWalle, 2001).

As for antecedents, one's attitude about learning, efficacy in learning effectiveness, and the norms about learning could all influence one's commitment to a learning goal-orientation (VandeWalle, 2001). For instance, if individuals have the attitude that competence is malleable, they are more likely to be intrinsically motivated to learn (A. J. Elliot et al., 2000). Furthermore, situational characteristics, which may influence subjective norms, have been shown to affect one's goal orientation (Button, Mathieu, & Zajac, 1996).

Commitment to Intangible Group/Organizational Targets

When targets exist for a group or organization, and yet these targets are relatively intangible and implicit, commitment to such targets falls into the fourth category of action commitments: commitment to intangible group/organization targets such as a group's or organization's climate or culture. One's commitment to group norms is an exemplar of this category of action commitments.

Exemplar

Group norms are shared beliefs among the team members regarding expected social behaviors (Vroom, 1969). They are not explicitly codified as written policies or rules, but they are a common, shared mentality among the team members. Group norm commitment is different from the mere existence of group norms. For example, members of a group may be aware of the conventional and agreed-upon behavioral patterns in the group, but they individually choose to conform or not to conform to this norm. Thus, group norm commitment is an individual-level commitment to a group-level norm and can be distinguished from the level of agreement within the group. As an example, Ehrhart and Naumann (2004) propose that the greater the dispersion in group members' perception and agreement with the OCB norm, the less likely that the group OCB norm would lead to individual OCB. In this example, the level of dispersion of agreement within the group is the notion of group norm strength, whereas any one individual's agreement with the norm is his or her group norm commitment.

Based on our proposed general model of action commitment, group norms commitment would be impacted by antecedents associated with attitudes toward the norms, efficacy in carrying out the norms, and social influences (i.e., subjective norms) related to norms. Attitudes toward a group norm are likely influenced by congruence with an individual's values, whereas an individual's efficacy is likely related to the extent to which one feels confident performing behaviors associated with group norms (Tasa, Taggar, & Seijts, 2007). An important social antecedent to group norms is likely to be the social cohesion of the group. Cohesion has been defined as the group members' tendency to stay with the group or a larger social entity (Bollen & Hoyle, 1990; Dion, 2000), which results primarily from the interpersonal attraction of group members (Mullen & Copper, 1994). Bollen and Hoyle (1990) contended that an individual group member's perception of cohesion captures the role the group plays in that member's life, and therefore it influences other subjective phenomena (such as group norms commitment).

Although norms do not always boost group performance, particularly when the agreed-upon group behaviors are counterproductive (Gersick & Hackman, 1990), commitment to group norms that are functional tend to improve group effectiveness because they facilitate group survival, provide regularity, help the group avoid inadequate interpersonal problems, and signify the group's identity (Feldman, 1984). Taggar and Ellis (2007), for example, found that collaborative problem-solving norms are positively related to nondiscretionary behaviors such as group problem-solving, communication, and planning/task coordination. Furthermore, we expect that group norm commitment will impact individual group member behavior. Given individual group norm commitment and individual behavior operate at the same level, group norm commitment is likely to be a better predictor of individual performance than group norm strength. Nonetheless, the relative effects of variables from multiple levels on commitment are important and discussed in chapter 12.

Other Targets

When the focus moves from formal organizational policies or targets to informal practices, the targets of action commitments become less tangible and more implicit, suggesting that it falls in the category of group- or organization-level intangible targets. As this relates to ethics, informal ethical principles are referred to as "the subtle messages that are received regarding ethical norms, or what is 'really' appropriate from an ethical perspective" (Tenbrunsel et al. [2003], p. 291). Victor and Cullen (1988) describe these prevailing assumptions about ethics as the organization's ethical climate. The ethical climate of the work context is largely shaped by organizational leaders (Treviño, Hartman, & Brown, 2000). This informal understanding about ethics may be more potent than formal codes in shaping behavior because it reflects what leaders actually do instead of what they say is important (Tenbrunsel et al., 2003).

A broader implicit organizational target of action commitment is organizational culture. Organizational culture is defined as "a pattern of shared basic assumptions that was learned by a group as it solved its problems of external adaptation and internal integration, that has worked well enough to be considered valid, and therefore, to be taught to new members as the correct way to perceive, think, and feel in relation to those problems" (Schein, 2004, p.17). Culture usually reflects the founders' or managements' values that later on are transformed and transmitted into shared values and assumptions among employees in the organization (Schein, 2004). These unwritten values and beliefs can be powerful influences that guide and constrain behavior. Nonetheless, an individual's commitment to this organizational culture should influence whether his or her behaviors are consistent with what is implied by the organization's culture.

Our general model of action commitment suggests that individuals' attitudes toward the culture the organization embraces, individuals' efficacy in their ability to perform up to organizational culture expectations, and the existence of subjective norms endorsing the culture are likely to influence their commitment to their organizational culture. For example, individuals who enjoy and believe in the value of innovation may have a higher commitment to an innovative organization culture, which subsequently results in their generation of creative ideas and demonstration of exploratory behaviors. In addition, when individuals believe that they can demonstrate the level of innovation portrayed by the innovative culture, they are likely to be more committed to such a culture. Furthermore, the endorsement by a transformational leader or a cohesive group also will likely enhance employees' commitment to the culture of innovation through such leaders' idealized influence and role modeling for innovation, as well as the group members' mutual influence among each other.

Organizational culture influences the behavior of individuals within an organization (Schein, 2004). Although we are not aware of studies that specifically examine individuals' organizational culture commitment, a related area of research is culture strength (Schneider, Salvaggio, & Subirats, 2002). Generally, the stronger the culture strength, the greater its impact on behavior. Because culture strength reflects the dispersion of individuals perceptions of culture, the degree to which individuals' commit to the organizational culture may moderate the effect culture strength has on individual behavior. This suggests that future research investigating the effects of culture strength would benefit from considering the multilevel interplay of organizational culture commitment and culture strength.

Future Research

In many ways, this chapter has covered new ground. First, we introduced action commitments as a set of commitments with action as their focus. An action commitment was defined as an attachment or bond to an action. The bond to action can be to a particular and identifiable action or to the actions necessary to achieve a particular target. Before reviewing research on action commitments, we also proposed a general model for discussing current and future research related to the antecedents and outcomes of action commitments. Finally, we proposed categories of action commitments and reviewed research related to an exemplar of each category as well as other examples that require additional research. In this section we propose future research in two areas. In the first area, we discuss aspects of the general model that were not discussed sufficiently earlier and are in need of further attention. In the second area, we discuss temporal issues related to action commitments that might stimulate future research.

Extensions to the General Model of Action Commitments

Although the antecedents of attitudes (attractiveness), efficacy (expectancy, perceived behavioral control), and subjective norms all relate, studies have demonstrated that each antecedent explains unique variance in intentions, but the relative strength of each differs across individuals (Ajzen, 2002). For example, when a person's attitude toward an action differs from what he or she expects others' attitudes to be, the perceived expectations of others can be a stronger influence on behavioral intentions than personal attitudes. Research from the theory of planned behavior indicates that this occurs more so with women than men (Grogan, Bell, & Conner, 1997), more so with people from collectivist cultures than those from individualist cultures (Abrams, Ando, & Hinkle, 1998; Conner & Heywood-Everett, 1998), and more so with those who strongly identify with a group than those who do not (Terry & Hogg, 1996). Similarly, we expect that the relative strength of each antecedent in affecting action commitment is likely to vary across individuals and cultures, but future research is needed to test this assertion.

In our general model of action commitments, we proposed that action commitment was both a conscious and an unconscious bond to an action or a series of actions necessary to achieve a target. Furthermore, we proposed a set of unconscious antecedents to action commitment. We based our assertions on the emerging research on unconscious activation of goals (Bargh et al., 2001; Stajkovic et al., 2006) and the role of unconscious emotions in influencing behavior (Winkielman & Berridge, 2001). Nonetheless, due to the limited research in this area, we did not discuss the potential unconscious antecedents in our review of categories of action commitments. Echoing Locke and Latham's (2004) call to investigate unconscious factors in motivation, we encourage future research to further study the effect of unconscious emotion on action commitments.

Action Commitments Over Time

With a few notable exceptions (Jansen, 2004; Neubert & Cady, 2001), very little research on action commitments has investigated commitment over time. Paralleling decision-making research on adoption and progress decisions (Beach, 1998), we propose that action commitments can be expressed as moving through phases that can be delineated as an adoption phase and then sequential progress phases. Action commitment during the adoption phase reflects initial acceptance of the goal, while action commitment during progress phases reflects ongoing cost-benefit and efficacy assessments related to continuing commitment during the implementation of the goal. Furthermore, additional research on escalation of commitment provides insight into the dynamics of commitment during phases.

Adoption and Progress Decisions

The initial adoption decision or action commitment is often influenced by relatively naïve personal answers to questions such as, "Do I like this goal or change?" and "Will my actions be successful?" Furthermore, initial commitment is influenced by the persuasion tactics involved in announcing the goal or change (Jansen, 2004; Locke, Latham, & Erez, 1988). In contrast, action commitment during progress phases is a consideration of answers to questions related to "How is it going?" and "How am I doing?"—answers that are informed by feedback and experience (Jansen, 2004; Klein, 1989). Furthermore, Jansen (2004) described differences in change momentum and commitment as fluctuating over time based on attentional processing and social information. In the process of persisting in action it is common for an individual's cognitive attention to the goal or change to wane in response to other attention-demanding events (Kanfer & Ackerman, 1989). Moreover, as actions are taken to pursue a goal or support a change, individuals take cues from the social environment that impact their attitudes (Salancik & Pfeffer, 1978). Whereas some of the cues are informal, others take the form of direct feedback that, according to control theory, regulates commitment and effort (Klein, 1989).

Evidence for differences in the antecedents of action commitment across phases is apparent in Neubert and Cady's (2001) longitudinal assessment of change commitment, in which some personal variables initially had strong associations with change commitment, but with progress in the change, the influence of personal variables decreased, whereas a situational variable (reward systems) became a significant influence on change commitment. In total, research on action commitment over time is limited. One exception is research on escalation of commitment in the decision-making literature.

Escalation of Commitment

Staw's (1976, 1997) seminal work describes how individuals unwisely continue in a course of action despite failure or deteriorating conditions. Defying the logic of rational utility estimates, escalation typically involves inappropriately considering prior investments, refusing to acknowledge evidence of the likelihood of unfavorable outcomes, or minimizing cognitive dissonance by sticking to earlier decisions (Brockner, 1992; McNamara, Moon, & Bromiley, 2002). Furthermore, individuals are more likely to escalate commitment in the face of negative consequences such as losing face or incurring punishment (McNamara et al., 2002) when they were the primary initiator of the action (Staw, 1976) and when alternative options are limited (Zardkoohi, 2004). Greer and Stephens (2001) also demonstrated that Mexican decision makers exhibit significantly greater escalation of commitment in comparison with U.S. decision makers. The difference was explained as related to the cultural tendency of Mexican decision makers to use more impression management to avoid perceptions of failure and lose face. Although escalation of commitment has been used to explain a variety of decisions from government policies to individual decisions, direct application to understanding action commitments over time has been limited.

During the adoption phase, personal characteristics such as self-efficacy and personality have been shown to influence goal and action commitments (Klein et al., 1999; Neubert & Cady, 2001). Whereas self-efficacy is a dynamic construct that changes based on direct and vicarious experience (Bandura, 1986), personality is stable and relatively unaffected by situational conditions (e.g., Mount & Barrick, 1995). As such, the influence of personality may remain constant over all phases, whereas self-efficacy may decrease through experiencing difficulties or decreased likelihood of goal achievement, and thereby reduce commitment over time.

Research on the links between personality and escalation of commitment shows that this effect depends on the trait and facet investigated (Moon, 2001). Specifically, the conscientiousness facet of achievement-striving was positively related to escalation of commitment, while the facet of duty was negatively related to escalation, perhaps due to its other-centered orientation (Moon, 2001). The achievement-escalation relationship also was found in studies of Type A personalities (Schaubroeck & Williams, 1993). Investigating facets of neuroticism found that anxiety was positively related to escalation, whereas depression was negatively related to escalation (Moon, Hollenbeck, Humphrey, & Maue, 2003). When an individual is personally responsible for the initial decision, the negative relationship between neuroticism and escalation of commitment has been described as resulting from high-neurotic individuals seeking ways to withdraw from stressful situations (Wong, Yik, & Kwong, 2006).

A situational recipe for escalation of commitment is the "tragedy of commons," where personal responsibility in the form of costs is diffused across a group or organization, while the benefits of the action accrue to a specific decision maker (Staw & Ross, 1987; Zardkoohi, 2004). A manager who sets stretch-goals for a department that requires workers to increase their hours and pace, or a manager who initiates major changes to "right size" an organization, may be examples of the tragedy of commons at work. In such cases, their action commitments may be subject to escalation because these managers may benefit greatly by their decisions, but the costs of the decision are diffused across many employees. In contrast, escalation is not likely for those employees who, as a result of managers' decisions, endure the costs and experience minimal benefits from working longer hours or with fewer colleagues.

Another area in which escalation may influence action commitments over time is ethics. Street, Robertson, and Geiger (1997) have argued that as commitment escalates over time, the likelihood of unethical behavior also increases. At Fortune 500 companies, escalation of commitment by the management team was significantly associated with ethical violations (Armstrong, Williams, & Barrett, 2004). In a laboratory simulation, the magnitude of the escalation situation—as measured by the discrepancy between expectations and performance—was associated with unethical behavior (M. Street & V. L. Street, 2006). Also in a laboratory context, Schweitzer, Ordonez, and Douma (2004) found that participants with specific and difficult unmet goals were more likely than participants with "do your best" goals to be unethical, although in their situation unethical behavior was more evident when individuals fell just short of achieving their goal.

Although only briefly reviewed here (see Staw, 1997, for a more comprehensive review), escalation of commitment theory and research offers alternative explanations for why individuals may indicate high levels of action commitment during progress phases despite difficulties or failures in the pursuit of a target. Nonetheless, these explanations should be considered with caution when attempting to explain organizational action commitments during progress phases. Much of the research on escalation of commitment has occurred in laboratory settings where participants had little or nothing at stake in acting out their commitments (Zardkoohi, 2004). Alternatively, organizations have built-in checks and monitoring processes that attenuate escalation of commitment (McNamara et al., 2002). As such, escalation of commitment and its associated personal and situational antecedents should be considered in longitudinal field studies. Furthermore, whereas the assertion that escalation should be avoided is common to escalation of commitment research, future research should investigate how to strengthen commitment over time, particularly as it relates to persisting during difficult or challenging times in the progress phase of pursuing a target.

Conclusion

This chapter reviewed existing research and future research opportunities related to action commitments to both intangible and tangible targets, with a focus on individual as well as group- and organization-level targets. In comparison to the foci of commitment discussed in previous chapters, there appears to be a greater need for advances in fundamental research and theory related to action commitments. With the exception of the goal commitment literature, which is well established, there is a great deal yet to be learned about change commitments and other group-/organizational-level targets and commitment to intangible targets at both the individual and group/organizational levels. Furthermore, research should explore how all action commitments change over time.

Action commitments research also is in need of the infusion of additional theory to supplement existing frameworks for antecedents and outcomes and to stimulate new directions. In this chapter, a model was presented for identifying and explaining antecedents that was based largely on the theory of planned behavior (Ajzen, 1991). In doing so, the antecedent of subjective norms was proposed as a potential source of action commitments, which, in turn, also raised the issue of multilevel influences on individual action commitment. This suggests the need for more multilevel theory to guide future research on action commitments.

Theoretical extensions of existing research coupled with rigorous empirical tests of theory in laboratory and field settings have great utility for practitioners. As noted in the introduction of this chapter, action commitments are fundamentally related to getting things done in organizations and achieving competitive advantage. As more research is brought to bear on understanding the nature of action commitments, their antecedents, and how they change over time, this research is likely to offer many practical benefits for managers in organizations. Although most practitioners readily agree with the necessity of gaining the commitment of employees to goals, values, changes, policies, and visions, fewer are aware of and apply the research findings related to these action commitments. Perhaps with the exception of the research on goal commitment, where some application is apparent, advances in action commitment research offer great promise for practical prescriptions that improve learning, persistence, and performance.

References

Abrams, D., Ando, K., & Hinkle, S. (1998). Psychological attachment to the group: Cross-cultural differences in organizational identification and subjective norms as predictors of workers' turnover intentions. *Personality and Social Psychological Bulletin, 24,* 1027–1039.

Ajzen, I. (1991). The theory of planned behavior. *Organizational Behavior and Human Decision Processes, 50,* 179–211.

Ajzen, I. (2002). Percieved behavioral control, self-efficacy, locus of control, and the theory of planned behavior. *Journal of Applied Social Psychology, 32*(4), 665–683.

Ajzen, I., & Fishbein, M. (1980). *Understanding attitudes and predicting social behavior.* Englewood Cliffs, NJ: Prentice Hall.

Allen, N. J., & Meyer, J. P. (1996). Affective, continuance, and normative commitment to the organization: An examination of construct validity. *Journal of Vocational Behavior, 49,* 252–276.

Armstrong, R. W., Williams, R. J., & Barrett, J. D. (2004). The impact of banality, risky shift and escalating commitment on ethical decision making. *Journal of Business Ethics, 53,* 365–370.

Aube, C., & Rousseau, V. (2005). Team goal commitment and team effectiveness: The role of task interdependence and supportive behaviors. *Group Dynamics: Theory, Research, and Practice, 9*(3), 189–204.

Bandura, A. (1977). Toward a unifying theory of behavioral change. *Psychological Review, 84,* 191–215.

Bandura, A. (1986). *Social foundations of thought and action: A social cognitive theory.* Englewood Cliffs, NJ: Prentice Hall.

Bargh, J., Gollwitzer, P. M., Lee-Chai, A., Barndollar, K., & Trötschel, R. (2001). The automated will: Nonconscious activation and pursuit of behavioral goals. *Journal of Personality and Social Psychology, 81*(6), 1014–1027.

Barrick, M. R., Mount, M. K., & Strauss, J. P. (1993). Conscientiousness and performance of sales representatives: Test of the mediating effects of goal setting. *Journal of Applied Psychology, 78,* 715–722.

Beach, L. (1998). *Image theory: Theoretical and empirical foundations.* Mahwah, NJ: Lawrence Erlbaum Associates.

Becker, H. S. (1960). Notes on the concept of commitment. *American Journal of Sociology, 66*(1), 32–40.

Becker, T. E., Randall, D. M., & Riegel, C. D. (1995). The multidimensional view of commitment and the theory of reasoned action: A comparative evaluation. *Journal of Management, 21,* 617–638.

Bollen, K. A., & Hoyle, R. H. (1990). Perceived cohesion: A conceptual and empirical examination. *Social Forces, 69*(2), 479–504.

Brockner, J. (1992). The escalation of commitment to a failing course of action: Toward theoretical progress. *Academy of Management Review, 17*(1), 39–61.

Brockner, J., & Higgins, E. T. (2001). Regulatory focus theory: Implications for the study of emotions at work. *Organizational Behavior and Human Decision Processes, 86*(1), 35–66.

Button, S. B., Mathieu, J. E., & Zajac, D. M. (1996). Goal orientation in organizational research: A conceptual and empirical foundation. *Organizational Behavior and Human Decision Processes, 67,* 26–48.

Cady, S. H., Grey-Boyd, D., & Neubert, M. J. (2001). Multilevel performance probability: A meta-analytic integration of expectancy and self-efficacy. *Psychological Reports, 88,* 1077–1090.

Cannon-Bowers, J. A., Rhodenizer, L., Salas, E., & Bowers, C. A. (1998). A framework for understanding pre-practice conditions and their impact on learning. *Personnel Psychology, 51,* 291–320.

Clore, G. L., Gasper, K., & Garvin, E. (2001). Affect as information. In J. P. Forgas (Ed.), *Handbook of affect and social cognition* (pp. 121–144). Mahwah, NJ: Lawrence Erlbaum Associates.

Cohen, A. (2003). *Multiple commitments in the workplace: An integrative approach.* Mahwah, NJ: Lawrence Erlbaum Associates.

Conner, M., & Heywood-Everett, S. (1998). Addressing mental health problems with the theory of planned behaviour. *Psychology, Health & Medicine, 3,* 87–95.

Cunningham, G. B. (2006). The relationships among commitment to change, coping with change, and turnover intentions. *European Journal of Work and Organizational Psychology, 15*(1), 29–45.

Davis, F. (1989). Perceived usefulness, perceived ease of use, and user acceptance of information technology. *MIS Quarterly, 13,* 318–341.

Davis, F., Bagozzi, R., & Warshaw, P. (1989). User acceptance of computer technology: A comparison of two theoretical models. *Management Science, 35,* 982–1003.

Davis, F. D., & Warshaw, P. R. (1992). What do intention scales measure? *The Journal of General Psychology, 119*(4), 391–407.

DeShon, R. P., & Gillespie, J. Z. (2005). A motivated action theory account of goal orientation. *Journal of Applied Psychology, 90*(6), 1096–1127.

DeShon, R. P., Kozlowski, S. W. J., Schmidt, A. M., Milner, K. R., & Wiechmann, D. (2004). A multiple-goal, multilevel model of feedback effects on the regulation of individual and team performance. *Journal of Applied Psychology, 89,* 1035–1056.

Diefendorff, J. M., & Gosserand, R. H. (2003). Understanding the emotional labor process: A control theory perspective. *Journal of Organizational Behavior, 24,* 945–959.

Dion, K. L. (2000). Group cohesion: From "field of forces" to multidimensional construct. *Group Dynamics, 4*(1), 7–26.

Dooley, R. S., & Fryxell, G. E. (1999). Attaining decision quality and commitment from dissent: The moderating effects of loyalty and competence in strategic decision-making teams. *Academy of Management Journal, 42*(4), 389–402.

Dweck, C. S., & Leggett, E. L. (1988). A social-cognitive approach to motivation and personality. *Psychological Review, 95,* 256–273.

Ehrhart, M. G., & Naumann, S. E. (2004). Organizational citizenship behavior in work groups: A group norms approach. *Journal of Applied Psychology, 89*(6), 960–974.

Elliot, A. J., Faler, J., McGregor, H. A., Campbell, W. K., Sedikides, C., & Harackiewicz, J. M. (2000). Competence valuation as a strategic intrinsic motivation process. *Personality and Social Psychology Bulletin, 26,* 780–794.

Elliot, E. S., & Dweck, C. S. (1988). Goals: An approach to motivation and achievement. *Journal of Personality and Social Psychology, 54,* 5–12.

Fedor, D. B., Caldwell, S., & Herold, D. M. (2006). The effects of organizational changes on employee commitment: A multilevel investigation. *Personnel Psychology, 59,* 1–29.

Feldman, D. C. (1984). The development and enforcement of group norms. *Academy of Management Review, 9,* 47–53.

Fishbein, M., & Ajzen, I. (1975). *Beliefs, attitudes, intention, and behavior.* Reading, MA: Addison-Wesley.

Fishbein, M., & Stasson, M. (1990). The role of desires, self-predictions, and perceived control in the prediction of training session attendance. *The Journal of Applied Social Psychology, 20,* 173–198.

Ford, J. K., Weissbein, D. A., & Plamondon, K. E. (2003). Distinguishing organizational from strategy commitment: Linking officers' commitment to community policing to job behaviors and satisfaction. *Justice Quarterly, 20,* 159–185.

Forgas, J. P. (2001). Affect, cognition, and interpersonal behavior: The mediating role of processing strategies. In J. P. Forgas (Ed.), *Handbook of affect and social cognition* (pp. 293–318). Mahwah, NJ: Lawrence Erlbaum Associates.

Gersick, C. J. G., & Hackman, J. R. (1990). Habitual routines in task-performing groups. *Organizational Behavior and Human Decision Processes, 47,* 65–97.

Giberson, T. R., Resick, C. J., & Dickson, M. W. (2005). Embedding leader characteristics: An examination of homogeneity of personality and values in organizations. *Journal of Applied Psychology, 90*(5), 1002–1010.

Gist, M. (1989). The influence of training method on self-efficacy and idea generation among managers. *Personnel Psychology, 42,* 787–805.

Gist, M. E., & Mitchell, T. R. (1992). Self-efficacy: A theoretical analysis of its determinants and malleability. *Academy of Management Review, 17,* 183–211.

Gosserand, R. H., & Diefendorff, J. M. (2005). Emotional display rules and emotional labor: The moderating role of commitment. *Journal of Applied Psychology, 90*(6), 1256–1264.

Greer, C. R., & Stephens, G. K. (2001). Escalation of commitment: A comparison of differences between Mexican and U.S. decision-makers. *Journal of Management, 27,* 51–78.

Grogan, S. C., Bell. R., & Conner, M. (1997). Eating sweet snacks: Gender differences in attitudes and behaviour. *Appetite, 28,* 19–31.

Guthrie, J. P., & Hollensbe, E. C. (2004). Group incentives and performance: A study of spontaneous goal setting, goal choice and commitment. *Journal of Management, 30*(2), 263–284.

Hamel, G., & Prahalad, C. K. (1989). Strategic intent. *Harvard Business Review, 67*(3), 63–76.

Hardy, S. A., & Carlo, G. (2005). Identity as a source of moral motivation. *Human Development, 48,* 232–256.

Herscovitch, L., & Meyer, J. P. (2002). Commitment to organizational change: Extension of a three-component model. *Journal of Applied Psychology, 87*(3), 474–487.

Higgins, E. T. (1997). Beyond pleasure and pain. *American Psychologist, 52*(12), 1280–1300.

Higgins, E. T. (1998). Promotion and prevention regulatory focus as a motivational principle. *Advances in Experimental Social Psychology, 30,* 1–41.

Hofmann, D. A., & Morgeson, F. P. (1999). Safety-related behavior as a social exchange: The role of perceived organizational support and leader-member exchange. *Journal of Applied Psychology, 84*(2), 286–296.

Hofmann, D. A., & Stetzer, A. (1996). A cross-level investigation of factors influencing unsafe behaviors and accidents. *Personnel Psychology, 49*(2), 307–339.

Hollenbeck, J. R., & Klein, H. J. (1987). Goal commitment and the goal-setting process: Problems, prospects, and proposals for future research. *Journal of Applied Psychology, 72,* 212–220.

Hollenbeck, J. R., Klein, H. J., O'Leary, A. M., & Wright, P. M. (1989). Investigation of the construct validity of a self-report measure of goal commitment. *Journal of Applied Psychology, 74,* 951–956.

Hollenbeck, J. R., Williams, C. R., & Klein, H. J. (1989). An empirical examination of the antecedents of commitment to difficult goals. *Journal of Applied Psychology, 74,* 18–23.

Hyatt, D. E., & Ruddy, T. M. (1997). An examination of the relationship between work group characteristics and performance: Once more into the breech. *Personal Psychology, 50,* 553–585.

Hyde, R. E., & Weathington, B. L. (2006). The congruence of personal life values and work attitudes. *Genetic, Social, and General Psychology Monographs, 132*(2), 151–190.

Jaccard, J., & King, G. (1977). A probabilistic model of the relationship between beliefs and behavioral intentions. *Human Communication Research, 3,* 332–342.

Jansen, K. (2004). From persistence to pursuit: A longitudinal examination of momentum during the early stages of strategic change. *Organizational Science, 15*(3), 276–294.

Judge, T. A., Thoresen, C. J., Pucik, V., & Welbourne, T. M. (1999). Managerial coping with organizational change: A dispositional perspective. *Journal of Applied Psychology, 84*(1), 107–122.

Kanfer, R., & Ackerman, P. L. (1989). Motivation and cognitive abilities: An integrative/aptitude-treatment interaction approach to skill acquisition. *Journal of Applied Psychology, 74*(4), 657–690.

Kark, R., & Van Dijk, D. (2007). Motivation to lead, motivation to follow: The role of the self-regulatory focus in leadership processes. *Academy of Management Review, 32,* 500–528.

Kavanagh, M. H., & Ashkanasy, N. M. (2006). The impact of leadership and change management strategy on organizational culture and individual acceptance of change during a merger. *British Journal of Management, 17,* S81–S103.

Kiesler, C. (1971). *The psychology of commitment.* New York: Academic Press.

Kiesler, C. A., & Sakamura, J. (1966). A test of a model for commitment. *Journal of Personality and Social Psychology, 3,* 349–353.

Klein, H. J. (1989). An integrated control theory model of work motivation. *Academy of Management Review, 14*(2), 150–172.

Klein, H. J. (1991). Further evidence on the relationship between goal setting and expectancy theories. *Organizational Behavior and Human Decision Processes, 49*(2), 230–257.

Klein, H. J., Brinsfield, C. T., & Molloy, J. C. (2006). *Understanding workplace commitments independent of antecedents, foci, rationales, and consequences.* Paper presented at the Academy of Management Annual Meeting, Atlanta, GA.

Klein, H. J., & Lee, S. (2006). The effects of personality on learning: The mediating role of goal setting. *Human Performance, 19*(1), 43–66.

Klein, H. J., Wesson, M. J., Hollenbeck, J. R., & Alge, B. J. (1999). Goal commitment and the goal setting process: Conceptual clarification and empirical synthesis. *Journal of Applied Psychology, 84,* 885–896.

Klein, H. J., Wesson, M. J., Hollenbeck, J. R., Wright, P. M., & DeShon, R. P. (2001). The assessment of goal commitment: A measurement model meta-analysis. *Organizational Behavior and Human Decision Processes, 85,* 32–55.

Lado, A. A., & Wilson, M. C. (1994). Human resource systems and sustained competitive advantage: A competency-based perspective. *Academy of Management Review, 19,* 699–727.

Lazarus, R. S. (1991). *Emotion and adaptation*. New York: Oxford University Press.

Li, A., & Butler, A. B. (2004). The effects of participation in goal setting and goal rationales on goal commitment: An exploration of justice mediators. *Journal of Business and Psychology, 19*(1), 37–51.

Liu, X., & Kaplan, H. B. (2001). Role strain and illicit drug use: The moderating influence of commitment to conventional values. *Journal of Drug Issues, 31*(4), 833–856.

Locke, E. A., Bryan, J. F., & Kendall, L. M. (1968). Goals and intentions as mediator of the effects of monetary incentives on behavior. *Journal of Applied Psychology, 52,* 104–121.

Locke, E. A., & Latham, G. P. (1990). *A theory of goal setting and task performance.* Englewood Cliffs, NJ: Prentice Hall.

Locke, E. A., & Latham, G. P. (2002). Building a practically useful theory of goal setting and task motivation. *American Psychologist, 57*(9), 705–717.

Locke, E. A., & Latham, G. P. (2004). What should we do about motivation theory? Six recommendations for the twenty-first century. *Academy of Management Review, 29,* 388–403.

Locke, E. A., & Latham, G. P. (2006). New directions in goal-setting theory. *Current Directions in Psychological Science, 15*(5), 265–268.

Locke, E. A., Latham, G. P., & Erez, M. (1988). The determinants of goal commitment. *Academy of Management Review, 13,* 23–39.

Mayer, R. C., & Schoorman, F. D. (1992). Predicting participation and production outcomes through a two-dimensional model of organizational commitment. *Academy of Management Journal, 35,* 671–684.

McNamara, G., Moon, H., & Bromiley, P. (2002). Banking on commitment: Intended and unintended consequences of an organization's attempt to attenuate irrational commitment. *Academy of Management Journal, 45,* 443–452.

Meyer, J. P., & Allen, N. J. (1991). A three-component conceptualization of organizational commitment. *Human Resource Management Review, 1,* 61–89.

Meyer, J. P., & Allen, N. J. (1997). *Commitment in the workplace*. Thousand Oaks, CA: Sage.

Meyer, J. P., Becker, E., & Vandenberghe, C. (2004). Employee commitment and motivation: A conceptual analysis and integrative model. *Journal of Applied Psychology. 89*(6), 991–1007.

Meyer, J. P., & Herscovitch, L. (2001). Toward a general model of commitment. *Human Resource Management Review, 11,* 299–326.

Mintzberg, H. (1990). The design school: Reconsidering the basic premises of strategic management. *Strategic Management Journal, 11,* 171–195.

Moon, H. (2001). The two faces of conscientiousness: Duty and achievement striving in escalation of commitment dilemmas. *Journal of Applied Psychology, 86*(3), 533–540.

Moon, H., Hollenbeck, J. R., Humphrey, S. E., & Maue, B. (2003). The tripartite model of neuroticism and the suppression of depression and anxiety within an escalation of commitment dilemma. *Journal of Personality, 7*(3), 347–368.

Morris, M., & Venkatesh, V. (2000). Age differences in technology adoption decisions: Implications for a changing work force. *Personnel Psychology, 53,* 375–394.

Mount, M. K., & Barrick, M. R. (1995). The Big Five personality dimensions: Implications for research and practice in human resource management. *Research in Personnel and Human Resources Management, 13,* 153–200.

Mullen, B., & Copper, C. (1994). The relation between group cohesiveness and performance: An integration. *Psychological Bulletin, 115*(2), 210–227.

Mulvey, P. W., & Klein, H. J. (1998). The impact of perceived loafing and collective efficacy in group goal processes and group performance. *Organizational Behavior and Human Decision Processes, 74*(1), 62–87.

Neubert, M. J. (1996). Commitment to a program of continuous quality improvement. *Academy of Management Meetings,* Cincinnati. OH.

Neubert, M. J., & Cady, S. (2001). Program commitment: A multi-study longitudinal field investigation. *Personnel Psychology, 54,* 421–448.

Neubert, M. J., Wong, D., Hartley, J., & Hofmann, D. (2002). Program commitment in strategy implementation. *Academy of Management Meetings,* Denver, CO.

Neubert, M. J., & Wu, C. (2005). Commitment to change in China. *Conference on Commitment,* Columbus, OH.

Nielsen, K. J., Carstensen, O., & Rasmussen, K. (2006). The prevention of occupational injuries in two industrial plants using an incident reporting scheme. *Journal of Safety Research, 37*(5), 479–486.

Olver, J. M., & Mooradian, T. A. (2003). Personality traits and personal values: A conceptual and empirical integration. *Personality and Individual Differences, 35*(1), 109–125.

O'Reilly, C. A., & Pfeffer, J. (2000). Unlocking the hidden value in organizations. *Employment Relations Today, 27,* 63–80.

Phillips, J. M., & Gully, S. M. (1997). Role of goal orientation, ability, need for achievement, and locus of control in the self-efficacy and goal-setting process. *Journal of Applied Psychology, 82,* 792–802.

Piccolo, R., & Colquitt, J. (2006). Transformational leadership and job behaviors: The mediating role of core job characteristics. *Academy of Management Journal, 49*(2), 327–340.

Podsakoff, P. M., MacKenzie, S. B., Paine, J. B., & Bachrach, D. G. (2000). Organizational citizenship behaviors: A critical review of the theoretical and empirical literature and suggestions for future research. *Journal of Management, 26,* 513–563.

Reichers, A. E. (1985). A review and reconceptualization of organizational commitment. *Academy of Management Review, 10,* 465–476.

Reichers, A. E., Wanous, J. P., & Austin, J. T. (1997). Understanding and managing cynicism about organizational change. *Academy of Management Executive, 11,* 48–59.

Renn, R. W. (2003). Moderation by goal commitment of the feedback-performance relationship: Theoretical explanation and preliminary study. *Human Resource Management Review, 13,* 561–580.

Riedel, J. A., Nebeker, D. M., & Cooper, B. L. (1988). The influence of monetary incentives on goal choice, goal commitment, and task performance. *Organizational Behavior and Human Decision Processes, 42*(2), 155–180.

Rokeach, M. (1973). *The nature of human values.* New York: Free Press.

Salancik, G. R. (1977). Commitment is too easy! *Organizational Dynamics, 6,* 62–80.

Salancik, G. R., & Pfeffer, J. (1978). A social information processing approach to job attitudes and task design. *Administrative Science Quarterly, 23*(2), 224–253.

Schaubroeck, J., & Williams, S. (1993). Type A behavior pattern and escalating commitment. *Journal of Applied Psychology, 78,* 862–867.

Schein, E. H. (2004). *Organizational culture and leadership* (3rd ed.). San Francisco: Jossey-Bass.

Schneider, B., Salvaggio, A. N., & Subirats, M. (2002). Climate strength: A new direction for climate research. *Journal of Applied Psychology, 87*(2), 220–229.

Scholl, R. W. (1981). Differentiating commitment from expectancy as a motivating force. *Academy of Management Review, 6,* 589–599.

Schwartz, S. H. (1992). Universals in the content and structure of values: Theoretical advances and empirical tests in 20 countries. In M. P. Zanna (Ed.), *Advances in experimental social psychology, Vol. 25* (pp. 1–65). San Diego, CA: Academic Press.

Schweitzer, M. E., Ordonez, L., & Douma, B. (2004). Goal setting as a motivator for unethical behavior. *Academy of Management Journal, 47,* 422–432.

Seijts, G. H., & Latham, G. P. (2001). The effect of distal learning, outcome, and proximal goals on a moderately complex task. *Journal of Organizational Behavior, 22*(3), 291–307.

Sommers, S., & Scioli, A. (1986). Emotional range and value orientation: Toward a cognitive view of emotionality. *Journal of Personality and Social Psychology, 51*(2), 417–422.

Stajkovic, A. D., Locke, E. A., & Blair, E. S. (2006). A first examination of the relationships between primed subconscious goals, assigned conscious goals, and task performance. *Journal of Applied Psychology, 91*(5),1172–1180.

Staw, B. M. (1976). Keep deep in the big muddy: A study of escalating commitment to a chosen course of action. *Organizational Behavior and Human Performance 16,* 27–44.

Staw, B. M. (1997). The escalation of commitment: An update and appraisal. *Organizational Decision Making,* 191–215.

Staw, B. M, & Ross, J. (1987). Behavior in escalation situations: Antecedents, prototypes, and solutions. *Research in Organizational Behavior, 9,* 39–78.

Street, M., & Street, V. L. (2006). The effects of escalating commitment on ethical decision-making. *Journal of Business Ethics, 64,* 343–356.

Street, M. D., Robertson, C., & Geiger, S. (1997). Ethical decision making: The effect of escalating commitment. *Journal of Business Ethics, 16,* 1153–1161.

Sue-Chan, C., & Ong, M. (2002). Goal assignment and performance: Assessing the mediating roles of goal commitment and self-efficacy and the moderating role of power distance. *Organizational Behavior and Human Processes, 89,* 1140–1161.

Taggar, S., & Ellis, R. (2007). The role of leaders in shaping formal team norms. *Leadership Quarterly, 18,* 105–120.

Tasa, K., Taggar, S., & Seijts, G. H. (2007). The development of collective efficacy in teams: A multilevel and longitudinal perspective. *Journal of Applied Psychology, 92*(1), 17–27.

Tenbrunsel, A. E., Smith-Crowe, K., & Umphress, E. E. (2003). Building houses on rocks: The role of the ethical infrastructure in organizations. *Social Justice Research, 16*(3), 285–307.

Terry, D. J., & Hogg, M. A. (1996). Group norms and the attitude-behavior relationship: A role for group identification. *Personality and Social Psychology Bulletin, 22*, 776–793.

Thoms, P., & Greenberger, D. B. (1995). Training business leaders to create positive organizational visions of the future: Is it successful? *Academy of Management Journal, 38*(1), 212–216.

Tolman, E. C. (1932). *Purposive behavior in animals and men.* New York: Appleton-Century Crofts.

Treviño, L. K., Hartman, L. P., & Brown, M. (2000). Moral person and moral manager: How executives develop a reputation for ethical leadership. *California Management Review, 42*, 128–142.

Treviño, L. K., Weaver, G. R., & Reynolds, S. J. (2006). Behavioral ethics in organizations: A review. *Journal of Management, 32*(6), 951–990.

Triandis, H. C. (1977). *Interpersonal behavior.* Monterey, CA: Brooks/Cole.

Tsai, W.-C. (2001). Determinants and consequences of employee displayed positive emotions. *Journal of Management, 27*, 497–512.

Tsai, W.-C., & Huang, Y.-M. (2002). Mechanisms linking employee affective delivery and customer behavioral intentions. *Journal of Applied Psychology, 87*(5), 1001–1008.

VandeWalle, D. (1997). Development and validation of a work domain goal orientation instrument. *Educational & Psychological Measurement, 57*, 995–1015.

VandeWalle, D. (2001). Goal orientation: Why wanting to look successful doesn't always lead to success. *Organizational Dynamics, 30*(2), 162–171.

VandeWalle, D., Brown, S. P., Cron, W. L., & Slocum, J. W., Jr. (1999). The influence of goal orientation and self-regulation tactics on sales performance: A longitudinal field test. *Journal of Applied Psychology, 84*, 249–259.

VandeWalle, D., & Cummings, L. L. (1997). A test of the influence of goal orientation on the feedback-seeking process. *Journal of Applied Psychology, 82*, 390–400.

Venkatesh, V., & Davis, F. (1996). A model of the antecedents of perceived ease of use: Development and test. *Decision Sciences, 27*, 451–482.

Venkatesh, V., & Davis, F. (2000). A theoretical extension of the technology acceptance model: Four longitudinal field studies. *Management Science, 46*, 186–105.

Victor, B., & Cullen, J. B. (1988). Organizational bases of ethical work climates. *Administrative Science Quarterly, 33*, 101–125.

Vroom, V. (1964). *Work and motivation.* New York: Wiley.

Vroom, V. (1969). Industrial social psychology. In G. Lindzey & E. Aronson (Eds.), *The handbook of social psychology.* Reading, MA: Addison-Wesley.

Weaver, G. R., & Agle, B. R. (2002). Religiosity and ethical behavior in organizations: A symbolic interactionist perspective. *Academy of Management Review, 27*(1), 77–97.

Weaver, G. R., Treviño, L. K., & Cochran, P. L. (1999). Corporate ethics practices in the mid-1990's: An empirical study of the Fortune 1000. *Journal of Business Ethics, 18*, 283–294.

Williams, L. J., & Anderson, S. E. (1991). Job satisfaction and organizational commitment as predictors of organizational citizenship and in-role behaviors. *Journal of Management, 17,* 601–617.

Winkielman, P., & Berridge, K. C. (2004). Unconscious emotion. *American Psychologist Society, 13*(3), 120–123.

Wofford, J. C., Goodwin, V. L., & Premack, S. (1992). Meta-analysis of the antecedents of personal goal level and of the antecedents and consequences of goal commitment. *Journal of Management, 18,* 595–615.

Wong, K. F. E., Yik, M., & Kwong, J. Y. Y. (2006). Understanding the emotional aspects of escalation of commitment: The role of negative affect. *Journal of Applied Psychology, 91*(2), 282–297.

Wooldridge, B., & Floyd, S. W. (1990). The strategy process, middle management involvement, and organizational performance. *Strategic Management Journal, 11*(3), 231–241.

Wright, P. M., O'Leary-Kelly, A. M., Cortina, J. M., Klein, H. J., & Hollenbeck, J. R. (1994). On the meaning and measurement of goal commitment. *Journal of Applied Psychology, 6,* 795–803.

Zardkoohi, A. (2004). Do real options lead to escalation of commitment. *Academy of Management Review, 29*(1), 111–119.

Section 3

Building and Maintaining Commitments

7

The Role of Individual Differences as Contributors to the Development of Commitment

Mindy E. Bergman and Justin K. Benzer
Texas A&M University

Jaime B. Henning
Eastern Kentucky University

Little empirical work has focused on individual difference influences on workplace commitments, and it has focused almost exclusively on organizational commitment. Recent meta-analyses (Cooper-Hakim & Viswesvaran, 2005; Meyer, Stanley, Herscovitch, & Topolnytsky, 2002; Riketta, 2002; Riketta & Van Dick, 2005) summarized empirical evidence regarding organizational commitment, yet few individual difference variables beyond simple demographics have been included, suggesting that they have not been studied frequently in the primary literature—an issue not lost on the meta-analysts (Meyer et al., 2002). This is not to suggest that individual differences have been ignored in the commitment literature. A handful of studies have examined the five-factor model and organizational commitment (Erdheim, Wang, & Zickar, 2006; Naquin & Holton, 2002). Lee, Ashford, Walsh, and Mowday (1992) were interested in a trait-like "commitment propensity." Hochwarter, Perrewé, Ferris, and Guercio (1999) suggested that if there is a commitment propensity, it might look something like conscientiousness. Some attention has been given to positive affectivity/negative affectivity (Thoresen, Kaplan, Barsky, Warren, & de Chermon, 2003). Self-efficacy is occasionally studied, although it is not clear whether it is an antecedent, a correlate, or an outcome of commitment (Judge, Thoresen, Pucik, & Welbourne, 1999; Sue-Chan & Ong, 2002; Whyte, Saks, & Hook, 1997). Relational demographics have also received some attention (Bacharach & Bamberger, 2004; Iverson & Buttigieg, 1997; Iverson & Kuruvilla, 1995). Finally, Wasti (2003a, 2003b) has developed a program of research on idiocentrism/allocentrism.

One of the problems with the scant research on individual differences and commitment is that they do not really describe *why* individual differences should be related to commitment. (A notable exception is idiocentrism/allocentrism; Berg, Janoff-Bulman, & Cotter, 2001; Janoff-Bulman & Leggatt, 2002; Wasti, 2003a, 2003b). Although these studies have a priori hypotheses or post hoc consideration of the relationships found, there is little in the way of broader theory. Klein, Molloy, and Cooper (chapter 1) trace the development of commitment as a construct in our field, reviewing major theoretical developments. Although many of the theories identify some individual difference influences (e.g., Mowday, Porter, & Steers, 1982), conspicuously absent are theories that hone in on specific individual differences as antecedents of commitment.

The aim of this chapter is to describe how individual differences could be related to commitment in the workplace. We borrow from personality psychology the metatheoretical framework of McCrae and Costa (1996), which describes the necessary components of a theory of individual differences and their roles in individuals' lives (McAdams & Pals, 2006). After establishing this framework in relation to commitment, we draw on several individual difference constructs to illustrate how potential influences on commitment. These are not meant as an exhaustive list, but rather as promising areas for future research.

McCrae and Costa's (1996) Metatheoretical Framework

McCrae and Costa (1996) described a metatheoretical framework of six components necessary for individual difference theories to be complete in their description of human nature:

Basic tendencies: the dispositions and abilities that are present in but vary across all individuals, such as temperament, creativity, cognitive ability, and physical strength.

External influences: the environment surrounding individuals and the experiences they have during their lives, including specific situations (e.g., work events) and global influences (e.g., national culture). In the context of commitment, external influences are foci-relevant situations that contribute to commitment development and maintenance.

Characteristic adaptations: "acquired skills, habits, attitudes, and relationships that result from the interaction of individual and environment; they are the concrete manifestations of basic tendencies" (McCrae & Costa, 1996, p. 69). Basic tendencies are inferred from characteristic adaptations, because many basic tendencies (but not all) cannot be directly measured. For example, it is possible to directly measure hormone levels by taking a sample of blood or saliva, but not to directly measure sexual drive, which must be assessed by self-report or observation. However, characteristic adaptations are not merely the behavioral outcomes of basic tendencies, because they are also influenced by the environment. Characteristic adaptations develop as basic tendencies direct individuals to situations and mold the responses that they make in them; such responses can become entrenched in the individual as they make similar responses across various situations. As we will describe below, commitment, as a mindset "binding an individual to a course of action" (Meyer & Herscovitch, 2001, p. 301), is a characteristic adaptation.

Self-concept: a special kind of characteristic adaptation that encompasses the individual's identity and sense of meaning in life. McCrae and Costa included this special category, separate from the more general characteristic adaptation component, because of the importance of the "self" in several subfields of psychology. Organizational identification* (Ashforth & Mael, 1989) is part of the self-concept.

Objective biography: the events, actions, and experiences throughout a lifetime. These are "objective" in the sense that they are activities that others could observe (and not only internal events, such as emotions). Objective biographies are multiply determined, such that any action an individual engages in rests upon a variety of characteristic adaptations as well as external influences. In work-life, objective biographies include completing training programs, leaving organizations and joining others, and day-to-day workplace events. It is important to note that any event can be either or both an objective biography (as an outcome of commitment) and an external influence on commitment.

---

* Organizational identification (Ashforth & Mael, 1989; Mael & Ashforth, 1992; 1995; Mael & Tetrick, 1992) is also a characteristic adaptation. It develops from basic tendencies (i.e., social categorization; self-enhancement and -consistency motives; Tajfel & Turner, 1985) and experiences in situations or with groups. It is probably best classified in the self-concept because identification refers to how individuals define themselves in terms of an object or group (Ashforth & Mael, 1989). It is not transportable to others, and changes in membership result in changes in how individuals perceive themselves (Ashforth & Mael, 1989). Note that the social cognitive process of identification is a basic tendency distinct from identification cognitions.

Dynamic processes link the previous five components together. The content of the five components (like boxes in a figure) and the dynamic processes (like arrows in a figure) together explain human nature. A broad array of dynamic processes exists; their nature depends on the specific constructs in question, not the general components listed above.

Although McCrae and Costa (1996) proposed one particular arrangement among the six components, they did not claim that their described arrangement was necessary or sufficient. Instead, their point was that a variety of dynamic processes link the other components together, resulting in multiple ways to conceptualize and configure human experience. This model is explicitly dynamic with multiple feedback loops, not the least of which is the influence of the individual's personal history (i.e., the guiding story of one's own life experiences and consistency of self over time; McAdams & Pals, 2006). For the purposes of this chapter, Figure 7.1 demonstrates an arrangement that elucidates how individual differences influence commitment.

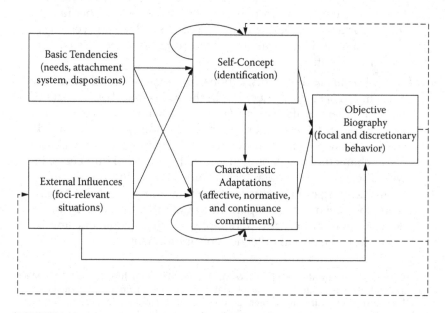

FIGURE 7.1
Arrangement of the six components from McCrae and Costa (1996). Curved arrows (emanating from and terminating in a single box) indicate that there are intermediate characteristic adaptations that influence the focal characteristic adaptations. Terms in parentheses indicate exemplars of the categories highlighted in this chapter. Dashed arrows indicate nonrecursive relationships.

Commitment as a Characteristic Adaptation

We consider commitment to be a characteristic adaptation. According to Meyer and Herscovitch (2001), the commitment mindset binds an individual to foci or to courses of action. Meyer and Allen (1991, 1997) proposed three different mindsets of commitment. *Affective commitment* (AC) is the mindset of wanting to stay in a relationship because of an emotional tie. *Continuance commitment* (CC) is the mindset of needing to stay because of the investments that would have to be forfeited if the relationship ended. Traditionally, *normative commitment* (NC) has been conceived as a mindset of obligation (Meyer & Allen, 1991; 1997). However, Meyer, Becker, & Van Dick (2006) theorized that NC could also be construed as a moral imperative, such that relationships are maintained because they allow the expression of deeply held values.

We conceptualize the commitment mindset (whether AC, CC, or NC) as a characteristic adaptation because it is developed through experiences with foci in situations that satisfy needs or otherwise provide positive experiences (Meyer & Allen, 1997). Each mindset is a distinct characteristic adaptation, with different environmental and basic tendency antecedents and associated with distinct dynamic processes and objective biographies. The dynamic process emanating from commitment is *binding*, described in detail in Meyer, Becker, and Vandenberghe (2004). In brief, the binding of an individual to an entity is a motivational force that directs attention to the entity and encourages intensity and persistence of activity toward that entity. Further, objective biography relevant to commitment could contain a variety of activities. In organizational commitment research, the most commonly studied objective biography is turnover; individuals who have lower organizational commitment are more likely to leave (Mathieu & Zajac, 1990; Meyer et al., 2002). Meyer and Herscovitch (2001) posited how each mindset might differentially affect focal (i.e., direct objectives) and discretionary (i.e., auxiliary objectives) behavior. These differential effects on behavior are concomitant with our argument that the dynamic processes of binding are separate for each commitment mindset, which are also distinct. This is not to suggest that there are not interactions among mindsets (Gellatly, Meyer, & Luchak, 2006; Meyer & Herscovitch, 2001; Wasti, 2005). Instead, the objective biography that arises from these motivational forces differs because the cognitive rationale behind these ties differs.

Basic tendencies that develop commitment. The relationship between individual differences (i.e., basic tendencies) and commitment (as a characteristic adaptation) will depend in part on the basic tendency, the mindset of commitment, and the focus of commitment. We could construct a laundry list of individual differences that might be fruitful for understanding commitment, including self-esteem (Kernis, Paradise, Whitaker,

Wheatman, & Goldman, 2000; Leary, Tambor, Terdal, & Downs, 1995), self-efficacy (Bandura & Locke, 2003; Gardner & Pierce, 1998), actual/ideal/ought selves (Higgins, Roney, Crowe, & Hymes, 1994), moral reasoning (Kohlberg, 1984; Schminke, Ambrose, & Neubaum, 2005), and regulatory focus (Shah & Higgins, 1997), among others (e.g., Edwards, 1991; Judge, Bono, Erez, & Locke, 2005). However, we focus instead on three exemplar areas of basic tendencies, allowing us to mine deeper theoretical issues. To that end, the remainder of this chapter focuses on three distinct areas of basic tendencies: need satisfaction, attachments, and dispositions.

Need Satisfaction and Self-Determination Theory

Self-determination theory (SDT; Deci & Ryan, 1985, 2000; Gagné & Deci, 2005) is one of the more recent attempts to describe fundamental psychological needs. SDT is based on the proposition that human beings are born with the tendency to seek out new and challenging situations, to grow, to learn, and to adapt, but that they require supportive conditions to reach their potential. Among the many needs that individuals have, SDT posits three as among the most important (Deci & Ryan, 2002), a proposition that has received some empirical support (Sheldon, Elliot, Kim, & Kasser, 2001). *Competence* refers to aspirations to have an effect on one's environment and to attain valued outcomes. *Autonomy* refers to a perception that one's activities are congruent with one's self-concept. *Relatedness* refers to a desire to establish a connection with relevant others (Deci & Ryan, 2002). Within McCrae and Costa's (1996) framework, these needs are basic tendencies. According to SDT, these needs drive behavior and must be satisfied for optimal functioning and well-being.

SDT states that the process of engaging in challenging acts can be enjoyable and rewarding even (and maybe especially) in the absence of external rewards. However, the extent to which behaviors are perceived to be autonomous is an important part of fulfilling needs. In addition to truly intrinsic motivation (i.e., engaging in tasks due to enjoyment of the act itself), the degree to which one experiences intrinsic rewards for competent activity depends on the degree to which external requirements have been internalized into one's self-concept (consistent with McCrae and Costa's [1996] definition) and thus are experienced as autonomously chosen. Internalization is defined as an intermediary process by which external, social requirements are assimilated into one's self-concept. Any action that is motivated by some instrumental, rather than purely intrinsic, interest is externally motivated. However, these external motivators can be experienced differently depending on the degree to which social requirements have been internalized into one's self-concept. Extrinsic motivation falls along a dimension of autonomous regulation ranging from *external* (i.e., to obtain a reward, no internalization; least autonomous), *introjected* (i.e., to boost perception of self-worth), *identified* (i.e., to support personal goals and values), to *integrated* (i.e., to meet fully assimilated goals; most autonomous). SDT proposes that externally generated behavioral regulation requirements are most likely to be internalized—and therefore to be perceived as autonomous—when individuals have a sense of security and relatedness either to the person assigning the task or to the task itself.

Recent research hints at a relationship between need satisfaction and commitment. As an acquired attitude, need satisfaction is categorized as a characteristic adaptation of the basic tendency of psychological needs. While no studies of need satisfaction to date have included all of AC, NC, and CC, several studies suggest need satisfaction is linked to AC and possibly to other mindsets. Need satisfaction has been linked to work engagement, which can be construed as AC to do the work at hand, among both American and Bulgarian workers (Deci et al., 2001). Bettencourt and Sheldon (2001) found a positive correlation between each of autonomy and relatedness need satisfaction and commitment (most like AC) to a group. Additionally, some evidence for a relationship between need satisfaction and turnover can be inferred from a study of high school dropouts, in which perceptions of competence and autonomy were related to intentions to leave school (Vallerand, Fortier, & Guay, 1997). There is some evidence that need satisfaction is important to turnover in the context of the theory of planned behavior (Ajzen, 1991), as need satisfaction has been shown to have direct effects on behavioral intentions and actual behaviors, as well as indirect effects through mediation by perceived autonomy, attitudes, and perceived behavioral control (Haggar, Chatzisarantis, & Harris, 2006).

Some research has linked psychological need satisfaction to traditional work outcome variables. Autonomy need satisfaction has been shown to have an incremental effect on mental health, job satisfaction, and satisfaction with work, beyond the effect of pay and job title (Ilardi, Leone, Kasser, & Ryan, 1993). Baard, Deci, and Ryan (2004) showed that performance evaluations of factory workers were positively correlated with relatedness need satisfaction, which could be accounted for, in part, by a positive relationship between need satisfaction and prosocial behavior (Gagné, 2003). More research is needed in this area.

Self-Determination and Commitment Mindsets

The work organization is a particularly promising arena for SDT research, because workplaces are filled with external regulatory requirements (e.g., rules) as well as acts that could be engaged for either intrinsic or extrinsic motives (Gagné & Deci, 2005). SDT proposes that need satisfaction promotes the internalization of regulatory requirements along a continuum ranging from no internalization (i.e., external regulation), to complete, integrated regulation. Over repeated exposures to activities that satisfy needs, individuals' motives for engaging in those behaviors will seem more internalized; that is, the more a behavior satisfies an individual's needs, the more it will seem to be freely chosen by the individual, regardless of the external regulatory control that actually occurs. The extent to which behavioral regulations are internalized is an intermediate characteristic adaptation linking psychological need satisfaction to commitment. This is not a static relationship, but a dynamic feedback process whereby behavioral regulation and commitment affect the satisfaction of psychological needs (Figure 7.2). For example, having low autonomy need satisfaction may prompt workers to regulate behaviors externally more frequently, but activities that are of intrinsic interest to the person would likely still be associated with a more internalized regulation. Over time, engaging in these internalized behavioral regulations should increase satisfaction of the need for autonomy, which should lead to an increased frequency of internal regulation for other, nonintrinsically interesting workplace activities.

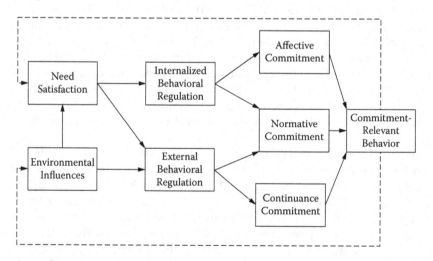

FIGURE 7.2
Nonrecursive relationships in the need satisfaction–commitment process. Dashed arrows indicate a positive feedback loop where the enactment of commitment-relevant behaviors can satisfy psychological needs. Need satisfaction leads to increased internalization and decreased external behavioral regulation. Environmental influences can promote external behavioral regulation, but are thought to only affect internalized behavioral regulation through the mediation of need satisfaction. The relationship between behavioral regulations and commitment is described in detail in the text.

It is important to note that in practice, many foci have complex behavioral regulations due to the many sources of regulation that can be associated with a single activity (Reichers, 1985). For example, commitment to a team goal that is associated with a pay-for-performance system could primarily be externally regulated, but could also be introjected (e.g., guilt in letting the team down), or identified or integrated if the team goal was associated with personal goals and values. Thus, the exact mindset in any circumstance would depend on the relative salience of regulatory factors associated with the commitment-relevant behavior. Following the previous example, a team member may work long hours to finish a project ahead of schedule, but the mindset that drove that behavior must be ascertained in order to understand how it was regulated.

From an SDT perspective, AC would occur when the individual identifies with and/or integrates the organizationally imposed behavioral requirements. Thus, AC is likely associated with high competence, autonomy, and relatedness need satisfaction. While need satisfaction itself has not often been examined in the context of workplace commitments, this reasoning is consistent with hypotheses regarding the contribution of positive workplace experiences to the presence of AC to the organization (Meyer & Allen, 1997; Meyer et al., 2002). Although need satisfaction has been the expository rationale for this relationship, the developmental contributions of need satisfaction based on positive workplace experiences to the internalization of workplace regulations and the subsequent rise of AC have not been investigated.

Whereas need satisfaction is proposed to be an antecedent of AC, it is likely to have a more complicated relationship to CC. CC is characterized by an awareness of the externally imposed costs and benefits of courses of action; however, the degree to which people are consciously aware of these costs will likely vary. For example, workers may acknowledge that leaving an organization would result in a great sacrifice, but if those employees are satisfied with their positions, their CC would likely not affect daily cognitions or behavior. Situations where these costs are more frequently made salient would likely increase the level of CC through the promotion of an external or introjected behavioral regulation. It is possible that high need satisfaction may attenuate this relationship by promoting an internalized regulation (see Figure 7.2), but this would depend on the strength of the external force.

Need satisfaction research could further illuminate the NC construct. Following the two-factor model of NC proposed by Gellatly et al. (2006) and elaborated by Meyer et al. (2006), NC based on indebted obligation would be associated with lower internalization (i.e., introjected regulation) than NC based on moral imperative (i.e., identified regulation). Furthermore, the greater internalization of moral imperatives (compared to obligations) would likely be related to both higher autonomy and relatedness need

satisfaction than commitment based in indebted obligation. As relatedness need satisfaction is thought to be important in the internalization
of job requirements, integration of organizational behavioral regulations
with the self-concept could lead to increased performance and a more
internalized form of commitment. This view is foreshadowed by Meyer
et al. (2004, 2006).

Foci and Need Satisfaction

Elsewhere in this book are chapters on organizational (Vandenberghe,
chapter 4), interpersonal (Becker, chapter 5), and action (Neubert & Wu,
chapter 6) foci. All are likely to provide experiences that influence behavioral regulation and need satisfaction. It is tempting to think that some
foci categories are more likely to meet particular needs—interpersonal
foci and relatedness need, or organizational and action foci and competence and autonomy needs. However, a priori categorization of foci and
needs would be erroneous. First, behaviors—and not foci themselves—
are regulated. Second, foci within each category could be more or less
composed of relatedness, competence, and autonomy facilitators; complex
foci could easily have many of these. For example, supervisors are foci
of commitment associated with relatedness, competence, and autonomy
facilitators such as attachment, similarity, feedback, and self-direction.

Further, as noted above, the "focus" of commitment and the relevant
focal and discretionary behavior must be carefully documented. Many
behaviors can be produced from a specific focus, and a single behavior
could be produced through different behavioral regulations. As commitment foci become more complex (i.e., commitment to people likely
involves multiple goals, and commitment to organizations likely involves
multiple people as well as abstract values), regulatory internalizations
likely become more complex as well. Thus, one may have AC to an organization and an overall integrated regulation, but the regulation of specific
organizational requirements could still range across the continuum of
internalization possibilities. Behavior in a given situation would likely be
influenced by the behavioral regulations that are most salient, rather than
a general overall internalization. Examination of these discontinuities
may yield insights into the processes by which different internalizations
lead to commitment. Thus, research involving multiple foci nested within
a broad focus (such as tasks, coworkers, and workgroups within an organization) may be especially useful for understanding how need satisfaction, internalization and identification, and commitment are related. The
hierarchical arrangement of these foci or goals, and the associated array of
behavioral regulations, may be especially important to understanding the
relationships among commitments to nested foci. Without clearly identifying the actual commitment focus and behavioral regulation, research

may yield uninterpretable and discrepant findings in the mindset-need satisfaction relationship.

One distinction among foci that may be important is *concreteness*. It is certainly likely that individuals make abstract foci more concrete by focusing on specific exemplars such as a supervisor (concrete) representing the organization (abstract; Reichers, 1985). However, it is also likely that people generate commitment mindsets to abstract foci themselves, without needing commitment to related concrete foci. For example, organizational membership may increase feelings of self-worth leading to increased commitment, and commitment to an organization may be increased by perceived value congruence to the organization as a whole, and these commitments can occur without a commitment to more concrete foci such as specific coworkers, the work itself, or a supervisor.

While commitment to concrete foci will likely influence commitment to relevant abstract foci (e.g., commitment to a supervisor influences commitment to an organization), commitment to abstract foci may be more strongly related to need satisfaction. This is because abstract foci may be more internally regulated, which better satisfies needs than does externally regulated behavior. For example, an organization could implement an external regulation such as a pay-for-performance system, which would increase commitment to concrete organizational goals and tasks, but not necessarily to an abstract organizational value change. This distinction may also be seen in the moral imperative/indebted obligation distinction of NC. Indebted obligation is likely associated with a more external regulation and is also likely concrete, while moral imperative is a more abstract construct and may have a greater association with internalized regulation. For example, individuals typically feel indebted to other, specific people (i.e., concrete foci) to whom investments should be repaid. The norm of reciprocity (Gouldner, 1960) mandates that obligations should be repaid to ensure smooth social functioning; this norm is an external regulation on behavior. Moral imperative NC, however, might be felt toward more abstract constructs—such as one's own values and beliefs—and might be regulated internally more so than externally.

Thus, the extent to which concreteness of foci influences behavioral regulation and commitment is an important avenue for future research. More important, however, is the issue that foci themselves are important to future research on commitment and needs. The quest is not to determine which particular foci from the universe of foci are most likely to be satisfying—a patently Quixotic task—but rather to understand what features of foci lead to internal regulation and commitment. Some possible features of foci might be less likely to coincide with work-related foci. Therefore, future research on commitment and behavioral regulation should include many foci from different life arenas and not narrowly fixate only on organizational research.

Future Research Directions

As described above, SDT behavioral regulation in specific situations is likely related to the development of longer term commitment mindsets. To start research in this area, several questions could be addressed. First, to what extent does one have to internalize behavioral regulations to experience AC, and on how many of the relevant behaviors (both focal and discretionary) must this internalization occur? That is, people who report high AC to a focus are probably not integrated in all related activities and engage in some behaviors because they "must" rather than because they "want to." So, what proportion of behaviors must be experienced as desired rather than required for the development or maintenance of AC at a high level? Further, if it is the case that concrete activities subsumed under more abstract foci help induce internalization of those abstract foci, then which types of concrete activities most support internalization? For example, it may be the case that formal training programs do not induce individuals to internalize broad organizational values, but that mentoring on projects, with its interpersonal contact and opportunities to achieve work goals, does.

SDT suggests that need satisfaction is important for both individual (e.g., well-being) and organizational (e.g., turnover) outcomes, but it is unclear how much control an organization has over the need satisfaction of its employees. Need satisfaction is to some degree a disposition (cf. Arvey, Bouchard, Segal, & Abraham, 1989), but it is also influenced by environmental changes. Initial research might examine how need satisfaction develops during organizational socialization processes, examining the influence of motivational and relational variables on the development of work-based need satisfaction compared to general need satisfaction at the time of hire. For established employees, one might examine how organizational change initiatives impact both need satisfaction at work and in life in general, and how organizations could promote long-term increases in need satisfaction.

Both need satisfaction and behavioral regulations are basic constructs that may be very important for organizational research in general and for commitment research in particular. This chapter suggests that while there are several behavioral regulations that may potentially lead to a commitment-relevant behavior, it may be possible to influence the type of regulation by increasing need satisfaction at work and in general. It is possible that the aggregated effect of increased individual need satisfaction on both turnover and performance could be substantial. It is clear that this is an area that both has high potential impact for organizational research, and is virtually unexplored by organizational researchers. The most potential impact will likely be in longitudinal, developmental, and multilevel studies. While cross-sectional studies are needed to establish the effect sizes of these variables with different outcomes, the most interesting questions will be answered with more sophisticated methodologies.

Attachment Theory

When commitment is described in general terms, the word "attachment" is often invoked (e.g., Meyer & Allen, 1991, 1997; Meyer et al., 2004, O'Reilly & Chatman, 1986). But there is a literature around this term in clinical, developmental, and social psychology that has largely been ignored in organizational research. In these fields, an *attachment* is the bond emanating from an individual toward another, based on experiences with the other and in expectations of security and comfort the other can provide (Bartholomew, 1990; Bowlby, 1969; Hazan & Shaver, 1987; Simpson & Rholes, 1998). Modern attachment research stems from Bowlby's (1969, 1973, 1988) work on child personality and behavior development. Bowlby argued that there is an innate, evolved system of behaviors and cognitions that helps individuals elicit care from others, keeping caregivers close when threat arises. Infants are not able to care for themselves and therefore must rely on others (adults) to provide protection and comfort in times of threat and distress. Adults can typically take care of themselves, but they also have deep-rooted tendencies to elicit care from others; caregiving is mutually provided in adult relationships (Ainsworth, 1989; Hazan & Shaver, 1987; Shaver, Hazan, & Bradshaw, 1988). Within the McCrae and Costa (1996) framework, the attachment system is a basic tendency, as all individuals have a native tendency to elicit security and comfort from others (Hinde & Stevenson-Hinde, 1991).

When threats arise, the individual initiates attachment behaviors (e.g., crying, among infants) that are intended to elicit caregiving responses from others (Bowlby, 1969, 1973; Kobak, 1994). If these responses are reliably provided and soothing,* over time the caregiver becomes a *secure base* for the individual. In addition to the actual person providing safety, a secure base is a set of cognitions that includes representations of the caregiver, the comfort provided, and the self as an object worthy of care (Ainsworth, Blehar, Waters, & Wall, 1978; Bowlby, 1988). But some attachment-eliciting behaviors are ignored or responded to without care and comfort (Ainsworth et al., 1978). Such responses can create schemas of the self as not worthy of attention and/or the caregiver as unreliable, not helpful, or even hurtful (Belsky, 1999; Bowlby, 1969, 1988). Bartholomew

---

* It is possible for others to respond reliably but without providing care and comfort, such as in abusive situations.

(1990) referred to these schemas as the *model of self* and the *model of others*.* When both are positive, a secure base is achieved. However, if either or both are not positive, dysfunctional attachment exists (Ainsworth et al., 1978; Bartholomew, 1990).

These models of others and of self have also been described in terms of the patterns of cognitions and behavior they produce (Bartholomew & Horowitz, 1991; Brennan, Clark, & Shaver, 1998; Fraley & Waller, 1998). *Anxiety*, based in the model of self, is characterized by anxious fear of abandonment, preoccupation with the relationship and the attachment object, and hyperactivation of attachment behaviors (e.g., clinging; Dozier & Kobak, 1992; Shaver & Mikulincer, 2002). Low-anxiety individuals see themselves as worthy of care. They do not worry about abandonment and are confident that others will accept them. High-anxiety individuals perceive themselves as unworthy of care, yet desperately want close relationships and thus become preoccupied with obtaining and maintaining them. *Avoidance*, based in the model of others, is characterized by dismissiveness of relationships and intimacy, emotional distancing, excessive self-reliance, and deactivation of attachment seeking (Bartholomew & Horowitz, 1991; Dozier & Kobak, 1992; Shaver & Mikulincer, 2002). Low-avoidance individuals view others as reliable sources of security and seek them for comfort. In contrast, because prior attachment seeking has not been successful or because others have intrusively activated caregiving and attachment systems in their mutual relationship, some individuals reduce attachment seeking and minimize their acceptance of others' interest and intimacy (i.e., high avoidance).

Attachment or attachments? Thus far, we have described attachment as a general way of approaching relationships that are rooted in cognitions about early experiences with caregivers (Bowlby, 1969; Collins & Read, 1994; Klohnen & John, 1998; Main, 1991). These experiences can be self-fulfilling, as they are schematized into expectations about the type of care that others provide and the type of care that the individual deserves; these schemas guide actions in future relationships (Benoit & Parker, 1994; Bowlby, 1969; Klohnen & John, 1998). Thus, a general attachment orientation can be viewed as a characteristic adaptation, arising from interactions between individuals and others in the environment, rooted in early life interactions.

However, any relationship could be an attachment (although not all relationships are), and there can be many attachments at a single time (Bridges, Connell, & Belsky, 1988; Hazan, Gur-Yaish, & Campa, 2004; Lewis, 1994). Any particular attachment relationship can be distinct from any and every other bond; early attachment experiences and subsequent

---

* Although these models are distinct theoretically, in actual experiences they are linked due to interactions among the attachment-eliciting and caregiving behavioral systems (Bowlby, 1969).

orientations do not fatalistically determine the nature of future relation-ships. If the style of caretaking changes early in life, then the general attachment style that children exhibit changes concomitantly (Bowlby, 1969; Davila & Cobb, 2004; Egeland & Farber, 1984). Further, individuals have multiple mental models of relationships (Baldwin et al., 1996; Collins, Guichard, Ford, & Feeney, 2004; Collins & Read, 1994; Simpson & Rholes, 2002). Although these appear to be organized hierarchically from general and abstract expectations about a group of objects to specific and detailed models of particular attachment objects (Collins & Read, 1994), individuals at any age can develop mental representations of new objects—even those that are similar to prior ones (e.g., a new dating partner)—that diverge from previous mental models (Baldwin et al., 1996; Collins & Read, 1994; Kobak, 1994; Lewis, 1994; Main, 1991; Simpson & Rholes, 2002). Mental models later in life can even compensate for earlier, insecure attachments (Kirkpatrick & Shaver, 1990).

The hierarchical organization of attachment mental models, as well as the ability to create new attachments that deviate from previous mental models, might be useful in understanding how commitments to different foci—especially nested or interrelated foci (Reichers, 1985)—are related. Although general attachment orientations make particular bonds more likely, not all commitments will be the same across foci. The need for secure relationships persists regardless of the individual's attachment orienta-tion, so commitments to foci in the absence of enjoyment might be explain-able when other attachments are considered. For example, commitment foci and mindsets might usefully compensate for each other (e.g., CC to a dreaded job, to support AC and NC to family), much as new attachments can compensate for previous insecure experiences. Finally, it is important to recognize that the general attachment orientation antecedes specific attachments to specific objects. It may be difficult to predict the attitudes and behaviors that individuals have toward a particular target directly from general attachment, because specific attachment interactions medi-ate these relationships. However, it is likely that (a) specific attachments to similar objects will be related, (b) general attachment orientations will be related to specific attachments, and (c) attachment orientations explain a significant portion of the variance between specific attachments to similar objects.

Whether considering specific attachment relationships or the broader orientations that are the summary of experiences (heavily weighted by early life experiences), attachments are characteristic adaptations. All are developed through the basic tendency of the attachment system and the environmental influence of actual caretaking experiences (Belsky, 1999; Kobak, 1994; Marvin & Britner, 1999). Although there are personality-like attachment tendencies, these are developed over time and experiences and not innate dispositions (Marvin & Britner, 1999). Instead, the basic tendency is the biological drive to obtain comfort and care when threatened (Bowlby, 1969; Hinde & Stevenson-Hinde, 1991).

Attachment to Various Foci

Most research on attachments has examined attachment to people; some researchers have argued that individuals attach only to people (e.g., Ainsworth, 1989). However, foci other than individual others can be interpersonal. Smith, Murphy, and Coats (1999) demonstrated that individuals attach to and develop mental models about relationships with social groups in ways consistent with attachment theory. It is likely that the extent to which foci are interpersonal will be a boundary condition on the relationship between attachment and commitment. For example, supervisors and coworkers are more interpersonal than are unions, change programs, and the organization. This is not to suggest that unions and organizations are not populated by people, but rather that these foci are less saturated by interpersonal features. Although the extent to which foci are interpersonal is likely to be related to the breadth or abstraction of the object or action, they are not the same. For example, one's family is a rather broad focus, yet it is clearly interpersonal; whereas one's work tasks are a narrow focus, yet (depending on the tasks) may not be very interpersonal. The interpersonal nature of foci is expected to be a boundary condition on the expected relationships because attachment cognitions are related to interpersonal interactions. The abstracted internal working models of others and of self (i.e., avoidance and anxiety), as orientations that individuals have toward expecting and acting in relationships, are more likely to be activated when interpersonal situations arise. Avoidant individuals do not need to avoid others and anxious individuals do not need to be worried or preoccupied when others are not present (e.g., working alone) or are not relevant (e.g., others concurrently shopping in a store).

There is evidence that attachment style influences behavior and commitment to a number of different foci beyond other people. Wolfe and Betz (2004) found that attachment orientation was related to fear of choosing a career. Kirkpatrick (1997) found that attachment style was related to important religious experiences and conversion. Hazan and Shaver (1990) showed that attachment styles were related to the relative priority of and perceptions of interference between work and love relationships. Hazan and Shaver also found differences across attachment styles in the social and exploratory natures of preferred and typical leisure activities. Thus, it is not necessarily the case that foci must be interpersonal to be subject to the attachment system.

Further, the presence of multiple foci could influence commitment to any foci. As Hazan and Shaver (1990) demonstrated, avoidant individuals tended to spend more time at work yet were less satisfied with their jobs, whereas anxious individuals tended to believe that work interfered with their personal relationships, possibly because of their tendency toward preoccupation with relationships that is based in their hyperactivation of the attachment system (Shaver & Mikulincer, 2002). Secure individuals prized relationships over work and believed they would sacrifice work rather than relationships if they were forced to choose (Hazan & Shaver, 1990). Thus, it is important to understand the interactive influence of attachments to multiple foci and their bearings on each other in the development of commitment and the objective histories of individuals.

Future Research Directions

Future research on attachment and commitment should consider both the specific attachment bond emanating from an individual to a focus and the general orientation that individuals develop due to early life interactions. The general attachment orientation should be viewed as an intermediate characteristic adaptation that partially mediates the influence of the attachment behavioral system (a basic tendency) and specific attachments (as characteristic adaptations). The primacy of the attachment behavioral system suggests that specific attachments would develop ahead of commitments to those objects, although there is probably a recursive developmental pattern such that as attachments strengthen, commitments grow, leading attachments to become more solidified. However, in cross-sectional views, it is probably best to consider specific attachments as antecedents of commitment. Initial studies of attachment and commitment should include multiple foci and measure general attachment orientation, specific attachment bonds toward each focus, and commitment toward each focus.

When considering the pair-bond or specific attachment, avoidance is likely to be especially important to the development—or lack thereof—of commitment. Avoidance reflects deactivation of the attachment system, so the attachment object is not sought when security is desired (Shaver & Mikulincer, 2002). Individuals high in avoidance tend to minimize the importance of others and can be pathologically self-reliant. Further, avoidant individuals engage in exploration, not because they are secure and can fulfill this inborn tendency, but rather to avoid interpersonal interactions (Simpson & Rholes, 2002). Therefore, individuals high in avoidance might actively seek out new commitment foci when they need to avoid interpersonal interactions with current commitment objects. Thus, AC is likely to develop when avoidance is low, because low avoidance represents a view that the other in the relationship is reliable and dependable in providing comfort; this emotional investment in the other contributes to the individual's well-being, which is best preserved when the relationship with the attachment object continues.

Additionally, at least when considering adult attachments, the attachment system interacts with the caregiving system (Shaver et al., 1988); adults tend to care for those who care for them. This give-and-take mirrors obligation NC, the sense that one should stay with and contribute to a commitment object when that object stays with and contributes to the person. Thus, individuals low in avoidance are likely to develop obligation NC. If the attachment system influences the development of both AC and NC, it may help explain why AC and NC of obligation have been so strongly related in previous research (Bergman, 2006).

Although CC could also be influenced by avoidance, these relationships are not likely to be strong. The calculative nature of CC could be enhanced by low avoidance, as those individuals will not be afraid of relying on the commitment object. Additionally, avoidance could help explain why CC has little effect on most focal and discretionary behaviors, other than turnover (which is also a relatively small effect, compared to AC; Meyer et al., 2002). CC is high when individuals recognize that they have invested so much in a relationship (e.g., hard work, learning, time for an organization) that leaving would mean forgoing some good outcomes (e.g., future stock options). However, when avoidance is low, the individual could frame the investments in a focus as contributions to a positive relationship rather than sunk costs that could be lost; low-avoidance individuals might perceive that those investments have less to do with future paybacks and more to do with caregiving—the give-and-take of the attachment and caregiving systems.

Anxiety might also be important to the development of commitment, but more complex relationships may be seen. Anxiety reflects relationship preoccupation and hyperactivation of the attachment system (Shaver & Mikulincer, 2002). Thus, it seems possible that anxiety could be related negatively or positively to commitment. On one hand, individuals who are low in anxiety have models of themselves as objects worthy of care and attention from others. They would not be concerned about the continuation or the costs to others of their relationships. Therefore, they would perceive an ongoing mutual relationship, developing commitment. On the other hand, high anxiety and its attendant hyperactivation could lead to commitment, especially AC and NC of obligation. High-anxiety individuals tend to cling to their relationship objects and are intensely emotionally invested in them. Thus, AC might be related to attachment-anxiety because of this emotional involvement. Further, NC of obligation might arise because the model of self among anxious individuals contain worry about their worth in the relationship. To increase their perceptions of their worth to the other—or at least to avoid decreasing their perceptions of their worth to the other—highly anxious individuals are likely to be very sensitive to give-and-take, especially their own giving. This may become especially important in unstable environments—such as when layoffs are threatened—as the uncertainty of the continuation of the relationship could lead anxious individuals to become intensely interested in maintaining the relationship.

The previous paragraphs describe issues when considering specific attachment bonds. But general orientations toward anxiety and avoidance could also contribute to commitment. Specifically, as individuals enter and become socialized in relationships with people, groups, or organizations, their attachment orientations guide their behavior in self-fulfilling ways (Bowlby, 1969). Individuals are likely to be attracted to targets based on their attachment orientation; some targets may be especially well suited to match the cognitions and interaction styles of particular attachment orientations. For example, high-avoidance individuals might be well suited to jobs that have few team interactions or are solo-practiced, or to jobs that require only short-term interactions with customers. Finally, these expectations shape the perceptions that individuals have of interactions, thus influencing the specific pair-bond relationship developed with any specific attachment object (Collins et al., 2004). That is, when individuals approach organizational relationships with avoidant cognitions, they may act in ways that will encourage them to be perceived as less valuable organizational members, such as avoiding discretionary events or not helping others, because the individual will not want to get "too close" to the organization or the people in it. If the organization must reduce the number of employees, the insecurely attached individuals who have failed to enact discretionary and citizenship behaviors will be more likely to be let go, thus fulfilling their own expectations and further fortifying their attachment orientations.

Thus, future research on attachment and commitment should carefully consider the longitudinal and developmental effects of attachment on commitment, as well as the recursive influence emanating from interactions with attachment objects/commitment foci. Additionally, both general attachment orientations as well as specific attachment bonds should be considered when researching attachment and commitment.

Dispositions

Interest in dispositional antecedents of work-related attitudes and behavior is generally quite high, making the lack of research on dispositional antecedents of commitment surprising. The relatively small amount of research on the dispositional antecedents of commitment has generally focused on AC, with significantly less attention on either CC or NC. Dispositional research on commitment has examined variables such as trait affectivity (e.g., Cropanzano, James, & Konovsky, 1993; Kim, Price, Mueller, & Watson, 1996; Payne & Morrison, 2002; L. J. Williams, Gavin, & M. L. Williams, 1996), locus of control (e.g., Macan, Trusty, & Trimble, 1996; Meyer et al., 2002; Tang, Baldwin, & Frost, 1997), and self-efficacy (e.g., Lee et al., 1992; Meyer et al., 2002). Dispositions are basic tendencies in the McCrae and Costa (1996) framework. We focus on two general dispositions, trait affectivity (Watson & Tellegen, 1985) and Five Factor Model (FFM) personality traits (Costa & McCrae, 1992), because they are promising areas for future research and because other related topics in organizational psychology—such as job satisfaction and citizenship performance (Hoffman, Blair, Meriac, & Woehr, 2007; LePine, Erez, & Johnson, 2002; Mathieu & Zajac, 1990; Meyer et al., 2002; Organ & Ryan, 1995)—have already begun to deliver on this promise (Judge, Heller, & Mount, 2002; Organ & Ryan, 1995).

Affectivity and commitment. Following research relating dispositional (especially negative) affectivity to job satisfaction, Cropanzano et al. (1993) examined the relationships between trait positive and negative affect (PA/NA) and commitment, finding PA positively and NA negatively related to commitment. Cropanzano et al. further suggested that organizational commitment mediates the relationship between each of PA and NA and turnover intentions. Thoresen et al. (2003) included PA, NA, and AC in their quantitative review of affect and job attitudes. As expected, PA was positively and NA negatively related to AC. They also examined studies that operationalized PA and NA in the forms of extraversion and emotional stability,* respectively. Although the estimated correlations were somewhat lower than those found for PA and NA, the results suggest extraversion and emotional stability are positively related to AC; it should be noted that these findings are based on a total of three studies.

Thus, although several studies have demonstrated significant correlations between affectivity and commitment (e.g., Cropanzano et al., 1993; Kim et al., 1996; Thoresen et al., 2003; Williams et al., 1996) and are an important and useful beginning, they offer little help in describing *why* these individual differences should be related to commitment. It may be the case that these dispositional variables influence workplace commitment indirectly through their effect on the appraisal of job characteristics. Trait affectivity is an important determinant of the experience of positive and negative affective states (Costa & McCrae, 1980; Tellegen, 1985; Watson & Clark, 1984) and may predispose individuals to evaluate their working conditions in a PA-induced positive (or NA-induced negative) light, thereby increasing (or decreasing) job satisfaction and producing

---

* In order to improve readability, we refer to "emotional stability" rather than "neuroticism" (and correspondingly adjusted the directions of the relationships described), despite the fact that previous research used the term "neuroticism."

higher (or lower) commitment. Weiss and Cropanzano (1996) and Brief (1998), for example, each proposed models of job attitudes that suggest dispositions influence job attitudes through the interpretation of objective job circumstances; Weiss and Cropanzano (1996) further argued that dispositions influence affective reactions to objective work events. Although these models were proposed in relation to job satisfaction and other attitudes, they are likely appropriate for understanding the motivational cognitions of commitment.

Affective experiences could be both a cause and a consequence of commitment. Dispositions could predispose individuals to develop commitment or could influence individuals' perceptions of foci, thus indirectly influencing commitment. Dispositions could also guide individuals to situations that best serve those dispositions, making individuals committed to those situations because they are pleasurable and enjoyable, they allow people to achieve, or they meet some social need; commitment arises because people are motivated to remain in satisfying situations. Herrbach (2006) examined affective outcomes of commitment beyond the influence of trait affectivity. He proposed that "commitment reflects a stabilized evaluation of one's work environment" (p. 639), positing AC as a favorable evaluation and CC as a defensive evaluation; therefore, high AC and CC would be related to experiencing more positive and negative affective states, respectively, above and beyond the influence of trait affectivity. Herrbach found that AC predicted positive affect at work beyond the influence of dispositional affect.

Thus, if PA and NA do direct individuals to and affect evaluations of situations, then they are likely to influence the development of some commitment mindsets. PA is likely to contribute to the development of AC. High-PA individuals appraise a greater number of situations more positively than their low-PA counterparts. Positive workplace experiences are an important contributor to AC (Meyer & Allen, 1997; Stinglhamber & Vandenberghe, 2003), so individuals who dispositionally perceive greater positivity in their workplace experiences would be more likely to develop AC. In contrast, high-NA individuals tend to evaluate their experiences negatively. Negative appraisals of workplace situations should dampen the development of AC, as individuals are motivated to minimize contact with undesirable outcomes. Finally, the correspondence of AC and trait affectivity to emotions suggests that these relationships will be stronger than relationships between affectivity and the other commitment mindsets.

PA and NA could also contribute to NC as obligations. There is some evidence that NC develops in response to positive workplace experiences (Meyer et al., 2002), which would be facilitated by high PA. Following social and gift exchange models (Belk, 1979; Blau, 1986), individuals who have positive workplace experiences may develop a sense of indebtedness to repay the organization or its members for these experiences.

Further, high-PA individuals may be less likely to view these obligations as demands for repayment (a negative, externally controlling experience) and more likely to view them as an opportunity to express gratitude, to contribute to a valued organization, or to further enmesh themselves into organizational life. However, although high-NA individuals can also develop a sense of obligation, the negative perceptions corresponding to high NA could result in obligations that are resented rather than respected and respectful (Berg et al., 2001; Janoff-Bulman & Leggatt, 2002). Thus, the evaluation of obligations—as an opportunity to give back or as a debt that one is required to repay—is likely to be influenced by affectivity and ultimately affect the behaviors enacted (Meyer & Herscovitch, 2001).

CC might be positively related to NA because high-NA people perceive their circumstances negatively, yet must still meet the instrumental demands of life. The instrumental reasons for work—notably, pay—are not ignored by workers, regardless of their evaluation of the content of work experiences, and can keep individuals in an organizational role even when they do not enjoy it, especially when alternatives are perceived as rare and low quality (Hulin, 1991). When individuals are tied to their foci due only to instrumentalities, CC is likely to form. This proposed influence of NA on the development of CC may explain why CC is related to low turnover (focal behavior) but rarely to positive discretionary behaviors (Becker & Kernan, 2003; Meyer & Herscovitch, 2001; Meyer et al., 2002).

FFM traits and commitment. The few studies examining the FFM-commitment relationship suggest that some personality traits are related to some commitment mindsets. In the only study published to date examining the FFM and all three of AC, NC, and CC, Erdhiem et al. (2006) found that conscientiousness correlated positively with AC and CC, extraversion correlated with all three mindsets (negatively with CC), emotional stability correlated negatively with CC, agreeableness correlated positively with NC, and openness correlated negatively with CC. Furthermore, all of these relationships remained significant after controlling for age, sex, job and organizational tenure, and the remaining personality dimensions. However, it should be noted that a number of these relationships were found despite the fact that they were not hypothesized; future research will bear out whether these are chance effects. Additionally, Naquin and Holton (2002) found positive correlations between each of the FFM traits and AC, and negative correlations between each of extraversion, openness, and emotional stability and CC. In structural-modeling analyses, both conscientiousness and agreeableness predicted a broad work commitment variable that included hard work, job involvement, AC, and CC.

A handful of unpublished studies also suggest that FFM traits are important predictors of organizational commitment. Watrous and Bergman (2004) examined the relationships among AC, NC, and CC and

FFM dimensions using multisource data. Their findings suggest conscientiousness is a predictor of AC and NC. Additionally, agreeableness was related to AC; however, agreeableness was only related to NC when both the predictor and criterion measures were obtained from the same source. Finkelstein, Protolipac, and Stiles (2006) found that all FFM traits were positively related to NC; extraversion, agreeableness, and emotional stability were related positively with AC; and agreeableness was positively whereas emotional stability was negatively related to CC. Additionally, they found that perceptions of job characteristics partially mediated the effect of the FFM on commitment. Finally, Leiva et al. (2004) examined personality and commitment to two foci (a university and a service provider—a hairstylist). After controlling for several situational variables, they found that extraversion and agreeableness predicted AC to the university, but only extraversion predicted AC to the service provider; additionally, agreeableness and emotional stability predicted NC to the university. Each of these latter studies (Finkelstein et al., 2006; Leiva et al., 2004) suggest that personality (a basic tendency) and external factors combine to influence commitment (a characteristic adaptation).

Thus, it seems that conscientiousness shows promise for predicting commitment, particularly AC (Erdhiem et al., 2006; Naquin & Holton, 2002; Watrous & Bergman, 2004). Hochwarter et al. (1999) argued that commitment has a dispositional root, and—using logic strikingly similar to McCrae and Costa (1996)—that conscientiousness may be this base. Given the findings of Thoresen et al. (2003), it is also likely that extraversion and emotional stability will be related to AC. Other research (Erdhiem et al., 2006; Finkelstein et al., 2006; Leiva et al., 2004; Naquin & Holton, 2002) lends further support to these speculations, particularly regarding extraversion.

Conscientious people seem predisposed to develop commitment (Hochwarter et al., 1999). The conscientious tend to be dependable. Commitment is displayed through a willingness to exert effort—also a conscientiousness marker—on behalf of foci. Conscientious people might develop CC because they should be sensitive to the maintenance of the organization's instrumental contributions to their lives. Conscientious people are also dutiful, making them likely to experience obligation-NC. Further, NC as a moral imperative may be influenced by conscientiousness, as the ability to work in organizations that allow for the achievement of goals and the expression and support of important personal values will be a dutiful act as well as an efficient use of time. However, conscientiousness may be most important for the development of AC. Conscientious individuals tend to be achievement oriented; workplaces allow achievements both small (accomplishing daily tasks and goals) and large (earning a promotion). This is reinforced because competently resolving activities is pleasing and satisfies psychological needs (Deci & Ryan, 2000), and individuals tend to want to remain in situations that are satisfying.

Extraversion and emotional stability also appear to be important to the development of commitment (Thoresen et al., 2003). Extraversion and emotional stability have much in common with PA and NA, respectively, but are not completely concomitant with them and therefore probably will not have identical influences on commitment. Unlike PA, extraversion includes sociability and risk taking. Extraverted individuals may develop more social ties though their assertive, sociable nature, therefore developing AC to others, such as coworkers. By extension, these individuals may develop AC to their organization because of its provision of these coworkers and a productive social environment. Finally, extraversion may be negatively related to CC—even though we do not predict that PA would be—because of its risk-taking component. Extraverts may be less sensitive to the cost of forgoing investments yet to be reaped in the organization; they may also have an extensive social network that provides greater alternative opportunities than introverts enjoy. Thus, extraverts may be less likely to experience CC. It may be important to investigate particular facets of extraversion, especially dividing between the risk-taking and sociability components, to understand its relationship with commitment.

Additionally, neuroticism (low emotional stability) might suppress the development of AC and NC, as neurotic individuals tend to view the world negatively. Further, neuroticism might contribute to the development of CC, as neurotic individuals would be highly sensitive to the costs of ending their organizational memberships, especially because they are also likely to denigrate alternative opportunities. Further, previous experiences as a job-seeker (as well as their perceptions of these experiences) would likely be more negative than those of more emotionally stable individuals, leading to a stronger sense of needing to remain in the organization.

Given the scant research on agreeableness and openness in relation to job attitudes and motivation, we can only speculate as to what relationships might be worth investigating. Agreeableness could lead to NC as an obligation. As agreeableness subsumes the tendencies to be cooperative and compassionate, agreeable individuals may be more likely to feel obligated in general and also might be more sensitive to obligations because of their penchant for harmonious relationships. High openness to experience may dispose individuals to seek out situations that allow imagination, creativity, and variety. When an organization, supervisor, or workgroup provides these, then the individual may develop AC and NC because of the positive experiences they have had. However, open individuals may also be less likely to develop CC, as they are not as constrained by conventional reasons for working (McCrae & John, 1992).

Future Research Directions

The interpersonal nature of foci might influence the extent to which some dispositions are related to commitment. For example, agreeableness and extraversion might be more important to the development of commitment to interpersonal foci than to other foci because agreeableness and extraversion are personality traits that explain interpersonal behavior (see Becker's chapter 5). In contrast, conscientiousness, openness, emotional stability, PA, and NA all influence behavior that does not have to refer to others (although it can). However, organizational and action foci can have interpersonal content to them as well. Actions could be committed to because they benefit particular individuals. For example, an employee might become committed to corporate-sponsored volunteering because the employee's supervisor benefits from employee participation; outside the workplace, adults might be committed to taking care of ailing in-laws because they care about their life partner's well-being. Further, some organizationally related actions (e.g., representing the workgroup on a corporate committee) might allow individuals to expand their social networks, which is likely to be enjoyable for an extrovert. Thus, it is important to be specific about the focus of commitment when considering dispositional influences; researchers must be careful to ensure that the root focus of commitment that drives behavior is identified. And, as noted in the previous sections, including multiple foci in any research on dispositions and commitment is important to demonstrating the universality of the influence of dispositions on commitment as well as to determining the existence of boundary conditions based on features of foci.

It is also likely that conscientiousness will be important for commitments to any foci, especially when considering behavioral outcomes of commitments. Conscientiousness, with its root in reliability, dependability, and striving for accomplishment, should (a) encourage the development of commitments and (b) fortify the positive effect of those commitments on relevant focal and discretionary behaviors. However, this latter issue—the moderating effect of conscientiousness on the commitment-behavior relationship—could actually be more important than the initial effect of conscientiousness on commitment. Commitments can occur with the best of intentions, but conscientious individuals are most likely to fulfill those intentions. Thus, future research should examine the direct, indirect, and moderating effects of conscientiousness on the commitment-behavior (focal and discretionary) relationship. Such research should go beyond organizational foci, and certainly go beyond the organization as a focus, to demonstrate whether conscientiousness is a general commitment propensity (Hochwarter et al., 1999). Although we have posited possible direct, indirect, and moderating effects only for conscientiousness, such effects could also occur with the other dispositions. Thus, we recommend that research not become slavishly devoted to conscientiousness, but rather consider at least all of the FFM.

Finally, we have focused here on dispositions from the FFM and the trait affectivity literatures, because the literature on other, related constructs such as job satisfaction has demonstrated that these are important dispositional predictors. However, other dispositions might prove fruitful for understanding commitment. For example, interpersonal theory (cf. Wiggins & Trapnell, 1996), with its focus on dynamic interpersonal interactions characterized by dominance and warmth behaviors in dyads, might well explain commitment to other individuals. We were limited in our ability to address the myriad conceptualizations of dispositions in this chapter and therefore want to reiterate that our work is illustrative, not exhaustive, of the potential influences of individual difference on commitment. However, it is important that researchers not just throw sundry dispositions at the commitment wall to see what sticks; choice of which dispositions to examine should follow through on the characteristic adaptations point of view. Hypothesized relationships, such as those posited here, should be based on the specific natures of the commitment mindsets, the dispositions, and the foci, rather than on some general concept that dispositions predict commitment.

Conclusions

Before closing this chapter, a few final remarks are needed. First, nearly all of the individual influences on commitment proposed in this chapter also referenced situational effects. McCrae and Costa (1996) argued that characteristic adaptations arise from the interactions of basic tendencies and external influences (cf. Judge & Kristof-Brown, 2004). Our work agrees with that position. Although some basic tendencies might more directly influence commitment (for example, conscientiousness), the role of situations is paramount. We have suggested that basic tendencies guide individuals to situations and that the experiences in those situations along with basic tendencies determine whether individuals develop commitment. Needs are satisfied by the provision of particular experiences; attachments develop through interactions with others; dispositions affect the evaluations that we make in the workplace and also contribute to fit within organizational contexts. In all of these conceptualizations, external influences cannot be ignored.

Further, we suggested that some basic tendencies, such as the attachment behavioral system, lead individuals to develop intermediate characteristic adaptations, such as attachment orientations, due to interactions with the environment. These intermediate characteristic adaptations may have direct influence on commitment, but again the more distal cause is an interactive experience between basic tendencies and external influences. Articulating the full network of dynamic relationships among basic tendencies, external influences, and characteristic adaptations (both focal and intermediary)—as well as self-concept and objective history—in the study of commitment will highlight where relationships can be expected, but could also explain why some plausible relationships might not be as strong as expected, because the basic tendencies might not be the direct antecedent of commitment.

Although we emphasize the conjunction of basic tendencies and external influences as antecedents of commitment, we are not suggesting that researchers should look for their simple interactive effects on characteristic adaptations. Although interactions might be useful in predicting commitment in linear regression analyses, especially in some initial investigations of these phenomena, the relationships that we have described are explicitly *developmental*. Commitment builds over time as a basic tendency keeps a person in a particular situation that provides experiences leading to the development of commitment. Cross-sectional studies of individual differences and organizational commitment are likely to spark some interest and attention in our journals, but only for so long. For a real, sustainable program of research on individual difference influences in commitment in organizations, developmental—not merely longitudinal—research is needed. Vandenberg and Stanley (chapter 12) review a number of analytic techniques, such as latent growth modeling, that address change over time and correspond to our distinction between developmental and longitudinal research.

Additionally, we must note that many of the experiences that individuals have can be construed in terms of any of several of the components in McCrae and Costa's (1996) framework. For example, objective histories can also be construed either as external influences or as having very tight linkages with external influences. As an illustrative example, turnover from one organization to another is an objective history, but it also changes the environment the individual is embedded in. Additionally, the move from one organization to another is filled with change and uncertainty—which are also important external influences. Thus, commitment—or any other characteristic adaptation—is subject to continual nonrecursive feedback effects.

At first blush much of what we've said about characteristic adaptations and dynamic processes may seem trivial—that commitment binds people to actions and "binding" is a dynamic process, or that individual differences "develop" commitment—except that when we consider a coherent framework of what it means to be bound (Meyer et al., 2004) or what it means for something to be "developed" (Beck & Wilson, 2001), the contribution is much clearer. These are terms that are not trivial in psychology. They have rich histories that point us to theoretical and methodological traditions. Our point is that when commitment researchers think about the individual differences that might lead to commitment, we must consider what commitment and these individual influences do in the lives of individuals. To acknowledge that definitions are similar is not enough; if we take such a path, we will accumulate correlations but we will not accumulate knowledge. Instead, we must consider the purpose commitment serves in the formation of and reaction to objective life experiences and external influences in the context of our basic tendencies. Then we might begin to understand.

References

Ainsworth, M.D.S. (1989). Attachments beyond infancy. *American Psychologist, 44,* 709–716.

Ainsworth, M. D. S., Blehar, M. C., Waters, E., & Wall, S. (1978). *Patterns of attachment: A psychological study of the Strange Situation.* Hillsdale, NJ: Lawrence Erlbaum.

Ajzen, I. (1991). The theory of planned behavior. *Organizational Behavior and Human Decision Processes, 50,* 179–211.

Arvey, R. D., Bouchard, T. J., Segal, N. L., & Abraham, L. M. (1989). Job satisfaction: Environmental and genetic components. *Journal of Applied Psychology, 74,* 187–192.

Ashforth, B. E., & Mael, F. (1989). Social identity theory and the organization. *Academy of Management Review, 14,* 20–39.

Baard, P. P., Deci, E. L., & Ryan, R. M. (2004). Intrinsic need satisfaction: A motivational basis of performance and well-being in two work settings. *Journal of Applied Social Psychology, 34,* 2045–2068.

Bacharach, S. B., & Bamberger, P. A. (2004). Diversity and the union: The effect of demographic dissimilarity on members' union attachment. *Group and Organization Management, 29,* 385–418.

Baldwin, M.W., Keelan, J.P.R., Fehr, B., Enns, V., & Koh-Rangarajoo, E. (1996). Social-cognitive conceptualization of attachment working models: Availability and accessibility effects. *Journal of Personality and Social Psychology, 71,* 94–109.

Bandura, A., & Locke, E. A. (2003). Negative self-efficacy and goal effects revisted. *Journal of Applied Psychology, 88,* 87–99.

Bartholomew, K. (1990). Avoidance of intimacy: An attachment perspective. *Journal of Social and Personal Relationships, 7,* 147–178.

Bartholomew, K., & Horowitz, L. M. (1991). Attachment styles among young adults: A test of a four-category model. *Journal of Personality and Social Psychology, 61,* 226–244.

Becker, T. E., & Kernan, M. C. (2003). Matching commitment to supervisors and organizations to in-role and extra-role performance. *Human Performance, 16,* 327–348.

Beck, K., & Wilson, C. (2001). Have we studied, should we study, and can we study the development of commitment? Methodological issues and the developmental study of work-related commitment. *Human Resource Management Review, 11,* 257–278.

Belk, R. W. (1979). Gift-giving behavior. In J. Sheth (Ed.), *Research in marketing,* Vol. 2 (pp. 95–126). Greenwich, CT: JAI Press.

Belsky, J. (1999). Interactional and contextual determinants of attachment security. In J. Cassidy & P. R. Shaver (Eds.), *Handbook of Attachment: Theory, research, and clinical applications* (pp. 249–264). New York: Guilford.

Benoit, D., & Parker, K. C. H. (1994). Stability and transmission of attachment across three generations. *Child Development, 65,* 1444–1456.

Berg, M. R., Janoff-Bulman, R., & Cotter, J. (2001). Perceiving value in obligations and goals: Wanting to do what should be done. *Personality and Social Psychology Bulletin, 27,* 982–995.

Bergman, M. E. (2006). The relationship between affective and normative commitment: Review and research agenda. *Journal of Organizational Behavior (Special Issue on Workplace Commitment and Identification), 27,* 645–663.

Bettencourt, B. A., & Sheldon, K. M. (2001). Social roles as mechanisms for psychological need satisfaction within social groups. *Journal of Personality and Social Psychology, 81(6),* 1131–1143.

Blau, P. M. (1986). *Exchange and power in social life.* New Brunswick, NJ: Transaction Publishers.

Bowlby, J. (1969). *Attachment and loss; Volume I: Attachment.* New York: Tavistock Institute of Human Relations.

Bowlby, J. (1973). *Attachment and loss; Volume II, Separation: Anxiety and anger.* New York: Tavistock Institute of Human Relations.

Bowlby, J. (1988). *A secure base: Parent-child attachment and healthy human development.* New York: Basic Books.

Brennan, K. A., Clark, C. L., & Shaver, P. R. (1998). Self-report measurement of adult attachment: An integrative overview. In J. A. Simpson and W. S. Rholes (Eds.), *Attachment theory and close relationships* (p. 46–76). New York: Guilford.

Bridges, L., Connell, J. P., & Belsky, J. (1988). Similarities and differences in infant-mother and infant-father interaction in the Strange Situation. *Development Psychology, 24,* 92–100.

Brief, A. P. (1998). *Attitudes in and around organizations.* Thousand Oaks, CA: Sage.

Collins, N. L., Guichard, A. C., Ford, M. B., & Feeney, B. C. (2004). Working models of attachment: New developments and emerging themes. In W. S. Rholes & J. A. Simpson (Eds.), *Adult attachment: Theory, research, and clinical implications* (pp. 196–239). New York: Guilford.

Collins, N. L., & Read, S. J. (1994). Cognitive representations of attachment: The structure and function of working models. *Advances in Personal Relationships, 5,* 53–90.

Cooper-Hakim, A., & Viswesvaran, C. (2005). The construct of work commitment: Testing an integrative framework. *Psychological Bulletin, 131,* 241–259.

Costa, P. T., & McCrae, R. R. (1980). Influence of extraversion and neuroticism on subjective well-being: Happy and unhappy people. *Journal of Personality and Social Psychology, 38,* 36–51.

Costa, P.T., & McCrae, R.R. (1992). Four ways five factors are basic. *Personality and Individual Differences, 13,* 653–665.

Cropanzano, R., James, K., & Konovsky, M. A. (1993). Dispositional affectivity as a predictor of work attitudes and job performance. *Journal of Organizational Behavior, 14,* 595–606.

Davila, J., & Cobb, R. J. (2004). Predictors of change in attachment security during adulthood. In W. S. Rholes & J. A. Simpson (Eds.), *Adult attachment: Theory, research, and clinical implications* (pp. 133–156). New York: Guilford.

Deci, E. L., & Ryan, R. M. (1985). *Intrinsic Motivation and Self-Determination in Human Behavior.* New York: Plenum Press.

Deci, E. L., & Ryan, R. M. (2000). The "what" and "why" of goal pursuits: Human needs and the self-determination of behavior. *Psychological Inquiry, 11(4),* 227–268.

Deci, E. L., & Ryan, R. M. (2002). An overview of self-determination research: An organismic-dialectical perspective. In E. L. Deci & R. M. Ryan (Eds.), *Handbook of Self-Determination Research* (pp. 3–33). New York: University of Rochester Press.

Deci, E. L., Ryan, R. M., Gagné, M., Leone, D. R., Usunov, J., & Kornazheva, B. P. (2001). Need satisfaction, motivation, and well-being in the work organizations of a former eastern bloc country: A cross-cultural study of self-determination. *Personality and Social Psychology Bulletin, 27(8),* 930–942.

Dozier, M., & Kobak, R.R. (1992). Psychophysiology in attacment interviews: Converging evidence for deactivating strategies. *Child Development, 63,* 1473–1480.

Edwards, J. A. (1991). The measurement of type A behavior pattern: An assessment of criterion-oriented validity, content validity, and construct validity. In C. L. Cooper & R. Payne (Eds.), *Personality and stress: Individual differences in the stress process.* New York: John Wiley and Sons.

Egeland, B., & Farber, E. A. (1984). Infant-mother attachment: Factors related to its development and changes over time. *Child Development, 55,* 753–771.

Erdhiem, J., Wang, M., & Zickar, M. J. (2006). Linking the Big Five personality constructs to organizational commitment. *Personality and Individual Differences, 41,* 959–970.

Finkelstein, L., Protolipac, D., & Stiles, P. (2006). Personality and organizational commitment: Mediational role of job characteristics perceptions. Poster presented at the 21st annual meeting of the Society for Industrial and Organizational Psychology, Dallas, TX.

Fraley, R. C., & Waller, N. G. (1998). Adult attachment patterns: A test of the typological model. In J. A. Simpson and W. S. Rholes (Eds.), *Attachment theory and close relationships* (p. 77–114). New York: Guilford.

Gagné, M. (2003). The role of autonomy support and autonomy orientation in prosocial behavior engagement. *Motivation and Emotion, 27(3),* 199–223.

Gagné, M., & Deci, E. L. (2005). Self-determination theory and work motivation. *Journal of Organizational Behavior, 26,* 331–362.

Gardner, D. G., & Pierce, J. L. (1998). Self-esteem and self-efficacy within the organizational context. *Group and Organization Management, 23,* 48–70.

Gellatly, I. R., Meyer, J. P., & Luchak, A. A. (2006). Combined effects of the three commitment components on focal and discretionary behaviors: A test of Meyer and Herscovitch's propositions. *Journal of Organizational Behavior, 69,* 331–345.

Gouldner, A. W. (1960). The norm of reciprocity: A preliminary statement. *American Sociological Review, 25,* 161–178.

Haggar, M. S., Chatzisarantis, N. L. D., & Harris, J. (2006). From psychological need satisfaction to intentional behavior: Testing a motivational sequence in two behavioral contexts. *Personality and Social Psychology Bulletin, 32(2),* 131–148.

Hazan, C., Gur-Yaish, N., & Campa, M. (2004). What does it mean to be attached? In W. S. Rholes & J. A. Simpson (Eds.), *Adult attachment: Theory, research, and clinical implications* (pp. 55–85). New York: Guilford.

Hazan, C., & Shaver, P. R. (1987). Romantic love conceptualized as an attachment process. *Journal of Personality and Social Psychology, 52,* 511–524.

Hazan, C., & Shaver, P. R. (1990). Love and work: An attachment-theoretical perspective. *Journal of Personality and Social Psychology, 59,* 270–280.

Herrbach, O. (2006). A matter of feeling? The affective tone of organizational commitment and identification. *Journal of Organizational Behavior, 27,* 629–643.

Higgins, E. T., Roney, C. J. R., Crowe, E., & Hymes, C. (1994). Ideal versus ought predilections for approach and avoidance: Distinct self-regulatory systems. *Journal of Personality and Social Psychology, 66,* 276–286.

Hinde, R. A., & Stevenson-Hinde, J. (1991). Perspectives on attachment. In C. M. Parkes, J. Stevenson-Hinde, & P. Marris (Eds.), *Attachment across the life cycle* (pp. 52–65). London: Routledge.

Hochwarter, W. A., Perrewé, P. L., Ferris, G. R., & Guercio, R. (1999). Commitment as an antidote to the tension and turnover consequences of organizational politics. *Journal of Vocational Behavior, 55,* 277–297.

Hoffman, B. J., Blair, C. A., Meriac, J. P., & Woehr, D. J. (2007). Expanding the criterion domain? A quantitative review of the OCB literature. *Journal of Applied Psychology, 92,* 555–566.

Hulin, C.L. (1991). Adaptation, persistence, and commitment in organizations. In M.D. Dunnette & L. Hough (Eds.), *Handbook of industrial and organizational psychology* (pp. 445–506). Palo Alto: Consulting Psychologists Press.

Ilardi, B. C., Leone, D. R., Kasser, T., & Ryan, R. M. (1993). Employee and supervisor ratings of motivation: Main effects and discrepancies associated with job satisfaction and adjustment in a factory setting. *Journal of Applied Social Psychology, 23,* 1789–1805.

Iverson, R. D., & Buttigieg, D. M. (1997). Antecedents of union commitment: The impact of union membership differences in vertical dyads and work group relationships. *Human Relations, 50,* 1485–1510.

Iverson, R. D., & Kuruvilla, S. (1995). Antecedents of union loyalty: The influence of individual dispositions and organizational context. *Journal of Organizational Behavior, 16,* 557–582.

Janoff-Bulman, R., & Leggatt, H. K. (2002). Culture and social obligation: When "shoulds" are perceived as "wants." *Journal of Research in Personality, 36,* 260–270.

Judge, T. A., Bono, J. E., Erez, A., & Locke, E. A. (2005). Core self-evaluations and job and life satisfaction: The role of self-concordance and goal attainment. *Journal of Applied Psychology, 90,* 257–268.

Judge, T. A., Heller, D., & Mount, M. K. (2002). Five-factor model of personality and job satisfaction: A meta-analysis. *Journal of Applied Psychology, 87,* 530–541.

Judge, T. A., & Kristof-Brown, A. L. (2004). Personality, interactional psychology, and person-organization fit. In B. Schneider & D. B. Smith (Eds.), *Personality and organizations.* Mahwah, NJ: Lawrence Erlbaum.

Judge, T. A., Thoresen, C. J., Pucik, V., & Welbourne, T. M. (1999). Managerial coping with organizational change: A dispositional perspective. *Journal of Applied Psychology, 84,* 107–122.

Kernis, M. H., Paradise, A. W., Whitaker, D. J., Wheatman, S. R., & Goldman, B. N. (2000). Master of one's psychological domain? Not likely if one's self-esteem is unstable. *Personality and Social Psychology Bulletin, 26,* 1297–1305.

Kim, S., Price, J. L., Mueller, C. W., & Watson, T. W. (1996). The determinants of career intent among physicians at a U.S. Air Force hospital. *Human Relations, 49,* 947–976.

Kirkpatrick, L. A. (1997). A longitudinal study of changes in religious belief and behavior as a function of individual differences in adult attachment style. *Journal for the Scientific Study of Religion, 36,* 207–217.

Kirkpatrick, L. A., & Shaver, P. R. (1990). Attachment theory and religion: Childhood attachments, religious beliefs, and conversion. *Journal for the Scientific Study of Religion, 29,* 315–334.

Klohnen, E. C., & John, O. P. (1998). Working models of attachment: A theory-based prototype approach. In J. A. Simpson and W. S. Rholes (Eds.), *Attachment theory and close relationships* (p. 115–140). New York: Guilford.

Kobak, R. (1994). Adult attachment: A personality or relationship construct? *Psychological Inquiry, 5,* 42–44.

Kohlberg, L. (1984). *The psychology of moral development.* San Francisco: Harper & Row.

Leary, M. R., Tambor, E. S., Terdal, S. K., & Downs, D. L. (1995). Self-esteem as an interpersonal monitor: The sociometer hypothesis. *Journal of Personality and Social Psychology, 68,* 518–530.

Lee, T. W., Ashford, S. J., Walsh, J. P., & Mowday, R. T. (1992). Commitment propensity, organizational commitment, and voluntary turnover: A longitudinal study of organizational entry processes. *Journal of Management, 18,* 15–32.

Leiva, P. I., Gaulke, K. M., Watrous, K. M., Huffman, A. H., Payne, S. C., & Webber, S. S. (2004). Personality correlated of commitment: An investigation of two foci of commitment. In M. E. Bergman (Chair), *Organizational commitment: Construct refinements and expansions.* Symposium presented at the 19th annual meeting of the Society for Industrial and Organizational Psychology, Chicago, IL.

LePine, J. A., Erez, A., & Johnson, D. E. (2002). The nature and dimensionality of organizational citizenship behavior: A critical review and meta-analysis. *Journal of Applied Psychology, 87*, 52–65.

Lewis, M. (1994). Does attachment imply a relationship or multiple relationships? *Psychological Inquiry, 5*, 47–51.

Macan, T. H., Trusty, M. L., & Trimble, S. K. (1996). Spector's work locus of control scale: Dimensionality and validity evidence. *Educational and Psychological Measurement, 56*, 349–357.

Mael, F. A., & Ashforth, B. E. (1992). Alumni and their alma mater: A partial test of the reformulated model of organizational identification. *Journal of Organizational Behavior, 13*, 103–123.

Mael, F. A., & Ashforth, B. E. (1995). Loyal from day one: Biodata, organizational identification, and turnover among newcomers. *Personnel Psychology, 48*, 309–333.

Mael, F. A., & Tetrick, L. E. (1992). Identifying organizational identification. *Educational and Psychological Measurement, 52*, 813–824.

Main, M. (1991). Metacognitive knowledge, metacognitive monitoring, and singular (coherent) vs. multiple (incoherent) model of attachment: Findings and directions for future research. In C. M. Parkes, J. Stevenson-Hinde, & P. Marris (Eds.), *Attachment across the life cycle* (pp. 127–159). London: Routledge.

Marvin, R. S., & Britner, P. A. (1999). Normative development: The ontogeny of attachment. In J. Cassidy & P. R. Shaver (Eds.), *Handbook of Attachment: Theory, research, and clinical applications* (pp. 44–67). New York: Guilford.

Mathieu, J. E., & Zajac, D. M. (1990). A review and meta-analysis of the antecedents, correlates, and consequences of organizational commitment. *Psychological Bulletin, 108*, 171–194.

McAdams, D. P., & Pals, J. L. (2006). A new big five: Fundamental principles for an integrative science of personality. *American Psychologist, 61*, 204–217.

McCrae, R. R., & Costa, P. T. (1996). Toward a new generation of personality theories: Theoretical contexts for the five-factor model. In J.S. Wiggins (Ed.), *The five-factor model of personality* (pp. 51–87). New York: Guilford.

McCrae, R. R., & John, O. P. (1992). An introduction to the five-factor model and its applications. *Journal of Personality, 2*, 175–215.

Meyer, J. P., & Allen, N. J. (1991). A three-component conceptualization of organizational commitment. *Human Resource Management Review, 1*, 61–89.

Meyer, J. P., & Allen, N. J. (1997). *Commitment in the workplace*. Thousand Oaks, CA: Sage.

Meyer, J. P., Becker, T. E., & Vandenberghe, C. (2004). Employee commitment and motivation: A conceptual analysis and integrative model. *Journal of Applied Psychology, 89*, 991–1007.

Meyer, J. P., Becker, T. E., & Van Dick, R. (2006). Social identities and commitments at work: Toward an integrative model. *Journal of Organizational Behavior, 27*, 665–683.

Meyer, J. P., & Herscovitch, L. (2001). Commitment in the workplace: Toward a general model. *Human Resource Management Review, 11*, 299–326.

Meyer, J. P., Stanley, D. J., Hercovitch, L., & Topolnytsky, L. (2002). Affective, continuance, and normative commitment to the organization: A meta-analysis of antecedents, correlates, and consequences. *Journal of Vocational Behavior, 61,* 20–52.

Mowday, R. T., Porter, L. W., & Steers, R. M. (1982). *Employee-organization linkages: the psychology of commitment, absenteeism, and turnover.* New York: Academic Press.

Naquin, S. S., & Holton, E. F., III. (2002). The effects of personality, affectivity, and work commitment on motivation to improve work through learning. *Human Resource Development Quarterly, 13,* 357–376.

O'Reilly, C. A., III, & Chatman, J. (1986). Organizational commitment and psychological attachment: The effects of compliance, identification, and internalization on prosocial behavior. *Journal of Applied Psychology, 71,* 492–499.

Organ, D. W., & Ryan, K. (1995). A meta-analytic review of attitudinal and dispositional predictors of organizational citizenship behavior. *Personnel Psychology, 48,* 775–802.

Payne, R. L., & Morrison, D. (2002). The differential effects of negative affectivity on measures of well-being versus job satisfaction and organizational commitment. *Anxiety, Stress, and Coping, 15,* 231–244.

Reichers, A. R. (1985). A review and reconceptualization of organizational commitment. *Academy of Management Review, 10,* 465–476.

Riketta, M. (2002). Attitudinal organizational commitment and job performance: A meta-analysis. *Journal of Organizational Behavior, 23,* 257–266.

Riketta, M., & Van Dick, R. (2005). Foci of attachment in organizations: A meta-analytic comparison of the strength and correlates of workgroup versus organizational identification and commitment. *Journal of Vocational Behavior, 65,* 490–510.

Schminke, M., Ambrose, M. L., & Neubaum, D. O. (2005). The effect of leader moral development on ethical climate and employee attitudes. *Organizational Behavior and Human Decision Processes, 97,* 135–151.

Shah, J., & Higgins, E. T. (1997). Expectancy X value effects: Regulatory focus as determinant of magnitude and direction. *Journal of Personality and Social Psychology, 73,* 447–458.

Shaver, P. R., Hazan, C., & Bradshaw, D. (1988). Love as attachment: The integration of three behavioral systems. In R. Sternberg & M. Barnes (Eds.), *The psychology of love* (pp. 69–99). New Haven, CT: Yale University Press.

Shaver, P. R., & Mikulincer, M. (2002). Attachment-related psychodynamics. *Attachment and Human Development, 4,* 133–161.

Sheldon, K. M., Elliot, A. J., Kim, Y., & Kasser, T. (2001). What is satisfying about satisfying events? Testing 10 candidate psychological needs. *Journal of Personality and Social Psychology, 80(2),* 325–339.

Simpson, J. A., & Rholes, W. S. (1998). Attachment in adulthood. In J. A. Simpson and W. S. Rholes (Eds.), *Attachment theory and close relationships* (p. 3–24). New York: Guilford.

Simpson, J. A., & Rholes, W. S. (2002). Fearful-avoidance, disorganization, and multiple working models: Some directions for future research and theory. *Attachment and Human Development, 4,* 223–229.

Smith, E. R., Murphy, J., & Coats, S. (1999). Attachment to groups: Theory and measurement. *Journal of Personality and Social Psychology, 77,* 94–110.

Stinglhamber, F., & Vandenberghe, C. (2003). Organizations and supervisors as sources of support and targets of commitment: A longitudinal study. *Journal of Organizational Behavior, 24,* 251–270.

Sue-Chan, C., & Ong, M. (2002). Goal assignment and performance: Assessing the mediating roles of goal commitment and self-efficacy and the moderating role of power distance. *Organizational Behavior and Human Decision Processes, 89,* 1140–1161.

Tajfel, H., & Turner, J. C. (1985). The social identity theory of intergroup behavior. In S. Worchel & W. Austin (Eds.), *Psychology of intergroup relations.* Chicago: Nelson-Hall.

Tang, T. L., Baldwin, L. J., & Frost, A. G. (1997). Locus of control as a moderator of the self-reported performance feedback-personal sacrifice relationship. *Personality and Individual Difference, 22,* 201–211.

Tellegen, A. (1985). Structures of mood and personality and their relevance to assessing anxiety, with an emphasis on self-report. In A. H. Tuma & J. D. Maser (Eds.), *Anxiety and the anxiety disorders* (pp. 681–706). Hillsdale, NJ: Erlbaum.

Thoresen, C. J., Kaplan, S.A., Barsky, A. P., Warren, C. R., & de Chermon, K. (2003). The affective underpinnings of job perceptions and attitudes: A meta-analytic review and integration. *Psychological Bulletin, 129,* 914–945.

Vallerand, R. J., Fortier, M. S., & Guay, F. (1997). Self-determination and persistence in a real-life setting: Toward a motivational model of high school dropout. *Journal of Personality and Social Psychology, 72(5),* 1161–1176.

Wasti, S. A. (2003a). Organizational commitment, turnover intentions and the influence of cultural values. *Journal of Occupational and Organizational Psychology, 76,* 303–321.

Wasti, S. A. (2003b). The influence of cultural values on antecedents of organisational commitment: An individual level analysis. *Applied Psychology: An International Review, 52,* 533–554.

Wasti, S. A. (2005). Commitment profiles: Combinations of organizational commitment forms and job outcomes. *Journal of Vocational Behavior, 67,* 290–308.

Watrous, K. M., & Bergman, M. E. (2004). Organizational commitment, organizational identification, and personality: An examination of interrelationships among three related constructs. In M. E. Bergman (Chair), *Organizational commitment: Construct refinements and expansions.* Symposium presented at the 19th annual meeting of the Society for Industrial and Organizational Psychology, Chicago, IL.

Watson, D., & Clark, L. A. (1984). Negative affectivity: The disposition to experience aversive emotional states. *Psychological Bulletin, 96,* 465–490.

Watson, D., & Tellegen, A. (1985). Toward a consensual structure of mood. *Psychology Bulletin, 98,* 219–235.

Weiss, H. M., & Cropanzano, R. (1996). Affective events theory: A theoretical discussion of the structure, causes and consequences of affective experiences at work. *Research in Organizational Behavior, 18,* 1–74.

Whyte, G., Saks, A. M., & Hook, S. (1997). When success breeds failure: The role of self-efficacy in escalating commitment to a losing course of action. *Journal of Organizational Behavior, 18,* 415–432.

Wiggins, J. S., & Trapnell, P. D. (1996). A dyadic-interactional perspective on the five factor model. In J. S. Wiggins (Ed.), *The five factor model of personality: Theoretical perspectives* (pp. 88–162). New York: Guilford Press.

Williams, L. J., Gavin, M. B., & Williams, M. L. (1996). Measurement and nonmeasurement processes with negative affectivity and employee attitudes. *Journal of Applied Psychology, 81,* 88–101.

Wolfe, J. B., & Betz, N. E. (2004). The relationship of attachment variables to career decision-making self-efficacy and fear of commitment. *The Career Development Quarterly, 52,* 363–369.

8

Social Influences

Sandy J. Wayne*
University of Illinois at Chicago

Jacqueline A.-M. Coyle-Shapiro
London School of Economics and Political Science

Robert Eisenberger
University of Delaware

Robert C. Liden
University of Illinois at Chicago

Denise M. Rousseau
Carnegie Mellon University

Lynn M. Shore
San Diego State University

The purpose of this chapter is to examine social antecedents of commitment. Social antecedents include organizational justice, trust, politics, and relationships with coworkers, team, leader, and organization. We have narrowed our focus by examining three antecedents that are based on social exchange theory, consisting of leader-member exchange (LMX), perceived organizational support (POS), and psychological contract (PC) theory. Compared to the other chapters in this section, our focus is on specific relationships as antecedents of commitment rather than individual (chapter 7), organizational (chapter 9), or cultural characteristics (chapter 10). For example, we examine how the employee-organization relationship in terms of POS impacts employee commitment rather than separately examining characteristics of the employee or characteristics of the organization, which is the focus of chapters 7 and 9, respectively.

---

* The authors contributed equally to this chapter.

LMX is the quality of the exchange relationship that develops between a member and his/her leader ranging from low- to high-quality (Liden, Sparrowe, & Wayne, 1997). Low-quality LMX relationships are based on compliance with job descriptions, tend not to evolve beyond what is specified in the employment contract, and have been identified as economic exchanges. Conversely, high-quality LMX relationships are characterized as social exchange relationships that involve exchange of resources and support that extend beyond contractual agreements (Settoon, Bennett, & Liden, 1996). POS is a global belief that employees form based on the extent to which they believe their organization cares about them and values their contributions (Eisenberger, Huntington, Hutchison, & Sowa, 1986). PC theory argues that employees form beliefs about what they have promised to provide their organization and what the organization has promised to provide them (Rousseau, 1995). LMX, POS, and PC theory are conceptually similar in that they are all based on social exchange theory (Blau, 1964). Thus, all three theories discuss how resource exchange within a relationship and the norm of reciprocity influences employee attitudinal and behavioral outcomes. All three constructs have a relationship component, with LMX focusing on the employee-leader relationship, whereas POS and PC theory are primarily concerned with the employee-employer relationship. In terms of level of analysis, LMX, POS, and PC theory primarily focus on the individual, and thus, this has been the predominant level of theory building and measurement. Psychological mechanisms, therefore, form the basis of most theory building in these areas.

These three social influences were selected because they are prominent theories in the field of organizational behavior and numerous empirical studies testing these theories have included commitment as a consequence. Thus, these social antecedents appear to play a prominent role in understanding commitment. Within each area, prior research on the link between the social antecedent (LMX, POS, or PC) and foci and mindsets of commitment is reviewed. This is followed by a discussion of suggestions for future research.

Commitment and LMX

Current Knowledge Regarding the Link Between LMX and Commitment

Initial studies as well as virtually all subsequent investigations of commitment and LMX have focused on affective commitment. Results have consistently demonstrated a positive association between LMX and affective commitment (e.g., Basu & Green, 1997; Liden, Wayne, & Sparrowe, 2000; Schriesheim, Castro, & Yammarino, 2000; Schyns, Paul, Mohr, & Blank, 2005; Tierney, Bauer, & Potter, 2002). Out of 29 studies that we located, 23 examined correlations between LMX and affective commitment and all found either direct or mediated positive relationships. Generalizability appears to be unquestioned as these studies involved a wide range of samples, including employees engaged in manufacturing, sales, police work, nursing, research and development, and management, and representing multiple countries in addition to the U.S., such as China (Law, Wong, D. Wang, & L. Wang, 2000), Great Britain (Epitropaki & Martin, 2005) and Singapore (Lee, 2005). Despite the consistent support for correlations between LMX and affective commitment, in studies that have also included POS, relationships between POS and affective commitment have been stronger than those between LMX and affective commitment (Masterson, Lewis, Goldman, & Taylor, 2000; Settoon et al., 1996; Wayne, Shore, & Liden, 1997; Wayne, Shore, Bommer, & Tetrick, 2002). Wayne and her colleagues (1997) found evidence for a reciprocal relationship between LMX and POS.

We identified nine studies that examined relationships between LMX (or closely related constructs involving the dyadic relationship between leader and member) and mindsets of commitment other than affective commitment (e.g., normative or continuance commitment). Only one study examined all three mindsets of commitment in organizations: affective, continuance, and normative (Self, Holt, & Schaninger, 2005). As expected, these researchers found that the source of support paralleled the foci of commitment. Specifically, workgroup support was tied to affective and normative commitment to the workgroup, and organizational support (POS) was linked to affective and normative commitment to the organization. Other research has demonstrated that individuals reporting higher quality LMX relationships are more committed to engaging in safe work behaviors (Hofmann & Morgeson, 1999). It has also been found that member commitment toward goal fulfillment is increasingly higher as LMX increases (Klein & Kim, 1998; Piccolo & Colquitt, 2006).

Utility of Current Knowledge on LMX and Commitment

Research has consistently shown that LMX is positively related to a number of foci and mindsets of commitment. Much of the support for LMX-commitment associations has been based on attitudinal models of commitment (see chapter 1), where LMX is an antecedent of commitment. As noted by Oliver (1990), there is a "black box" in terms of *how* and *why* the relationships that leaders form with subordinates translate into affective commitment and goal commitment, as well as subsequent outcomes such as safety behavior and intentions to remain in the organization.

So, although LMX and commitment have been linked empirically, current commitment theory has been insufficient in explaining why LMX is linked to certain foci and mindsets of commitment.

Affective commitment. Although research has shown that POS is more strongly related to affective commitment than LMX, Eisenberger, Stinglhamber, Vandenberghe, Sucharski, and Rhoades (2002) established that leaders serve as the most critical agent of the organization in the eyes of many followers. These researchers found in a longitudinal cross-panel study that perceptions of supervisor support preceded POS, suggesting that the support that leaders provide to subordinates largely determines their perceptions of the extent to which they are supported by the organization. In turn, when employees feel supported by the organization, they tend to reciprocate by being committed to the organization (Eisenberger et al., 1986) and through in-role and extra-role behaviors (Masterson et al., 2000; Settoon et al., 1996; Wayne et al., 1997). So, even though the direct relationship between POS and affective commitment is stronger than the relationship between LMX and affective commitment, it appears that POS is largely based on support provided by the leader.

Goal commitment. Piccolo and Colquitt (2006) found support for their reasoning that leaders may affect subordinate goal commitment through perceptions of job characteristics, of which autonomy and feedback may be most directly tied to goal commitment. These researchers argued that when employees receive performance feedback and have control over how and when they complete their tasks, they become more committed to performance goals. Through feedback and provision of empowerment, which are clearly forms of support provided by the leader, subordinates reciprocate by being committed to the organization (Arnold, Arad, Rhoades, & Drasgow, 2000; Liden et al., 2000). Expanding on the influence of feedback on goal commitment, Henderson, Dulac, and Liden (2006) contended that LMX is positively related to communication richness, which in turn enhances the degree to which members understand the goal and perceive greater value in attaining the goal. These authors further argued that understanding the goal and desiring goal attainment lead to high levels of goal commitment. Consistent with the goal-setting literature (Locke & Latham, 2002), Klein and Kim (1998) found that goal commitment, in turn, is positively related to goal attainment, operationalized as sales performance. But interestingly, these researchers found that although goal commitment is positively related to sales performance for high-LMX members, it is not related to sales performance for low-LMX members.

Safety commitment. Hofmann and Morgeson (1999) hypothesized that when employees feel supported by the leader, as evidenced by high-LMX quality, they reciprocate by being more committed to engaging in safe behaviors and in turn are involved in fewer accidents than employees who are less supported, as reflected in lower LMX quality. Consistent with their hypotheses, Hofmann and Morgeson found LMX to be positively related to safety commitment and negatively related to accidents. Furthermore, they found support for leader safety communication as a mediator between LMX and safety commitment. This finding is consistent with LMX research showing LMX to be positively related to frequency of communication with the leader (Kacmar, Witt, Zivnuska, & Gully, 2003).

Future Research on LMX and Commitment

We suggest additional research on mindsets of commitment beyond affective commitment, which has been extensively studied with respect to LMX. We currently know relatively little about LMX as it relates to the mindsets of normative and continuance commitment, as well as the relation between LMX and the commitment foci of safety and goals. It would also be useful for research to be conducted that includes multiple commitment mindsets within the same study so that relative comparisons may be made. Foci of commitment, such as commitment to the supervisor, might help to untangle the overlap between POS and LMX. Research has suggested that employees differentiate between commitment to different foci, including commitment to the immediate supervisor versus commitment to others (Becker, 1992; Bentein, Stinglhamber, & Vandenberghe, 2002; Redman & Snape, 2005; Vandenberghe, Bentein, & Stinglhamber, 2004). This implies that when the immediate supervisor is seen as the main agent of the organization, employee perceptions of the organization are based on support provided by the supervisor (Eisenberger et al., 2002). Support from the supervisor would therefore present an obligation to reciprocate to the supervisor via supervisor commitment, but would also create an implied obligation to be committed to the organization. This is because support from the supervisor would be interpreted as indirectly coming from the organization through the supervisor, as an agent of the organization.

We encourage a continuation of recent research that has contributed toward a better understanding of how and why LMX relates to commitment. Examination of mediating and moderating variables that help to explain the relation between LMX and affective commitment offers promise. For example, research on goal orientations (Janssen & Van Yperen, 2004) might be integrated into a model of LMX, goal commitment, and goal attainment. LMX may interact with goal orientations in determining the degree of goal commitment and subsequent goal attainment. Specifically, the greatest commitment to goals should occur with the combination of high LMX and member mastery orientation, and the lowest goal commitment should be present with combined low LMX and a performance orientation.

Another largely unexplored avenue for future research is to examine multilevel issues surrounding the relationship between LMX and commitment. For example, Sherony and Green (2002) found among engineering and health services employees that although LMX and organizational commitment were positively correlated as in previous studies, variance in the quality of exchange relationships with coworkers was negatively related to organizational commitment. Similarly, the greater the variance in LMX across group members, the lower the mean commitment level for the group (Schyns, 2006). It would be interesting to extend this research by exploring in multilevel models the extent to which exchange relationships between leaders and their bosses (Tangirala, Green, & Ramanujam, 2007) and others in larger social networks (Sparrowe & Liden, 2005) influence individual levels of organizational commitment. Specifically, when the immediate leader has a high-quality relationship with his or her boss, more resources and support should be available to subordinates, which may increase the correlation between LMX and commitment to the organization via a desire to reciprocate for support received. Similarly, commitment to the organization may be more highly related to LMX when the leader is central in advice networks, as these leaders have more information to share with followers (cf. Sparrowe & Liden, 2005).

We recommend research that explores other contextual variables, such as organizational culture discussed in chapter 9, as they relate to associations between LMX and commitment (cf. Erdogan, Liden, & Kraimer, 2006). For example, we expect that in aggressive cultures, correlations between LMX and organizational commitment are weaker than in cultures that are characterized by high levels of respect for people. In the latter organizations, relationships between leaders and members are more likely to be driven by a concern for benefitting others, which is manifested in organizational commitment.

A final topic for future research is to explore cross-cultural differences in the association between LMX and commitment (see chapter 10). Do social exchange relationships between leader and member relate to commitment across national cultures? We suggest that several variables that have been shown to underlie differences between national cultures may influence the magnitude of correlations between LMX and commitment. For example, in collectivistic cultures, we expect the relationship between LMX and organizational commitment to be stronger than it is in relatively more individualistic cultures. This is because organizational commitment is characterized by concerns for the collective or the success of the larger entity to which all employees belong. In relatively individualistic cultures, members would tend to develop relationships with leaders for personal gains, such as personal career advancement, with relatively less concern for the organization.

Commitment and POS

Current Knowledge Regarding the Link Between POS and Commitment

Many employers value the benefits that accrue from employees' commitment to the organization. Employees often take the converse perspective, being concerned with the organization's commitment to their welfare. The organization serves as an important source of the employees' socioemotional resources, such as respect and caring, and tangible benefits, such as wages and medical insurance. Being regarded highly also indicates that increased effort will be noted and rewarded. Employees therefore develop general beliefs concerning the extent to which the organization cares about their well-being and values their contributions (Eisenberger et al., 1986; Rhoades & Eisenberger, 2002).

Organizational support theory considers the development, nature, and outcomes of POS (e.g., Eisenberger, Armeli, Rexwinkel, Lynch, & Rhoades, 2001; Rhoades & Eisenberger, 2002; Rhoades, Eisenberger, & Armeli, 2001; Shore & Shore, 1995). A key feature of POS is that it represents the employee's perceptions of the benevolent intentions of the organization based on the organization's discretionary acts. In contrast, employees' commitment reflects their intentions toward the organization. Thus, these two sets of constructs represent each exchange partner's contribution to the employee-organization relationship. Organizational support theory views POS as a relatively stable cognition based on a history of treatment by the organization (Shore & Shore, 1995). Likewise, Meyer and Herscovitch (2001) view affective, normative, and continuance commitment as three employee mindsets providing persisting motivation that may be distinguished from the short-term motivation associated with incentives. Yet, there are important differences between the constructs. First, POS lacks the affect directed at the organization that is implicit in Meyer and Herscovitch's three mindsets of affective, normative, and continuance commitment. POS is an affect-free cognition with motivational consequences to the extent that an employee has strong socio-emotional needs and/or accepts the norm of reciprocity as being relevant to the employee-employer relationship. Thus, socio-emotional need strength and reciprocity norm acceptance strongly influence employees' reactivity to POS (Armeli, Eisenberger, Fasolo, & Lynch, 1998; Eisenberger et al., 2001).

Second, while employee commitment has a long and diverse history influenced by varied perspectives (see Klein, Molloy, & Cooper in this volume), POS has developed based on a single formulation by Eisenberger and his colleagues (Eisenberger et al., 1986). Each of these construct histories has both benefits and liabilities. On the one hand, the diversity of perspectives in the employee commitment literature has created construct confusion but has also provided a rich and thought-provoking literature with extensive debate among scholars. On the other hand, the clarity in the POS literature has created continuity across scholars in their understanding and approach but has perhaps produced somewhat narrow conclusions in a construct domain that may be equally rich and broad as that for employee commitment. This latter point is especially relevant to linking POS with varied targets and mindsets of commitment, as we discuss below.

Organizational support theory builds on the central premise that workers act in accord with the norm of reciprocity, trading their effort and dedication to the organization for POS and its associated promise of future benefits (Blau, 1964; Eisenberger et al., 1986). A considerable body of evidence indicates that employees with POS experience their employment more favorably (e.g., demonstrating increased job satisfaction and positive mood and reduced stress) and are more invested in their work organization (e.g., demonstrating increased affective organizational commitment, increased performance, and reduced turnover; see review by Rhoades & Eisenberger, 2002).

Organizational support theory holds that POS fosters affective commitment by meeting employees' socio-emotional needs and creating a felt obligation to the organization (Armeli et al., 1998; Eisenberger et al., 1986). The fulfillment of socio-emotional needs is assumed to facilitate the incorporation of employees' organizational membership and role status into their social identity, thereby creating a strong affective commitment to the organization. Additionally, on the basis of the reciprocity norm, POS is held to create a felt obligation to care about the organization's welfare and help the organization reach its objectives. Employees could fulfill this debt through greater affective commitment and greater efforts to aid the organization. Accordingly, many studies have reported that POS and affective commitment are strongly associated yet empirically distinct (e.g., Shore & Tetrick, 1991; Shore & Wayne, 1993).

Consistent with these views, the relationship between POS and employee turnover was found to be greater among employees who strongly embraced the norm of reciprocity as applied to work (Eisenberger et al., 1986). Further, POS was positively related both to felt obligation and to affective commitment (Eisenberger et al., 2001). Likewise, POS has been found to influence turnover through its influence on affective commitment (D. G. Allen, Shore, & Griffeth, 2003). Because felt obligation is very similar to Meyer and Herscovitch's (2001) current conceptualization of normative commitment, these findings suggest that POS can be considered a major antecedent of both affective and normative commitment.

POS provides an important mechanism by which positive work experiences lead to affective commitment (Meyer & Allen, 1997). Three major categories of work experiences—organizational rewards, procedural justice, and supervisor support—have been found to be positively related to affective commitment. By indicating the organization's positive evaluation of employees, POS appears to mediate the relationships between such work experiences and affective commitment (Wayne et al., 1997). Consistent with this view, using a diverse sample of employees, POS was found by Rhoades et al. (2001) to mediate positive associations of the three major work experiences with affective commitment.

Shore and Shore (1995) argued that employee perceptions of justice should contribute to the development of POS. Such fair treatment suggests to employees that the organization cares about their well-being (Rhoades & Eisenberger, 2002). This link has been supported in a number of studies. Fasolo (1995) found that distributive and procedural justice of performance appraisals enhanced POS. Moorman, Blakely, and Niehoff (1998) and Masterson et al. (2000) found that justice predicted POS. Wayne et al. (2002) showed that justice influences affective commitment indirectly through its effects on POS.

A longitudinal panel study (Rhoades et al., 2001) examined changes in POS and affective commitment in retail employees over spans of two and three years. POS was found to be positively related to changes in affective commitment at both intervals, with no reverse relationship observed. A third study found a negative relationship between POS and subsequent voluntary employee turnover that was mediated by affective commitment both among retail employees and poultry- and feed-processing workers. These findings support the view that favorable job conditions operate on POS to influence affective commitment and its consequences.

Organizational support theory applies to the support received from supervisors, workgroups, top management, other organizational units, and representatives at various levels of the organizational hierarchy. In most organizations, both the overall organization and the lower-level embedded organizational units contribute to perceptions of support and the development of affective commitment. The decision to focus on a particular organizational unit, with respect to perceived support, will depend on the nature of the organization and the purposes of the analysis. In some organizations, such as conglomerates, the subsidiary for which the employee works may retain primary identity as *the organization*. For example, a small engineering firm studied by one of the authors was acquired by Hewlett Packard yet retained its original name and identity except for a few standardized human resource functions. For these employees, *the organization* remained the original company.

The significance of support received from, and consequent commitment to, workgroups and divisions seems to vary across organizations. For example, many small organizations are so well integrated that informal and fluctuating work arrangements dominate formal units and lines of authority, allowing little independent identity for workgroups or departments. On the other hand, in large organizations the manager and the unit may take on the "face" of the organization for individual employees, so that support at the local unit level may be viewed as representing support from the organization more generally.

Of particular theoretical and practical interest are findings that organizational support at one level in the organizational hierarchy can influence affective commitment at other levels. Mueller and Lawler (1999) have argued that lower-level organizational units (e.g., supervisor, workgroup) are usually more strongly involved in daily interactions with employees than are higher-level units, and thus strongly influence job satisfaction. However, to some degree, employees identify embedded lower-level units with higher levels and generalize experiences accordingly. Thus, Heffner and Gade (2003) showed that satisfaction with special operations forces (a lower-level unit) increased not only affective commitment to special operations forces, but also satisfaction with the military in general. Both of these, in turn, were positively related to military affective commitment. And military affective commitment was positively related to long-term military career intentions.

As noted in the prior section on LMX, the extent that employees identify their supervisor with the organization, perceived supervisor support should be positively associated with POS, a finding which has been repeatedly replicated (e.g., Kottke & Sharafinski, 1988; Malatesta, 1995; Rhoades et al., 2001; Shore & Tetrick, 1994; Yoon & Lim, 1999). Rhoades et al. (2001) showed in longitudinal studies that such perceived supervisor support was related to changes in POS over time, suggesting a causal relationship. Support from another important organizational unit, the workgroup, also has been found to be related to POS (Buffardi, Baughman, & Vagalebre, 2002).

The preceding findings suggest that employees generalize their experiences regarding supportive treatment from lower-level nested organizational units (e.g., supervisor, workgroup) to higher-level units, including the organization as a whole. Thus, the development of affective commitment does not depend solely on benefits received directly from the entire organization. Rather, organization members assign credit to higher order units both for the support received directly from those units and for some of the support received from the lower order units. According to Stinglhamber et al. (2006), the influence of perceived support received from lower-level organizational units on affective and normative commitment should depend on the extent to which employees identify lower-level units with the higher-level entities (organizational embodiment). These authors found with pharmaceutical employees that perceived supervisor support was related to POS, which carried through to affective commitment, and that these relationships were stronger when employees closely identified their supervisor with the organization.

Herscovitch and Meyer (2002) suggested that one way to distinguish the impact of different forms of commitment is to examine their combinatory effects. Gellatly, Hunter, Luchak, and Meyer (2007) recently examined the likelihood of academic physicians having various combinations of commitment (termed *commitment profiles*) as a function of POS. POS was related positively to the high-affective/high-normative commitment profile and negatively to the low-affective/low-normative commitment profile. This is consistent with prior findings that POS is related to felt obligation and affective commitment, and that felt obligation leads to affective commitment (Eisenberger et al., 2001). Interestingly, the relationships of POS with the affective/normative commitment combinations, found by Gellatly et al., appeared stronger in the positive direction with high continuance commitment and stronger in the negative direction with low continuance commitment. Thus, although POS is normally found to be slightly negatively related to continuance commitment, for some employees POS seems strongly related to a profile of mindsets involving the affect, obligation, and perceived implicit and explicit ties to the organization that would make it difficult for them to leave.

Utility of Current Knowledge on POS and Commitment

The literature we have reviewed suggests that work experiences provided by organizations operate through POS to influence affective commitment. Favorable organizationwide human resource policies, as well as beneficial treatment received from organizational agents (supervisors) and other embedded organizational units (e.g., workgroups and departments/divisions), should contribute to POS and therefore affective commitment. It has also been found that felt obligation mediates the relationship between POS and affective commitment (Eisenberger et al., 2001). Research needs to be done in which actual interventions are applied to see which types of experiences are most conducive to the development of POS and associated felt obligation. Such research on new hires would be especially useful in understanding how POS develops. Since POS has many positive effects, understanding its early development would be very valuable.

Employees infer the favorableness of treatment from the context in which it occurs. Sociologist Alvin Gouldner (1960) reasoned that favorable treatment received from others conveys positive regard for the recipient to the extent that the treatment is viewed as a discretionary or voluntary action rather than being impelled by circumstances. Eisenberger, Cummings, Armeli, and Lynch (1997) found that the positive association between the favorableness of various job conditions and POS was over six times greater when the organization was seen as having high discretion over carrying out the treatment, as opposed to little discretion. These findings indicate that favorable treatment by organizations is a necessary but not sufficient condition for establishing high POS. To the extent that an organization effectively conveys favorable treatment as a discretionary act, POS will be strongly enhanced. Similarly, Koys (1991) found that the strength of employee beliefs that personnel policies were intended to accord fair treatment was important for the development of affective commitment. In contrast, the belief that such policies were required by legal regulations was not related to affective commitment. Thus, a core element of organizational support theory is that beneficial treatment indicates the organization values the employee by providing discretionary positive treatment. Such discretionary treatment enhances affective commitment through its effect on POS. This literature also suggests the need to further understand different kinds of employee treatment, including such aspects as discretionary/mandated, organizational benevolence/harmfulness, economically/socially motivated. Such exploration may allow for additional understanding of associations between POS and employee commitment mindsets.

Future Research on POS and Commitment

Organizational support theory assumes that employees form generalizations concerning their valuation by organizational entities that hold significance for employees. While the focus was initially on perceived support from the entire organization, it was recognized and supported by empirical evidence that employees formed distinct support perceptions about workgroups (Buffardi et al., 2002; Self et al., 2005) and supervisors (e.g., Kottke & Sharafinski, 1988; Eisenberger et al., 2002). As previously discussed, it was further found that support from these embedded organizational units generalized to POS. The mechanism for this generalization is organizational embodiment, involving the extent to which employees identify the embedded organizational unit with a larger organizational unit (Stinglhamber et al., 2006). These findings suggest that employees generalize their experiences concerning support and commitment from lower order organizational units to higher order units.

Research on other relevant constituents of the employment relationship (Reichers, 1985) such as the union also suggests the need for additional development of constituent-generalizable and -specific conceptualizations. In the union setting, research has shown that union instrumentality (i.e., the extent to which the union is instrumental in obtaining desired benefits for members, such as pay and working conditions) and perceived union support are antecedents of union commitment (affective commitment to the union) and union participation (Barling, Fullagar, & Kelloway, 1992; Fullagar & Barling, 1991; Fullagar, Gallagher, Clark, & Carroll, 2004; Fuller & Hester, 2001; Sinclair & Tetrick, 1995; Tetrick, Shore,

McClurg, & Vandenberg, 2007). Tetrick (1995) pointed out that there is a fundamental difference in the relationship between individuals and their unions compared to individuals and their employers. While employees receive compensation from their employers for their contributions, members pay their unions for services and benefits received through their union dues. These differences suggest that affective, normative, and continuance commitment are likely to take on somewhat dissimilar meanings in a union setting than in an employer setting. In addition, as argued by Tetrick et al. (2007), the union represents all individuals in the bargaining unit, whether or not they are members of the union, and all members of the bargaining unit enjoy the rewards and favorable working conditions attained without differentiation among the members based on their contributions. Thus, organizational discretionary treatment, which plays an important role in employer-employee relations, is not an element of the union-member relationship. These differences between the employee-organization relationship and member-union relationship suggest that future research linking support and commitment should consider which features of organizational support theory and commitment theory are generalizable across contexts and targets, and which need revision or refinement to incorporate important features of the particular relationship of interest.

Progress in future research on the relationship between POS and affective commitment might benefit from the study of individual characteristics (see chapter 7), such as dispositional moderating variables that involve socio-emotional needs. Because organizational support theory assumes that POS contributes to affective commitment in part through the fulfillment of socio-emotional needs, employees with high needs should show a strong POS–affective commitment relationship. For the relationship between POS and normative commitment, other dispositional moderating variables might be influential, such as conscientiousness. That is, the relationship between POS and normative commitment might be stronger for individuals with high levels of conscientiousness because such individuals also are likely to expect conscientiousness from others, including organizational representatives. POS, which is associated with attributions of caring and value, may serve as an indicator of likely conscientious treatment of employees.

Another important topic involves group- and organization-level effects on POS and therefore affective commitment. To the extent that organizations adopt strategic policies that communicate positive valuation of employees, affective commitment should be enhanced. Finally, a clearer conceptual analysis is needed for the relationships of POS with continuance and normative commitment. Might the perception of "being trapped" in the organization, as related to continuance commitment, lessen POS because of a reduction of perceived self-determination? Normative commitment, as recently formulated by Meyer and Herscovitch (2001), has moved away from the heavy emphasis on obligation to remain with the organization and to a more diverse set of obligations to the organization. Thus, normative commitment has grown more similar to organizational support theory's concept of a felt obligation to help the organization reach its goals. This raises the question of whether the concepts of normative commitment and felt obligation should be merged. Finally, though we expect POS to be primarily associated with affective organizational commitment, many questions remain as to whether POS might also influence other targets of commitment, such as commitment to the supervisor and the workgroup, by enhancing employee feelings of being valued and cared about. Though presumably the organization would be the primary target of such support, employees may also choose to reciprocate to other organizational members whom they view as representatives of the organization.

While organizational support theory provides a strong basis for links between POS and both affective and normative commitment, more research is needed that seeks to expand understanding of these associations. For example, why might POS have stronger links with affective than with normative commitment, especially given that the basis for predicting POS effects is a sense of employee obligation, which is reflected in normative commitment? One possibility is POS's impact on affective commitment through the fulfillment of socio-emotional needs. It is also the case that a felt obligation to help the organization reach its objectives resulting from favorable treatment is somewhat similar to normative commitment, even if the constructs have been used in separate streams of research. Specifically, felt obligation is viewed as an outcome of POS and depends on employees' acceptance of the reciprocity norm as applied to work, and normative commitment has evolved into a concept focusing on multiple potential bases of obligation. Thus, until there is more evidence about the distinctiveness of these concepts, we feel it is premature to pose specific relations between POS and normative commitment.

Organizational support theory has had little to say concerning the link between POS and continuance commitment, and yet prior research does suggest that these concepts are related. Continuance commitment generally is found to have a small negative relationship to POS (Shore, Tetrick, Lynch, & Barksdale, 2006), although previously discussed evidence suggests that for some employees, high POS is strongly positively related to a high-affective, -normative, and -continuance commitment profile, and low POS is strongly negatively related to a low-affective, -normative, and –continuance commitment profile (Gellatly et al., 2007). How might we account for these relationships of POS with continuance commitment? Organizational support theory supposes that POS increases reward expectancies (Eisenberger et al., 1986), and research supports this view. For employees showing the cluster effects, POS might enhance perceived entitlements and opportunities specific to the organization that would be difficult to duplicate elsewhere. Continuance commitment in the context of high affective and normative commitment might be experienced positively. On the other hand, the negative overall correlation between POS and continuance commitment suggests that for many employees, POS reduces continuance commitment. Thus, outside the context of high affective and normative commitment, continuance commitment might be experienced negatively.

One avenue for future research regarding this suggestion takes into account the distinction between affective and normative commitment's focus and concern with the organization's welfare and goals and considers continuance commitment's relationship to self-interested motives (R. E. Johnson & Chang, 2006; Meyer & Herscovitch, 2001; Meyer, Becker, & Vandenberghe, 2004). More attention might be given to ways in which POS causes employees to become more involved in their work activities and take a greater intrinsic interest in them, resulting in greater affective and normative commitment. In contrast, without the favorable context of affective and normative commitment, continuance commitment may be more related to feelings of entrapment and loss of self-determination, which might be lessened by POS. Consistent with this possibility, Gellatly et al. (2007) reported that POS was positively related to perceived job autonomy and that job autonomy was negatively related to continuance commitment. Gellatly et al. suggested that job autonomy might mitigate aversive feelings of control and perceived low self-determination associated continuance commitment.

As with organizational support theory, recent conceptualizations by Meyer and Herscovitch (2001) and Klein, Molloy, and Cooper (chapter 1) note that commitment can be formed to organizational units at different levels of specificity in the organization. Yet, these theories do not deal with the relationships of organizational support at one organizational level (e.g., supervisor) to commitment at a different organizational level (e.g., organization), as found by Stinglhamber et al. (2006), nor does it deal with generalization of commitment from lower-level organizational units to higher-level organizational units (Heffner & Gade, 2003). The organizational support theory construct of organizational embodiment, or something like it, would help these theories explain the integration of commitment across organizational units. Likewise, organizational strategies that encourage consistent expectations and treatment of employees may serve to create uniformity in employee perceptions of support and commitment to different targets (Shore, Porter, & Zahra, 2004). Cross-level research is clearly needed to better understand how managerial policies and philosophies, along with strategies and organizational culture, influence consistency and distinctiveness in relations between support and commitment across levels.

Commitment and PCs

Current Knowledge Regarding the Link Between PCs and Commitment

The empirical evidence tying PCs to organizational commitment centers around the link affective commitment has with PC fulfillment and breach (negative fulfillment). Contract breach occurs "when one party in a relationship perceives another to have failed to fulfil promised obligations" (Robinson & Rousseau, 1994, p. 247). Although researchers have measured contract breach in different ways, the empirical evidence is fairly consistent in supporting a negative relationship between contract breach and affective commitment (Bunderson, 2001; Coyle-Shapiro & Kessler, 1998; W. E. Hopkins, S. A. Hopkins, & Mallette, 2001; Kickul, 2001; Lester, Turnley, Bloodgood, & Bolino, 2002; Restubog, Bordia, & Tang, 2006; Robinson, 1996; Robinson & Rousseau, 1994; Turnley & Feldman, 1999). (Note: contract breach is commonly defined and operationalized in terms of the lower range of the fulfillment continuum, the latter ranging from highly unfulfilled to highly fulfilled.) Employees who perceive that their employer has failed to fulfill one or more obligations are expected to respond by lowering their affective commitment to the organization. In comparison, employees who perceive their employer to have fulfilled its obligations are likely to increase their affective commitment.

Although contract breach has negative ramifications for affective commitment, little is known about the conditions under which the impact of contract breach on affective commitment is exacerbated or mitigated. Conditions such as the employment exchange's prior history (Rousseau, 1995) and the nature or content of the PC itself (relational or transactional; (Robinson & Rousseau, 1994; Zhao, Wayne, Glibkowski, & Bravo, 2007) can strengthen or weaken the impact of contract breach on worker attachment to the firm.

An individual's evaluation of how well his/her employer fulfills the PC is an important although not an exclusive basis for the development of affective commitment. The nature of the PC and degree of convergence between the employee and employer in terms of their respective obligations have also been linked to affective commitment, although studies that focus on the actual obligations the PC entails are less common than evaluations of PC breach or fulfillment (Rousseau & Tijoriwala, 1998). Sels, Janssens and van den Brande (2004) found that the dimensions of long-term mutual obligations, acceptance of an unequal employment relationship, and a collective contract level were positively associated with affective commitment. Dabos and Rousseau (2004a) report that the degree of agreement in the PCs of worker and employer is positively related to worker attachment to the firm, at least with respect to those PCs incorporating relational terms. Agreement with regard to more monetary or transactional features was found to have no relationship to worker attachment.

A dominant explanation put forward for the negative relationship between contract breach and affective commitment is the norm of reciprocity. However, this explanation is rarely empirically examined, and furthermore, little consideration has been given to different forms of reciprocity that may underpin the process of psychological contracting. Sahlins (1972) distinguished three forms of reciprocity: generalized, balanced, and negative, based on three dimensions of equivalence of the returns, immediacy of returns, and the degree and nature of the interests of the exchange partners. Generalized reciprocity captures an exchange in which the equivalence and timing of the returns are less important and the interests of the exchange party is altruistic (Sparrowe & Liden, 1997). Balanced reciprocity is characterised by fixed or close timing of returns, exchanges of equal value, and mutual interest, whereas negative reciprocity differs on the dimension of interest in which exchange partners are driven by complete self-interest (Sparrowe & Liden, 1997). Parzefall (2005) found that generalized reciprocity fully mediated the relationship between PC fulfillment and affective commitment in a sample of Finnish knowledge workers. No relationship between balanced reciprocity and affective commitment was found. These findings suggest that employees' perception of their employer's contractual behavior influences the type of reciprocity governing the exchange.

Although the norm of reciprocity seems to be a dominant explanation for the relationship between fulfillment or breach of PCs and affective commitment, others exist. For example, J. L. Johnson and O'Leary-Kelly (2003) found that affective cynicism partially mediated the relationship between contract breach and organizational commitment (the authors combine affective and normative commitment). Other potential factors include the magnitude of the loss workers experience as a function of contract breach, and mitigating factors such as procedural and interactional justice (Masterson et al., 2000).

Little empirical work exists on the potential link of PC fulfillment or breach to continuance commitment. One study failed to find a significant relationship between PC fulfillment and continuance commitment (Parzefall, 2005). Although this study did not distinguish between transactional and relational contracts, transactional contracts are thought to be tied to continuance commitment, particularly on the part of marginalized workers and those with limited opportunities elsewhere (Rousseau, 1995).

Normative commitment captures the feeling of obligation to stay in the organization (Meyer & Allen, 1991) and thus can be construed as a component of an individual's PC. Though the PC comprises reciprocal obligations between employees and their employer (Rousseau, 1995), it is surprising that empirical studies have not examined normative commitment. Meyer, Allen, and Topolnytsky (1998) suggest that normative commitment might reflect an employee's recognition of his/her obligation within their PC. Furthermore, Meyer, Stanley, Herscovitch, and Topolnytsky (2002) suggest that normative commitment may develop in consequence of benefits workers receive from the employer, which in turn create a felt obligation to reciprocate. Thus, normative commitment can function both as a term of an individual's PC as well as a consequence of employee reciprocity for previous employer contract fulfillment.

Reflecting upon commitment from a PC perspective surfaces some unsettled issues. First, the link between PC fulfillment and affective commitment is based on the involvement, shared values, and identification through which fulfilled PCs give rise to affective commitment (Meyer & Herscovitch, 2001). The affective commitment research is silent with regard to reciprocity. This is contrary to the implicit assumption adopted by PC researchers that affective commitment is in some way driven by the norm of reciprocity. Second, normative commitment may overlap with PC obligations such that it has no surplus or distinct meaning. This is discussed in a later section.

Utility of Current Knowledge on PC Theory and Commitment

Joining PC theory to commitment research highlights reciprocity as the underlying mechanism for enhancing affective commitment. With this in mind, employers seeking to promote affective commitment need to take steps that minimize employees' experience of contract breach while enhancing perceptions of contract fulfillment. Affective attachment is a consequence of the psychological experience of the employment relationship, and its value to the firm derives from the ways in which it motivates employees to reciprocate.

Contract fulfillment signals the employer's future intent toward the employee. In particular, fulfilling the employee's PC derives from a shared understanding by employer and worker regarding the employer's obligations (as worker fulfillment reflects mutuality regarding the employee's obligations to the firm). Mutuality is likely based on frequent interaction between the parties and the attention each party gives to the needs of the other (a condition of a mutual relational agreement; Rousseau, 2001; Wade-Benzoni, Rousseau, & Li, 2006). It is also facilitated by public communications that reinforce shared perspectives among coworkers regarding the organization's commitments and fulfillment of its obligations (e.g., Ho, Rousseau, & Levesque, 2006).

Future Research on PCs and Commitment

In reflecting on the need for further theory development, an obvious concern is the meaning of commitment in the context of the dynamic contemporary workplace, as discussed in chapter 2. Despite the increasing prevalence of layoffs, short-term employment arrangements, independent contractors, and labor force disruption, it is apparent that workers continue to prize employment based upon long-term commitments and mutual support, while more firms offer such arrangements, if at all, to only their most highly valued employees (Groysberg, Ashish, & Nitin, 2004; Rousseau, 2005a) or where they derive strategic value from building workforce problem-solving capacity over time (e.g., Shaw, 2006). However, research on shorter term employment arrangements involving limited obligations on the part of both worker and employer yields a mix of findings. Interim managers hired as temporary executives with limited term financial contracts nonetheless vest socio-emotional attachment to the firm, particularly when the relationship is viewed as fair (Rybnikova, 2006). Similarly, Van Dyne and Ang (1998) found that outsourced workers hired back as contractors had more positive reactions to the workplace than their former full-time counterparts still employed in the company. Lastly, a seven-country study found that contingent workers experience different types of PCs, which are likely to account for differential workplace responses (Schalk, de Jong, & Linde, 2006). Thus, the shift to a more formalized, explicit economic contract does not necessarily mean low job attitudes, limited contributions, or the absence of affective commitment. What is less clear, however, is the form that affective commitment takes in the contemporary workplace.

Affective commitment may be enhanced by employers who provide socio-emotional support to workers (Eisenberger et al., 1986; Eisenberger et al., 1997; Eisenberger et al., 2001), regardless of the expected duration of the employment relationship. Moreover, support in the form of career development opportunities can be especially valued by workers challenged to maintain their employability in the face of absent or uncertain employer commitments with regard to future employment prospects. Similarly, consistent with Groysberg et al. (2004), high-performing workers who are successful in bargaining for individual employment conditions that provide developmental opportunities or signal future promising prospects with the firm can respond with greater affective commitment as well as a greater sense of obligation to remain with the supportive employer (normative commitment; Rousseau, 2005b).

Our review of the PC-commitment connections suggests the importance of examining the content and conditions of the psychological contract in understanding the nature of commitment among workers across the broad spectrum of contemporary work arrangements. In particular, the induction of the normative commitment to remain with the firm due to valued resources that reinforce the employment relationship is an important focus for future research. Given the link between normative commitment and reciprocal obligations, and the dearth of research on normative commitment, more research into its dynamics and overlap with other constructs is critical.

One question a PC perspective raises is the conceptualization of the other party in the worker's PC. Traditional commitment theories focus on the employee-firm relationship. However, PC research suggests that other parties might be one's immediate manager, acting as an agent of the employer; one's team members in a decentralized firm (Rousseau, 1995); or other entity such as patient, client, or profession (Bunderson, 2001). Commitment research recently has paid more careful attention to the target of the commitment, operationalizing it with respect to workgroups, managers, and the organization itself. Research linking PCs and commitment needs to focus more carefully on the target of each.

Although the relationship between PC and affective commitment has received greater attention vis-à-vis other forms of commitment, gaps remain in our understanding of this relationship. Additional research could explore the role of negative emotions in the relationship between breach and affective commitment following Zhao et al. (2007). Other potential mechanisms include trust (Robinson & Rousseau, 1994), perceived inequity (Robinson, Kraatz, & Rousseau, 1994), and impediment to goal progression (Conway & Briner, 2002); examination of these would expand the potential mechanisms through which breach has a negative effect on affective commitment.

Future research could explore the relationship between PCs and normative commitment in terms of whether it represents a term of an individual's PC or an outcome based on employees reciprocating employer contract fulfillment. A priori, the lack of discrimination between the constructs of affective and normative commitment needs to be addressed (Ko, Price, & Mueller, 1997). This is partly a measurement issue, as normative commitment items seem to be worded in a way that evokes respondents' affective bond (Bergman, 2006). However, it is also a conceptual issue in terms of the psychological processes that differentiate the development of affective and normative commitment. Although Meyer et al. (2002) argue that the bases for developing each differ, Bergman (2006) argues that this may not be so clear-cut. She proposes that affective commitment itself could be viewed as a positive work experience that prompts employees to reciprocate through normative commitment. N. J. Allen and Meyer (1990) speculate that moral obligations might influence feelings about what is desired, and hence normative commitment may lead to the development of affective commitment. In view of the potential reciprocal relationship between affective and normative commitment and the potential overlap in the underlying psychological processes, additional theorizing is needed in terms of how PCs are related to both.

One suggestion that may unite the opposing positions of PC and commitment researchers is to differentiate between the universal norm of reciprocity, which captures how individuals should behave following the receipt of benefits, and individual reciprocity orientation (the extent to which individuals value reciprocity). Individuals who value reciprocity may be more likely to hold the desire to benefit the other (affective commitment), irrespective of their personal obligation to do so (normative commitment). In addition, the type of reciprocity (balanced, negative, and generalized) may have stronger/weaker effects on different forms of organizational commitment.

One last area for future research is, as in the case of LMX above, to examine multilevel issues surrounding the relationship between PCs and commitment. Early research from a multilevel perspective indicates that the obligations employees believe themselves party to (i.e., PCs) are shaped by their relative standing in the informal social structure of the organization (Dabos & Rousseau, 2004b). Employees central to the advice network, that is, whom other workers seek out for work-related advice and information, are more likely to believe they have a relational (socio-emotional) or balanced contract (socio-emotional obligations conditioned on individual and firm performance) with the employer than do their less central peers. Both relational and balanced obligations are associated with higher affective commitment, suggesting that higher informal social standing can induce greater commitment to the organization.

Moreover, employees have been found to hold similar PCs with their friends in the organization, particularly with regard to resources promised by the employer to all organization members (e.g., benefits). For resources accessed competitively within the firm (e.g., promotion), related PC beliefs depend on the beliefs of those to whom the individual goes to for work-related advice (Ho et al., 2006). Thus, social ties and standing appear to impact employee PC beliefs.

Lastly, although no evidence has been found of between-supervisor differences in their employees' PCs (e.g., Dabos & Rousseau, 2004a), employees sharing the same boss can develop different PCs, and different degrees of affective commitment, based on whether the supervisor has granted some of them special idiosyncratic employment conditions (Rousseau, 2005b). In particular, workers with granted special opportunities for development (e.g., challenging projects, training) are more likely to report relational and/or balanced contracts with the employer, resulting in higher levels of affective commitment than their less privileged counterparts. This finding raises the issue of whether differential treatment within a group might enhance the commitment of some workers at the expense of that of others. With respect to LMX, it raises the issue of how subordinates of the same manager respond to differences in his/her exchange relationships among them (Rousseau, 2000).

Conclusion

Empirical research on LMX, POS, and PCs has primarily focused on affective commitment toward the organization. Theoretical arguments across all three areas for why the employee-leader or employee-organization relationship impacts affective commitment focus on exchange theory and the norm of reciprocity. That is, employees are indebted to their leaders or organizations because of favorable treatment they receive, which creates a felt obligation to reciprocate by increasing their affective commitment to the organization. Across all three areas there is strong support for a positive relationship between LMX, POS, and PCs and affective commitment toward the organization. Thus, there is compelling evidence that the social influences of LMX, POS, and PCs are critical predictors of affective commitment to the organization.

Although the three areas have focused on affective commitment toward the organization, there are a number of differences across these areas in the study of commitment as well. In contrast to the LMX and PCs research, POS has often been examined as a mediator between major categories of work experiences (organizational rewards, procedural justice, and supervisor support) and affective commitment. A distinction in the LMX area is that studies have examined other foci of commitment such as goal and safety commitment, which has not been the case in the POS and PC literatures. Finally, a distinctive feature of the PC is its focus on obligations based on the belief that a promise had been made. The potential explanations of how individuals respond to perceived broken promises extend beyond the norm of reciprocity. Therefore, the relationship between PC breach and affective commitment may draw upon a broader range of explanations than that of POS and LMX.

It should be noted that LMX, POS, and PCs are conceptually distinct constructs but related. As noted in this chapter, an employee's leader may be viewed as the "face of the organization" or a key organizational agent and thus is the primary determinant of the employee's perceptions of organizational support. Linking POS and PCs, Aselage and Eisenberger (2003) developed an integrated model that provides a more comprehensive understanding of the employee-organization relationship. Despite the relationships among LMX, POS, and PCs, there have been few attempts to explore the relative importance of these exchange relationships on commitment. One exception is a study by Wayne et al. (1997) that examined both LMX and POS as predictors of affective commitment. Thus, although individual studies on affective commitment within the LMX, POS, and PCs literatures have been informative, we recommend that future research examine multiple exchange relationships in understanding affective, normative, and continuance commitment.

References

Allen, N. J., & Meyer, J. P. (1990). The measurement and antecedents of affective, continuance and normative commitment. *Journal of Occupational Psychology, 63*, 1–18.

Allen, D. G., Shore, L. M., & Griffeth, R. W. (2003). The role of perceived organizational support and supportive human resource practices in the turnover process. *Journal of Management, 29*, 99–118.

Armeli, S., Eisenberger, R., Fasolo, P., & Lynch, P. (1998). Perceived organizational support and police performance: The moderating influence of socioemotional needs. *Journal of Applied Psychology, 83*, 288–297.

Arnold, J. A., Arad, S., Rhoades, J. A., & Drasgow, F. (2000). The Empowering Leadership Questionnaire: The construction and validation of a new scale for measuring leader behaviors. *Journal of Organizational Behavior, 21*, 249–269.

Aselage, J., & Eisenberger, R. (2003). Perceived organizational support and psychological contracts: A theoretical integration. *Journal of Organizational Behavior, 24*, 491–509.

Balfour, D. L., & Wechsler, B. (1996). Organizational commitment: Antecedents and outcomes in public organization. *Public Productivity & Management Review, 19*, 256–277.

Barling, J., Fullagar, C., & Kelloway, K. (1992). *The union and its members: A psychological approach.* New York: Oxford University Press.

Basu, R., & Green, S. G. (1997). Leader-member exchange and transformational leadership: An empirical examination of innovative behaviors in leader-member dyads. *Journal of Applied Social Psychology, 27*, 477–499.

Becker, T. E. (1992). Foci and bases of commitment: Are they distinctions worth making? *Academy of Management Journal, 35*, 232–244.

Becker, T. E., Billings, R. S., Eveleth, D. M., & Gilbert, N. L. (1996). Foci and bases of employee commitment: Implications for job performance. *Academy of Management Journal, 39*, 464–482.

Bentein, K., Stinglhamber, F., & Vandenberghe, C. (2002). Organization-, supervisor-, and workgroup-directed commitments and citizenship behaviours: A comparison of models. *European Journal of Work and Organizational Psychology, 11*, 341–362.

Bergman, M. E. (2006). The relationship between affective and normative commitment: Review and research agenda [Special Issue]. *Journal of Organizational Behavior, 27*, 645–663.

Blau, P. M. (1964). Exchange and power in social life. New York: Wiley.

Buffardi, L. C., Baughman, K., & Vagalebre, M. (2002, August). *Perceived support and affective commitment at the organizational and local work unit levels.* Paper presented at the 62nd annual meeting of the Academy of Management, Denver, CO.

Bunderson, J. S. (2001). How work ideologies shape the psychological contracts of professional employees: Doctors' responses to perceived breaches. *Journal of Organizational Behavior, 22,* 717–741.

Conway, N., & Briner, R. B. (2002). A daily diary study of affective responses to psychological contract breach and exceeded promises. *Journal of Organizational Behavior, 23,* 287–302.

Cook, J., & Wall, T. (1980). New work attitude measures of trust, organizational commitment and personal need non-fulfillment. *Journal of Occupational Psychology, 53,* 39–52.

Coyle-Shapiro, J., & Kessler, I. (1998, August). *The psychological contract in the UK public sector: Employer and employee obligations and contract fulfillment.* Paper presented at the 58th annual meeting of the Academy of Management, San Diego, CA.

Coyle-Shapiro, J., & Kessler, I. (2000). Consequences of the psychological contract for the employment relationship: A large scale survey. *Journal of Management Studies, 37,* 903–930.

Dabos, G. E., & Rousseau, D. M. (2004a). Mutuality and reciprocity in the psychological contracts of employee and employer. *Journal of Applied Psychology, 89,* 52–72.

Dabos, G. E., & Rousseau, D. M. (2004b, August). *Social interaction patterns shaping employee psychological contracts: Network-wide and local effects.* Paper presented at the 64th annual meeting of the Academy of Management, New Orleans, LA.

Duchon, D., Stephen, G. G., & Taber, T. D. (1986). Vertical dyad linkage: A longitudinal assessment of antecedents, measures, and consequences. *Journal of Applied Psychology, 71,* 56–60.

Eisenberger, R., Armeli, S., Rexwinkel, B., Lynch, P. D., & Rhoades, L. (2001). Reciprocation of perceived organizational support. *Journal of Applied Psychology, 86,* 42–51.

Eisenberger, R., Cummings, J., Armeli, S., & Lynch, P. (1997). Perceived organizational support, discretionary treatment, and job satisfaction. *Journal of Applied Psychology, 82,* 812–820.

Eisenberger, R., Huntington, R., Hutchison, S., & Sowa, D. (1986). Perceived organizational support. *Journal of Applied Psychology, 71,* 500–507.

Eisenberger, R., Stinglhamber, F., Vandenberghe, C., Sucharski, I. L., & Rhoades, L. (2002). Perceived supervisor support: Contributions to perceived organizational support and employee retention. *Journal of Applied Psychology, 87,* 565–573.

Epitropaki, O., & Martin, R. (1999). The impact of relational demography on the quality of leader-member exchanges and employees' work attitudes and well-being. *Journal of Occupational and Organizational Psychology, 72,* 237–240.

Epitropaki, O., & Martin, R. (2005). From ideal to real: A longitudinal study of the role of implicit leadership theories on leader-member exchanges and employee outcomes. *Journal of Applied Psychology, 90,* 659–676.

Erdogan, B., Liden, R. C., & Kraimer, M. L. (2006). Justice and leader-member exchange: The moderating role of organization culture. *Academy of Management Journal, 49*, 395–406.

Fasolo, P. M. (1995). Procedural justice and perceived organizational support: Hypothesized effects on job performance. In R. Cropanzano & K. M. Kacmar (Eds.), *Organizational politics, justice, and support: Managing social climate at work* (pp. 185–195). Westport, CT: Quorum Press.

Flaherty, K. E., & Pappas, J. M. (2000). The role of trust in salesperson-sales manager relationships. *Journal of Personal Selling and Sales Management, 20*, 271–278.

Fullagar, C. J., & Barling, J. (1991). Predictors and outcomes of different patterns of organizational and union loyalty. *Journal of Occupational Psychology, 64*, 129–143.

Fullagar, C. J., Gallagher, D. G., Clark, P. F., & Carroll, A. E. (2004). Union commitment and participation: A 10-year longitudinal study. *Journal of Applied Psychology, 89*, 730–737.

Fuller, J. B., Jr., & Hester, K. (2001). A closer look at the relationship between justice perceptions and union participation. *Journal of Applied Psychology, 86*, 1096–1105.

Ganesan, S., Weitz, B., & John, G. (1993). Hiring and promotion policies in sales force management: Some antecedents and consequences. *The Journal of PersonalSelling and Sales Management, 13*, 15–26.

Gellatly, I. R., Hunter, K. H., Luchak, A. A., & Meyer, J. P. (2007, April). *Predicting commitment profile membership: the role of perceived organizational support and autonomy.* Paper presented at the 22nd annual meeting of the Society for Industrial and Organizational Psychology, New York.

Gouldner, A. W. (1960). The norm of reciprocity: A preliminary statement. *American Sociological Review, 25*, 161–178.

Graen, G. B., & Cashman, J. F. (1975). A role-making model of leadership in formal organizations: A developmental approach. In J. G. Hunt & L. L. Larson (Eds.). *Leadership frontiers* (pp. 143–165). Kent, OH: Kent State University Press.

Graen, G. B., Novak, M., & Sommerkamp, P. (1982). The effect of leader-member exchange and job design on productivity and satisfaction: Testing a dual attachment model. *Organizational Behavior and Human Performance, 30*, 109–131.

Graen, G. B., & Uhl-Bien, M. (1995). Relationship-based approach to leadership: Development of leader-member exchange (LMX) theory of leadership over 25 years: Applying a multi-level multi-domain perspective. *The Leadership Quarterly, 6*, 219–247.

Green, S. G., Anderson, S. E., & Shivers, S. L. (1996). Demographic and organizational influences on leader-member exchange and related work attitudes. *Organizational Behavior and Human Decision Processes, 66*, 203–214.

Groysberg, B., Ashish, N., & Nitin, N. (2004). The risky business of hiring stars. *Harvard Business Review, 82*, 92–100.

Heffner, T. S. & Gade, P. A. (2003). Commitment to nested collectives in special operations forces. *Military Psychology, 15*, 209–224.

Henderson, D. J., Dulac, T., & Liden, R. C. (2006). The role of LMX and communication in the goal setting process. In G.B. Graen (Ed.), *LMX: The Series, IV.* Greenwich, CT: Information Age Publishing.

Herscovitch, L., & Meyer, J. P. (2002). Commitment to organizational change: Extension of a three-component model. *Journal of Applied Psychology, 87*, 474–487.

Ho, V. T., Rousseau, D. M., & Levesque, L. L. (2006). Social networks and the psychological contract: Structural holes, cohesive ties, and beliefs regarding employer obligations. *Human Relations, 59*, 459–481.

Hochwarter, W. A. (2003). The interactive effects of pro-political behavior and politics perceptions on job satisfaction and affective commitment. *Journal of Applied Social Psychology, 33*, 1360–1378.

Hofmann, D. A., & Morgeson, F. P. (1999). Safety-related behavior as a social exchange: The role of perceived organizational support and leader-member exchange. *Journal of Applied Psychology, 84*, 286–296.

Hollenbeck, J. R., Williams, C. R., & Klein, H. J. (1989). An empirical examination of the antecedents of commitment to difficult goals. *Journal of Applied Psychology, 74*, 18–23.

Hopkins, W. E., Hopkins, S. A., & Mallette, P. (2001). Diversity and managerial value commitment: A test of some proposed relationships. *Journal of Managerial Issues, 13*, 288–306.

Janssen, O., & Van Yperen, N. W. (2004). Employees' goal orientations, the quality of leader-member exchange, and the outcomes of job performance and job satisfaction. *Academy of Management Journal, 47*, 368–384.

Johnson, R. E., & Chang, C. H. (2006). "I" is to continuance as "We" is to affective: The relevance of the self-concept for organizational commitment. *Journal of Organizational Behavior, 27*, 549–570.

Johnson, J. L., & O'Leary-Kelly, A. M. (2003). The effects of psychological contract breach and organizational cynicism: Not all social exchange violations are created equal. *Journal of Organizational Behavior, 24*, 627–647.

Kacmar, K. M., Carlson, D. S., & Brymer, R. A. (1999). Antecedents and consequences of organizational commitment: A comparison of two scales. *Educational and Psychological Measurement, 59*, 976–994.

Kacmar, K. M., Witt, L. A., Zivnuska, S., & Gully, S. M. (2003). The interactive effect of leader-member exchange and communication frequency on performance ratings. *Journal of Applied Psychology, 88*, 764–772.

Kickul, J. (2001). Promises made, promises broken: An exploration of small business attraction and retention practices. *Journal of Small Business Management, 39*, 320–335.

Kinicki, A., & Vecchio, R. (1994). Influences on the quality of supervisor-subordinate relations: The role of time-pressure, organizational commitment, and locus of control. *Journal of Organizational Behavior, 15*, 75–82.

Klein, H. J., & Kim, J. S. (1998). A field study of the influence of situational constraints, leader-member exchange, and goal commitment on performance. *Academy of Management Journal, 41*, 88–95.

Klein, H. J., Wesson, M. J., Hollenbeck, J. R., Wright, P. M., & DeShon, R. P. (2001). The assessment of goal commitment: A measurement model meta-analysis. *Organizational Behavior and Human Decision Processes, 85*, 32–55.

Ko, J. W., Price, J. L., & Mueller, C. W. (1997). Assessment of Meyer and Allen's three-component model of organizational commitment in South Korea. *Journal of Applied Psychology, 82*, 961–973.

Kottke, J. L., & Sharafinski, C. E. (1988). Measuring perceived supervisory and organizational support. *Educational and Psychological Measurement, 48,* 1075–1079.

Koys, D. J. (1991). Fairness, legal compliance, and organizational commitment. *Employee Responsibilities and Rights Journal, 4,* 283–291.

Kumar, N., Scheer, L. K., & Steenkamp, J.-B. E. N. (1991). The effects of supplier fairness on vulnerable resellers. *Journal of Marketing Research, 32,* 54–65.

Law, K. S., Wong, C. S., Wang, D., & Wang, L. (2000). Effect of supervisor–subordinate guanxi on supervisory decisions in China: An empirical investigation. *International Journal of Human Resource Management, 11,* 751–765.

Lee, J. (2005). Effects of leadership and leader-member exchange on commitment. *Leadership & Organization Development Journal, 26,* 655–672.

Lester, S. W., Turnley, W. H., Bloodgood, J. M., & Bolino, M. C. (2002). Not seeing eye to eye: Differences in supervisor and subordinate perceptions of and attributions for psychological contract breach. *Journal of Organizational Behavior, 31,* 39–56.

Liden, R. C., & Maslyn, J. M. (1998). Multidimensionality of leader-member exchange: An empirical assessment through scale development. *Journal of Management, 24,* 43–72.

Liden, R. C., Sparrowe, R. T., & Wayne, S. J. (1997). Leader-member exchange theory: The past and potential for the future. *Research in Personnel and Human Resources Management, 15,* 47–119.

Liden, R. C., Wayne, S. J., & Sparrowe, R. T. (2000). An examination of the mediating role of psychological empowerment on the relations between the job, interpersonal relationships, and work outcomes. *Journal of Applied Psychology, 85,* 407–416.

Locke, E. A., & Latham, G. P. (2002). Building a practically useful theory of goal setting and task motivation: A 35-year odyssey. *American Psychologist, 57,* 705–717.

Major, D. A., Kozlowski, S. W. J., Chao, G. T., & Gardner, P. D. (1995). Newcomer expectations and early socialization outcomes: The moderating effect of role development factors. *Journal of Applied Psychology, 80,* 418–431.

Malatesta, R. M. (1995). *Understanding the dynamics of organizational and supervisory commitment using a social exchange framework.* Unpublished doctoral dissertation, Psychology Department, Wayne State University, Detroit, Michigan.

Mansour-Cole, D. M., & Scott, S. G. (1998). Hearing it through the grapevine: The influence of source, leader-relations, and legitimacy on survivors' fairness perceptions. *Personnel Psychology, 51,* 25–54.

Martin, R., Thomas, G., Charles, C., Epitropaki, O., & McNamara, R. (2005). The role of leader-member exchanges in mediating the relationship between locus of control and work reactions. *Journal of Occupational and Organizational Psychology, 78,* 141–147.

Masterson, S. S., Lewis, K., Goldman, B. M., & Taylor, M. S. (2000). Integrating justice and social exchange: The differing effects of fair procedures and treatment on work relationships. *Academy of Management Journal, 43,* 738–748.

Meyer, J. P., & Allen, N. J. (1984). Testing the "side-bet theory" of organizational commitment: Some methodological considerations. *Journal of Applied Psychology, 69,* 372–378.

Meyer, J. P., & Allen, N. J. (1991). A three-component conceptualization of organizational commitment. *Human Resource Management Review, 1*, 61–89.

Meyer, J. P., & Allen, N. J. (1997). *Commitment in the workplace: Theory, research, and application.* Newbury Park, CA: Sage.

Meyer, J. P., Allen, N. J., & Smith, C.A. (1993). Commitment to organizations and occupations: Extension and test of a three-component conceptualization. *Journal of Applied Psychology, 78,* 538–551.

Meyer, J. P., Allen, N. J., & Topolnytsky, L. (1998). Commitment in a changing world of work [Special Issue]. *Canadian Psychology, 39,* 83–93.

Meyer, J. P., Becker, T. E., & Vandenberghe, C. (2004). Employee commitment and motivation: A conceptual analysis and integrative model. *Journal of Applied Psychology, 89,* 991–1007.

Meyer, J. P., & Herscovitch, L. (2001). Commitment in the workplace: Toward a general model [Special Issue]. *Human Resource Management Review, 11,* 299–326.

Meyer, J. P., Stanley, D. J., Herscovitch, L., & Topolnytsky, L. (2002). Affective, continuance and normative commitment to the organization: A meta-analysis of antecedents, correlates and consequences. *Journal of Vocational Behavior, 61,* 20–52.

Moorman, R. H., Blakely, G. L., & Niehoff, B. P. (1998). Does perceived organizational support mediate the relationship between procedural justice and organizational citizenship behavior? *Academy of Management Journal, 41,* 351–357.

Mowday, R. T., Porter, L. W., & Steers, R. M. (1982). *Employee–organization linkages: The psychology of commitment, absenteeism, and turnover.* New York: Academic Press.

Mowday, R. T., Steers, R. M., & Porter, L. W. (1979). The measurement of organizational commitment. *Journal of Vocational Behavior, 14,* 224–247.

Mueller, C. W., & Lawler, E. J. (1999). Commitment to nested organization units: Some basic principles and preliminary findings. *Social Psychology Quarterly, 62,* 325–346.

Oliver, N. (1990). Rewards, investments, alternatives and organizational commitment: Empirical evidence and theoretical development. *Journal of Occupational Psychology, 63*(1), 19–31.

O'Reilly, C., & Chatman, J. (1986). Organizational commitment and psychological attachment: The effects of compliance, identification, and internalization on prosocial behavior. *Journal of Applied Psychology, 71,* 492–499.

Parzefall, M. R. (2005, August). *Psychological contract fulfillment and the form of reciprocity: Examining the sense of indebtedness.* Paper presented at the 65th annual meeting of the Academy of Management, Honolulu, HI.

Piccolo, R. F., & Colquitt, J. A. (2006). Transformational leadership and job behaviors: The mediating role of core job characteristics. *Academy of Management Journal, 49,* 327–340.

Porter, L. W., & Smith, F. J. (1970). *The etiology of organizational commitment.* Unpublished manuscript, University of California at Irvine.

Porter, L. W, Steers, R. M., Mowday, R. T., & Boulian, P. V. (1974). Organizational commitment, job satisfaction, and turnover among psychiatric technicians. *Journal of Applied Psychology, 59,* 603–609.

Redman, T., & Snape, E. (2005). Unpacking commitment: Multiple loyalties and employee behaviour. *Journal of Management Studies, 42*, 301–328.

Reichers, A. (1985). A review and reconceptualization of organizational commitment. *Academy of Management Review, 10*, 465–476.

Restubog, S. L. D., Bordia, P., & Tang, R. L. (2006). Effects of psychological contract breach on performance of IT employees: The mediating role of affective commitment. *Journal of Occupational and Organizational Psychology, 79*, 299–306.

Rhoades, L., & Eisenberger, R. (2002). Perceived organizational support: A review of the literature. *Journal of Applied Psychology, 87*, 698–714.

Rhoades, L., Eisenberger, R., & Armeli, S. (2001). Affective commitment to the organization: The contribution of perceived organizational support. *Journal of Applied Psychology, 86*, 825–836.

Robinson, S. L. (1996). Trust and breach of the psychological contract. *Administrative Science Quarterly, 41*, 574–599.

Robinson, S. L., Kraatz, M. S., & Rousseau, D. M. (1994). Changing obligations and the psychological contract: A longitudinal study. *Academy of Management Journal, 37*, 137–152.

Robinson, S. L., & Rousseau, D. M. (1994). Violating the psychological contract: Not the exception but the norm. *Journal of Organizational Behavior, 15*, 245–259.

Rousseau, D. M. (1995). *Psychological contract in organizations: Understanding written and unwritten agreements.* Newbury Park, CA: Sage.

Rousseau, D. M. (2000). LMX meets the psychological contract: Looking inside the black box of leader-member exchange. In F. Dansereau and F. Yammarino (Eds.), *Leadership: The multilevel approaches* (Vol. B, pp. 149–154), Greenwich, CT: JAI Press.

Rousseau, D. M. (2001). Schema, promises, and mutuality: The psychology of the psychological contract. *Journal of Organizational and Occupational Psychology, 24*, 511–541.

Rousseau, D. M. (2005a). Developing psychological contract theory. In K. G. Smith & M. Hitt (Eds.), *Master in organizational research* (pp. 190–214), New York: Oxford University Press.

Rousseau, D. M. (2005b). *I-deals: Idiosyncratic deals employees bargain for themselves.* New York: M.E. Sharpe.

Rousseau, D. M., & Tijoriwala, S. (1998). Assessing the psychological contract. *Journal of Organizational Behavior, 19*, 679–698.

Rybnikova, I. (2006, August). How to ensure the high performance of interim managers. Paper presented at the 66th annual meeting of the Academy of Management, Atlanta, GA.

Sahlins M. D. (1972). *Stone age economics.* New York: Aldine Publishing Company.

Scandura, T. A., & Graen, G. B. (1984). Moderating effects of initial leader-member exchange status on the effects of a leadership intervention. *Journal of Applied Psychology, 69*, 428–436.

Schalk, R., de Jong, J., & Linde, B. (2006, August). More than transactional? The diversity of psychological contracts among contingent workers: A seven country study. Paper presented at the 66th annual meeting of the Academy of Management, Atlanta, GA.

Schriesheim, C. A., Castro, S. L., & Yammarino, F. J. (2000). Investigating contingencies: An examination of the impact of span of supervision and upward controllingness on leader-member exchange using traditional and multivariate within- and between-entities analysis. *Journal of Applied Psychology, 85,* 659–677.

Schriesheim, C. A., Neider, L. L., Scandura, T. A., & Tepper, B. J. (1992). Development and preliminary validation of a new scale (LMX-6) to measure leader-member exchange in organizations. *Educational and Psychological Measurement, 52,* 135–147.

Schriesheim, C. A., Scandura, T. A., Eisenbach, R. J., & Neider, L. L. (1992). Validation of a new leader-member exchange scale (LMX-6) using hierarchically-nested confirmatory factor analysis. *Educational and Psychological Measurement, 52,* 983–992.

Schyns, B. (2006). Are group consensus in leader-member exchange (LMX) and shared work values related to organizational outcomes? *Small Group Research, 37,* 20–35.

Schyns, B., Paul, T., Mohr, G., & Blank, H. (2005). Comparing antecedents and consequences of leader-member exchange in a German working context to findings in the US. *European Journal of Work and Organizational Psychology, 14,* 1–22.

Self, D. R., Holt, D. T., & Schaninger, W. S. Jr. (2005). Work-group and organizational support: A test of distinct dimensions. *Journal of Occupational and Organizational Psychology, 78,* 133–140.

Sels, L., Janssens, M., & van den Brande, I. (2004). Assessing the nature of psychological contracts: A validation of six dimensions. *Journal of Organizational Behavior, 25,* 461–488.

Settoon, R. P., Bennett, N., & Liden, R. C. (1996). Social exchange in organizations: Perceived organizational support, leader-member exchange, and employee reciprocity. *Journal of Applied Psychology, 81,* 219–227.

Shaw, K. (2006). The value of innovative human resource management practices. In E. E. Lawler & J. O'Toole (Eds.), *America at Work: Choices and Challenges* (pp. 227–240). New York: Palmgrave Macmillan.

Sherony, K. M., & Green, S. G. (2002). Coworker exchange: Relationships between coworkers, leader-member exchange, and work attitudes. *Journal of Applied Psychology, 87,* 542–548.

Shore, L. M., Porter, L. W., & Zahra, S. A. (2004). Employer-oriented strategic approaches to the employee-organization relationship (EOR). In J. Coyle-Shapiro, L. M. Shore, S. Taylor, & L. E. Tetrick (Eds.), *The employment relationship: Examining psychological and contextual perspectives* (pp. 135–160), Oxford: Oxford University Press.

Shore, L. M., & Shore, T. H. (1995). Perceived organizational support and organizational justice. In R. Cropanzano and K. M. Kacmar (Eds.), *Organizational politics, justice, and support: Managing social climate at work* (pp. 149–164). Westport, CT: Quorum Press.

Shore, L. M., & Tetrick, L. E. (1991). A construct validity study of the Survey of Perceived Organizational Support. *Journal of Applied Psychology, 76,* 637–643.

Shore, L. M., & Tetrick, L. E. (1994). The psychological contract as an explanatory framework in the employment relationship. In C. L. Cooper and D. M. Rousseau (Eds.), *Trends in organizational behavior* (Vol. 1, pp. 91–99). New York: Wiley.

Shore, L. M., Tetrick, L. E., Lynch, P., & Barksdale, K. (2006). Social and economic exchange construct development and validation. *Journal of Applied Social Psychology, 36,* 837–867.

Shore, L. M., & Wayne, S. J. (1993). Commitment and employee behavior: Comparison of affective commitment and continuance commitment with perceived organizational support. *Journal of Applied Psychology, 78,* 774–780.

Sinclair, R. R., & Tetrick, L. E. (1995). Social exchange and union commitment: A comparison of union instrumentality and union support perceptions. *Journal of Organizational Behavior, 16,* 669–680.

Sparrowe, R. T., & Liden, R. C. (1997). Process and structure in leader-member exchange. *Academy of Management Review, 22,* 522–552.

Sparrowe, R. T., & Liden, R. C. (2005). Two routes to influence: Integrating leader-member exchange and network perspectives. *Administrative Science Quarterly, 50,* 505–535.

Stinglhamber, F., Eisenberger, R., Aselage, J., Jones, J. R., Eder, P., Sucharski, I. L., et al. (2006). Supervisor's organizational embodiment. Unpublished manuscript, Psychology Department, University of Delaware.

Tangirala, S., Green, S. G., & Ramanujam, R. (2007). In the shadow of the boss's boss: Effects of supervisors' upward exchange relationships on employees. *Journal of Applied Psychology, 92,* 309–320.

Tetrick, L. E. (1995). Developing and maintaining union commitment: A theoretical framework. *Journal of Organizational Behavior, 16,* 583–595.

Tetrick, L. E., Shore, L. M., McClurg, L., & Vandenberg, R. J. (2007). A model of union participation: The impact of perceived union support, union instrumentality, and union loyalty. *Journal of Applied Psychology, 92,* 820–828.

Tierney, P., Bauer, T. N., & Potter, R. E. (2002). Extra-role behavior among Mexican employees: The impact of LMX, group acceptance, and job attitudes. *International Journal of Selection and Assessment, 10,* 292–303.

Truckenbrodt, Y. B. (2000). The relationship between leader-member exchange and commitment and organizational citizenship behavior. *Acquisition Review Quarterly, 7,* 233–244.

Turnley, W. H., & Feldman, D. C. (1999). The impact of psychological contract violations on exit, voice, loyalty, and neglect. *Human Relations, 52,* 895–922.

Vandenberghe, C., Bentein, K., & Stinglhamber, F. (2004). Affective commitment to the organization, supervisor, and work group: Antecedents and outcomes. *Journal of Vocational Behavior, 64,* 47–71.

Van Dyne, L., & Ang, S. (1998). Organizational citizenship behavior of contingent workers in Singapore. *Academy of Management Journal, 41,* 692–703.

Wade-Benzoni, K. A., Rousseau, D. M., & Li, M. (2006). Managing relationships across generations of academics: Psychological contracts in faculty-doctoral student collaborations. *International Journal of Conflict Management, 17,* 4–33.

Wayne, S. J., Shore, L. M., Bommer, W. H., & Tetrick, L. E. (2002). The role of fair treatment and rewards in perceptions of organizational support and leader-member exchange. *Journal of Applied Psychology, 87*, 590–598.

Wayne, S. J., Shore, L. M., & Liden, R. C. (1997). Perceived organizational support and leader-member exchange: A social exchange perspective. *Academy of Management Journal, 40*, 82–111.

Yoon, J., & Lim, J. C. (1999). Organizational support in the workplace: The case of Korean hospital employees. *Human Relations, 52*, 923–945.

Zhao, H., Wayne, S., Glibkowski, B., & Bravo, J. (2007). The impact of psychological contract breach on work-related outcomes: A meta-analysis. *Personnel Psychology, 60*, 647–680.

9

Organizational-Level Antecedents and Consequences of Commitment

Patrick M. Wright and Rebecca R. Kehoe
Cornell University

The construct of commitment has increasingly become of interest to organizations. While the construct has a long and voluminous history within the academic realm, business leaders' recognition of the importance of human capital has focused their attention on the attitudes of people within their firms. In particular, *The War for Talent*, popularized by McKinsey & Company (Michaels, Handfield-Jones, & Axelrod, 2001), directed business leaders' efforts toward the issue of how to "attract, motivate, and retain" those most critical to their firm's success. Consequently, these leaders sought to build processes and characteristics in their organizations that would facilitate attracting, motivating, and retaining key talent.

The focus on attraction, motivation, and retention leads directly to an understanding of commitment. Commitment in organizations has been defined as "the relative strength of an individual's identification with and involvement in a particular organization" (Mowday, Porter, & Steers, 1982, p. 27). It entails an identification with the organization's goals, a willingness to exert extra effort for the organization, and a desire to remain with the organization (Whitener, 2001). As an attitude, it has often been treated as implying a cognitive (belief), affective (emotion), and behavioral (action) reaction to an object such as an organization. The purpose of this chapter is to review the organizational correlates of commitment in order to provide some ideas regarding future research avenues that would result in fruitful theoretical and practical knowledge of the commitment process.

To achieve this purpose we will first discuss some definitional and operational issues that are relevant to understanding how we have approached this review on organizational correlates of commitment. We will then review the major studies that have examined some of these correlates. Then we will explore some of the theoretical issues inherent in this research. Finally, we will examine the methodological and future research issues on organizational correlates of commitment.

Definitions

In discussing organizational influences on commitment, we first want to clarify what we mean by *organizational, influences,* and *commitment.* By *organizational* we mean characteristics of the organizational context in which respondents work, which might either influence or be impacted by commitment. This does not require that the organization be the level of analysis, but rather that the focal construct be a real or perceived characteristic of the organization. This perception component leads to some potential overlap with chapter 8, by Wayne, Coyle-Shapiro, Eisenberger, Liden, Rousseau, and Shore, who focus on the social influences. While the social influences may often shape the perceptions of the organizational characteristics, we hope to focus more on those characteristics than on the social processes.

By *influences* we specifically recognize the difficulty in inferring cause from the vast majority of studies in this area. While authors and papers often refer to constructs that they posit either "cause" or "influence" commitment, or that are "outcomes" of commitment, our observation is that such statements are based in theoretical, rather than empirical, groundings. However, consistent with the ubiquitous causal language used in both theorizing and empirical research, we refer to "influences" even though the causal direction may not have been proven. Finally, we will use a broad definition with regard to commitment. Generally, *commitment* has been defined as a willingness to persist in a course of action, often because of some sense of obligation; hence, it has both rational and emotional components (Vance, 2006). More recently, Klein, Molloy, and Brinsfield (chapter 1) define commitment as "an individual's perception that they are bound to a given target," and persuasively argue that commitment can vary in terms of its target (organization, goal, etc.), strength, and rationale (i.e., attribution for why they are committed to a target). We will tend to treat commitment as the outcome or process through which individuals become cognitively, affectively, and/or behaviorally bound to an object or a course of action.

However, defining the right object or course of action is where the definition becomes broad to the point of almost unwieldy. First, commitments can vary in terms of their target (Klein et al., chapter 1). Within the organizational literature alone, researchers have examined commitment to organizations (e.g., Meyer & Allen, 1991; Mowday et al., 1982), unions (Barling, Fullagar, & Kelloway, 1992), teams and leaders (e.g., Becker, 1992, Hunt & Morgan, 1994), careers (e.g., Hall, 1996), and goals (e.g., Locke, Latham, & Erez, 1988). In addition, even commitment to the same basic focus can vary widely in operationalization. For instance, the organizational commitment construct is strongly related to a number of other constructs in the academic and practitioner literatures. For instance, of recent interest in the practitioner literature is the concept of "employee engagement." Vance (2006) examined the variety of definitions that companies and consultants have used and found that virtually all either use the term "commitment" in their definitions, or have components that overlap with commonly used items that comprise organization commitment scales. In addition, a number of studies on "climate" entail measures such as service climate that often look like a form of commitment to serving the customer because of a commitment to make the organization successful. Thus, while we recognize Klein et al.'s valid case that such measures confound the cause and effect of commitment with its definition, because previous literature has not made such distinctions, we will broadly define commitment to include research that has used some form of employee engagement measure.

Levels of Analysis Issues

Before getting into the details of our review, we must specifically address the levels of analysis issues in this area to explain how we focused our literature search. Because of the nature of commitment, it is largely an individually based construct. Individuals, through their beliefs, emotions, and/or behaviors can come to some degree of commitment strength. Consequently, commitment is almost universally measured at the individual level of analysis, usually by asking individual respondents to indicate their commitment on some survey-type instrument.

While the actual measurement of commitment happens at the individual level, the construct can be conceptualized and/or operationalized at multiple levels of analysis. For instance, individual survey responses can comprise the commitment measure. Or, those individual responses can be aggregated across individuals within a particular group or job (e.g., Wright, Gardner, Moynihan, & Allen, 2005). Finally, commitment may be aggregated to an even higher level such as the business unit or organization (e.g., Fulmer, Gerhart, & Scott, 2003). This, of course, begs the question as to the best level of analysis at which commitment should be operationalized. Because of the inherently individualistic nature of the construct, obviously, the vast majority of commitment research has focused on the individual level of analysis. When examining issues such as goal commitment (Hollenbeck & Klein, 1987), one can hardly argue with the appropriateness of such a level of analysis. However, because we are focused on "organizational" correlates of commitment, the question of the best level presents additional problems in that some of these organization-level variables should have effects on aggregated individual measures of commitment. We will address this level issue more specifically later in the chapter.

By focusing on organizational predictors of commitment, we automatically load one side of the equation with what is, by definition, an organizational-level phenomenon. One can allegedly ask individuals about a particular organizational characteristic, but if more than one individual within the same organization are responding, and the analyses are performed at the individual level, the organizational nature of the variable is lost.It becomes an individual's perception of the characteristic rather than the characteristic itself. If one aggregates to the organizational or unit level, then while the organizational aspect of the characteristic gains validity, this validity comes at the loss of the individual nature of commitment (chapter 7, by Bergman, Benzer, and Henning, provides a detailed discussion of how individual differences influence commitment). We hold off a detailed analysis of the "cross-level" nature of the organizational correlates of commitment for later, but suffice to say here that the very nature of the relationship is problematic.

Organizational Correlates of Commitment

The organizational correlates of commitment that we discuss in this chapter fall under five general categories: structure, climate, culture, human resource (HR) practices, and performance. These correlates seemed most appropriate for review based on their broad presence in the existing literature and their potential fruitfulness in future research.

Structure

Characteristics of organizational structure have received less attention than many other variables of interest in the realm of commitment. *Structure* has been defined as the distribution of authority, organization of tasks, and patterns of relationships across departments and functional units in an organization (Power, 1988, p. 67) and has been described in terms of various components. Structure may be of interest in commitment research because of its inherent role in shaping employees' relationships with their organizations through its influences on interpersonal relationships, work design, and employee voice mechanisms. When structure has been considered as a correlate of commitment, two structural components that have commonly appeared together have been organizational size and centralization, which refers to the concentration of power within an organization. Both of these variables have yielded inconsistent results when examined as antecedents of commitment.

Specifically, organizational size was found to be significantly negatively related to affective commitment ($r = -.31$) when used as a control by Rhoades, Eisenberger, and Armeli (2001) in a study of electronics and appliance sales employees, but was found to have no significant relationship when considered as a predictor of commitment in a sample of federal government managers by Stevens, Beyer, and Trice (1978). Mathieu and Zajac (1990) also found no significant relationship in a meta-analysis of correlates of commitment.

The relationship between centralization and commitment has been found to be even less consistent. Morris and Steers (1980) found a positive relationship between decentralization (the opposite of centralization) and commitment ($r = .33$) in a study of public sector employees. Similarly, Glisson and James (2002) found a significant negative relationship between centralization and commitment ($r = -.3$) in a sample of case managers for child welfare. On the other hand, a significant positive centralization-commitment association was reported in a study of nursing department employees ($r = .44$) by Bateman and Strasser (1984), and a nonsignificant relationship was found when centralization was used as a control by Stevens et al. (1978). Reflecting this inconsistency, Mathieu and Zajac (1990) found a nonsignificant association between centralization and commitment in their meta-analytic review.

Another aspect of organizational structure that may relate to commitment but has thus far not been directly addressed in the literature is communication structure. Organizations' formal and informal communication structures may reflect employees' voice mechanisms and hence the extent to which organizations value input and feedback from non-managerial employees. For example, a sole emphasis on downward communication may send signals to employees about the lack of value placed on their concerns, which may in turn cause employees to feel detached and less committed to their organization. On the other hand, employees in organizations encouraging both horizontal and vertical communication are likely to have the opportunity to play a more significant role in the planning of their organizations' strategic goals. This is likely to cause employees to better understand and feel more connected to organizational goals, in turn leading to greater commitment to both the goals and the organization as a whole (Wright, Gardner, & Moynihan, 2003).

Climate

A more frequently studied correlate of commitment is climate. Climate has been defined as the shared perceptions of organizational policies, practices, and procedures, both formal and informal (Reichers & Schneider, 1990). It is usually conceptualized as a shared perception with regard to a particular referent or strategic objective, such as climate for service, innovation, safety, and so forth, although sometimes this target is the entire organization. Climate has been examined as both a single- and multifaceted construct and has been analyzed at various levels within an organization. For instance, climate can be shared among workgroup members, job group members, or organizational members. However, we distinguish this from *psychological climate*, which refers to an individual's perception of the work environment, perceptions that need not be shared across individuals. In this section we first review studies employing various operationalizations of climate in several settings, followed by studies examining concepts that seem to fall under the climate definition without having been labeled as climate by their authors. Specifically, we include studies involving justice, perceived organizational support, and organizational politics in this review.

In an organizational-level analysis involving 42 manufacturing organizations, Patterson, Warr, and West (2004) found a positive relationship between a number of dimensions of climate (e.g., concern for employee welfare, effort, skill development, innovation and flexibility, quality) and a concurrent measure of organizational commitment. In the same study, commitment was found to mediate the relationship between climate and productivity in the following year. Climate was similarly related to commitment in a sample of clinical and case management service providers nested in 49 mental health service organizations (Aarons & Sawitzky, 2006). In an individual-level study, Glisson and James (2002) showed that work unit climate predicted individual-level organizational commitment in a sample of case managers in child welfare and juvenile teams. In a different approach, Carr, Schmidt, Ford, and DeShon (2003) demonstrated in a 70-sample meta-analysis that three facets of climate—affective, cognitive, and instrumental—were all positively related to affective organizational commitment.

Organizational justice, perceived organizational support, and organizational politics qualify under the definition of climate in that they all reflect formal or informal practices or procedures of an organization as perceived by its employees. Simons and Roberson (2003) explain that collective justice perceptions are likely to emerge among a group of employees in a work unit in very much the same way that we understand general perceptions of climate to emerge, because employees are likely to share similar experiences with work rules and management and to interpret these experiences in comparable ways. In both a department and business unit-level study of hotels, these authors found support for a relationship between procedural justice and concurrent measures of organizational commitment. Additionally, they demonstrated that interpersonal justice was positively related to commitment at the unit level, with the relationship mediated by satisfaction with employees' supervisors. At the individual level of analysis, Liden, Wayne, and Kraimer (2003) also found a positive relationship between procedural justice in client organizations and organizational commitment, with the relationship mediated by perceived organizational support. Interestingly, in the same study, contingent workers' commitment to their staffing agency was negatively related to commitment to the client organization.

Perceived organizational support was also found to be a significant correlate of organizational commitment in individual-level analyses of electronics and appliance sales (Rhoades et al., 2001), manufacturing, and public-sector employees (Randall et al., 1999) In a meta-analysis of 42 studies with an N in excess of 11,000, Rhoades and Eisenberger (2002) found that perceived organizational support was correlated .60 with all commitment measures, .65 with affective commitment, and –.13 with continuance commitment. Perceived organizational support can be considered a climate type in that employees' perception of it in a workplace is thought to emerge not from individual employees' characteristics but from higher-level decisions by an organization to create a supportive environment for its employees. For a more detailed discussion of the relationship between perceived organizational support and commitment, see chapter 8, by Wayne et al.

The presence of organizational politics can also be understood as a type of climate in that it is a perception of how the organization operates at a level beyond the individual. Randall et al. (1999) found that the perception of organizational politics was negatively related to organizational commitment at the individual level of analysis across three organizations.

It is important to note that the climate construct has the potential to be confounded with commitment. Climate measures may often contain commitment items (e.g., "I am committed to serving our customers"), and conceptualizing climate with regard to a target almost inherently assumes some binding to the target or behavior.

Overall, the research on climate and organizational commitment has demonstrated that employees' commitment to an organization is directly related to the organizational climate—the sets of policies, practices, and procedures that employees experience and perceive at work. It should be noted that the bulk of this research has focused on the affective commitment mindset, a conceptualization that may limit generalizability to other mindsets. A related concept to climate in the literature is organizational culture, which also involves the environment in which employees work. Not surprisingly, researchers have investigated the relationship between culture and organizational commitment as well.

Culture

For the purpose of this chapter we focus on organizational, as opposed to ethnic or country-based, culture. The latter concept is covered in chapter 10, by Wasti and Önder. While organizational culture has been conceptualized in several ways, a definition consistent with the studies we review specifies culture as the organizational norms and expectations regarding how people behave and how things are done in an organization. This definition encompasses norms, values, shared behavioral expectations, and assumptions that guide the behaviors of employees in a work unit (Glisson & James, 2002; Aarons & Sawitzky, 2006). We include in this review studies involving overarching organizational cultures, subcultures within organizations, and person-organization fit, a concept that we classify under our definition of culture.

Aarons and Sawitzky (2006) found that culture was related to organizational commitment in a sample of mental health service employees and that this relationship was partially mediated by climate. Similarly, in a sample of child welfare and juvenile justice case management teams, Glisson and James (2002) found that team-level culture predicted individual-level commitment. In another analysis of organizational subcultures, Lok, Westwood, and Crawford (2005) demonstrated that nurses' perceptions of the ward-level cultures in a hospital setting were more predictive of their organizational commitment than were their perceptions of hospital-level (organization–level) culture. In an individual-level study conducted across 68 organizations in the Netherlands, Van Vianen (2000) found that person-organization fit was not related to organizational commitment for newly hired employees, but person-people fit within the organization was. In contrast, Silverthorne (2004) found that person-organization fit was a significant predictor of commitment, as were different types of organizational culture. Specifically, Silverthorne found that different cultural types could be ranked in terms of their associations with commitment. A supportive culture was strongest, an innovative culture second, and a bureaucratic culture weakest in predicting high levels of organizational commitment of employees across organizations.

The results of studies linking climate and culture to commitment suggest the importance of considering employees' perceptions of their work environments and experiences when studying commitment. It has been consistently demonstrated and makes sense that the way employees perceive their workplace and workday is related to the attitudes they hold toward their organization.

HR Practices

HR practices are another set of factors that have been found to relate to the everyday work experiences of employees in organizations. Ties to organizational commitment have been demonstrated both with individual HR practices and with entire bundles of practices working together and reinforcing each other in an overarching HR management system. The significance of commitment studies involving individual HR practices is that they enable researchers to identify some of the circumstances under which specific practices are most likely to be valued by employees. Studies of entire HR systems and their relationships with commitment are important in allowing researchers to examine how systems of interacting practices combine to influence employee attitudes. We review both types of studies here.

In an individual-level, cross-organizational study of general managers, Scandura and Lankau (1997) found that the availability of flexible work hours was positively related to organizational commitment. Flexible work hours allow employees some degree of discretion in the particular hours that they work. In this sample, the relationship between flexible work hours and commitment was moderated by gender and employees' family responsibilities. Specifically, the positive relationship was stronger for female managers and employees with family obligations.

Mentoring is another HR practice that has been tied to commitment. Specifically, in a sample of U.S. army officers, Payne and Huffman (2005) found in a cross-sectional, individual-level study that both career and psychosocial mentoring were positively related to organizational commitment. The relationship was moderated by the source of mentoring, with officers mentored by their supervisors showing greater commitment than officers mentored by sources other than their supervisors.

Systems of HR practices have been demonstrated to relate to organizational commitment across a variety of employee and organizational samples. Specifically, in individual-level studies, HR systems have been found to relate to commitment in samples of frontline employees from car rental, retail, and hospitality organizations in South America (Browning, 2006) as well as in a sample of software professionals in the U.S. (Paul & Anantharaman, 2004). Additionally, in a business-unit-level analysis, Wright et al. (2005) demonstrated a similar relationship between a system of HR practices and a concurrent commitment measure in their study of a large food service organization.

These studies illustrate that, whether considering individual practices or systems of practices, HR management is an important correlate of commitment. While theory would suggest that HR management influences commitment within an organization through shaping employees' experiences and work environment, this area in particular is in need of longitudinal empirical support to confirm the causal direction of this relationship.

What has been missing within this literature, however, is a specific examination of the different mindsets of commitment, and how those might be differentially related to HR practices. For instance, while only examining the affective commitment mindset, Gardner, Moynihan, and Wright (2007) found that bundles of HR practices focused on enhancing motivation and empowerment were positively related to commitment, but those focused on enhancing skills were unrelated to such commitment. One could imagine that practices enhancing skills actually reduce affective commitment as they provide employees with more marketable skills. In addition, some HR practices such as stock options and not-yet-portable pensions may be negatively related to the affective mindset, but positively related to continuance commitment.

Turnover

Within the practitioner literature, particularly the employee engagement and "war for talent" areas, the concept of commitment has been advocated for its ability to retain employees. While the practitioner literature has recently seen this upsurge in popularity, one must note that academic researchers have been interested in this relationship since the 1970s (Porter & Steers, 1972), albeit largely at the individual level of analysis. At this level, Hom and Griffeth (1995) reviewed the literature and concluded that organizational commitment was negatively related to turnover intentions and to subsequent turnover behavior.

While employee turnover may be considered an individual-level phenomenon, it is a real problem for organizations at both the organization and the unit level, evidenced by organization-wide initiatives directed at employee retention. Recent research has also focused on aggregated commitment and its relationship to turnover. Ostroff (1992) theorized and found that a group's level of commitment was related to the group's level of turnover. Simons and Roberson (2003) found a weak negative relationship between collective commitment and organizational turnover rates. Angle and Perry (1981), in a study of bus company employees, found a strong negative relationship between affective commitment and turnover. Gardner et al. (2007) found a strong negative relationship between affective commitment and turnover.

In a unit-level study of a financial service organization, Ryan, Schmit, and Johnson (1996) found a significant negative relationship between shared, work-related employee attitudes and branch-level turnover rates over a two-year period. Additionally, in a unit-level, cross-industry meta-analysis based on about 8,000 business units in 36 organizations, Harter, Schmidt, and Hayes (2002) similarly found a negative commitment-turnover relationship.

Again, this literature has tended to focus only on the affective commitment mindset, and could be improved considerably by expanding to explore different mindsets. Individuals' departure decisions are certainly influenced by their affective perceptions about the organization, but may be influenced by normative or continuance mindsets as well.

Performance

Organizational performance has been conceptualized in a variety of ways. Ultimately, many organizations aim to achieve excellence in terms of financial performance. However, other performance indicators, such as customer satisfaction and (reduced levels of) employee turnover, have been shown to be important for organizations both as ends in themselves and as means to achieving both financial and other end goals. Several indicators of firm performance, some of which we review in this section, have repeatedly been shown to relate to organizational commitment.

Financial measures are perhaps the most commonly used indicators of overall firm performance. In both organization and business-unit-level studies, commitment and financial performance have been shown to be related across multiple settings. Across a diverse sample of organizations appearing on the Best Companies list and additional organizations matched to these, Fulmer et al. (2003) found that employee attitudes were related to both return on assets and book-to-market value in an organization-level analysis. Similarly, in another organization-level study across firms of various industries, Schneider, Hanges, Smith, and Salvaggio (2003) demonstrated a relationship between employee attitudes and return on assets and earnings per share. Profit and productivity have been linked to commitment across diverse organizational samples as well (Harter et al., 2002; Patterson et al., 2004; Wright et al., 2005). Additionally, in a business-unit-level study, Wright et al. (2005) linked commitment to additional operational performance measures, including shrinkage, quality, workers compensation, and expenses.

Both unit and organization-level studies have demonstrated a relationship between customer satisfaction and organization commitment. In a unique sample of school teachers, Ostroff (1992) found that teachers' reported work attitudes were associated with student satisfaction in an organization-level analysis of schools. Similar relationships have been found between employee attitudes and satisfaction of more traditional customer groups in unit-level studies of financial service organizations (Ryan et al., 1996) and restaurants (Koys, 2001), as well as in a cross-industry meta-analysis (Harter et al., 2002).

Overall, the studies reviewed in this section have illustrated the importance of considering both financial and nonfinancial indicators of performance in investigations of commitment. Additional research would be useful in determining whether working in an organization that achieves superior performance causes employees to be more committed or committed employees work together in ways that drive organizations to succeed.

Conceptual Issues

Causal Theories

One major conceptual issue in this literature deals with the causal direction of a number of the relationships cited. Implicit in many of the organization-level studies is an assumption that most of the organizational correlates such as climate, culture, structure, HR practices, and so forth are determinants of commitment, while most assume performance as an outcome of commitment. However, consistent with the theoretical debate concerning the attitudinal and behavioral perspectives outlined in chapter 1 of this book, it is likely that some of these causal relationships are more complex than such unidirectional assumptions reflect. On the determinant side, while it might be difficult to suggest that structure stems from commitment, some other determinants may actually be influenced by commitment. For instance, when employees feel emotionally committed to the organization, they will likely interpret organizational actions and practices in a positive manner. They also may speak positively about these characteristics to coworkers, influencing their perceptions and reports of organizational characteristics. Thus, one could easily posit a reverse, or at least dual, causality.

On the outcome side, again, while most authors imply that commitment leads to performance, the opposite may be likely as well (Wright et al., 2005), further demonstrating the possibility of reciprocal causality. Just as everyone likes to be part of a winning team, when individuals or organizations perform well, the respondents' reports of commitment can increase. Thus, while the causal nature of the determinants and outcomes of commitment are often assumed, if not stated explicitly, conceptually the causal nature of these relationships may not be as straightforward as the authors suggest.

This leads to the implication that commitment may indeed relate to multiple organizational phenomena through patterns of reciprocal causality. While some objective characteristics such as size may not be influenced by commitment, others may be. For instance, as companies decentralize, employees may feel enhanced commitment owing to their autonomy. If such commitment leads to better productivity, decision making, and performance, it may enable the firm to further decentralize. Thus, what seems like a simple, one-way relationship can, over time, become reciprocal. However, to date, while some theoretical work has begun to address the potential complexity of the causal relationships between commitment and other organizational factors, empirical research has continued to assume simpler patterns reflecting one-way causation.

Concerns Regarding Individual Level of Analysis

The most obvious problem with the individual level of analysis is that it requires drawing cross-level conclusions from within-level data. While not impossible, one certainly finds it difficult to design studies that examine organizational characteristics at the individual level of analysis. For instance, one approach would be to ask respondents to report characteristics of the organization that can then be correlated with their commitment. However, using an individual to report data on the organization raises the issue of reliability. For instance, Gerhart (1999) found extremely low levels of interrater reliability among respondents to strategy measures. Later, Gerhart et al. (2000) and Wright, Gardner, Moynihan, and Park (2001) found low levels of reliability among respondents reporting HR practices that existed at the organization and even job level. Thus, depending upon the nature of the construct being measured, it appears that individual respondents can be notoriously poor sources of organizational characteristic data.

In addition, when multiple respondents vary in their reports, the mere fact that they vary reveals that any observed relationships will be (a) with regard to *perceived* organizational characteristics, and (b) consequently subject to at least some level of percept-percept bias. While this provides variability for the purposes of predicting individual-level commitment, it calls into question the validity of using aggregated measures.

An additional problem with the use of the individual level of analysis stems from more practical considerations, particularly with regard to examining performance as a correlate. Research has generally found only weak relationships between individual-level attitudes and individual performance. Ostroff (1992) suggested that one reason for this is that, in addition to individual attitudes, individual performance is likely to be affected by a variety of other factors that are unique to the individual, such as situational influences, ability, and personality. Thus, a particular employee's performance has several additional correlates, which may prevent the detection of a strong commitment-performance relationship at this level of analysis. However, when aggregated to higher levels, many of these other influences are likely to wash out, allowing for detection of the commitment-performance relationship at the group or organization level. In another argument against the individual level of analysis, Ryan et al. (1996) contended that performance measured at higher (e.g., organizational) levels is likely to be affected by factors that cannot be accounted for by individual performance, such as interactions in employee workgroups and the organizational social climate in the workplace, both of which may be linked to levels of commitment. Hence, the authors argue, productivity is not an individual construct, but a group- or organization-level construct, and should be measured, along with its correlates, at the appropriate corresponding level of analysis.

In addition to the cited problems associated with analyzing commitment at the individual level, several advantages to group- or organization-level analysis of the construct have been suggested. For example, James et al. (1988) noted that groups of employees consistently share social interactions. These interactions, they argue, should naturally lead to shared meanings and consequently to shared attitudes. It has been added that employees in a work unit are also subjected to the same environmental influences and experiences (Gutek & Winter, 1992; Judge & Hulin, 1993). With already shared meanings and attitudes, employees are likely to interpret these work experiences in a similar way, thus reinforcing their common attitudinal ground. Additionally, Ostroff (1992) contends that employees are as a whole affected by their coworkers' attitudes and behaviors, especially when they depend on each other in their work tasks. As a result, a group of employees that is generally high in commitment is more likely to be generally high in the correlates of commitment than is any one of the group's individual members. In sum, several scholars have argued that many of the circumstances that are likely to influence employees' commitment to an organization are likely to occur and take effect not at the individual level but at the group or organizational level. For this reason, despite the traditional use of individual-level measures, some scholars contend that commitment is most appropriately operationalized at one of these higher levels of analysis.

Aggregational Theories

If one assumes that there is conceptual validity in aggregations of commitment across individuals in workgroups, business units, or organizations, this leads to questions as to the aggregational theories that make such operationalizations valid. Note that chapter 12 in this book addresses a number of these issues in more detail, but we cover them here specifically with regard to the organizational influences on commitment.

Chan (1998) suggested five different aggregational models that can exist. First, an additive model consists of summing and/or averaging lower-level scores into a unit-level variable, regardless of the within-unit variance. Such a model assumes that individuals within a unit need not agree, but that the mean differences across units contain meaningful variation.

Second, a direct consensus model averages lower-level scores, but requires consensus or agreement on the within-unit scores. Thus, the model suggests that the variable is one that is shared among members of the unit, and thus, one must demonstrate the shared nature of the variable before being able to look at variation across units as being meaningful.

Third, a referent shift model is like a direct consensus model in that it (a) uses an aggregation of the lower-level scores and (b) requires consensus or agreement on the within-unit scores, but, instead of individuals responding as to their own psychological state, they are responding as to their perceptions of the unit (e.g., "members of this department focus on customers"). Thus, rather than having an affective component, a referent shift model assumes a "belief" about a characteristic of the group.

Fourth, a dispersion model focuses on the variance within the unit rather than the consensus within the unit (e.g., diversity). In this model, it is actually the differences among individuals that comprise the construct or variable of interest.

Finally, a process model proposes similar relationships among composition variables at one level that are also present at another level. In essence, this model goes beyond looking at the focal variable to examine the relationship between the focal variable and some other variable(s) at a different level of analysis.

Because the aggregation of commitment has only begun relatively recently, less attention has been paid to aggregational concerns. For instance; while one could certainly hope that organizational phenomena lead to similar reactions in terms of commitment, there is not reason to believe that this has to be the case. A recent model proposed by Wright and Nishii (forthcoming), depicted in Figure 9.1, describes the problematic nature of current examinations of the HR–firm performance relationship. As can be seen from this model, the problems stem from the fact that HR practices and firm performance measures are both organization-level

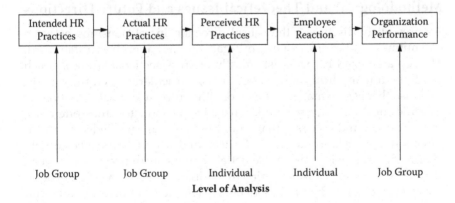

FIGURE 9.1
A process model of the relationship between HR practices and performance. *Note.* Adapted from "Strategic HRM and Organizational Behavior: Integrating Multiple Levels of Analysis," by P. Wright & L. Nishii, 2006. CAHRS Working Paper WP06-05 Center for Advanced Human Resource Studies, School of ILR, Cornell University.

(or at least job-level) phenomenon, but that the mediation mechanisms require individual-level experiences, interpretations and reactions. Based in the HR–performance literature, their argument is that while an empirical relationship has been established between HR practices and distal firm performance outcomes, organizational characteristics such as HR practices can be perceived, interpreted, and reacted to differently by different individuals. In their process model, they note that while the firm may have a policy regarding what practices should exist, supervisors may vary greatly in whether and how they actually implement them. Then, employees must perceive the practices, and they may vary in how they perceive the practices. Having perceived the practices, they must interpret the purpose of the practices, in essence making some kinds of positive or negative attributions as to what the firm hopes to accomplish from those practices. Finally, those interpretations may dictate how employees react affectively, cognitively, and behaviorally. This has two implications: First, there may be meaningful variance across units, even when individuals within units may not agree. Second, the variance in commitment to the same organizational phenomenon may be an interesting focus of exploration for bridging the micro-macro divide (Wright & Boswell, 2002).

The conceptual issues with regard to the level of analysis lead to a discussion about the methodological issues which stem from this level problem.

Methodological and Theoretical Issues and Future Directions

As previously discussed, the causal direction in relationships between commitment and various aspects of organizations has not been established. The research cited here consists mostly of cross-sectional studies, which preclude drawing firm causal conclusions, particularly given the conceptual case that can be made as above for either reverse or dual causation.

While some longitudinal studies have been conducted, they often lack robust design and analyses that would further our knowledge of causal direction. For instance, Ryan et al. (1996) and Koys (2001) collected data at only two points in time. While better than most studies, this is a weak design for inferring causal priority. In addition, Wright et al.'s (2005) organization-level study had a reasonably short time span between data collection (i.e., performance data was collected 3–9 months prior to and 9–15 months following collection of commitment data). This possibly did not provide enough time for real change to occur. Finally, in what is probably the most rigorous longitudinal study, Schneider et al. (2003) used questionnaire items on attitudes that varied across time period and organizations (though this problem is somewhat mitigated by stability and internal consistency of items). Also, we must note that their results led them to conclude that the relationship between commitment and performance at the organization level was one of dual causation.

In studies at the individual level of analysis, the major problem we see deals with common method bias. Because individual-level studies often use multiple individuals within a work unit or organization, variations in responses to the organization characteristics are error variance (because there is one true level of the characteristic). This error is likely due to the perceptions of individuals, and can lead to the potential for the relationships observed to be a form of a mental model of the phenomenon that individuals hold. This does not preclude research at the individual level; individual variance and theories of how organizational characteristics influence individual commitment can help move the field forward. However, such research would require that the measures of organizational commitment come from some source (e.g., archival, peer, supervisor) other than the individual providing the commitment measure.

An additional issue that concerns research at all levels of analysis is that the commitment construct has been operationalized in dissimilar ways across studies. Specifically, several empirical studies that are grounded in the theory developed for commitment have measured variables that actually represent other constructs. For example, Ryan et al. (1996), Fulmer et al. (2003), and Schneider et al. (2003) examined relationships of correlates with more general attitudinal measures as opposed to commitment. Koys (2001) measured employees' job satisfaction rather than commitment. Finally, Harter et al. (2002) included studies measuring employee engagement in their meta-analysis on commitment. However, while this inconsistency may initially appear to be a cause for concern, two studies have revealed that, in reviewing studies examining job satisfaction, engagement, and commitment, the relationships of these variables with various correlates have been nearly identical (Ryan et al., 1996; Fulmer et al., 2003). This does not imply that these differences in constructs are trivial or irrelevant. It may be that the relationships will differ when examining different targets of commitment, different causes, or different outcomes. This is certainly an area for future research to examine.

Having identified some concerns with the present state of commitment research, we suggest that the greatest opportunities for future work on commitment will be in addressing the current issues of eliminating common method bias and determining directions of causality. Specifically, one way in which common method bias can be eliminated is by splitting a participant sample such that half of the sample responds to questions regarding commitment, while the other half responds to questions concerning the predicted correlates (Wright et al., 2005). Alternatively, a longitudinal design could be used to minimize the effects of common method bias as well as to begin to analyze directions in proposed causal relationships (Simons & Roberson, 2003).

In addition to addressing the noted limitations of existing research, future studies of commitment could benefit from extending the current findings across settings and from specifying paths through which commitment might impact broader organizational outcomes. For example, several authors have noted the need for studies of commitment conducted across a wider range of industries, organizational contexts, and employee populations, noting that the relationships observed in single industry or single organization studies may prove to be more complex when examined across a greater variety of contexts (Ostroff, 1992; Koys, 2001; Simons & Roberson, 2003). Additionally, Harter et al. (2002) proposed a need for study of a mediated model, where commitment mediates the relationship between specified organizational antecedents and firm-level financial outcomes.

Third, future research should address the organizational influences on different targets of commitment. We have largely focused on organizational commitment because this is the target that has received the lion's share of empirical attention. However, researchers have examined other targets such as commitment to an organizational change (Fedor, Caldwell, & Herold, 2006), commitment to unions (Barling et al., 1992), and commitment to professions (Hall, 1996). One could also conjecture that organization-level variables might influence commitment to targets such as supervisors or the job.

Fourth, the present research has often been plagued by a lack of specificity on both the commitment and the influence variables. For instance, HR practices are often grouped as an overall index, in spite of the fact that different practices might differentially affect commitment. In addition, as noted before, much of the organization-level research has focused primarily on the affective mindset, to the neglect of other mindsets. More specifically measuring influences (e.g, motivation, empowerment, and skill-enhancing HR practices) and commitment mindsets (affective, normative, and continuance) may lead to deeper theorizing and understanding of the organizational influences on commitment. For instance, Gardner, Moynihan, and Wright (2007) found that skill-enhancing HR practices were unrelated to an affective organizational commitment measure, but that motivation-enhancing and opportunity-enhancing practices were positively related.

Finally, the relationships between organization characteristics and commitment can certainly benefit from multilevel theorizing and research. As discussed previously with regard to aggregational theories and models, there does not seem to be consensus regarding whether or not consensus in commitment is required, whether the variance in commitment within groups is a meaningful focal construct, or whether relationships between commitment and certain variables at the individual level are the same at the unit level. It appears to us that current, individual-level commitment theories may not make sense at the organizational level, and the research suggests that commitment is not just an individual-level construct. However, considerably more work must be done both at theorizing about differences at different levels and across levels, and at conducting research aimed at revealing these multilevel phenomena. Klein, Molloy, and Brinsfield's (2006) general heuristic model of commitment provides an effective starting point for sparking both organization-level and multilevel theory and research on organizational influences on commitment.

Conclusion

While the commitment construct has increased in importance to organizations, its usefulness has not been matched by well-designed research that is as applicable to organization-level decision making. The use of individual level of analysis studies most often leads to the problem of percept-percept correlations in research on organizational characteristics related to commitment, which precludes drawing firm conclusions regarding these relationships. Conducting more research at the unit or business level, longitudinal research, and research using objective or other sources of data for measures to be related to commitment should enable our field to provide strong data that can lead to better prescriptions for how firms might increase the commitment of their workforces.

References

Aarons, G. A., & Sawitzky, A. C. (2006). Organizational climate partially mediates the effect of culture on work attitudes and staff turnover in mental health services. *Administration and Policy in Mental Health, 33*(3), 289.

Angle, H. L., & Perry, J. L. (1981). An empirical assessment of organizational commitment and organizational effectiveness. *Administrative Science Quarterly, 26*(1), 1.

Barling, J., Fullagar, C., & Kelloway, E. K. (1992). *The union and its members: A psychological approach.* New York: Oxford University Press.

Bateman, T. S., & Strasser, S. (1984). A longitudinal analysis of the antecedents of organizational commitment. *Academy of Management Journal, 27*(1), 95.

Becker, T. E. (1992). Foci and bases of commitment: Are they distinctions worth making? *Academy of Management Journal, 35*(1), 232.

Bergman, M., Benzer, J., and Henning, J. (in press). The role of individual differences as contributors to the development of commitment. In H. J. Klein, T. E. Becker, & J. P. Meyer (Eds.), Commitment in Organizations: Accumulated Wisdom and New Directions, Psychology Press.

Browning, V. (2006). The relationship between HRM practices and service behaviour in South African service organizations. *The International Journal of Human Resource Management, 17*(7), 1321.

Carr, J. Z., Schmidt, A. M., Ford, J. K., & DeShon, R. P. (2003). Climate perceptions matter: A meta-analytic path analysis relating molar climate, cognitive and affective states, and individual level work outcomes. *The Journal of Applied Psychology, 88*(4), 605.

Chan, D. (1998). Functional relations among constructs in the same content domain at different levels of analysis: A typology of composition models. *The Journal of Applied Psychology, 83*(2), 234.

Fedor, D. B., Caldwell, S., & Herold, D. M. (2006). The effects of organizational changes on employee commitment: A multilevel investigation. *Personnel Psychology, 59,* 1–29.

Fulmer, I. S., Gerhart, B., & Scott, K. S. (2003). Are the 100 best better? An empirical investigation of the relationship between being a "great place to work" and firm performance. *Personnel Psychology, 56*(4), 965.

Gardner, T. M., Moynihan, L. M., & Wright, P. M. (2007). *The influence of human resource practices and collective affective organizational commitment on aggregate voluntary turnover.* Unpublished manuscript.

Gerhart, B. (1999). Human resource management and firm performance: Measurement issues and their effect on causal and policy inferences. In P. M. Wright, L. D. Dyer, J. W. Boudreau, & G. T. Milkovich (Eds.), *Research in personnel and human resource management, supplement 4* (pp. 31). Greenwich, CT: JAI Press.

Gerhart, B., Wright, P. M., McMahan, G. C., & Snell, S. A. (2000). Measurement error in research on human resources and firm performance: How much error is there and how does it influence effect size estimates? *Personnel Psychology, 53*(4), 803.

Glisson, C., & James, L. R. (2002). The cross-level effects of culture and climate in human service teams. *Journal of Organizational Behavior, 23*(6), 767.

Gutek, B. A., & Winter, S. J. (1992). Consistency of job satisfaction across situations: Fact or framing artifact. *Journal of Vocational Behavior, 41,* 61–78.

Hall, D. T. (1996). *The Career is Dead—Long Live the Career: A Relational Approach to Careers.* San Francisco: Jossey-Bass Publishers.

Harter, J. K., Schmidt, F. L., & Hayes, T. L. (2002). Business-unit-level relationship between employee satisfaction, employee engagement, and business outcomes: A meta-analysis. *The Journal of Applied Psychology, 87*(2), 268.

Hollenbeck, J. R., & Klein, H. J. (1987). Goal commitment and the goal-setting process: Problems, prospects, and proposals for future research. *The Journal of Applied Psychology, 72*(2), 212.

Hom, P. W., & Griffeth, R. W. (1995). *Employee turnover.* Cincinnati, OH: South-Western College Pub.

Hunt, S. D., & Morgan, R. M. (1994). Organizational commitment: One of many commitments or key me. *Academy of Management Journal, 37*(6), 1568.

James, L. R. (1988). Comment: Organizations do not cognize. *Academy of Management Review, 13,* 129–132.

Judge, T. A., & Hulin, C. L. (1993). Job satisfaction as a reflection of disposition: A multiple source causal analysis. *Organizational Behavior and Human Decision Processes, 56*(3), 388.

Klein, H. J., Molloy, J. C., & Brinsfield, C. T. (2006). Understanding workplace commitments independent of antecedents, foci, rationales, and consequences. Paper presented at the academy of management annual meeting, Atlanta, GA.

Koys, D. J. (2001). The effects of employee satisfaction, organizational citizenship behavior, and turnover on organizational effectiveness: A unit-level, longitudinal study. *Personnel Psychology, 54*(1), 101.

Liden, R. C., Wayne, S. J., & Kraimer, M. L. (2003). The dual commitments of contingent workers: An examination of contingents' commitment to the agency and the organization. *Journal of Organizational Behavior, 24*(5), 609.

Locke, E. A., Latham, G. P., & Erez, M. (1988). The determinants of goal commitment. *Academy of Management.the Academy of Management Review, 13*(1), 23.

Lok, P., Westwood, R., & Crawford, J. (2005). Perceptions of organisational subculture and their significance for organisational commitment. *Applied Psychology, 54*(4), 490.

Mathieu, J. E., & Zajac, D. M. (1990). A review and meta-analysis of the antecedents, correlates, and consequences of organizational commitment. *Psychological Bulletin, 108*(2), 171.

Meyer, J. P., & Allen, N. J. (1991). A three-component conceptualization of organizational commitment. *Human Resource Management Review, 1,* 61–89.

Michaels, E., Handfield-Jones, H., & Axelrod, B. (2001). *The war for talent.* Boston: Harvard Business School Press.

Morris, J. H., & Steers, R. M. (1980). Structural influences on organizational commitment. *Journal of Vocational Behavior, 17,* 50–57.

Mowday, R. T., Porter, L. W., & Steers, R. M. (1982). *Employee-organization linkages: The psychology of commitment, absenteeism, and turnover.* New York: Academic Press.

Ostroff, C. (1992). The relationship between satisfaction, attitudes, and performance: An organizational level analysis. *The Journal of Applied Psychology, 77*(6), 963.

Patterson, M., Warr, P., & West, M. (2004). Organizational climate and company productivity: The role of employee affect and employee level. *Journal of Occupational and Organizational Psychology, 77,* 193.

Paul, A. K., & Anantharaman, R. N. (2004). Influence of HRM practices on organizational commitment: A study among software professionals in India. *Human Resource Development Quarterly, 15*(1), 77.

Payne, S. C., & Huffman, A. H. (2005). A longitudinal examination of the influence of mentoring on organizational commitment and turnover. *Academy of Management Journal, 48*(1), 158.

Porter, L. W., & Steers, R. M. (1972). *Organizational, work and personal factors in turnover and absenteeism.* Washington, D.C.: U.S. Office of Naval Research.

Power, D. J. (1988). Anticipating organizational structures. In J. Hage (Ed.), *Futures of organizations: Innovating to adapt strategy and human resources to rapid technological change* (pp. 67–80). Lexington, MA: Lexington Books.

Randall, D. M. (1990). The consequences of organizational commitment: Methodological investigation. *Journal of Organizational Behavior (1986–1998), 11*(5), 361.

Randall, M. L., Cropanzano, R., Bormann, C. A., & Birjulin, A. (1999). Organizational politics and organizational support as predictors of work attitudes, job performance, and organizational citizenship behavior. *Journal of Organizational Behavior, 20*, 159–174.

Reichers, A. E., & Schneider, B. (1990). Climate and culture: An evolution of constructs. In B. Schneider (Ed.), *Organizational culture and climate* (1st ed.). San Francisco: Jossey-Bass.

Rhoades, L., & Eisenberger, R. (2002). Perceived organizational support: A review of the literature. *The Journal of Applied Psychology, 87*(4), 698.

Rhoades, L., Eisenberger, R., & Armeli, S. (2001). Affective commitment to the organization: The contribution of perceived organizational support. *The Journal of Applied Psychology, 86*(5), 825.

Ryan, A. M., Schmit, M. J., & Johnson, R. (1996). Attitudes and effectivness: Examining relations at an organizational level. *Personnel Psychology, 49*(4), 853.

Scandura, T. A., & Lankau, M. J. (1997). Relationships of gender, family responsibility and flexible work hours to organizational commitment and job satisfaction. *Journal of Organizational Behavior, 18*(4), 377.

Schneider, B., Hanges, P. J., Smith, D. B., & Salvaggio, A. N. (2003). Which comes first: Employee attitudes or organizational financial and market performance? *The Journal of Applied Psychology, 88*(5), 836.

Silverthorne, C. (2004). The impact of organizational culture and person-organization fit on organizational commitment and job satisfaction in Taiwan. *Leadership & Organization Development Journal, 25*(7/8), 592.

Simons, T., & Roberson, Q. (2003). Why managers should care about fairness: The effects of aggregate justice perceptions on organizational outcomes. *The Journal of Applied Psychology, 88*(3), 432.

Stevens, J. M., Beyer, J. M., & Trice, H. M. (1978). Assessing personal, role, and organizational predictors of managerial commitment. *Academy of Management Journal, 21*(3), 380.

Van Vianen, A. E. M. (2000). Person-organization fit: The match between newcomers' and recruiters' preferences for organizational cultures. *Personnel Psychology, 53*(1), 113.

Vance, R. J., & SHRM Foundation (2006). *Employee engagement and commitment: A guide to understanding, measuring and increasing engagement in your organization.* Alexandria, VA: SHRM Foundation.

Wasti, S., & Önder, C. (in press). Commitment across cultures: Progress, pitfalls, and propositions. In H. J. Klein, T. E. Becker, & J. P. Meyer (Eds.), Commitment in Organizations: Accumulated Wisdom and New Directions, Psychology Press.

Wayne, S., Coyle-Shapiro, J., Eisenberger, R., Liden, R., Rousseau, D., & Shore, L. (in press). Social Influences. In H. J. Klein, T. E. Becker, & J. P. Meyer (Eds.), Commitment in Organizations: Accumulated Wisdom and New Directions, Psychology Press.

Whitener, E. M. (2001). Do "high commitment" human resource practices affect employee commitment? A cross-level analysis using hierarchical linear modeling. *Journal of Management, 27*(5), 515.

Wright, P. M., & Boswell, W. R. (2002). Desegregating HRM: A review and synthesis of micro and macro human resource management. *Journal of Management, 28*(3), 247.

Wright, P. M., Gardner, T. M., & Moynihan, L. M. (2003). The impact of HR practices on the performance of business units. *Human Resource Management Journal, 13*(3), 21.

Wright, P. M., Gardner, T. M., Moynihan, L. M., & Allen, M. R. (2005). The relationship between HR practices and firm performance: Examining causal order. *Personnel Psychology, 58*(2), 409.

Wright, P. M., Gardner, T. M., Moynihan, L. M., & Park, H. J. (2001). Measurement error in research on human resources and firm performance: Additional data and suggestions for future research. *Personnel Psychology, 54*(4), 875.

10

Commitment Across Cultures: Progress, Pitfalls, and Propositions

S. Arzu Wasti
Sabanci University, Turkey

Çetin Önder
Başkent University, Turkey

The definition of culture has been controversial in the social sciences; yet, there is considerable agreement that culture consists of shared elements that provide the standards for perceiving, believing, communicating, evaluating, and acting among those who share a language, a historical period, and a geographic location (Triandis, 1996). Culture is argued to manifest itself in terms of self-definitions, assumptions, beliefs, values, attitudes, norms, and overt behavior at the individual level and in structures, practices, and rituals at the organizational level (Aycan, 2000). As such, culture emerges as an important variable in terms of shaping the meaning, development, and implications of commitment. In this chapter, we critically review the growing cross-cultural commitment literature with a focus on methodological issues that may threaten the validity of explanations regarding the influence of culture on commitment. The term *cross-cultural* refers to comparative as well as single-country studies conducted outside North America, because single-country studies often implicitly deal with cross-cultural differences as they compare extant (usually American) findings with non-American data (Schaffer & Riordan, 2003). Next, we offer a theoretical model that seeks to delineate the ways that commitment can vary across national boundaries, and finally we conclude with future research directions.

Commitment Across Cultures: The Journey So Far

Preliminary Explorations

Since the endorsement of the view that perhaps was most prominently expressed by Hofstede (1980) that management structures and processes are culturally contingent, cross-cultural research has flourished. Indeed, the growing number of studies and the need for a theoretical framework to make sense of them was the impetus for Randall (1993), who conducted the first systematic review of the cross-cultural organizational commitment literature. Drawing on Hofstede's framework, Randall suggested that individualism-collectivism, with its implications for the importance of pursuing individual versus group priorities, could be especially relevant for organizational commitment researchers. In particular, she predicted greater affective attachment in collectivist cultures due to stronger ties with managers and coworkers, in contrast to greater calculative involvement in individualistic cultures, where the job itself or the compensation system was expected to be the primary antecedent. Randall further argued that high uncertainty avoidance cultures, characterized by a tendency to stay with the same employer and to treat loyalty as a virtue, would depict higher levels of affective commitment. Regarding the power distance dimension, which reflects the emphasis given to hierarchical relations in a society, she anticipated that the greater decentralization attributed to low power-distant countries would be associated with higher levels of affective commitment. Finally, she hypothesized that in feminine cultures, where individuals are more concerned with the quality of life, employees may have stronger affective ties to the organization, while in masculine cultures, characterized by assertiveness and higher need for achievement, employees may express more calculative involvement.

Through a computerized literature search, Randall (1993) identified 27 empirical studies exploring organizational commitment in countries other than the United States or across two or more cultures. However, only four studies, all of which were conducted in Japan, explicitly addressed the impact of culture on commitment. Moreover, 12 of the remaining studies were conducted in Canada, which can be argued to be similar to the United States on a number of dimensions, such as individualism and level of industrialization. In addition to finding little support for the theoretical predictions regarding the influence of culture, Randall concluded that due to the limited number of studies reporting comparable statistics, different nature of samples across countries, wide reliance on different instruments for measuring commitment, as well as inadequate construct validation information, it was difficult to compare the antecedents and consequences of commitment across cultures.

Current View of the Commitment Scene

We embarked on an update and reviewed the comparative and non–North American articles published between 1991 and 2007 in journals listed in the Social Sciences Citation Index under social psychology, applied psychology, management, and industrial relations. We selected a sample of 152 empirical articles (159 studies) that explicitly dealt with the construct, antecedents, or outcomes of organizational commitment. We content analyzed each article to ascertain its approach to cross-cultural research design and the methodological practices with respect to sampling, instrumentation (focusing on the organizational commitment scale), and data collection. A list of the articles as well as more detail on article selection, coding criteria, final coding, and effect sizes for comparative studies can be obtained from the first author.

Our review confirmed that the interest in culture and commitment was continuing to grow. For instance, while only 12% of studies reviewed were published in the early 1990s, the corresponding percentages were 31 and 57 for the late 1990s and the 2000s. In total, there were samples from 56 countries, comparing favorably to the figure (10) reported by Randall (1993). The majority of the samples were from the United Kingdom (UK; 30 studies), followed by Israel and the Netherlands (both 17), Australia (15), China and the United States (both 14), South Korea (13), and Belgium (12).

Nevertheless, there was modest progress in terms of explicating the influence of culture on commitment because much of this research endorsed an *imposed-etic* approach. This approach assumes culture-specific (emic) theories, constructs, and measures (usually developed in the United States or Canada) to be universal (etic) and is criticized with respect to limiting researchers to Western constructs of uncertain cross-cultural relevance and impeding the discovery of consequential culture-specific constructs or relationships (e.g., Katigbak, Church, Guanzon-Lapeña, Carlota, & del Pilar, 2002). Indeed, as seen in Table 10.1, almost half (41%) of the organizational commitment studies, which we labeled "no context," not only adopted an imposed-etic design but also failed to point out relevant contextual information. For instance, the national origin of the samples was typically mentioned in passing in the methods section, and information on methodological practices such as translation, validation of the scale in the new context, or macro variables such as the economic system, labor laws, or culture were often unreported. Most of these studies were from Israel (20%), Australia (18%), the Netherlands (9%), and the United Kingdom (9%).

One can make a case that industrially advanced societies produce knowledge that is easily transferable to each other, thereby mitigating concerns about contextual differences. Yet, this position is questionable in view of well-documented institutional differences in human resource systems (e.g., Gooderham, Nordhaug, & Ringdal, 1999). In the case of Israel, the

TABLE 10.1

Cross-Cultural Research Design

	1991–1995	1996–2000	2001–2007	Total
Imposed-etic: No context	6	23	36	65
	(32)	(46)	(40)	(41)
Imposed-etic: Generalizability	6	14	25	45
	(32)	(28)	(28)	(28)
Imposed-etic: One-way	5	6	13	24
	(26)	(12)	(14)	(15)
Derived etic	1	4	14	19
	(5)	(8)	(16)	(12)
Emic	1	3	2	6
	(5)	(6)	(2)	(4)
Total	19	50	90	159
	(100)	(100)	(100)	(100)

Note: The numbers represent the number of articles, and the percentages are provided in parentheses.

No context: Imposed-etic studies that do not explicitly mention the (national) context of the study setting.

Generalizability: Exploratory imposed-etic studies with no explicit hypotheses based on cultural theories or only ex post facto treatment of culture.

One-way: Imposed-etic studies advancing theoretical hypotheses based on culture theories.

Derived etic: Studies adapting imported theories and methods to better suit the local context, including studies carried out by a multicultural team of scholars attempting to incorporate both universal and culture-specific perspectives.

Emic: Studies that draw on indigenous theories and methods.

argument is debatable also with respect to cultural differences (e.g., House, Hanges, Javidan, Dorfman, & Gupta, 2004). This raises the question, therefore, as to why there has been such a lack of motivation to investigate cross-national differences. Wasti (2006) argued that, to the extent that academic reward structures around the world consider publication in U.S. journals to be indicative of good research, knowledge production will be geared toward the endorsement of universalistic assumptions, as acceptance in U.S. journals oftentimes necessitates adherence to mainstream (i.e., North American) paradigms (see Collin, Johansson, Svensson, & Ulvenblad, 1996; Leong & Leung, 2004; and Smith, 2005, for supporting arguments and evidence). In this regard, it is noteworthy that the aforementioned countries producing the bulk of the (decontextualized) commitment research represent the highest international penetration to top-tier American management journals (see for example, Kirkman & Law, 2005).

Of the imposed-etic studies that explicitly acknowledged their national context, many (28% in total) were observed to be exploratory, despite the availability of cultural theories. These studies, labeled "generalizability," sought to assess generalizability typically by general references to differences between East and West or on the basis that the study had not been done in that part of the world before. Only 15% of all studies, while imposed-etic in approach, developed a priori hypotheses regarding how cultural differences would manifest themselves on the commitment process. These studies, labeled "one-way" (Brett, Tinsley, Janssenns, Barsness, & Lytle, 1995), typically tested the boundary conditions of North American management theories by drawing on individualism, collectivism, power distance, and to a lesser extent, uncertainty avoidance and masculinity. Of note, less than half of the generalizability and one-way studies in total (43%) reported information about the institutional differences in comparison to North America.

Arguably, an imposed-etic strategy is inevitable in the first stages of cross-cultural inquiry (Berry, 1989). However, the high number of studies that provided no validation evidence for imported scales or relied on imported validation evidence suggests that an imposed-etic approach was not taken as an initial step toward testing external validity, but rather the generalizability of the extant knowledge was assumed. In fact, echoing Randall (1993) more than a decade ago, the instrumentation practices had much room for improvement when compared with Schaffer and Riordan's (2003) recommended procedures for cross-cultural research. Table 10.2 presents our assessment of the existing practices. While many investigators who employed imported scales undertook the preferred practice of translation and back-translation (40%), in more than one-quarter (27%) of the studies with non-English-speaking samples, the researchers provided no information regarding translation. The reported reliability and validity evidence was not impressive (we rated 63 and 41%, respectively, as satisfactory). Finally, in 88% of comparative studies, the investigators did not report or account for response bias, and only 39% established measurement invariance across their samples.

The unfortunate consequence of such careless instrumentation is that it impedes the accumulation of cross-cultural construct validation information and blocks the way for the investigation of more substantive issues. Imposed-etic studies with satisfactory instrumentation practices, on the other hand, do provide evidence about the transferability of North American models and measures of commitment. For instance, there seems to be stronger support for Meyer and Allen's (1991) three-component model in Western Europe (e.g., Vandenberghe, Stinglhamber, Bentein, & Delhaise, 2001) than in contexts considerably different from North America. In particular, Cheng and Stockdale's (2003) data from China yielded a modest fit, primarily due to the poor performance of the continuance commitment (CC) scale. Gautam, Van Dick, and Wagner's (2001) assessment in Nepal revealed that no demographic or organizational variable was associated

TABLE 10.2

Methodological Practices: Instrumentation

	1991–1995	1996–2000	2001–2007	Total
Translation				
Translation information not relevant	3	7	7	17
	(25)	(28)	(13)	(19)
No translation information provided	2	4	14	20
	(22)	(22)	(30)	(27)
Translation	1	1	2	4
	(11)	(6)	(4)	(5)
Translation/back-translation	3	8	18	29
	(33)	(44)	(39)	(40)
Adaptation/semantic-equivalence	0	2	2	4
	(0)	(11)	(4)	(5)
Bilingual subjects	2	1	3	6
	(22)	(6)	(7)	(8)
Reference to previous translation	0	2	1	3
	(0)	(11)	(2)	(4)
Combination of methods	1	0	6	7
	(11)	(0)	(13)	(10)
Pilot test information provided	2	5	6	13
	(17)	(20)	(11)	(14)
Satisfactory reliability reported	6	17	34	57
	(50)	(68)	(64)	(63)
Response bias mentioned/accounted for	2	0	1	3
	(33)	(0)	(7)	(12)
Satisfactory validation reported	5	7	25	37
	(42)	(28)	(47)	(41)
Measurement equivalence investigated	3	1	6	10
	(50)	(17)	(43)	(39)
Total	12	25	53	90

Note: The numbers represent the number of articles, and the percentages are provided in parentheses. The percentages reported for various translation practices are adjusted to reflect the proportion of studies for which translation was relevant. Response bias and measurement equivalence counts and percentages relate to comparative studies. No-context studies and four of the emic studies (further coded as universalistic, i.e., treating constructs of interest as universally relevant without evidence) were not considered to be informative from the point of cross-cultural research and were excluded from this analysis.

with affective commitment (AC), which nonetheless was the only form of commitment relating significantly to search and turnover intentions. Ko, Price, and Mueller's (1997) test in Korea revealed that the three scales had acceptable reliability, but the AC and normative commitment (NC) scales lacked discriminant validity, and the construct validity of NC and CC were questionable. To investigate whether this was due to culturally irrelevant items, Lee, Allen, Meyer, and Rhee (2001) administered a set of items written by an international team (Meyer, Barak, & Vandenberghe, 1996) to another Korean sample and found support for the three-component model. In the same way, Wasti (2003) adapted Meyer, Allen, and Smith's (1993) scales by adding culture-specific items that she developed through interviews with Turkish employees and validated the three-factor conceptualization. Thus, notwithstanding the potential benefits of developing culturally appropriate operationalizations (i.e., going beyond imposed-etic approaches), taken together with Stanley et al.'s (2007) meta-analysis on the cross-cultural validity of Meyer and Allen's (1991) model, the three components appear distinguishable across cultures.

Some antecedents and outcomes that are well established in the North American literature also appear to generalize across cultures, although such confirmation is mostly from industrialized Western countries and limited to AC. Specifically, the results of several comparative studies suggest that interesting work (e.g., Hult, 2005), investment in employees (e.g., Lee & Bruvold, 2003), promotion opportunities (e.g., Roe, Zinovieva, Dienes, & Horn, 2000), and participation (e.g., Palich, Hom, & Griffeth, 1995) are generalizable antecedents of AC.

Interestingly, studies at the individual level show moderating effects of cultural values on the relationship between various antecedents and outcomes of organizational commitment. For instance, Brockner et al. (2001) reported a stronger positive correlation between voice and AC for individuals endorsing lower levels of power distance values, a finding they further validated at the national level with samples from the United States, China and Mexico. Walumbwa and Lawler (2003), across Kenyan, Indian, and Chinese samples, showed that the relationship between transformational leadership and AC was stronger for individuals who endorsed collectivistic values. Lastly, Wasti (2003) showed that the relationship between NC and turnover intentions was stronger for Turkish individuals who endorsed collectivistic values to a greater extent.

Indeed, regarding turnover intentions, the meta-analysis by Stanley et al. (2007) indicated that neither cultural values nor practices as measured by the GLOBE Project (House et al., 2004) moderated the relationship between AC and turnover intentions, but the negative relations between turnover intentions and both CC and NC were greater in cultures with stronger in-group as well as institutional collectivism and power distance practices. With respect to job performance, Jaramillo, Mulki, and Marshall's (2005) meta-analysis, which used Hofstede's (1980) rankings, showed stronger correlations between AC and salesperson performance in collectivist than individualistic nations.

Lastly, the discriminant validity of AC toward various foci such as supervisor, workgroup and occupation has also been supported across several contexts (e.g., Boshoff & Mels, 2000; Cohen, 2000; Stinglhamber, Bentein, & Vandenberghe, 2002). For instance, in addition to developing a five-dimensional commitment-to-supervisor scale in Chinese, Chen, Tsui, and Farh (2002) confirmed mainstream findings that show commitment to supervisor to be more strongly associated with in-role and extra-role performance than commitment to organization (Becker, Billings, Eveleth, & Gilbert, 1996). Indeed, drawing on collectivism and power distance, Cheng, Jiang, and Riley (2003) proposed the "cultural hypothesis," which argues that values upholding submission to authority and personalized loyalty render the supervisor a more significant focus of commitment, and that commitment to supervisor, in addition to explaining local outcomes (i.e., supervisor-relevant outcomes such as in- and extra-role performance), will strongly predict global outcomes (i.e., organization-relevant outcomes like turnover intentions). While Cheng et al. (2003) confirmed the cultural hypothesis in Taiwan, a study in China by Snape, Chan, and Redman (2006) failed to replicate their findings.

While these latter studies on commitment to supervisor present personalized loyalty as a reflection of cultural values, it should be noted that such loyalty is also institutionally perpetuated in the context of these studies. For instance, research from China draws attention to the weak legal system, which fosters reliance on personal contacts rather than the rule of law (Chen & Francesco, 2003). Indeed, it is the interplay of cultural and institutional factors that shapes the nature of commitment across contexts. Yet, in most cross-cultural organizational commitment research, pertinent institutional variables are often dismissed, and any observed difference is quickly attributed to cultural values. As aptly put by Rousseau and Schalk (2000, p. 15), "Culture, when used to explain everything, may wind up explaining nothing—unless we more carefully address the societal institutions that compose and support it and their link to employment practices and individual experiences." In the next section, we present a model of commitment that aims to bring these together.

Culture, Context, Commitment: Charting the Terrain

As emphasized by Redding, Norman and Schlander (1994), the study of organizational commitment across cultures cannot be limited only to the notion of commitment, but necessitates a comparative analysis of the concept of organization, which is a product of the particular sociological, political, legal, and economic milieu. To illustrate, Wang (2004) argued that the focus of commitment has traditionally been the State in China, and therefore affect-based commitment resulting from an equitable and contractual exchange between workers and an organization may be new to Chinese workers. More recently, Gelfand, Nishii, and Raver (2006) noted that cross-cultural research has increasingly become reductionist due to a focus mainly on culture inside the head of the individuals, and underlined the importance of examining the nature of societal institutions across cultures. Aycan (2005) also pointed out that the incorporation of socio-institutional and organizational variables allows for an explanation of organizational variation within societies, which is typically overlooked in cross-cultural investigations. The model we propose in Figure 10.1 tries to make constructive use of these criticisms.

Overview of the Model

In this model we treat culture as qualitatively different from, but reciprocally connected with, institutions (Redding, 2008). We propose that the social-institutional context, as shaped to some extent by culture, influences the organizational context, which in turn impinges on the human resource (HR) system of the organization (Hamilton & Biggart, 1988; Whitley, 1999; Wilkinson, 1996). Social-institutional factors also directly influence the HR system, as when the law stipulates particular HR practices. The HR system, mediated by the psychological climate (individuals' perceptions of what the organization is like and how they are to perform their daily activities; Bowen & Ostroff, 2004), influences employees' perceptions of the terms of exchange between employees and employers (psychological contract) and organizational support (i.e., social antecedents, chapter 8, this volume). In congruence with social exchange theory (Blau, 1964), the nature of these perceptions predicts commitment forms and foci. *Forms* refers to AC, NC, and CC; whereas *foci* refers to the targets of commitment like the organization, supervisor, coworkers, and labor union. With multiple forms and foci, it is possible to consider "profiles of commitment" along these two attributes. Commitment profiles in turn predict focal and discretionary behaviors, which ultimately determine organizational productivity. Focal behaviors are those to which an individual is bound by his or her commitment (e.g., in the case of organizational commitment the act of staying); discretionary behaviors fall within the domain of contextual performance (Meyer & Herscovitch, 2001).

An important variable in the model, which we propose is influenced by social-institutional factors, is HR strength. A strong HR system is characterized by distinctiveness, consistency, and consensus (Bowen & Ostroff, 2004). To the extent that the HR system is strong, there will be less variance across employees with respect to interpreting their work experiences. Shared interpretations in effect constitute the organizational climate and

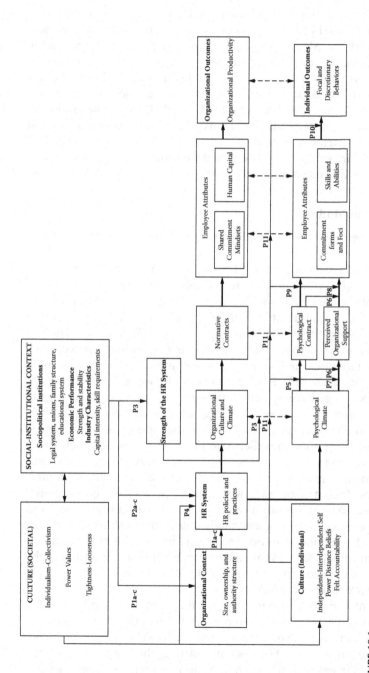

FIGURE 10.1

An integrated model of cultural and social-institutional influences on commitment. Propositions presented in the text are denoted by P1 to P11. Block arrows represent HR-system-mediated influences of societal culture and social-institutional context, referred to as P1 to P5. The model draws on Ostroff and Bowen (2000) regarding the multilevel relations between climate, contracts, commitment, and outcomes (represented by dashed arrows), Aselage and Eisenberger (2003) in terms of the relationship between POS and psychological contracts, and Gelfand et al. (2006) regarding the relationship between societal culture and its manifestations at the individual level.

culture, which lead to normative contracts, shared mindsets, collective behavior, and eventually to organizational outcomes. The model further depicts reciprocal relations between levels for the perceptual variables and employee attributes. It is argued that individual-level perceptions will be influenced in part by the existing organizational climate and culture as well as normative contracts; individual mindsets and behaviors will be influenced in part by shared mindsets and collective behaviors.

Culture, operationalized along specific dimensions (namely, individualism-collectivism, tightness-looseness, and power distance) is argued to have cross-level effects both at the organizational and the individual levels (Gelfand et al., 2006). At the organizational level, these dimensions are proposed to influence the HR system in terms of the prevalence as well as purpose of various HR practices and policies. Through socialization practices endorsed in the family, school, and other domains of public life, societal culture is argued to influence the psychology of the individual in terms of self-construals (e.g., independent versus interdependent self; Markus & Kitayama, 1991), values (e.g., power; Schwartz, 1994) and cognitive mechanisms (e.g., felt accountability; Gelfand et al., 2006). These psychological syndromes are expected to moderate the relationships between the psychological climate and social antecedents, and social antecedents and commitment, as well as commitment and behavior. They are also expected to moderate the reciprocal relations between individual and collective levels of climate, contracts, and commitment.

In sum, our model is based on the multiple bases, multiple foci conceptualization of commitment offered by Meyer and Herscovitch (2001) and Reichers (1985), and largely echoes Klein, Brinsfield, and Molloy's (2006) heuristic model of workplace commitments in terms of antecedent variables (see also chapter 1, this volume). Drawing on the contributions by Ostroff and Bowen (2000; see also chapter 9, this volume), Aselage and Eisenberger (2003; see also chapter 8, this volume), it further explains the multilevel relationships among antecedent variables. Thus, our model expands existing commitment theories by explicating the cross-level effects of societal factors on the commitment process. Although the model does not do justice to recent contributions by Meyer and his colleagues (e.g., Meyer, Becker, & Vandenberghe, 2004) that further explicate the development and consequences of commitment, we allude to some key constructs (e.g., goal regulation) in their work and recommend the interested reader to consult these articles.

In what follows, we offer specific propositions regarding the influence of social-institutional and cultural factors on the commitment process. To ease the cognitive demand on the reader, we stick to the societal-level labels of cultural dimensions throughout the text but clarify which level we are referring to. By drawing on specific examples, we then discuss how social-institutional and cultural factors interactively shape organizational- and individual-level variables to determine the nature and consequences of commitment within and across national contexts.

Effects of Social-Institutional Factors on Commitment Forms and Foci

In the model, social-institutional context comprises sociopolitical institutions (namely, the legal system, unions, family structure, and the educational system), economic performance in terms of strength and stability, and industry characteristics regarding capital and skill requirements. These social-institutional factors essentially determine the zone of negotiability within which psychological contracts of employees are formed (Thomas, Au, & Ravlin, 2003). That is, these factors set limits on what employees can expect from the employing organization and shape employee perceptions as to the extent to which various HR practices are undertaken with discretion. For instance, laws stipulate standards as to minimum wage or hours of work; educational systems shape skills and abilities of employees, determining their career prospects; unions protect employees against undue dismissal and bargain for higher wages. We further acknowledge that there may be strong interdependencies between our select aspects of social-institutional environment (e.g., economic performance and legal system strength) and that many of the distinctions we introduce below (e.g., strong versus weak legal systems) coarsely map onto the difference between developed and developing countries. Yet, for the purposes of discussion we ignore the interdependencies and refer to prior research, which used continuous measures to capture variance in similar aspects of the social-institutional environment (e.g., Parbooteah & Cullen, 2003). Also, we note that there may be significant within-country heterogeneity regarding social-institutional factors. For instance, there may still be a sizable nonunion workforce in a country where the unionization rate is higher compared with other countries.

Our model depicts that social-institutional factors influence the development of commitment forms and foci primarily as mediated by organizational-level variables, namely, the organizational context and the HR system. Organizational context comprises size, ownership, and authority structure, that is, whether power is positional or personal, and its degree of centralization. Size, ownership, and authority structure determine features of coordination and control systems, first and foremost the HR system, which ultimately influences commitment forms and foci as mediated by employees' perceived organizational support (POS) and psychological contracts. Below, we focus on strength of the legal system, family structure, legal regulation of employee participation, and industry characteristics, which arguably relate closely to features of the organizational context and the HR system (Fligstein, 1996; Hamilton & Biggart, 1988; Whitley, 1992). In the interest of space, we do not incorporate the implications of the

HR system on commitment forms and foci in this set of propositions, but allude to them under the section regarding cultural factors.

The strength of the legal system determines enforceability of contracts and the prevalence of formal versus informal contracts. Weak legal systems, such as those in ex-communist or developing countries, lack both the elaborate rules that constrain power holders in organizations and the capacity to intervene when existing rules are circumvented (Fligstein, 1996). As a result, weak legal systems translate into authority structures that are particularistic. Such organizations display concentration of power in the hands of a few individuals (e.g., members of the same political party) and arbitrary use of power. Employees in these organizations depend on particular individuals rather than formal rules or procedures for recruitment, promotion, or other rewards. As argued by Pearce, Branyiczki, and Bigley (2000), employees in particularistic organizations are more likely to trust their in-group and unlikely to be committed to the organization (however, they may be committed to the persons on whom they depend).

Another instance of particularistic organization, a product of historical patterns of economic development, is the family business (Whitley, 1992). In countries where the family structure is more traditional, the importance of family identity and the concomitant distrust of nonfamily members reinforce small-scale family business ownership. Family organizations are characterized by informal authority structures based on persons, not position, leading to particularistic HR practices, which as argued above fosters commitment to particular individuals rather than the organization. Further, particularism (i.e., nepotism), which promotes a concentration of power at the top of the familial hierarchy, lowers expectations with respect to autonomy or recognition among employees not connected to the owners (Kickul, Lester, & Belgio, 2004). These employees may primarily develop transactional contracts, and consequently, economic cost-based organizational commitments, whereas members of the owning family or employees in their network may feel obligated toward their in-group and perceive social costs associated with quitting (i.e., letting down the in-group) or develop affect-based commitment due to their privileged status.

Proposition 1a: The strength of the legal system and family structure have cross-level effects on organizational context regarding size, ownership, and authority structure, which in turn influence the particularism versus universalism of the HR system.

Countries also differ with respect to legal regulation of subordination relations between employees and employers, which reflects on authority structures of organizations. In developed countries, employees are granted extensive rights and protection against employers, partly through formal means of employee representation, such as the works councils in European Union countries or in the form of employee representatives

sitting on corporate boards. Employee representation generates HR policies and practices, which accommodate employees' need for voice, thereby
increasing organizational AC (Meyer & Allen, 1997).

Proposition 1b: The legal system has cross-level effects on organizational
context in terms of authority structure, which shapes the HR system
regarding practices pertaining to employee representation.

Finally, countries differ with respect to the portion of the labor force
employed in establishments that use capital- and skill-intensive technologies (Scott, 2006). Organizations using capital- and skill-intensive technologies, which are more prevalent in developed economies, tend to be
larger and managed by formal authority structures. Such organizations
have elaborate HR systems geared toward developing a skilled workforce
able to use discretion in work-related matters. Members of these organizations therefore expect higher job security, more career opportunities, and
better pay and benefits when compared with employees of organizations
that invest little in capital and employee skills. Due to smaller size and
lack of formal HR systems, these latter organizations, which are more
prevalent in developing economies, tend to comprise short-term employment, little training, and lower wages and benefits, causing employees
to develop psychological contracts that are more transactional in nature.
Arguably, transactional contracts are tied to CC, particularly on the part
of marginalized workers and those with limited opportunities elsewhere
(Rousseau, 1995).

Proposition 1c: Industry characteristics have cross-level effects on organizational context in terms of size and authority structure, which influence the
HR system regarding the prevalence of high-performance work systems.

The social-institutional context also has a direct effect on the HR system
through the legal framework, educational system, prevalence of unions,
and the family structure. In some countries HR practices are extensively
controlled through laws and regulations, whereas in others legal frameworks are sources of general guidelines, giving management a wider scope
of choice (Gooderham et al., 1999). Regarding the educational system,
countries vary on the division of labor in the provision of technical and
practical training (Dobbin & Boychuk, 1999; Hult, 2005; Whitley, 2003). In
some countries (e.g., Germany and Nordic countries) state-controlled educational systems have created a sizeable workforce with general technical
and practical training as well as certified skills. In other countries (e.g.,
Japan) training has been the employer's responsibility, and consequently,
is more geared toward developing company-specific (nontransferable)
skills. Coupled with seniority-based rewards and other practices that foster long-term employment, the Japanese HR system, possibly along with
other forms and foci of commitment, is conducive to the development of
CC to the organization.

Proposition 2a: The legal and educational systems have cross-level effects on the HR system in terms of determining managerial discretion and responsibility regarding the endorsement of various HR practices.

Another sociopolitical factor of relevance is the unionization of the workforce. Trade unions foster mechanisms for voice, representation, and protection of employees (Freeman & Medoff, 1984); therefore, in countries where unions have no presence, employees are more likely to be excluded from managerial hierarchies and vulnerable to arbitrary management practices. Perceiving lower levels of organizational support and higher probabilities for contract breaches, these employees are less likely to be affectively committed to their organizations. However, union presence may not always bring about a positive climate. In some countries with a long-standing tradition of union organization, labor-management relations have been antagonistic. In these countries, such as France, the relatively militant union movements engage the State rather than directly involving the employers, and bargaining is based on rule-oriented job control rather than codetermination of workplace practices (Dobbin & Boychuk, 1999). In other countries, unions either directly interact with management or are represented in management, and codetermination is prevalent. Workers in these countries are more likely to experience higher levels of POS as well as commitment and reciprocate by accepting flexible work arrangements and high internal mobility (Streeck, 1992).

In countries where unions have a strong presence, unions also emerge as entities to which employees may be committed. An important issue in these contexts is whether commitment to union undermines commitment to organization. Prior research points to the moderating role of union-management relations climate. Where union-management relations are cooperative and nonadversarial, employees are found to be committed to both their employing organizations and unions, whereas adversarial union-management relations are argued to be detrimental to organizational commitment (Kim & Rowley, 2006).

Proposition 2b: Unionization of the workforce has cross-level effects on the HR system in terms of governing employee representation.

We further propose that societal differences in gender roles and familial obligations have implications for the HR system. In countries where there is a stronger expectation that women will leave employment upon marriage and assume traditional household roles (e.g., taking care of children and the elderly), companies tend to discriminate against female employees by paying less and offering little training and fewer career opportunities, which results in transactional contracts among women (Whitley, 1992).

Proposition 2c: The family structure has cross-level effects on the HR system with respect to practices prohibiting gender discrimination.

It should be noted that in societies with traditional gender roles, the male members of the family are expected to provide for an extended family (Özkan & Lajunen, 2005). Considering that traditional countries frequently undergo economic crises, experience higher levels of unemployment, and offer little social security, the male employees, coupled with perceived in-group pressure as well as less mobility (Diaz-Saenz & Witherspoon, 2000), may be more concerned about transactional (i.e., economic exchange) rather than relational obligations in their employment relationship.

Finally, we contend that social-institutional factors, particularly the legal system and the country's economic performance, have a bearing on strength of the HR system. Regarding HR strength, we focus on consistency, which refers to consistency of HR practices across persons, contexts, and time (Bowen & Ostroff, 2004). In developing countries, lack of equal opportunity clauses, which limit discrimination by race, religion, gender, and the like, and suboptimal supervision of basic HR practices that pertain to benefits, occupational health, and safety, damage the consistency and thus the strength of the HR system. Moreover, developing economies frequently undergo economic crises, which result in economic stagnation and consequently force organizations to restructure themselves (Hoskisson, Johnson, Tihanyi, & White, 2005). Frequent organizational restructurings harm the consistency of HR systems as organizations terminate employment relationships or change the terms of employment, for example, by lowering wages. In these countries, alternative employment opportunities are typically scarce and employment contracts tend to be relatively short-term, earnings are unstable, and organizations offer little more than basic pay (Hamilton & Kao, 1990), which limits employees to transactional psychological contracts (Cappelli, 1999).

Proposition 3: The legal system and the country's economic performance influence the strength of the HR system in terms of consistency of HR practices across employees, situations, and time.

Effects of Cultural Factors on Commitment Forms and Foci

Regarding cultural factors, individualism and collectivism are arguably not only the most potent dimensions in terms of theoretical development and empirical evidence, but also key factors impinging on commitment. In individualist cultures, social behavior is guided primarily by attitudes, personal needs, and rights, and individuals in such cultures favor contractual relationships based on the principles of exchange (Triandis, 1995). On the other hand, collectivists tend to behave in keeping with the norms of their in-group as well as obligations and duties that are designed to maintain social harmony among the members of the in-group. Whereas in-groups tend to be *achieved* (through similar beliefs, attitudes, values, and occupations) in individualistic cultures, they are typically *ascribed* (e.g., kin, religion, village, and nation) and defined through tradition in collectivist cultures (Triandis, 1994). Thus, for example, coworkers may be considered an in-group in one culture and an out-group in another. As Tayeb (1994) pointed out, although Japan, India, and Iran are collectivist nations, the kin collectivist Iranian and Indian employees have as individualistic a relationship with their workplaces as those in any individualistic nation; whereas in Japan, the organization manifests itself as the primary in-group. Furthermore, although individualists treat in-groups and out-groups similarly to some extent, collectivists differentiate the two very clearly and treat the latter harshly in cases of conflict (Triandis, 1995). Accordingly, an accurate understanding of the organizational implications of collectivism involves identifying the in-groups and out-groups of relevance (Rhee, Uleman, & Lee, 1996).

Other cultural dimensions of importance are power distance and tightness-looseness. In a culture with large power distance, there is stronger adherence to authoritarian norms as well as greater dependence on and acceptance of authority, whereas low power-distance cultures are characterized by more egalitarian relationships (Hofstede, 1980). Cultural tightness-looseness is defined as the strength of social norms and the degree of sanctioning within societies (Gelfand et al., 2006). Societal tightness-looseness is proposed to have cross-level effects on a psychological syndrome of felt accountability at the individual level, which is the subjective experience that one's actions are subject to evaluation and that there are potential punishments based on these evaluations (Gelfand et al., 2006). In other words, individuals in tight societies expect violations of norms to be met with stronger punishments as compared with individuals in loose societies.

Organizations are open systems that perpetuate and reinforce societal norms. As such, organizational cultures and HR practices that support them, generally speaking, reflect the larger societal cultural values (Aycan, 2000; Gelfand et al., 2006). For instance, in individualist cultures, reward systems that stress individual merit are likely to prevail; in low power-distance cultures, job designs facilitating employee autonomy might be common. By increasing feelings of self-worth and fulfillment, such HR practices are expected to foster affective commitment to the organization or the supervisor (Meyer & Allen, 1997). Similarly, in collectivist cultures the prevalence of in-group recruitment may generate a strong pressure to meet the expectations of both the reference person and the recruiter regarding continued employment in the organization, thereby elevating social costs associated with quitting (Powell & Meyer, 2004; Wasti, 2002) and leading to higher levels of NC and CC toward these foci. In tight cultures, the concern for conformity might lead to extensive and formal socialization practices. This concern with person-organization fit may signal a relational employment contract and generate higher levels of NC as well as AC toward the organization.

Proposition 4: Societal culture has cross-level effects on the prevalence of HR practices, which, mediated by employees' perceptions as to their favorability (POS) or their reciprocal obligations (psychological contracts), influence commitment forms and foci.

At the individual level, cultural variation in perception and interpretation of signals from the organization can influence the formation of the psychological contract (Thomas et al., 2003). For instance, compared with loose cultures, individuals in tight cultures are likely to be highly sensitive to organizational norms as well as sanctions (Gelfand et al., 2006). Collectivists may be more sensitive to information regarding relational obligations (i.e., exchange of socioemotional resources), whereas individualists may be attuned to transactional obligations (i.e., exchange of economic resources). We further speculate that the emphasis on the transactional aspects might render the organization, top management, or supervisor more salient organizational constituents for individualists, whereas collectivists may largely register mutual obligations with their supervisors and coworkers rather than the abstract organization. Likewise, the supervisor or top management would be critical referents in high power-distance cultures. Indeed, recruitment, selection, and socialization strategies prevalent in different cultural and institutional contexts, as described previously, may reinforce this tendency.

We further argue that individuals with different cultural profiles may interpret the same piece of information differently (Thomas et al., 2003). For example, training opportunities may be interpreted in transactional terms (e.g., their immediate performance implications) by individualists as opposed to relational terms (e.g., a long-term mutual investment) by collectivists. Cultural variation will influence the formation of the psychological contract also in connection with differing motives in social exchange (Thomas et al., 2003). For instance, Kickul et al. (2004) argued that collectivist employees working for their in-group (e.g., family firm) would be concerned about intrinsic outcomes, but those working for an out-group would be primarily concerned about extrinsic outcomes. More generally, for collectivists, transactional forms may take precedence over relational forms when dealing with out-group organizations or out-group members (Lee, Tinsley, & Chen, 2000). In contrast, individualists may seek to establish balanced forms, which combine the open-ended relational emphasis with the transactional feature of well-specified performance-reward contingencies (Hui, Lee, & Rousseau, 2004).

Proposition 5: Individual-level manifestations of societal culture moderate the relationship between an employee's psychological climate and psychological contract in terms of determining the nature (e.g., transactional vs. relational) and the referents of the contract.

As discussed below, cultural differences in cognition and motivation will have implications regarding perceptions of contract fulfillment. For example, Kickul et al. (2004) argued that in high power-distance cultures, employees would expect fewer promises regarding intrinsic outcomes such as autonomy or participation and therefore experience fewer breaches of this nature or react less negatively to such breaches. Conversely, Hui et al. (2004) noted that in such cultures, for a powerful employer (or supervisor) to commit to certain psychological contract obligations may exceed employees' expectations, eliciting a very positive response and generating a strong willingness to reciprocate. This contention is in line with Aselage and Eisenberger (2003), who argued that the receipt of a favorable benefit without prior promise would more greatly enhance POS than if the organization was expected to provide that benefit. Similarly, unfavorable treatment would result in diminished POS, more so when that treatment violated a promise to the employee. Aselage and Eisenberger further proposed that the psychological contract, by virtue of informing employees of the behaviors they owe the organization, would guide employees' reciprocation of POS. Accordingly, we offer the following:

Proposition 6: An employee's psychological contract, shaped by the cultural and institutional framework as to what constitutes mutual obligations and what is discretionary, moderates the relation between psychological climate and POS as well as POS and commitment.

We further argue that the primary antecedents of POS, namely, fairness, supervisor support, and job conditions, will bear differential importance across individuals with different cultural profiles (e.g., Robert, Probst, Martocchio, Drasgow, & Lawler, 2000). For instance, job security may be a stronger predictor of POS for collectivists than individualists; autonomy may be more significant for employees with low rather than high power-distance values. Evidence suggests that collectivists, being less attuned to their individual rights and more concerned with maintaining harmony, give less weight to fairness perceptions in their relationship with their supervisor than do individualists (Erdogan & Liden, 2006). Besides, in different cultures perceptions of fairness or supervisor support may be formed by reference to different aspects of the HR system. In other words, while perceptions of job conditions, fairness, or supervisor support may be universally relevant antecedents of POS, their operationalization may be highly culture-bound (e.g., Greenberg, 2001). For example, Ohbuchi, Suzuki, and Hayashi (2001) showed that Japanese employees' perception of justice was more correlated with attainment of group rather than personal goals. Likewise, for vertical (i.e., high power-distant) collectivists, favorable supervisor support, in addition to being the most significant antecedent of POS, might mean a paternalistic leadership style (Aycan,

2000), which involves high levels of concern with the personal life of the employee (i.e., the welfare of the employee's in-group).

Proposition 7: Individual-level manifestations of societal culture moderate the relationship between psychological climate and POS regarding what constitutes favorable organizational treatment.

Rhoades and Eisenberger (2002) argued that POS would be more strongly associated with job outcomes for employees with higher needs for affiliation, esteem, approval, and support, leading us to speculate that the relationship between POS and commitment will be stronger for collectivists compared with individualists. Research evidence demonstrates felt obligation to be mediating the relationship between POS and affective organizational commitment (Eisenberger, Armeli, Rexwinkel, Lynch, & Rhoades, 2001). However, we agree with Eisenberger and his colleagues (chapter 8, this volume) that this construct overlaps highly with NC. Accordingly, we propose that collectivism will moderate the relationship between POS and NC (the underlying mechanism being felt obligation to reciprocate) as well as the relationship between POS and AC (the underlying mechanism being fulfillment of socioemotional needs). We also speculate that collectivist employees' in-group–out-group perceptions will be a further moderating variable such that the proposed relationships will be stronger if the organization or the supervisor is considered to be an in-group. For employees high in power distance, while we expect that POS will have a stronger association with commitment to supervisor rather than the organization (Hui et al., 2004), recent evidence indicates that such employees, because of their strong deference to authority figures, are less reliant on the reciprocity norm with respect to their performance contributions than their counterparts with low power-distance scores, rendering the relationship between POS and commitment weaker for the former case (Farh, Hackett, & Liang, 2007). In sum, we advance the following argument:

Proposition 8: Individual-level manifestations of societal culture moderate the relationship between POS and commitment with respect to the nature of the psychological processes underlying this association, which in turn influences commitment forms and foci.

Regarding the relationship between psychological contracts and commitment, we argue that fulfillment of relational obligations will be better predictors of commitment for collectivists (particularly for those working with in-groups) compared with individualists, whose behavior may be better predicted by fulfillment of balanced contracts, or collectivists working for out-groups, who might be more concerned with the transactional aspects of their psychological contracts (e.g., Lee et al., 2000; Thomas et al., 2003). We propose that fulfillment of relational obligations will be more strongly related to NC and social-cost-based CC (i.e., CC developing from perceived costs of not fulfilling expectations of others) for collectivists than individualists, and that fulfillment of balanced obligations will be more strongly related to AC and possibly economic-cost-based CC for individualists than collectivists. As mentioned, we predict that coworkers and supervisors will be more relevant foci for collectivists' commitment in comparison to individualists, who may tend to view the organization, top management, and supervisor as salient constituents. We also predict fulfillment of relational obligations to be more strongly predictive of AC, NC, and social-cost-based CC to supervisor in high as opposed to low power-distance cultures. We further speculate that for employees in tight cultures, who have high attentiveness regarding normative requirements as well as greater need for predictability, fulfillment of either form of contract obligations will be stronger predictors of NC as well as CC when compared to employees from loose cultures.

In agreement with Thomas et al. (2003), we also argue that individualists, being more attentive to information regarding equity and immediate compensation for effort, will have lower thresholds for perceiving violations, whereas collectivists, who are more motivated to create long-term obligations by keeping relations open, will be less likely to expect immediate contract fulfillment. This, and the relative difficulty involved in assessing whether relational obligations have been met, suggest that collectivists, on the whole, will have higher thresholds for perceiving contract breaches. Likewise, employees high as opposed to low in power distance may feel stronger motivation for conformity, and thus may have higher thresholds for perceiving contract breaches from those with authority. We further expect that individuals in loose cultures will have higher thresholds to breaches, whereas in tight cultures, in addition to fewer instances of contract breaches due to incongruence (i.e., misunderstanding regarding mutual obligations), we anticipate lower thresholds to violations from any organizational constituency.

Proposition 9: Individual-level manifestations of societal culture moderate the relationship between psychological contracts and commitment by shaping perceptions regarding contract violation and fulfillment, which in turn influence commitment forms and foci.

As regards the relationship between commitment and behavior, for employees high on power distance, we argue that both AC and NC to supervisor will be more predictive of focal and discretionary behaviors than commitment to the organization. For collectivist or tight employees, NC or social-cost-based CC might be better predictors of focal employee behavior than for individualist or loose individuals, where AC is proposed to be a stronger predictor of both focal and discretionary behavior. Regarding discretionary behavior, obligation- or cost-based commitment has been argued to be less desirable than affect-based commitment (Gellatly, Meyer, & Luchak, 2006; Meyer et al., 2004). The contention is that employees with high levels of NC or CC toward a particular organizational focus feel somewhat pressured or trapped, and consequently do not experience high levels of intrinsic motivation to pursue goals associated with that focus. However, this observation may not generalize to collectivists for whom living up to in-group expectations is found to be more intrinsically motivating than personal choice (Iyengar & Lepper, 1999). More generally, individuals from different cultures differ in terms of the extent to which they internalize constraints imposed by their in-groups (Chirkov, Ryan, Kim, & Kaplan, 2003). In a collectivist culture, if the organization or any constituency within it is perceived as the in-group, employees will feel higher levels of NC toward that in-group and also experience greater intrinsic motivation with respect to complying with in-group goals. Indeed, Triandis (1983) noted that when the organization overlaps with the in-group (e.g., collectivists running a family restaurant), there is great mobilization of effort toward the success of the enterprise. Yet, where there is no correspondence between in-group and organization (e.g., collectivists in bureaucracies), suspicion, lack of communication, and little cooperation abound.

Based on Markus and Kitayama (1991), the argument here is that collectivists internalize the goals of their in-group so much that fulfilling significant others' expectations in effect becomes equivalent to fulfilling personal goals, and thus is conducive to behaviors that are typically associated with AC. Even when they do not fully internalize in-group goals, collectivists may experience the feeling of fulfilling obligations (i.e., NC per se) more positively. For the collectivist mindset, being cognizant of and receptive to significant others' expectations is a source of self-esteem and fulfills important motivations such as belonging, engaging in appropriate action, and maintaining harmony. Also, a collectivist in a collectivist context engages in fulfilling obligations with the expectation that they will be reciprocated.

Proposition 10: Individual-level manifestations of societal culture moderate the relationship between commitment forms and foci, and employee (focal and discretionary) behaviors.

At this point, it should be noted, however, that what constitutes focal or discretionary behavior appears to be largely context-bound. Research suggests that employees' ability to maintain cordial working relationships with coworkers and supervisors, willingness to accept orders without questioning, respectful attitude, and gratitude constitute focal behaviors in high power-distance and collectivist cultures (Aycan, 2000; Hui et al., 2004). Further, especially under weak legal systems and particularistic authority structures, many aspects of performance are neither clearly defined, nor contractually rewarded (e.g., Farh, Zhong, & Organ, 2004). Thus, in certain circumstances, when NC is experienced without complete internalization of significant others' goals, behaviors that are more socionormative or visible (e.g., not criticizing in meetings) may be enacted more, compared with those that relate to task completion or are difficult to observe.

Finally, compared with individualistic and/or loose cultures, we posit that the reciprocal links between levels will be stronger for collectivist and/or tight cultures. In such cultures, selection and socialization systems are geared toward restricting the variance of individuals who enter the organization and ensuring the match of the individual to organizational norms (e.g., Aycan, 2000; Gelfand et al., 2006). Such practices are conducive to the development of strong organizational cultures (i.e., clear and agreed-on organizational norms) that guide employees' perceptions of appropriate actions. At the individual level, in collectivist cultures, employees are predicted to experience higher degrees of social interaction and stronger motivation to seek harmony; and likewise, in tight cultures, employees are likely to experience a stronger pressure to fit in, suggesting that individual-level perceptions and mindsets may have stronger reciprocal relations with collective perceptions and mindsets as compared with loose or individualist cultures. Thus, in tight and/or collectivist cultures, we speculate less variance in observed commitment profiles compared with individualist and/or loose cultures, where more idiosyncrasy or expression of personal preferences is expected.

Proposition 11: Organizational- and individual-level manifestations of societal culture moderate the reciprocal links between individual- and organizational-level climate, contract, and commitment, which determine the variance in observed commitment profiles.

This proposition, however, should be considered by taking into account in-group–out-group perceptions of collectivists. If the organizational composition is heterogeneous (and/or the HR system is weak), collectivists may experience the dynamics described above only within their in-groups, which may lead to the emergence of distinct subcultures across the organization, where some are completely incongruent with organizational goals or in conflict with other subcultures. Such situations may foster commitment to local foci at the expense of the organization.

Discussion

With the proposed model, while by no means flawless or final, we hope to provide a more complete map to explore commitment across contexts. The model's complexity in effect allows for clarity in terms of not only guiding future research but also explaining the contradictions in the accumulated literature. Consider, for example, the earlier findings on Japan, which indicated an incongruity between expressed and observed commitment (i.e., turnover) as evaluated from an American perspective (Besser, 1993). A more accurate interpretation is possible by taking into account the institutional differences along with their interactions with culture, such as lifetime employment policies and their implications for primary work relationships. On the one hand, as Atsumi (1979) argued, the real reason for not changing companies is not that the Japanese employees feel loyal to the company, but rather they cannot sacrifice the *tsukiai* (obligatory personal) relationships that they have painfully cultivated over the years with their fellow workers and other work-related people to ensure getting work done efficiently. On the other hand, in a collectivist and tight culture, where there is much emphasis on interdependence among in-group members as well as very high opportunity costs to defection, there are also strong normative (if not affective, as measured by North American scales) pressures to stay (Near, 1989; Yamagishi, 1988). The integration of institutional and cultural factors will allow researchers to recognize the implicit assumptions underlying organizational behavior models generated in North America, such as behavior being a consequence of individual choice (Maertz, Stevens, & Campion, 2003) or the foundation of the employment contract being "employment at will" (Rousseau, 2000), and to address cross-national generalizability a priori as well as more precisely.

The incorporation of institutional factors further permits an explanation of the observed differences in commitment among nations that appear to cluster together along broad cultural dimensions. For instance, consider the variations in organizational structure across contexts that arguably have a common cultural heritage, such as the Japanese *kaisha*, the Korean *chaebol*, and the Chinese family firm. Within this group of societies influenced by Confucian ethical codes, historically different authority patterns have led to variation in the role of the State and its relations with business enterprises (Hamilton & Biggart, 1988). Arguably, these differences have notable implications for commitment: Whereas in the Japanese case, the separation of ownership and control and delegation to managers and workgroups has been conducive to greater levels of company commitment, the Korean *chaebols*, which operate under a "strong State" model characterized by centralized economic planning and aggressive implementation procedures, depict more authoritarian leadership structures with lower trust in and commitment to employees. In the case of Taiwan, on the other hand, the government promotes virtually free-trade conditions, allowing familial patterns to shape the course of Taiwan's industrialization. This has in turn led to decentralized patterns of industrialization and a predominance of small- and medium-sized family firms. In the family firm, organizational commitment of nonkin employees is highly limited, and the employment relationship is very idiosyncratic along the lines of kin, close friendships versus nonkin relations. This analysis further underlines the tenet of our model that the implications of cultural values can be predicted accurately only when the institutional and organizational structure in which they are experienced are taken into account.

Finally, the proposed model also allows an assessment of intra-national variation. Although much comparative work treats any sample to be nationally representative as well as comparatively equivalent, the impact of culture may be less evident in large organizations, organizations operating in high-tech industries, or multinational corporations compared with small organizations, organizations operating in the service industry, or those owned by families. For instance, in Turkey, as in many developing countries, only a small portion of the workforce is well educated and thereby able to procure a relational or balanced employment contract, typically offered by large or multinational corporations (Aycan, 2005). The majority of the workforce is relatively unskilled or uneducated, with little to offer to and expect from their employers. Furthermore, the bulk of Turkish employees are employed by nonunionized, small- or medium-sized organizations, almost all of which are family owned and owner managed (Paşa, Kabasakal, & Bodur, 2001). As discussed previously, such organizations may be best characterized by a duality of commitment profiles along the lines of kin (and connections) and nonkin members. Management typically tries to secure commitment by creating a surrogate family through personalistic recruitment, paternalistic management, and seniority-based reward systems. Yet, in implementation there is much arbitrariness across employees (also triggered by chronic economic instability and coupled with the weak legal system). Collectivism on the part of the nonkin employees may manifest itself in terms of AC or NC to immediate supervisors or coworkers, as they also will be primary sources of social capital (e.g., information on job opportunities elsewhere). Thus, the nature of the employment relationship and its psychological implications may differ significantly, depending on the employee's position in the national labor market and the relational networks within which the individual is embedded, as well as the industrial and organizational attributes. Highlighting these factors, we hope our model will guide cross-cultural research in terms of ensuring equivalent samples from each country for the purposes of comparison.

Commitment Across Cultures: The Journey Ahead

Conceptualizing Commitment: Definitions, Dimensions

Looking forward, we feel that the initial step to be taken involves refining the existing operationalizations of the key commitment constructs. At this point, we feel that it is safe to conclude that the AC construct and the most commonly used scales (e.g., ACS by Meyer et al., 1993) are generalizable across contexts. Yet, CC and NC not only have been understudied cross-culturally, but also may be more consequential in terms of capturing cultural and institutional variation. The current operationalization of CC represents perceptions of high personal sacrifice associated with quitting. When measured as vaguely, affective, normative, and calculative costs all serve as antecedents to CC (Powell & Meyer, 2004), making it impossible to predict its outcomes other than turnover. To complicate matters further, items in Meyer et al.'s (1993) NC scale seem to overlap with those in Powell and Meyer's Expectations of Others subscale, which is proposed as an antecedent to CC (as well as NC). As such, the construct validity of CC is at risk, more so perhaps in cross-cultural research. In particular, we contend that for the collectivist mindset, being cognizant of normative obligations means being cognizant of the costs involved in violating them, and we argue for the need to develop a scale that differentiates the type of costs (i.e., mindsets) involved.

We feel that attempts to revise both the CC and NC scales (see also Bergman, 2006) will greatly benefit from cross-cultural theory and evidence. In the current NC scale, items that allude to personal norms coexist with items that refer to staying out of an obligation to other people. Our analysis suggests that for collectivists, scales that combine items that tap these two aspects of NC, in particular with vague references to "people," will fail to capture the proposed dynamics of NC. As suggested by Wasti (2002), a useful distinction in terms of understanding NC may involve viewing it as comprising two components: personal norms and social factors. This distinction parallels Triandis's theory of interpersonal behavior (1980), which proposes that an individual's behavioral intention is a function of (1) his/her affect toward performing the act; (2) his/her beliefs about the consequences of performing that behavior and the evaluation of those consequences; (3) social factors, that is, the perceived appropriateness of a particular behavior for members of specific reference groups (normative beliefs) and occupants of specific positions in the social structure; and (4) the subject's personal normative beliefs about what he or she should or ought to do with regard to the behavior of interest. Such a conceptualization may better reflect the "two faces" of NC proposed by Gellatly et al. (2006), where personal norms would measure "moral imperative," and social factors would capture "indebted obligation." Furthermore, it could allow an assessment of NC as experienced differentially by individualists (more a function of personal norms) and collectivists (a function of social factors and personal norms depending on the context, i.e., in-group–out-group). Social factors may also explain variance across high versus low power distance, tight versus loose cultures.

Contextualizing Commitment: Collectivism and Beyond

Future research should prioritize incorporating the proximal context such as the nature of group memberships, particularly when analyzing the implications of collectivism. While most cross-cultural research has treated collectivism as the major cultural dimension impinging on commitment, all studies have either ignored the in-group–out-group distinction or simply assumed the organization to be an in-group. Furthermore, studies have relied extensively on Hofstede's (1980) rankings, which do not take into account the "species" of collectivism involved. Indeed, recent work has largely sought to clarify the construct by delineating which collective is of relevance, when and where. To this end, Brewer and Chen (2007) differentiated between the individual, the relational, and the collective levels of self. The relational self incorporates dyadic relations between the self and particular close others, whereas the collective self involves depersonalized relationships with others by virtue of common membership in a symbolic group. Brewer and Chen (2007) further argued that East Asians, who are typically relational collectivists, are more likely to feel committed to specific individuals in organizations and not necessarily the institution they belong to. For North Americans, on the other hand, the collective self can be highly salient, and can translate into a sense of belonging to and connecting with the organization. This argument is in line with Rousseau (2000), who noted that Americans hold the cultural value of associability. Different from collectivism in Japan or China, which comprises subordination, American associability emphasizes active participation, cooperation, and attachment to address shared social problems that cannot be undertaken by an individual. Rousseau (2007) further noted that, unlike the East Asian variant, the collective to whom the individual is attached need not be stable or enduring.

This analysis suggests that future conceptualizations should refrain from treating collectivism as a stable, target-independent orientation and also recognize that individualism does not preclude social identification with social groups and collectives albeit with different dynamics in terms of duration and intensity. The American associability value can also have implications regarding action commitments such as commitment to goals, projects, change, and strategy (see chapter 6, this volume), which are not social per se, but often times require task-oriented collective action. While Rousseau (2000) noted that both American individualism and associability are task-oriented, her diagnosis in effect may be pointing to another cultural dimension worthy of exploration: performance orientation, which reflects the extent to which a society encourages and rewards performance improvement (House et al., 2004), may also be relevant regarding action commitments. Likewise, dimensions such as future orientation or uncertainty avoidance (House et al., 2004) may have further implications for action commitments across cultures.

Finally, there is much value in undertaking studies that explore definitions of a "committed" employee in various contexts, as well as question the universality of the content and relevance of outcome variables, such as performance or discretionary behaviors. Being the product of a culture characterized by specificity (Trompenaars, 1993), which refers to the extent to which personal and professional matters are separated, North American organizational behavior theories typically treat professional relationships as limited to the workplace (Sanchez-Burks, 2005). In contrast, diffuse cultures are characterized by a spillover of personal and professional life domains, which means that individuals develop intimate friendships with colleagues, or prefer to work with friends to begin with. As such, in diffuse cultures, employees tend to be evaluated with respect to broader character attributes (e.g., integrity, family values, kindness) rather than their task performance (e.g., Farh et al., 2004). The meaning, nature, and implications of commitments to social foci may be more complex in diffuse as compared with specific cultures, rendering mainstream theories as well as methodologies (e.g., surveys) insufficient for the cross-cultural adventure.

Concluding Remarks

While our model provided a framework to investigate the influence of institutional and cultural factors on commitment, it did not fully address all possible linkages among the proposed variables. There are solid cross-national analyses on various institutional factors affecting psychological contracts (e.g., Rousseau & Schalk, 2000), HR practices (e.g., Aycan, 2005), and empirical findings regarding the moderating influence of cultural values on antecedents of POS (e.g., Greenberg, 2001), which may serve as starting points in grounding the model. Our model also solely focused on the institutional factors influencing the strength of the HR system. For instance, Gelfand et al. (2006) proposed tightness-looseness to have implications with respect to the consistency of the HR system, manifesting in terms of greater internal alignment of various HR practices. Future research may investigate the potential implications of culture on HR-system strength, also in terms of distinctiveness and consensus.

As lucidly expressed by Greenfield (2000, p. 229), "only data that enables us to challenge universalistic theories (as opposed to data alone)" will contribute to the incorporation of culture into mainstream organizational theories. At this point, we feel that the greatest contribution may come from indigenous, single-country studies that seek to understand the meanings of the key constructs of organizational commitment (i.e., organization, its constituents, and commitment) and their interactions. To this end, we advocate consultation of disciplines such as sociology, economics, political science, and history, which provide frameworks for the contextualization of organizational phenomena.

In advocating single-country "case" studies, we agree with Berry (2000, p. 197) that "one has to be 'cultural' before being 'cross'" and argue that investigations in different contexts, without extensive reliance on imported theory or measurement, are essential for the discovery of both universal and culture-specific aspects related to organizational commitment. Such an endeavor undoubtedly calls for different research strategies, such as qualitative inquiry. However, it is only through treading new methodological and theoretical territories that commitment research will travel across borders.

References

Aselage, J., & Eisenberger, R. (2003). Perceived organizational support and psychological contracts: A theoretical integration. *Journal of Organizational Behavior, 24*, 491–509.

Atsumi, R. (1979). *Tsukiai*—Obligatory personal relationships of Japanese white-collar company employees. *Human Organization, 38*, 63–70.

Aycan, Z. (2000). Cross-cultural industrial and organizational psychology: Contributions, past developments and future directions. *Journal of Cross Cultural Psychology, 31*, 110–128.

Aycan, Z. (2005). The interplay between cultural and institutional/structural contingencies in human resource management practices. *International Journal of Human Resource Management, 16*, 1083–1119.

Becker, T. E., Billings, R. S., Eveleth, D. M., & Gilbert, N. L. (1996). Foci and bases of commitment: Implications for performance. *Academy of Management Journal, 39*, 464–482.

Bergman, M. E. (2006). The relationship between affective and normative commitment: Review and research agenda. *Journal of Organizational Behavior, 27*, 645–663.

Berry, J. W. (1989). Imposed-etics-emics-derived etics: The operationalization of a compelling idea. *International Journal of Psychology, 24*, 721–735.

Berry, J. W. (2000). Cross-cultural psychology: A symbiosis of cultural and comparative approaches. *Asian Journal of Social Psychology, 3*, 197–205.

Besser, T. L. (1993). The commitment of Japanese workers and U.S. workers: A reassessment of the literature. *American Sociological Review, 58*, 873–881.

Blau, P. M. (1964). *Exchange and power in social life.* New York: Wiley.

Boshoff, C., & Mels, G. (2000). The impact of multiple commitments on intentions to resign: An empirical assessment. *British Journal of Management, 11,* 255–272.

Bowen, D. E., & Ostroff, C. (2004). Understanding HRM-firm performance linkages: The role of the "strength" of the HRM system. *Academy of Management Review, 29,* 203–221.

Brett, J. M., Tinsley, C. H., Janssens, M., Barsness, Z. I., & Lytle, A. L. (1995). New approaches to the study of culture in industrial/organizational psychology. In P. C. Earley & M. Erez (Eds.), *New perspectives on international industrial/ organizational psychology* (pp. 75–129). San Francisco: New Lexington Press.

Brewer, M., & Chen, Y.-R. (2007). When (who) are collectives in collectivism? Toward conceptual clarification of individualism and collectivism. *Psychological Review, 114,* 133–151.

Brockner, J., Ackerman, G., Greenberg, J., Gelfand, M. J., Francesco, A. M., Chen, Z. X., et al. (2001). Culture and procedural justice: The influence of power distance and reactions to voice. *Journal of Experimental Social Psychology, 37,* 300–315.

Cappelli, P. (1999). *The new deal at work: Managing the market-driven workforce.* Boston: Harvard Business School Press.

Chen, Z. X., & Francesco, A. M. (2003). The relationship between the three components of commitment and employee performance in China. *Journal of Vocational Behavior, 62,* 490–510.

Chen, Z. X., Tsui, A. S., & Farh, J. L. (2002). Loyalty to supervisor vs. organizational commitment: Relationships to employee performance in China. *Journal of Occupational and Organizational Psychology, 75,* 339–356.

Cheng, B. S., Jiang, D. Y., & Riley, H. J. (2003). Organizational commitment, supervisory commitment, and employee outcomes in Chinese context: Proximal hypothesis or global hypothesis? *Journal of Organizational Behavior, 2,* 313–334.

Cheng, Y., & Stockdale, M. S. (2003). The validity of the three-component model of organizational commitment in a Chinese context. *Journal of Vocational Behavior, 62,* 465–489.

Chirkov, V., Ryan, R. M., Kim, Y., & Kaplan, U. (2003). Differentiating autonomy from individualism and interdependence: A self-determination theory perspective on internalization of cultural orientations and well-being. *Journal of Personality and Social Psychology, 84,* 97–110.

Cohen, A. (2000). The relationship between commitment forms and work outcomes: A comparison of three models. *Human Relations, 53,* 387–417.

Collin, S.-O., Johansson, U., Svensson, K., & Ulvenblad, P.-O. (1996). Market segmentation in scientific publications: Research patterns in American vs. European management journals. *British Journal of Management, 7,* 141–154.

Diaz-Saenz, H. R., & Witherspoon, P. D. (2000). Psychological contracts in Mexico: Historical, familial, and contemporary influences on work relationships. In D. M. Rousseau & R. Schalk (Eds.), *Psychological contracts in employment: Cross-national perspectives.* (pp. 87–103). Thousand Oaks, CA: Sage.

Dobbin, F., & Boychuk, T. (1999). National employment systems and job autonomy: Why job autonomy is high in the Nordic countries and low in the United States, Canada, and Australia. *Organization Studies, 20,* 257–291.

Eisenberger, R., Armeli, S., Rexwinkel, B., Lynch, P. D., & Rhoades, L. (2001). Reciprocation of perceived organizational support. *Journal of Applied Psychology, 86,* 42–51.

Erdogan, B., & Liden, R. C. (2006). Collectivism as a moderator of responses to organizational justice: Implications for leader-member exchange and ingratiation. *Journal of Organizational Behavior, 27,* 1–17.

Farh, J. L., Hackett, R. D., & Liang, J. (2007). Individual-level cultural values as moderators of perceived organizational support-employee outcome relationships in China: Comparing the effects of power distance and traditionality. *Academy of Management Journal, 50,* 715–729.

Farh, J.-L., Zhong, C.-B., & Organ, D. W. (2004). Organizational citizenship behavior in the People's Republic of China. *Organization Science, 15,* 241–253.

Fligstein, N. (1996). Markets as politics: A political-cultural approach to market institutions. *American Sociological Review, 61,* 656–673.

Freeman, R. B., & Medoff, J. L. (1984). *What do unions do?* New York: Basic Books.

Gautam, T., Van Dick, R., & Wagner, U. (2001). Organizational commitment in Nepalese settings. *Asian Journal of Social Psychology, 4,* 239–248.

Gelfand, M. J., Nishii, L. H., & Raver, J. L. (2006). On the nature and importance of cultural tightness and looseness. *Journal of Applied Psychology, 91,* 1225–1244.

Gellatly, I. R., Meyer, J. P., & Luchak, A. A. (2006). Combined effects of the three commitment components on focal and discretionary behaviors: A test of Meyer and Herscovitch's propositions. *Journal of Vocational Behavior, 69,* 331–345.

Gooderham, P. N., Nordhaug, O., & Ringdal, K. (1999). Institutional and rational determinants of organizational practices: Human resource management in European firms. *Administrative Science Quarterly, 44,* 507–532.

Greenberg, J. (2001). Studying organizational justice cross-culturally? Fundamental challenges. *The International Journal of Conflict Management, 12,* 365–375.

Greenfield, P. M. (2000). Three approaches to the psychology of culture: Where do they come from? Where can they go? *Asian Journal of Social Psychology, 3,* 223–240.

Hamilton, G. G., & Biggart, N. W. (1988). Market, culture, and authority: A comparative analysis of management and organization in the Far East. *American Journal of Sociology, 94,* S52–S94.

Hamilton, G., & Kao, C.S. (1990). The institutional foundation of Chinese business: The family firm in Taiwan. *Comparative Social Research, 12,* 95–112.

Hofstede, G. (1980). *Culture's consequences: International differences in work-related values.* Beverly Hills, CA: Sage.

Hoskisson, R. E., Johnson, R. A., Tihanyi, L., & White, R. E. (2005). Diversified business groups and corporate refocusing in emerging economies. *Journal of Management, 31,* 941–965.

House, R. J., Hanges, P. J., Javidan, M., Dorfman, P. W., & Gupta, P. (Eds.) (2004). *Culture, leadership, and organizations: The GLOBE Study of 62 Societies.* Thousand Oaks, CA: Sage.

Hui, C., Lee, C., & Rousseau, D. M. (2004). Psychological contract and organizational citizenship behavior in China: Investigating generalizability and instrumentality. *Journal of Applied Psychology, 89,* 311–321.

Hult, C. (2005). Organizational commitment and person-environment fit in six Western countries. *Organization Studies, 26,* 249–270.

Iyengar, S. S., & Lepper, M. R. (1999). Rethinking the value of choice: A cultural perspective on intrinsic motivation. *Journal of Personality and Social Psychology, 76,* 349–366.

Jaramillo, F., Mulki, J. P., & Marshall, G. W. (2005). A meta-analysis of the relationship between organizational commitment and salesperson job performance: 25 years of research. *Journal of Business Research, 58,* 705–714.

Katigbak, M. S., Church, A. T., Guanzon-Lapena, M. A., Carlota, A. J., & del Pilar, G. H. (2002). Are indigenous personality dimensions culture specific? Philippine inventories and the five-factor model. *Journal of Personality and Social Psychology, 82,* 89–91.

Kickul, J., Lester, S. W., & Belgio, E. (2004). Attitudinal and behavioral outcomes of psychological contract breach: A cross-cultural comparison of the United States and Hong Kong Chinese. *International Journal of Cross-Cultural Management, 4,* 229–252.

Kim, J.-W., & Rowley, C. (2006). Commitment to company and labor union: Empirical evidence from South Korea. *International Journal of Human Resource Management, 17,* 673–692.

Kirkman, B. L., & Law, K. (2005). International management research from AMJ: Our past, present and future. *Academy of Management Journal, 48,* 377–386.

Klein, H. J., Brinsfield, C. T., & Molloy, J. C. (2006, August). *Understanding workplace commitments independent of antecedents, foci, rationales, and consequences.* Paper presented at the Academy of Management Annual Meeting, Atlanta, GA.

Ko, J. W., Price, J. L., & Mueller, C. W. (1997). Assessment of Meyer and Allen's three-component model of organizational commitment in South Korea. *Journal of Applied Psychology, 82,* 961–973.

Lee, K., Allen, N. J., Meyer, J. P., & Rhee, K. Y. (2001). The three-component model of organisational commitment: An application to South Korea. *Applied Psychology: An International Review, 50,* 596–614.

Lee, C. H., & Bruvold, N. T. (2003). Creating value for employees: Investment in employee development. *International Journal of Human Resource Management, 14,* 981–1000.

Lee, C., Tinsley, C. H., & Chen, G. Z. X. (2000). Psychological and normative contracts of work group members in the United States and Hong Kong. In D. M. Rousseau, & R. Schalk (Eds.), *Psychological contracts in employment: Cross-national perspectives* (pp. 87–103). Thousand Oaks: Sage.

Leong, F. T. L., & Leung, K. (2004). Academic careers in Asia: A cross-cultural analysis. *Journal of Vocational Behavior, 64,* 346–357.

Maertz, C., Stevens, M., & Campion, M. (2003). A turnover model for the Mexican maquiladoras. *Journal of Vocational Behavior, 63,* 111–135.

Markus, H. R., & Kitayama, S. (1991). Culture and the self: Implications for cognition, emotion, and motivation. *Psychological Review, 98,* 224–253.

Meyer, J. P., & Allen, N. J. (1991). A three-component conceptualization of organizational commitment. *Human Resource Management Review, 1,* 61–89.

Meyer, J. P., & Allen, N. J. (1997). *Commitment in the workplace: Theory, research and application.* Thousand Oaks, CA: Sage.

Meyer, J. P., Allen, N. J., & Smith, C. A. (1993). Commitment to organizations and occupations: Extension and test of a three-component conceptualization. *Journal of Applied Psychology, 78,* 538–551.

Meyer, J. P., Barak, I., & Vandenberghe, C. (1996). *Revised measures of affective, continuance and normative commitment to organizations.* Unpublished manuscript. Department of Psychology, The University of Western Ontario.

Meyer, J. P., Becker, T. E., & Vandenberghe, C. (2004). Employee commitment and motivation: A conceptual analysis and integrative model. *Journal of Applied Psychology, 89,* 991–1007.

Meyer, J. P., & Herscovitch, L. (2001). Commitment in the workplace: Towards a general model. *Human Resources Management Review, 11,* 299–326.

Near, J. P. (1989). Organizational commitment among Japanese and U.S. workers. *Organization Studies, 10,* 281–300.

Ohbuchi, K., Suzuki, M., & Hayashi, Y. (2001). Conflict management and organizational attitudes among Japanese: Individual and group goals and justice. *Asian Journal of Social Psychology, 4,* 93–101.

Ostroff, C., & Bowen, D. E. (2000). Moving HR to a higher level: HR practices and organizational effectiveness. In K. J. Klein & S. W. J. Kozlowski (Eds.), *Multilevel theory, research, and methods in organizations: Foundations, extensions, and new directions* (pp. 211–266). San Francisco: Jossey-Bass.

Özkan, T., & Lajunen, T. (2005). Masculinity, femininity, and the Bem sex role inventory. *Sex Roles, 52,* 103–110.

Palich, L. E., Hom, P. W., & Griffeth, R. W. (1995). Managing in the international context: Testing cultural generality of sources of commitment to multinational enterprises. *Journal of Management, 21,* 671–690.

Parbooteah, K. P., & Cullen, J. B. (2003). Social institutions and work centrality: Explorations beyond national culture. *Organization Science, 14,* 137–148.

Paşa, S. F., Kabasakal, H., & Bodur, M. (2001). Society, organizations, and leadership in Turkey. *Applied Psychology: An International Review, 50,* 559–589.

Pearce, J. L., Branyiczki, I., & Bigley, G. A. (2000). Insufficient bureaucracy: Trust and commitment in particularistic organizations. *Organization Science, 11,* 148–162.

Powell, D. M., & Meyer, J. P. (2004). Side-bet theory and the three-component model of organizational commitment. *Journal of Vocational Behavior, 65,* 157–177.

Randall, D. (1993). Cross-cultural research on organizational commitment: A review and application of Hofstede's value survey module. *Journal of Business Research, 26,* 91–110.

Redding, S. G. (2005). Separating culture from institutions: The use of semantic spaces as a conceptual domain, and the case of China. *Management and Organization Review, 4,* 257–289.

Redding, S. G., Norman, A., & Schlander, A. (1994). The nature of individual attachment to the organization: A review of East Asian variations. In H. C. Triandis, M. Dunnette, & L. Hough (Eds.), *Handbook of industrial and organizational psychology* (2nd ed., Vol. 4, pp. 557–607). Palo Alto, CA: Consulting Psychologists Press.

Reichers, A. E. 1985. A review and reconceptualization of organizational commitment. *Academy of Management Review, 10,* 465–476.

Rhee, E., Uleman, J. S., & Lee, H. K. (1996). Variations in collectivism and individualism by ingroup and culture: Confirmatory factor analyses. *Journal of Personality and Social Psychology, 1,* 1037–1054.

Rhoades, L., & Eisenberger, R. (2002). Perceived organizational support: A review of the literature. *Journal of Applied Psychology, 87,* 698–714.

Robert, C., Probst, T. M., Martocchio, J. J., Drasgow, F., & Lawler, J. J. (2000). Empowerment and continuous improvement in the United States, Mexico, Poland, and India: Predicting fit on the basis of dimensions of power distance and individualism. *Journal of Applied Psychology, 85,* 643–658.

Roe, R. A., Zinovieva, I. L., Dienes, E., & Horn, L. A. T. (2000). A comparison of work motivation in Bulgaria, Hungary, and the Netherlands: Test of a model. *Applied Psychology: An International Review, 49,* 658–687.

Rousseau, D. M. (1995). *Psychological contract in organizations: Understanding written and unwritten agreements.* Newbury Park, CA: Sage.

Rousseau, D. M. (2000). Psychological contracts in the United States. In D. M. Rousseau, & R. Schalk (Eds.), *Psychological contracts in employment: Cross-national perspectives* (pp. 250–282). Thousand Oaks, CA: Sage.

Rousseau, D. M., & Schalk, R. (2000). Introduction. In D. M. Rousseau & R. Schalk (Eds.), *Psychological contracts in employment: Cross-national perspectives* (pp. 1–28). Thousand Oaks, CA: Sage.

Sanchez-Burks, J. (2005). Protestant relational ideology: The cognitive underpinnings and organizational implications of an American anomaly. *Research in Organizational Behavior, 26,* 265–305.

Schaffer, B. S., & Riordan, C. M. (2003). A review of cross-cultural methodologies for organizational research: A best-practices approach. *Organizational Research Methods, 6,* 169–215.

Schwartz, S. H. (1994). Beyond individualism and collectivism: New cultural dimensions of values. In U. Kim, H. C. Triandis, C. Kagitcibasi, S.-C. Choi, & G. Yoon (Eds.). *Individualism and collectivism: Theory, method, and applications* (pp. 85–122). Newbury Park, CA: Sage.

Scott, A. J. (2006). The changing global geography of low-technology, labor-intensive industry: Clothing, footwear, and furniture. *World Development, 34,* 1517–1536.

Smith, P. B. (2005). Is there an indigenous European social psychology? *International Journal of Psychology, 40,* 254–262.

Snape, E., Chan, A. W., & Redman, T. (2006). Multiple commitments in the Chinese context: Testing compatibility, cultural and moderating hypotheses. *Journal of Vocational Behavior, 69,* 302–314.

Stanley, D. J., Meyer, J. P., Jackson, T. A., Maltin, E. R., McInnis, K., Kumsar, A. Y., et al. (2007, April). *Cross-cultural generalizability of the three-component model of commitment.* Poster presented at the Twenty-Second Annual Conference of the Society for Industrial and Organizational Psychology, New York.

Stinglhamber, F., Bentein, K., & Vandenberghe, C. (2002). Extension of the three-component model of commitment to five foci. *European Journal of Psychological Assessment, 18,* 123–138.

Streeck, W. (1992). *Social institutions and economic performance: Studies of industrial relations in advanced capitalist economies.* London: Sage.

Tayeb, M. H. (1994). Organization and national culture: Methodology considered. *Organization Studies, 15,* 429–446.

Thomas, D. C., Au, K., & Ravlin, E. C. (2003). Cultural variation and the psychological contract. *Journal of Organizational Behavior, 24*, 451–471.

Triandis, H. C. (1980). Values, attitudes, and interpersonal behavior. In H. E. Howe & M. M. Page (Eds.), *Nebraska symposium on motivation 1979* (pp. 195–259). Lincoln, NE: University of Nebraska Press.

Triandis, H. C. (1983). Dimensions of cultural variation as parameters of organizational theories. *International Studies of Management and Organizations, 12,* 139–169.

Triandis, H. C. (1994). Cross-cultural industrial and organizational psychology. In H. C. Triandis, M. Dunnette, & L. Hough (Eds.), *Handbook of industrial and organizational psychology*, (2nd ed., Vol. 4, pp. 103–172). Palo Alto, CA: Consulting Psychologists Press.

Triandis, H. C. (1995). *Individualism and collectivism*. Boulder, CO: Westview Press.

Triandis, H. C. (1996). The psychological measurement of cultural syndromes. *American Psychologist, 51*, 407–415.

Trompenaars, F. (1993). *Riding the waves of culture*. London: The Economist Books.

Vandenberghe, C., Stinglhamber, F., Bentein, K., & Delhaise, T. (2001). An examination of the cross-cultural validity of a multidimensional model of commitment in Europe. *Journal of Cross-Cultural Psychology, 32, 322–347.*

Walumbwa, F. O., & Lawler, J. J. (2003). Building effective organizations: Transformational leadership, collectivist orientation, work-related attitudes and withdrawal behaviors in three emerging economies. *International Journal of Human Resource Management, 14*, 1083–1101.

Wang, Y. (2004). Observations on the organizational commitment of Chinese employees: Comparative studies of state-owned enterprises and foreign-invested enterprises. *International Journal of Human Resource Management, 15,* 649–669.

Wasti, S. A. (2002). Affective and continuance commitment to the organization: Test of an integrated model in the Turkish context. *International Journal of Intercultural Relations, 26*, 525–550.

Wasti, S. A. (2003). Organizational commitment, turnover intentions and the influence of cultural values. *Journal of Occupational and Organizational Psychology, 76,* 303–321.

Wasti, S. A. (2006, July). *Clusters of cross-cultural research on organizational commitment: Analysis of publication priorities, patterns and progress.* Paper presented at the Eighteenth International Congress of the International Association for Cross-Cultural Psychology, Spetses, Greece.

Whitley, R. (1992). *Business systems in East Asia. Firms, markets and societies.* Thousand Oaks, CA: Sage.

Whitley, R. (1999). *Divergent capitalisms: The social structuring and change of business systems.* Oxford: Oxford University Press.

Whitley, R. (2003). The institutional structuring of organizational capabilities. The role of authority sharing and organizational careers. *Organization Studies, 24,* 667–695.

Wilkinson, B. (1996). Culture, institutions and business in East Asia. *Organization Studies, 17,* 421–447.

Yamagishi, T. (1988). The provision of a sanctioning system in the United States and Japan. *Social Psychology Quarterly, 51,* 265–271.

Section 4

Methodological Issues and Challenges

11

Measurement of Commitment

Stephen Jaros
Southern University and A&M College

Accurate measurement is a prerequisite for advancing our understanding of work commitment, because it helps us achieve objectivity in the interpretation of data about the nature of commitment: what it is, how it develops, and what it affects (Schwab, 1980). In this chapter, what we know about commitment measurement will first be assessed from different theoretical perspectives, some of which are discussed by Klein, Molloy, and Cooper in chapter 1. Then, general technical issues related to commitment measurement methods will be addressed, and techniques useful for developing new commitment measures and improving the construct validity of existing measures will be described. I conclude with a discussion of the contention that there is a core essence of commitment that is common to all theoretical formulations, and how measurement can contribute to addressing this issue.

Measurement Issues in Alternative Theoretical Perspectives

In chapter 1, Klein et al. discuss differences among various theoretical formulations of work commitment. In this section, I briefly analyze the adequacy of measures used to tap these and other alternative conceptualizations.

Adequacy of Behavioral-Theory Measures

Klein et al. (this volume) discuss H. Becker's (1960) side-bet theory, Salancik's (1977) model, and Staw's (1997) "escalation of commitment" model as examples of behavioral-based theories of commitment. Ritzer and Trice (1969) and Hrebiniak and Alutto (1972) developed measures to tap H. Becker's concept of commitment with scale items that asked respondents whether they would remain organizational members in the face of escalating levels of inducements to leave. Meyer and Allen (1984) showed that these scales were saturated with affective commitment and thus were not adequate measures of H. Becker's theory. Other scales assessing H. Becker's theory have used organizational tenure as a proxy for commitment (cf. Rusbult & Farrell, 1983), on the grounds that higher tenure reflects higher sunk costs and putative satisfaction with the exchange relationship. But, length of tenure can be a product of nonexchange factors, so these measures are suspect as well. Since then, work on H. Becker's theory has been dominated by Meyer and Allen's (1984) concept of *continuance* commitment. The research stream that followed focused on the attitudinal aspect of H. Becker's theory, which emphasizes the employee's *awareness* of the costs of leaving, as measured with the continuance commitment scale (CCS), the original 1984 version of which has been critiqued for including "low alternatives" items that do not fall within the commitment domain as theorized by H. Becker (cf. McGee & Ford, 1987; Jaros, 1997).

Recently, Powell and Meyer (2004) accepted this critique and redesigned the CCS to include only "high sacrifice" items. This scale consists of six items, three of which are adaptations of high-sacrifice items from the original CCS, and three of which were newly written for the study. Their acceptance was based primarily on meta-analytic evidence showing that the high-sacrifice subscale has a much stronger negative (and thus theoretically correct) relationship with turnover cognitions than does the low-alternatives subscale (Meyer, Stanley, Herscovitch, & Topolnytsky, 2002). However, Luchak & Gellatly (2007), using a revised version of the CCS developed by Meyer, Allen, and Smith (1993) that includes three low-alternatives items, two high-sacrifice items, and one indeterminate item, recently found that when curvilinear effects were modeled, continuance commitment was a stronger predictor of turnover cognitions than indicated by past, linear-effects research. This finding might cause Powell and Meyer to rethink their acceptance of the idea that low-alternatives items do not belong in the CCS, but in my view the issue is theoretical, not empirical; H. Becker's theory is compatible with high-sacrifice items, not low-alternatives items. The low-alternatives items are better thought of as reflecting a separate construct: an employee's perceived employment alternatives.

Also, contrary to prior research, Powell and Meyer (2004) found that their revised CCS correlated positively with measures of both affective and normative commitment, which could indicate that this measure is more consistent with the concept of commitment as a positive mindset, as opposed to alienation (cf. T. Becker, 2005).

Finally, Meyer, Becker, and Van Dick (2006) have proposed that continuance commitment has an affective dimension reflecting feelings of security or anxiety about losing one's investments in the organization. If so, these feelings are explicitly tapped by the wording of only two of the eight original CCS items, and by none of the revised Powell and Meyer (2004) items (Jaros, 2007). This reflects a theme in commitment measurement research: construct validity problems arise because refinement of measures tends to lag behind conceptual refinement.

Another behavioral approach to commitment conceptualizes it as a binding of the individual to behavioral acts. Salancik (1977), drawing on Keisler and Sakamura's (1966) earlier work and applying it to the realm of the organization, defined commitment as one's psychological obligation to behave consistent with one's prior actions, and he conceived that commitment to behavior results to the extent that the behavior is associated with volition, revocability, and publicness, processes closely associated with the self-justification and dissonance-reduction concepts linked with Staw's escalation theory.

Thus, a measure that taps Salancik's concept of *behavioral* commitment should (a) be strongly predicted by measures of volition, publicness, and revocability, (b) reflect a sense of psychological obligation, and (c) strongly predict future behavior to the course of action posited to be the target of the commitment. O'Reilly and Caldwell (1980) defined behavioral commitment in terms of "tenure intention" and measured it with a scale written for the study that asked employees how long they intended to remain with the organization. The measure correlated with other variables as predicted by the behavioral theory. Kline and Peters (1991) tested Salancik's model with an author-developed scale that tapped "perceived obligation to follow through on their actions," and included items such as "I do not feel obligated to stick with this job" (reverse keyed). As predicted, the scale was found to have a positive relationship with volition and publicness, and a negative relationship with revocability.

The two studies cited here are exemplary of how behavioral commitment has been measured. The scales have generally performed as theorized in substantive research, probably due to the strength of the underlying theoretical model. But whereas behavioral commitment figured prominently in Mathieu and Zajac's (1990) meta-analysis of organizational commitment, it was only briefly mentioned in Cooper-Hakim and Viswesvaran's (2005) meta-analysis: because of its operationalization in terms of one's obligation or intent to act, behavioral commitment has been absorbed by concepts such as withdrawal or staying intentions (cf. Jaros, Jermier, Koehler, & Sincich, 1993), and as such isn't often viewed these days as a distinct form of commitment.

Finally, Staw and colleagues' *escalation* concept of commitment is purely behavioral, defined as persisting in a course of action in the face of negative feedback about its utility. Conceptually, the escalation concept appears to be a special case of Salancik's behavioral commitment construct, one limited to instances of behavioral persistence in the face of negative feed-back, and lacking the "intent" dimension. The psychological processes that influence escalation commitment are complex, but its measurement is relatively straightforward, since behavioral persistence can usually be directly and unambiguously observed (cf. Haslam et al., 2006).

Adequacy of Attitude-Theory Measures

Attitudinal commitment is usually defined as a mental state in which individuals identify with and are involved with a target, and thus have a positive evaluation of it, perhaps based on target-self values congru-ence (Mowday, Porter, & Steers, 1982). Thus, it includes constructs such as *affective* commitment (e.g., "cohesion" commitment, Kanter, 1968; and the commitment constructs developed by Buchanan, 1974, and Porter, Steers, Mowday, & Boulian, 1974) and *normative* commitment, and as noted above, arguably aspects of continuance commitment as well. However, exchange notions have crept into our understanding of attitudinal commitment via the concepts of perceived organizational support, which is a power-ful predictor of affective commitment (Lamastro, 2006), psychological contracts (Coyle-Shapiro & Morrow, 2006), and reciprocity norm, which Meyer and Herscovitch (2001) recently posited as a basic cause of norma-tive commitment.

Affective commitment is usually measured with the Organizational Commitment Questionnaire (OCQ; Porter et al., 1974) or a scale that has been to some degree derived from it, such as Meyer and Allen's (1984) Affective Commitment Scale (ACS); Gordon, Philpot, Burt, Thompson, and Spiller's (1980) measure of union commitment; Cook and Wall's (1980) British Organizational Commitment Scale; and O'Reilly and Chatman's (1986) measure of internalization/identification commitment (OCI). Recently, Jaussi (2007) identified several ways in which measures of affec-tive-attitudinal commitment are at variance with their conceptualiza-tions. For example, Meyer and Allen (1997) define affective commitment in terms of emotional attachment to, identification with, and involvement in the organization, but Jaussi argues that neither emotional attachment or involvement are tapped by any of the eight ACS items, and identifica-tion by only two of them. Similar disconnections between concept defini-tion and measures were found for the OCQ and OCI.

One can take issue with some of Jaussi's (2007) specific claims. For example, Jaussi argues that the ACS item "I would be very happy to spend my career with this organization" taps something she calls "attachment," not positive affect or emotions. In my view, this item, via its reference to happiness, does tap positive affect. However, her overall argument is com-pelling: each of these scales either omits definitional concepts from its items or has items that tap concepts not referred to in the construct definition.

Jaussi's (2007) solution is to theorize that *involvement, identification,* and *willingness to exert effort* are common to all of these conceptualizations, and thus constitute core dimensions of affective-attitudinal commitment. She then created scales for each dimension by combining items from the OCQ, ACS, and OCI, plus some author-written items. While these sub-scales were distinguishable in her empirical analysis, in my view Jaussi's solution is conceptually problematic. First, recent research (see Riketta & Van Dick, this volume; Gautam, Van Dick, & Wagner, 2004) has established the *distinctiveness* of identification and commitment as psychological processes, so identification should probably be purged from our concepts and measures of commitment. Also, as argued by Klein et al. (this volume), "willingness to exert effort" is better labeled an outcome or behavioral expression of commitment, not a part of the construct itself. Thus, affective commitment should be defined in terms of one's awareness of a positive emotional bond with the target, as per Kanter's (1968) and Buchanan's (1974) seminal definitions. This could be measured with modified versions of Likert-type scales such as the ACS and OCQ, or with semantic-differential scales that prompt the respondent to think of their feelings and strength of attachment toward the organization via affective anchors (e.g., good-bad, pleasant-unpleasant, strong-weak), as per H. McCaul, Hinsz, and K. McCaul (1995) and Jaros et al. (1993). See Al-Hindawe (1996) for technical issues in constructing semantic-differential scales.

Beyond the problems identified by Jaussi (2007), existing measures of affective commitment tend to be characterized by the inclusion of "intent to quit" items (Bozeman & Perrewe, 2001) and negative-wording method effects (Magazine, L. Williams, & M. Williams, 1996; Mathews & Shepherd, 2002). However, despite these flaws, in empirical research affective commitment scales tend to have high internal reliability and fit as hypothesized within their nomological net (cf. Hartog & Belschak, 2007). Thus, if scales such as the ACS and OCQ were modified to fit the recommendations made here, overall construct validity would likely be even higher.

The concept of normative commitment, and its measurement via the normative commitment scale (NCS), has been even more problematic (Bergman, 2006; Cohen, 2007; Jaros, 2007). Bergman notes that despite changes in construct definition, the NCS, introduced by Allen and Meyer (1990) and modified by Meyer et al. (1993), has not been revised to reflect the reciprocity-norm thesis proposed by Meyer and Herscovitch (2001) or the "indebted obligation" and "moral imperative" dimensions proposed by Meyer et al. (2006). Thus, item-level refinement of the NCS is needed to align it with current conceptualizations of the construct.

Also, in Western cultural settings, the 1990 and 1993 versions of the NCS have tended to add little to prediction of behaviors beyond what is predicted by affective commitment (Meyer et al., 2002). However, recently, Gellatly, Meyer, and Luchak (2006) found that when modeled as part of a commitment "profile" with affective and continuance commitment, the NCS did play a key role in predicting citizenship behaviors. Notably, Gellatly et al. used truncated versions of the ACS and NCS composed of the three items from each scale that had the highest factor loadings in their data set. They reported that these three-item scales had higher reliabilities than the reliabilities for the full scales reported in the Meyer et al. (2002) meta-analysis. Likewise, using three-item versions of the ACS and NCS, Boezeman and Ellemers (2007) found that among volunteer workers, the NCS significantly predicted "intent to remain a volunteer," whereas the ACS did not. These findings suggest that affective and normative commitment might be distinct constructs, but that the full versions of the NCS do not do a good job of operationalizing the distinction.

Finally, when studied in Eastern cultures, the NCS (typically the 1993 version) *has* tended to be a significant predictor of outcomes (cf. Wasti, 2003, $r = -.54$ with turnover intentions; Gautam, Van Dick, Wagner, Upadhyay, & Davis, 2005, $r = .33$ with compliance), which could mean the salience of NC is greater in "collectivist" cultures characterized by strong reciprocal obligation norms. Support for this notion lies in the fact that the NCS and CCS also tend to correlate significantly and positively in Asian samples (Cheng & Stockdale, 2003, $r = .37$; Chen & Francesco, 2003,; $r = .48$ in Chinese samples), suggesting that in Eastern cultures NC is experienced as a kind of "binding obligation." Thus, the weak findings associated with normative commitment to date could be a product of not only how it has been measured but also where it has been measured (Western vs. Eastern cultures).

Adequacy of Cognitions-Theory Measures

Cognitive approaches conceptualize commitment as being characterized by conscious, rational, largely nonaffective mental processes and deciding to commit to something as a result. Hollenbeck and Klein's (1987) model of goal commitment, as measured by the Hollenbeck, Williams, and Klein (HWK, 1989) scale (refined by DeShon & Landis, 1997; and Klein, Wesson, Hollenbeck, Wright, & DeShon, 2001), is arguably exemplary of this approach, because it posits goal commitment as a person's determination to reach a goal, characterized by willingness to exert effort to achieve it, and persistence in doing so. Alternatively, Wright, O'Leary-Kelly, Cortina, Klein, and Hollenbeck (1994) argue that the original HWK scale was designed to reflect commitment as an "attitude about a goal" and that its items were designed to reflect cognitive, affective, and behavioral-intent components of commitment, per the traditional tripartite construction of an attitude. Nevertheless, the cognitive dimension is sufficiently present in this scale to be used as an example in this discussion.

Note that cognitions commitment overlaps with behavioral commitment to the extent that it is defined in terms of persistence, particularly since persistence in pursuing a goal is held to be influenced by the volition, publicness, and revocability factors identified by Salancik in the behavioral model. Also, the "willingness to exert effort" dimension reflects a behavioral-intent aspect of the model, and indeed, two of the nine items that make up the original HWK scale are adapted from the OCQ.

Meta-analytic confirmatory factor analysis (CFA) has shown that a refined five-item HWK scale (Klein et al., 2001) has generally sound psychometric properties, but nevertheless one may doubt whether this unidimensional scale captures the multifaceted cognitions (willingness to exert effort, persistence, determination to achieve the goal) that comprise the definition of goal commitment. However, in this case, the construct, not the scale, should be revised: the five items in the revised HWK scale appear to more closely focus on *determination* to achieve a goal, which is the core of the concept (cf. Locke & Latham, 1990). Effort, willingness, and persistence are behavioral expressions of commitment and should be omitted from its definition.

Yet recently, Aube and Rousseau (2005), in assessing commitment to team goals, used somewhat modified versions of three of the five items in the revised HWK scale, rejecting two of them on the grounds that they tapped non-goal-commitment domains, including perceptions of goal difficulty. One of the items they omitted was an item identified by Wright et al. (1994) as being behavioral-intent in nature. Despite having just three items, this scale had a coefficient alpha of .85 in their study, better than what Klein et al. (2001) found for the five-item scale, and performed as expected in substantive analyses. Thus, this three-item version might be even better at tapping the core goal commitment construct.

Adequacy of Multiple-Target Models

As discussed in other chapters (T. Becker, chapter 5; Vandenburghe, chapter 4), some researchers have developed perspectives that integrate multiple targets into a model of work commitment, raising the issue of how they should be simultaneously measured. Morrow (1983) advocated the development of a Job Diagnostic Index (JDI)-analogue scale to measure the five forms of commitment in her model. Morrow's approach suggests the existence of an overall, global work commitment, reflecting the "sum total" of the five commitment facets. In her revision of this model, Morrow (1993) suggested that measuring multiple forms of commitment from the same source and using the same paper-pencil method would likely create a "halo effect" that would preclude respondents from distinguishing among them, resulting in apparently inflated inter-relationships. Consistent with Morrow's fear, research that has tested and developed multi-target, JDI-type general indexes of work commitment (cf. Blau, Paul, and St. John, 1993; Cohen, 1993) has reported results indicating a significant amount of construct overlap.

In contrast to Morrow, who posited targets of commitment that she believed were salient to employees everywhere, Reichers (1985) argued that target salience would to an extent be unique at the organizational level. Thus, the first step in measuring commitment to multiple targets should be to conduct interviews with employees to find out what the relevant targets are in their organization. Then, a valid organizational commitment scale could be adapted to measure commitment to each, and these target-specific scales should correlate highly with a measure of overall organizational commitment. Reichers also suggested that perhaps commitment scales with forced-choice formats that require employees to indicate whether they would commit to the goals of target X over target Y or vice-versa should be used to model the conflicting goals that often characterize different parts of the organization. This has never been done, probably because forced-choice formats do not measure commitment constructs per se, but they measure the relative strengths of those commitments.

However, multiple commitments can conflict with each other, and thus measuring how employees prioritize competing commitments is a worthwhile (but largely neglected) aspect of commitment research. In addition to the forced-choice approach, a way to address this issue would be to adopt the approach used by Ravlin, Meglino, and colleagues (cf. Ravlin & Meglino, 1989) in the work-values area: ask respondents to rank-order their commitments and subject the top-ranked one to further analysis. Or, one could measure conflict directly via a Likert-type scale that asks respondents the degree to which they experience conflict among their commitments, including commitments to work and nonwork domains. These methods will not allow one to assess the absolute level of different commitments, but if the purpose of the research is to study conflicts among commitments, they can be appropriate.

Ideally, multitarget models of commitment should be tested in their entirety. This is almost never done (for an exception, see Lee, Carswell, & Allen, 2000) because of survey space and/or completion time concerns. Thus, one potentially fruitful approach to measuring several targets of commitment in a single study is the matrix method developed by Cohen (1993; see Cohen, 2003, p. 86, for an example). The vertical axis of the matrix is titled "statements" and includes a list of scale items to tap commitment, and the different targets to be assessed are arrayed along the top horizontal axis. The matrix structure saves space and allows respondents to work through the questionnaire quickly. Van Dick, Wagner, Stellmacher, and Christ (2004) used a similar measurement tool, a version of the Repertory Grid Technique, to measure multiple forms of organizational identification.

One potential criticism of matrix/grid approaches is that because the questions used to tap commitment to each target are identical, the concepts might tend to blur into each other, creating consistency and priming artifacts that could lead to empirical results that falsely suggest concept redundancy. Cohen (1993) did find some evidence of concept redundancy. Similarly, Van Dick et al.'s (2004) data showed that the average correlation among four identification targets was .41 using the grid method, compared with .28 when using nongrid measures of the same targets.

Alternatively, Allen (2003) has argued that the bias might work in the opposite direction: making all of the questions identical *except* for the word that labels the target might make each stand out in greater relief to the respondent, such that the respondent may feel pressure to provide responses that exaggerate the differences they actually perceive between them. Therefore, researchers who adopt a matrix/grid or other same-wording approach for practical reasons must be particularly mindful of the need to identify and control for response biases. Pilot studies could analyze commitment data collected using standard, differently worded measures and matrix/grid measures, and compare their intercorrelations (e.g., Van Dick et al., 2004). If this analysis reveals that the grid/matrix scales have the same psychometric properties as the standard scales, our confidence in their construct validity will be enhanced and we can use grid-only measurement in future research.

Overall, if the researcher concludes that a particular multitarget model correctly conceptualizes commitment and is thus worthy of investigation, then Cohen (2003), following Morrow (1993), describes what I believe to be the best *process* for measurement: choose and/or develop highly reliable, valid measures of commitment for each of the relevant targets. Once that's accomplished, these measures can be studied in different combinations to test the multitarget models of Morrow, Reichers, and others. Cohen's (2006, 2007) recent work is exemplary of this approach.

Adequacy of Multiple-Bases Models

Although others (e.g., Kelman, 1958; Jahoda, 1956; Etzioni, 1961) preceded her in the development of multiple bases of attitudes more generally, Kanter (1968) represented the first attempt to define commitment as having multiple bases. Later three-component conceptualizations, such as those put forth by O'Reilly and Chatman (1986), Allen and Meyer (1990), Penley and Gould (1988), and Jaros et al. (1993) owe much to Kanter's work. Despite their considerable differences, each of these models is composed of a combination of exchange-based, affect-based, and moral-normative-based commitments, all similar to what Kanter theorized. Indeed, when measured in the same study, researchers have often found considerable empirical overlap between some constructs from these different models.

Jaros et al. reported a correlation of .76 between their measure of affective commitment and Meyer and Allen's ACS, while T. Becker (2006) reported correlations ranging from the .80s to the .90s between different combinations of Meyer and Allen's NCS and ACS and the OCI scale.

Of these models, the Meyer and Allen (1997) formulation is characterized by the richest integrative conceptual work, and has thus come to dominate the multiple-bases literature. The strengths and weaknesses of their measures, the ACS, NCS, and CCS, were discussed above. As noted by Klein, Brinsfield, and Molloy (2006), conceptual work is still needed to sort out exactly what "bases" of commitment exist before definitive measures can be developed to tap and assess them.

While this section has addressed measurement issues from *within* the context of various theoretical perspectives, recently some researchers (T. Becker, this volume; Brown, 1996; Klein et al., 2006 and this volume; Meyer, this volume; Meyer & Herscovitch, 2001) have attempted to distill a conception of commitment that is common to all of them. These efforts, and the measurement issues that arise as a result, are addressed in the conclusion of this chapter.

General Commitment Measurement Issues

This section addresses non-theory-specific commitment measurement issues. Among other issues, these include insights that organizational psychologists can gain from sociological, qualitative studies of commitment, the adaptation of organizational commitment measures to multiple targets in singles studies, and how to improve the validity and reliability of commitment scales and their component items.

Sociological Approaches to the Measurement of Commitment

While sociological theories of commitment have been impactful in the field of I/O psychology (e.g., H. Becker, 1960; Kanter, 1968), sociological measurement methods have not. I/O psychologists are trained in the use of statistical methods, while sociologists often study work commitment by using qualitative methods. Examples include Barker's (1993) three-year participant observation study of the development of commitment in self-managing teams, Kunda's (1992) observational study of commitment and alienation at a high-tech organization, and Adler and Adler's (1988) five-year participant observation study of "intense loyalty" in a college athletic program. The longitudinal nature of these sociological studies allowed for the measurement of commitment as an unfolding process (see

Vandenburg & Stanley, this volume) whereby different goals, values, and norms emerged over time, and commitments to them arose and ebbed.

Of course, qualitative assessments are not without their limitations. No scalar metric is employed, making descriptions such as "intense" loyalty in the Adler and Adler study difficult to interpret because they lack a basis of comparison beyond the impressions of the researcher. In essence, we have a single individual or team "rater," albeit one who is more deeply immersed in the organization than is typical in quantitative research, assessing commitment via impressionistic description. In contrast, traditional commitment scales are designed to capture level shadings directly expressed by the respondent, and to generate numerical data that allows for cross-organizational comparisons. Thus, qualitative analysis can be viewed as a supplement/complement to quantitative assessment, working together (cf. Jick, 1979) to enhance our understanding of work commitment. Qualitative assessment could be used to build theory for later quantitative measurement or could be done concurrently as part of a true multimethod assessment of commitment.

Appropriateness of Adapting Measures of Organizational Commitment to Serve as Measures of Other Targets

Commitment researchers often adapt scales originally designed to measure organizational commitment to tap commitment to other targets. Examples include Stinglhamber, Bentein, and Vandenberghe's (2002) extension of the Meyer and Allen organizational commitment model to four other targets; T. Becker and colleagues' adaptation of the OCI scales (O'Reilly & Chatman, 1986) to targets such as supervisors and top management (T. Becker, 1992; T. Becker, Randall, & Riegel, 1995; T. Becker, Billing, Eveleth, & Gilbert, 1996); and Bishop and colleagues' (Bishop, Scott, & Burroughs, 2000; Bishop, Scott, Goldsby, & Cropanzano, 2005) modification of the OCQ to measure team commitment.

As noted earlier, sometimes, researchers retain the exact wording of the organizational commitment measure, changing only the focal term from "organization" to whatever other target is being studied (e.g., Clugston, Howell, & Dorfman, 2000), and sometimes the scales are substantially reworded or new items are written for different targets (e.g., Meyer et al., 1993). Particularly in the former case but also sometimes in the latter, strengths and weaknesses of the organizational commitment measures tend to get passed on to the other-target measures created from them. For example, although outside the commitment domain there is strong empirical evidence for the distinction between identification and internalization (cf. Ashforth & Mael, 1989) as bases of attitudes, in most commitment studies the OCI scale items (O'Reilly & Chatman, 1986) tend to load together (cf. O'Reilly, Chatman, & Caldwell, 1991; Sutton & Harrison, 1993;

Malhotra & Galleta, 2005), and they tend to load together and/or be highly correlated when adapted as measures of other targets (Cohen, 2003). In the Meyer and Allen model of organizational commitment, the ACS tends to have higher predictive power than the CCS and NCS, and the NCS tends to be highly correlated with the ACS (Meyer et al., 2002); and some extensions of this model to the occupational domain have reported similar results (Blau & Holladay, 2006; Chang, Chi, & Miao, 2007).

But, when developing scales to measure commitment to new targets, one has to start somewhere, and existing organizational commitment items are in some cases as good a place to start as any (Reichers, 1985). What matters is whether the items fit our conceptualization of the commitment construct and how well the items perform in substantive research.

Formative Versus Reflective Indicators

In traditional measurement theory, a *reflective* construct is empirically defined by the common variance among its scale indicators (Mackenzie, Podsakoff, & Jarvis, 2005; Edwards & Bagozzi, 2000). Thus, when using CFA notation, paths run from the construct to the scale items, such that the items reflect the latent construct. But for a *formative* construct, the scale items determine the latent construct, which is theorized as the aggregate of its indicators. As Mackenzie et al. noted, modeling a construct as reflective when it is really formative can result in mistakes such as eliminating scale items because they are uncorrelated with other scale items or result in lower internal consistency scores (intercorrelations and high internal consistency are evidence of good fit for reflective constructs, but are irrelevant to formative constructs) or result in significant bias to parameter estimates if the mis-specified construct is included in a structural model with other variables.

Is this issue a problem in commitment research? The key here is to reflect on theory that describes the nature of the commitment construct. If one theorizes that as an employee's commitment increases, their response to a question such as, "I feel pride in being a member of this organization" should go up, then commitment is a reflective construct and the traditional approach to measurement is appropriate. But if one believes that as pride increases, commitment will rise, then a formative model is appropriate. Some researchers have begun to reevaluate commitment constructs that have typically been modeled as reflective. For example, Law and Wong (1999) proposed that Cook and Wall's (1980) commitment construct—comprised of loyalty, identification, and involvement dimensions measured with separate subscales—is formative, not reflective, in nature and should be modeled as such. These propositions should be tested via empirical research, and other commitment measures should be similarly reevaluated if the construct definition indicates formative, rather than reflective, logic. See Edwards (2001) for a technical description of how to empirically assess whether a construct is formative or reflective.

Reverse Coding of Commitment Scale Items

Reverse coding of some scale items is a common practice in commitment research, rooted in a desire to avoid acquiescence bias. However, recent research (Magazine et al., 1996; Mathews & Shepherd, 2002; Bozeman & Perrewe, 2001; Culpepper, 2000) suggests that reverse-coding-method factors are present in many commonly used measures of commitment, including the Meyer and Allen scales and the OCQ. Reverse-coding effects have been found to affect measurement model fit in CFAs, and may "impair the reliability and validity of a measure and... thereby decrease the observed relationships with constructs of interest" (Magazine et al., 1996, p. 247).

Schriesheim and Eisenbach (1995) noted that there are actually four kinds of item formats: regular (e.g., I am happy), negated regular (e.g., I am not happy), polar opposite (I am sad), and negated polar opposite (I am not sad). Their study found that while each of the four formats produces its own "method effect," regular-worded items were characterized by significantly higher trait variance, significantly lower error variance, less method variance, and the highest reliability coefficient. And, citing Nunnally's (1978) analysis of acquiescence bias, they argued that the "overwhelming weight" of evidence shows that agreement tendency is of minor importance as a source of measure invalidity. Thus, given the substantial costs of using mixed-format scale items, and the scant benefit of doing so, they concluded that scales should be composed of regular-worded items—unless the research has a strong theoretical rationale for using mixed format in their particular study. Note that Schriescheim and Eisenbach's analysis was conducted on Likert-type scales, so it is an open question as to whether reverse-coded items present the same kind of problems for other types of scales, such as bipolar adjective scales (e.g., whether it matters if a bipolar item is presented as ranging from happy to sad, or vice versa).

One way to address this problem in existing scales is to simply eliminate reverse-coded items. But, as Bayazit, Hammer, and Wazeter (2004) noted, this might mean eliminating items that would otherwise be highly reliable and valid indicators. So the best solution is to reformat commitment scales with negated regular, polar opposite, and negated polar opposite items as regular items.

Similarly, Barnette (2000) investigated the use of reverse-coded items and *response-option formatting*, which refers to whether response options to a Likert-scale item are listed from strongly agree to strongly disagree, or vice versa, by comparing a unidirectional response option format (all items SA–SD or SD–SA) with a mixed-response option format. Six formats were tested: three item-response options (all SA–SD, all SD–SA, and half SD–SA/half SA–SD) for two-item formats (all positively worded; mixed positively and negatively worded).To avoid respondent confusion, in the mixed-response conditions a warning statement was given immediately before the beginning of the items, telling respondents about the mixed-response format. To control for past research findings that a respondent's ability to accurately respond to reverse-coded items depends in part on their level of cognitive development, Barnette's study was conducted in classrooms with high school students, college undergraduate and graduate students, and teachers. Barnette found that using all positively worded items with a mixed-response format, with half of the scale items having response options of agree to disagree and the other half going from disagree to agree via random ordering, produced higher reliability estimates and higher item variance than any other combination, and also acts as a check on agreement-response bias if the researcher has a reason to fear it in his/her research context.

Behavioral Intent Items as Part of Commitment Scales

To an extent, this is a special instance of debates about what an attitude is (cf. Clark & Fiske, 1982). If commitment is conceptualized as a traditional attitude, with cognitive, affective, and behavioral intent components (cf. Wright et al., 1994), then including behavioral intent items in a measure of commitment is arguably necessary, because behavioral intentions are a part of the definition of the attitude itself. Within the commitment literature, some researchers argue that behavioral "terms" of a commitment— the behaviors implied by the commitment—should be included in scale items (e.g., Brown, 1996; Meyer & Herscovitch, 2001), and others argue that they should not (e.g., McCaul et al., 1995; Klein et al., 2006 and this volume). Bozeman and Perrewe (2001), in arguing against the inclusion of intent-to-remain wording in the OCQ, noted that including items with this wording resulted in an "inflated" correlation between the OCQ and turnover cognitions. In contrast, Meyer and Herscovitch (2001) argue for "specifying the behavior of interest" in commitment items, at least with respect to focal behaviors, precisely *because* it will improve the predictive power of commitment measures and because of a belief that a commitment's behavioral terms (e.g., in the case of organizational commitment, remaining with the organization) are integral to the concept of commitment.

Nevertheless, I believe that the Bozeman and Perrewe (2001) stance against including behavioral wording in commitment measures is the better practice. As they note, behavioral intent items are difficult to justify as exclusively or integrally a part of a commitment construct, since those intentions are likely influenced by other factors, such as job satisfaction, as well. This recommendation is particularly salient for items that load on a behavioral intentions factor and not on the commitment factor, such as the three OCQ items that loaded exclusively on turnover cognitions in the Bozeman and Perrewe study. It is also salient if one is interested in testing a theoretical model, such as Mobley, Horner, and Hollingsworth (1978) or Hom and Griffith (1995), that posits turnover intentions as mediators between factors such as commitment and turnover behavior, because including behavioral intentions wording in commitment scale items prevents us from assessing whether behavioral intentions mediate the commitment-behavior relationship, or at least it confounds the issue.

Additionally, Meyer (1997) has argued that scales such as the OCQ (and Meyer & Allen's ACS) do not actually contain "intent to" items. He argues that they contain items reflecting a "mindset associated with intention to remain," and intentions and mindsets are not the same thing. To an extent, I agree: the OCQ doesn't contain any items that literally say, "I intend to remain with this organization." Also, Bozeman and Perrewe's empirical analyses are partially supportive of this position. Their CFA found that of the six OCQ items that their expert panel said reflected intent to remain, three loaded exclusively with other, non-OCQ turnover cognitions items, but three cross-loaded significantly with both commitment and turnover cognition items, and more so with commitment, indicating greater commitment content than turnover cognitions content.

Thus, Meyer's (1997) argument that some commitment items that are referred to as reflecting behavior intentions but actually reflect behavioral terms or mindsets can seemingly be assessed empirically: if these items load with established behavior-intent scales and not with commitment items, then that would suggest that they really are behavioral intent items. If they load more strongly on a commitment factor than with behavior-intent items, then this is perhaps suggestive of a "behavioral terms" designation. But even then, one can question the appropriateness of specifying behavioral terms in a definition of commitment to an entity. For example, in the Meyer and Allen model, remaining with the organization is the focal behavior of normative organizational commitment, and NCS items include wording about remaining with the organization. Yet one can imagine circumstances in which an employee could best express loyalty or obligation to the organization by leaving (e.g., someone who resigns "for the good of the company"). Thus, it seems unwise to measure an employee's level of normative commitment in terms of any particular behavior. The commitment is to an entity, such as the organization, and under different circumstances that might mean many different kinds of behaviors, even leaving. Thus, behaviors are better thought of as *expressions* of commitment (cf. Randall, Fedor, & Longenecker, 1990) rather than elements of commitment. Of course, if the target of the commitment is itself a behavior (e.g., see Neubert & Wu, this volume) then the behavior should be included in the item wording, as the target.

Cross-Cultural Measurement Issues

Cross-cultural measurement issues in commitment research, such as the use of etic or emic scale items, back-translation, and cross-cultural measurement equivalence, are addressed in Wasti and Onder (this volume).

Measurement of Commitment Using Multiple Sources

Typically, an employee's work commitment is measured by asking the employee about his/her commitment. This makes sense, because it seems putatively correct that no one can know employee X's commitment level better than employee X. It exists inside his or her heart and mind. But, people aren't always honest about themselves (perhaps due to social desirability bias), or some employees might not be available to report on themselves, so alternative sources can possibly serve as a surrogate for or check on self-reported commitment, or may possibly reveal facets of that commitment the employee is unaware of.

For example, Gade, Tiggle, and Schumm (2003) collected data on soldiers' affective and continuance commitment by conducting telephone surveys of soldiers and their spouses. Spouses were asked to give their perception of their soldier's commitment, via questions such as, "It would be too costly for my spouse or fiancé to leave the military in the near future" (a CCS item). Gade et al.'s results showed that the spousal data was similar in some respects to the data collected directly from the soldiers, but there were differences as well. Compared to soldiers' self-report data, spousal perception of soldier affective and continuance commitment had higher reliability estimates, but measurement models assessing the factor structure of these scales had slightly inferior CFA-model fit. Spousal perceptions of affective and continuance commitment were also more highly correlated ($r = .38$) than in the soldiers' self-report data ($r = .17$) and as reported by research on these constructs more generally. Moreover, the correlations between spousal-perceived and soldier affective commitment and spousal and soldier continuance commitment, while statistically significant, were modest ($r = .26$, $p < .05$, for both affective and continuance commitment) and less than we would expect if spousal and soldier perceptions of the soldier's commitment were nearly identical.

In her commentary on the Gade et al. study, Allen (2003, p. 242) asks, "What does it mean to describe another person's commitment?" and suggests that the wording of the CCS items used to assess spousal perceptions seemed to tap both the spouse's perceptions of their partner's commitment to the military, but also, and mistakenly, the spouse's own commitment to their partner's commitment to the military. This could possibly account for the relatively low correlations found between the spousal- and soldier-rated commitments.

Goffin and Gellatly (2001) also measured affective and continuance commitment via multiple sources, in their case from employees, their supervisors, and their coworker peers. They posited that peer perceptions of the employee's commitment and the employee's self-rating should be very similar, perhaps even converge, but that supervisor's assessment of the employee's commitment should be significantly different from the employee's self-rating, since supervisors and employees don't share work experiences to the same degree as do peers and employees.

Results showed that while mean levels of affective commitment were statistically the same across all three raters, employee continuance commitment was significantly higher than peer- or supervisor-rated continuance commitment. By adding supervisor-rated affective and continuance commitment to self-rated affective and continuance commitment, variance explained in employee job performance rose from 15% to 39%. Data were also analyzed by using multitrait (affective and continuance commitment), multirater (peer, self, supervisor) analysis to compare mean levels of each commitment type for each rating method, which indicated moderate convergence across the three rating sources.

With the caveat that two studies is too few to draw definitive conclusions, taken together the results of the Gade et al. and Goffin and Gellatly studies suggest that if, for whatever reason, commitment data can't be gathered from the employee, then close significant others such as peers, spouses, classmates, or teammates can *perhaps* serve as viable surrogates. Also, the Goffin and Gellatly (2001) finding that supervisory ratings explained additional variance in job performance beyond that explained by self-rater commitment is important because one of the holy grails of commitment research is the search for additional explained variance in behaviors. It implies that not everything about one's commitment is known by oneself. Significant others may understand aspects of our commitment that we are unaware of.

Scale Reporting

Most journals require that authors report a correlation or covariance matrix so as to facilitate scale-level meta-analyses or independent analysis of substantive tests. But with the development of item-level analyses, such as CFA/Item Response Theory and item-level meta-analytic techniques (cf. Klein et al., 2001), the following recommendations would enhance our ability to accumulate knowledge about commitment measures. First, if space permits, publish item-level intercorrelations, not just scale intercorrelations (e.g., Ugboro 2006; Dawley, R. Stephens, & D. Stephens, 2005). If space doesn't permit, calculate them and in the paper note that they are available upon request. Second, if CFA modification indices are used to identify commitment scale items with correlated errors and high cross-loadings and then eliminate them from the scales so as to improve measurement model fit, then report (or make available upon request) the unmodified CFA fit statistics as well. This will aid in gauging the construct validity and generalizability of the unmodified scales across studies.

Single-Item Measures of Commitment

Single-item measures are always viewed with some amount of skepticism, because of our inability to calculate internal consistency ratings for them (though their internal reliability *can* be assessed using factor analysis— see Wanous & Hudy, 2001). Thus, they are scarce in the commitment literature. T. Becker (1992) used single-item measures of commitment to supervisor, to workgroup, and to top management, all of which successfully predicted outcome variables; and Johnson, Caughlin, and Huston (1999), in their study of marriage commitment, used single-item scales of "want to," "have to," and "need to" commitment to stay married. Johnson et al. concluded that the single-item measures were "too global," such that respondents might have found it difficult to distinguish among them, but their interrcorrelations never exceeded a modest .34. Also, Tubbs (1994) argued that goal commitment should perhaps be conceptualized not as a traditional attitude (with cognitive, evaluative, and behavioral intent components) but as strictly a behavioral intent concept. He suggested that a single item, such as "How committed are you to your goal?" could capture this. Thus, perhaps additional empirical research would reveal single-item measures of organizational commitment, such as "How committed are you to your organization?" as having the same reasonable amount of robustness that Wanous, Reichers, and Hudy (1997) found for single-item measures of job satisfaction.

Phone and Internet Measurement

Traditionally, work commitment has been measured by administering paper-and-pencil questionnaires, filled out either at work or via mail. But recently researchers have begun to use alternative technologies to gather commitment data, such as telephone (Gade et al., 2003) and Internet surveys (cf. Dawley et al., 2005) as a means of reaching large numbers of respondents at low cost, particularly compared to mail surveys. Substantively, Internet surveys probably don't differ from paper-and-pencil scales (Cole, Bedeian, & Field, 2006). Telephone measures raise trickier issues: voice contact with another person could create social desirability response biases. Or, answering questions while talking on the phone at home might put the respondent more at ease than they might feel while in the midst of one's boss, customers, and so forth at work, thus generating more honest responses. Until these potential response-bias issues are sorted out, caution has to be maintained when using telephone surveys.

Item Parceling

Item parceling involves combining scale items into parcels, which are then subject to analysis. It may be done to increase the stability of parameter estimates in a structural equation model, or to reduce the number of parameters that need to be estimated and thus permit analysis to proceed with smaller samples. Parceling will usually improve the fit of a CFA measurement model and may be more likely than individual items to meet the multivariate-normality assumption, and will always improve reliability scores (MacCallum, Widaman, Zhang, & Hong, 1999; Sass & Smith, 2006).

However, while parceling can improve model fit, it can distort the fit of our measurement or structural models as well. As Kim and Hagtvet (2003) note, "The use of item parcels is appropriate only when the parcels retain all the common information from single items and do not distort factor content" (p. 103). They recommend a two-factor CFA method that allows the researcher to compare various parceling methods (e.g., random assignment, matching high- and low-loading items, matching items based on impact on reliability) and choose one that best meets the information retention and nondistortion criteria. Also, Sass and Smith (2006) found that if normality assumptions are met and a scale is unidimensional, various parceling methods tend to produce the same structural-model (not measurement-model) parameters, and these are the same structural-model parameters produced by using single items as indicators of a latent construct.

Note that item parceling is inappropriate if we are conducting tests of measure invariance/equivalence. Meade and Kroustalis (2006) found that "combining item-level data into parcels prior to conducting measurement equivalence tests can greatly mask a lack of invariance that can be detected with item-level data" (p.370). If the research question relates to the measurement model's validity, as it does in tests of measurement equivalence, then the individual items, not parceling, should be used. Finally, if a scale is multidimensional, the parcels for the scale cannot be formed by using items that come from separate dimensions: each dimension must have its own parcel created by items linked to that dimension.

Use of MRI Spectroscopy (MRS) to Link Commitment to Brain Structure or Chemical Reactions

One trend in the development of the study of work attitudes over the past 20 years has been the search for underlying dispositional/trait antecedents. In commitment research, Williams and Anderson (1994) and Chan (2001) have found that affective commitment items (from the OCI scale and the OCQ, respectively) were saturated with positive affectivity; Erdheim, Wang, and Zickar (2006) found linkages between Big Five personality factors and Meyer and Allen commitment constructs; and Meyer (this volume) suggests that people might be genetically predisposed to commit. Taking this notion of an inherent basis for commitment a step further, it might be the case that commitment is rooted in chemical-neurological processes in the brain, and technologies such as MRS could be used to measure these.

MRS measurement is currently impractical in field studies of commitment, but it could potentially be useful in experimental studies, perhaps in goal commitment or escalation-of-commitment research. MRS readings of brain activity could be taken as experimental subjects electronically submit their responses to self-report measures such as the HWK goal-commitment scale, or as they react to feedback about progress they are making toward a goal, or how they respond to negative feedback in escalation experiments. Thus, MRS might help us measure any chemical and neurological processes that underlie the experience of commitment.

Measurement of Commitment Across Time

Recently, researchers have developed latent growth and latent curve models for the assessment of commitment over time (cf. J. Tisak & M. Tisak, 2000; Bentein, Vandneberghe, Vandenberg, & Stinglhamber, 2005). See Vandenberg and Stanley, this volume, for a discussion of these techniques.

Best Practices in Developing Measures of Commitment

In this section, recent scale-development research is drawn upon to make recommendations for best practice procedures for developing new commitment measures and refining existing ones. First, a three-stage process of scale development based on Hinkin (1995), but updated with findings since then, is presented. Second, some methods for refining existing commitment scales are discussed. Finally, I conclude with a discussion of the measurement implications of recent attempts to conceptualize a core or essence common to all forms and bases of commitment.

Developing New Commitment Measures

According to Hinkin (1995), the development of a new scale should proceed through the following steps: item generation, scale development, and scale evaluation. In the *item generation* stage, the key issue is content validity—making sure that the items tap, and only tap, the domain of interest (cf. Messick, 1995). This first requires an "understanding of the phenomenon to be investigated and a thorough review of the literature to develop the theoretical definition of the construct ..." (Hinkin, p. 969). The definition is then used as a guide for the generation of items (cf. Schwab, 1980). After items are chosen from existing scales that seemingly tap the relevant domain, or are written, other raters, such as scholars and organizational constituents who have experiential knowledge of the conceptual domain, should be used to validate our work. Interrater reliability values can be used to select the most promising items for further analysis.

In the *scale development* stage, the pool of items identified as a scale in item generation is subject to analyses intended to reveal its psychometric properties. This involves conducting pretests on representative samples of the population being studied. In finalizing the scale for analysis, we should seek to keep scale length short to minimize response fatigue while keeping in mind that scales can be too short to have the necessary content validity or have adequate internal consistency. The response options for the scale should be at least five to capture all the nuances/levels of response, but diminishing returns make more than seven unnecessary (Lissitz & Green, 1975). As noted earlier, if we are using a Likert-type response scale, the direction of response options should be mixed (Barnette, 2000), and to avoid item-wording-method effects, items should be regularly worded (Schriesheim & Eisenbach, 1995).

Pretest samples should be carefully chosen to reflect the population that we expect the construct to apply to, and the sample size should be large enough to meet the five-data-points-per-parameter rule of thumb for CFA. CFA and Item Response Theory can be used in conjunction, the former to determine factor structure, and the latter to identify item response patterns (Meade & Lautenschlager, 2004; Stark, Chernyshenko, & Drasgow, 2006). It is at this stage that reliability estimates should be calculated for the scale. In addition to coefficient alpha, Cooksey and Soutar (2006) make a strong case for calculating coefficient beta scores, since a unitary scale can report a high alpha coefficient even if it actually has an unintentionally multidimensional structure (cf. Meyer & Allen's original CCS). Cooksey and Soutar define coefficient beta as the "worst split-half reliability of a scale" (p.80), in contrast to alpha, which is the mean of all possible split-half reliabilities of a scale. Unlike coefficient alpha, which assumes that a scale is unidimensional, coefficient beta can help identify the presence of subdimensions in a scale designed to be unidimensional. However, beta is not recommended as a replacement for alpha, because they provide different, complementary information: "beta gives a better estimate of the test's homogeneity, while alpha is the more appropriate estimate of how a test will correlate with another test sampled from the same domain" (p. 81).

In the *scale evaluation* stage, we assess the criterion, convergent, and dis-criminant validity of the scale by studying its relationships with theo-rized antecedents and outcomes, and how it compares to other measures of the same construct, the idea being to determine whether the scale fits into the theorized nomological net. Multitrait/multimethod CFA is an appropriate method to test convergent/discriminant validity. The sample providing the data to be analyzed should not be the same sample used during the scale development analyses. Also, measurement invariance using CFA and Item Response Theory analyses should be assessed across different demographic, institutional, or cultural groups. Once these steps are taken and the scale's construct validity is established, it is ready for use in substantive research, though findings from that research might point out the need for yet further refinements in the measure.

Refinement of Existing Measures

In our efforts to improve the measurement of work commitment, some techniques can be used to make existing scales more valid and reliable measures of their underlying constructs:

Meta-analytic, item-level CFA. As demonstrated by Klein et al. (2001), who used this method to refine the HWK scale, this technique can be used to leverage data that has been generated by prior research to conduct item-level refinements of a commitment scale. Of course, no purely quan-titative method can address every refinement issue: Klein et al. noted that several combinations of items were of equal statistical fit, but the final five-item scale was chosen in part on judgment calls such as limiting the scale length while maintaining high internal reliability and sufficient content coverage. Also, this method improves a scale by a process of item elimi-nation. Sometimes, though, a scale can be improved even more by the inclusion of new items, either as additions to or replacements of existing items.

Development of truncated measures. A truncated measure is a shortened version of a standard scale. A good example of this is the short-form OCQ, a 9-item version of the full 15-item scale. Item elimination to cre-ate a shorter scale might be desirable to save space on a survey, to reduce the number of parameters needed to be estimated in a structural model, or if we're concerned about a longer version taxing the attention span of some category of respondents. Truncation might also result from efforts to refine a measure by eliminating items that reduce reliability or other-wise have poor construct validity (cf. Boezeman & Ellemers, 2007) and thus result in an improved version of an existing scale. In doing so, we have to ensure that we don't sacrifice adequate content coverage. In par-ticular, if the construct is formative, truncation for reasons other than to improve construct validity will damage the validity of the scale, since each indicator contributes unique information to the construct.

Use of archival data to create analogue scales. Tremble, Payne, Finch, and Bullis (2003) employed a novel method for measuring commitment in governmental databases, which tend to be large and longitudinal but often do not include formal measures of commitment. Essentially, creating an *analogue* scale amounts to scouring the scales that were actually administered for items that appear to tap the commitment construct of interest; once a pool of possible commitment items is identified, methods discussed earlier for developing new measures can be used to create an analogue, or surrogate, scale of the construct. But, one issue to be mindful of is that this approach involves modeling the surrogate on an existing measure of the construct, and thus presumes that this existing scale is itself a valid measure. If it's not, then a surrogate will duplicate its weaknesses as well. For example, Tremble et al. (2003), following Meyer and Allen (1984), sought out surrogate continuance commitment items that tapped both the "high sacrifices" and "low alternatives" dimensions of the CCS scale, and succeeded. But, since the low-alternatives items probably measure another construct, they should have just included high-sacrifice items in their surrogate scale.

Conclusion: Measuring What's Inside the "Black Box" of Commitment

This chapter has sought to review what we know about the measurement of work commitment and offer ideas about how we can add to what we know. However, in doing so, we must bear in mind that as we employ methods to close the gap between what our instruments measure and what the underlying commitment construct is, we could be trying to hit a moving target. As the nature of work changes, work commitment targets and outcomes may change as well. Thirty years ago, when many employees expected to spend their careers at a single firm, a "desire to remain" in one's organization or union might have been the most salient outcome of commitment, but today it might be a willingness to innovate during the short time that both the employee and the organization expect to be together. Thus, if one believes that commitment constructs and measures should include behavioral terms or intentions (cf. Brown, 1996), then scales that were valid measures of organizational commitment at one point in time, may, as time goes by, reflect it less and less accurately. Also, these developments could mean that employees are experiencing commitment to new targets, such as commitment to change initiatives (Herscovitch & Meyer, 2002; Meyer et al., 2007), commitment to customers (Vandenberghe et al., 2007), or commitment to Web site use (Li, Browne, & Chau, 2006), which weren't viewed as salient in earlier times. This implies the need to develop commitment measures that reflect these new workplace realities.

The possibility that traditional theories and measures of commitment, most of which were developed between the 1960s and 1980s, might be out of touch with changing employment conditions underlies the recent development of work-related attitudes that appear to be closely related to organizational commitment, such as job embeddedness (Mitchell, Holtom, Lee, Sablynski, & Erez, 2001), global job attitude (Harrison, Newman, & Roth, 2006), job engagement (Vinje & Mittelmark, 2007), the psychological contract (Rousseau & Wade-Benzoni, 1995), and psychological collectivism (Jackson, Wesson, Colquitt, & Zapata-Phelan, 2006). To an extent, each has emerged in response to perceived deficiencies in how well longstanding conceptualizations of attitudes such as commitment and job satisfaction fit today's changing work environment. It is also a chief concern of this volume, which has focused on the adequacy of our theories of commitment.

By providing the data that act as feedback in the theory refinement process, measurement plays a key role in keeping our commitment theories relevant. Research results, particularly those that don't comport with theorized expectations, provide feedback about the validity of our theories of work commitment. Thus, perhaps the most important current contribution measurement could make is to help us refine theory about exactly what "commitment" is. Almost 50 years ago, H. Becker (1960) noted that commitment "has been treated as a primitive concept, introduced as the need is felt without examination of its character... and made to cover a wide range of common-sense meanings, with predictable ambiguities" (p.32). Today, there is still a sense that at the core of existing models of commitment is a theoretical "black box" (Swailes, 2002): the concept of commitment itself has been undertheorized.

As reviewed by Klein et al. (this volume), that has begun to change. Brown (1996) defined commitment as, in essence, an "obliging force" that leads to continuity of action in the face of changing circumstances, and said that it has focus, strength, and terms. Meyer and Herscovitch (2001) argue that the essence of commitment is a "force that binds" one to a course of action of relevance to a target. Klein et al. (2006) and T. Becker (2005) define commitment as a psychological state reflecting a "bond" with a target. All definitions share in common the notions that commitment (1) is something that is *binding* for the employee, (2) varies in *strength*, and (3) has a *target*. The latter two are relatively unproblematic: measuring the target is a matter of including item wording that specifies whether the commitment is to the organization, the team, a change initiative, a project, and so forth. Measuring strength means tapping shadings, for example, by offering response options such as "strongly agree" and "somewhat disagree" that allow us to gauge the intensity of the commitment.

However, differences revolve around (a) the issue of behavioral referents as part of commitment, as discussed earlier, and (b) whether commitment is a force or a bond. Klein et al. (2006) and T. Becker (2005) argue that behavioral terms are outcomes of commitment, not part of the construct, and thus, such wording should be omitted from commitment scale items. This argument also pertains to item wording that reflects *antecedents* of commitment, such as value congruence or identification with the organization (as in the OCQ); item wording should reflect commitment itself, not causes or consequences. In contrast, Meyer and Herscovitch (2001) and Brown (1996) argue that behavioral terms are characteristic of commitment itself and thus should be included in item wording. Earlier in this paper, I discussed why I believe that on this point, the Klein et al. and T. Becker approach is better.

T. Becker (2005) and Klein et al. (2006) emphasize that commitment is a *bond* one has with a target, and agree that the bond should be measured. Klein et al. also posit that employees develop rationales for their commitment and that these rationales interact with the bond to influence outcomes. To both Klein et al. and T. Becker, the bond may be either perceived or not perceived. Measuring a bond that is not perceived might be problematic, in that the act of asking an employee to respond to a commitment questionnaire item will seemingly either prompt them to reflect on their bond, at which point they become aware of it and it is no longer unperceived, or else the bond is so deeply unconscious that the prompt fails to cause them to think of the bond, which therefore remains unperceived, and in which case the employee likely will answer the item with a response such as "disagree," which the researcher will then mistakenly interpret as indicating a lack of commitment. Perhaps an unperceived bond can only be measured indirectly, via its effect on behavior. Alternatively, it might be possible to use other raters, such as supervisors or coworkers, to assess a given employee's unperceived bond (cf. Goffin & Gellatly, 2001).

In contrast, Brown (1996) and Meyer and Herscovitch (2001) define the essence of commitment as the *force* that binds one to a target, but between these researchers there are differences as well: Meyer and Herscovitch propose that (a) commitment is experienced by the employee as one of three "mindsets," (b) the force is difficult to measure, and even if it can be measured, doing so would be moot, because (c) the force is always experienced as a mindset (e.g., desire, obligation, need), and it is the mindset that influences behavior. Thus, they argue we should devote our efforts to measuring the mindsets. In contrast, Brown says that the force can and should be measured, albeit using wording that reflects a sense of pledge and obligation, which Meyer would consider reflective of a mindset.

Though inherently theoretical in nature, the resolution of the bond/ force issue might be assisted by measurement. First, those who think it is worthwhile to measure either the "binding force" or the "bond," be it perceived or not, such as Brown (1996), T. Becker (2005), and Klein et al. (2006), have to succeed in doing so, and with or without reference to any behavioral or antecedent terms. Perhaps a single item measure, such as "I am committed to this organization" or "I am pledged to this organization," could suffice to measure these theorized essences. But in practice, until either is accomplished, the Meyer and Herscovitch (2001) position will likely be the default position adopted by researchers, since they have provided measures of their key constructs. It could be that the essence of commitment is not so much a "black box" but a "black hole," an object that cannot be measured directly, but only indirectly via mindsets.

If scales that tap the binding force or bond are developed, then the competing positions can be assessed empirically. We could construct substantive models that compare the relative efficacy of Meyer & Herscovitch's (2001) mindsets + target scale items against Brown's (1996) obliging force + target scale items, Klein et al.'s (2006) perceived bond + target and rationales scales, and T. Becker's (2005) bond + target scale, all on relevant outcomes. By thus penetrating the black box and determining what commitment *is*, we'd be addressing the greatest measurement challenge in commitment research.

References

Adler, P., & Adler, P. (1988). Intense loyalty in organizations: A case study of college athletics. *Administrative Science Quarterly, 33*, 401–417.

Al-Hindawe, J. (1996). Considerations when constructing a semantic-differential scale. *La Trobe Papers in Linguistics, 9*, 1996.

Allen, N. (2003). Organizational commitment in the military: A discussion of theory and practice. *Military Psychology, 15*, 237–253.

Allen, N. J., & Meyer, J. P. (1990). The measurement and antecedents of affective, continuance and normative commitment to the organization. *Journal of Occupational Psychology, 63*, 1–18.

Ashforth, B., & Mael, F. (1989). Social identity theory and the organization. *Academy of Management Review, 14*, 20–39.

Aube, C., & Rousseau, V. (2005). Team goal commitment and team effectiveness: The role of task interdependence and supportive behaviors. *Group Dynamics: Theory, Research, and Practice, 9*, 189–204.

Barker, J. R. (1993). Tightening the iron cage: Concertive control in self-managing teams. *Administrative Science Quarterly, 38*, 408–437.

Barnette, J. (2000). Effects of stem and Likert response option reversals on survey internal consistency: If you feel the need, there is a better alternative to using those negatively worded stems. *Educational and Psychological Measurement, 60,* 361–370.

Bayazit, M., Hammer, T., & Wazeter, D. (2004). Methodological challenges in union commitment studies. *Journal of Applied Psychology. 89,* 738–747.

Becker, H. S. (1960). Notes on the concept of commitment. *American Journal of Sociology, 66,* 32–42.

Becker, T. E. (1992). Foci and bases of commitment: Are they distinctions worth making? *Academy of Management Journal, 35,* 232–244.

Becker, T. E. (2005). *Problems of commitment.* Paper presented at the Conference on Commitment, Columbus, OH.

Becker, T. E. (2006). Concept *redundancy among forms and bases of commitment.* Paper presented at the 21st Annual Conference of the Society for Industrial and Organizational Psychology, Dallas, TX.

Becker, T. E. Interpersonal commitments (this volume).

Becker, T. E., Billing, R. S., Eveleth, D. M., & Gilbert, N. L. (1996). Foci and bases of employee commitment: Implications for job performance. *Academy of Management Journal, 39,* 464–482.

Becker, T. E., Randall, D. M., & Riegel, C. D. (1995). The multidimensional view of commitment and the theory of reasoned action: A comparative evaluation. *Journal of Management, 21,* 617–638.

Bentein, K., Vandenberghe, C., Vandenberg, R., & Stinglhamber, F. (2005). The role of change in the relationship between commitment and turnover: A latent growth modeling approach. *Journal of Applied Psychology, 90,* 468–482.

Bergman, M. (2006). The relationship between affective and normative commitment: Review and research agenda. *Journal of Organizational Behavior, 27,* 645–663.

Bishop, J. W., Scott, K. D., & Burroughs, S. M. (2000). Support, commitment, and employee outcomes in a team environment. *Journal of Management, 26,* 1113–1132.

Bishop, J., Scott, J., Goldsby, M., & Cropanzano, R. A. (2005). Construct validity study of commitment and perceived support variables: A multifoci approach across different team environments. *Group and Organization Management, 30,* 153–180.

Blau, G., & Holladay, E. (2006). Testing the discriminant validity of a four dimensional occupational commitment measure. *Journal of Occupational and Organizational Psychology. 79,* 691–704.

Blau, G., Paul, A., & St. John, N. (1993). On developing a general index of work commitment. *Journal of Vocational Behavior, 42,* 298–314.

Boezeman, E., & Ellemers, N. (2007). Volunteering for charity: Pride, respect, and the commitment of volunteers. *Journal of Applied Psychology, 92,* 771–785.

Bozeman, D. B., & Perrewe, P. L. (2001). The effect of item content overlap on Organizational Commitment Questionnaire-turnover cognitions relationships. *Journal of Applied Psychology, 86,* 16–25.

Brown, R. (1996). Organizational commitment: Clarifying the concept and simplifying the existing construct typology. *Journal of Vocational Behavior, 49,* 230–251.

Buchanan, B. (1974). Building organizational commitment: The socialisation of manners in work organizations. *Administrative Science Quarterly, 19,* 533–546.

Chan, D. (2001). Method effects of positive affectivity, negative affectivity, and impression management in self-reports of work attitudes. *Human Performance, 14,* 77–96.

Chang, H., Chi, N., & Miao, M. (2007). Testing the relationship between three component organizational/occupational commitment and organizational/occupational turnover intention using a non-recursive model. *Journal of Vocational Behavior, 70,* 352–368.

Chen, Z., & Francesco, A. (2003). Relationship between the three components of commitment and employee performance in China. *Journal of Vocational Behavior, 62,* 490–510.

Cheng, Y., & Stockdale, M. S. (2003). The validity of the three-component model of organizational commitment in a Chinese context. *Journal of Vocational Behavior, 62,* 465–489.

Clark, M. S., & Fiske, S. T. (1982). Affect and cognition. Hillsdale, NJ: Erlbaum.

Clugston, M., Howell, J. P., & Dorfman, P. W. (2000). Does cultural socialization predict multiple bases and foci of commitment? *Journal of Management, 26,* 5–30.

Cohen, A. (1993). Work commitment in relation to withdrawal intentions and union effectiveness. *Journal of Business Research, 26,* 75–90.

Cohen, A. (2003). *Multiple commitments at work: An integrative approach.* Hillsdale, NJ: Lawrence Erlbaum.

Cohen, A. (2006). The relationship between multiple commitments and organizational citizenship behaviors in Arab and Jewish cultures. *Journal of Vocational Behavior, 69,* 105–118.

Cohen, A. (2007). An examination of the relationship between commitments and culture among five cultural groups of Israeli teachers. *Journal of Cross-Cultural Psychology, 38,* 34–49.

Cohen, A. (2007). Commitment before and after: An evaluation and reconceptualization commitment. *Human Resource Management Review, 17,* 336–354.

Cole, M., Bedeian, A., & Field, H. (2006). The measurement equivalence of web-based and paper-and-pencil measures of transformational leadership. *Organizational Research Methods, 9,* 339–368.

Cook, J., & Wall, T. (1980). New work attitude measures of trust, organisational commitment and personal need non-fulfillment. *Journal of Occupational Psychology. 53,* 39–52.

Cooksey, R., & Soutar, G. (2006). Coefficient Beta and hierarchical item clustering. *Organizational Research Methods, 9:* 78–98.

Cooper-Hakim, A., & Viswesvaran, C. (2005). The construct of work commitment: Testing an integrative framework. *Psychological Bulletin, 131,* 241–59.

Coyle-Shapiro, J. A.-M., Morrow, P. C. (2006). Organizational and client commitment among contracted employees. *Journal of Vocational Behavior. 68,* 416–431.

Culpepper, R. (2000). A test of revised scales for the Meyer and Allen (1991) three-component commitment construct. *Educational and Psychological Measurement, 60,* 604–616.

Dawley, D., Stephens, R., & Stephens, D. (2005). Dimensionality of organizational commitment in volunteer workers: Chamber of commerce board members and role fulfillment. *Journal of Vocational Behavior, 67*, 511–525.

DeShon, R., & Landis, R. S. (1997). The dimensionality of the Hollenbeck, Williams, and Klein (1989) measure of goal commitment on complex tasks. *Organizational Behavior and Human Decision Processes, 70*, 105–116.

Edwards, J. (2001). Multidimensional constructs in organizational behavior research: An integrative framework. *Organizational Research Methods, 4*, 144–192.

Edwards, J. R., & Bagozzi, R. P. (2000). On the nature and direction of relationships between constructs and measures. *Psychological Methods, 5*, 155–174.

Erdheim, J., Wang, M., & Zickar, M. (2006). Linking the Big Five personality constructs to organizational commitment. *Personality and Individual Differences, 41*, 959–970.

Etzioni, A. (1961). *A comparative analysis of complex organizations.* New York: Free Press.

Gade, P., Tiggle, R., & Schumm, W. (2003). The measurement and consequences of military organizational commitment in soldiers and spouses. *Military Psychology, 15*, 191–207.

Gautam, T., Van Dick, R., & Wagner, U. (2004). Organizational identification and organizational commitment: Distinct aspects of two related concepts. *Asian Journal of Social Psychology, 7*, 301–315.

Gautam, T., Van Dick, R., Wagner, U., Upadhyay, N., & Davis, A. J. (2005). Organizational citizenship behavior and organizational commitment in Nepal. *Asian Journal of Social Psychology, 8*, 305–314.

Gellatly, I., Meyer, J., & Luchak, A. (2006). Combined effects of the three commitment components on focal and discretionary behaviors: A test of Meyer and Herscovitch's propositions. *Journal of Vocational Behavior, 69*, 331–345.

Goffin, R., & Gellatly, I. (2001). A multi-rater assessment of organizational commitment: Are self-report measures biased? *Journal of Organizational Behavior, 22*, 437–451.

Gordon, M. E., Philpot, J. W., Burt, R. E., Thompson, C. A., & Spiller, W. E. (1980). Commitment to the union: Development of a measure and an examination of its correlates [Monograph]. *Journal of Applied Psychology, 65*, 479–499.

Harrison, D. A., Newman, D. A., & Roth, P. L. (2006). How important are job attitudes? Meta-analytic comparisons for integrative behavioral outcomes and time sequences. *Academy of Management Journal, 49*, 305–326.

Hartog, D., & Belschak, F. (2007). Personal initiative, commitment, and affect at work. *Journal of Occupational and Organizational Psychology, 80*, 601–622.

Haslam, S., Ryan, M., Postmes, T., Spears, R., Jetten, J., & Webley, P. (2006). Sticking to our guns: Social identity as a basis for the maintenance of commitment to faltering organizational projects. *Journal of Organizational Behavior, 27*, 607–628.

Herscovitch, L., & Meyer, J. P. (2002). Commitment to organizational change: Extension of a three-component model. *Journal of Applied Psychology, 87*, 474–487.

Hinkin, T. (1995). A review of scale development practices in the study of organizations. *Journal of Management, 21*, 967–988.

Hollenbeck, J., & Klein, H. (1987). Goal commitment and the goal-setting process: Problems, prospects, and proposals for future research. *Journal of Applied Psychology, 72*, 212–220.

Hollenbeck, J. R., Williams, C. L., & Klein, H. J. (1989). An empirical examination of the antecedents of commitment to difficult goals. *Journal of Applied Psychology, 74*, 18–23.

Horn, P. W., & Griffith, R. W. (1995). *Employee turnover.* Cincinnati, OH: South-Western College Publishing.

Hrebiniak, L., & Alutto, J. (1972). Personal and role-related factors in the development of organizational commitment. *Administrative Science Quarterly, 17*, 555–573.

Jackson, C., Wesson, M., Colquitt, J., & Zapata-Phelan, C. (2006). Psychological collectivism: A measurement validation and linkage to group member performance. *Journal of Applied Psychology, 91*, 884–899.

Jahoda, M. (1956). Psychological issues in civil liberties. *American Psychologist, 11*, 234–240.

Jaros, S. (1997). An assessment of Meyer & Allen's (1991) three-component model of organizational commitment and turnover intentions. *Journal of Vocational Behavior, 51*, 319–337.

Jaros, S. (2007). Measurement issues in the Meyer and Allen model of organizational commitment. *ICFAI Journal of Organizational Behavior, 6*: 7–25.

Jaros, S. J., Jermier, J. M., Koehler, J. W., & Sincich, T. (1993). Effects of continuance, affective, and moral commitment on the withdrawal process: An evaluation of eight structural equation models. *Academy of Management Journal, 36*, 951–995.

Jaussi, K. (2007). Attitudinal commitment: A three-dimensional construct. *Journal of Occupational and Organizational Psychology, 80*, 51–61.

Jick, T. (1979) Mixing qualitative and quantitative methods: Triangulation in action. *Administrative Science Quarterly, 24*, 602–611.

Johnson, M., Caughlin, J., & Huston, T. (1999). The tripartite nature of marital commitment: Personal, moral, and structural reasons to stay married. *Journal of Marriage and the Family, 61*, 160–177.

Kanter, R. (1968). Commitment and social organization: A study of commitment mechanisms in utopian communities. *American Sociological Review, 33*, 499–517.

Keisler, C., & Sakamura, J. (1966). A test of a model for commitment. *Journal of Personality and Social Psychology, 3*, 349–353.

Kelman, H. (1958). Compliance, identification, and internalization: Three processes of attitude change. *Journal of Conflict Resolution, 2*, 51–60.

Kim, S., & Hagtvet, K. (2003). The impact of misspecified item parceling on representing latent variables in covariance structure modeling: A simulation study. *Structural Equation Modeling, 10*, 101–127.

Klein, H., Brinsfield, C., & Molloy, J. (2006). *Understanding workplace commitments independent of antecedents, targets, rationales, and consequences.* Paper presented at the 2006 Academy of Management Meetings, Atlanta, GA.

Klein, H., Molloy, J., & Cooper, J. Conceptual foundations: Construct definitions and theoretical representations of workplace commitment (this volume).

Klein, H. J., Wesson, M. J., Hollenbeck, J. R., Wright, P. M., & DeShon, R. P. (2001). The assessment of goal commitment: A measurement model meta-analysis. *Organizational Behavior and Human Decision Processes, 85,* 32–55.

Kline, C., & Peters, L. (1991). Behavioral commitment and tenure of new employees: A replication and extension. *Academy of Management Journal, 34,* 194–204.

Kunda, G. (1992). *Engineering culture: Control and commitment in a high-tech corporation.* Philadelphia: Temple University Press.

Lamastro, V. (2006). Commitment and perceived organizational support. *National Forum of Applied Educational Research Journal-Electronic.* 20, 3.2.

Law, K., & Wong, C. (1999). Multidimensional constructs in structural equation analysis: An illustration using the job perception and job satisfaction constructs. *Journal of Management, 25,* 143–160.

Lee, K., Carswell, J., & Allen, N. (2000). A meta-analytic review of occupational commitment: Relations with person- and work-related variables. *Journal of Applied Psychology, 85,* 799–811.

Li, D., Browne, G., & Chau, P. (2006). An empirical investigation of web-site use using a commitment-based model. *Decision Sciences, 37,* 427–444.

Lissitz, R. W., & Green, S. B. (1975). Effect of the number of scale points on reliability: A Monte Carlo approach. *Journal of Applied Psychology, 60,* 10–13.

Locke, E. A., & Latham G. P. (1990). *A theory of goal setting and task performance.* Englewood Cliffs, NJ: Prentice Hall International.

Luchak, A., & Gellatly, I. (2007). A comparison of linear and non-linear relations between organizational commitment and work outcomes. *Journal of Applied Psychology, 92,* 786–793.

MacCallum, R. C., Widaman, K. F., Zhang, S., & Hong, S. (1999). Sample size in factor analysis. *Psychological Methods, 4,* 84–99.

Mackenzie, S., Podsakoff, P., & Jarvis, C. (2005). The problem of measurement model misspecification in behavioral and organizational research and some recommended solutions. *Journal of Applied Psychology, 90,* 710–730.

Magazine, S. L., Williams, L. J., & Williams, M. (1996). A confirmatory factor analysis examination of reverse-coding effects in Meyer and Allen's affective and continuance commitment scales. *Educational and Psychological Measurement, 56,* 241–245.

Malhotra, Y., & Galleta, D. (2005). A multidimensional commitment model of volitional systems adoption and usage behavior. *Journal of Management Information Systems, 22,* 117–151.

Mathews, B., & Shepherd, J. (2002). Dimensionality of Cook and Wall's (1980) British Organizational Commitment Scale revisited. *Journal of Occupational and Organizational Psychology, 75,* 369–375.

Mathieu, J., & Zajac, D. (1990). A review and meta-analysis of the antecedents, correlates, and consequences of organizational commitment. *Psychological Bulletin, 108,* 171–194.

McCaul, H., Hinsz, V., & McCaul, K. (1995). Assessing organizational commitment: An employee's global attitude toward the organization. *Journal of Applied Behavioral Science, 31,* 80–90.

McGee, G. W., & Ford, R. C. (1987). Two (or more?) dimensions of organizational commitment: Reexamination of the affective and continuance commitment scales. *Journal of Applied Psychology, 72,* 638–642.

Meade, A., & Kroustalis, C. (2006). Problems with item parceling for CFA tests of measurement invariance. *Organizational Research Methods, 9,* 369–403.

Meade, A., & Lautenschlager, G. (2004). A comparison of item response theory and confirmatory factor analytic methodologies for establishing measurement equivalence/invariance. *Organizational Research Methods, 7,* 361–388.

Messick, S. (1995). Validity of psychological assessment. *American Psychologist, 50,* 741–749.

Meyer, J. P. (1997). Organizational commitment. In C. L. Cooper & I. T. Robertson (Eds.), *International Review of Industrial Organizational Psychology, 12,* 176–228.

Meyer, J. The relevance of commitment in the changing world of work. (This volume).

Meyer, J., & Allen, N. (1984). Testing the "side bet theory" of organizational commitment: Some methodological considerations. *Journal of Applied Psychology, 69,* 372–378.

Meyer, J. P., & Allen, N. J. (1997). *Commitment in the workplace: Theory, research, and application.* Newbury Park, CA: Sage.

Meyer, J. P., Allen, N. J., & Smith, C., (1993). Commitment to organizations and occupations: Extension and test of a three-component conceptualization. *Journal of Applied Psychology, 78,* 538–551.

Meyer, J., Becker, T., & Van Dick, R. (2006). Social identities and commitments at work: Toward an integrative model. *Journal of Organizational Behavior, 27,* 665–683.

Meyer, J. P., & Herscovitch, L. (2001). Commitment in the workplace: Toward a general model. *Human Resource Management Review, 11,* 299–326.

Meyer, J., Srinivas, E., Lal, J., & Topolyntsky, L. (2007). Employee commitment and support for organizational change: Test of the three-component model in two cultures. *Journal of Occupational and Organizational Psychology, 80,* 185–211.

Meyer, J. P., Stanley, D. J., Herscovitch, L., & Topolnytsky, L. (2002). Affective, continuance and normative commitment to the organization: A meta-analysis of antecedents, correlates, and consequences. *Journal of Vocational Behavior, 61,* 20–52.

Mitchell, T. R., Holtom, B. C., Lee, T. W., Sablynski, C. J., & Erez, M. (2001). Why people stay: Using job embeddedness to predict voluntary turnover. *Academy of Management Journal, 44,* 1102–1121.

Mobley, W. H., Horner, S. O., & Hollingsworth, A. T. (1978). An evaluation of the precursors of hospital employee turnover. *Journal of Applied Psychology, 63,* 408–414.

Morrow, P. C. (1983). Concept redundancy in organizational research: The case of work commitment. *Academy of Management Review, 8,* 486–500.

Morrow, P. C. (1993). *The theory and measurement of work commitment.* Greenwich, CT: JAI Press.

Mowday, R. T., Porter, L. W., & Steers, R. M. (1982). *Employee-organizational linkages: The psychology of commitment, absenteeism, and turnover.* New York: Academic Press.

Neubert, M., & Wu, C. Action commitments (this volume).

Nunnally, J. (1978). *Psychometric theory, 2nd Edition.* New York: McGraw-Hill.

O'Reilly, C., & Caldwell, D. (1980). Job choice: The impact of intrinsic and extrinsic factors on subsequent satisfaction and commitment. *Journal of Applied Psychology, 65,* 559–565.

O'Reilly, C., & Chatman, J. (1986). Organizational commitment and psychological attachment: The effects of compliance, identification, and internalization on prosocial behavior. *Journal of Applied Psychology, 71,* 492–499.

O'Reilly, C., Chatman, J., & Caldwell, D. (1991). People and organizational culture: A profile-comparison approach to assessing person-organization fit. *Academy of Management Journal, 34,* 487–516.

Penley, L., & Gould, S. (1988). Etzioni's model of organizational involvement: A perspective for understanding commitment to organizations. *Journal of Organizational Behavior, 9,* 43–59.

Porter, L. W., Steers, R. M., Mowday, R. T., & Boulian, P. V. (1974). Organizational commitment, job satisfaction, and turnover among psychiatric technicians. *Journal of Applied Psychology, 59,* 603–609.

Powell, D., & Meyer, J. (2004). Side-bet theory and the three-component model of organizational commitment. *Journal of Vocational Behavior, 65,* 157–177.

Randall, D. M., Fedor, D. B., and Longenecker, C. O. (1990). The behavioural expression of organizational commitment. *Journal of Vocational Behavior, 36,* 210–224.

Ravlin, E. C., & Meglino, B. M. (1989). The transitivity of work values: Hierarchical preference ordering of socially desirable stimuli. *Organizational Behavior and Human Decision Processes, 44,* 494–508.

Reichers, A. E. (1985). A review and reconceptualization of organizational commitment. *Academy of Management Review, 10,* 465–476.

Riketta, M., & Van Dick, R. Commitment's place in the literature (this volume).

Ritzer, G., & Trice, H. M. (1969). An empirical study of Howard Becker's side-bet theory. *Social Forces, 47,* 475–479.

Rousseau, D. M., & Wade-Benzoni, K. A. (1995). Changing individual-organizational attachments: A two-way street. In A. Howard (Ed.), *The changing nature of work.* New York: Jossey-Bass.

Rusbult, C., & Farrell, D. (1983). A longitudinal test of the investment model: Impact on job satisfaction, job commitment, and turnover of variations in rewards, costs, alternatives, and investments. *Journal of Applied Psychology, 68,* 429–438.

Salancik, G. R. (1977). Commitment and the control of organizational behavior and belief. In B. Staw & G. Salancik (Eds.), *New directions in organizational behavior* (pp. 1–54). Chicago: St. Clair.

Sass, D., & Smith, P. (2006). The effects of parceling unidimensional scales on structural parameter estimates in structural equation modeling. *Structural Equation Modeling, 13,* 566–586.

Schriesheim, C. A., & Eisenbach, R. J. (1995). An exploratory and confirmatory factor-analytic investigation of item wording effects on the obtained factor structures of survey questionnaire measures. *Journal of Management, 21,* 1177–1193.

Schwab, D. (1980). Construct validity in organizational behavior. *Research in Organizational Behavior, 2*, 3–43.

Stark, S., Chernyshenko, O., & Drasgow, F. (2006). Detecting differential item functioning with CFA and IRT: Toward a unified strategy. *Journal of Applied Psychology, 91*, 1292–1306.

Staw, B. (1997). The escalation of commitment: an update and appraisal. In Z. Shapiro (Ed.), *Organizational Decision Making* (pp. 191–215). Cambridge, UK: Cambridge University Press.

Stinglhamber, F., Bentein, K., & Vandenberghe, C. (2002). Extension of the three-component model of commitment to five foci: development of measures and substantive test. *European Journal of Psychological Assessment, 18*, 123–138.

Sutton, C., & Harrison, W. (1993). Validity assessment of compliance, identification, and internalization as dimensions of organizational commitment. *Educational and Psychological Measurement, 53*, 217–223.

Swailes, S. (2002). Organizational commitment: A critique of the construct and measures. *International Journal of Management Reviews, 4*, 155–178.

Tisak, J., & Tisak, M. S. (2000). Permanency and ephemerality of psychological measures with application to organizational commitment. *Psychological Methods, 5*, 175–198.

Tremble, T., Payne, S., Finch, J., & Bullis, R. 2003. Opening organizational archives to research: Analog measures of organizational commitment. *Military Psychology, 15*, 167–190.

Tubbs, M. (1994). Commitment and the role of ability in motivation: Comment on Wright, O'Leary-Kelly, Cortina, Klein, and Hollenbeck (1994). *Journal of Applied Psychology, 79*, 804–811.

Ugboro, I. (2006). Organizational commitment, job redesign, employee empowerment and intent to quit among survivors of restructuring and downsizing. *Journal of Behavioral and Applied Management, 7*, 232–256.

Van Dick, R., Wagner, U., Stellmacher, J., & Christ, O. (2004). The utility of a broader conceptualization of organizational identification: Which aspects really matter? *Journal of Organizational and Occupational Psychology, 77*, 171–191.

Vandenburg, R., & Stanley, L. Methodological issues and opportunities: What evil lurks in the shadows of commitment research? (This volume).

Vandenberghe, C., Bentein, K., Michon, R., Chebat, J., Tremblay, M., & Fils, J. (2007). An examination of the role of perceived support and employee commitment in employee-customer encounters. *Journal of Applied Psychology, 92*, 1177–1187.

Vandenburghe, C. Organizational commitments (this volume).

Vinje, H., & Mittelmark, M. (2007). Job engagement's paradoxical role in nurse burnout. *Nursing and Health Sciences, 9*: 107–111.

Wanous, J., & Hudy, M. (2001). Single-item reliability: A replication and extension. *Organizational Research Methods, 4*, 361–375.

Wanous, J., Reichers, A., & Hudy, M. (1997). Overall job satisfaction: How good are single-item measures? *Journal of Applied Psychology, 82*, 247–252.

Wasti, S. (2003). Organizational commitment, turnover intentions, and the influence of cultural values. *Journal of Occupational and Organizational Psychology, 76*, 303–321.

Wasti, S., & Onder, C. Commitment across cultures (this volume).

Williams, L. J., & Anderson, S. E. (1994). An alternative approach to method effects by using latent-variable models: Applications in organizational behavior research. *Journal of Applied Psychology, 79,* 323–331.

Wright, P. M., O'Leary-Kelly, A. M., Cortina, J. M., Klein, H. J., & Hollenbeck, J. R. (1994). On the meaning and measurement of goal commitment. *Journal of Applied Psychology, 79,* 795–803.

12

Statistical and Methodological Challenges for Commitment Researchers: Issues of Invariance, Change Across Time, and Profile Differences

Robert J. Vandenberg and Laura J. Stanley
University of Georgia

A common theme underlying several of the substantively oriented chapters of this volume (chapter 1, Klein, Molloy, & Cooper; chapter 2, Meyer; chapter 3, Riketta & Van Dick; chapter 13, Becker, Klein, & Meyer) is the need to align our theoretical systems describing the role of commitment in a way that more accurately represents the nature of today's employer-employee relationships than is currently the case. Collectively, the chapters of this volume denote that understanding commitment's theoretical role in the contemporary workplace is complex. While this complexity is obvious, what may not be is that the adequate examination and testing of the proposed systems may not be undertaken solely using conventional (i.e., old) methodologies and analytical schemes.

Many of the complexities surrounding the theoretical role of commitment and its operationalization are due to changes in the definition of commitment. Early definitions focused on the behavioral nature of commitment. Becker (1960) suggests that "commitment comes into being when a person, by making a side bet, links extraneous interests with a consistent line of activity" (p. 32). However, recent definitions focus on the psychological nature of commitment. O'Reilly & Chatman (1986) suggest that commitment is "the psychological attachment felt by the person for the organization" (p. 493). Similarly, Meyer and Herscovitch (2001) state that "commitment is a psychological stabilizing or obliging force that binds individuals to courses of action relevant to the target of the force" (p. 358). Recognizing that many commitment measures capture behaviors rather than the psychological mindsets that determine behaviors, commitment researchers have stressed the need for new commitment measures (Meyer

& Herscovitch, 2001). However, they know that developing new commitment measures will be difficult.

One of the difficulties associated with measuring commitment is that it may consist of multiple mindsets. Meyer and Herscovitch (2001) suggest that "the psychological force [of commitment] is experienced as a mindset that can take different forms. These mindsets reflect distinguishable components of the underlying commitment construct" (p. 358). They suggest that the mindsets can be combined to reflect an individual's "commitment profile" (p. 308). Many commitment researchers endorse a multidimensional conceptualization of commitment that operationalizes the mindsets as affective, continuance, and normative commitment (Meyer & Allen, 1991). In addition, commitment researchers acknowledge that individuals experience commitment to multiple foci (organization, supervisor, workgroup, etc.). Measuring the commitment profile entails capturing all possible combinations of mindsets and foci and the interplay between them. Current commitment measures distinguish between the mindsets but fail to capture the complex interplay among them (Meyer & Herscovitch, 2001). As such, acknowledging commitment's theoretical role as a complex psychological state consisting of multiple mindsets requires an analytical scheme that operationalizes this complexity. For the purposes of this chapter, we adopt the Meyer and Herscovitch (2001) view that commitment consists of multiple mindsets, although this definition is not universally accepted (e.g., see chapters 1 and 5 of this volume).

Acknowledging commitment as a process also implies the notion of change. For example, Meyer and Allen (1991) suggest that an individual's organizational commitment develops over time. Similarly, other researchers suggest that individuals adjust their level of commitment based on organizational characteristics (Brockner, Tyler, & Cooper-Schneider, 1992; Meyer & Allen, 1991; Mowday, Porter, & Steers, 1982) and exchanges with the organization (Meyer & Allen, 1991). However, research regarding how commitment develops has been unsystematic (Meyer & Herscovitch, 2001; Meyer & Allen, 1991; Mowday et al., 1982; Reichers, 1985) in terms of the methods and models used. In addition, while several researchers have examined the interplay among commitment mindsets using cross-sectional research designs (Jaros, 1997; Watsi, 2005), few have examined the interplay among the different mindsets as they change over time. In sum, acknowledging commitment's theoretical role as a process requires that commitment researchers use methodologies that capture how commitment unfolds over time.

In addition, there is increasing recognition of the need to compare different groups due to the hypothetical differences between those groups that may make them differ in their commitment to the organization or some other target. However, as noted by Vandenberg and Lance (2000), a researcher should not simply assume that the measurement and structural properties of the commitment measure are the same (i.e., invariant) between the groups without first testing that assumption. If those properties are not invariant, then interpreting any observed differences in commitment scores between the groups, for example, becomes highly problematic. Vandenberg and Lance (2000) suggest that researchers perform measurement invariance tests before making cross-group comparisons. Otherwise, they may make a false inference concluding that the groups differed in some meaningful conceptual manner, when in reality the observed differences are due to a lack of measurement and/or structural invariance.

The overriding goal of the current chapter is to review developments within the methodological and statistical arenas that can perhaps meet these challenges. First, we review measurement invariance. We cover this topic first because measurement invariance is a necessary condition for many analyses, particularly those in which the conceptual premises entail comparing groups or involve some aspect of change across time within a group. Second, we will discuss latent growth modeling (LGM) as a method for analyzing longitudinal data, and in particular, as a means for operationalizing change as a latent variable. Third, we discuss latent variable mixture modeling approaches to analyzing cross-sectional and longitudinal data. We start with a review of latent profile analysis (LPA), a technique commonly used with cross-sectional data, and end with latent class growth modeling (LCGM).

Measurement Invariance

In several chapters of this volume (chapter 2, Meyer; chapter 4, Vandenberghe; chapter 5, Becker; chapter 7, Bergman, Benzer, & Henning; chapter 8, Wayne, Coyle-Shapiro, Eisenberger, Liden, Rousseau, & Shore; chapter 9, Wright & Kehoe; chapter 10, Wasti & Önder) the authors recognize the need for research in which there is an expectation about group differences, and thus, that the groups should be compared. Regardless of the conceptual reasons as to why groups may differ, the concern of this section is that testing many of the premises regarding group differences requires the use of identical measures or indicators in multiple samples. We illustrate this concern with the hypothetical model in Figure 12.1, in which three commitment mindsets (AFF = affective; NORM = normative; CONT = continuance) negatively impact turnover intention (TI), which in turn is expected to increase job search behaviors (JS).

Latent variables in Figure 12.1 are represented by ellipses, and individual response items are represented by boxes. Further, assume Group 1 in

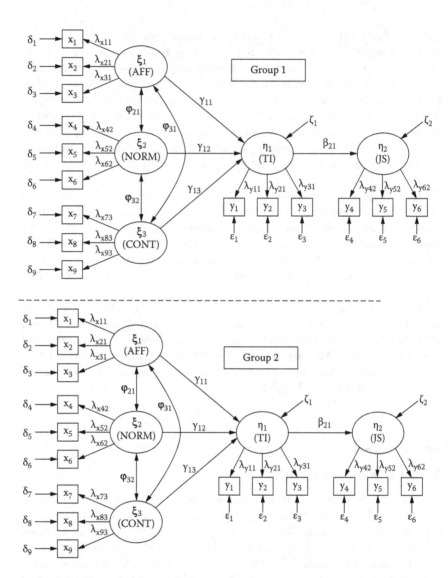

FIGURE 12.1
Structural model for cross-group comparisons.

Figure 12.1 consists of individuals at the start of their professional careers, and Group 2 consists of individuals near the end of their professional careers. Due to these career stage differences, our hypothetical researcher expects that the commitment mindsets are more meaningful to Group 1 than to Group 2. As such, it is also expected that the commitment mindsets will be stronger drivers of turnover intention in Group 1 than in Group 2. Let's assume the researcher tests this expectation by examining whether the paths from the mindsets to turnover intention in Group 1 differ significantly from the corresponding paths in Group 2. These paths are represented by γ_{11}, γ_{12}, and γ_{13} for both groups in Figure 12.1. Indeed, our fictitious researcher supports that expectation.

Unbeknownst to this researcher, however, is the fact that the factor loadings for the three commitment measures (Λg, or λ_{x11}, λ_{x21}, ... λ_{x93} from Figure 12.1) are much stronger in Group 1 than they are in Group 2. Therefore, it is highly likely that these differences in factor loadings caused the observed difference in the paths γ_{11}, γ_{12}, and γ_{13}. That is, because of the lack of invariance in factor loadings between the two groups, our researcher may inaccurately conclude that the differences between the groups in paths are due to some meaningful conceptual difference, when in reality it is due to the *undetected differences* in the factor loadings between the two groups. This lack of invariance presents a confound that precludes making meaningful substantive inferences because of the differences in the properties of the measures defining the constructs.

"Undetected differences" is emphasized because this is the typical state of affairs in most research even today. "Collectively, the crux of all of the research on measurement invariance is that cross-group comparisons, regardless of whether through traditional tests (e.g., regression) or for differences in structural equation modeling (SEM) parameters, *require* (i.e., demand) prerequisite assumptions of invariant measurement operations across the groups being compared" (Williams, Edwards, & Vandenberg, 2003, p. 921). It is beyond the scope of this chapter to provide a thorough technical treatment of the measurement invariance issues. Such a treatment is found in Vandenberg and Lance (2000), and in Ployhart and Oswald (2004; see also, Steenkampf & Baumgartner, 1998; Vandenberg, 2002). These references also include example syntax using the SEM package referred to as LISREL (Jöreskog & Sörbom, 1996). Further, the first author may be contacted for other examples using syntax from both LISREL and another statistical analysis with latent variables program, M*plus* (B. O. Muthén & L. K. Muthén, 1998–2006).

The reader may be wondering why these issues are not just applicable to SEM forms of analyses. As stated by Vandenberg and Lance (2000, p. 40), there are at least four reasons. First, if substantial measurement inequivalence exists across groups, it is inappropriate to compare the groups using nonequivalent measures even when the comparison may be between regression coefficients. Second, even if measurement equivalence exists, tests that are more traditional are rarely (if ever) preceded by tests of measurement invariance. Thus, tests of measurement invariance that support equivalence provide the justification for group differences tests because one enters the latter tests with a high degree of confidence that the groups were using identical cognitive frames of reference and were responding to items using the same metric. Third, tests of differences between latent means are disattenuated for measurement error because the latent means are derived from a measurement model in which both the true and error scores underlying item responses are accounted for in the analyses. Corrections for attenuation due to unreliability are rarely effected in more traditional tests (Schmidt & Hunter, 1996). Finally, in cases where perhaps only a few items do not possess invariance such as in the case of metric invariance, then a researcher may use a partial metric invariance strategy whereby those few items are freely estimated while the others are constrained to be invariant. (Byrne, Shavelson, & B. Muthén, 1989). This is just not possible in more traditional analytic approaches (Cole & White, 1993).

Thus, in the space allotted, what are our recommendations to the reader, particularly if the reader is unfamiliar with the issues? The first step is to read Vandenberg and Lance (2000), and Ployhart and Oswald (2004). These articles will help the reader become grounded and familiar with the language and the conceptual issues underlying the various tests for invariance. The second step is to conduct most of the invariance tests using a measurement model approach. That is, even if the ultimate goal is to test a conceptual model as presented in Figure 12.1, we recommend first examining the measurement model as presented in Figure 12.2.

Figure 12.2 is simply a reconfiguration of Figure 12.1 into what is commonly referred to as a confirmatory factor analysis (CFA) model. The terms "measurement model" and "CFA" are used interchangeably by many. A detailed explanation with syntax of CFA models is provided by Lance and Vandenberg (2001). In our hypothetical example, there would actually be two such measurement models, one for Group 1 and another for Group 2.

While many researchers regularly conduct CFAs, they are usually completed to demonstrate how well items hang together, and/or to point out evidence of convergent-discriminant validity. The latter uses are important, but they do not establish invariance as implied here even if the factor loadings (the λ values) appear the same. Rather, our recommendation stems purely from the fact that the very first invariance test between our fictitious groups is a test for configural invariance (Vandenberg & Lance, 2000). This is a test of the null hypothesis that the a priori pattern (i.e., configuration) of free and fixed factor loadings imposed on the measures' components (e.g., items) is equivalent across groups (Horn & McArdle, 1992). This test is based on the premise that the factor structure is a reasonable empirical map of the underlying conceptual or cognitive frame of reference used to make item responses (Vandenberg & Self, 1993). Therefore, if the null hypothesis fails, this means that members of both groups were responding to the same items *using different constructs*. For example, individuals from high and low power-distance countries may have very different conceptualizations of affective commitment to their supervisors. The items, "I enjoy discussing my supervisor with people

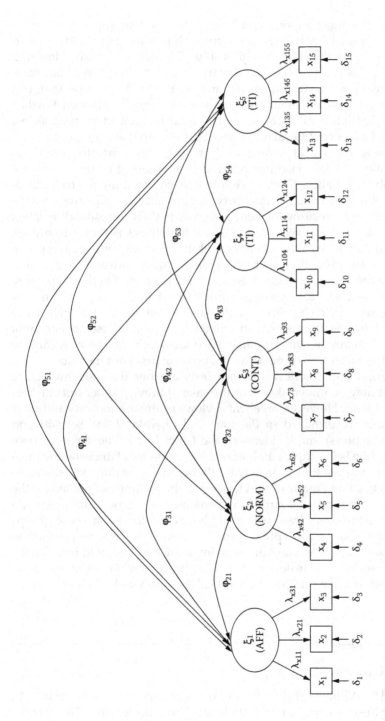

FIGURE 12.2
Measurement model for cross-group comparisons.

outside of the organization," and "I really feel as if my supervisor's problems are my own," may be meaningful to those possessing a low power-distance because they have a relationship with their supervisor. However, for those possessing high power distance, a frame of reference connoting an affective bond to the supervisor may not exist. Most important, this means that the researcher may not compare the groups as planned. Further, resorting to traditional regression analysis, as mentioned above, does not make the lack of configural invariance between groups disappear.

Assuming configural invariance is tenable, the next step examines the equality of factor loadings referred to as a test of metric invariance (Vandenberg & Lance, 2000). It is effected by constraining the factor loading (λ_{ik}) of like items to be equal between groups. Factor loadings are the regression slopes relating the item responses to their corresponding latent variables, ξ_j (Bollen, 1989). Thus, the null hypothesis is that both groups calibrated their items to the latent variable in the same way (e.g., a response of 3 means the same thing to both groups). If metric invariance is untenable, then the researcher cannot assume that members of both groups were using the same metric when responding to the items (e.g., a 3 rating means different things). Depending on the severity of the metric invariance issue (one item vs. the majority in a given measure), the researcher cannot proceed with any meaningful analysis from which inferences regarding group differences will be made without coping first with the issue.

Configural and metric invariance tests are not the only invariance tests that may be undertaken. For the sake of brevity, other tests are not presented here. However, excellent reviews of invariance tests and their sequencing are provided in Ployhart and Oswald (2004), Schmitt and Kuljanin (in press), and Vandenberg and Lance (2000). The major purpose of this section is to simply emphasize the importance of undertaking measurement invariance tests. As noted at the beginning of this chapter, a common theme among many of the chapters in this volume is broadening the scope of commitment research into domains where group differences are expected. At the very least, we should have confidence that these groups are using the same conceptual frame of references when responding to our measures. Further, measurement invariance tests should be required (i.e., demanded), regardless of whether the researcher ultimately tests hypotheses using a traditional analytical approach such as regression.

Latent Growth Modeling

As noted by Williams et al. (2003), one of the advanced applications of SEM has been the modeling of intraindividual change across time. This form of modeling has been variably called latent growth model (LGM), the latent growth curve model, level and shape model, latent trajectory model, random effects model, and random coefficients modeling (Hamaker, 2005). The names simply reflect that interest in the analysis of intraindividual change has two historical roots: one out of the random coefficients/multilevel modeling tradition (the last two names), and another from an SEM perspective (the first three names). The former tradition is best represented contemporarily by Singer and Willet (2003), while the latter is best represented by Bollen and Curran (2006). We use the name latent growth modeling throughout this section, reflecting that we follow an SEM tradition.

In chapter 11 of this volume, Jaros identified a key issue underlying the measurement of commitment: the need for longitudinal studies that capture how the process of becoming more or less committed across time is driven by other constructs and/or is a driver of other constructs. Examples of LGM in the study of the commitment process are emerging (Tisak & Tisak, 2000; Bentein, Vandenberg, Vandenberghe, & Stinglhamber, 2005; Lance, Vandenberg, & Self, 2000). In all cases, the authors focused on isolating intraindividual trajectories of change in commitment or commitment mindsets, and examining whether explanatory variables accounted for the individual differences in the rate of change and/or whether the differences in the rate of change accounted for variability in a set of criterion variables. What makes LGM fundamentally different from traditional longitudinal approaches is that "change" is captured as a latent variable in and of itself; that is, the dynamic nature of the construct is operationalized. No other analytical technique does this (see pp. 3–4 of Duncan, Duncan, Strycker, Li, & Alpert, 1999).

The following is a summary of the fundamentals underlying LGM. Excellent comprehensive technical treatments are provided in Bollen and Curran (2006), Duncan et al. (1999), and Singer and Willet (2003). Further, Chan (1998, 2002), and Lance, Meade, and Williamson (2000) provide less technical, yet excellent, overviews of LGM as well. Also, the first author may be contacted if the reader would like to request example syntax using both LISREL (Jöreskog & Sörbom, 1996) and another statistical analysis with latent variables program called M*plus* (L. K. Muthén & B. O. Muthén, 1998–2006).

The model in Figure 12.3 is overly simplistic and used here to simply familiarize the reader with underlying terminology and basic principles. Ellipses denote latent variables, while boxes represent observed variables. There are three observed variables in this example, one each for a measure of affective commitment taken at three time periods (AFF – T1, etc.). There could be as many time periods as desired, but three is the minimum (Bollen & Curan, 2006). The two latent variables are initial status (also referred to as an intercept) and change (also referred to as a slope). Initial status represents the level of the affective commitment latent variable at

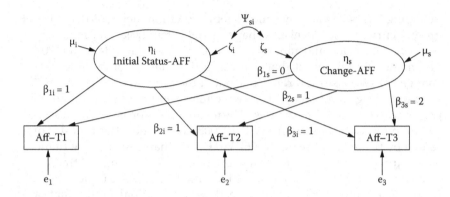

FIGURE 12.3
Hypothetical LGM with observed scores.

baseline (i.e., Time is 0 in the sense that no time has yet passed). Change represents the unit change (increase or decrease) in the affective commitment latent variable per every unit change in time.

As seen in Figure 12.3, to fix the loadings of the initial status latent variable to the three observed variables, a 1 is used (e.g., $\beta_{1i} = \beta_{2i} = \beta_{3i} = 1$). In addition, loadings of the change latent variable are fixed to 0 (β_{1s}), 1 (β_{2s}), and 2 (β_{3s}). This loading pattern serves two purposes. It fixes the mean of the initial status latent variable (μ_i) to Time 1. Further, it establishes the time metric underlying the mean change (μ_s). The 0, 1, and 2 pattern of our fictitious example denotes that there were equal intervals between the Times 1 through 3 administrations of the commitment measure (e.g., baseline, 6 months from baseline, 12 months from baseline). As such, we can eventually make statements such as, "We can expect a μ_s change in affective commitment every six months." Finally, ψ_{si} in Figure 12.3 indicates the covariance between the disturbance terms of the two latent variables. When standardized, this value represents the correlation between initial status and change.

The example in Figure 12.3 illustrates a linear model where the intraindividual trajectories of change in affective commitment are straight lines. If a fourth (or more) period of measurement had been undertaken, the model could be extended to include a third latent variable, η_q, where "q" symbolizes a quadratic component; that is, a turn in the line. A fourth measurement is required because adding a quadratic latent variable to the model in Figure 12.3 would result in an underidentification problem (Duncan et al., 1999). Using a quadratic latent variable permits modeling, for example, in cases when commitment is expected to increase (or decrease) to some maximum (minimum) level before flattening out. The loadings of the quadratic latent variable to the observed affective commitment measures are the squared values of the linear loadings. Other

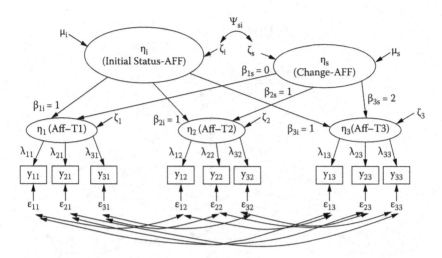

FIGURE 12.4
Hypothetical LGM—latent variable approach.

turns in the lines (e.g., tertiary) may be operationalized as well. While the reader may opt to conduct LGM using an observed variables model as in Figure 12.3, our recommendation is to adopt the perspective in Figure 12.4.

The LGM in Figure 12.4 represents the latent variable approach to LGM technically referred to as a curve-of-factors model (Duncan et al., 1999). The major difference between it and Figure 12.3 is in the operationalization of affective commitment at the three time points. In Figure 12.3, the boxes denote that the observed mean or summed score was used. By contrast, the ellipses in Figure 12.4 indicate that affective commitment is viewed as a latent variable at each time point. If the initial status and change latent variables were removed, one would recognize this as a repeated-measures CFA. The curved arrows between the uniqueness terms of like items across time recognizes that there may be an autoregressive component to repeated measures that systematically influences responses, and thus, should be controlled. The autoregressive component is the potential item's effect on itself across time. The model in Figure 12.4 is representative of the ones used by Bentein et al. (2005), and Lance, Vandenberg, & Self (2000). Among the advantages of Figure 12.4 over Figure 12.3 is the fact that measurement error is accounted for by using a measurement model to define each occasion of affective commitment.

Most useful perhaps to the reader, however, is the model shown in Figure 12.5. Figure 12.5 extends Figure 12.4 by indicating that one's initial status and change in affective commitment influences job search or JS (β_{4i} and β_{4s}, respectively), which in turn influences turnover intention or TI (β_{54}). Other examples could have been presented, such as a model that includes

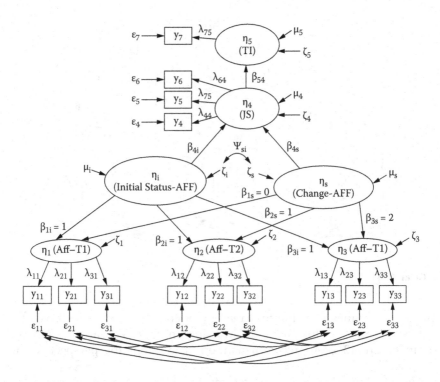

FIGURE 12.5
Hypothetical LGM—initial status and change as predictors.

antecedents of change, or a model that examines the impact of change in one variable on change in another variable (see Bentein et al., 2005).

These types of models are interpretatively much more exciting than the cross-sectional ones typically presented in the research literature. For example, let's assume from Figure 12.5 that μ_s, the mean change in affective commitment, was statistically significant and positive. Hence, there is an increase in commitment for each unit change in time. Further, let's assume that JS was measured four months after the T3 collection of affective commitment, and β_{4s} was significant and negative. This literally means that as one's commitment strengthens over time, there will be a decrease in that individual's job search activities. Terms such as "strengthen," "change," "weaken," and the like imply something about the dynamic property of the focal construct—a property that cannot be captured using cross-sectional designs or even in a design where commitment may be measured at Time 1 and JS behavior at Time 2 (again see Duncan et al., 1999, for excellent explanations for the latter statement).

The researcher should be aware of several issues before engaging in LGM analyses. First, measurement invariance must be established before undertaking the LGM (Bollen & Curran, 2006; Chan, 1998, 2002; Lance,

Meade & Williamson, 2000; Lance, Vandenberg & Self, 2000). Second, before proceeding to tests of models such as Figure 12.5, the researcher should establish whether or not change has occurred. This is referred to as a first-order, or unconditional, model (Bollen & Curran, 2006). It would not make sense to test the model in Figure 12.5, for example, if change in affective commitment was not present. Thus, models such as that represented in Figure 12.4 should be undertaken first on all variables in which change is hypothesized to occur. Third, as part of the latter step, tests for the presence of quadratic or other nonlinear forms of change should be established after detecting the presence of linear change, assuming the data are appropriate for doing so. Further, if nonlinear change is detected and brought into models such as that in Figure 12.5, then the interpretation of outcomes is not as straightforward as would be with just linear change (Bollen & Curran, 2006, p. 94, provide an excellent explanation).

In closing, the reader may be wondering, "Why is the ability of LGM to operationalize change of such importance to commitment research?" Our answer is simple. Namely, in even the most carefully planned longitudinal studies, we have not effectively operationalized change. Yet, over the years there have been several references to the importance of studying how commitment develops over time (Mowday et al., 1982; Mathieu & Zajac, 1990; Meyer & Allen, 1991, 1997), or how we may intervene to change commitment (Salancik, 1977). Our point is that change is an integral part of current conceptualizations of commitment, but we have not effectively tested the role of change. LGM is the strongest statistical procedure for doing so, relative to other approaches (Burr & Nesselroade, 1990; Cronbach & Furby, 1970; Duncan et al., 1999; Rogosa, 1995; Lance, Vandenberg & Self, 2000).

Latent Variable Mixture Modeling

As noted earlier, a major challenge within commitment research is capturing the complex interplay among the multiple mindsets (Meyer & Herscovitch, 2001; Sinclair, Tucker, Cullen, & Wright, 2005). From our perspective, the situation is much more intricate than is readily apparent. Specifically, the actual needs of commitment researchers are not just limited to identifying the appropriate analytical tool for combining the different mindsets of commitment. Rather, the outcome of that tool (the actual value or values reflecting the interplay among the commitment mindsets) must meet other requirements as well. One requirement is the outcome must possess the properties that permit its use as an antecedent, consequence, mediator, or moderator—just like any other construct.

A second requirement is that the analytical tool captures the interplay among the mindsets as they change across time.

Our point is that analytical tools for combining variables have existed for decades. Yet, if we view the research requirements above as criteria for usefulness, these tools have severe limitations. For example, cluster analysis has existed for decades (Tryon, 1939). Cluster analysis is an exploratory technique for grouping similar objects or individuals. Researchers define clusters such that the distance between values within a cluster is minimized and the distance between values in different clusters is maximized. Sinclair et al. (2005) and Wasti (2005) recently used cluster analysis to create commitment profiles, and demonstrated differences between profiles on performance ratings, levels of antisocial and organizational citizenship behavior, and desirable work behaviors. While useful findings emerged from these studies, the problem remains that the only outcome from cluster analysis is a classification index (an index of 1 may be assigned to those who are high on all variables, a 2 to those who are low, etc.). This outcome, though, does not possess the type of measurement properties required to fulfill the two requirements outlined above.

Another commonly suggested method for operationalizing the synergy or interplay among the commitment mindsets is the use of interaction terms (Meyer & Allen, 1991; Meyer & Herscovitch, 2001). Interactions are thought to operationalize the synergy among mindsets because they capture the potential moderator effects that the different mindsets may have on the relationship between other mindsets and behavioral outcomes. Several studies have examined interactions between commitment mindsets (Jaros, 1997; Meyer, Paunonen, Gellatly, Goffin, & Jackson, 1989; Randall, Fedor, & Longenecker, 1990; Somers, 1995). These studies provide evidence that when one commitment mindset is strong, it can attenuate the relationship between behavior and other commitment mindsets (Somers, 1995; Jaros, 1997). Interactions may not be an option for many researchers due to the statistical and power requirements to detect a significant interaction (Cronbach, 1987). They are high even in simple, two-variable cases. However, as noted in the chapters in this volume, a number of the interesting research questions will entail the use of three or more mindsets or foci, increasing the statistical demands even more. Examples in the current volume are chapters 4 (Vandenberghe), 5 (Becker), and 6 (Neubert & Wu).

Our primary point, like it was with cluster analysis, is that the outcome from an interaction perspective does not possess the measurement properties to meet the research requirements presented above. It is not feasible to use the outcomes associated with testing all possible interactions of three or more commitment mindsets as antecedents, consequences, mediators, or moderators. Further, the interaction approach is basically a regression analysis, which is variable- rather than person-focused. Variable-focused techniques focus on relationships between variables, but person-focused, or configural, techniques focus on classes of individuals who share similar characteristics or patterns of variables (Craig & Smith, 2000). For example, a researcher using a variable-focused technique may test for the interactive effects of affective and normative commitment on turnover intentions. Conversely, a researcher using a person-focused technique such as latent profile analysis (LPA) focuses on how a class of individuals characterized by high levels of both affective and normative commitment is different from a class of individuals characterized by a profile of high affective and low normative commitment. Given the increased complexity associated with new conceptualizations of commitment and the overwhelming number of possible combinations of commitment mindsets and of targets or foci of commitment, taking a configural approach to commitment research is appropriate.

The question before us is, "What type of configural approach meets most, if not all, of the research requirements confronting contemporary commitment researchers?" The answer resides in finite mixture modeling (McLachlan & Peel, 2000; L. K. Muthén & B. O. Muthén, 1998–2006). As with all sections of this chapter, it is our intent to give the reader an appreciation of the potential underlying this approach. Excellent technical treatments are provided by Hagenaars and McCutcheon (2002), Magidson and Vermunt (2002, 2004), McLachlan and Peel (2000), B. O. Muthén (2001, 2004), and Vermunt and Magidson (2002). In brief, mixture modeling is actually a set of techniques. A common aspect across them is modeling with categorical latent variables representing homogenous subsets of individuals or cluster membership. The operative term is *latent*, in that the variable consists of K number of categories or clusters. Individuals' category or cluster values on the latent variable are presumed to cause their levels on the observed indicators, which in commitment research would be the measures operationalizing the commitment mindsets (Pastor, Barron, Miller, & Davis, 2006). "The term *mixture* is referring to the notion that the data are not being sampled from a population that can be described by a single probability distribution. Instead, the data are conceived as being sampled from a population composed of a mix of distributions, one for each cluster, with each cluster distribution characterized by its own unique set of parameters" (Pastor et al., 2006, p. 15).

A key phrase from the above quote is "characterized by its own unique set of parameters." Paraphrasing from the Measurement Invariance section of this chapter, we noted that while the reader may be unfamiliar with the Greek symbols, what is important to understand is that each one represents some quantifiable aspect of the properties of the measures or the latent variables. Emphasized there as well is the fact that one can freely estimate those properties within each group and/or make those properties invariant/equal between the groups. The same is true in the context of latent mixture modeling; that is, one may parameterize the properties such that they are unique to each cluster and/or are assumed to be equal or invariant between clusters.

Latent modeling is important because it allows the researcher to develop analytical models in such a way that the outcome meets many of the research requirements stated at the start of this section (L. K. Muthén & B. O. Muthén, 1998–2006). Briefly, those requirements entail having an outcome representing the synergy of the commitment mindsets that can be used in various capacities, such as an antecedent, an outcome, a mediator, and the like. In the following pages, we focus on two types of mixture modeling. One is a type of latent class analysis (LCA) referred to as latent profile analysis (LPA) which may be an appropriate tool for cross-sectional forms of data. The other is latent class growth modeling (LCGM), which is appropriate for identifying classes of individuals homogenous with respect to change across time on the commitment mindsets.

Latent Profile Analysis

LCA and LPA are forms of mixture modeling that use latent categorical variables to identify groups or classes of individuals who share similar relationships between observed variables. However, LPA uses continuous observed variables, and LCA uses categorical observed variables. Both analyses are similar to factor analysis in that relationships among a set of observed variables are assumed to be caused by a common factor, or a latent variable, that cannot be directly observed (B. O. Muthén & L. K. Muthén, 2000). In LCA and LPA, the common factor is a latent class representing a homogeneous group of individuals. In factor analysis, the common factor is a latent variable, which represents a group of observed variables that share similar properties. In sum, researchers use factor analysis to reduce large amounts of data into meaningful constructs. In contrast, LCA and LPA reduce large amounts of data into meaningful classes of individuals. As such, analyzing classes of individuals may provide more meaningful results than analyzing groups of observed variables. This is because the synergistic effects of combinations of variables exist within individuals, not within the variables themselves. For a good example of the application of LPA, see Pastor et al. (2006), who used it to capture combinations of four conceptually different goal orientations in their sample.

Even though LCA and LPA have similar analytical cores, discussion from this point forward is limited to LPA, given that commitment variables are viewed as continuous or continuouslike by most researchers. Using actual data, we start by using LPA in a measurement model context, and subsequently present it in a test of an SEM. Figure 12.6 illustrates the measurement model.

There are two latent variables and one latent categorical variable (all denoted by circle) in Figure 12.6. The latent variables labeled SYN COMM

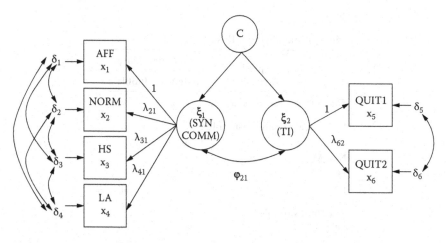

FIGURE 12.6
Illustration of a general latent profile model.

and TI are the commitment and turnover intention constructs, respectively. The other, labeled "c," is the latent class. To keep our example simple, we operationalized four forms of commitment (Dunham, Grube, & Castañada, 1994; Hackett, Bycio, & Hausdorf, 1994; Meyer, Allen, & Gellatly, 1990) using means which in turn acted as the manifest or observed variables for the latent variable SYN COMM. Turnover intention was operationalized using two items. Our premise is that SYN COMM represents the synergy among the four commitment mindsets.

The arrow from the latent class variable, "c," to the latent variables, SYN COMM and TI, in Figure 12.6 connotes that the linear combination of the observed variables onto their respective latent constructs varies as a function of latent class membership. We specified that the properties of the measurement models be freely estimated within each category of the latent class variable. As stated earlier, the factor pattern is the best empirical representation of individuals' cognitive frames of reference (Vandenberg & Self, 1993). Therefore, we are assuming that there are multiple probability distributions. As such, members of a given class have a greater probability of sharing a given frame of reference than of sharing the frame of reference characterizing members of other classes.

We will address the topic of "how many classes" at the end of this section when we present recommendations. For current purposes, however, we specified that there were two classes underlying the latent profile variable, "c." Data analyses were completed using M*plus* (L. K. Muthén & B. O. Muthén, 1998–2006), and the syntax from these analyses is available upon request from the first author. In addition to the LPA, we conducted a typical analysis (CFA) of the measurement model in Figure 12.6, which excludes the "c" latent profile variable. The factor loadings, factor correlations, and

TABLE 12.1

Measurement Model Results

Variables	Typical Analysis	Latent Profile Analysis	
		Profile 1	Profile 2
Standardized Factor Loadings			
SYN COMM Latent Variable			
AFF	.68[a]	.66[a]	.66[a]
NORM	.59[b]	.60[b]	.55[b]
HS	.30[b]	.32[b]	.45[b]
LA	−.15[b]	−.19[b]	.11
TI Latent Variable			
QUIT1	.85[a]	.89[a]	.81[a]
QUIT2	.87[b]	.80[b]	.95[b]
Standardized Factor Covariances			
SYN COMM With			
TI	−.67[b]	−.65[b]	−.75[b]
Intercepts of the Indicators[c]			
AFF	3.2	3.1	3.3
NORM	2.3	2.3	2.4
HS	2.7	3.0	2.4
LA	1.8	2.4	1.1
QUIT1	2.7	2.8	2.6
QUIT2	2.4	2.5	2.3

Note: [a] = referent indicator, and thus, no significance test; [b] = statistically significant at $p < .05$
or smaller; [c] = all intercepts were statistically
significant from 0 at $p < .05$ or smaller.

item intercepts are presented in Table 12.1, and the posterior probabilities of profile or class membership are presented in Table 12.2.

The results of our analyses indicated that the two-class LPA was superior to the typical analysis presented in Table 12.1. Of interest is whether the combination of the four commitment mindsets differed by class. Examination of the factor loadings in Table 12.1 clearly shows that while SYN COMM in Profile 1 is a function of all four mindsets, only affective, normative and high-sacrifice commitments in Profile 2 seem to underlie the SYN COMM latent variable. Low-alternatives commitment possessed a

TABLE 12.2

Classification Posterior Probabilities for the LPA Model

Profiles	Profile 1	Profile 2
Profile 1	.99	.01
Profile 2	.13	.87

nonsignificant factor loading on SYN COMM in Profile 2. With respect to the intercepts (means) of the profile indicators, a post hoc test of mean differences indicated that affective and normative commitment did not differ significantly between profiles, but high-sacrifice commitment for Profile 1 was significantly greater than that for Profile 2. Finally, the results in Table 12.2 indicated "clean" classification of individuals, or clearly defined classes. The posterior probabilities describe the homogeneity of individuals within the class and are used to assign individuals to classes. Interpretatively, this means that there was 99% confidence that individuals in Profile 1 ($n = 374$) belong to that profile, and only a 1% chance of belonging to the other profiles. Similarly, there was 87% confidence that individuals in Profile 2 ($n = 338$) belong to it and no other profiles.

While measurement models are interesting, they are not subject to the forms of interpretation in which commitment researchers are interested. Most interest resides in models such as that presented in Figure 12.7.

There are three substantive questions being addressed in Figure 12.7: (1) the arrow from "c" to SYN COMM addresses the question of whether there are latent mean differences between the classes/profiles; (2) similarly, the arrow from "c" to TI addresses whether there are latent intercept differences between the profiles; and (3) the broken arrow from "c" to the SYN COMM – TI path addresses whether the path is moderated by profile classification. For purposes of clarification, the reason why the term *latent mean* is used in reference to SYN COMM and *latent intercept* in reference to TI is that the former is an exogenous variable and the latter an endogenous variable. In short, the latent intercept is the latent mean of TI when SYN COMM is at zero. Please note that even in the presence of an interaction, SYN COMM remains as an exogenous variable to the endogenous variable, TI. The arrow from "c" to it doesn't change that status—it simply

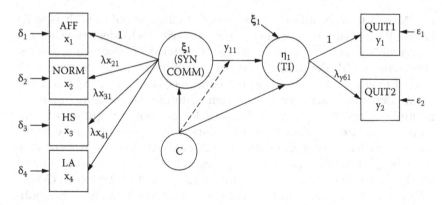

FIGURE 12.7
Illustration of SEM mixture modeling.

reflects that there may be mean differences on SYN COMM between the classes of "c."

All of the statistics (see Nylund, Asparouhov, & Muthén, 2007, for a review of the statistical criteria for determining the best-fitting model) indicated that a two-class/-profile model was superior to a single-class model (the typical SEM analyses). With respect to the first two questions, Profile 1 possessed a significantly lower SYN COMM latent mean and significantly greater TI latent intercept than did Profile 2. Most importantly, the SYN COMM to TI path was moderated by the latent profile variable. For Profile 1, the standardized path was $-.90$ ($p < .0000$), accounting for 82% of the variance in the TI latent variable. By contrast, the standardized path was $-.24$ ($p < .005$) for Profile 2, accounting for 6% of the variance in the TI latent variable.

Recall that the major differences between profiles were (a) all four mindsets were associated with SYN COMM for Profile 1 individuals but not for Profile 2, (b) the level of high-sacrifice commitment was significantly greater in Profile 1 than Profile 2 but the levels of affective and normative commitment did not differ between profiles, and (c) low alternatives did not play a role in defining SYN COMM for Profile 2. Regardless of how one might substantively interpret this, our major point is that LPA provides a viable alternative for operationalizing the synergy among the commitment mindsets, and does so in a way that meets many of the research requirements outlined above; that is, the value of the resulting latent categorical variables lies in the researcher's ability to use the latent variables as outcome variables, mediators, or moderators. This point is reinforced again in the following pages, as we turn attention now to latent class growth modeling analysis (LCGM).

Latent Class Growth Modeling

LCGM is a form of mixture modeling for longitudinal data. It is similar to LPA in that it uses latent categorical variables to identify groups of individuals who are similar in terms of patterns of observed variables. However, LCGM identifies groups of individuals who are similar with respect to change trajectories in the variable(s) of interest. In LCGM, the researcher infers latent variables from commitment measures taken at multiple points in time. The estimated classes represent groups of individuals who are homogeneous with respect to vectors of change in the outcome variable or combinations of vectors of change in several outcome variables. For detailed technical reviews of LCGM, see Nagin and Land (1993), Nagin (1999), Nagin and Tremblay (2001), and B. O. Muthén (2001).

Figure 12.8 illustrates an LCGM for affective commitment. It is identical to Figure 12.4 except there is now the inclusion of the "c," or categorical latent variable. Please refer back to Figure 12.4 for a full description.

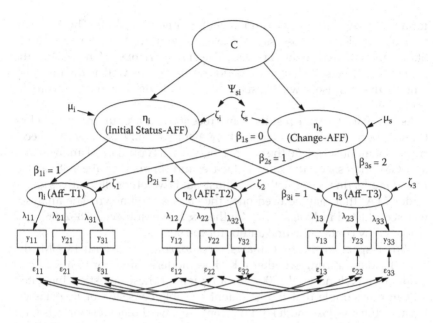

FIGURE 12.8
Hypothetical LCGM—affective commitment only.

Recall, though, that perhaps the most important latent variable from a theory-testing standpoint is that representing intraindividual trajectories of change (η_s in both figures). The arrows from the latent variable "c" to the Initial Status and Change latent variables suggest that one expects the data are not being sampled from a population that can be described by a single probability distribution (i.e., that there are relatively uniform types of change or everyone starts at similar levels). Instead, it is now assumed the data are sampled from a population composed of a mix of distributions, one for each cluster, with each cluster distribution characterized by its own unique set of parameters representing initial status and change (Pastor et al., 2006). Further, as discussed in the LGM section and assuming the data are appropriate for doing so, we could enter a quadratic latent variable representing a change in the curve of the trajectory. What we may discover in undertaking the LCGM, therefore, are meaningful subgroups of individuals: some changing upward, others downward, others downward-leveling off, or others slowly increasing and then accelerating at some later point. These represent very different characterizations of change that may have their own driving forces or outcomes.

Perhaps the most important application here is to broaden the model to include multiple mindsets, and in doing so, to capture the interplay among the mindsets as they change across time. Figure 12.8, for example, would be modified to include Initial Status and Change latent variables for normative, high-sacrifice and low-alternatives mindsets. The "c" latent variable would now possess eight arrows pointing to each set of Initial Status and Change latent variables. The class variable, "c," represents the synergistic effects of change in the four mindsets as well as the interplay among the mindsets with respect to individuals' initial status on the mindsets.

As an illustration, the results from a recent paper are summarized below (Vandenberg, Stanley, Vandenberghe, & Bentein, 2007). We took two pieces from that manuscript: (a) the contrast between a typical LGM analysis and a LCGM analysis on the same database, and (b) another alternative analytical model (in the sense that we illustrated two other alternatives above under LPA) that may be used once the classes are known. The analyses were conducted in M*plus* (B. O. Muthén & L. K. Muthén, 1998–2006), and readers may contact the first author for the syntax.

With respect to the first analysis, comparing LGM with LCGM, the statistics determining whether a K class model is superior to a K-1 class model (see Nylund et al., 2007, for a review of these statistics) indicated that in our sample that the "c" latent variable consisted of five classes. Because the six-class model did not converge, we did not test models with six or more classes. The posterior probabilities for class membership are presented in Table 12.3, and the results of the growth analyses are presented in Table 12.4.

As seen in Table 12.3, the posterior probabilities indicated strong support for the classification. The probability values representing the likelihood of an individual belonging to the class to which he or she was assigned were 88% or higher in each class. The probability of belonging to other classes was not greater than 8%. These results indicate that the classes were distinguishable.

TABLE 12.3

Classification Posterior Probabilities for the LCGM Model

Class	n	1	2	3	4	5
1	100	**0.88**	0.03	0.01	0.00	0.08
2	73	0.05	**0.88**	0.01	0.01	0.06
3	75	0.01	0.00	**0.92**	0.02	0.04
4	165	0.01	0.01	0.02	**0.90**	0.06
5	299	0.07	0.03	0.00	0.01	**0.89**

Note: Values in bold are the average posterior probabilities associated with the classes to which individuals were assigned.

TABLE 12.4

Growth Parameter Estimates for the Entire Sample
and the 5 LCGM Classes

Class	Initial Status $(\mu_{IS})^b$	Change (μ_{CH})	Class	Initial Status $(\mu_{IS})^b$	Change (μ_{CH})
Entire Sample			*Static*		
AFF	3.16	0.07[a]	AFF	2.53	0.00
NORM	2.35	−0.06[a]	NORM	1.22	−0.09
HS	2.75	0.04[a]	HS	2.68	0.00
LA	1.86	0.02	LA	2.72	−0.04
TI	2.57	0.01	TI	3.11	0.06
Decreasing			*Socio-Emotionally Decreasing*		
AFF	3.40	−0.26[a]	AFF	3.34	−0.09[a]
NORM	2.82	−0.46[a]	NORM	2.41	−0.10[a]
HS	3.16	−0.26[a]	HS	2.50	0.04
LA	2.56	−0.26	LA	1.08	−0.01
TI	2.62	0.21[a]	TI	2.37	−0.03
Increasing			*Stuck*		
AFF	2.61	0.23[a]	AFF	3.27	−0.09[a]
NORM	1.73	0.57[a]	NORM	2.59	−0.04
HS	2.52	0.28[a]	HS	2.80	0.10[a]
LA	2.23	0.05	LA	1.78	0.14[a]
TI	3.51	−0.70[a]	TI	2.28	0.13[a]

Note: [a] = statistically significant at $p < .05$ or smaller; [b] = all Initial Status means were statistically significant from 0 at $p < .05$ or smaller.

Looking first at the LGM results on the entire sample in Table 12.4 (this is the typical analysis that most researchers would undertake), we observe statistically significant support for positive change in affective commitment (.07). This value represents a small to moderate positive change. This result, along with the initial status, means the individuals in this sample started out at the mid-range of affective commitment (3.16) and increased positively from that initial status during the duration of the study. A similar increase in high-sacrifice commitment was also observed, but normative commitment decreased significantly during this time. Further, there were no changes in either low-alternatives commitment or turnover intention. Interpreting these findings would be difficult at best. Yet, our main point is that perhaps these findings are the consequence of incorrectly assuming that there is a single probability distribution underlying this sample; that is, all individuals belong to the same profile of Change and Initial Status on the variables. Even a cursory glance at the Initial Status and Change values for the five classes of the latent categorical variable in Table 12.4, however, indicates that there are vast differences between the classes in the "c" latent variable—in short, there are multiple probability distributions underlying this sample.

Specifically, each class represents a different profile of change. In other words, the results indicate that the latent "c" variable in Figure 12.8 moderated the growth parameters. Specifically, Class 1 consists of individuals characterized by statistically significant linear decreases in affective, normative, and high-sacrifice commitment, and no change in lack of alternatives commitment. As such, we labeled this class Decreasing in order to reflect the diminishing attachment with respect to three of the four commitment mindsets. Also, as would be expected by theory, the change in turnover intention for this class was positive and statistically significant. Individuals in Class 2 possessed a very different pattern: statistically significant increases in affective, normative, and high-sacrifice commitment, and no change in lack of alternatives commitment. In contrast to individuals in Class 1, those in Class 2 started with low levels of affective, normative, and high-sacrifice commitment (Initial Status values of 2.61, 1.73, 2.52) and increased over time. Additionally, as might be expected by theory, the change in turnover intention in this class was negative and statistically significant. Therefore, we labeled this class Increasing in order to reflect increases in attachment with respect to the three commitment mindsets. Individuals in Class 3 were labeled Static, because as seen in Table 12.4, there were no statistically significant changes in the four commitment mindsets across time. Thus, they remained at low to slightly below mid-range levels of commitment (1.22–2.72) throughout the duration of the study.

Individuals in Class 4 were given the title Socio-Emotionally Decreasing to reflect that their levels of affective and normative commitments decreased significantly over time, but their levels of high-sacrifice and lack of alternative commitments did not change. Thus, there was a weakening of the emotional and social forces binding individuals to the organization in this class across time. Given that affective and normative commitments are typically considered the strongest forms of commitment, we would have expected a corresponding increase in the turnover intention of individuals in this class. However, as seen in Table 12.4, turnover intention did not change over time in this class. Finally, Class 5 individuals possessed statistically significant decreasing levels in affective commitment, but significant increases in high-sacrifice and lack of alternatives commitments across time. Normative commitment did not change significantly. We labeled this class Stuck in order to reflect diminishing emotional attachment to the organization and increasing attachment due to lack of employment alternatives and high costs associated with leaving. Interestingly, the turnover intention within this group increased positively over time.

One interesting finding to emerge from the current results is that change in turnover intention, whether increasing or decreasing, may not be simply a function of the so-called strongest forms of commitment—affective and normative commitments. Rather, the only time turnover intention changed in a class above was when affective and/or normative commitment changed in combination with one or both of the remaining two forms of commitment. The results using the entire sample are also interesting. We would be hard pressed, for example, to explain why affective commitment increased over time, but normative decreased, given that those two commitments are typically highly positively correlated. Our primary point is that most applied researchers get their data by asking an organization for permission to collect data, and settle for data from anyone who will complete the measures. Alternatively, the researchers may simply ask individuals from several organizations (as was done here) to complete the measures, and thus, the data better represents general employee populations. Regardless, the most common analytical approach, even with sophisticated statistical control procedures, is to use the complete sample in the analysis and thereby automatically assume that the constructs, the associations among them, and/or the change in them across time can be described by a single probability distribution (Pastor et al., 2006). The current findings, instead, indicate that the data are best conceived as being sampled from a population composed of a mix of distributions, one for each cluster, with each cluster distribution characterized by its own unique set of parameters.

In the previous overview of LPA, we illustrated how the latent categorical variable could be used in an SEM context. While a similar analysis could have been undertaken using the latent class variable from the LCGM, we took a non-SEM approach to illustrate the flexibility of this approach once the latent class variable has been defined. Specifically, within the current database, the actual turnover of individuals was noted for a time period (Time 4) following the last (Time 3) collection of the commitment and turnover intention measures. We then conducted a series of logistic regressions within each class using the change (or no change) in turnover intention within a class as a predictor of turnover in that class. These results are presented in Table 12.5.

Using Time 4 turnover as the dependent variable, and given that we found statistically significant change in turnover intention in the Decreasing, Increasing, and Stuck classes, we entered their Time 1 turnover intentions in the first step of a hierarchical analysis, followed by their Time 3 turnover intentions in the second step. Given that the change in intention for these three classes was linear, Time 2 intention could be excluded (Bentein et al., 2005). Given that we did not find change in turnover intentions in

TABLE 12.5

Logistic Regression of Actual Turnover at Time 4 Onto Turnover Intention at Times 1 and 3 Within Each Class

		Beta Coefficients		Chi-	Nagelkerke
Class	Constant	T1 Intention	T3 Intention	square	r-square
1. Decreasing	−7.09[a]	0.36	1.37[a]	27.19[a]	0.54
2. Increasing	−3.98	0.80	−0.35	3.99	0.17
3. Static	−6.54[a]	—	1.33[a]	8.99[a]	0.31
4. Socio-emotionally decreasing	−4.94[a]	—	1.11[a]	18.19[a]	0.32
5. Stuck	−6.10[a]	−0.24	1.26[a]	9.77[a]	0.19

Note: Only the T3 TI was included as a predictor of turnover in the Static and Socio-Emotionally Decreasing classes because these groups did not show statistically significant change in TI over time. Because there was no change, we could use TI at T1, T2, or T3 to predict actual turnover. We chose T3 because it is the most salient. T1 = Time 1; T2 = Time 2; T3 = Time 3; TI = Turnover Intentions

[a] $p < .05$.

the Static and Socio-Emotionally Decreasing classes, only their Time 3 turnover intentions was entered to predict turnover at Time 4.

The logistic regressions of the change in turnover intention from Time 1 to Time 3 onto turnover were statistically significant for the Decreasing ($\chi^2 = 27.19$, $p < .00$) and Stuck ($\chi^2 = 9.77$, $p < .01$) classes, but not for the Increasing class. The positive change coefficients for the Decreasing and Stuck classes from Table 12.5 indicated that as turnover intention increased across time, there was a greater probability of leaving the organization at Time 4. Specifically, 54% of the variance in turnover was accounted for by the change in intention for the Decreasing class, and 19% of the variance in turnover in the Stuck class was accounted for by the increase in intention. The logistic regression of only Time 3 turnover intention onto Time 4 turnover was statistically significant for both the Static ($\chi^2 = 8.99$, $p < .00$) and Socio-Emotionally Decreasing ($\chi^2 = 18.19$, $p < .00$) classes. The positive coefficients indicate that the higher the level of Time 3 intention, the greater the probability of leaving the organization at Time 4. Indeed, intention at Time 3 explained 31% of the variance in turnover at Time 4 in the Static class and 32% of the variance in the Socio-Emotionally Decreasing class.

Our goal through all of the illustrations above was simply to introduce readers to an alternative analytical process. Driving this goal was the need for commitment researchers to adopt analyses permitting us to capture the interplay among the different commitment mindsets in such a way that the interplay is a construct itself. The LPA examples demonstrated how one might approach the issue using cross-sectional data. In contrast, the LCGM examples exhibited how the issue may be incorporated into longitudinal designs where interest resides in how the commitment mindsets change across time. Given that the purpose of this chapter is to demonstrate new analytical approaches, the use of theory was admittedly "thin" in these examples. However, theory could easily be applied to many of the relationships observed in these examples (e.g., the relationship of commitment to intention, or of intention to turnover).

General Recommendations for Using LPA and LCGM

What the reader has encountered in reviewing this section is literally our own experiences and struggles in understanding latent mixture modeling—a fledgling understanding at best. Based on our limited experiences, we make the following recommendations.

At the top of our list is to allow theory to be the driving force for making decisions about measures and their conceptual associations. Theory is central to issues such as determining the number of clusters, classes, or profiles that underlie the latent categorical variable, and the characteristics of those classes. While fit indices clearly indicate the number of classes providing the best fit, researchers must ensure that the resulting classes are theoretically meaningful. As pointed out by the first author in his keynote address at the Ohio State University Conference on Organizational Commitment (Vandenberg, 2005), one of the "evils" underlying the commitment research literature in general has been the overwhelming analytical treatment of the different mindsets as independent of one another across the vast majority of studies to date. While a few studies have emerged or are emerging in which authors are evaluating combinations (Wasti, 2005; Jaros, 1997; Meyer et al., 1989; Randall et al., 1990; Somers, 1995), the major point of Vandenberg's statement is that our conceptual knowledge of how the mindsets combine and the implications of those combinations are very immature at best. Hence, establishing theory as a driving force for the number of profiles and what they look like is going to be a struggle at first, but one that is sorely needed to take commitment research to the next level. Perhaps commitment research will need to go through a period of *informed* exploratory research until we have gained enough confidence to know and understand how the different mindsets combine with one another.

Informed is a key term in the previous sentence. Not unlike other analytical tools, LPA and LCGM could be misused to first identify the classes and then attach a post hoc explanation to them. To avoid this, we recommend that researchers exercise sound research practices such as using one sample to identify profiles, and then cross-validating the existence of those profiles in another sample (Pastor et al., 2006). Further, researchers should observe whether the theoretical associations prescribed to the profiles generalize across other samples and in different contexts.

Another recommendation from our experiences is to develop a comprehensive understanding of the empirical criteria used to identify the number of profiles. The use of such criteria is an advantage that latent mixture modeling has over other techniques such as specifying interactions and cluster analysis. Nylund et al. (2007) provide an excellent review of these criteria, and Pastor et al. (2006) provide an excellent application. We followed the approach detailed in those sources. Specifically, the goal is to address whether a latent variable with K classes is better than K-1 classes. The ensuing statistics identify the point at which the addition of another profile or class results in degradation of model fit. Thus, the optimal number is the latent variable with the number of classes before degradation occurs. Like all such criteria, though, this does not mean the profiles or classes are theoretically meaningful. One would hope, however, that as this line of work progresses in commitment research, the number and types of profiles are stated a priori, and the application of the criteria becomes more of a hypothesis test, or at a minimum, a test of the assumption that the theoretically established profiles exist within one's own database.

Our third recommendation is to be very clear in advance as to how the analyses of primary interest (i.e., hypothesis testing) will be undertaken. As noted previously, there are many options as to how one might incorporate the results from the LCA; that is, one is not bound to using only SEM. Further, there are a number of parts to the LCA, some of which may or may not be of interest. For example, one can save each individual's posterior probabilities of belonging to the classes and profiles, and use those as predictors, criteria, mediators, or moderators. Using the posterior probabilities to represent cluster membership means that the accuracy of classifying persons into clusters can be incorporated into the analyses (Pastor et al., 2006).

Our final recommendation is to start simply and gradually. That is, do not leap into analyzing a complex model without first understanding the variables and how they combine (e.g., doing the analyses underlying Figure 12.8 before testing Figure 12.7). Latent mixture models are computationally complex and prone to convergence issues. A number of those issues may be circumvented by understanding how the variables behave individually before attempting to test hypotheses in which the variables are combined.

Conclusion

While commitment may be conceptually viewed quite differently among the authors of this volume, a common thread tying the chapters together is that commitment is conceptually complex and multifaceted, and may take different roles. The adequate testing of the premises presented in these chapters, therefore, will present a number of methodological and analytical challenges. We have attempted to deal with three such challenges in the current chapter: (1) addressing the invariance of the measurement properties underlying the scales when comparing groups or within a group across time; (2) operationalizing change in commitment as a construct in and of itself that in turn may be used as an antecedent, outcome, mediator, or moderator; and (3) accounting for the interplay among commitment mindsets or forms.

With respect to invariance issues, our primary point is that one cannot merely assume that the same commitment scale applied to different groups (even in the same language) or to the same group across time is being interpreted in the same manner. As noted by Vandenberg and Lance (2000), the assumptions of invariance need to be examined in each and every case. Otherwise, there is a risk that the lack of invariance may confound the ability to make meaningful inferences from the findings, or may even prevent a comparison of groups or the test of change across time.

With respect to capturing the change in commitment mindsets as a construct in and of itself, this is not only an issue with the chapters in this volume but in reality has been a long-standing one in the commitment research literature for decades (Meyer & Herscovitch, 2001; Meyer & Allen, 1991). Namely, commitment has always been viewed as a process variable with expectations that it may increase, decrease, or otherwise change over time. Yet, with a few exceptions (Tisak & Tisak, 2000; Bentein et al., 2005; Lance, Vandenberg & Self, 2000; Vandenberg & Self, 1993), the vast majority of studies to date have been cross-sectional in nature, and as such, have failed to operationalize commitment as a process. LGM is presented as one of the best means for capturing change in a variable as a latent construct. Thus, it may be used as other latent constructs as an antecedent, consequence, mediator, or moderator.

Finally, with respect to examining the interplay among the various commitment mindsets, this is viewed by us to be one of the most critical challenges, and one, like above, that is not only limited to the current chapters but has been a long-standing one. Across the vast majority of published studies utilizing multiple forms of commitment or multiple mindsets of one target of commitment, each form or mindset has been treated independently of other forms or mindsets in the same study. Yet, we recognize conceptually that within any given individual, the forms or mindsets work together, in unison. Further, within the context of change, this means that the forms or mindsets may increase and/or decrease and/or remain the same simultaneously across time. As noted in the review of latent mixture modeling, one of the problems with common approaches (e.g., cluster analysis, or creating interaction terms) is that they fail to capture a construct representing the interplay. Representing the interplay through a construct is important because it may be conceptually modeled as an antecedent, outcome, moderator, or mediator. Two forms of latent mixture modeling, LPA and LCGM analyses, were presented as a potential means of achieving the latter.

In sum, this chapter builds on other chapters of this volume (chapter 1, Klein, Molloy, & Cooper; chapter 2, Meyer; chapter 3, Riketta & Van Dick; chapter 13, Becker, Klein, & Meyer) by emphasizing new theoretical roles of commitment and offering techniques for capturing commitment based on these roles. We hope that commitment researchers will heed the calls for more longitudinal studies and more studies examining combinations of commitment. The purpose of this chapter was to provide commitment researchers with the tools necessary to heed these calls.

References

Becker, H. S. (1960). Notes on the concept of commitment. *American Journal of Sociology, 66,* 32–42.

Bentein, K., Vandenberg, R. J., Vandenberghe, C., & Stinglhamber, F. (2005). The role of change in the relationship between commitment and turnover: A latent growth modeling approach. *Journal of Applied Psychology, 90,* 468–482.

Bollen, K. A. (1989). *Structural equations with latent variables.* New York: Wiley-Interscience Publications.

Bollen, K. A., & Curran, P. J. (2006). *Latent curve models: A structural equation perspective.* New York: John Wiley & Sons, Inc.

Brockner, J., Tyler, T. R., & Cooper-Schneider, R. (1992). The influence of prior commitment to an institution on reactions to perceived unfairness: The higher they are, the harder they fall. *Administrative Science Quarterly, 37,* 241–261.

Burr, J. A., & Nesselroade, J. R. (1990). Change measurement. In A. von Eye (Ed.), *Statistical methods in longitudinal research* (Vol. 1, pp. 3–34). Boston: Academic Press.

Byrne, B. M., Shavelson, R. J., & Muthén, B. (1989). Testing for the equivalence of factor covariance and mean structures: The issue of partial measurement invariance. *Psychological Bulletin, 3,* 456–466.

Chan, D. (1998).The conceptualization and analysis of change over time: An integrative approach incorporating longitudinal means and covariance structures analysis (LMACS) and multiple indicator latent growth modeling (MLGM). *Organizational Research Methods, 1,* 421–483.

Chan, D. (2002). Latent growth modeling. In F. Drasgow & N. Schmitt (Eds.), *Measuring and Analyzing Behavior in Organizations: Advances in Measurement and Data Analysis* (pp. 302–349, Volume in the Organizational Frontier Series). San Francisco: Jossey-Bass.

Cole, D. A., & White, K. (1993). Structure of peer impressions of children's competence: Validation of the peer nomination of multiple competencies. *Psychological Assessment, 5,* 449–456.

Craig, S. B., & Smith, J. A. (2000, April). *Integrity and personality: A person-oriented investigation.* Paper presented at the 15th Annual Conference of the Society for Industrial and Organizational Psychology, New Orleans, LA.

Cronbach, L. J. (1987). Statistical tests for moderator variables: Flaws in analyses recently proposed. *Psychological Bulletin, 102,* 414–417.

Cronbach, L. J., & Furby, L. (1970). How should we measure "change"—Or should we? *Psychological Bulletin, 74,* 68–80.

Duncan, T. E., Duncan, S. C., Strycker, L. A., Li, F., & Alpert, A. (1999). *An introduction to latent variable growth modeling: Concepts, issues and applications.* Mahwah, NJ: Lawrence Erlbaum.

Dunham, R. B., Grube, J. A., & Castañada, M. B. (1994). Organizational commitment: The utility of an integrative definition. *Journal of Applied Psychology, 79,* 370–380.

Hackett, R. D., Bycio, P., & Hausdorf, P. A. (1994). Further assessments of Meyer and Allen's (1991) model of organizational commitment. *Journal of Applied Psychology, 79,* 15–23.

Hagenaars, J. A., & McCutcheon, A. L. (Eds.). (2002). *Applied latent class analysis.* Cambridge: Cambridge University Press.

Hamaker, E. L. (2005). Conditions for the equivalence of the autoregressive latent trajectory model and a latent growth curve model with autoregressive disturbances. *Sociological Methods & Research, 33,* 404–416.

Horn, J. L., & McArdle, J. J. (1992). A practical and theoretical guide to measurement invariance in aging research. *Experimental Aging Research, 18,* 117–144.

Jaros, S. J. (1997). An assessment of Meyer and Allen's (1991) three-component model of organizational commitment and turnover intentions. *Journal of Vocational Behavior, 51,* 319–337.

Jöreskog, K. G., & Sörbom, D. (1996). *LISREL 8: User's reference guide.* Chicago: Scientific Software International, Inc.

Lance, C. E., Meade, A. W., & Williamson, G. M. (2000). We should measure change—And here's how. In G.M. Williamson & D.R. Shaffer (Eds.), *Physical illness and depression in older adults: Theory, research, and practice,* (pp. 201–235). New York: Plenum.

Lance, C. E., & Vandenberg, R. J. (2001). Confirmatory factor analysis. In Drasgow & N. Schmitt (Eds.), *Measuring and analyzing behavior in organizations: Advances in measurement and data analysis* (Volume in the Organizational Frontier Series, pp. 221–256). San Francisco: Jossey-Bass.

Lance, C. E., Vandenberg, R. J., & Self, R. M. (2000). Latent growth models of individual change: The case of newcomer adjustment. *Organizational Behavior and Human Decision Processes, 83,* 107–140.

Magidson, J., & Vermunt, J. K. (2002). Latent class models for clustering: A comparison with K-means. *Canadian Journal of Marketing Research, 20,* 37–44.

Magidson, J., & Vermunt, J. K. (2004). Latent class models. In D. Kaplan (Ed.), *The Sage handbook of quantitative methodology for the social sciences* (pp. 175–198). Thousand Oaks, CA: Sage Publications, Inc.

Mathieu, J. E., & Zajac, D. (1990). A review and meta-analysis of the antecedents, correlates, and consequences of organizational commitment. *Psychological Bulletin, 108,* 171–194.

McLachlan, G., & Peel, D. (2000). *Finite mixture models.* New York: John Wiley & Sons, Inc.

Meyer, J. P., & Allen, N. J. (1991). A three-component conceptualization of organizational commitment. *Human Resource Management Review, 1,* 61–89.

Meyer, J. P., & Allen, N. J. (1997). *Commitment in the workplace: Theory, research, and application.* Thousand Oaks, CA: Sage.

Meyer, J. P., Allen, N. J., & Gellatly, I. R. (1990). Affective and continuance commitment to the organization: Evaluation of measures and analysis of concurrent and time-lagged relations. *Journal of Applied Psychology, 75,* 710–720.

Meyer, J. P., & Herscovitch, L. (2001). Commitment in the workplace: Towards a general model. *Human Resources Management Review, 1,* 299–326.

Meyer, J. P., Paunonen, S. V., Gellatly, I. R., Goffin, R. D., & Jackson D. N. (1989). Organizational commitment and job performance: It's the nature of the commitment that counts. *Journal of Applied Psychology, 74,* 152–156.

Mowday, R. T., Porter, L. W., & Steers, R. (1982). *Organizational linkages: The psychology of commitment, absenteeism, and turnover.* San Diego, CA: Academic Press.

Muthén, B. O. (2001). Latent variable mixture modeling. In G. A. Marcoulides & R. E. Schumacker (Eds.), *New developments and techniques in structural equation modeling* (pp. 1–33). Hillsdale, NJ: Lawrence Erlbaum Associates.

Muthén, B. O. (2004). Latent variable analysis: Growth mixture modeling and related techniques for longitudinal data. In D. Kaplan (Ed.), *The Sage handbook of quantitative methodology for the social sciences* (pp. 345–368). Thousand Oaks, CA: Sage Publications, Inc.

Muthén, B. O., & Muthén, L. K. (2000). Integrating person-centered and variable-centered analyses: Growth mixture modeling with latent trajectory classes. *Alcoholism: Clinical and Experimental Research, 6,* 882–891.

Muthén, L. K., & Muthén, B. O. (1998–2006). *Mplus User's Guide.* Fourth Edition. Los Angeles: Muthén & Muthén.

Nagin, D. S. (1999). Analyzing developmental trajectories: A semi-parametric, group-based approach. *Psychological Method, 4,* 139–157.

Nagin, D. S., & Land, K. C. (1993). Age, criminal careers, and population heterogeneity: Specification and estimation of a nonparametric, mixed Poisson model. *Criminology, 31,* 327–362.

Nagin, D. S., & Tremblay, R. E. (2001). Analyzing developmental trajectories of distinct but related behaviors: A group-based method. *Psychological Methods 6,* 18–34.

Nylund, K. L., Asparouhov, A., & Muthén, B. (2007). Deciding on the number of classes inlatent class analysis and growth mixture modeling. *Structural Equation Modeling, 14,* 535–569.

O'Reilly, C. A., & Chatman, J. (1986). Organizational commitment and psychological attachment: The effects of compliance, identification, and internalization on prosocial behavior. *Journal of Applied Psychology, 71,* 492–499.

Pastor, D. A., Barron, K. E., Miller, B. J., & Davis, S. L. (2006). A latent profile analysis of college students' achievement goal orientation. *Contemporary Educational Psychology, 32,* 8–47.

Ployhart, R. E., & Oswald, F. L. (2004). Applications of mean and covariance structure analysis: Integrating correlational and experimental approaches. *Organizational Research Methods, 7,* 27–65.

Randall, D. M., Fedor, D. B., & Longenecker, C. O. (1990). The behavioral expression of organizational commitment. *Journal of Vocational Behavior, 36,* 210–224.

Reichers, A. E. (1985). A review and reconceptualization of organizational commitment. *Academy of Management Review, 10,* 465–476.

Rogosa, D. R. (1995). Myths and methods: "Myths about longitudinal research" plus supplemental questions. In J. Gottman (Ed.), *The Analysis of Change,* (pp. 2–65). Mahwah, NJ: Lawrence Erlbaum Associates.

Salancik, G. R. (1977). Commitment and the control of organizational behavior and belief. In B. M. Staw and G. R. Salancik (Eds.). *New directions in organizational behavior.* Chicago: St. Clair Press.

Schmidt, F. L., & Hunter, J. E. (1996). Measurement error in psychological research: Lessons from 26 research scenarios. *Psychological Methods, 1,* 199–223.

Schmitt, N., & Kuljanin, G. (in press). Measurement invariance: Review of practice and implications. *Human Resource Management Review.*

Sinclair, R. R., Tucker, J. S., Cullen, J. C., & Wright, C. (2005). Performance differences among four organizational commitment profiles. *Journal of Applied Psychology, 90,* 1280–1287.

Singer, J. D., & Willet, J. B. (2003). *Applied longitudinal data analysis: Modeling change and event occurrence.* New York: Oxford University Press.

Somers, M. J. (1995). Organizational commitment, turnover, and absenteeism: An examination of direct and interaction effects. *Journal of Organizational Behavior, 16,* 49–58.

Steenkampf, J. E. M., & Baumgartner, H. (1998). Assessing measurement invariance in cross-national consumer research. *Journal of Consumer Research, 25,* 78–91.

Tisak, J., & Tisak, M. S. (2000). Permanency and ephemerality of psychological measures with application to organizational commitment. *Psychological Methods, 5,* 175–198.

Tryon, R. C. (1939). *Cluster Analysis.* Ann Arbor, MI: Edwards Brothers, Inc.

Vandenberg, R.J. (2002). Toward a further understanding of and improvement in measurement invariance methods and procedures. *Organizational Research Methods, 5,* 139–159.

Vandenberg, R. J. (2005). *The diary of a "mad" methodologist: What evils lurk in the shadows of commitment research?* Presented at The Ohio State University Conference on Organizational Commitment , Columbus, OH.

Vandenberg, R. J., & Lance, C. E. (2000). A review and synthesis of the measurement invariance literature: Suggestions, practices, and recommendations for organizational research. *Organizational Research Methods, 3,* 4–69.

Vandenberg, R. J., & Self, R. M. (1993). Assessing newcomers' changing commitments to the organization during the first six months of work. *Journal of Applied Psychology, 78,* 557–568.

Vandenberg, R. J., Stanley, L. J., Vandenberghe, C., & Bentein, K. (2007, August). *On the applicability of latent class growth analysis.* Paper presented at the meeting of the Academy of Management, Philadelphia, PA.

Vermunt, J. K., & Magidson, J. (2002). Latent class cluster analysis. In J. A. Hagenaars & A. L. McCutcheon (Eds.), *Applied latent class analysis* (pp. 89–106). Cambridge, UK: Cambridge University Press.

Williams, L. J., Edwards, J. R., & Vandenberg, R. J. (2003). Recent advances in causal modeling methods for organizational and management research. *Journal of Management, 29,* 903–936.

Wasti, S. A. (2005). Commitment profiles: Combinations of organizational commitment forms and job outcomes. *Journal of Vocational Behavior, 67,* 290–308.

Section 5

Integration and Future Directions

13

Commitment in Organizations: Accumulated Wisdom and New Directions

Thomas E. Becker*
University of Delaware

Howard J. Klein
The Ohio State University

John P. Meyer
The University of Western Ontario

As editors of this book, we had a core set of objectives that we presented to the authors as questions to be answered in their chapters: What do we know now? How useful is what we know? Are current commitment theories adequate, and if not, what theoretical developments are needed? What can we learn from relevant theory and research outside of commitment within industrial/organizational (I/O) psychology, and from theory and research on commitment outside of I/O psychology? What do we need to know and do? In this concluding chapter, we review and synthesize the information compiled by the authors in addressing these questions. We deal with each in turn, with emphasis on the final question. Our objectives are to demonstrate the importance of commitment for organizations and their employees, to identify key gaps in our current understanding of the commitment process, and to provide an agenda for future research.

What We Know About Commitment

After more than 40 years of theory development and research, there is now a very large body of work from which we can learn, and meta-analytic reviews of the research reveal a number of consistent patterns.

* The authors contributed equally to this chapter.

In short, we know a great deal about commitment, and that knowledge is reflected throughout the pages of this book. In considering the chapters in this volume as a whole, it is clear that the topic of employee commitment remains a relevant and vibrant topic of research and a continuing practical concern. As Meyer argued in chapter 2 and as we discuss later in this chapter, it is likely that cultural and structural changes in organizations have made commitment more pertinent than ever. No brief summary can do justice to the breadth of what we know about commitment, but we offer here some insights gleaned from considering the chapters in this volume as a whole. These chapters reflect, in large measure, the accumulated wisdom of the field, and we present the corresponding findings as touchstones for subsequent discussion of what we need to know and how we might go about expanding our understanding of the commitment process. As we discuss what we know, we must be mindful that the research base is largely nonexperimental; and therefore the implied causal directionality, although consistent with commitment theories, is often inconclusive (see chapter 12).

Nature of Commitment

In general, we know that commitment is something that exists within individuals that has important implications for themselves and for the targets of their commitment. We know that numerous antecedents to commitment have been identified and that there are multiple bases (e.g., internalization, identification, compliance; O'Reilly & Chatman, 1986) that can lead to the formation of commitment. We also know that employees have a multitude of work-related commitments, not just commitment to the organization that employs them. Those commitments can be to other organizations (e.g., unions, professional associations, client organizations), individuals within or outside the organization (e.g., coworkers, supervisors, suppliers, customers), groups (e.g., work teams), and various ideas and initiatives (e.g., values, goals, decisions, policies, change programs). Finally, we know that, regardless of target, commitments can be experienced differently and that how one experiences a given commitment has implications for the individual's reactions and responses to that commitment in terms of affective, cognitive, and behavioral outcomes.

With respect to multiple targets, we know that employees develop and simultaneously experience multiple work-relevant commitments (in addition to numerous nonwork commitments). Those workplace commitments can conflict with one another or, when compatible, create synergy. Interestingly, meta-analytic evidence (Cooper-Hakim & Viswesvaran, 2005) indicates that these commitments generally relate positively to one another, suggesting that compatibility may be the rule rather than the exception (although we cannot say whether this is because incompatibilities are rare or get resolved). Research has shown that individuals can distinguish among their multiple commitments and that they account for unique variance in organization-relevant outcomes such as retention and performance (e.g., Lee, Carswell, & Allen, 2000). In addition, investigators who have conducted systematic investigations in this area have shown that multiple commitments (e.g., organization, supervisor, team, customer) often combine to influence behavior (e.g. Becker, 1992; Becker, Billings, Eveleth, & Gilbert, 1996; Vandenberghe, Bentein, & Stinglhamber, 2004).

This research consistently demonstrates that the strongest relations between commitment and behavior result when there is congruence between the target of the commitment and the beneficiary of the behavior. Consequently, the best predictor of organization-relevant outcomes (e.g., organizational citizenship behavior, OCB, directed toward the organization) is likely to be the employees' commitment to the organization, whereas the best predictor of team effectiveness is likely to be commitment to the team or team leader. It also appears that the impact of commitments to less congruent targets are channeled through their effects on commitment to more congruent targets (Bentein, Stinglhamber, & Vandenberghe, 2002; Maertz, Mosley, & Alford, 2002). That is, the impact of supervisor commitment on retention is mediated by its effect on organizational commitment, and the impact of organizational commitment on team performance is mediated by its effect on team commitment. In sum, we know that employees form multiple commitments and that this has implications for work behavior. However, evidence concerning the nature of the interactions among commitments and the mechanisms by which multiple commitments exert joint effects is preliminary. As we discuss later in this chapter, this is an important area for future research.

Turning to the multiple ways a commitment can be experienced, the most widely adopted model of these alternative beliefs and feelings about a commitment is Meyer and Allen's (1991, 1997) three-component model of affective, normative, and continuance mindsets. These different mindsets reflect general perceptions of desire, obligation, or cost and are not exclusive as all three can be experienced in combination and to differing degrees for any given commitment (Meyer & Herscovitch, 2001). As discussed later, there is not complete consensus on whether these three mindsets adequately reflect the different ways people can experience a commitment or whether the notion of mindsets is the best depiction of the alternative ways individuals experience commitment. What is known, however, is that people experience commitments differently and that different mindsets (or profiles of mindsets) are associated with different commitment outcomes (Gellatly, Meyer & Luchak, 2006; Meyer, Stanley, Herscovitch, & Topolnytsky, 2002). There is also some evidence that these patterns differ in different cultural contexts (Stanley et al., 2007).

Development of commitment. Early research conducted to identify the antecedents of commitment, regardless of the target, tended to be relatively unsystematic and not particularly informative (Hollenbeck & Klein, 1987; Meyer & Allen, 1997; Reichers, 1985). This was due, in part, to the wide array of factors that have the potential to influence commitment and the absence of a coherent organizational framework. There is still much work to be done in the development of such a framework (see subsequent discussion), but we have made some strides in that direction. For example, we now recognize that, regardless of the target, antecedent variables can be classified into several broad categories reflecting level of origin: target characteristics; individual differences; and social, organizational, and cultural determinants. Indeed, the structure of chapters 7–10 in this volume reflects such a categorization. Antecedents can also be categorized according to the bases (O'Reilly & Chatman, 1996) or mindsets (Allen & Meyer, 1990) characterizing the commitment. That is, the personal or situational factors contributing to the internalization of organizational values or an affective mindset are quite different from those that lead to compliance or a continuance mindset.

Another potentially useful way to categorize antecedent variables is in terms of proximity—some antecedents appear to be more distal and influence commitment through more proximal factors. For example, in the goal commitment literature, the likelihood and attractiveness of goal attainment are thought to be the most proximal antecedents and to mediate the influence of a host of other situational and individual difference variables (Hollenbeck & Klein, 1987; Klein, Wesson, Hollenbeck, & Alge, 1999). For union commitment, pro-union attitude and beliefs about union instrumentality have been identified as the two most predominant predictors (Bamberger, Kluger, & Suchard, 1999). In the case of organizational commitment, distal influences such as transformational leadership, organizational climate, and specific human resource management (HRM) practices likely operate through their effects on more proximal influences such as perceived organizational support (Rhoades & Eisenberger, 2002), organizational justice (Colquitt, Conlon, Wesson, Porter, & Ng, 2001), organizational identification (Riketta, 2005), and person-organization fit (Kristof-Brown, Zimmerman, & Johnson, 2005; Verquer, Beehr, & Wagner, 2003). In sum, the list of variables that have the potential to influence commitment is lengthy, and research on commitment antecedents continues to be somewhat unsystematic. This need not be the case, however, as antecedents can be classified in terms of level of origin, basis/mindset, and proximity. Admittedly, however, the development of a comprehensive framework for the classification of the antecedents of commitment is still a work in progress and is discussed further later in this chapter.

Consequences of commitment. Across targets, commitment appears to have three primary outcomes: a reluctance to withdraw, a willingness to put forth effort on behalf of the target, and affectivity toward the target. The strength and direction of these outcomes depends, in part, upon how the commitment is experienced (e.g., commitment mindsets). There is the least empirical evidence for the affective consequences of commitment. There is some recent work, however, which points to commitment being highly beneficial for employees (and indirectly so for employers) through its influence on positive affect and, in turn, physical and psychological well-being through reduced negative affect and various indices of stress (Meyer et al., 2002; Thoresen, Kaplan, Barsky, Warren, & de Chermont, 2003). Herrbach (2006), for example, found that commitment, and in particular, the affective mindset, accounted for variance in positive and negative state affect experienced at work beyond what was explained by dispositional affect. In addition, goal commitment has been shown to be negatively related to stress (Klein et al., 1999).

The largest body of evidence pertains to the reluctance to withdraw. Interest in organizational commitment was stimulated primarily because of its promise to explain employee turnover better than job satisfaction, and meta-analytic findings clearly support the negative relationship between organizational commitment and turnover (e.g., Cooper-Hakim & Viswesvaran, 2005; Mathieu & Zajac, 1990). Meta-analyses further reveal that the linkage is mediated by turnover intention (Tett & Meyer, 1993), and that the correlation is strongest when the commitment reflects an affective mindset (Meyer et al., 2002). Organizational commitment has also been shown to predict other withdrawal behaviors such as absenteeism and tardiness. The reluctance to withdraw is evident for other targets as well. For example, goal commitment has been shown to predict the unwillingness to change or abandon a goal, union commitment predicts continued union membership, and commitment to one's occupation relates to remaining in that line of work. The above are all examples of reluctance to behaviorally withdraw from the commitment target. Withdrawal can also take the form of psychological disengagement, and the reluctance to withdraw behaviorally or psychologically is a key reason why commitment is usually cited as a major component of engagement (e.g., Macey & Schneider, 2008).

The final category of commitment consequences centers on a willingness to put forth effort toward the target, and the consequences of that effort, including job performance. Job performance is arguably the consequence of greatest interest to employers, and empirical evidence suggests that organizational commitment does relate to performance, albeit weakly (Riketta, 2002). When this link is examined over time, it appears that commitment is indeed antecedent to performance and that the strength of that association is greater when the time lag is relatively short (Riketta, 2008). Commitments to other targets, such as teams and supervisors, have similarly been shown to be positively related to job performance, sometimes to a greater extent than organizational commitment (e.g., Becker et al., 1996; Bishop, Scott, & Burroughs, 2000). In addition, team commitment has been shown to predict team performance, and goal commitment has been found to have both main and interactive effects on task performance (Klein et al., 1999; Locke & Latham, 1990). Job behavior is certainly dependent on a number of factors unrelated to commitment, so it is not surprising that organizational commitment has been found to relate more strongly to behaviors that are more discretionary in nature, such as OCB (LePine, Erez, & Johnson, 2002; Riketta, 2002), and negatively with counterproductive work behaviors (Dalal, 2005).

In terms of other targets, commitment to supervisors and teams (e.g., Becker & Kernan, 2003; Bentein et al., 2002) has also been shown to be related to OCB, commitment to organizational programs and change initiatives has been shown to be associated with higher levels of behavioral support for those efforts (e.g., Neubert & Cady, 2001; Herscovitch & Meyer, 2002), union commitment has been shown to result in a willingness to work for the union and to actively participate in union activities (Snape, Redman, & Chan, 2000), and occupational commitment has been shown to result in the continued development of relevant knowledge and skills (Meyer, Allen, & Smith, 1993; Snape & Redman, 2003). Studies that have examined multiple commitment mindsets (for both performance and behavioral outcomes) have generally found differences in the strength of relations, with an affective mindset consistently demonstrating the strongest and most positive associations, at least in North America and other individualist cultures (Cooper-Hakim & Viswesvaran, 2005; Meyer et al., 2002). There is recent evidence suggesting that a normative mindset might relate more strongly to work behavior in collectivist cultures (Stanley et al., 2007; also see chapter 10).

How Useful Is What We Know About Commitment?

The simple answer to this question is that what we know is very useful, but that there is much that we still need to know. Indeed, one important use of what we know is to provide guidance for future research, and we attend to that application in the concluding section of this chapter. Another important use is to guide practice, and it is to this purpose that we direct our attention here. We need to be cautious in making recommendations when our knowledge is admittedly incomplete, but that can be said about the application of knowledge in any scientific discipline. There has been a clarion call for a more evidence-based approach to management (Pfeffer & Sutton, 2006; Rousseau, 2006), and we believe that the accumulated knowledge generated in over 40 years of commitment research can provide a wealth of such evidence. Therefore, with due caution to limitations in current theory and research (as discussed later in this chapter), we believe the following advice can be offered to managers.

First, as argued in chapter 2, employee commitment is important, perhaps even more so in a changing world of work where things are becoming less predictable and long-term employment relationships are becoming more difficult to establish. In this regard, it is important to keep in mind that employees can commit to more than their employing organization. They can commit to their own careers and occupation, people (e.g., supervisor, coworkers, teams, customers), goals, policies, programs, and change initiatives (see chapters 4–6). To the extent that the targets of these commitments share goals in common with the organization, the organization as a whole can benefit. However, when in conflict, these other commitments could lead employees to behave in ways that are detrimental to the organization. Therefore, it is important to manage these alternative commitments carefully to ensure goal alignment.

Second, commitments can be experienced in different ways (i.e., accompanied by different mindsets), and this can have important implications for the consequences of those commitments. A recent meta-analytic review of the relations between commitment and behavior demonstrated that although affective, normative, and continuance mindsets all relate negatively with turnover intention and turnover, only affective and normative mindsets related positively to other desirable behaviors, including attendance, job performance, and OCB. Indeed, the benefits of commitment experienced with affective and normative mindsets appear to be greatest for behaviors like OCB that are considered discretionary. Similar findings have been reported in studies involving other targets of commitment. For example, affective, normative, and continuance mindsets for commitment to a change initiative were all found to correlate positively with compliance with the requirements for change, but only affective and normative mindsets were positively related to more discretionary forms of support such as willingness to champion the change (Herscovitch & Meyer, 2002; Meyer, Srinivas, Lal, & Topolnytsky, 2007). Therefore, organizations that rely heavily on employees to make decisions or take personal initiative may find it particularly important to foster a strong affective mindset in its employees. One way to do this is for managers to provide the material and psychological support required by employees to effectively perform their jobs.

Third, it is important to look beyond outcomes of immediate benefit to organizations (e.g., retention, job performance) when considering the relevance of commitment. A growing body of research has found positive relations between organizational and occupational commitment experienced with an affective mindset and various indices of employee health and well-being (Maltin & Meyer, in press). Relations with measures of various stressors, strains, and indices of burnout tend to be negative. Interestingly, correlations between a continuance mindset and indices of well-being and strain tend to be the reverse of those for an affective mindset. Consequently, the evidence suggests that the commitment mindsets that have the most positive implications for organizations also appear to have the greatest benefits for employees. There is also growing evidence that a healthier workforce benefits the organization through reduced absenteeism and lower insurance claims and premiums (e.g., Goetzel et al., 1998).

Fourth, we have learned a great deal about the key drivers of commitment, particularly when experienced as an affective mindset. As noted earlier, research has now identified several proximal antecedents of commitment. These include perceived organizational support, organizational justice, organizational identification, and person-organization fit. There are many other HRM practices, work experiences, and climate factors that have been found in individual studies to relate to commitment. We suspect that many of these more specific factors operate in large part through their effects on the more proximal influences. However, the impact of specific practices is likely to be more situation specific, and organizations should be cautious in adapting "best practices" without due consideration of contextual differences. For example, the introduction of childcare benefits might help foster commitment in an organization where a large majority of employees are likely to take advantage of such benefits, but could create resentment in another organization where relatively few would find value in that benefit. The latter situation might be avoided by evaluating policies and practices in terms of the implications for perceived support, justice, or fit (Meyer & Topolnytsky, 2000). Although the research evidence is limited, we suspect that this core set of proximal antecedents can be applied or adapted to other targets of commitment as well. For example, perceived supervisor support has been found to relate to goal commitment and supervisor commitment just as organizational support relates to organizational commitment (e.g., Stinglhamber & Vandenberghe, 2003; Vandenberghe et al., 2004). Principles of justice have also been shown to influence reactions to organizational change (Novelli, Kirkman, & Shapiro, 1995), including commitment to the change (Fedor, Caldwell, & Herold, 2006).

Finally, we have learned that commitment is relevant across cultures, but that commitments can develop, be experienced, and influence behavior somewhat differently in different cultures (see chapter 10). Cross-cultural research is still in its infancy, so it is difficult to provide specific guidance beyond a simple caution that management strategies found to be effective in fostering commitment in one culture may be less effective in others. Similarly, these same practices may be differentially effective within organizations where there is considerable diversity in cultural back-ground. Our recommendation, therefore, is that organizations be aware of cultural differences and that they conduct their own investigations to assess cultural norms to gauge how these might influence receptiveness to management practices.

In sum, not only do we know a good deal about commitment, what we know is very useful. That said, there are gaps in what we know, and the usefulness of what we know is limited by not having a better understand-ing of the interplay among commitments to multiple targets and mind-sets and not fully understanding exactly what commitments (i.e., to what targets) experienced in what ways (e.g., mindsets) are most desirable in what contexts. Indeed, as we note in the next section, there are still some basic disagreements about the meaning of commitment and how it should be operationalized. Resolving these issues will have implications for our pursuit of further knowledge and for the application of that knowledge.

Are Current Commitment Theories Adequate?

Whether or not current theories are adequate depends upon the criteria used. The authors of each section were asked to consider the adequacy of current theories from their perspectives and with reference to the substan-tive issues under review. The predominant viewpoint was that authors were able to understand, explain, and predict the aspects of commitment germane to their chapter using the array of theories and models currently available. Therefore, it appears that there is value in the current theories. However, the fact that there are multiple commitment frameworks in oper-ation (see chapter 1) can be viewed as either a benefit or a concern. On the one hand, the existence of multiple approaches is advantageous because it introduces diversity into our thinking about what commitment is, how it develops, and how it impacts employees and the organizations in which they work. On the other hand, the lack of consensus on a number of issues regarding the meaning, structure, and measurement of commitment can create barriers to communication and the cross-fertilization of ideas and thereby hinder progress in our understanding of how commitment devel-ops and how it relates to important outcomes. Space does not permit us to fully debate each area of disagreement, but for the sake of increasing awareness, we briefly point out some of the key issues so that they can be addressed in future research as discussed later in this chapter.

What type of concept is commitment? Commitment has historically been depicted as an attitude (Mowday, Porter, & Steers, 1982), and still is by some (e.g., Solinger, Van Olffen, & Roe, 2008). Yet more recently, authors (e.g., Meyer & Herscovitch, 2001) have argued that commitment is a psychological state that is distinct from an attitude. As discussed in chapter 1, current definitions of attitudes as a summary judgment (e.g., Ajzen & Fishbein, 2000) do not adequately describe the concept of commitment. Because commitment is both more than a summary judgment and is not conditional on such a judgment, we are in agreement that commitment is a psychological state but that it is not an attitude and should not be described as an attitude. As such, we also do not believe commitment and attitudinal variables such as job satisfaction should be viewed as interchangeable or overlapping to the extent that they can be combined into a single "job attitudes" variable (e.g., Harrison, Newman, & Roth, 2006).

We agree with the authors of chapter 1 that commitment is most appropriately viewed as either a psychological bond to a target or as a force binding one to a target. However, we are not in agreement on which of these two conceptualizations is most viable. This is a nontrivial issue because these two conceptualizations involve alternative definitions of commitment, each supported by prior conceptual and empirical work and each with different implications for the role and measurement of commitment. We return to this difference of opinion later in this chapter when discussing needed future research.

The extent to which commitment is a motivational construct is a final aspect of the nature of commitment on which we disagree. Meyer, Becker, and Vandenberghe (2004) present commitment as a unique type of motivational force. One perspective, therefore, is that commitment, by its nature, is motivation and should be considered with other motivation theories. This is an implicit assumption underlying definitions of commitment as a binding force. A second view is that commitment, because it affects the direction, amplitude, and persistence of behavior, is motivational and that defining where commitment ends and motivation begins would be arbitrary. A third position is that commitment and motivation are distinct concepts and that boundaries are necessary to adequately define a construct. Along these lines, Klein et al. in chapter 1 argue that commitment is distinct from, and an antecedent of, motivation. Whether or not commitment is motivation has implications for how commitment should be measured and its expected relationships with other variables. For example, motivation is widely viewed as not directly observable, needing to be inferred from measures of attention, effort, or persistence (Kanfer, Chen, & Pritchard, 2008). Viewing commitment as motivation would seem to imply that commitment, similarly, would need to be measured indirectly.

What is the dimensionality of commitment? Commitment is widely viewed as multidimensional in the literature, yet most recent definitions of commitment (e.g., Meyer & Herscovitch, 2001) present the core essence of commitment as unidimensional. Much of the confusion regarding dimensionality comes from the multiple perspectives from which it has been studied (e.g., attitudinal, behavioral), the multiple targets of commitment (e.g., organization, supervisor), the multiple bases that can lead to the formation of commitment (e.g., identification, compliance), and the multiple mindsets that can characterize a commitment (e.g., normative, affective). We are in agreement that, despite these multiple perspectives, antecedents, targets, and interpretations, the core essence of commitment is a singular concept. That is, commitment, whether defined as a bond or force, is a unidimensional concept that can result from and be shaped by multiple factors, be directed at multiple targets, and be experienced in multiple ways (e.g., different mindsets) with different consequences. Thus, although commitment at its core is unidimensional, there are several aspects of the commitment phenomenon that are multidimensional.

We are not in agreement regarding the implications of the dimensionality issue for the measurement of commitment. On the one hand, Meyer and Herscovitch (2001) suggest that a measure of the core essence of commitment is unnecessary because it is the accompanying mindsets that are most important in determining behavior. Meyer and Herscovitch (2001) further argue that it might not be possible to measure commitment directly without using language that implies one or more of the mindsets that accompany that commitment. The counterargument is that if there is a unidimensional core essence of commitment, then a unidimensional measure of that overall level of commitment is needed (Klein, Brinsfield, & Molloy, 2006). Specifically, although the accompanying mindsets matter, having a separate measure of commitment strength would (a) provide a single indicator of the overall level of commitment to a target across mindsets, (b) allow for the examination of how strength and mindsets may change and influence each other over time, and (c) allow researchers to examine the unique and potential interactive contributions of each in determining commitment outcomes.

The dimensionality of the most commonly used typology of commitment mindsets has also been a debated issue. Meyer and Allen's (1991) framework suggests three alternative mindsets (affective-desire/want to, continuance-perceived cost/need to, normative-obligation/ought to) and has received substantial, but not universal, support. Several studies have demonstrated high overlap between normative and affective mindsets (e.g., Allen & Meyer, 1990; Becker, 2006; Ko, Price, and Mueller, 1997), and others have found that the continuance mindset consists of two separate dimensions: high investments versus few alternatives (e.g., McGee & Ford, 1987; Meyer, Allen, & Gellatly, 1990; Stinglhamber, Bentein, & Vandenberghe, 2002). In addition, recent research suggests that the normative mindset can be experienced as a "moral imperative" when combined with a strong affective mindset and as an "indebted obligation" when paired with a weak affective and strong continuance mindset (e.g., Gellatly et al., 2006).

A related issue is whether all of these mindsets should be considered commitment. Specifically, behavioral consistency driven by sunk costs or perceived necessity is considered commitment (e.g., calculative involvement, continuance mindset, or compliance) in some models. On the other hand, Becker (2005) has argued that because the continuance mindset is typically unrelated to the other commitment mindsets and often correlates with other variables in the opposite direction from other commitment mindsets, it should be considered a separate concept distinct from commitment (cf. Powell & Meyer, 2004, for a contrasting perspective). We are in agreement that the continuance mindset is quite different from the affective and normative mindsets, but we disagree as to whether that difference is great enough to warrant being defined as a distinct construct, separate from commitment.

Do mindsets best capture the different ways individuals experience their commitments? Commitment mindsets reflect a person's beliefs and feelings about the nature of his or her commitment. Meyer and Allen's (1991) affective, normative, and continuance mindsets were presented as a way to integrate the different ways commitment had been viewed and studied in the literature. These three mindsets reflect general perceptions of desire, obligation, or cost (or combinations thereof) and, hence, are distinct from the bases or antecedents of commitment (Meyer & Herscovitch, 2001). Commitment rationales were proposed by Klein et al. (2006) as an alternative way of describing the possible explanations one may have for a given commitment. Commitment rationales refer to the different possible self-explanations one may have for a given commitment, and reflect how an individual makes sense of their commitment to a target at a particular point in time. Rationales are based on both past and current perceptions of the target and environment.

Rationales and mindsets are similar in a number of ways, but there are differences between the two perspectives. First, mindsets, or at least their measurement, typically include both how individuals view their commitment and how strongly they are committed. Rationales, on the other hand, are presented as a distinct construct from commitment strength. Klein et al. (2006) argued that rationales thus convey more clearly than mindsets that there is a singular commitment to a particular target that can be experienced in multiple ways. Second, each mindset is thought to be shaped by different bases and antecedent factors reflected in those bases (e.g., Meyer & Allen, 1991; Meyer & Herscovitch, 2001). Rationales, because they are more explicitly defined in terms of sense making, hold that an individual's self-explanations for their commitment to a given target may or may not reflect the factors that led to that commitment.

Should behavioral inclination be included within the construct definition of commitment? We are in agreement that commitment definitions and corresponding measures should not include intentions or behavior, as these are outcomes of commitment that researchers and practitioners want to predict, and their inclusion would confound commitment with its consequences. We are not in agreement, however, as to whether a desire to act or an implied course of action should be included in the definition of commitment (and hence in commitment measures). From the perspective that commitment is a binding force, it is argued that the behavioral terms of a commitment are an important part of the construct and its measurement (Brown, 1996; Meyer & Herscovitch, 2001). These terms can be very specific (e.g., meet a goal) or quite general (e.g., provide needed support) and are implied or made explicit when the commitment is made. The value of a commitment therefore is in the assurance (or at least increased likelihood) that the individual will behave in the agreed upon manner (e.g., stay with the organization). From this perspective, the behavioral terms, through the different mindsets (desire, obligation, need), are distinguishable from and shape specific intentions with regard to how the terms of the commitment will be carried out.

If one instead views commitment as a bond rather than a force, then there is no need to include a desire to engage in a specific course of action. Furthermore, from this perspective the inclusion of a desire to act, as with intentions, unnecessarily confounds commitment with its primary outcomes. The value of a commitment is still the increased likelihood that the individual will behave in a particular manner, but those terms are not viewed as a part of the commitment construct. That is, although commitment is likely to result in the intention to take action, it does not necessarily entail desire, intention, or behavior. From this perspective, there can be a bond to a target without there also being a bond to a course of action. Commitments manifest themselves in multiple ways, not all of which are behavioral. For example, there are numerous forms of withdrawal, not all of which involve actions (e.g., one can cognitively or emotionally "check out" while going through the motions behaviorally).

What We Can Learn From Theory and Research in Other Areas

The study of commitment began outside of the workplace in the fields of psychology and sociology. Currently, commitment is studied in numerous disciplines and in a multitude of contexts in and outside of the workplace. As noted in Klein et al. (2006), commitment is studied in areas as diverse as fitness routines in health management (e.g., Poole, 2001); religious beliefs and practices in religion and philosophy (e.g., Kahn & Greene, 2004); love relationships in interpersonal counseling (e.g., Johnson, Caughlin, & Huston, 1999); volunteer service in social psychology (e.g., Matsuba & Walker, 2004); consumer brands in marketing (e.g., Rust, Lemon, & Zeithaml, 2004); positions, candidates, and parties in political science (e.g., Crosby & Taylor, 1983); and sports teams in sports management (e.g., Wann & Pierce, 2003). In many of these disciplines and others, researchers have borrowed heavily from the work conducted in workplace contexts and thus often do not provide unique theoretical perspectives.

Even in such cases, however, because commitment models are modified and adapted to reflect the phenomenon of interest, additional insights can be gained from these literatures regarding commitment antecedents, processes, and outcomes. For example, research in marketing has examined the relationship between commitment and forgiveness with respect to consumer relationships with brands (e.g., Aaker, Fournier, & Brasel, 2004). Such research could be extended to workplace contexts in examining trust repair with respect to commitment to coworkers or supervisors and organizational targets following psychological contract violations. As another example, research on commitment in interpersonal relationships has focused on the interplay of sacrifice and self-interest in the development of commitment (e.g., Whitton, Stanley & Markman, 2007). More explicit consideration of such concepts may enrich our understanding of the development of workplace commitments.

In addition, as noted in several places in this volume, streams of research exist in other disciplines that, although not specifically directed at the study of commitment, have implications that may be valuable for understanding commitment. For example, evolutionary psychology may better inform us about the fundamental reasons that humans form commitments, including insights into social exchange and the formation of group hierarchies. Research on interpersonal attraction has the potential to more thoroughly explain to whom employees become committed, and attachment theory can probably elucidate individual differences in the nature of workplace bonds. For more on these and other promising leads, see the discussions on evolutionary psychology (chapters 2 and 5), interpersonal attraction (chapter 5), developmental psychology (chapter 7), as well as sociology, economics, political science, and history (chapter 10).

From these areas and others, a number of theoretical perspectives have been suggested in the literature as being useful for explaining workplace commitments. The theories most often mentioned in this volume as having value for explaining and understanding commitments in the workplace are social exchange theories (chapters 4, 5, 8, and 10), self-determination theory (chapters 2, 4, 7, and 8), attachment theory (chapters 5 and 7), regulatory focus theory (chapters 4 and 6), and the theory of planned behavior (chapters 6 and 7). In sum, further theoretical development is clearly encouraged and warranted. It also appears that an increased understanding of commitment is best achieved by continuing to examine commitment through existing models and the lens of multiple theories from multiple disciplines, at least until the above conceptual issues can be resolved. At that point, a new encompassing theory of commitment may be warranted or an existing theory may more clearly emerge as worthy of widespread acceptance.

What Do We Need to Know and Do?

As we noted above, we have learned a great deal about workplace commitments, both directly and by extrapolating from theory and research in other areas. However, we also have a great deal more to learn. Therefore, we conclude this chapter by identifying key gaps in our theory, research methodology, and research findings and by providing an agenda for future research. We begin by addressing ways that we might resolve basic disagreements concerning the conceptualization and measurement of commitment (also see chapters 1 and 11). As long as these differences exist, the commitment literature is likely to be fractionated with less cross-fertilization than might be desirable. We then address some of the major limitations in the way commitment research has been conducted in the past. This has important implications for what we can conclude from our findings regarding the development and consequences of commitment and its relations with other variables (see chapters 3 through 9). Here we borrow heavily from the discussion of methodological issues and developments in chapter 12. Finally, we focus on issues that have become particularly salient as the result of the increasing prevalence of change (see chapter 2), and the spread of interest in commitment to countries with very different cultures than those where most of the theoretical and empirical work has been conducted (see chapter 10).

Conceptualization and Measurement of Commitment

As noted above and in chapter 1 of this volume, commitment has been conceptualized and studied in a variety of ways, and this has resulted in multiple, sometimes incompatible, perspectives. These differences may appear subtle but have important implications for the way in which commitment is measured (see chapter 11) and, thus, for the substantive findings accumulated in research using those measures. In this section we return to five such issues and describe the research needed to address them. Resolving these issues is critical for progress in commitment research, particularly with regard to better communication among researchers studying commitment to different targets.

Commitment as a bond versus a force that binds. As noted earlier, some theorists define commitment as a bond, whereas others consider it to be a force that binds. These are philosophical differences in the nature of the construct—differences that are not likely to be resolved by persuasive argument or a few well-conducted studies. Such definitional differences do not easily lend themselves to competitive empirical testing. However, resolution should be possible when accumulated research provides evidence regarding the value of each perspective for understanding commitment phenomenon across foci and generating valuable implications for practice. Several steps must be taken, however, before the accumulation of evidence can be objectively assessed to evaluate the merits of conceptualizing commitment as a bond versus a binding force. First, consistent with a goal of this book, awareness of alternative definitions needs to be increased. Second, state-of-the-art measures of commitment accurately reflecting each definition must be used to examine the nomological network surrounding commitment. Although the bond-versus-force debate and several other issues in this section are conceptual in nature, they can only be resolved at the operational level. For that to occur, it is critical that operationalizations accurately reflect each conceptual position. Chapter 11 discusses commitment measurement issues in depth.

Inclusion of behavioral terms in definitions of commitment. As discussed above and in chapter 11, some authors (e.g., Brown, 1996; Meyer & Herscovitch, 2001) argue that commitments by their very nature include behavioral implications. According to Meyer and Herscovitch (2001), the terms of a commitment serve to identify the behavioral outcomes that can be expected. For example, if the terms of the commitment are to remain with the organization, then retention becomes the relevant criterion. If on the other hand the commitment is to achieve a goal, then goal attainment becomes the outcome of interest. In cases where the terms of the commitment are very general (e.g., wedding vows), the outcomes of interest will also be broad (e.g., maintaining the relationship and satisfying the needs of the target). From this perspective, precisely how a commitment is defined and enacted depends upon the commitment mindset(s). Meyer and Herscovitch (2001) further argue that, in the measurement of commitment, the mindsets (want to, ought to, have to) pertaining to the behavioral terms of a commitment are distinguishable from the behaviors or behavioral intentions they are theorized to predict (see Meyer, 1997).

On the other hand, others (Becker, 2005; Klein et al., 2006) argue that behavioral terms need not and should not be included in the definition of commitment. Although both views recognize that behaviors and intentions should be external to the definition of commitment, this perspective would exclude all behavioral terms, arguing that the same rationale for excluding intentions and behaviors applies to a desire, an obligation, a need to act, or a specific course of action. That is, these are the outcomes that researchers and practitioners want to predict, and incorporating them into the definition of commitment and its measures confounds predictors and criteria. As with the bond-versus-force discussion above, this is a basic philosophical difference that does not easily lend itself to a single competitive test. Rather, accumulated evidence using measures that appropriately include and exclude behavioral terms will likely lead to one approach or the other being chosen as most useful.

Experiencing commitment. A final disagreement that is largely definitional in nature is how to best represent the different ways individuals can experience a commitment. Mindsets are best reflected by Meyer and Allen's (1997) three-component framework. Klein et al. (2006) suggested rationales as an alternative perspective but did not identify exactly what those rationales are, instead suggesting that qualitative research is needed to identify the different ways individuals make sense of the full range of multiple commitments in the contemporary workplace. As discussed earlier, there are substantial similarities but a few key differences between these perspectives, both in terms of how this aspect of commitment is depicted, and potentially in terms of the set of distinct experiences represented. Before the mindset-versus-rationales issue can be properly evaluated, the set of rationales that best describes the range of ways employees make sense of their multiple commitments needs to be identified, and then valid measures need to be created to reflect those rationales. At that point, empirical research can be accumulated to examine whether using rationales instead of—or in addition to—mindsets helps to account for more variance in important outcome variables.

A third alternative to needing either mindsets or rationales should also be noted. Specifically, commitment could conceivably be defined more narrowly such that only some or even just one mindset or rationale is considered to be commitment, with other mindsets or rationales defined as distinct constructs, separate from commitment. Just as identification, previously viewed as an element of commitment, is now recognized as a distinct construct, other aspects of commitment could similarly be defined instead as related but distinct phenomenon. For example, attachments experienced primarily as sunk costs or a lack of alternatives could be defined separately, perhaps as a concept termed "alienation." To support such distinctions, construct definitions would need to be put forth that clearly distinguish how these psychological states are experienced, and empirical evidence would need to be provided that such distinctions are warranted in terms of divergence and differential patterns of relationships with antecedent and outcome variables. The latter would require that existing measures be reinterpreted in light of the new conceptualizations or new measures of the concepts created and validated.

The dimensionality of commitment. There are multiple commitment targets, bases, and mindsets, and as such these phenomena can legitimately be labeled multidimensional. At its core, however, several authors have argued that commitment is unidimensional. We come back to the implications of this assertion in the next section. In terms of targets and bases, the implications are not for measurement but for the development of parsimonious frameworks for organizing and studying all of the different things to which individuals can be committed and all the antecedent factors that can influence the development of commitment. In terms of mindsets, as noted earlier, there is some debate as to dimensionality of commitment mindsets, with arguments made that there should be between two and five distinct mindsets instead of the three components articulated by Meyer and Allen (1991). Research is needed to resolve this issue and to develop measures that adequately capture the underlying dimensionality of the different mindsets.

It has also been suggested that new qualitative work is needed to determine whether changes in the employment context or employee expectations have altered the way employees interpret the multitude of workplace commitments (Klein et al., 2006). For example, researchers could ask individuals in a wide variety of positions to talk about how they experience and make sense of the full range of commitments they have relating to their work lives. Asking about why they are committed and how that commitment developed would also be valuable. Results of such studies may demonstrate that a different configuration of mindsets or additional mindsets are required. As a result, additional work may be needed to ensure that measures of commitment adequately reflect the different ways commitment can be experienced. Any new or refined measures of commitment should reflect, or at least be clear about, the above conceptual issues. It is also important for new or revised measures to facilitate the examination of commitment across targets and cultures.

Singular measure of commitment strength. There has been debate as to whether it is necessary, desirable, or even possible to have a separate measure of the unidimensional core essence of commitment (i.e., the overall level of commitment toward a particular target) independent of the mindsets or rationales that may accompany that commitment. The resolution to this debate will depend on the development and validation of a measure of commitment strength that does not induce or reflect a particular mindset. We do not necessarily view new commitment scales as invalidating the extensive body of research that has been accumulated using existing measures. Rather, the validation process for any new scale should include an examination of convergence and divergence from existing commitment measures to determine how the accumulated research using prior measures should be reinterpreted within any new measurement framework. Readers are also referred to chapter 11 for a more detailed discussion of the issues surrounding the measurement of commitment.

In answering the question of what we need to know and do, we have first addressed issues pertaining to the conceptualization and measurement of commitment, because they have important implications for whether the field moves toward greater unification or remains fragmented. As discussed above, resolving these issues may take some time. However, research on substantive issues concerning commitment need not be put on hold in the interim, and there are a number of pressing issues we would like to see commitment researchers address. The following were selected for discussion because they reflect common themes in the recommendations made by the various chapter authors. We refer the reader to the chapters themselves for elaboration on how these themes apply with regard to the various content areas and for recommendations that are more specific to a particular area.

Application of New Methodologies

Vandenberg and Stanley, in chapter 12, observe that there is often a mismatch between the questions commitment researchers ask and the research methods they use to answer those questions. Practical and sometimes ethical considerations preclude the use of quasi-experimental studies, let alone randomized, double-blind experiments; yet nonexperimental methods and correlational analyses have not always been applied to full advantage. For example, several of the chapter authors note that, despite the belief that commitment is a "process," there has been relatively little longitudinal research conducted to examine how commitment develops and exerts its influence over time. Similarly, in spite of the long-standing belief that commitment is influenced by organizational policies and practices and has the potential to contribute to organizational effectiveness, there has been relatively little research conducted at the organizational level or using cross-level analyses. Therefore, more longitudinal research is required, as well as a shift in attention from individual-level studies to higher-level and cross-level research. In this section we want to draw readers' attention to more appropriate methodologies and analyses and encourage the creative use of these strategies in addressing both old and new questions regarding the development and consequences of commitment.

Commitment is, at first blush, an individual-level variable, and our theories of commitment have generally focused on how employees become committed and how this commitment influences their behavior at work. Nevertheless, implied in our theories of commitment is the belief that it develops over time through a complex interplay of individual difference and situational variables. Individual differences in personality, values, and attachment styles (see chapter 7) presumably predispose an individual's willingness to commit, and this predisposition interacts with pre- and post-entry work experiences (see chapters 7–9) to shape the strength and nature of the various workplace commitments that develop. Furthermore, these commitments are subject to change as conditions at work, in the economy, or in the person's life in general change. However, the vast majority of research conducted to examine the development of commitment has been cross-sectional, typically with commitment, personal characteristics, or perceptions of situational factors measured on a single occasion. Clearly, the correlations produced in these studies (and summarized in meta-analyses) do not allow us to evaluate the complex processes implied in our theories. Longitudinal studies and time-lagged panel designs are better but are still limited in their ability to address questions pertaining to change over time. Fortunately, as Vandenberg and Stanley explain in chapter 12, developments in structural equation modeling (SEM) techniques, most notably latent growth modeling (LGM) and related analyses, provide more appropriate ways for us to test hypotheses concerning how individual difference and situational variables, as well as changes in these variables, relate to changes in commitment over time. Similarly, they can be applied to examine how changes in commitment relate to changes in behavior over time. We strongly encourage greater use of these more sophisticated analytic strategies in future research.

Although commitment is something experienced by individuals, its implications for organizational effectiveness are arguably most clearly reflected at an organizational level of analysis (see chapters 2 and 9). Moreover, many of the factors presumed to influence commitment (e.g., HRM policies and practices) are organization-level variables (although they influence individuals via perceptions). Nevertheless, there has been a relative paucity of organization-level research conducted to examine the development or implications of commitment. Similarly, despite the recent interest in the development of commitment to teams and its implications for team effectiveness, there has been little team-level research. There has also been very little cross-level research conducted, despite the fact that our theories imply such cross-level effects. For example, based on theories of commitment and strategic HRM, we would expect HRM policies and practices (an organization-level variable) to influence perceptions of these practices (e.g., fairness) and the organization (e.g., perceived organizational support), which, in turn, shape employee commitment (individual-level variables). In addition, we expect that employees' commitment influences their behavior and performance and that, when aggregated to an organizational level, has implications for organizational effectiveness. We need more cross-level analyses to test these hypotheses. Fortunately, there are data-analytic techniques such as hierarchical linear modeling to assist in this process. Therefore, we strongly encourage more multi- and cross-level research.

As noted above, it is now widely accepted that commitment can be characterized by different mindsets and can be directed at multiple targets. Furthermore, those multiple commitment mindsets and commitments to multiple targets often combine to influence behavior. However, the vast majority of research continues to examine relations involving individual mindsets or commitments to individual targets, occasionally looking at additive effects and, even more rarely, interactive effects. Thus, most research has not captured the complexity of the potential interplay among the multiple mindsets and targets reflected in theory and experienced by employees. For example, Meyer and Herscovitch (2001) recently argued that the strength of any given commitment mindset will influence the relation between another mindset and any behavioral outcome. In testing this hypothesis, Gellatly et al. (2006) discovered that the three mindsets within Meyer and Allen's three-component model provide a "context" for one another. This context effect was most clearly illustrated in the case of the normative mindset, which, it seemed, could be experienced either as a "moral imperative" (when combined with a strong affective mindset) or as an "indebted obligation" (when combined with a weak affective and strong continuance mindset). It is conceivable that commitments to various targets also provide a context for one another. For example, commitment to a team or a union might be experienced differently, and influence behavior differently, depending on whether employees have a strong or weak commitment to their organization. The more widespread use of techniques such as latent class analysis (LCA) and latent growth class analysis (LGCA) described in chapter 12 may help facilitate the examination of profiles of commitment mindsets and multiple commitment targets.

Finally, we want to draw attention to the importance of the issue of measurement equivalence as interest in commitment spreads outside of North America and other Western countries (see chapter 10) and as researchers increasingly study commitment in a greater variety of cultures. In chapter 12, Vandenberg and Stanley note that it is essential that researchers wanting to make cross-cultural comparisons first demonstrate that they are using equivalent measures. In the absence of such evidence, it is impossible to draw firm conclusions about similarities and differences across cultures. Of course, as Wasti and Önder point out in chapter 10, there are many other methodological issues that arise in cross-cultural research. Many of these issues have been addressed by research in other domains, so we encourage commitment researchers who are conducting research in other cultures and/or want to make cross-cultural comparisons to consult these literatures to identify potential problems and solutions.

In sum, we encourage commitment researchers to make a more con-
certed effort to apply methods and data-analytic techniques that are well
matched to their research questions. As discussed in chapter 12, tremendous strides have been made in recent years to develop new data-analytic
strategies that should allow us to get closer to our quest for causal inference
and to address complex questions about the commitment process. Not all
of these developments originate in the I/O psychology literature, so we
also encourage researchers to look to other literatures for innovations in
methodology that can be imported to address substantive issues such as
those described below. It is similarly important that as journal reviewers
we begin to demand that the concerns outlined in chapter 12 (e.g., proper
treatment of measurement invariance, multiple dimensions, and change)
be appropriately addressed in empirical commitment research.

Development of Commitment

The authors of chapters 7 through 9 address the individual, social, and
organizational influences on commitment. The authors of chapters 4
through 6 also address developmental issues in their treatment of organizational, social, and action commitments. Collectively, there has been
a great deal of research on the antecedents side of the commitment process, and as we noted above, we have learned a great deal. However, there
is still much to be learned, and the learning process should be greatly
facilitated by application of the new methodologies described in the previous section. In this section we highlight a few of what we consider to
be among the more important issues to be addressed in future research
relating to the development of commitment.

Even a cursory review of the development literature reveals that interest
and research on potential antecedents of commitment has been somewhat
uneven. For example, as noted in chapters 6 and 7, and consistent with
the larger trend in I/O psychology and organizational behavior, greater
attention needs to be given to the role of affect in the development of commitment. In addition, there has been far less attention given to individual
and organizational variables than to social factors and general work experiences. Much of the attention given to the influence of personal characteristics has been in the context of person-organization fit research. We
now have considerable evidence that person-organization fit, particularly
values fit, relates positively to commitment experienced with an affective mindset (Kristof-Brown et al., 2005; Verquer et al., 2003). However,
there may be other individual differences (e.g., personality, attachment
style) that contribute to assessments of fit and would be worth exploring. Individual differences might also play a more direct role in shaping
commitment, or at least the predisposition to commit, and therefore we
encourage additional research to identify these characteristics and to

determine whether it might be possible to select employees based on their ability and willingness to make commitments. Such research should be guided by theory along the lines demonstrated by Bergman, Benzer, and Henning in chapter 7. We also encourage researchers to look beyond the I/O psychology literature for relevant variables and theory. Attachment theory as described by Bergman et al. and evolutionary psychology as discussed by Becker (chapter 5) are good illustrations of how we might benefit from looking beyond the confines of I/O psychology.

There has also been relatively little research conducted to examine the influence of organizational (see chapter 9) or cultural (see chapter 10) variables on the development of commitment. The relative exclusion of these more macro influences may be because commitment researchers tend to view commitment as an individual-level variable that is primarily responsive to immediate work experiences. Nevertheless, it can be argued that these immediate experiences are greatly influenced by national culture and organizational factors, policies, and procedures. As such, these influences deserve greater research attention. We do not currently know enough about how cultural factors affect the development of commitment (see chapter 10). With more organizations operating on a global scale, this is a critical gap in our knowledge. Organizational factors are equally important, as they may be the key levers that organizations can use in managing commitment (see chapter 9). As such, we need to know more about when and how these levers exert their effects, even if they are indirect. As Meyer noted in chapter 2, if we hope to convince organizations to invest in the development of commitment-oriented HRM initiatives, it will be necessary to demonstrate that these initiatives pay dividends. This evidence will be best accumulated through additional organization- and cross-level research.

It is also clear from the reviews in chapters 4 through 6 that there has been far more research on the development of organizational commitments than on social or action commitments. Even within the category of organizational commitments, there has been more research on commitment to employers than on commitments to unions, occupations, professions, and other types of organizations. The authors of these chapters suggest a number of directions for future research that, if followed, should help to address these gaps. We focus here on two general issues that became apparent to us as we reviewed these chapters: the need for more attention on commitment as a process and the identification of common antecedents or antecedent categories.

First, research should shift from simply identifying correlates of commitment that are likely antecedents to examining the development of commitment as a process that unfolds over time. Commitment theory is richer in its description of process than is apparent from the current body of research. For example, Meyer and Allen (1997) drew on existing theory to identify a number of mechanisms (e.g., attributions, perceptions of justice, organizational support) that might help to explain how work experiences exert their influence on commitment. More recently, there have been additional process theories proposed to guide research on the development of commitment (e.g., Meyer et al., 2004; Meyer, Becker, & Van Dick, 2006). In chapter 6, Neubert and Wu suggest that we may want to look beyond conscious processes to unconscious processes such as those implicated in the escalation of commitment.

Commitment theorists have recognized that commitment is a process that develops over time, yet researchers have predominantly examined commitment as a static construct. As a psychological state, commitment can ebb and flow in its levels, but there has been little research on such changes in commitment. Indeed, since commitments do not simply develop and then exist forever, the examination of how commitment dissipates or is lost may yield valuable insights into the commitment process. We therefore encourage additional theory development to account for such dynamism, with efforts to incorporate theory from other branches of psychology, as well as research that tests the temporal aspects of commitment. Analytic techniques such as LGM, described in chapter 12, are ideally suited to such process-focused research.

Second, our understanding of the development of commitment would be greatly aided by identifying a core set of antecedents or antecedent categories. As noted earlier, a large number of different commitment antecedents have been identified in the literature, and the examination of those antecedents has tended to be unsystematic. As also previously discussed, antecedents can be classified in terms of level of origin, basis/mindset, and proximity. The future research needs are to determine which of these organizing frameworks are most useful; to develop integrative frameworks that account for differences in level, basis, and proximity; and to evaluate these frameworks. Commitment to any given target in a particular context will undoubtedly have its unique determinants. Nevertheless, there may be common sets or general types of antecedents that operate across targets and contexts. Examples of research questions to be examined in testing these frameworks include, "Do similarly grouped antecedents operate similarly?" and "Do more distal antecedents operate through more proximal ones as proposed?" It is also important to recognize that regardless of how antecedents are categorized, those different categories are unlikely to be simply additive in influencing the development of commitment. For example, as noted earlier and as discussed in chapters 7 and 8, individual differences are thought to interact with situational factors to influence the development of commitment over time. As such, future research systematically examining both main and interactive effects of antecedents from different categories is also needed.

Consequences of Commitment

Interest in organizational commitment was stimulated to a large degree by its implications for employee retention (Mowday et al., 1982). The sustained interest in commitment over the last 40 years is attributable, at least in part, to its implications for behavior, including retention, attendance, job performance, and OCB. Indeed, research has consistently demonstrated modest, albeit meaningful, relations with all of these outcomes (Meyer et al., 2002; Riketta, 2002, 2008). Interest in other commitment targets has similarly been driven by the ability of commitment to explain outcomes important in the study of those targets. However, there are several ways in which research on the consequences of commitment can and needs to be enriched.

A first way in which our understanding of commitment consequences can be improved is through the examination of an expanded range of outcome variables. As noted earlier, there are three primary categories of commitment outcomes, and in each category there are unexplored or underexplored outcomes. For example, withdrawal has been frequently examined, but the different forms that withdrawal can take have not been fully examined with respect to the complete set of commitment targets. Further, a better understanding is needed of the direct behavioral outcomes of commitment versus secondary outcomes such as performance, the important contextual moderators of those relationships, and when behavioral outcomes are more likely to involve extra- versus in-role activities.

Counterproductive work behavior is another potentially important consequence of commitment, though the link between commitment and counterproductive work behavior has only recently been examined (e.g., Becker & Bennett, 2007; Dalal, 2005). Preliminary research, largely unpublished, suggests that organizational commitment with an affective mindset is negatively associated with the tendency to behave in ways that are harmful to coworkers or to the organization itself. We need additional research on counterproductive work behavior, including studies that examine links with other commitment targets and mindsets. In addition, given that change has become increasingly prevalent in the world of work, job performance should be expanded to include such aspects as adaptability, resilience, creativity, and innovation.

The last category, affective outcomes, probably has the most room for expansion. As mentioned earlier, emerging evidence suggests that organizational commitment experienced with affective and normative mindsets relates positively to measures of employee health and well-being and negatively to strain and burnout, while commitment with a continuance mindset has the opposite relations. Some research has shown that the affective mindset has a buffering effect on the impact of stressors on strain (e.g., Begley & Czajka, 1993; Schmidt, 2007). Interestingly, however, other studies have found that stressors have stronger relations among those who are highly committed than those who are not (e.g., Irving & Coleman, 2003; Reilly, 1994). Presumably the moderating effect of commitment on the stressor-strain relationship is itself moderated, but we know little or nothing about the mechanisms involved.

For all three of the above outcome categories, it has not been sufficiently recognized that the implications can be either positive or negative for the individual, the target, or both. The potential "dark side" of commitment has been discussed in the organizational and goal commitment literatures (e.g., Klein et al., 1999; McElroy, Morrow, & Laczniak, 2001; Randall, 1987), but, with the exception of work on the escalation of commitment, most of the research to date has focused on positive outcomes. Commitment to a target can potentially be detrimental when the target is problematic (as with an unethical organization or abusive supervisor), or when commitment becomes sufficiently strong as to bias judgment and decision making. Negative outcomes are also likely whenever a commitment results in an individual's expending excessive levels of time and effort on behalf of a target, levels that are not sustainable without experiencing high levels of stress or producing great difficulties in satisfying competing commitments. The conditions under which different workplace commitments conflict, the effects of such conflicts, and the processes by which those conflicts are resolved represent other pressing needs for future research.

A second way our understanding of commitment consequences can be improved, as was the case with the development of commitment, is to give greater attention to process issues. Meyer et al. (2004) recently proposed a process model linking commitment to task performance through its implications for self-regulation and task motivation. This model builds on a large body of research on motivation, both within (e.g., Locke, 1997) and outside the field of I/O psychology (e.g., Higgins, 1997; Ryan & Deci, 2000). These authors offer a number of new propositions that need to be evaluated, and complementary models might need to be developed and tested to address other process variables. For example, as noted above, we need a better understanding of how commitment relates to employee-relevant outcomes such as health and well-being or burnout (see Maltin & Meyer, in press) and to counterproductive work behaviors (see Becker & Bennett, 2007). We also need a better understanding of how conscious and unconscious processes combine to influence commitment (see chapter 6).

Third, we know that employees develop commitments to multiple targets. However, we don't know enough about how these commitments relate to one another and how they combine to shape behavior. As we discuss below, this becomes increasingly important as we consider the implications of change on commitment. If it is indeed the case that organizations are finding it increasingly difficult to make long-term commitments to their employees and to expect long-term commitments from employees in return (see chapter 2), then we need to know more about "substitutes for organizational commitment." Such substitutes would involve alternative ways that organizations can achieve similar, desirable outcomes by fostering commitment to other targets (e.g., goals, supervisors, teams, customers). To understand these substitutes, we need a better understanding of how commitments to various targets relate individually, and in combination, to desired organizational outcomes.

Finally, we need more research examining the links between commitment and its outcomes at higher levels of analysis (e.g., team, organizations). As we noted above, convincing organizations to invest in initiatives designed to foster commitment will require evidence that these initiatives pay off. To date, making a convincing case requires piecing together findings from different literatures (see chapter 2). What is needed is a systematic program of causal organizational-level research examining the role of commitment in the black box between HRM systems and organizational effectiveness, as well as cross-level research linking the commitment of organizational members with organizational outcomes. Such research should examine the influence of commitment-oriented management practices on various workplace commitments and the influence that a committed workforce has on organizational effectiveness. That effectiveness should be measured using indices meaningful to organizations, including absenteeism and retention rates, customer satisfaction and retention, return on investment, profit margin, and the like (see chapter 9).

Implications of Change

We conclude our discussion of a future research agenda with issues arising from changes in the workplace (see chapter 2). We include globalization and increasing cultural diversity within Western countries among those changes. Fortunately, researchers are beginning to study commitment in a variety of countries and cultures outside of North America and the Western world (see chapter 10).

One of the most basic issues that needs to be addressed is how change affects the nature of employer-employee relations. This includes large-scale changes within a single organization (e.g., restructuring, downsizing, merger or acquisition) as well as the prevalence of organizational change in general. Such research should focus not only on the effects that these changes can have on commitments but on the mechanisms involved (e.g., contract violation, loss of trust) and the effectiveness of strategies to mitigate the likely negative impact of such changes (see Schweiger & DeNisi, 1991, as an example). If it is commitment to the organization that is primarily affected by large-scale changes, this again argues for the

need to better understand how commitments to other targets might substitute for organizational commitment to help organizations meet their
objectives. In addition to targets such as goals, teams, and projects, other
largely unexplored targets such as the organization's mission or values
(e.g., community or environmental support) should also be examined as
potential substitutes for organizational commitment. Of course, we also
need to know a great deal more about the development and impact of
commitment to the change itself (see chapters 2 and 6).

It is important to recognize that not only is the workplace changing—
but so is the worker. Therefore, we need more research to understand how
changing demographics are likely to affect the nature, development, and
consequences of commitment. Age, gender, and education have all been
studied in the past, and the relations with commitment have generally
been found to be weak or inconsistent. However, we have yet to take a
systematic look at how these and other demographic factors might relate
to various commitment targets. For example, the implications of an aging
workforce and generational differences among employees have not been
sufficiently explored. Similarly, workgroup homogeneity or heterogeneity
with respect to the full range of diversity dimensions has not been examined in relation to team commitment. In addition, changing career expectations and norms (e.g., more frequent job and career transitions) as well
as trends toward higher levels of education need to be studied relative to
professional and occupational commitment. There are other demographic
variables, including cultural and ethnic backgrounds, that have received
very little attention. This brings us to the question of the cross-cultural
generalizability of our commitment theories.

Wasti and Önder (chapter 10) provide a comprehensive review of the
cross-cultural research on commitment. They also provide a detailed and
complex model to illustrate the many ways that culture and other societal
variables are likely to affect the nature, development, and consequences of
commitment. A comparison of what we know (from the review) and what
we need to know (from the model) make it clear that we have a great deal
to learn about culture and commitment. First, although some research
suggests that commitment models and measures developed in the
Western world transfer reasonably well when applied in other cultures,
Wasti and Önder question whether the samples included in these studies
are truly representative of the native culture. More important, they argue
that we need to do more than simply evaluate the transportability of existing models—we should begin with more qualitative research to discover
what commitment means to individuals within these cultures. It is possible that we will discover new meanings, some of which might be unique
to a particular culture, and others that might indicate the need to revise
our general models. There are clearly many new and exciting directions
for research in this area. Our only caution to those who are interested

in pursuing cross-cultural research is that they make themselves aware of the potential pitfalls (e.g., translation difficulties, nonequivalence of samples, confounding societal differences) and become well versed in the strategies and techniques that have been developed to avoid or address these problems.

Conclusion

As expatiated by the chapters of this book, a great amount of progress has been made in understanding the nature of commitment, its anteced-ents and consequences, and the processes through which commitment has its effects. Equally exciting, we believe, is the work yet to be done. In this chapter we have tried to summarize the former and promote the lat-ter. The chapter authors represented in this volume are some of the best theorists and researchers in the field, and we look forward to seeing their work and the work of their students in the journals in the near future. There are untold others who could easily have been selected as authors, who also have important contributions to make. We encourage readers to consider our recommendations but to also apply their own judgment and creativity to moving the commitment literature forward. We believe workplace commitments to be more important now than ever and, there-fore, there is a profound need to further advance our knowledge. A sound scientific agenda, not a concern for fads and fashions, is needed to produce something of lasting value to the academic and practitioner communities. We hope that this volume will help facilitate that endeavor.

References

Aaker, J., Fournier, S., & S. Brasel. (2004). When good brands do bad. *Journal of Consumer Research, 31*, 1–18.

Ajzen, I., & Fishbein, M. (2000). Attitudes and the attitude-behavior relation: Rea-soned and automatic processes. In W. Strobe & M. Hewstone (Eds.), *European Review of Social Psychology*. New York: John Wiley & Sons.

Allen, N. J., & Meyer, J. P. (1990). The measurement and antecedents of affective, continuance and normative commitment to the organization. *Journal of Occu-pational Psychology, 63*(1), 1–18.

Bamberger, P. A., Kluger, A. N., & Suchard, R. (1999). The antecedents and con-sequences of union commitment: A meta-analysis. *Academy of Management Journal, 42*(3), 304–318.

Becker, T. E. (1992). Foci and bases of commitment: Are they distinctions worth making? *Academy of Management Journal, 35,* 232–244.

Becker, T. E. (2005). *Problems of commitment: Three dilemmas regarding the nature of employee attachment.* Presented at the first Conference on Commitment, Ohio State University, Columbus, OH.

Becker, T. E. (2006, May). *Concept redundancy among forms and bases of commitment.* Paper presented at the 21st Annual Conference of the Society for Industrial and Organizational Psychology, Dallas.

Becker, T. E., & Bennett, R. J. (2007). Employee attachment and deviance in organizations. In J. Langan-Fox, C. Cooper, and R. Klimoski (Eds.), *Research companion to the dysfunctional workplace: Management challenges and symptoms* (pp. 136–151). New Horizons Management Series. (Cary L. Cooper, Ed.). Northampton, MA: Edward Elgar.

Becker, T. E., Billings, R. S., Eveleth, D. M., & Gilbert, N. L. (1996). Foci and bases of employee commitment: Implications for job performance. *Academy of Management Journal, 39,* 464–482.

Becker, T. E., & Kernan, M. C. (2003). Matching commitment to supervisors and organizations to in-role and extra-role performance. *Human Performance, 16*(4), 327.

Begley, T. M., & Czajka, J. M. (1993). Panel analysis of the moderating effects of commitment on job satisfaction, intent to quit, and health following organizational change. *Journal of Applied Psychology, 78,* 552–556.

Bentein, K., Stinglhamber, F., & Vandenberghe, C. (2002). Organization-, supervisor-, and workgroup-directed commitments and citizenship behaviours: A comparison of models. *European Journal of Work & Organizational Psychology, 11*(3), 341–362.

Bishop, J. W., Scott, K. D., & Burroughs, S. M. (2000). Support, commitment, and employee outcomes in a team environment. *Journal of Management, 26*(6), 1113.

Brown, R. B. (1996). Organizational commitment: Clarifying the concept and simplifying the existing construct typology. *Journal of Vocational Behavior, 49,* 230–251.

Colquitt, J. A., Conlon, D. E., Wesson, M. J., Porter, C. O. L. H., & Ng, K. Y. (2001). Justice at the millennium: A meta-analytic review of 25 years of organizational justice research. *Journal of Applied Psychology, 86,* 425–445.

Cooper-Hakim, A., & Viswesvaran, C. (2005). The construct of work commitment: Testing an integrative framework. *Psychological Bulletin, 131*(2), 241–259.

Crosby, L. A., & Taylor, J. R. (1983). Psychological commitment and its effects on post-decision evaluation and preference stability among voters. *Journal of Consumer Research, 9*(4), 413–431.

Dalal, R. S. (2005). A meta-analysis of the relationship between organizational citizenship behavior and counterproductive work behavior. *Journal of Applied Psychology, 90*(6), 1241–1255.

Fedor, D. B., Caldwell, S., & Herold, D. M. (2006). The effects of organizational changes on employee commitment: A multilevel investigation. *Personnel Psychology, 59,* 1–29.

Gellatly, I. R., Meyer, J. P., & Luchak, A. A. (2006). Combined effects of the three commitment components on focal and discretionary behaviors: A test of Meyer and Herscovitch's proposition. *Journal of Vocational Behavior, 69,* 331–345.

Goetzel, R. Z., Anderson, D. R., Whitmer, R. W., Ozminkowski, R. J., Dunn, R. L., & Wasserman, J. Health Enhancement Research Organization (HERO) Research Committee. (1998). The relationship between modifiable health risks and health care expenditures: An analysis of the multi-employer HERO health risk and cost database. *Journal of Occupational and Environmental Medicine, 40*(10), 843–854.

Harrison, D. A., Newman, D. A., & Roth, P. L. (2006). How important are job attitudes? Meta-analytic comparisons of integrative behavioral outcomes and time sequences. *Academy of Management Journal, 49,* 305–325.

Herrbach, O. (2006). A matter of feeling? The affective tone of organizational commitment and identification. *Journal of Organizational Behavior, 27,* 629–643.

Herscovitch, L., & Meyer, J. P. (2002). Commitment to organizational change: Extension of a three-component model. *Journal of Applied Psychology, 87,* 474–487.

Higgins, E. T. (1997). Beyond pleasure and pain. *American Psychologist, 52*(12), 1280–1300.

Hollenbeck, J. R., & Klein, H. J. (1987). Goal commitment and the goal-setting process: Problems, prospects, and proposals for future research. *Journal of Applied Psychology, 72*(2), 212–220.

Irving, P. G., & Coleman, D. F. (2003). The moderating effect of different forms of commitment on role ambiguity–job tension relations. *Canadian Journal of Administrative Sciences, 20,* 97–106.

Johnson, M. P., Caughlin, J. P., & Huston, T. L. (1999). The tripartite nature of marital commitment: Personal, moral, and structural reasons to stay married. *Journal of Marriage & the Family, 61,* 160–177.

Kahn, P. J., & Greene, A. L. (2004). Seeing conversion whole: Testing a model of religious conversion. *Journal of Pastoral Psychology, 52,* 233–258.

Kanfer, R., Chen, G., & Pritchard, R. D. (2008). The three C's of work motivation: Content, context, and change. In R. Kanfer, G. Chen, & R. D. Pritchard (Eds.) *Work Motivation: Past, Present, and Future.* 1–16. New York: Routledge/Taylor & Francis Group.

Klein, H. J., Brinsfield, C. T., & Molloy, J. C. (2006). *Understanding workplace commitments independent of antecedents, foci, rationales, and consequences.* Paper presented at the Academy of Management Annual Meeting, Atlanta, GA.

Klein, H. J., Wesson, M. J., Hollenbeck, J. R., & Alge, B. J. (1999). Goal commitment and the goal-setting process: Conceptual clarification and empirical synthesis. *Journal of Applied Psychology, 84*(6), 885–896.

Ko, J. W., Price, J. L., & Mueller, C. W. (1997). Assessment of Meyer and Allen's three-component model of organizational commitment in South Korea. *Journal of Applied Psychology, 82,* 961–973.

Kristof-Brown, A., Zimmerman, R., & Johnson, E. (2005) Consequences of individuals' fit at work: A meta-analysis. *Personnel Psychology, 58,* 281–342.

Lee, K. L., Carswell, J. J., & Allen, N. J. (2000). A meta-analytic review of occupational commitment: Relations with person- and work-related variables. *Journal of Applied Psychology, 85,* 799–811.

LePine, J. A., Erez, A., & Johnson, D. E. (2002). The nature and dimensionality of organizational citizenship behavior: A critical review and meta-analysis. *Journal of Applied Psychology, 87,* 52–65.

Locke, E. A. (1997). The motivation to work: What we know. *Advances in Motivation and Achievement, 10,* 375–412.

Locke, E. A., & Latham, G. P. (1990). *A theory of goal setting and task performance.* Englewood Cliffs, NJ: Prentice Hall.

Macey, W. H., & Schneider, B. (2008). The meaning of employee engagement. *Industrial and Organizational Psychology: Perspectives on Science and Practice,1,* 3–30.

Maertz, C. P., Mosley, D. C., & Alford, B. L. (2002). Does organizational commitment fully mediate constituent commitment effects? A reassessment and clarification. *Journal of Applied Social Psychology, 32,* 1300–1313.

Maltin, E. A., & Meyer, J. P. (in press). Engagement et bien-être des employés (Commitment and employee well-being). In J. Rojot, P. Roussel, & C. Vandenberghe (Eds.), *Comportement organizationnel, Volume 3: perspectives en théories des organisations, motivation au travail, engagement dans l'organisation.* Bruxelles: De Boeck. (English version available from the authors.)

Mathieu, J. E., & Zajac, D. M. (1990). A review and meta-analysis of the antecedents, correlates, and consequences of organizational commitment. *Psychological Bulletin, 108*(2), 171–194.

Matsuba, M. K., & Walker, L. J. (2004). Extraordinary moral commitment: Young adults involved in social organizations. *Journal of Personality, 72,* 413–436.

McElroy, J. C., Morrow, P. C., & Laczniak, R. N. (2001). External organizational commitment. *Human Resource Management Review, 11*(3), 237–256.

McGee, G. W., & Ford, R. C. (1987). Two (or more?) dimensions of organizational commitment: Rexamination of the Affective and Continuance Commitment Scales. *Journal of Applied Psychology, 72,* 638–642.

Meyer, J. P. (1997). Organizational commitment. In I. T. Robertson & C. L. Cooper (Eds.), *International review of industrial and organizational psychology,* (Volume 12, pp. 175–228). New York: John Wiley & Sons.

Meyer, J. P., & Allen, N. J. (1991). A three-component conceptualization of organizational commitment. *Human Resource Management Review, 1*(1), 61–89.

Meyer, J. P., & Allen, N. J. (1997). *Commitment in the workplace: Theory, research, and application.* Thousand Oaks, CA: Sage.

Meyer, J. P., Allen, N. J., & Gellatly, I. R. (1990). Affective and continuance commitment to the organization: Evaluation of measures and analysis of concurrent and time-lagged relations. *Journal of Applied Psychology, 75,* 710–720.

Meyer, J. P., Allen, N. J., & Smith, C. A. (1993). Commitment to organizations and occupations: extension and test of a three-component conceptualization. *Journal of Applied Psychology, 78*(4), 538–551.

Meyer, J. P., Becker, T. E., & Van Dick, R. (2006). Social identities and commitments at work: Toward an integrative model. *Journal of Organizational Behavior, 27,* 665–683.

Meyer, J. P., Becker, T. E., & Vandenberghe, C. (2004). Employee commitment and motivation: A conceptual analysis and integrative model. *Journal of Applied Psychology, 89*(6), 991–1007.

Meyer, J. P., & Herscovitch, L. (2001). Commitment in the workplace: Toward a general model. *Human Resource Management Review, 11*(3), 299–326.

Meyer, J. P., Srinivas, E. R., Lal, J. B., & Topolnytsky, L. (2007). Employee commitment and support for an organizational change: Test of the three-component model in two cultures. *Journal of Occupational and Organizational Psychology*. *80*, 185–211.

Meyer, J. P., Stanley, D. J., Herscovitch, L., & Topolnytsky, L. (2002). Affective, continuance, and normative commitment to the organization: A meta-analysis of antecedents, correlates, and consequences. *Journal of Vocational Behavior*, *61*, 20–52.

Meyer, J. P., & Topolnytsky, L. (2000). *Best practices: Employee retention*. Toronto, Canada: Carswell.

Mowday, R. T., Porter, L. W., & Steers, R. M. (1982). *Employee-organization linkages: The psychology of commitment, absenteeism, and turnover*. New York: Academic Press.

Neubert, M. J., & Cady, S. H. (2001). Program commitment: A multi-study longitudinal field investigation of its impact and antecedents. *Personnel Psychology*, *54*(2), 421–448.

Novelli, L., Jr., Kirkman, B. L., & Shapiro, D. L. (1995). Effective implementation of organizational change: An organizational justice perspective. In C. L. Cooper and D. M. Rousseau (Eds.), *Trends in Organizational Behavior* (Vol. 2, pp. 15–36). Bognor Regis, UK: John Wiley & Sons Limited.

O'Reilly, C., & Chatman, J. (1986). Organizational commitment and psychological attachment: The effects of compliance, identification, and internalization on prosocial behavior. *Journal of Applied Psychology*, *71*(3), 492–499.

Pfeffer, J., & Sutton, R. I. (2006). *Hard facts, dangerous half-truths and total nonsense: Profiting from evidence-based management*. Boston: Harvard Business School Press.

Poole, M. (2001). Fit for life: Older women's commitment to exercise. *Journal of Aging and Physical Activity*, *9*, 300–312.

Powell, D., & Meyer, J. (2004). Side-bet theory and the three-component model of organizational commitment. *Journal of Vocational Behavior*, *65*, 157–177.

Randall, D. M. (1987). Commitment and the organization: The organization man revisited. *Academy of Management Review*, *12*(3), 460–471.

Reichers, A. E. (1985). A review and reconceptualization of organizational commitment. *Academy of Management Review*, *10*(3), 465–476.

Reilly, N. P. (1994). Exploring the paradox: Commitment as a moderator of the stressor–burnout relationship. *Journal of Applied Social Psychology*, 24, 397–414.

Rhoades, L., & Eisenberger, R. (2002). Perceived organizational support: A review of the literature. *Journal of Applied Psychology*, *87*, 698–714.

Riketta, M. (2002). Attitudinal organizational commitment and job performance: A meta-analysis. *Journal of Organizational Behavior*, *23*, 257–266.

Riketta, M. (2005). Organizational identification: A meta-analysis. *Journal of Vocational Behavior*, *66*, 358–384.

Riketta, M. (2008). The causal relation between job attitudes and performance: A meta-analysis of panel studies. *Journal of Applied Psychology*, *93*(2), 472–481.

Rousseau, D. M. (2006). Is there such a thing as "evidence-based management?" *Academy of Management Review*, *31*(2), 256–269.

Rust, R. T., Lemon, K. N., & Zeithaml, V. A. (2004). Return on marketing: Using customer equity to focus marketing strategy. *Journal of Marketing*, *68*, 109–127.

Ryan, R. M., & Deci, E. L. (2000). Self-determination theory and the facilitation of intrinsic motivation, social development, and well-being. *American Psychologist, 55,* 68–78.

Schmidt, K.-H. (2007). Organizational commitment: A further moderator in the relationship between work stress and strain? *International Journal of Stress Management, 14,* 26–40.

Schweiger, D. M., & DeNisi, A. S. (1991). Communication with employees following a merger: A longitudinal field experiment. *Academy of Management Journal, 34,* 110–135.

Snape, E., & Redman, T. (2003). An evaluation of a three-component model of occupational commitment: Dimensionality and consequences among United Kingdom human resource management specialists. *Journal of Applied Psychology, 88*(1), 162–159.

Snape, E., Redman, T., & Chan, A. W. (2000). Commitment to the union: A survey of research and the implications for industrial relations and trade unions. *International Journal of Management Review, 2,* 205–230.

Solinger, O., Van Olffen, W., & Roe, R.A. (2008). Beyond the three-component model of organizational commitment. *Journal of Applied Psychology, 93,* 70–83.

Stanley, D. J., Meyer, J. P., Jackson, T. A., Maltin, E. M., McInnis, E., Kumsar, Y., et al. (2007, April). Cross-cultural generalizability of the three-component model of commitment. Presented at the annual meeting of the Society for Industrial and Organizational Psychology, New York.

Stinglhamber, F., Bentein, K., & Vandenberghe, C. (2002). Extension of the three-component model of commitment to five foci. *European Journal of Psychological Assessment, 18*(2), 123–138.

Stinglhamber, F., & Vandenberghe, C. (2003). Organizations and supervisors as sources of support and targets of commitment: A longitudinal study. *Journal of Organizational Behavior, 24,* 251–270.

Tett, R. P., & Meyer, J. P. (1993). Job satisfaction, organizational commitment, turnover intention and turnover: Path analyses based on meta-analytic findings. *Personnel Psychology, 46,* 259–293.

Thoresen, C. J., Kaplan, S. A., Barsky, A. P., Warren, C. R., & de Chermont, K. (2003). The affective underpinnings of job perceptions and attitudes: A meta-analytic review and integration. *Psychological Bulletin, 129,* 914–945.

Vandenberghe, C., Bentein, K., & Stinglhamber, F. (2004). Affective commitment to the organization, supervisor, and work group: Antecedents and outcomes. *Journal of Vocational Behavior, 64,* 47–71.

Verquer, M. L., Beehr, T. A., & Wagner, S. H. (2003). A meta-analysis of relations between person-organization fit and work attitudes. *Journal of Vocational Behavior, 63,* 473–489.

Wann, D. L., & Pierce, S. (2003). Measuring sport team identification and commitment: An empirical comparison of the Sport Spectator Identification Scale and the Psychological Commitment to Team Scale. *North American Journal of Psychology, 5,* 365–372.

Whitton, S., Stanley, S., & Markman, H. (2007). If I help my partner, will it hurt me? Perceptions of sacrifice in romantic relationships. *Journal of Social and Clinical Psychology, 26,* 64–92.

Subject Index

Figures are in italics, tables in bold

Author Index

Wright, C., 102, 395–396
Wright, P.M., 23, 47, 48, 119, 123, 180,
    181, 191, 285–308, 299, 352, 352–353,
    360, 363, 368, 385
Wright, T.A., 47, 102
Wu, C., 116, 119, 179–216, 226, 257, 361,
    396, 442
Wu, T., 89

Y

Yamagishi, T., 332
Yammarino, F.J., 255
Yik, M., 119, 202
Yoon, J., 12, 110, 155, 262
Young, W.R., 106
Youngcourt, S.S., 118
Yuschenkova, D.V., 156

Z

Zaccaro, S.J., 6, 23, 159
Zahra, S.A., 267
Zajac, D.M., 3, 9, 16, 41, 47, 69, 71, 76,
    101–103, 111, 138, 196, 221, 236, 289,
    349, 395, 423
Zapata-Phelan, C., 370
Zardkoohi, A., 201, 202, 203
Zeithaml, V.A., 432
Zeitz, G., 51, 58
Zhang, S., 365
Zhao, H., 268, 272
Zhong, C.-B., 330, 336
Zickar, M.J., 217, 238–239, 366
Zimmerman, R., 422, 440
Zinovieva, I.L., 315
Zivnuska, S., 156, 257

Printed in the United States
by Baker & Taylor Publisher Services